D1566286

Ana Pauker

Ana Pauker

*The Rise and Fall
of a Jewish Communist*

Robert Levy

UNIVERSITY OF CALIFORNIA PRESS
Berkeley · *Los Angeles* · *London*

Frontispiece: Ana Pauker, 1926. Courtesy
of Tatiana Brătescu and Gheorghe Brătescu.

University of California Press
Berkeley and Los Angeles, California

University of California Press, Ltd.
London, England

Library of Congress Cataloging-in-Publication Data

Levy, Robert, 1957–.
  Ana Pauker: the rise and fall of a Jewish
  Communist / Robert Levy.
      p.   cm.
    Includes bibliographical references and index.
    ISBN 0-520-22395-0 (cloth: alk. paper).
      1. Pauker, Ana, 1893–1960.   2. Romania—
  Politics and government—1944–1989.
  3. Cabinet officers—Romania—Biography.
  4. Communists—Romania—Biography.
  5. Jews—Romania—Biography.   I. Title.
  DR267.5.P38 L48   2001
  949.803′1′092—dc21
  [B]
                                    99-087890
                                         CIP

Manufactured in the United States of America

09   08   07   06   05   04   03   02   01

10   9   8   7   6   5   4   3   2   1

The paper used in this publication meets the
minimum requirements of ANSI/NISO
Z39.48-1992 (R 1997) (Permanence of Paper). ⊗

To Mary and Isaac Rosenberg

Last, but most certainly not least, there was Ana Pauker. . . .
I have always felt when I was with her that she was like a boa
constrictor which has just been fed, and therefore is not
going to eat you—at the moment! Heavy and sluggish as
she seemed, she had all that is repellent and yet horribly
fascinating in a snake. I could well imagine, simply from
watching her, that she had denounced her own husband, who
in consequence was shot; and my further acquaintance with
her showed me the cold and dehumanized brilliance by which
she had reached the powerful position she occupied.

Ileana, Princess of Romania,
Archduchess of Austria, I Live Again

Contents

Illustrations

Acknowledgments

This project has been long in the making and has benefited from the generous assistance of friends and colleagues on three continents. In Romania, I would like to cordially thank Marius Oprea, Claudiu Secaşiu, Professor Florin Constantiniu, Mircea Chiriţoiu, Mircea Suciu, Stelian Tanase, Dan Fârnoagă, Alice Dumitrache, Lya Benjamin, Harry Kuler, Alexandru Nistor, Alexandru Şiperco, Tania Şiperco, Eduard Mezincescu, Dr. Agnes Mureşan, George Macri, Rodica Radu, Mihai Pelin, Gheorghe Ţuţui, Gheorghe Niacşu, Florin and Liliana Balteanu, Mihaela Arsene, Aurelia Albu, Sorin Cozmanciuc, and the staffs of the foreign office of the Romanian Academy and the Nicolae Iorga Historical Institute. Particular thanks and appreciation go to Dr. Gheorghe and Tatiana Brătescu, whose support and assistance have been incalculable.

In Israel, I am deeply indebted to my brother Neal Levy, Orna Sasson, Ze'ev Dunie, Liviu Rotman, Shlomo Leibovici, Jean Coler, and particularly Sorin Toma. Heartfelt thanks also go out to Michel and Marie Birnbaum and Cristina Boico in Paris.

On this continent, I would first like to thank Professor Vladimir Tismaneanu, who has generously offered invaluable scholarly direction and assistance since the inception of this project in the 1980s. He has graciously shared vitally important documents from Ana Pauker's inquiry file, which had been denied me for more years than I care to remember. I am also very grateful to Sheryl Levy-North, Dumitru Cercel, Georgiana Fârnoagă, Barbara Bernstein, David Hirsch, Vera Wheeler,

Professor Anna Igra, Professor Sharon Gillerman, Professor Steven J. Zipperstein, Professor Barisa Krekic, Professor Michael Heim, Jane Stewart, Marcia Rorty, Ilie Zaharia, and Josef Bujes. Special thanks and appreciation go out to my mentors Professors Ivan T. Berend and Gail Kligman, for their enduring support and intellectual guidance.

Finally, I'd like to wholeheartedly thank my loving parents, Rose and Ben Levy, and my comrades-in-arms, Erica Silverman and Dorothy H. Rochmis, for everything.

Introduction

In September 1948 there appeared on the cover of *Time* magazine the portrait of a solid and imposing middle-aged woman—her expression stout and angry, her hair pushed back and unkempt, and her strong, almost menacing presence easily confirming the description *Time* would make of her: she was, it declared, "the most powerful woman alive." In a feature of its own a few months later, *Life* magazine would describe her as having "undeniable strength. . . . Her voice is deep, her tone confident, her manner brisk. She is an extraordinarily dynamic woman." [1] To a leading Israeli diplomat, she was "a true Minister" who conspicuously stood out from the many ministers he dealt with at that time; to a representative of an international Jewish organization, she was an "exceptional" figure next to whom Golda Meir paled in comparison; and to a Zionist activist who had been a childhood friend but was later imprisoned by her regime, "[s]he was fascinating—full of spirit and utterly devoted to her ideals. If [she] were alive now and came through this door into my house, I would welcome her with all my heart." [2] Other accounts were far less flattering: to one observer, she was "a grim, clever and evil woman"; to another, a "ruthless female . . . , a vain, violent and unprincipled figure." [3] From any perspective, however, she was an object of fascination whose story had all the makings of a good drama: the daughter of poor religious Jews rising to the pinnacle of power in a country traditionally disdainful of both Jews and women. She was, of course, Ana Pauker—then the great "Red Matron" of the Soviet bloc, and the star in the skies of Communist Romania.

Officially Romania's Foreign Minister from 1947 to 1952—the first woman in the modern world ever to hold such a post—Pauker was actually the unofficial head of Romania's Communist Party immediately after the war and for a number of years was the country's true behind-the-scenes leader. Always one of the first to be mentioned in the long list of outstanding revolutionary women, Pauker, unlike a Rosa Luxemburg or a Dolores "La Passionaria" Ibarruri, made it to "the top"—the first and the last woman to do so in the Communist world. Yet today, also unlike Luxemburg or Ibarruri, Pauker has all but disappeared from history. Discredited as a long-standing Stalinist leader, she is now barely known outside Romania. Few contemporary adherents of progressive or leftist politics seem ever to have heard of her, while many feminists, even those seeking to reclaim past matriarchs as today's role models, have no idea who she was.[4]

At the same time, Pauker is largely absent from Jewish historiography. This was, perhaps, a consequence of the conventional view of Jewish Communists as "non-Jewish Jews" who readily discarded their identities and abandoned their people for revolutionary universalism.[5] No longer Jewish protagonists pursuing particularly Jewish goals, they were considered outside the purview of Jewish history. Indeed, Jewish historians regarded Pauker much as Israeli Prime Minister David Ben-Gurion depicted her in 1949: "This daughter of a Jewish rabbi now living in Israel is endeavoring to destroy the Jewish community in her country. To her any Jew is a Fascist. She would like to bring famine to [Israel] in order to curb the wish of Jews to come here." As one scholar recently noted, Ana Pauker came to be known as an "archetype of self-hatred" among Jewish Communists.[6]

In Romania, on the other hand, Pauker has become a mythic figure symbolizing the perceived predominance of Jews in Romanian Communism, as well as the terror and repression of the Stalinist years. A key subject of the public discourse of post-Communist Romania, Pauker exemplifies what today is described as the "Cominternist" or foreign component in Romanian Communism, made up exclusively of ethnic minorities and always negatively contrasted with ethnic-Romanian "patriots" such as Gheorghe Gheorghiu-Dej or Nicolae Ceauşescu. This depiction of good and bad Communists is part of a long history of distrusting and blaming the "other"—be it foreigners or internal minorities—within the region. It is also part of a pattern of diversionist anti-Semitism in Romania, employed by the country's rulers, for instance, when dealing with the ever-explosive peasant question in the nineteenth and early twentieth centuries. But by "other," we also emphatically mean gender; Pauker was hated not only for being a "foreign" Jew, but also for being a woman who dared to rebel against traditional norms.

For over forty years, moreover, Romanian Communist propagandists carefully portrayed Ana Pauker as an extreme and dogmatic Stalinist who was the key promoter of Soviet-inspired policies in the early Romanian Communist regime. This characterization continues today, and a number of that regime's participants have recently articulated it. "Ana Pauker . . . ," one of them asserted, "excelled in implementing Stalinism in Romania as quickly as possible." Added another, "I would say that she was the most Stalinist-minded leader of the party at that time." Her actions, concluded a third, were guided by a simple and ruthless formula: "Terror, Divisiveness, and Pauperization."[7] This portrayal has been largely accepted by Western scholars, who, long denied access to Communist Party archives, had no way of gauging the satellite leaders' true reactions to the compulsory Stalinization of their regimes.[8] Yet, as opposed to several of those leaders, historians seem to have had little doubt of Pauker's submissiveness: amid persistent rumors that she denounced her own husband as a Trotskyist during the Great Terror of the late 1930s, "her fanatical subservience to Moscow was not only undisputed, it was legendary." One of the many jokes about this "describes Pauker promenading through the streets of Bucharest on a cloudless summer day with an umbrella opened over her head. On being asked why, she replied: 'Haven't you heard the Soviet radio today? It's raining in Moscow!'"[9]

This book reexamines Ana Pauker's life and career and finds much of the conventional wisdom to be largely myth. The evidence reveals a person characterized more by contradictions than by dogmatism: a Communist leader fanatically loyal to Stalin and the Soviet Union but actively opposing the Stalinist line and deliberately defying Soviet directives on a number of important fronts—uniquely, during the perilous period of Stalin's final years. Indeed, Pauker's actions provide the most striking instance of a satellite's noncompliance with the Stalinist *dictat* during the heyday of "high Stalinism" (that is, between Tito's expulsion from the Cominform in 1948 and Stalin's death in 1953), and they suggest a far more complex political dynamic in post–World War II Communism than is traditionally portrayed.

Likewise, the evidence presents Pauker as a Jewish Communist largely untainted by self-hatred. Although outwardly disconnected from Jews and Judaism, she promoted an independent line on Jewish issues that rejected orthodox Marxism-Leninism's class-based approach, and she sanctioned the unrestricted emigration of Romanian Jews to Israel after the Soviets adopted an increasingly hostile stance toward the Jewish state. She did so, moreover, while firmly committed to revolutionary internationalism and while earnestly identifying with the Romanian people.

This study began on the premise that Pauker's story, and that of Jewish Communists generally, is an important part not only of Communist and Romanian history but of contemporary Jewish history as well. As the late Israeli historian Jacob L. Talmon noted, "Hitler singled out the international Jewish-Marxist revolutionary as his main target, as the prototype of Jewish evil-doer, as the microbe destructive of all Aryan civilization" when he unleashed the Holocaust on European Jewry.[10] Further, these Jewish revolutionaries' fate ultimately reflected the tragedy of all European Jewry. In the end, no matter how aloof or remote they may have been to their fellow Jews, no matter how much they yearned to break from all things Jewish, these radicals connoted a clear continuity with the Jewish past.

The degree to which Ana Pauker has been stereotyped is emblematic of traditional inferences about Jewish Communists as a whole: the mythical "Judeo-Bolshevism" denoting the prevalence of Jews in the Communist movement. Like most stereotypes, this one is based on a grain of truth. Jaff Schatz's recent study on Polish Jewish Communists concisely summarizes a whole literature attributing the reasons for the Jewish presence in Communist and revolutionary politics generally. Schatz suggests that none of the various theories—all of which emphasize either psychological, cultural, or social factors—alone can explain a complex and diverse phenomenon that defies overgeneralization.[11] In Romania's case, Ana Pauker was one of a small coterie of Jews who joined the Romanian Workers' Social Democratic Party before World War I. In contrast, most Romanian Jews shied from revolutionary politics or joined Zionist movements in response to their increasing marginalization. As the political situation became more and more polarized with fascism's rise in the 1930s, a growing number of socialist Zionists went over to the Communists; indeed, the Marxist-Zionist *HaShomer HaTzair* movement became known to some party insiders as the primary training ground for Romanian Jewish Communists during that decade.[12]

Classified Romanian Communist Party (RCP) statistics listed the ethnic proportion of party members in 1933 as 26.58 percent Hungarian, 22.65 percent Romanian, and 18.12 percent Jewish; Jewish veterans of the RCP contend that the proportion of Jews during this period was actually much higher (roughly 50 percent), as a large number of those cited as Hungarians were in fact Magyarized Jews from Transylvania. Nevertheless, the numbers were hardly significant in comparison to Romanian Jewry as a whole (totaling roughly 800,000 by 1940): by the end of World War II, the RCP could claim a total of only 700–800 members and a few thousand sympathizers of *any* ethnicity.[13]

Immediately after the war, the numbers of Jews joining the RCP increased markedly, though, again, they by no means comprised a majority of Romanian Jewry. Many of these new recruits were apparently younger Jews attracted to the prospect of building a new "democratic" order after the horrors and destruction of the world war.[14] They proved vital in consolidating the new regime, given the sparsity of party members, the loss of Romanian professionals during the war, the extensive postwar purges, and the need for people who had not been implicated with the old order. This perhaps paralleled Soviet Russia soon after the October Revolution, when many Russian Jews, faced with the White armies' anti-Semitic onslaught, entered the government apparatus and replaced those of the old bureaucracy and intelligentsia who boycotted the Soviet regime; in fact, Lenin himself credited the Jews with having "sabotaged the saboteurs," in effect saving the revolution by neutralizing the boycott.[15] But if Jews were indispensable in Romania after World War II, they remained so only briefly: by the end of 1945, thanks to the RCP's mass-recruitment campaign, of more than 300,000 party members, no less than 71 percent were ethnic-Romanians and only 7 percent were Jews.[16]

Still, under the new regime Jews were conspicuous in positions of power for the first time in Romanian history. This led to a pronounced anti-Semitic backlash in the country, as it did in the Soviet Union in the 1920s. There the Jewish presence in government posts generated a maelstrom of resentment and animosity so great that even the Kremlin could not ignore it. According to one historian, the source of this anti-Semitism "lay among the dispossessed and declassed strata of the urban middle class, and penetrated into the upper strata of industrial workers, the university students, the membership of the Communist Youth, and, last but not least, into the Communist Party itself."[17] A major issue of contention was the Jews' social mobility in places where they had never been seen before. This had occurred in postrevolutionary France, where emancipated Jews flocked to the urban centers and appeared to adapt more easily to the free-enterprise economy of the new liberal order. Many saw the Jews as the main beneficiaries of the recent changes and assumed they must have been responsible for them. They believed the Jews had used the individualism and atomization of liberalism and the internationalism of revolutionary socialism to destroy traditional Christian society, while maintaining their own cohesion.[18] In other words, both liberalism and socialism were seen as a Jewish conspiracy.

Another factor in this backlash was what Talmon observed to have been a "recurrent pattern" in Jewish history, stemming from the Jews' role as pioneers in European society.

> In his famous work on the beginnings of urban life in eleventh- and twelfth-century Europe, Henri Pirenne propounded the thesis that its earliest pioneers were human flotsam, fugitives from the law, serfs who had run away from their villages, men without name, occupation, standards or reputation. He went on to offer the generalization that, in great social transformations and new ventures, it was precisely people of this kind who served as pioneers. The long-settled and the well-established clung to patrimony and privileges. They shunned novelty, since it entailed displacement, risk, and had something disreputable about it. It was therefore men who had no ties, no reputations to lose, and were not permanently and safely rooted, who flocked into the new occupations. Pirenne's observation can almost be taken as a constant recurring law of Jewish life in the Middle Ages and in modern times. In the Middle Ages the Jews chose or were driven to fill a vacuum and to play a necessary pioneering role. They were at first invited, welcomed and granted privileges by the princes, the great builders of towns, as money-lenders and international tradesmen. . . . In time . . . , the Christian populations lost their horror of usury and began to look upon trade and commerce with approval as both respectable and profitable. . . . They resorted to a well-tried expedient and expelled the usurpers and parasites who, though ostracized and defenseless, were able and had the audacity to hold the well-born by the throat. The Jews were thus driven out from all the countries of Western Europe in the later Middle Ages.[19]

A similar scenario subsequently played out in East-Central Europe, where Jews were encouraged to assume an important economic role in certain undeveloped and largely townless regions. The Polish-Lithuanian, Hungarian, and Romanian aristocracies sought to develop industry in their countries but feared the growth of a native middle class that might become a political rival. They therefore preferred a politically harmless "foreign" middle class and offered Jews positions such as innkeepers, craftsmen, and lessors of mills and breweries in newly emerging towns bordering their vast estates. Deteriorating economic conditions and a massive population explosion in the nineteenth century brought a huge migration of impoverished gentry and destitute peasants to these towns, where they found the Jews already established. The consequent competition and nationalist tensions would end only with the Jews' disappearance from the region.[20]

This pattern followed a general rule concerning "out-groups": when a new ethnic or religious group immigrates into an already settled land, penetrating the established economic and social positions is difficult. The majority will tolerate the minority and allow it to encroach upon its positions only if the newcomers satisfy economic needs that do not seriously compete with its own. The minority must therefore seek untapped sources of income (that is, become pioneers), but once the minority establishes itself, the majority begins to covet the new positions.[21]

Hence, when the illegal Romanian Communist Party of the interwar years emerged from the underground to become the new establishment, its Jewish pioneers began to be seen as undeservedly and disproportionately privileged. Calls for "proportionality" quickly followed, and acceding to the majority, the regime responded with the "Romaniazation" of the party ranks. "Jewish predominance," long the reality of the risk-prone underground, was no longer tolerated from the late 1940s on: a permanent purge of the Jewish old guard ensued, with those replacing them being exclusively ethnic-Romanians.[22]

The purge of Ana Pauker in May 1952 was part of this process, though it also resulted from her genuinely deviationist policy and an upsurge of arrant anti-Semitism in the Communist bloc. The evidence indicates that Pauker was slated for the same fate as Rudolf Slansky of Czechoslovakia (executed in December 1952) but that her show trial was abruptly canceled after Stalin's death. She remained, however, one of the principal victims of the great Jewish purge of Stalin's final years, which signified a continuation of opportunistic anti-Semitism in the revolutionary left. This was the "socialism of fools" that August Bebel had railed against, the use of Jew-hatred by part of the socialist movement beginning in the nineteenth century. A phenomenon to be distinguished from political anti-Semitism, it first appeared with the Enlightenment, as progressive rationalists and anticlerical leftists attacked Judaism rather than their real target, the Christian Church. The Deists, fervent believers in "natural religion" and bitter opponents of the clergy, blamed Judaism as the "root of evil" in the church. Likewise, the "young Hegelians," advocating separation of church and state and focusing on a radical critique of Christianity, bashed Judaism for causing everything despicable in the Christian religion. Beginning in the 1860s, Social Democratic parties applied similar tactics, including extensive acquiescence to right-wing anti-Semitism in the belief that it would ultimately benefit the socialist movement.[23] The German and Austrian Social Democrats eventually abandoned such strategies after losing ground to anti-Semitic parties in their countries. They continued in France and Western Europe, however, and they lay behind the Russian revolutionaries' praise of anti-Semitic pogroms in the 1880s. German Communists used them regularly during the Weimar Republic.[24]

When the Kremlin played the Jewish card for diversionist purposes after World War II, it signaled the end of Jewish attempts to integrate into East-Central European society through Communism. Assimilating out of the Jewish fold with particular fervency, Jewish Communists hoped to free themselves from nationalist oppression by eliminating or transcending nationalism through revolutionary internationalism. For them, "The Internationale" undoubtedly had far greater significance than for those who took their national rights for granted. This was, indeed, part of a long tradition within Jewish radicalism and was seen, for instance, among Jews in the *Narodnaia Volia* of nineteenth-century Russia, who practically alone among their fellow Populists embraced cosmopolitan socialism.[25] As Hebrew writer Chaim Hazaz wrote, while Russian, German, or French revolutionaries struggled to redeem the proletariat of their own countries, Jewish revolutionaries set out to save the entire world.[26] In the end, their hopes for redemption through revolution proved a tragic illusion.

The futility of Jewish integration under Communism, moreover, reflected the Jews' general failure to assimilate into European society. In parts of modern Europe, Jews were offered integration and acceptance consistent with the universalist tenets of the Enlightenment, but for a price: they must abandon their distinctiveness and way of life in exchange for an end to anti-Semitism and their pariah status.[27] This included giving up their traditional "parasitic" and "exploitative" occupations, as if they had chosen such positions in the first place. In offering this "assimilationist contract" to its Jewish minority, the majority group suggested that only the Jews' differences, their supposedly backward and unbecoming peculiarities, led to the prejudice and hostility against them and that individual Jews could gain acceptance by individually making themselves more acceptable.[28] Many Jews found this premise quite reasonable. After all, was not the axiom of the modern world that education and culture were all that mattered? Did not the principles of the Enlightenment suggest that one could transcend all obstacles and overcome all hostility simply by educating oneself and becoming sufficiently "cultured"? A large number of emancipated Jews, therefore, became cultural fanatics obsessed with improving and cultivating themselves. Only yesterday completely marginalized and estranged from the majority community, they seemingly overnight became the most devoted adherents to the national culture in nearly every country they inhabited.[29] At the same time, they were only too happy to dispense with occupations into which they had been forced for generations and to embrace the opportunity to pursue professions and areas of employment heretofore denied them.

An implicit clause in the contract, however, proved the assimilating Jews' Achilles' heel: the majority group reserved the sole right to determine when the Jews had rid themselves of distasteful "Jewish" traits sufficiently to satisfy the contract. It soon became clear that no matter what the Jews did, that determination was never coming.[30] Those who had eliminated their cultural differences with the majority were ironically considered more different than ever before.[31] An incessant enthusiasm for the national culture suddenly and paradoxically became a sign of foreignness. "What more than anything else kept the assimilating Jews apart from any established section of the majority was precisely their assimilatory zeal. . . ."[32] "Jewishness" itself, believed by many to be an inexorable part of every assimilated Jew's makeup, was now singled out as a vice that Jews were to be shunned for (or, for that matter, praised for within certain avant-garde circles), and Jews remained inexplicably other.[33] Moreover, Jews soon found that, despite changing to more acceptable occupations, they made no headway with the majority. Magically their new occupations became stigmatized as having been "Judaized" and hopelessly sullied, even though the positions previously were always respectable.[34] At the same time, the traditional, hated "Jewish" occupations suddenly became acceptable as soon as only Gentiles were working in them. It became clear that the problem was not the occupations but the workers; Jewish professions were hated because Jews pursued them, and not the other way around.[35]

All this is evident in the Jewish experience under Communism. While Jewish party activists discarded their identities, renounced their past, and embraced the majority culture under the guise of revolutionary internationalism, the Jewish community was systematically transformed into "productive" laborers, thus ending its previous socioeconomic role. But this did not prevent a resurgence of popular anti-Semitism in these societies; on the contrary, for the reasons noted, it enhanced it. The more assimilated the Jews became, the more cohesive and threatening they appeared to the majority, and the more productive they became, the more they were seen as usurping the majority.[36]

Ana Pauker's fate underscored not only this outcome but also women's ultimate failure under Communism to overturn their societies' traditional restrictions. Pauker's case is instructive, moreover, in that it sheds additional light on the topic of Jewish assimilation, which has undergone considerable revision of late among Jewish historians. At first glance, Pauker's position favoring Jewish emigration suggests that she had rethought the feasibility of revolutionary internationalism's solving the "Jewish Question," perhaps in response to the upsurge of popular and state anti-Semitism in the Soviet bloc during Stalin's later years. If so, it would add credence to the classic historiographical theory on Jewish assimilation emphasizing "bipolarity" in modern Jewish life. Originating from Jewish historian Simon Dubnov, the theory posited that the more open and tolerant a society became, the greater the danger of assimilation and internal disintegration within the Jewish minority; conversely, the more a society reverted to intolerance and Jew-hatred, the more the Jews responded with renewed solidarity.[37]

This dichotomy, however, fails to explain Pauker's continued association with Jewish groups during her early years in the socialist and Communist movement, when the party most accepted and tolerated Jews; nor does it explain Pauker's enduring respect for, and close relationship with, her Orthodox Jewish parents and brother throughout her Communist career. Here, it seems, was a case of a fully assimilated Jew's continued primordial loyalties—an anomaly that in other contexts led scholars to reject the "bipolarity" approach to Jewish assimilation and to stress a multiplicity of factors precluding sweeping generalizations on the issue.[38] Though Pauker's Jewish identity should not be overemphasized, her record further proves that Jewish assimilation, including the espousal of revolutionary internationalism, does not necessarily imply nonidentification with other Jews. Yet it is important to underscore Pauker's multifarious and contradictory loyalties. No matter how much her alienation as a Jew and a woman from Romanian society led her to Communism or how much her revolutionary internationalism eroded into a mechanical allegiance to the Soviet Union, in the end she proved a tenacious patron of the Romanian peasantry—and did so against the will of her Soviet masters. This is one of this study's most important findings.

Researching Ana Pauker was problematic from the outset—not only because of Romania's prolonged resistance to opening its archives but also because of the many pitfalls inherent in Communist Party research. Tony Judt, for one, recently warned of "the danger of overestimating the knowledge and understanding to be gained from newly opened [Communist] archives, however promising they may appear. An 'archive,' after all, . . . is not a fount of truth. The motives and goals of those creating the documents, the limits of their own knowledge, the incorporation of gossip or flattery into a report for someone senior, the distortions of ideology or prejudice have all to be taken into account." [39] Added to this is the reported tendency of Communist leaders, perhaps simply out of habit, initially to preserve conspiratorial methods of the underground when conducting business during the postwar period.[40] At times they resolved to leave no record of certain meetings or ordered stenographers to stop their work when discussions turned particularly sensitive. According to one source, the party leadership sometimes doctored archival material in its perennial pursuit to rewrite history.[41] But such tampering, it seems, usually consisted of "losing" documents. We know, for instance, that General Secretary Gheorghe Gheorghiu-Dej ordered archival documents destroyed on at least one occasion.[42]

Thus using multiple sources is imperative, to amass as much material from as many sources as possible in order to corroborate information as well as to fill in the inevitable gaps and lapses. The archival evidence documented here therefore includes the transcripts of the Politburo and Secretariat of the Central Committee of the RCP (renamed the Romanian Workers' Party in February 1948), as well as those of the plenaries of the Central Committee, the sessions of the Council of Ministers, the periodic gatherings of regional party secretaries, and meetings of various sections of the Central Committee apparat. Added to this are investigative documents of official party commissions, as well as penal interrogations and declarations from the archives of the former *Securitate* (known today as the Romanian Information Service). Finally, I supplemented archival research with extensive interviews of some eighty witnesses from the inner circle of the party elite—many of whom were able to speak freely for the first time.

Obtaining such vast material enabled me to check the veracity of certain documents—especially penal interrogations and declarations, which, for obvious reasons, are inherently dubious. In analyzing such sources, I followed several general rules of thumb. First, no penal interrogation can be taken at face value, unless corroborated by other sources. Second, the dates of prison interrogations are crucial. Torture began to be used on certain party members in Romania in the summer of 1952; hence, interrogations before that date are more reliable than those begun after. Third, interrogations by party commissions are more reliable than penal interrogations conducted in prison. This is not, however, foolproof: at times those questioned by party commissions tried to say precisely what their inquisitors wanted to hear, particularly in declarations made soon after being released from prison (perhaps as a condition of release). Thus, fourth, declarations to party commissions made before imprisonment are more reliable than, and take precedence over, those made after imprisonment. Fifth, in any declaration, testimony specifically involving a leader then in power is probably true, as both prisoners and interrogators were loath to misrepresent anything about a current leader for fear of repercussions (though attempts at flattery are always possible). Sixth, being simple propaganda devices, the considerable number of "recollective" declarations that from 1956 on were "requested" of witnesses explicitly to substantiate the party line blaming all Stalinist or leftist "deviations" on the Pauker faction are largely useless for our purposes. (Indeed, a list of leading questions provided to the declarants has been found in the archives.)[43] Still, in some instances declarants contradicted the obvious agenda of their "testimony," attributing a "right-wing" or liberal position to Pauker. I have accepted those accounts as more than likely true, for why would one fabricate such a statement and risk invoking the party leadership's wrath?

Likewise, oral sources have their own limitations: they are often subjective accounts of witnesses who might selectively remember only what most benefits them. Still, though they may be biased in certain areas, testimonials of direct participants provide a reservoir of information simply unavailable in "objective" written sources. "As Gibbon put it, the serious historian 'is obliged to consult a variety of testimonies, each of which, taken separately, is perhaps imperfect and partial'; he added that 'ignorance of this common principle' is itself a major cause of misunderstanding."[44] The challenge is to recognize oral sources' biases, separating the empirically verifiable from wishful thinking or outright falsehoods. I attempted to do this, first, by cross-checking oral testimony with archival sources and, second, by interviewing as many people as possible to corroborate all claims with those of other witnesses. In the end, excepting dates (which, after fifty years, were invariably problematic), the information I gained from interviews was generally accurate and confirmed by the documents.

The first two chapters of this political biography of Ana Pauker examine her childhood and early revolutionary career. The remainder of the study covers her years in power and subsequent purge. This is not a history of Romanian Communism, nor does it attempt to document Communist actions and policies during Pauker's tenure. Rather, it focuses on Pauker's personal role in the party leadership and her positions on a number of key issues: agrarian policy, party purges, and Jewish emigration. This is only one aspect of what would be a very complex comprehensive history. It must, therefore, be supplemented with a thorough accounting of Communist rule from the perspective of the Romanian people—who have paid, and continue to pay, a painful and bitter price for its imposition.

CHAPTER ONE

Early Years

Details of Ana Pauker's childhood are sketchy. She wrote no memoirs and was apparently reticent to speak at length about her past, even to her own family. Fortunately, several documents from her Comintern file in Moscow fill some of the many gaps in her biography. She was born Ana Rabinsohn on December 13, 1893, to Orthodox Jewish parents in the predominantly Jewish village of Codăeşti, Vaslui County, in Moldavia, where her grandparents resided, but she lived her entire childhood in Bucharest.[1]

Ana's parents had migrated to the Romanian capital in the late nineteenth century, as did large numbers of Jews who initially resided in the provinces. The Jewish population of Bucharest grew from 6,000 in 1859 to 43,274 in 1899, making it the largest Jewish community in the country.[2] Each of two separate Jewish entities lived in different neighborhoods—the larger being the Ashkenazi, with twenty-eight synagogues, and the smaller but better organized and more firmly established being the Sephardic, with only two synagogues.[3] By the end of the century, the Jewish community as a whole could also claim a vast array of institutions, organizations, and charities and was markedly less Orthodox than those in outlying areas.[4] In addition, Bucharest's Jews were decidedly divided by class, with a small, affluent bourgeoisie surrounded by an impoverished mass. The Rabinsohn family clearly fell in the latter category: as Pauker later related, she lived "under very difficult conditions" throughout her childhood.[5]

Ana's father, Hersh Kaufman Rabinsohn, had performed various religious functions as a young man, including that of Hebrew teacher and cantor; later he made his living in Bucharest as a ritual butcher (*shoychet*), while serving as a functionary at one of the city's synagogues.[6] The late Chief Rabbi Moses Rosen portrayed him as "an ultra-religious Jew, with many Jewish books, severe and principled concerning the respect of religious norms," who openly opposed the Bucharest rabbinate on the grounds that it did not sufficiently support Jewish religious life. Pauker herself reportedly described him as an unrealistic and "exalted romantic" who on temporal matters forever relied on her mother, Sarah Rabinsohn, an unassuming, enterprising woman, the soul and pillar of the family, and clearly the more practical, business-oriented of the two.[7] The parents generated a meager income, not nearly enough to support their four surviving children (two having died in infancy)[8] or to raise themselves out of extreme poverty. But this hardly seems a family that valued material comfort over religious piety.

Younger sister Bella Rabinsohn's written statement from Pauker's Comintern file reveals that Ana was particularly close to and greatly influenced by her paternal grandfather, "a very interesting rabbi, with culture, intelligence and humanity," and undoubtedly the patriarch of the family. He had personally named Ana at her birth, Bella recalled, "not after someone who had died, as is customary with the Jews, but after Anna [*Chanah* in Hebrew], the mother of the prophet Samuel, a symbol of the purity of the soul and of modesty, as well as after Anna, the woman from the epoch of the Maccabees, who, with a heroism worthy of history," watched before her own death her seven sons savagely murdered for refusing to disavow their God. The grandfather imparted to his young granddaughter his wish that she live a life "worthy of their name." Totally devoted to her erudite and charismatic grandfather, Ana, "not being more than 7 years old," convinced her parents to let her travel the 150-plus miles alone to Codăeşti to be with him.

From the beginning her exceptional intelligence stood out, and by the age of seven she already had learned from him what her sister whimsically described as "the most difficult parts of Jewish studies."[9] While reportedly clashing with her father over her unyielding demand to attend a boys-only *heder* (Hebrew school) in Bucharest, she found an enthusiastic ally in her otherwise tradition-conscious grandfather.[10] Impressed with young Ana's "logic, spirit of observation and *Scharfsinnul*" (sharp mind), the elderly rabbi broke with religious norms of educating only male children and insisted that his granddaughter be sent to school. She attended the Jewish community's Fraternitatea Zion primary school, one of the two Ashkenazi primary schools in Bucharest. Established in 1890, and with a student body of 400, the school was located on the grounds of the Templu Choral synagogue, the most important synagogue in the capital.[11] In 1905 Ana completed the four-year primary course at the top of her class, but despite insisting to her parents that she continue her education, she had to work as a seamstress when they could not pay for further schooling.[12]

Thanks to the intervention of the renowned Rabbi Dr. A. M. Beck, who had taken the precocious young student under his wing, the Raşela şi Filip Focşăneanu professional school soon allowed Ana to continue her studies at deferred cost.[13] This was the only Ashkenazi professional school in Bucharest, with a limited student body of 150.[14] When she completed the program, a combination of trade (tailoring) and scholarly studies, in 1909, Ana was again urged to continue her education, but once more could not afford it. She returned to working as a seamstress in a sweatshop while privately studying with Dr. Beck to take the entrance examinations of a Hebrew-language institute. After she passed the examinations on Hebrew and the Jewish religion, the Fraternitatea Zion school hired her to teach the first grade. She began teaching there in 1910, or possibly 1911.[15]

Though Ana Rabinsohn completed only eight years of formal schooling, she was nevertheless considerably ahead of the vast majority of Jewish women in Eastern Europe at that time. On the whole, in East European Jewish society formal education was the exclusive domain of Jewish males and consisted solely of religious study. This does not mean, however, that Jews necessarily adhered to these prescriptions or that Jewish women were not informally educated; on the contrary, literacy among nineteenth-century Jewish women in Eastern Europe was quite high. Some girls' *hederim* (plural for *heder*) did in fact exist, usually in a separate room of the same building as the boys', and some localities allowed girls to attend the boys' hederim. Moreover, the *Bais Ya'akov* movement, which provided schooling for Jewish girls, also had begun. But the girls as a rule had a different curriculum than did the boys: they were taught in Yiddish (as well as Russian in the Russian Empire), and regularly used Yiddish translations of biblical stories (the *Tse'na Ureena*) and other Yiddish texts written primarily for and read by women; the boys, on the other hand, always learned in Hebrew. Moreover, female hederim were rather rare, and female attendance in male hederim fairly insignificant. Instead, most literate Jewish women apparently learned how to read and write on their own or with the help of friends or relatives. A few of the wealthy had private tutors in their homes. By the 1860s a substantial number of Jewish girls had begun going to modern public and private schools in the various big cities of the region, but there, too, the high cost of tuition restricted attendance to the small affluent minority. In all cases, the education of Jewish girls was as a rule strictly utilitarian, a practical tool for the secular business world. This was true even of the wealthy girls with private tutors and of those attending hederim, where sewing was standard on the girls' curriculum. While boys' education on principle focused on the sacred texts and the spiritual realm, girls were schooled on the mundane issues of work and livelihood.[16]

At first glance it would seem that, despite significant variations, Ana Rabinsohn's experience roughly conformed with this scenario. That her grandfather ignored traditional precepts and tutored Ana as a young child and that she may have gone to a boys' heder briefly was unexceptional. Nor was the curriculum at either the primary or professional schools she attended in any way unique, for her instruction in both practical skills and scholarly subjects fit the current pattern of Jewish female schooling. Indeed, even her special tutorials with Dr. Beck basically fit the general rule, as she was in effect undergoing occupational training to teach at the Fraternitatea Zion school. But on closer examination Rabinsohn's education transcended certain restrictions on a girl's schooling, and she went a step further than practically all her peers. Her grandfather was no ordinary grandfather, but a rabbi, and he did not limit himself to teaching Ana to read and write, as was customary, but taught her an array of intricate Judaic subjects together with her male cousins. Even her mere attendance at a private primary school was unique, as poor families generally could not afford the fees. Her special deferred tuition at the professional school clearly underscores her exemplary, special status among her fellow students. Further, it was still unusual (though it was increasingly becoming less so at that time) that she not only was allowed to learn and matriculate in the Hebrew language but also was tutored in Hebrew only *after* being encouraged to pursue a higher education. True, the study of the sacred texts was still denied her, but otherwise Ana Rabinsohn's gender apparently did not inhibit her formal education, which was, to say the least, exceptional indeed.

What finally prevented Rabinsohn from continuing her studies was her poverty and, most particularly, the state's oppression of Romanian Jewry. In 1893, the year of Ana's birth, the Romanian government barred Jewish children from attending public elementary schools free of charge.[17] It also ruled that "strangers" (Jews) could enter state professional schools only when places were available and on payment of exorbitant fees. Moreover, strangers were permanently ineligible for state scholarships, their numbers could never exceed one-fifth of a school's student body, and they were precluded from attending all agricultural schools. Five years later, the government further excluded Jews from all secondary schools and universities.[18] Thus, if Rabinsohn were ever able to continue her education, she would have to have done so in another country.

This was a period of escalating state anti-Semitism in Romania, where Jews were officially stateless aliens. At the Congress of Berlin in 1878, which led to the creation of an independent Romanian state, the Romanian government rejected Western pressure to naturalize its Jews, adamantly insisting "that there were not, and that there have never been, any Romanian Jews; there were merely Jews, who had been born in the Principality, but who had never been assimilated, either in speech or in custom, by the Romanian nation." Eventually, however, it compromised, agreeing to naturalize Jews on a case-by-case basis. But, of the entire Romanian Jewish community, which numbered 240,000 in 1912, only about 1,000 "exceptions" had obtained Romanian citizenship by the beginning of the First World War.[19] As the Union of Native Jews declared to the Romanian parliament in 1910:

> We have long been the target of a fierce campaign of hatred and defamation, and subjected to legislation that, after declaring us foreigners, has been gradually impoverishing us. But never before has this offensive been conducted with such callousness as of late. For tens of years, law after law has cut down the occupations we are allowed to engage in. . . .
>
> All these measures have obviously been dictated by certain policies aimed at destroying us . . . , and with the ultimate goal of depriving us of any possibility of making a living, and therefore, living in this country. . . .
>
> A deadly war is being waged against us. . . . They sow hatred against us . . . in towns, boroughs and villages. . . . They openly incite violence against us. This is a campaign that uses any weapon and means. . . .
>
> With no reason whatsoever and led only by unsound hatred . . . , people are accusing us of being deadly enemies of whatever is not Jewish, of practicing a morality opposed to universal human principles, of dreaming to dominate the entire world, and, particularly, of seeking the destruction of this country.[20]

By the time this manifesto formally protested the policies of each successive government since 1864, Romania had become a symbol for uncompromising anti-Semitism. Ironically, though, that nation had not been known historically either for violence against Jews or for intolerance of its ethnic minorities.[21] Under various princes of the Wallachian and Moldavian Principalities, the Jews enjoyed many liberties up through the end of the eighteenth century and were, for the most part, living peacefully at the beginning of the nineteenth.[22] But in the early 1700s a long-festering religious Judeophobia led to outbreaks of church-inspired accusations of ritual murder.[23] The accusations reached epidemic levels by the end of the century and culminated in a bloody pogrom in Bucharest that killed 128 Jews in 1801.[24] This heritage assured a preponderance of anti-Jewish sentiment by the time modern anti-Semitism erupted as a major force of Romanian nationalism and as a corollary to nineteenth-century socioeconomic circumstances.

Romanian nationalism was intrinsically connected to one central fact: the lands comprising modern Romania had suffered under foreign domination for centuries and were subjected to successive waves of foreign rule. Even the most prominent families who made up the landed gentry in the country (the boyars) were in large part of Greek (Phanariot) extraction, having taken the place of the original Romanian nobility. Consequently, fear and loathing of foreigners—be they the Turks, who invaded and occupied the country; the Hungarians, who were seen as oppressors of Romanians in Transylvania; the Russians, the conquerors and occupiers of Romanian lands; or the Greeks (especially in the eighteenth century) and the Jews, who were both "imbued with all the moral defects of *the internal foreigner*"—were conspicuous in Romanian nationalism from the beginning. This was, moreover, characteristic of nationalism in Eastern Europe generally, where constant oppression created in its various peoples a pronounced suspicion (if not hatred) of anyone even nominally different, as well as an impassioned bitterness toward foreigners. But Romania clearly took it to an extreme. "Hostility to foreigners," Romanian essayist and philosopher Emil Cioran noted, "is so characteristic of Romanian national feeling that the two will always be inseparable. The first national reaction of the Romanian is not pride in the destiny of Romania, or a sentiment of glory, which is a hallmark of French patriotism, but revolt against foreigners, often aired as a swear word, and sometimes crystallized in a durable hatred. . . . We have lived under foreigners for 1,000 years; not to hate them and not to eliminate them would demonstrate an absence of national instinct." Or as historian and economist B. P. Haşdeu put it in 1871, "Foreigners at the head of the state, foreigners in the ministries, foreigners in parliament, foreigners in the magistracy, foreigners at the bar, foreigners in medicine, foreigners in finances, foreigners in trade, foreigners in publicism, foreigners in public works, foreigners up, foreigners down and yet—*Romanism is on the move.*" [25]

Modern Romanian nationalism, then, was a conscious rebellion against both external enemies and "foreign" elements residing in the country—elements that played a crucial socioeconomic role in the nineteenth century. The country's traditionally agrarian economy had long consisted almost exclusively of poor peasants living under the harsh rule of the boyars, with no significant middle class or urban life. But the 1829 Treaty of Adrianople changed this abruptly, ending Turkey's monopoly over commerce in the Danubian Principalities (Wallachia and Moldavia) and opening them to international trade in 1830. Romania's medieval socioeconomic order made trade with Western Europe even more difficult and had to be reformed as quickly as possible. The large landowners, moreover, found themselves in dire need of capital as Western imported goods became more readily available in Romania. They thus began to lease their land and contract out their monopoly rights on holding shops and stores and on selling meat and alcohol to a growing number of merchants and traders setting up marketplaces (*târguri*) on parts of the big estates. Romanians traditionally rejected trading. The peasants showed little inclination for it until the beginning of the twentieth century, and the boyars shunned it as demeaning, preferring absentee landowning or the civil service. An imported merchant class filled the role, settling in Romania under the protection of foreign emissaries. The few existing traditional artisan and trade guilds soon collapsed under the competition from these foreign traders, and the latter quickly emerged as the first true middle class in Romania's history, sandwiched between the boyars and the peasant masses. [26]

The foreign traders in Romania were overwhelmingly Greeks, Armenians, Bulgarians, and Serbs during the first half of the nineteenth century. They gradually assimilated into Romanian society (particularly the Greeks and Armenians) and entered politics and the liberal professions. [27] Increasingly taking their place in trade were three groups of Jews: the *pământeni,* or "native Jews," a well-established community who had lived in the principalities for centuries; the *hrişovelţi,* or "charter Jews," a number of Jewish merchants from the Russian Empire who between 1780 and 1850 were naturalized by special charters after certain boyars solicited their immigration to help establish small towns; and two waves of illegal Jewish immigrants, the first fleeing Russia during its occupation of Romania from 1829 to 1856, often to avoid the infamous Cantonists Decree (a Russian law that forcibly drafted Jews into the Russian army for twenty-five years), and the second, mostly from Galicia and Russia, arriving in ever greater numbers from the mid–nineteenth century on.[28] Barred from owning land (since 1830) and from entering nearly all professions (until 1919), the Jews were forced to engage in trading, moneylending, and particularly artisan work. In so doing they played a conspicuous and significant role in urbanizing and developing Moldavian markets.[29] Jews made up as much as 50 percent of the population of small Moldavian *bourgs* (villages) and 35 percent of the Moldavian towns throughout the nineteenth century (reaching no less than 57.7 percent of the population in the Moldavian capital of Iaşi by the end of the century). They often were the only people with trade contacts abroad. Moreover, newly constituted Jewish entrepreneurs owned most of Bukovinian industry, particularly lumber. At the same time, a small class of urban Jews, especially in Wallachia, underwent embourgeoisement and acculturation by excelling in commerce, industry, journalism, and medicine.[30] As in Poland, however, Jews generally comprised the urban bourgeoisie in Romania's most impoverished regions (northern Moldavia, Bukovina, Bessarabia, parts of northern Transylvania). Yet also as in Poland, their overwhelming majority nonetheless remained steeped in poverty.[31] Their poverty, however, had little impact on Romanian nationalist ideology, which exhibited an anti-Semitism with classic characteristics of a crisis of modernization. All the social tensions of modernization and newly emerging capitalism, deemed consequences of an "evil urbanization" and an erosion of a "spiritually pure" rural life, were blamed squarely on the Jewish minority.[32]

Center stage in Romania's nationalist indictment of Jews was the "Peasant Question." The British consul general observed in the early 1800s, "[t]here does not perhaps exist a people laboring under a greater degree of oppression from the effect of despotic power and more heavily burdened with impositions and taxes than the peasants of Moldavia and Wallachia." Little was done to alleviate the peasants' plight at any time in the nineteenth century. A partial land reform in 1864 did practically nothing to relieve their wretched poverty and dependence on the big landowners. The small plots many peasants received could hardly support a family, so the peasants had to labor on large estates simply to make ends meet. By 1907, fully 60 percent of Romania's peasants held such inadequate holdings or no land at all (including those whose plots produced a bare subsistence brings the number to 85 percent), while the latifundia of the boyars comprised no less than half of all arable and grazing land in the country.[33]

In many areas, particularly Moldavia, Romania's tormented and subjugated peasantry increasingly found themselves in direct contact more with Jewish middlemen than with the thriving boyar landlords. Jews were most likely the rural traders and merchants who provided household goods that the peasants could not obtain elsewhere and in turn bought their surplus produce for desperately needed hard currency; they were most likely the artisans upon whom the peasants relied in the newly emerging towns and urban communities, introducing a whole variety of trades to the agrarian landscape; they were most likely the tavern keepers, the distillers, and the mill and lumber operators; and they were most likely the moneylenders to whom the debt-ridden peasants must turn (the state would not lend them money) to pay off their meager and insufficient land holdings. The Jews thus introduced monetary exchange into rural Romania's traditional subsistence farming system, thereby contributing to its transformation into a modern, capitalistic economy. At the same time, they became, at least since the last third of the nineteenth century, the perfect scapegoat for Romanian nationalists, who disingenuously held all Jews uniformly responsible for the peasantry's tragic plight.[34]

"The Jewish population," a recent study noted, "became a *problem* the moment the upper class of Romanian society was fully aware of its inability to solve the serious social problems brought on by the political evolution of Romania in those years." Though the socioeconomic system was rapidly changing in a frenzied attempt to adapt to Western standards after the country was opened to international trade, many problems remained: the absolute power of the ruling circles, the corruption and graft in the government, the poverty of the peasants, and the wide-ranging discontent. Promises were routinely made to the peasants regarding impending land reform, such as an 1859 assurance of Ion Brătianu to a delegation of tenant farmers that they would definitely receive land once the principalities were unified. But the boyars, who never developed the slightest sense of noblesse oblige, refused to countenance such an improvement in the peasants' conditions, as it would have threatened their protracted class privileges. They unceremoniously overthrew Prince Alexandru Ion Cuza in 1866 after he dared to abolish serfdom officially and implemented a limited land reform despite their objections. Then they passed several regulations against the peasants in Parliament to undercut the prince's reforms—reforms they depicted as part of a "Jewish policy" harmful to the interests of the Romanian nation.[35]

As a result, spontaneous, violent peasant rebellions continuously erupted for the next forty-three years: between 1864 (the year of Cuza's ineffectual land reform) and 1907 thousands of local and regional uprisings shook the country, all calamitous precursors to Romania's Great Peasant Revolt of 1907.[36] Authorities responded with a twofold policy, forcefully crushing the *jacqueries,* often with great bloodshed, all the while striving to deflect peasant anger to a predictable, convenient target. The Jews were not only to serve as the boyars' middlemen, but also to take the blame for the neofeudal order the boyars fought to preserve.[37] At the same time nationalist intellectuals, who worried that the struggle for social reform would unduly weaken the precarious Romanian state, refused to jeopardize national cohesion by genuinely backing peasant rights.[38] Both groups commenced, therefore, to blame the Jews for Romania's agrarian problem. The Jews, they repeatedly declared, were the "bloodsuckers of the villages," the "sore of the peasantry," the "poisoners" of the peasants, "evil parasites" and "lepers" who "earn without working," the "village leeches" who live off the sweat of peasant labor.[39]

As an immediate, preliminary step to stop the rebellions, the authorities canceled all debts to Jewish moneylenders in areas affected by peasant unrest and then expelled the Jews wholesale from the villages in question.[40] The expulsions began in 1867, immediately after Interior Minister Ion Brătianu prohibited Jews from settling in the villages and rural regions and ordered "vagabond" Jews—he called them "helpless and filthy Jews" who could not find jobs—expelled forthwith.[41] The latter was essentially a reinstatement of Paragraph 94 of the 1834 Organic Laws instituted by the Russian occupying authorities, expelling vagabond Jews or Jews with "no useful trade."[42] The expulsions always occurred where peasants were rebelling, even in urban towns in the vicinity of the revolts (such as Ploeşti in 1870) that were arbitrarily reinvented as rural villages to drive out the Jews.[43] They were part of an ongoing process affecting a large number of mostly Moldavian Jews. The Romanian press never reported the process and successive Romanian regimes persistently disputed it, but it continued unabated until the First World War.[44] The expulsions led to countless horrific injustices, including a particularly odious 1867 incident in Galaţi, where Jewish vagabonds drowned while being forcibly deported across the Danube River.[45] In some areas Jews eventually were allowed to return to their homes, "until," one historian suggested, "the next diversion was needed. The continual expulsions from the villages," he added, "led to the impoverishment of the Jewish masses, and to a degradation and deterioration of their character. The insecurity at times caused certain Jews to be more grabbing and more predatory, seeking illicit profits, and thus providing new pretexts for xenophobia. This vicious circle continued until World War One."[46]

The situation deteriorated further when the Great Peasant Revolt in 1907 brought the issue of Jewish *arendaşi* (tenant contractors) to the fore.[47] The arendaşi became a Romanian institution when absentee landowning in the country escalated from the mid–nineteenth century on, as the boyars, who preferred to live in Bucharest and other European capitals, increasingly leased their estates to tenant contractors. "By 1900," Henry L. Roberts reported, "56 per cent of the area of properties over 50 hectares and more than 72 per cent of the vast estates over 5,000 hectares were being leased, for the most part not to individual peasants but to large tenants."[48] As for the Jews' specific role in this phenomenon, widely regarded as considerable and largely detrimental, scholarly research has determined that the vast majority (72.6%) of the country's arendaşi were in fact ethnic-Romanians. Indeed, Romanians comprised the majority of arendaşi even in Jewish-dominated Moldavia, though Jewish contractors were conspicuously prominent there.[49] (One Austrian-Jewish family, the Fischer brothers, controlled 75 percent of Suceava, Dorohoi, and Botoşani Counties.)[50] Research has also found that the Jewish arendaşi initially benefited the estates they administered. They were, in effect, agricultural entrepreneurs who invested either liquid capital or agricultural equipment, improved farming methods, hired workers, and overhauled the estates' mills and distilleries to maximize profits in domestic and foreign markets. In short, they tried to transform often moribund, revenue-depleting estates into viable, modern enterprises.[51]

After 1875, however, the Romanian economy suffered a severe downturn due to dropping agricultural prices throughout Europe and the United States' gradual dominance of the European wheat market. Romania's decreasing market share froze modernization on its estates, as both landowners and tenant contractors sought to make up for lost income by further exploiting peasant workers rather than expanding mechanization. Gross speculation proliferated as profit margins tumbled: the boyars hiked the leases of all tenant contractors, who in turn squeezed their peasant laborers or their renters, further worsening the peasants' predicament and adding to peasant unrest. Perhaps inevitably, the peasant was often more inclined to blame the middleman with whom he dealt than to blame the absentee landlord, probably even more so if that middleman were a Jew, whom he generally viewed as an alien intruder. Too, Christian arendași could own their own land and thus were often local farmers seeking to enhance their holdings through tenant contracting; the Jews, on the other hand, were prohibited from owning land and could only lease it for five years.[52]

One can only speculate whether these restrictions—as did the expulsions—led some Jewish arendași to turn quick, short-term profits and thus become more exploitative of a land and peasantry with whom they had less connection than did their Christian counterparts. Likewise, one can only speculate to what extent the increasing incitement by government propagandists as well as village priests and teachers[53] generated peasant hostility against the Jews. But one point is beyond conjecture: despite beginning in Moldavia on lands leased by a Jewish tenant contractor (Mochi Fischer), the Great Peasant Revolt ultimately was only indirectly connected to the Jews. It was instead a general social rebellion against neoserfdom and escalating poverty that quickly engulfed the entire country.[54] The Romanian authorities, who massacred thousands of peasants in their panic-stricken efforts to end the unrest, clearly understood this. King Carol in fact rejected the notion that the Revolt was fundamentally anti-Semitic, on the grounds that "for every two Jews assaulted there are 100 dead Christians" as a consequence of the unrest.[55] Nevertheless, the Revolt was predictably "interpreted by those responsible for [the country's] socioeconomic abuses as a victory for the cause of nationalism, as a patriotic manifestation by a Romanian peasantry against oppression by foreigners—the Jews."[56] Forever citing the Revolt's point of origin, the term *Fischerland* (for the Fischer brothers) was repeatedly employed to illustrate the extent of "Jewish exploitation."[57] Hastily enacted legislation again ordering the expulsion of all foreigners from Romania's villages was immediately carried out with unprecedented zeal. All Jews (some 2,800 people), for instance, were expelled from the villages in Iași and Dorohoi Counties; they were, moreover, given forty-eight hours to evacuate their homes in Bacău County; and their banishment from Vaslui County, where Pauker's grandparents resided, was particularly ruthless.[58]

Hence diversion was a key element in Romanian anti-Semitism, but it was by no means the only element. While the landlords and their allies opportunistically played the Jewish card for their own purposes, the most consistently avid anti-Semites appeared actually to come from other quarters, a nascent native middle class that coveted the very "parasitic" positions that Jews were condemned for holding in Romanian society. As in all of Europe, Romania's population exploded throughout the nineteenth century; this, coupled with the economic crisis of the 1870s and the resultant deteriorating conditions in the countryside, led to a mass peasant migration to the towns and cities. There, as elsewhere in East-Central Europe, these uprooted peasants became unskilled urban laborers and often worked under already established Jewish artisans, merchants, and businessmen. Resenting their subordinate position to an often unassimilated and Yiddish-speaking "alien" minority, they began to view the Jews as their principal enemy. Hence many began "making their way, with elbows and fists if necessary, soliciting, claiming, and imposing their presence with the supreme argument: I am Romanian! If this could not easily be demonstrated due to their ethnicity (be it Greek, Bulgarian, Armenian, etc.), their argument had to be more decisively stated: I am a Christian! . . . The Jews were the competitors. They *took* the positions that the Romanians wanted, and since the Romanians considered that those positions were theirs, the Jews had to be replaced by all means!" [59]

Nationalist elements immediately took up the call, demanding the wholesale removal of Jewish industrial and commercial pioneers to make way for this incipient Romanian middle class. Ion Brătianu candidly told members of his government in 1880, "Our goal must be to completely remove our Jews from the Romanian economic sphere." [60] Thus the state fully utilized its power to redistribute Jewish-held positions among ethnic-Romanians. In 1864, even before Cuza's overthrow, the Romanian Parliament prohibited Jews from working as peddlers, thereby depriving 20,000 of them of their only income.[61] On December 4 of that year, the Jews were forbidden to be lawyers; on December 27, 1868, they were officially excluded from Romania's state-administered medical profession; on January 15, 1869, they were barred from being tax-farmers in rural communes; on October 25, 1869, they were prevented from working as apothecaries except where no ethnic-Romanian ones could be found; on February 15, 1872, they were forbidden to be tobacco dealers; on April 1, 1873, they were precluded from selling liquor in rural areas; on August 4 and September 5, 1873, they were prohibited from being chief physicians of sanitary districts; on June 8–10, 1874, they were eliminated as chief physicians of districts and hospitals and told that "strangers" could remain directors of pharmacies only until

1878 (unless ethnic-Romanians were not available), when all new pharmacies were to be run solely by "Romanians"; on June 6, 1880, they
were barred from serving as directors and auditors of the National Bank
of Romania; on June 16, 1886, they were advised that henceforth drug-
gists could only be "Romanians" or naturalized citizens; on December 7, 1886, all businesses were forbidden from keeping their account
books in Yiddish; on February 28, 1887, they were officially banned from
being state employees of the Romanian kingdom; on May 22, 1887,
they learned that the majority of administrators of all private businesses
were henceforth to be "Romanians"; on May 24, 1887, they were apprised of a new law mandating that two-thirds of the work force of all
factories must be "Romanians" within five years of a factory's establishment; and on March 16, 1902, Jewish artisans, totaling 30,000
heads of families supporting 100,000 dependents, found their livelihood
suddenly threatened with the passage of the Artisan Bill, which would
preclude Jews from any kind of artisan or handicraft trade.[62]

"In Romania," noted one contemporary observer, "a Jew cannot
even be a street-sweeper, as this is a state job."[63] Even the Romanian
Orthodox Church, departing from standard procedure of proselytizing
non-Christians, "refused to convert Jews, lest they claim any economic
rights whatsoever"; instead, the church endorsed boycotting the Jews
and throwing them out of the country.[64] To be a Jew in Romania in the
late nineteenth and early twentieth centuries was to be a stateless outcast, an annoying impediment to national renewal to be excised from
the body politic like a malignant cancer. Anti-Semitism, often translating into violence, had become endemic to Romanian nationalists of all
persuasions.[65] Not in the least considered an extreme position during
this period, it "took its place matter of factly as a presupposed element
of the intelligentsia's outlook on life. To be Romanian," one scholar concluded, "was to be instinctively anti-Jewish."[66]

This hostility directly affected Ana Rabinsohn in more injurious
ways. Her father told political journalist Judd Teller in 1949 that Ana
fled an anti-Semitic disturbance in Bucharest in 1906, being only twelve
at the time. She arrived home sobbing and lay delirious in bed for almost
a week. "Thereafter," Hersh Rabinsohn added, "she refused to speak
Yiddish, which was the tongue our entire household spoke. It is then,
perhaps, that I should have sat 'shiva' [the Jewish mourning ritual for
relatives of the dead] for her." It was the old man's assumption, Teller
noted, that his daughter's traumatic encounter was "related to her ultimate defection from Jews." Whether Rabinsohn was actually referring

to Orthodox Jewry when speaking of his daughter's "defection" is not clear, but Teller concludes that Pauker's ordeal had the same impact that similar traumas had on Ferdinand Lasalle and Rosa Luxemburg and suggests that each of these experiences engendered a palpable self-hatred "characteristic to most Jews attracted to radicalism." [67]

These persistent claims about Ana Pauker fail to explain why she went on not only to learn Hebrew, but to teach it to others and to continue doing so for two years after joining the socialist movement, stopping only because she lost her job.[68] Likewise, attributing her refusal to speak Yiddish at home to simple self-hatred ignores an important point: Romania's political restrictions did *not* prevent Ana Rabinsohn (or a considerable number of other Romanian Jews, particularly in Bucharest) from assimilating into, and identifying with, Romanian society. This was apparently more pronounced among Jewish women than Jewish men.[69] Among other factors, the traditional Jewish practice of denying women the study of the sacred texts inadvertently facilitated their more rapid assimilation and secularization, for they were allowed instead to read literature and secular works while men were expected to read only the holy books. Thus precisely because of their limited educational opportunities, East European Jewish women were freer than men to pursue secular learning and were therefore more exposed to, and presumably more enamored with, the culture of the outside world.[70] This was certainly the case with Ana Rabinsohn, who, her sister Bella recalled, became an avid reader during childhood.[71] Ana's reading no doubt inspired her to venture beyond the confines of her Jewish environment. But since no Reform Judaism movement existed in Eastern Europe and Jews, therefore, were either Orthodox or secular but nothing in between, any Jew who sought a more modern or cosmopolitan life than found in the traditional, Jewish Orthodox world essentially had only one option: assimilating out of the Jewish fold.[72] A great many East European Jewish women chose to do exactly that, Rabinsohn clearly among them.

Assimilation's effect on Rabinsohn's self-image as a Jew is an open question, though a certain self-hating has been attributed to assimilated Jews of her generation—especially, though by no means exclusively, in Germany. During the twenty-year period between 1894 and 1914, the years when Rabinsohn was growing up, observers "had become painfully aware of a particularly unhealthy attitude among young Jews toward themselves as individuals, toward the Jewish group, its values and its preoccupations, and that many had inadvertently skidded into accepting the anti-Semites' stereotype of the Jew." [73] Rabinsohn, too, seems to have been influenced at the time by published anti-Semitic stereotypes of Jews in traditionally Jewish occupations. As her sister Bella recounted in her Comintern declaration, "at the age of 18 or 19 [in 1912 or 1913], under the influence of Freytag's book *Soll und Haben,* [Ana] was able to convince her mother to give up her 'hateful' occupation as a small-time food seller, and thus, snatching away the independence of mother, completely changed the financial situation of the family."[74]

The book in question, Gustav Freytag's *Debit and Credit (Soll und Haben)*, one of the most popular German novels of the nineteenth century, critically portrays a Jewish merchant house in a stereotypically horrendous light. The book's underlying message, effectively argued by Freytag, is that the only good Jew is the assimilating, disappearing Jew, as opposed to the contemptuous mass in the traditional Jewish milieu. This concept was widely subscribed to by German Jewry, who read the book and embraced its stereotypes with remarkable unanimity; indeed, doing so "became a sign of Jewish assimilation" in fin de siècle German society.[75] If her sister Bella's account is correct, this may have been true of Ana Rabinsohn, to some degree.

In addition, when she formally became a socialist in 1915, Rabinsohn was most likely influenced by the then near unanimous attitude on the Jewish Question within the socialist movement, which, like Freytag, favored the assimilation, and thus the disappearance, of the Jews into European society.[76] At that time the undisputed orthodox Marxist theoretician was Karl Kautsky of the Austrian Social Democratic Party, whom every socialist party in Europe considered the most respected interpreter of Marxism. Kautsky's theories were even more influential on the Jewish Question, as nearly all Marxists (including the Bolsheviks) regarded him as an authority on the subject.[77] In Kautsky's estimation, the Jews had no place in the future socialist world. They had survived as a nation throughout the centuries only because they performed exclusive economic functions in the countries where they lived. During the Middle Ages they were at once a nation and a class of merchants and usurers in Europe and thus became indispensable in precapitalist society.[78] "To be Jewish in the Middle Ages," Kautsky wrote, "did not mean only being a member of a particular nation but also of a particular profession. To be Jewish meant to be a usurer and vice versa; the Jewish character became that of the usurer and that of the usurer the Jew."[79] With capitalism's onset, however, the Jews became stratified into other occupations, thereby ending both their previous economic function and their raison d'être as a separate entity.[80] The only thing now uniting them, Kautsky reasoned, was anti-Semitism;[81] for they were not really a nation in the modern sense of the word, possessing no territory and speaking what he considered a "nonlanguage," but were instead a "caste."[82] Thus the Jews would quickly disappear with the complete emancipation that socialism undoubtedly would bring. Unlike the American Indians' disappearance, this was not to be regretted, because the Jews essentially would be rising to a higher level of human activity and progress.[83] "We will not have completely emerged from the Middle Ages," Kautsky concluded, "as long as Judaism still remains among us. The more quickly it disappears, the better it will be for society and for the Jews themselves."[84]

Kautsky was assuredly wrong both about the Jews' playing an exclusive economic role and about their inability to survive outside that role, but his position did not necessarily imply anti-Semitism or ill will.[85] Nor, for that matter, did Freytag's position when writing *Soll und Haben*. Neither Kautsky nor Freytag was an anti-Semite in the political sense of the term,[86] but both believed in and promoted anti-Jewish stereotypes that greatly detracted from the Jews' already degraded image. In truth, a vast number of European Jews who desired and actively worked for the betterment of world Jewry did precisely the same thing. Many in the Zionist movement, too, subscribed to the most appalling stereotypes of the very people for whom they struggled, as did persons of *all* modern Jewish ideologies. All evinced a "self-denigrating apologia regarding the image of the Jew in the modern world" that was the direct product of Jewish assimilation and that affected all types of assimilated Jews, not just those attracted to radicalism.[87] This self-denigration was discernible, therefore, not only among those who cut all ties with Jews and Judaism, but among any Jew who assimilated and struggled to integrate into the modern world—including those who continued to empathize with Jews and, indeed, even those who devoted their lives to them.

Likewise, the young Ana Rabinsohn may have been self-denigrating to a greater or lesser degree, but if she were, it did not prevent her from continuing to work in and sympathize with the Jewish milieu for a considerable time. In addition to teaching Hebrew, she enthusiastically collaborated with a group of young affluent Jews who established a hostel for poor Jewish children, working incessantly to keep the hostel running for several years after she became a socialist. In 1918, she personally took part in defense units protecting Jews against pogroms then breaking out in Bucharest. And during the first half of the 1920s, while firmly entrenched in the Communist movement, she continued to associate with Jewish intellectuals, frequenting an innovative Jewish bookstore called Hasefer.[88]

Still, as with many modern Jews, Rabinsohn's loyalties remained manifold and contradictory. In addition to her political allegiances, her continuing association with the Jewish community went hand in hand with an increasing identification with the Romanian people. This dichotomy was not unlike that of Rabinsohn's future husband, Marcel Pauker, whom she met in 1918.[89] In contrast with Ana, Marcel left a lengthy autobiography, intricately detailing his political beliefs and motivations. Born and raised in a "completely Romanianized" Jewish household in Bucharest, Marcel Pauker was assimilated to a much greater degree than Ana Rabinsohn. Although he insistently acknowledged his Jewish origins and participated in various acts of solidarity with the Jewish community, his sense of identity clearly lay elsewhere. Like Rabinsohn, he lived a great deal of time in the Romanian countryside throughout his childhood, spending "four or five months out of the year, working in the fields . . . , [and] participating in the life and pain of the village with youthful enthusiasm. . . . I was . . . able," he wrote, "to get to know from below the cannibalistic exploitation of the peasant . . . , and I developed a deep love for our gentle and tortured Romanian people." Indeed, his passion for the peasants' plight was his primary attraction to socialism, for while "the situation of the peasantry was very clear to me," he suggested, ". . . the secrets of capitalist production were less clear."[90] Considering her actions once in power, Ana Pauker seems to have shared these ideas to an extent. At the very least, they influenced her considerably, for she would emerge as the Romanian peasantry's principal defender among the country's Communist leaders.

CHAPTER TWO

In the Movement

In 1915 Ana Rabinsohn walked into a club of the Romanian Workers' Social Democratic Party (RWSDP) on 12 Sfântul Ionică Street in Bucharest and formally registered as a party member. "I entered the workers movement," she later declared, "revolted by the social injustice I saw and knew about, and because, from what I read, I viewed the working class as an oppressed class that was fighting against exploitation and social injustice." [1] Evidently she also did so under the influence of Henry Steinberg, a fellow teacher at the school where she taught. They met and became lovers in 1911, when she was seventeen. He regularly gave her socialist writings and accompanied her to May Day gatherings in the forests just outside Bucharest. [2] In joining the socialists, Rabinsohn became part of a coterie of young Jewish women who flocked to radicalism from the last third of the nineteenth century on. Specifically, she was one of a second generation of Jewish radical women who entered the General Jewish Labor Bund, the Mensheviks, the Bolsheviks, and various Marxist and Socialist Zionist parties at the turn of the century and later. These women came from Jewish *shtetls* in the Pale of Settlement and elsewhere and emerged from the heart of the Jewish community. That Rabinsohn came from Romania's impoverished Jewish masses undoubtedly added anti-Semitic persecution to her motives to join the socialists, for the myriad of anti-Jewish laws and decrees passed in the late nineteenth and early twentieth centuries in Romania was catastrophic for poor Jews, while hurting much less the majority of affluent and upper-middle-class Romanian Jewry.[3]

Unlike the Russian Empire, Romania completely lacked radical movements. The General Jewish Labor Bund, to which the vast majority of radical Jewish women then belonged,[4] did not exist in Romania (except for Bessarabia), and the Socialist Zionist parties in the country were still rudimentary. In any case, Ana Rabinsohn's preference for revolutionary internationalism typified many female members during the Bund's formative years. Women at that time comprised at least half, and possibly the majority, of the Bund's workers' circles, which staunchly advocated a more centralized, conspiratorial movement that focused on education as a prerequisite to revolutionary action.[5] Highly influenced by revolutionary internationalism, the workers' groups waged a two-year battle to maintain Russian as the language of use within the Bund, as they were primarily interested in bettering themselves personally and getting ahead in the non-Jewish, Russian world. Ironically, cosmopolitan intellectuals who had personally witnessed the Dreyfus Affair while in the West and thus were markedly disillusioned with the Left's failure to respond to anti-Semitic persecution, called for the Bund to focus on Yiddish-based agitation among the Jewish masses and to adopt a more Jewish-centered revolutionary program.[6] Hence Rabinsohn's attraction to revolutionary internationalism was hardly unique among radical Jewish women and poor Jewish workers of her generation.

Soon after registering as a member of the RWSDP, Rabinsohn was assigned to work at the party organization's disbursement office in Bucharest.[7] She continued working as a Hebrew and Jewish studies teacher for two years after joining the movement, having transferred from the primary school to the professional school she attended only a short time earlier. She was, her sister Bella recalled, highly popular among both colleagues and students, and was in fact "the most beloved professor the school ever had up till then." However, she soon refused, for ideological reasons, to continue to instruct her students in religion.[8] She was fired in 1917, after being warned, for teaching them revolutionary songs.[9] Thereupon she resorted to tutoring children from wealthy families, which she already had started doing to supplement her income from teaching , as more and more families hired a tutor rather than risk sending their children to school after the German bombardment of Bucharest in the fall of 1916.[10] At the time, Rabinsohn's Social Democratic activities were limited mostly to working in the party's disbursement office and attending various rallies and meetings in 1915 and 1916. When

the RWSDP was outlawed soon after Romania entered the war, Rabinsohn and other members were further confined to meeting at the party's
library, where they discussed and studied the war's progress and the February and October Revolutions in Russia.[11]

The RWSDP was a small and inconsequential movement when Rabinsohn formally joined, and socialism's success was consistently remote.
Both were first introduced in Romania by two disparate groups: one
made up of Russian immigrants, the most important of whom was Constantin Dobregeanu-Gherea (1855–1920), a Ukrainian Jew originally
named Nahum Katz;[12] the other comprised of young Romanian intellectuals from mostly aristocratic backgrounds (dubbed "The Generous"),
who brought their socialism back from their studies in France. The Generous soon became disillusioned with the country's backward social
conditions and abandoned the movement, leaving it to the "foreigners"
(Dobregeanu-Gherea, along with the Bulgarian Christian Rakovsky) to
rebuild the party during the first decade of the twentieth century. From
then on, however, the Social Democrats made little headway among the
ethnic-Romanians. They had few adherents among the Romanian intelligentsia, the great majority of whom supported the Rightist National
Liberal and Conservative parties for reasons that were as practical as
they were ideological: the intellectuals, who were repelled by the socialists' pronounced internationalism, were largely employed in a civil service controlled by the two ruling parties. The RWSDP, therefore, relied on
the working class for its membership much more than did similar parties elsewhere in East-Central Europe, but the industrial proletariat then
comprised only 2 percent of Romania's population (100,000 persons).[13]
On the eve of the First World War it included a large percentage of Jewish
workers and urban artisans.[14] Hence the socialists' insignificant numbers and non–ethnic-Romanian composition, and hence their virtual isolation from the Romanian masses and near total political irrelevance.

With the end of the war, the RWSDP resumed activity in Romania,
though it was now severely split between radicals and moderates. The
Social Democrats consistently opposed the war, and when Romania
broke its neutrality to declare war on Austria-Hungary in 1916, the
government subjected them to massive repression.[15] Consequently most
of the party's radical leaders fled to Russia, leaving the top posts to
the more moderate elements. At the same time, however, the repression further radicalized the party's rank and file. More and more activists openly identified with the October Revolution and favored adopting illegal, underground methods to start an immediate revolution in

Romania. These members established a pro-Bolshevik "Maximalist" faction—or what Ana Pauker labeled the *Sfatul secret* (Secret Council)—within the RWSDP ranks that challenged the party leadership's more orthodox-Marxist policies.[16]

At the same time, hundreds of thousands of Russian soldiers had inundated Romania, and their enthusiasm for the Bolshevik Revolution a few months earlier spread through the country like wildfire. With the nation's economy near the breaking point, conditions developed that both the socialists and the government recognized as truly revolutionary. Strikes broke out throughout the country, with 250 taking place in 1919, jumping to 750 in 1920, and all becoming "a battle ground between communist militants and the moderates of the Socialist Party." Though in no way controlling the strikes, the radicals set out to infuse them with their own political demands, issuing clandestine manifestos behind the backs of, and in open revolt against, the RWSDP leadership. Their efforts quickly bore results: by 1919 they had become the party's predominant force in Bucharest, the largest and most powerful section in the country.[17]

Participating in the Secret Council, Rabinsohn began to engage in various illegal activities during 1918—distributing illegal manifestos, working as a clandestine messenger in various parts of the country, assisting imprisoned party activists, and taking part in defense units battling pogromists then attacking Bucharest's Jewish community.[18] But she probably never was more than a marginal player during this period, as indicated by her soon leaving for Switzerland despite the acute and ever increasing revolutionary fervor. Learning that she could complete her secondary studies and take high school matriculation exams far more easily there, Rabinsohn resolved to leave for Switzerland, with the goal of entering medical school upon returning to Romania. In 1918 she took a job cataloging the library of industrialist Heinrich Fischer and began saving for the trip. Assisted by one of her younger brothers, she was able to leave for Switzerland in September 1919.[19]

Rabinsohn's departure, though perhaps oddly timed, is not altogether surprising, for she was always intensely preoccupied with finishing her education.[20] At the same time, however, her relationship with Marcel Pauker likely influenced her decision. She later wrote that she left for Switzerland "with the help of some party comrades at the time."[21] Marcel Pauker was most likely one of them. Coming from a well-off Romanian Jewish family, he was certainly in a position to help Rabinsohn financially, and he had left for Switzerland at the beginning of 1919 to complete his studies in engineering.[22] Rabinsohn's trip was hardly a matter of her simply following Pauker to Switzerland, as she clearly pursued her own agenda there and, moreover, lived in Geneva while he lived in Zurich. Yet he must have had a powerful pull on her. Pauker was handsome, dynamic, and self-assured. Passionate by nature, fervently idealistic, highly impulsive, and stubbornly independent, he was unflinching in his beliefs to the point of impudence. Though only in his mid-twenties when he became a leader of Romanian Communism in the early 1920s, he never hesitated to brashly criticize the more experienced and respected party veterans, be they fellow Romanians, renowned Bulgarian Communists who served as his mentors, the prominent Hungarian economist Eugen Varga (with whom he clashed on the issue of agrarian problems in Southeastern Europe at the Comintern's Fourth World Congress), or even high-level Comintern and Soviet functionaries; nor, when writing an autobiographical statement in Moscow in November 1937, at the height of the Great Terror in the Soviet Union, did he flinch from noting his "love of country and [Romanian] patriotism," or his reproach of his father "for having been ashamed of his Jewish origins," when both attitudes were clearly taboo under the rubric of full-fledged Stalinism.[23] Whatever led her to Switzerland, Rabinsohn would be indelibly influenced by this charismatic and controversial figure and was no doubt thoroughly enamored with him.

During her year and a half in Geneva, Ana Rabinsohn became acquainted with such leading socialists as Rene Lachenal, Humbert Droz, Henry Barbuse, Stasia Stanislavskaia, Platten Nicoll, and others. She also consorted with a group of Communist students—among whom, one account reported, was the Romanian Jew Tristan Tzara, soon to be known as the father of Dadaism.[24] Contradicting a 1921 report that she was the secretary of a group of Romanian Communist students in Geneva and in that capacity regularly corresponded by courier with party officials in both Romania and Russia, she later asserted that she kept no contact with the socialist movement in Romania, and limited her political activities in Geneva to occasional participation in meetings and rallies.[25]

Instead, it appears that Rabinsohn was mostly preoccupied with her studies and preparing for the matriculation exams, "which," her sister Bella recalled, "was extraordinarily difficult for her, as she was completely unprepared." Moreover, her tenuous financial situation soon worsened when Fischer failed to send salary payments he owed her, and her impoverished parents' meager contributions could hardly cover Geneva's high cost of living.[26] Despite receiving money from her brother, Marcel Pauker, and Stasia Stanislavskaia, Rabinsohn had to take a job at a factory, but frail health forced her to quit.[27] Her personal difficulties took another turn for the worse when the brother who had helped her leave for Switzerland, "a very delicate soul" to whom she was utterly devoted, committed suicide.[28] In the end she was forced to renounce her studies and left Geneva without having passed the matriculation exams at the beginning of 1921 to join Pauker in Zurich. They were married soon afterward, and both returned to Romania that summer following Marcel's June graduation.[29]

Arriving in Bucharest in August 1921, the two deemed the political situation quite propitious but found the Communist movement in deep crisis.[30] During their absence the pro-Bolshevik faction of the RWSDP continued to gain ground despite increasing repression by the government, which was determined to destroy the Communists by eliminating their leaders, either through arrest or murder.[31] As the Communists' position strengthened, it was only a matter of time before party unity would break down entirely. The official split finally came at an RWSDP Congress in May 1921, where a majority voted to affiliate with Lenin's Third International (Comintern) and establish the Socialist Communist Party of Romania (RSCP), later renamed the Communist Party in Romania (RCP); those voting in favor were immediately arrested and sentenced to prison.[32] This left a political vacuum within the Romanian Communist leadership that the Paukers, wholeheartedly joining the RSCP, promptly filled.

Propelled straight to the top, Marcel became a member of the provisional leadership.[33] Ana was given somewhat less important positions. She was made secretary of the party-affiliated Central Commission of Women, given responsibility over a number of party cells, organized a campaign to recruit new party members, worked at the union of a large tobacco factory, created a union at a second factory, and led a strike at a third. In October 1922 she was a delegate to the party's Second Congress, secretly held in Ploieşti, where she was elected to the General Council, an enlarged central committee of sorts within the party hierarchy.[34] One month later she traveled as a delegate to the Comintern's Fourth World Congress in Moscow, along with Marcel Pauker, Lucreţiu Patraşcanu, and two other delegates.[35] She also participated at an international women's conference while in Moscow and continued her work with women upon returning to Romania, taking part, for instance, at a conference of women from Transylvania and the Banat.[36] Moreover, at this time she and Patraşcanu reportedly joined the editorial staff of the party mouthpiece, *Socialismul,* edited by Marcel Pauker.[37] In 1923, she and her husband won election to the Committee of the Bucharest Section of the party.[38] Soon afterward, given her connections with clandestine circles of unorganized workers, the Bucharest Committee entrusted her to lead a three-week strike involving 1,600 workers and made her an official delegate (along with Marcel) at the fall 1923 Syndicates' Congress in Cluj.[39] Finally, Ana Pauker was appointed secretary of the Central Committee of the Red Aid (MOPR), where, once again, she worked alongside Marcel.[40]

Ana Pauker was first arrested for Communist activity in her capacity as secretary of MOPR. She was picked up at Bucharest party headquarters on Săgeţii Street in November 1923 and imprisoned for four months, during which she twice went on hunger strikes. She was released when the authorities suspended her trial. (The trial was held in 1928, long after she had left the country, and she was sentenced to twenty years in absentia.)[41] At the end of 1924 she was arrested again, along with Marcel Pauker and three others, in a government sweep that seized an estimated 800 Communists soon after the RCP was officially outlawed. During her interrogations, Ana Pauker submitted a written protest against the failure of the regal commissioner, who assisted in the inquiry, to counter threats made by her Siguranţă interrogator. Nevertheless, she later asserted, "I refused to make any declaration, written or verbal, about anything. In the five months of detention, we went on a ten-day hunger strike at one point, and a fourteen-day hunger strike at another. After the [one lasting] fourteen days, three of us women comrades were released. At that time very many men and women comrades were beaten horribly . . . , and I was the only one who could still stand on my feet when I was released."[42]

Coming on the heels of Ana's arduous existence in Geneva and the trauma of her brother's suicide, the ordeal of imprisonment only compounded the personal hardships Ana and Marcel Pauker endured after returning to Romania. In December 1921 Ana gave birth to their first child, a baby girl they named Tanio. The following spring Marcel was fired from his newly acquired engineering post because of his Communist activities, immediately throwing them into a financial tailspin. When the veterans of the movement, arrested at the May 1921 Party Congress, were amnestied several weeks later, Marcel naturally expected them to take over the party leadership, freeing him to seek employment elsewhere. Yet nearly everyone, he subsequently asserted, proceeded to abandon the movement upon their release, forcing him to continue his extensive duties in the party apparat. "[Ana] had to look for work," he related, "despite the fact that she was nursing a baby. We lived in the worst poverty, because I had my prejudices, and considered that now, as an adult and a father, I should no longer accept anything from my parents." Their material situation worsening daily, they were apparently in no position to cope when Tanio developed a serious case of dysentery and died "in complete misery" in July 1922.[43] The following January Marcel wrote of the tragedy in a letter to his parents:

> I don't know whether seven months of contact with a life, a life that still doesn't seem to be anything but an object, a doll of flesh, whether seven months are enough to create bonds of parental feelings of such intensity that their rupturing totally breaks you to pieces, like a woven cloth coming apart. But in those moments of turmoil, which had exceeded our strength for a long time and brought us to the brink of nervous exhaustion, this piece of painful reality has been more than one could bear. . . . Ana had one fainting spell after another. . . .
>
> I will always have that picture in my mind when the baby died. I seem to see that small room and the corner of the sofa where Ana was sitting, and that soft and burning, burning body. And Ana trying to talk about something else, and the tears from the baby's eyes, closed and closed only to reopen the next day, blue like the sky in the summer, which, with our help, killed her. I left for Braşov. How much torment can I take? And I hurried back home, being afraid for Ana, whom I left weak and broken after two consecutive fainting spells.[44]

In his 1937 autobiographical statement, Marcel Pauker acknowledged that his first reaction was to blame his situation in the party for the baby's death, and he angrily accused the party veterans of having "killed her through their desertion." [45] But if Marcel or Ana Pauker ever entertained the notion that party involvement demanded too high a personal price, they apparently did so only fleetingly. They were, after all, part of the first generation of Communists after the First World War, who dismissed the personal costs of their political stances; instead, "[e]very sacrifice was welcomed as a personal contribution to the 'price of collective redemption'; and it should be emphasized that the links which bound [them] to the Party grew steadily firmer, not in spite of the dangers and sacrifices involved, but because of them." [46]

The basis of this generation's mind-set remained relatively unchanged since it had led them to Bolshevism in the first place. Their outlook was in large part due to the untold suffering and bloodshed of the First World War, the impact of which was so devastating, the changes wrought so monumental, that it could easily be described as one of the "true great watersheds in history." This catastrophe, and the crisis of capitalism that followed, left all of them "convinced as they were of their own existence that only a revolution could free the world once and for all from want, oppression, humiliation, and war. . . . Even the most skeptical among [them] found a certitude here, the only certainty that seemed to be in no danger of being shaken."[47] As a result, following the October Revolution, many socialists such as Ana and Marcel Pauker, who had never evinced any prior attraction to Lenin and Bolshevism, were now eagerly enlisting in the Communist fold, more often than not quite ignorant of just what they were joining.[48] Often young, inexperienced idealists, enamored with activism and full of disdain for their respective parties' more reflective veterans, these recruits were particularly drawn to the Bolsheviks' prestige in having achieved the only successful revolution to date. For the most part the attraction was not ideological but strictly emotional.[49]

For many, the Bolsheviks provided an all-embracing solution to the hopelessness, anguish, and nihilism of the war: the shortcut to the revolution. This guide to action, the idea of not merely interpreting but changing the world, caught the imagination of a large number of traumatized intellectuals and socialist activists after the war.[50] "[W]e had," the former Polish Communist Aleksander Wat recalled, "a chasm in front of us, ruins, [which were] a cause for spiritual joy because here, precisely, something new could be built, the great unknown . . . the great hope that from this, these ruins . . . , everything could be made anew, the way you wanted it, that was fascinating, of course, to the imagination of intellectuals." What is more, Leninism afforded intellectuals a central role in this audacious enterprise. For Lenin, revolutionary "consciousness" stemmed not, as Marx believed, from the instincts and experiences of the workers themselves, but "from the outside"—the intelligentsia. Without intellectuals serving as professional revolutionaries in alliance with, and in leadership of, the proletariat, the revolution, Lenin insisted, would never take place. Herein, noted Manes Sperber, lay a profound contradiction that few seemed to heed in the midst of such exalted certitude: "we viewed everything in terms of what absolutely had to happen but would not happen if *we* did not bring it about."[51]

But, then again, ideological consistency was not a strong point among a great many of this generation, who, having impulsively flocked to Bolshevism, hardly realized the ideological implications of their conversion.[52] In the end, these ardent young radicals, who became Communists out of the need to create new realities, unwittingly joined a rigidly centralized movement designed to render them completely powerless. The party as envisioned by Lenin was tightly controlled by a leadership strategically adopting whatever posture suited the party's immediate interests at any given time—all to be obediently carried out by the party's rank and file.[53] Totally without political opportunism themselves, a significant number of these new recruits invariably opposed Lenin's cynical methods from the beginning. Consequently, Lenin placed his "21 Conditions," exceedingly stringent restrictions on Comintern membership, stipulating that "unconditional support of Soviet Russia remains as before the cardinal duty of Communists of all countries," and required, among other things, that Communists wage continual purges in their respective parties to assure the maintenance of "iron discipline" and complete subservience to the central command.[54] Once they accepted these conditions, given the central command's base in the only Communist state then in existence, sooner or later they inevitably would become idle servants to the interests of that state. "Internationalism and Communism," Adam Ulam observed, "could not co-exist. Soon all Communist parties, whether in France or in Iceland, became part of what Leon Blum called the 'Russian Nationalist Party.' . . . Only the appearance of Communism in another major state could have challenged this organic connection between Communism and Russian nationalism."[55] With practically all Communists' increasing financial dependence on Moscow, one can easily see how they became trapped in a new subservience that merely replaced "the subjugation to the bourgeoisie" that they never stopped accusing the Second International of having long endured.[56]

Still, this process would need nearly all of the 1920s to unfold, for this generation stubbornly maintained "a great deal of independence and initiative" during that decade, and its "constituent parties were by no means subject to mechanical, detailed central control." Counteracting this required the Soviets to take offensive action of sorts. For instance, Grigory Zinoviev launched his campaign to "Bolshevize the Comintern," which meant institutionally enforcing Soviet hegemony, and the Comintern leaders reverted to playing multiple factions against one another to assure complete control over any given party. "The history of the Communist International," Ignazio Silone concluded, "was therefore a history of schisms, a history of intrigues and of arrogance on the part of the directing Russian group toward every independent expression of opinion by the other affiliated parties."[57]

The postwar careers of Ana and Marcel Pauker clearly reflect these developments. Drawn to intellectual pursuits independent of Communism (an avid interest in Freud, for instance),[58] they emerged as oppositionists in party politics for much of the twenties. Their opposition was due in part to objective circumstances inside Romania. The arrests in May 1921 left the newly created RSCP with its designated leader, Gheorghe Cristescu, in prison and a muddled amalgam of region-specific splinter groups without a center; headed by Alexandru Bădulescu (Gelbert Moscovici), the official Romanian representative at the Comintern, an external faction in Vienna increasingly dictated policy; the party organization in the Dobrogea region officially aligned itself to the Bulgarian Communist Party; and the Bessarabian Communists were closely connected to, and considered themselves part of, the Communist Party (Bolshevik) (CP[b]) of the Ukraine.[59]

As a member of the provisional leadership of the RSCP, and under the influence of the Bulgarian leaders of the Communist Balkan Federation, Marcel Pauker immediately attempted to consolidate a central party command that would be free of Vienna's interference and wield effective authority over the regional bodies.[60] Opposing Bădulescu's promotion of terrorism such as Max Goldştein's bombing of the Senate on December 8, 1920, Pauker sought to abolish, at least temporarily, all clandestine, illegal groups linked to similar groups in Bessarabia that were in turn associated with the Soviet-Ukrainian *Zakordon* (Beyond the Borders) organization and the Odessa Section of the Comintern.[61] These Bessarabian groups apparently were instructed to impose a policy on the Romanian party that would give clandestine activity priority over legal organizing, implying that subversive operations aimed at securing Bessarabia's return to the USSR were of far greater value than the explicit recruitment of Romanian workers. Marcel Pauker ardently advocated just such legal recruitment activity, proposing (apparently with the backing of Lucreţiu Patraşcanu) to again issue a party press, promptly implement a mass recruitment campaign for the unions, and organize the unions in a united front with the then still radical Peasant Party.[62]

Resisting Pauker's proposal, however, was a majority of party leaders in Romania, including Elek Köblös, a leader of the party organization in Transylvania and (according to Marcel Pauker) a Soviet espionage agent, who pressed for the Communists to immediately abandon all legal activity and limit themselves to subversive acts; and General Secretary Cristescu (released in the amnesty in June of 1922), who

opposed Pauker's united front idea and generally considered any pro-
vocative undertaking such as a public political campaign against the
government "too dangerous" for the party cadres. Cristescu's preference for clandestine work over open agitation was perhaps one reason
he threw his support to the Bessarabians in their struggle with Marcel
Pauker and why, as Ana Pauker later acknowledged, both she and Marcel, from what was soon to be their base in the Bucharest section of the
party, openly "opposed the Central Committee headed at that time by
Cristescu," which, "to the extent that it functioned, took positions that
obstructed our work." [63] As for the Soviets, just where they stood on the
matter soon became clear: despite repeated assurances by the Comintern
that Ukrainian interference, through the Zakordon and the Bessarabian
groups, would cease, their meddling in Romanian party affairs continued; and despite Marcel Pauker's firm backing, "thanks to Bulgarian
coaching," of the Comintern's line of "self-determination up to separation" of national minorities (that is, Bessarabia's incorporation into the
Soviet Union), he was rebuked for "oppositionist activity" at the RCP's
Third Congress in August 1924 and summarily ousted from the party
leadership.[64]

Several weeks earlier Cristescu had himself been removed as general
secretary for opposing Bessarabian secession, which he argued would
not only lead the government to ban the RCP, but isolate the party further from the Romanian masses—a position soon proven prescient on
both counts. Replacing him was Köblös, who transferred the center of
what was now an illegal party underground from Bucharest to Transylvania. Stressing that the party avoid political issues and limit itself to the
"workers' movement," Köblös opposed engaging in ambitious schemes
on the lines of what he termed Marcel Pauker's "politics of balloons"
and effectively prevented Pauker from attaining anything approaching a
leadership role.[65] While Ana Pauker initially served under Köblös in a
reconstituted Central Committee (again being entrusted with organizing
women workers), her regular work alongside her husband, and her expression of views similar to his criticizing the new leaders, assured that
she, too, would quickly end up in the party doghouse.[66]

Ana Pauker said her opposition to the new party leadership and her
subsequent ostracism started during her second imprisonment, which
began at the end of 1924, only a few months after Köblös assumed control of the RCP. "We in prison were revolted by the passivity of the leadership of that time, and I made it a point to tell them" upon being re-

leased in mid-1925. Unable to find work after leaving prison, she set up a tailor shop in Bucharest and became active in a cell of the local tailors' union, in which capacity she was soon arrested a third time while distributing manifestos and imprisoned for ten days. "At that time," she added, "there were many party members who were dissatisfied with the opportunist, apolitical and false line of the party in union work, with the passivity of party work, and with the policies of fighting the government by bribing the Siguranță and the military tribunals for the release of our comrades. An open struggle was then carried out for the first time in front of the comrades of the union against [the party leadership]." It was therefore no surprise that Ana Pauker, then eight months pregnant, received the party leaders' blessing to leave the country in February 1926 for four months to deliver her baby and be with her husband, who was hospitalized in Prague with scarlet fever; nor was it any surprise that the RCP leadership soon ordered her to remain abroad, under the pretext that she would likely be arrested if she returned to Romania.[67]

During the German elections of 1926, she spent several months in Berlin, where she worked in a party electoral organization.[68] After that, she and Marcel were instructed during the summer to proceed to Paris, where she was assigned to "two [party] cells that weren't even functioning," and began working at an obscure committee in the French Communist Party for Romanian émigrés. Moving to Vienna in July 1927, she persistently asked party leaders to let her return to Romania but was rebuffed on the grounds that there she would engage in politics opposed to the Politburo.[69] The leadership "methodically refused to allow me to work in the country," she asserted, "based on its system of removing all those comrades who were not in agreement with its opportunistic line." Reduced to doing translation work in Vienna, she asked to be sent to the Lenin School in Moscow, but again was repeatedly refused because of her noted "oppositionist" posture.[70]

Ana Pauker maintained that oppositionist posture even though the Comintern had underscored its confidence in Köblös's leadership and prohibited opposition to it.[71] Her attitude was not in the least out of the ordinary for Romanian Communists during this period. For instance, the Fourth RCP Congress, June 28–July 7, 1928, triggered factional fighting within the Romanian party that embodied an outright rejection of the Comintern-imposed leadership—with Marcel Pauker leading the rebels. But this first generation of party activists, who were largely revolted by Stalin's methods and inclined to support Trotsky during his brief struggle against Stalin,[72] in the end yielded en masse to Stalinism. Their innate independence and rebelliousness would vanish with the movement's mounting Stalinization at the end of the decade.

The year 1928 was a crucial turning point in that process. It marked the termination of the New Economic Policy and the launching of Stalin's "revolution from above" in the Soviet Union, which included the forced collectivization of agriculture; rapid, massive industrialization; and a "cultural revolution" imposed upon society at large.[73] At the same time, it marked Ana Pauker's emergence from disgrace and obloquy within the RCP and the beginning of her galloping climb into the Comintern hierarchy. After the RCP leadership several times refused her requests to attend the Lenin School in Moscow, she traveled to the Soviet capital at the beginning of the year, ostensibly on vacation with her husband. There she obtained the intervention of the renowned German Communist Klara Zetkin, whom she personally knew from her work at MOPR. (Zetkin headed MOPR from 1924 to 1927.)[74] Though the Lenin School as a rule could not accept Pauker without the RCP leaders' recommendation and had already formally rejected her on the grounds that she was again pregnant, it reversed its decision and provisionally accepted her as an auditor. Pauker was allowed to enter the school in March, and soon after a new RCP leadership was appointed in the summer of 1928, she formally requested and received the required recommendation to become an official student in full standing.[75]

Opened in 1926, the Comintern's Lenin School trained the leadership of the various Communist parties, at that time under two separate curricula: an eight-month "short course" for lower-ranking activists returning to do party work in their home countries, and a comprehensive, three-year program restricted to Central Committee members or to those who had headed a regional party organization for at least four years and were now being groomed as high-level Comintern functionaries.[76] Placed in the higher-ranking three-year course, Pauker attended classes on such topics as Marxian economics, historical materialism, agrarian issues, military science, the history of the Communist and labor movements of every country, the creation and employment of party cadres, revolutionary methods, espionage, and sabotage.[77] Manual labor supplemented the theoretical studies, as all first-year students were mandated to work in a Soviet factory during the summer months; thus, Pauker was sent with a group of students to do such "practical work" in the city of Kalinin in the summer of 1929.[78] Quickly excelling in her studies, she was named head of the Kalinin group and was appointed the leader responsible (*staroste*) for the school's Romanian contingent, then comprised of ten students.[79] In December she was sent to France for one month to investigate and report on the situation within the French Communist Party, a task normally reserved for the most promising students during the last half of their third year.[80] After taking part in a commission of three students dispatched to the Volgan German Republic in March 1930 to assist "in correcting the mistakes" of the collectivization campaign there, Pauker was selected to work for several months as an adviser in the Comintern's Latin Secretariat, without having to attend the school's third year.[81]

It was most likely during her stint at the Latin Secretariat, which oversaw the French, Italian, Spanish, and Portuguese Communist parties, that Ana Pauker began what was to be a close and enduring friendship with Dimitri Manuilsky. If any leading Communist in Moscow could be said to have been Pauker's patron, it was Manuilsky, who presided over the Latin Secretariat and was the Kremlin's principal representative at the Comintern from 1931 on.[82] A highly controversial figure, he was often noted, Austrian former Communist Ernst Fischer observed, for "his intrigues, . . . his unpredictable changes of front, [and] his craftiness and ruthlessness with which he carried out the instructions of the central authority, making or breaking politicians." But behind what outwardly appeared as rank opportunism couched in jovial cynicism, there was, Fischer added, a far different persona—one that did not hesitate to hint at his dismissive dissent from particular party policies or fear to defend threatened comrades.[83] Moreover, Manuilsky, as another high-ranking Comintern official pointed out, was vastly more knowledgeable and sophisticated than the other Comintern leaders. Consequently, "his habit of thought was less dogmatic and less schematic than his colleagues', and in addition he had the courage to have thoughts, to express them, to discuss differences and really argue about them. You know, that was something really exceptional in the Comintern apparatus in the years after Lenin."[84] One is left to wonder whether, as was the case with Marcel Pauker, Manuilsky's contradictory character left its lasting imprint on his Romanian protégé's future.

In the fall of 1930, Manuilsky sent Ana Pauker (alias "Marina") to France as a special organizational instructor of the Comintern's Executive Committee (ECCI). This time she remained there two years.[85] Subsequently joining her was Eugen Fried, who became France's chief Comintern instructor for the rest of the decade. Employing the pseudonym Comrade Clement, Fried oversaw the systematic Stalinization of the French Communist Party (FCP), which included establishing an all-powerful cadres commission modeled after the Soviet prototype. Despite a reported propensity for secrecy and his imposition of Stalinist organizational norms, Fried was noted for a marked openness and promotion of free expression in his dealings with other activists. "He acquired the art of not squelching or stifling people, but of encouraging them to form grand theses of ideas," noted the FCP's preeminent historian, Philippe Robrieux. "And attaining such ideas, he believed, was the business of triumphing in the class struggle. He was always analyzing, explaining and correcting the line of movement," seemingly similar in this respect to Manuilsky.[86] Fried's enterprising intelligence, combined with an affecting charisma, assured him a formidable footing in the French Communist movement. Pauker, who was clearly drawn to men of such spirited dynamism, would inevitably fall for him. She had been separated from her husband ever since entering the Lenin School and was to some degree estranged from him after learning that he had fathered a child with a Bessarabian woman in 1931.[87] Her affair with Fried likewise resulted in a pregnancy, and she gave birth to a baby girl (Marie) in Moscow in 1932. Having been obliged by party duty to place her two other children (Vlad, born in 1925, and Tatiana, born in 1928) in an MOPR children's home in the Soviet Union, Pauker left her new baby in the care of Aurore Thorez, the former wife of FCP General Secretary Maurice Thorez, thus leading to the widespread rumor that he was actually the father. Aurore Thorez took Marie back to Paris in the fall of 1933.[88]

Pauker reportedly then worked at Comintern headquarters in Moscow for approximately the next two years (1932–34), though a precise accounting of her activities during this period is elusive. True to form with the workings of clandestine organizations, a number of official chronologies of Pauker's career from her Comintern file are purposely vague or erroneous from the time she left the Lenin School in 1930 to her arrest in Romania five years later. Exactly when she returned to Romania is therefore unclear. In a fall 1944 interview, Pauker suggested that she returned as early as 1932, while her brother-in-law, Eugen Iacobovici, maintained in his memoirs that she arrived in March 1933, just after the Grivița railroad strike in Bucharest. While she may have secretly traveled to Romania on various brief missions, she probably did not return there permanently until 1934, as specified in the report of a party commission investigating Pauker after her ouster. Corroborating this is the fact that Pauker, who operated in Romania at the time under

the pseudonym Maria Grigoraş, possessed an identity card issued with
that name on October 15, 1934. Indeed, it would seem that Pauker was
sent to Romania as a result of the Comintern's change of course in promoting a Popular Front in mid-1934, for she was specifically entrusted
with organizing the RCP's antifascist Popular Front campaign, again
working closely with Marcel Pauker, who headed the party's legal and
underground press at the time.[89]

On the night of July 12, 1935, Ana Pauker was arrested in Bucharest
while leaving a secret meeting of the RCP secretariat along with two
other party activists. In the process she was shot in both legs. (The bullet went through her left leg and embedded in her right leg, from which
it was never removed.) She was not taken to a hospital, but straight
to Siguranţă headquarters for immediate questioning. "I believe that I
was shot with the intention of killing me," Pauker declared in a subsequent interrogation. "And that was proven by the fact that, when I left
the Siguranţă to go to the War Council [where she was initially incar-
cerated], police inspector Turcu said to me: 'The agent who shot you
was an idiot for not shooting you through the heart. And if you fall into
my hands again I'll shoot to kill.' " [90]

Eleven months later, on June 5, 1936, Ana Pauker went on trial together with eighteen other RCP activists in a makeshift courthouse seven
kilometers outside Craiova, a middle-sized town that lacked a large antifascist movement.[91] The authorities had to move the trial to this remote
location from Bucharest, where three days earlier protests had become
so large that the magistrate canceled further proceedings there. Each
day the accused were brought into the hall in shackles, the women
chained in groups of three, the men chained separately. A defense team
of twenty-four attorneys took part, including at least seven from abroad,
among them Isabelle Blum Grégoire, a member of the Belgian Parliament and the daughter of Leon Blum.

Attendance was restricted almost exclusively to military officers,
Siguranţă agents, and the "blue shirts" of the fascist National Christian
League (LANC), thus assuring a specter of violence that was forever
present during the trial.[92] Chief defense attorney Lucreţiu Patraşcanu
was at one point ousted from the hall and prohibited from returning
on the grounds that he, too, was a Communist, and consequently had
to be replaced by Ion Gheorghe Maurer. In addition, attorney Ella Ne-
gruzzi, a member of the National Liberal Party, was forced to resign
from the defense team after receiving persistent death threats, and defense witnesses were often attacked outside the courtroom.[93] On one

occasion the tensions exploded during a dispute between the prosecution and defense attorney A. Nachtigal, as recorded by a journalist
covering the trial:

> Nachtigal was ordered by the chief magistrate to leave the hall. The attor-
> ney refused. Screaming, the judge again ordered him out. Refraining from
> screaming, the attorney again refused. An uproar ensues: the defense attor-
> neys rise to their feet in protest; the people in the hall rise to their feet,
> protesting the protesters. The judge orders regal commissioner Stavrache to
> physically remove the lawyer. The proceedings are suspended, the judges
> withdraw, and officers and troops enter the hall. The regal commissioner de-
> mands that the attorney leave the building. The other attorneys form a circle
> around Nachtigal, in solidarity with their colleague. All hell breaks loose.
>   "In the face of such force, there's nothing that can be done," says the law-
> yer. He leaves the hall together with the other attorneys, surrounded by sen-
> tinels in military uniform, bayonets drawn. The hall breaks out in applause.
> At that moment, shouts are heard from the defendants' box. The accused,
> "under the whip" of Ana Pauker, vehemently protest the attorneys' removal.
> The guards immediately intervene, slapping and kicking in all directions. . . .
> The women are hit with particular brutality, though not without reason, as
> they were the leaders of the "rebellion." And the one leading the leaders was
> Ana, and she was also the one who was struck the most. Orders are issued to
> remove the accused. There is a stampede towards them; the accused are hit
> from all sides and dragged out by their arms and legs as they defiantly resist.
> Two of them (Ana Czaszar and Estera Radoşoveţchi) have fainted, and are
> carried out by the others. Ana is handcuffed. . . .[94]

In another incident, a soldier attempted to strike Pauker with his bayo-
net, but one of her codefendants, Alexandru Moghioroş, blocked the
blow.[95]

Though RCP propagandists initially dubbed the hearing the Trial of
the 19 Anti-Fascists, it soon became universally known as the Trial of
Ana Pauker, given her prominence in the RCP and her central and com-
manding role throughout the proceedings. Methodically questioning
every witness and often asking more questions than the attorneys themselves, Pauker addressed the court with such passion that she quickly
drew comparisons with Georgi Dimitrov at Leipzig.[96] The accusation
against her, of course, was true: she was a Comintern agent actively
working against the Romanian government. But, at the same time, she
emerged as an unmistakable symbol for a large number of antifascist
democrats in a period when fascism and anti-Semitism had become an
explosive force throughout the country.

That summer of 1936 was a "turning point in bringing about a general anti-Jewish agitation" in Romania.[97] The extreme Right, which in-

cluded the fanatically anti-Semitic Iron Guard (also known as "the Legionaries") and the Nazi-affiliated LANC, connived with the National Liberal government of Gheorghe Tătărăscu to mount an all-out assault on the country's antifascist elements, employing anti-Semitism as its most important weapon.[98] At the same time, the moderate Right, which through the twenties had accepted Jews into its ranks, had by the mid-thirties completely broken with them and adopted its own anti-Semitic positions to counter the rising loss of its traditional constituents to fascist groups. " 'Taking the wind out of the extremists' sails' became the anti-Semitic watchword of the moderate Rightists. The ruling Romanian Right . . . did not attempt to counterbalance the alleged social radicalism of the extreme Right with a radical social policy [of its own], but rather by the radicalization of its anti-Jewish policy." [99] The extreme Right waged a furious campaign against the democratic press, arbitrarily labeling it Jewish in a determined effort to wipe it out; virtually every Jewish lawyer was removed from the Bucharest bar that year, with severe restrictions imposed in other professions as well; Jews were randomly beaten up in many parts of the country, and Jewish businesses regularly attacked; and in November the LANC staged a massive anti-Semitic demonstration in the capital, drawing over 100,000 swastika-bearing peasants from practically every corner of Romania.[100]

Pauker's trial struck a major propaganda coup for the extreme Right, with its pretenses of being the nation's sole protector against a "Jewish-Communist conspiracy," and it added fuel to the authorities' escalating anti-Semitic campaign. The mainstream's attempt to co-opt anti-Semitism failed to check the extremists' appeal, and in elections the following year support for the Iron Guard was six times what it had been in 1932, making it the third-largest party and "by far the most popular and most dynamic" political movement in the country. The results, moreover, spelled an end to Romania's parliamentary system: by February 1938 King Carol II had dissolved Parliament, banned all political parties, and established his own dictatorship. While suppressing the Iron Guard, whose popularity had clearly become a threat, the king at the same time institutionalized much of its anti-Semitism. Within a year some 120,000 Jews were stripped of their citizenship, with the remainder losing a substantial part of their political rights. " 'Romaniazation' of education and the professions began, excluding Jewish lawyers, teachers, and state employees, prohibiting Jewish ownership of certain enterprises, applying the numerus clausus in fact if not in name." Yet this proved child's play compared to what came afterward: though the

regime of the Legionaries that replaced the exiled Carol in September
1940 did not produce the degree of violence that most Jews expected,
the military junta of Ion Antonescu (established four months later)
would soon unleash a horrendous bloodbath.[101]

At the end of the trial Pauker received a maximum ten-year sentence.
Under these deteriorating circumstances, she presumably was at least
vulnerable in prison. When transferred with her female codefendants
from the Văcăreşti central jail in Bucharest to the Dumbrăveni women's
prison in Transylvania, however, she found the conditions there better
than they had been during her last incarceration in the mid-1920s. Communists and other political prisoners had been granted certain privileges
since 1930: they were no longer kept in separate individual cells or
obliged to wear standard prison uniforms; they were allowed to cook
their own meals, work in their own workshops, and correspond with the
outside world; and they were permitted to receive books and newspapers and to engage in intellectual pursuits of their own choosing. Heading a collective of some one hundred Communist and antifascist prisoners, Pauker helped organize a school preparing the women for high
school matriculation exams, and she taught French and German and
lectured on such subjects as Marxist-Leninist theory and political economics.[102] This would last until 1940, when the authorities abruptly rescinded all privileges. Pauker and all those serving maximum sentences
were then moved to Râmnicu-Sărat prison in Muntenia and placed under strict solitary confinement in cells two and a half steps long and wide
enough to fit only a small cot. Pauker was put in a windowless corner
cell away from the others. (The prisoners had taught themselves Morse
code at Dumbrăveni, but that was to be of no use to her now.) The food
was inedible, and the prisoners were denied books or writing materials.[103] "We were terrorized . . . ," a woman jailed with Pauker recalled.
"We were allowed to go out only one hour a day. There were five separate yards, and each one of us was taken out individually. . . . We almost
never saw the daylight."[104]

Ironically, this change for the worse did not occur with the Iron
Guard's rise to power that year, but during the final eight months of
Carol's rule. In the fall of 1940, soon after the king's ouster, some 2,000
Legionaries embarked on a pilgrimage to Râmnicu-Sărat, where many
had been jailed by the former regime. When they arrived at the prison
dressed in their green uniforms, the women were terrified. Immediately
upon entering, the Legionaries sought out Ana Pauker's cell, but to the
astonishment of all, they intended only to engage in a political discus-

sion, respectfully referring to her as the captain of the Communists. At one point, one of the Legionaries suddenly entered the cell of twenty-three-year-old Vilma Kajesco, but instead of a gun he held a camera, to photograph the hovel where he had spent five years of his life. "After [he] left," she related, "another one came to my cell and opened the peephole. He asked me: 'Were you a Communist?' I answered: 'I was, I am and I will be.' To which he retorted: 'Bravo.' . . . You should know that, to my surprise, they did not behave badly at all. On the contrary, they were quite nice." [105]

Having resolved to turn Râmnicu-Sărat into an Iron Guard museum, the Legionaries transferred the women to Caransebeş prison near Timişoara.[106] There Pauker secretly met for the first time with Gheorghe Gheorghiu-Dej, the leader of the men's Communist collective at Doftana prison, evacuated to Caransebeş when an earthquake destroyed Doftana in November 1940.[107] Soon after their meeting, Pauker and the women's collective were transferred back to Dumbrăveni, where Pauker remained until she was traded to the Soviets on May 7, 1941, six weeks before the Nazi invasion.[108] Since the Russians considered her the most important Communist in Romania, Pauker "was therefore the only personality of Romanian Communism accepted, and even demanded, by Moscow for an exchange with the Romanian government." [109] Not having anyone to trade for her, the Soviets arrested "Moş" Ion Codreanu, a prominent Romanian peasant leader from Bessarabia, "who was guilty of absolutely nothing, promising that he would later return (as they took him to Russia)—for him they got Pauker." [110]

Because the women's collective at Dumbrăveni maintained contact with the outside world during most of Pauker's prison term, she arrived in Moscow already aware of events there. She knew, for example, of the Nazi-Soviet pact of 1939, which had left her "totally shocked and disoriented"; [111] she knew of the Moscow show trials, and of the startling spectacle of practically the entire Bolshevik old guard in the dock for high treason; and she knew that her husband, Marcel, had been among the purged. News of his exclusion from the party as an "enemy of the people" arrived in 1938, when an article from the RCP mouthpiece *Scânteia* and a party brochure on Romanian Trotskyists were found hidden in the wooden crate of an MOPR food package. "[W]hen she read the material regarding Marcel Pauker," her fellow inmate Sara Alterescu revealed, "Ana locked herself in a small room and didn't come out of that room for three days. And when she did come out, her face was completely changed." Upon arriving in Moscow, Ana told Dimitri Manuilsky's wife, Varia, who had expected her own husband's arrest during the Terror, that she intended to request a meeting with Lavrenti Beria and ask him if Marcel were still alive; however, after consulting with others, Varia strongly urged her not to.[112]

Nevertheless, Pauker could not help but infer what happened to Marcel, given the Terror's shocking dimensions. Among countless others, no less than three-quarters of all foreign Communists living in or summoned to the Soviet Union had disappeared. This included all but a handful of her comrades from the Comintern hierarchy, as well as the Lenin School's administrative staff. Moreover, few Romanians were left alive to describe the massacre to her: Elena (Lenuța) Filipovici (who had gone on a hunger strike in prison with Ana Pauker in 1924, and was in the Romanian contingent at the Lenin School that Pauker headed), Elek Köblös, Alexandru Dobrogeanu-Gherea, Alexandru Bădulescu, David Fabian, Ecaterina Arbore, and many others had been liquidated. They were joined by almost all foreign Communists who were in Russia as refugees, having fled right-wing or fascist dictatorships in their own countries.[113] The most extreme case was that of the Polish Communist Party, which literally ceased to exist after every Polish Communist the NKVD could get its hands on was either shot or sent to a Siberian labor camp, where all but a few dozen died.[114] Also murdered were practically all Yugoslavs, Hungarians, Koreans, Latvians, Estonians, and even those in the tiny Palestinian Communist Party,[115] as well as Germans—with over two hundred German Communists (many of them Jews) taken out of the camps and put on a train straight to the Gestapo in Nazi-occupied Poland.[116] Also included were a large percentage of the foreign and Soviet veterans of the Spanish Civil War and many veterans of the failed socialist uprising in Austria, who arrived during the Great Terror.[117] Even ordinary foreign workers, who came to settle in the USSR only out of a desire to participate in its revolution, perished in the killing spree.[118] Finally there were those assassinated outside the USSR, whom Pauker believed to have included Eugen Fried, who was murdered in Brussels in 1943.[119] On a trip to Paris in 1945, when Pauker visited Aurore Thorez, who had witnessed Fried's demise, Thorez pointedly corrected her impression that the Nazis had killed him: "No, Ana," Thorez insisted. "*They* did it."[120] She and many others suspected (wrongly, it now turns out) that the NKVD had liquidated Fried for, among other transgressions, expressing doubts over the Nazi-Soviet pact.[121]

In the end, concluded Branko Lazitch, "[a]ll foreign Communists who had followed Lenin or had cooperated with him before October

1917, immediately after the victory and during the foundation of the Comintern in 1919, were exterminated." The Comintern to which Ana Pauker returned was nothing but an empty shell enveloping a mass grave. It was only a matter of time before Stalin, who murdered more Communists than all European police forces (including the Gestapo) combined, would officially declare its dissolution, to which Ana Pauker was a signatory in 1943.[122]

That Ana Pauker was a signatory to the Comintern's dissolution and remained a devoted party leader after learning of the Terror and continued working with the very murderers of her husband and comrades has, perhaps more than anything else, given her the widely held reputation of being the classic party hack—a fanatical Stalinist whose only interest was serving her masters in Moscow. Soon to follow were a host of rumors reportedly initiated by the Romanian authorities and the country's right-wing press that she not only had collaborated with Marcel Pauker's executioners but had actually denounced him before or soon after his arrest. This, of course, was a complete impossibility since she was in jail in Romania at the time. Nevertheless, these charges plagued her for the remainder of her career and persist even today, reflecting the general assumption regarding all Communist survivors of the Terror who did not subsequently leave the party: "Whatever their original revolutionary idealism and zeal might have been, they all became 'apparatchiks,' and in the process sacrificed their personalities to the machinery that had crushed so many of their comrades. Duplicity and demoralization, cynicism and corruption, became second nature to these servants of an absolute despotism." [123]

There is much to suggest that Pauker, too, made that inevitable journey from idealist to apparatchik. As with most Communists of her generation, she joined the party out of genuinely pure motives, for "one does not enter a revolutionary movement that is persecuted by the government for trivial or opportunistic reasons." [124] Hers was not a generation of calculating pragmatists or, as Pauker herself acknowledged, one guided primarily by class consciousness.[125] They were, more or less, simply selfless dreamers enraptured with their ideals.[126] "All we lived for," Victor Serge recalled, "was activity integrated into history. . . . None of us had, in the bourgeois sense of the word, any personal existence; we changed our names, our posting and our work at the Party's need; we had just enough to live on without real material discomfort, and we were not interested in making money, or following a career, or producing a literary heritage, or leaving a name behind us; we were interested solely in the difficult business of reaching Socialism." [127] Yet these same people readily acceded to the distinct moral relativism of Communist ideology, which applied one set of ethical standards solely to Communists and quite another to everyone else.

The Soviet regime's executions and atrocities apparently troubled few consciences in the party as long as the victims were exclusively non-Communists, as during the first decade and a half of Bolshevik rule. While Lenin forbade executions of his fellow Communists and tended to maintain an atmosphere of tolerance among them, he strictly adhered to the conviction that anything was permissible as long as it was applied to the "class enemy." He declared, "We repudiate all morality that proceeds from supernatural ideas or ideas that transcend class conceptions. In our opinion, morality is entirely identical to the interest of the class war." [128] Where were the cries of indignation when Lenin cynically classified the various socialist parties, as well as the sailors of Kronstadt, as counterrevolutionaries to justify crushing them? How was Stalin's adoption of these same methods really any different when he simply applied the class-enemy label to the Communists themselves?

True, Pauker had proved herself willing to suffer disgrace in the party for principle's sake when, Lenin's 21 Conditions notwithstanding, she openly opposed the RCP leadership on certain issues; indeed, she was labeled an oppositionist for this even during her first year at the Lenin School.[129] But she rapidly rose to the highest circles of the Comintern apparat precisely during the onset of Stalinism and precisely when the Soviets were achieving complete hegemony over the entire movement. She may or may not have approved of Stalin's "socialist offensive," launched during her tenure at the Lenin School, though, given her past criticisms of the RCP leadership's passivity, she more than likely approved. (After all, the New Economic Policy, we are told, had always "made every sincere Communist ashamed . . . [l]ike a disgrace in the family, a daughter going bad.")[130] However, it soon became clear that her personal positions were very much beside the point. In the end Ana Pauker fell victim, as did all her comrades, to an axiom of party life: having become Communists in the firm conviction of impending revolution, they came to believe that they could bring about the inevitable only within the framework of one specific organization.[131] Hence, they transferred on to the tangible body of the Communist Party their indignation over the injustices of capitalism and their belief in the coming revolution that would invariably eradicate those injustices. And hence, the party itself inherited the historically imminent new order's veneer of infallibility. "The Party," Leon Trotsky declared, "in the last analysis is always right, because the Party is the single historic instrument given to the proletariat for the solution of its fundamental problems"—that is, the single historic instrument that would bring about the desired and inevitable revolution. Or as the former Czechoslovak Communist Eduard Goldstücker ruefully acknowledged, "I was convinced that Lenin's Party could do no wrong and say nothing that was untrue." [132]

To be sure, the doctrine of Party = Truth was a powerful force that attracted many to Communism, for "it appealed to the deepest needs of faith and conversion, as opposed to other ideologies" and satisfied "the hunger for something all-embracing." Such unbounded allegiance served to create "a moral energy quite astonishing in its intensity" but was also "the spiritual source" of the party's inquisitional intolerance. "The terrible doctrine of infallibility," Ernst Fischer pointed out, "began to serve as justification for every arbitrary act, while any stirring of an individual conscience was reprobated as petit-bourgeois or as indicating susceptibility to the class enemy's propaganda. The victory of the October Revolution, the consolidation and stabilization of Soviet rule in spite of all prognostications to the contrary had, it was maintained, finally proved that everyone else was wrong and only the Bolsheviks were right, and that the party and Stalin were infallible." [133] Thus the impetus for many independent-minded activists to join the Bolsheviks itself became an unmitigating factor in their deepening servitude.

This scenario played out painfully among the foreign cadres attending the Lenin School, as Polish Communist Hersh Mendel, who studied there at the same time as Pauker, described:

> Life in the Soviet Union for foreign revolutionaries [during 1928–1930] was unbearable. It seemed as if everything was being done to degrade and dishonor each and every socialist who had not gone through the Russian school. It went badly for any Communist, for example, who praised his own party, who held that it was revolutionary and who, as a member, took pride in it. One could be certain in those days that such sentiments meant big trouble. The Soviet bigwigs even had a name for it: "underestimating the Soviet Union." [134]

For the vast majority of foreign Communists at the school, commitment to the Soviet Union was steadfast and unquestioning. Their resistance to equating solidarity with servility, however, had to be drummed out of their psyches. To that end, the Shakhty Trial must have been particularly helpful. Held in Moscow in May and June 1928, its key message was that neutrality in party politics invariably spelled sabotage. "Stalin's objective, in common with the Inquisition, was to force thinking people to desist from their independent thoughts and moral principles and identify with a party and with policies felt to be unacceptable or questionable." [135] Failing to do so, moreover, was tantamount to treason. It was during Pauker's tenure at the Lenin School that the equation "Doubt = Treason" began to be formidably enforced in Soviet (and thus International Communist) party politics. [136] To express any doubt whatsoever, indeed even to listen to such doubts, automatically became grounds for being considered an enemy. [137]

Equally significant, however, was the highly conspiratorial, impersonal interaction imposed at the school that was reportedly pervasive among all Communists in Moscow. As one veteran activist put it, "The rules were so conspiratorial that it was almost impossible to create a flow of communication with other comrades. . . . Only things that were absolutely necessary were ever discussed, and one never asked anything else. Questions aroused suspicion; that was the rule of the game." Students were prohibited from using their own names (Pauker was known as Sofia Marin), and admonished against making personal friendships. As Arthur Koestler once observed, "[F]riendships within the Party automatically aroused political suspicion. . . . The slogans of the Party emphasized the diffuse and impersonal 'solidarity of the working class' instead of individual friendship, and substituted 'loyalty to the Party' for loyalty to friends. Loyalty to the Party meant, of course, unconditional obedience, and meant, furthermore, the repudiation of friends who had deviated from the Party-line, or for some reason had fallen under suspicion." [138]

Added to this were the ubiquitous "self-criticisms" prescribed on sorrowful students at the slightest pretext, which proved highly effective controls. "Almost unconsciously I learnt to watch my steps, my words and my thoughts," Koestler recalled, describing his experience as part of a Communist cell in Germany in 1931.

> I learnt that everything that I said in the cell or in private . . . remained on record and could one day be held against me. I learnt that my relations with other members of the cell should not be guided by trust but by "revolutionary vigilance"; that reporting any heretical remark was a duty, failure to do so was a crime against the Party, and that to feel revulsion against this code was a sign of sentimental, petit-bourgeois prejudice. . . . I learnt to avoid any

original form of expression, any individual turn of phrase. Euphony, grada-
tions of emphasis, restraint, nuances of meaning, were suspect.

The constant intimidation, the dread of the slightest spontaneity, and
the anguished pondering over every gesture were all necessary in the
Stalinist system, for they were invaluable tools in eradicating the vestiges
of personal conscience and individual initiative, and for assuring the
complete submission of the party faithful.[139]

On the other side of this phenomenon were the privileges and status
of the closed circle of party activists. The bigger rations, the material com-
forts, the access to information, and the special facilities reserved for
high-level functionaries were not only corrupting influences, but highly
efficient controls, in that they reinforced the recipient's sense of belonging to the established order. To give but one example, Polish Communist
Wanda Pampuch-Bronska described the party's unegalitarian policies
during the Second World War—a time when one would expect the opposite: "[It was] disgusting the way the meager food supplies were distributed strictly according to rank in the Communist hierarchy. The
head of a section of the publishing office received two kilograms of butter and two of sugar while his deputy received only half as much, and so
on. Since they often lived together, the lower-ranking comrades, who
had received little or nothing in the distribution of food, could watch as
their comrade-chiefs consumed their 'due' rations before their eyes."
The ruling class's "us-them" mentality and their near-total isolation
from the masses also explain a great deal about the psychological makeup of the Stalinist apparatchik.[140]

Ultimately the most important factor was fear—a plentiful commodity at the Lenin School during Pauker's time there. To again quote
Mendel:

> [S]nooping at the Lenin School proceeded apace, and with it a sense of dread
> among us students intensified as well. One was afraid to utter a word. . . . It
> was not only dangerous to greet comrades on the street, it was also danger-
> ous to meet with them in our rooms. Whenever one wished to discuss even
> the most innocent of questions with another, he plugged up the keyhole of
> his door with a hand towel, stopped up the air duct which fed into the ad-
> joining room and whispered softly in the other comrade's ear. . . . The situa-
> tion grew worse as arrests and shootings began to take place. Not one single
> week went by without somebody being taken into custody.

At the same time, massive purges took place inside the Comintern shortly
before Pauker began working at the Latin Secretariat. The condemned

included celebrated leaders of the Comintern and the various Communist parties who became pariahs literally overnight—greeted by no one, "not even their closest personal friends of the day before." Such was the fate, for example, of RCP leader Elek Köblös, to which Pauker personally bore witness. Meeting him by chance in Moscow while she was at the Lenin School (most likely in 1930), she discovered that he had been reduced to working as a laborer in a factory. Apparently criticized for not having taken a harder line against him, she subsequently acknowledged having made the "mistake" of fostering a "passive attitude toward Köblös," whom she considered a personal friend despite their political differences. "Later I found out," she noted, "that he had been arrested as a provocateur." [141]

By 1932, with the Soviet Union in turmoil and increasing disenchantment among the party cadres, the regime responded by throwing "the entire country . . . into a paroxysm of persecution—foreign spies everywhere, in every Soviet plant, in every Soviet shop, in every Soviet office." This was apparently doubly true for the Comintern, as Pauker was to discover after she resumed working there upon her return from Paris. During the summer of 1932 when she arrived in Moscow, the secret police surreptitiously took over the Comintern's headquarters. Police guards were placed not only at the building's entrance, but in the corridors on every floor. Talking in the hallways was expressly forbidden. The entire staff was under constant watch, and all were suspect. Even the most innocent of discussions on Communist theory, which "had long since become taboo in the Comintern," were now categorically "branded with one label: Espionage!" [142]

The Soviet leadership's use of fear included its widespread practice of taking hostages from among foreign Communists, either disgraced officials themselves, large numbers of whom were held against their will in Moscow in a state of forced idleness, or members of their families. [143] The disgraced Marcel Pauker experienced both, first being detained himself and then seeing his children held hostage. He had trouble leaving the country in 1928 and again in 1932, after completing a two-year assignment as an engineer in the Soviet town of Magnitogorsk in the Urals. [144] Finally in the fateful year of 1937, when recalled from the safety of Prague, he ignored his friends' warnings not to go back to Moscow, probably in part because his children were being held there in an MOPR children's home. [145] Thus Ana Pauker clearly spoke from personal experience when she quipped to Milovan Djilas at a Cominform meeting after the war, "To Moscow whenever you please, from Moscow when they let go of you!" [146]

The net result of all this was a movement of fervent revolutionary idealists—altruistic, totally devoted to the working class, selfless bordering on the masochistic—surrendering to a Kremlin leadership increasingly made up of what Angelica Balabanoff described as the "scum of humanity." If Benjamin Gitlow, one of those idealists himself, is correct, the degenerating dynamic of party existence assured that, in the last analysis, the former ended up no different than the latter: "The radicals, who became communists," he tells us, "went through a personal metamorphosis so complete that they were mentally and morally changed into different human beings. . . . Dreamers and visionaries, the timid souls among the radicals, were transformed into machiavellian political tricksters and hardened conspirators." It was, Mendel confirmed, precisely such types at the Lenin School who rose to the top of the Comintern hierarchy. Students "who mastered Stalin's style" and "jeered at the terrible misery of the Russian masses in the crudest manner," while going "about sumptuously dressed and complain[ing] that the food at the Lenin School was not to their tastes," were all considered "the best Communists." [147]

Given Ana Pauker's fast rise up the Comintern pecking order, she presumably might have been among those "best Communists." Unfortunately, her Comintern file provides little information on her actions and attitudes after 1928, and memoirs of Comintern officials from that period are nearly nonexistent. We do know, however, that she emerged from her Comintern training exceedingly guarded and disciplined and faithfully willing to adhere to the Kremlin's ever-changing and contradictory policies. She was also sufficiently intimidated by 1930 that, when writing her party autobiography, she intentionally omitted the fact that she had taught in two Jewish schools and pretended that her brother who committed suicide had never existed, claiming her family had three, not four, children. The testimonials of two women imprisoned with Pauker further depict her as rigidly endorsing the forced collectivization campaign of 1929–33 and the execution of Marshal M. N. Tukhachevsky in 1937. When one woman dared wonder out loud how Tukhachevsky could possibly have been a traitor, Pauker was said to have scolded her for being "a wavering element who doesn't trust the Party" and insisted that her lack of faith be discussed before the entire collective.[148]

Nevertheless, as the earlier depictions of Manuilsky and Fried themselves indicate, Ana Pauker's actions on one issue while still at the Lenin
School suggest a far more contradictory and complex situation than
Gitlow and Mendel portray. In the summer of 1930, Pauker and a number of Romanian students at the Lenin School were summoned to a special meeting of the Comintern's Balkan Secretariat, then headed by Bela
Kun and Henryk Walecki.[149] The issue at hand: a bitter dispute between
two factions of the RCP inside Romania, a dispute that literally split the
interior party. The leader of one faction was Vitali Holostenko (Barbu),
a Bessarabian-born Ukrainian appointed general secretary of the RCP at
the Fourth Party Congress in June–July 1928, having been transferred
from his post as head of the Agit-Prop Section of the Moldavian Regional Committee of the Ukrainian CP(b).[150] Leading the opposing faction was Marcel Pauker (Luximin), whose return to Romania after the
congress Holostenko himself had approved and who now had delibera-
tive voting rights in the Politburo, Secretariat, and Central Committee.[151] The two clashed over various policies almost immediately. At the
end of 1928, for example, Pauker rejected Holostenko's sweeping depiction of the just-elected National Peasant government as fascist, and
instead insisted on building "a mass movement" utilizing front organizations like the recently formed Workers-Peasants Bloc to influence
the new regime; in turn, Holostenko accused Pauker of fostering a
"right-wing" orientation, in apparent contradiction of the Comintern's
leftward turn at the Sixth World Congress of July–September 1928.[152]
Not surprisingly, a Comintern dictat settled the matter by sustaining
Holostenko.[153]

But the first clue of a "fractionalist fight" actually arose at the end of
1929.[154] Receiving news that Köblös had recently been released from a
Soviet prison, the Politburo was evenly split over whether to demand his
rearrest. Those voting in favor soon formed the Holostenko faction, and
those against formed the Pauker faction.[155] The rupture took place in
January 1930, when Holostenko unilaterally convened a truncated Central Committee limited mostly to his allies, in order to elect three new
CC members who would assure him a majority.[156] At first limited to
the RCP's highest circles, the dispute became public by the end of February and continued full force throughout March and April. Backing
Holostenko were the Bessarabian-Ukrainian wing of the party, the Bukovinian regional party organization, the party committees of Con-
stanța, Cluj, Brașov, and Arad, and RCP activists Ștefan Foriș and Constantin Pârvulescu, among others. Actively allied with Marcel Pauker

were Politburo members Dori (Rudi) Goldstein and Vasile Luca (Luca Laszlo); his supporters included all party organizations in Bucharest except the MOPR Central Committee, as well as the Bucharest, Galaţi, Iaşi, Timişoara, Oradea, and Târgu Mureş party committees.[157] Remaining neutral throughout was Lucreţiu Patraşcanu.[158]

As Marcel Pauker firmly emphasized in 1937, the dispute sprang from the intervention of various Ukrainian organizations and the Ukrainian CP(b) in Romanian Party affairs at the Fourth RCP Congress. His reading of the Congress, moreover, was ironically quite similar to that of his old nemesis, Elek Köblös, who, when appealing for Luca's support during the Congress's proceedings, exclaimed, "Don't you see that this group, led by Holostenko, with the support of Ukrainian nationalists, is seeking to put their hands on our party in order to use it for their own goals?"[159] Behind the Ukrainians from the very beginning, Marcel Pauker insisted (and Vasile Luca later corroborated), was the Comintern's Balkan Secretariat, which joined the Ukrainians in imposing Holostenko as the general secretary, designated a place in both the RCP's Politburo and Secretariat for a Ukrainian CP(b) representative, and sought to isolate resistant RCP members. "[T]hat Bela Kun . . . poked his nose in our affairs in an assault against the Communist Party in Romania, I have no doubt," Marcel Pauker declared. "And I said so [at the Balkan Secretariat] in 1930, though, naturally, not in such a manner."[160] This distrust of the Comintern seemingly was but an extension of Pauker's earlier positions when battling Ukrainian interference in the early 1920s. It is also discernible in Dori Goldstein's orders to Luca when they left for Moscow to confer with the Comintern in 1929: he was not to discuss the already existent divergencies between the Luximin and Barbu factions with Comintern officials, as it was a problem to be resolved solely within the RCP without involving the Comintern.[161]

In June 1930, the Comintern summoned the factions' leaders to appear before the Balkan Secretariat in Moscow.[162] At the meeting, which Ana Pauker and the other Lenin School students attended, Marcel Pauker quickly found himself raked over the coals by the Comintern's representatives. In Bela Kun's estimation, the guilty party was first and foremost Marcel Pauker. The first draft of the Secretariat's resolution cited evidence that Holostenko had started the dispute, but Kun deleted it soon afterward. Kun was making every effort, Marcel Pauker later wrote, to maintain Holostenko in the RCP leadership, while attributing the whole affair to the machinations of the Luximin faction.[163] The Secretariat sanctioned Pauker for his part in the "unprincipled fractionalist

fight" and ordered him to do "low-level work" at the Magnitogorsk factory. In a move to restore unity, the Secretariat removed Holostenko as
General Secretary and transferred him back to the Ukrainian CP(b).[164]

Clearly this was a golden opportunity for Ana Pauker to prove that
her party loyalties transcended any personal ties, as was indeed expected
of all the "best Communists." Moreover, as Marcel Pauker certainly appeared to be challenging Comintern control, for her to oppose him
openly would seem doubly imperative. She failed miserably. Her 1932
self-criticism on the matter acknowledged that her entire position at the
Balkan Secretariat meeting "was actually an act of solidarity with the
Luximin faction." This included rejecting the notions in the Comintern's
final resolution that the fractionalism had been "unprincipled" or that
Marcel Pauker's actions had no basis. It further included proposing that
the "fractionalists" be allowed to remain in the RCP leadership, which
in reality "was a show of support for the Luximin faction." Ten years
later Manuilsky would candidly remark to her that she was lucky not to
have been in Romania during the fractionalist infighting, as she undoubtedly would have been caught up in it more than anyone.[165]

Not surprisingly, the Comintern was quite interested in Ana Pauker's
reaction to the news of Marcel's "unmasking" in 1938. Her Comintern
file contains two reports on the issue, both sent to Moscow in 1940.
One provides a vague account of the discussion on the matter within
the party cell. While some one hundred women made up the "antifascist" collective at Dumbrăveni, a much smaller number of actual
party members comprised the Communist cell that led the collective. In
this latter body Pauker finally addressed the news that her husband was
a "people's enemy" and "Trotskyist traitor." One of the women present
was Sara Alterescu:

> We read the material that had arrived. And everyone who spoke up was, in
> an obligatory fashion, indignant and revolted. . . . Then Liuba [Chişinevschi]
> said: "Look, I criticize Ana that she, being the wife of Marcel Pauker, did not
> warn the party that he's an *agent provocateur*." And Ana replied: "I am now
> wracking my brain to find something, a sign of any kind, that would have led
> me to believe that he was an enemy of the people. I'm not placing any doubt
> on the party's decision; the party knows better than I. But I did not see any-
> thing; and as much as I search my soul, my recollections, my memory, I don't
> find anything that could prove such a thing."

The report disclosed that ultimately the only suspicious sign Ana Pauker
could remember from her husband's past was that he had maintained
contact with the Trotskyist Christian Rakovsky when the latter was the

Soviet ambassador to France—a point already cited in the *Scânteia* article's reprint of the Comintern resolution denouncing Marcel and an act of which she, too, probably was guilty. Ana Pauker knew Rakovsky from her RWSDP days and was in Paris with Marcel in 1926 while Rakovsky was ambassador there. The report concluded by noting the party had written Ana Pauker at Dumbrăveni, asking that the matter be discussed not only in the smaller Communist cell, but in the entire women's collective. In reality, the party had not just requested, but actually criticized Ana Pauker for "not [having] contribut[ed] to a prompt and sweeping denunciation of M[arcel] P[auker]," as she herself later acknowledged in a written response. Her reason for not doing so, she wrote, was that, "[i]n the special conditions that I find myself in, I was not aware of his recent activities against the Party except for what I read in *Scânteia* and the brochure against the Trotskyists from Romania." [166]

Moscow duly noted Ana Pauker's second refusal to openly denounce Marcel, for in 1940 the Comintern dispatched RCP General Secretary Ştefan Foriş to Râmnicu-Sărat to discuss the issue with her and perhaps to give her another chance. The second report in her file, however, recounts that she was staid and unresponsive to Foriş's inquiries on the Romanian Trotskyists and quotes her as mechanically retorting, "If the Party considers them enemies, then that's what they are." The report concluded, "It's clear from this response that Ana Pauker has not expressed her opinion on the matter." Adding that Liuba Chişinevschi's challenge to Pauker at the cell meeting "was not to Pauker's liking one bit," the report critically noted that "the Party organization in the prison, which is under the influence of Ana Pauker, has itself not adopted a well-defined position on this question." This was indeed the case, as Zina Brâncu, another member of the party cell, acknowledged, for the cell had decided to ask the party whether they could report the news to the larger collective without revealing the actual names of the accused, which put everything on hold for a considerable period. When they finally presented the material, Brâncu added, they were forced to appoint another cell member to take Pauker's place in addressing the issue. "[Ana] told me several times, and repeated it when I left prison, that she doesn't think that he's a traitor or an agent of the Siguranţă; she thinks him capable of fractionalism, and knows that he's very ambitious, but she nevertheless believes that he's an honest man. For that reason, she didn't want to discuss the news that arrived about Luximin before the [entire] collective." [167]

Ana Pauker largely confirmed Brâncu's account in a self-criticism written in September 1952. As she later confided to Lucreţiu Patrăşcanu, she was convinced that the Soviets had "unjustly set up" Marcel and "d[id] not believe what [was] said about him in the USSR." Ana Pauker's attitude is noteworthy not merely because she refused to openly attack her husband or because she did not believe what was obviously a typical Stalinist contrivance. It is truly noteworthy because, having worked closely with Marcel as late as 1935 in Bucharest, she must have known certain particulars in his political outlook. In October 1934, Marcel and three other Secretaries, one of whom was Alexandru Sencovici, were appointed to the RCP Secretariat. In a 1993 interview, Sencovici, then in his nineties, described Marcel Pauker precisely and at length, repeatedly stressing his principal point: by 1934 Marcel, who always had a penchant for pronouncing strong opinions, had openly expressed ambivalence toward the Soviets. After the fractionalist fight in 1930, and after his two-year stay in the Soviet Union immediately thereafter, Marcel returned to Romania, Sencovici asserted, highly critical of Soviet practices and stubbornly opposed to Soviet domination. While perhaps exaggerated, Sencovici's account nonetheless seems to correspond with Marcel's actions. That Ana Pauker did not see this as "enemy activity" or "treachery to the Party" is significant and no doubt foreshadowed her future behavior.[168]

Hence, the second, more critical, report on Ana Pauker ends with the following disclosure: "At the beginning of the war, Ana Pauker, receiving information regarding the French Communist Party's position (its initial mistaken position) on the defense of France [that is, the FCP's support of France's war against Nazi Germany in contradiction to the Nazi-Soviet pact], said that the comrades of the F.C.P. were right; that is, she justified their mistaken position." In addition, though no documentation exists in her Comintern file, Moscow must have been informed of another episode at Caransebeş prison in the fall of 1940: when asked, as head of the collective, to isolate a certain Tereza Simon on the grounds that she was a known Trotskyist, Pauker refused to do so and suggested instead the collective should seek to "enlighten her."[169]

Ana Pauker had retained, therefore, vestiges of independence and remained faithful to certain principles when she returned to the Soviet Union in May 1941. She was, moreover, clearly vulnerable as the wife of an "enemy of the people" the minute she stepped foot there, even more so given her insufficient response to Marcel's purge. But once she left Soviet soil in September 1944, her actions could no longer be attributed simply to self-preservation. Her decision to continue following

Stalin after the Great Terror was psychologically complicated. Suffice it to say that by so doing Ana Pauker proved herself an exemplary Lenin School graduate: the disciplined and loyal soldier readily serving those who she believed had "set up" her husband. At the same time, however, she never distanced herself from the Pauker family once back in Romania; on the contrary, her first stop upon arriving in Bucharest was not at party headquarters, but at Marcel's parents, and she delighted in her son Vlad's refusal to change his last name when pressured to do so soon after the war.[170] The contradictions and ambiguities evident throughout her career continued, and they would intensify in the years to follow.

CHAPTER THREE

In Power

Ana Pauker returned to the Soviet Union on May 7, 1941.[1] The Soviet press did not report her arrival, but word of it quickly spread among the Romanians residing there,[2] a majority of whom were Spanish Civil War veterans brought from French internment camps in 1939 or 1940.[3] Pauker was feted at a festive Moscow reception in her honor and immediately appointed as the RCP's representative to the Comintern. She was also provided a residence "in the building where all the high chiefs of the Comintern reside[d],"[4] which underscored her prominence as a select member of the Comintern hierarchy. She once confided to a colleague that she had noticed German and Romanian troops amassing at the border when she crossed it but, true to the times, was advised to keep her mouth shut;[5] six weeks later, the Nazi blitzkrieg against the USSR began. On October 16, Pauker and other Comintern officials were evacuated by train to the eastern city of Ufa. "The whole trip to the other end of the Volga took one week," a fellow passenger related. "There was nothing to eat. At some points people would get off the train to beg for food. Whatever we said, that we have sick or wounded people on the train, would not work. But, at one village, the moment they heard that Ana Pauker was aboard, there was food for the entire train."[6] By then Pauker was a celebrated Soviet propaganda symbol, and her name was well-known even among simple villagers in the Russian countryside.

In Ufa, Pauker directed the Comintern's *România liberă* (Free Romania) radio station, which based its reports on Romanian newspapers that rarely arrived. One of her wartime secretaries, Natalia Scurtu, subsequently revealed that Pauker appeared listless and depressed throughout this period and had to be prodded to answer the many letters she received from RCP members in remote parts of the country. "[M]y impression was that she was . . . sad and embittered from a lack of information, a lack of connections, and a lack of work," Scurtu related. "Her material life was not very easy, despite her privileged situation, because she had two children to support."[7] Returning to Moscow in 1942, Pauker and RCP activists Vasile Luca and Manole H. Manole formed a committee mandated to draw up a platform for a National Democratic Front in Romania.[8] She began working at Institute No. 205 after the Comintern's 1943 dissolution,[9] also collaborating with Luca to organize the first divisions of volunteers among Romanian prisoners of war, under the auspices of the general directorate of the Red Army,[10] and presiding over the Congress of Romanian Prisoners at Krasnogorsk in September of 1943.[11] Her emotional state seeming to have "changed overnight," Pauker proposed naming one of the divisions after the Romanian national figure Tudor Vladimirescu and reportedly played a key role in its formation, having convinced the first Romanian officers to take its command.[12] In spring 1944, she was sent, again with Luca, to the liberated towns of Bălți and Botoșani on the Romanian front, spending two months in the latter,[13] and was then briefly placed in the Marx-Engels-Lenin Institute in Moscow.[14] On September 16, 1944, she flew back to Bucharest.[15]

In Romania Pauker kept a low profile—limiting her public functions to heading an innocuous women's organization (the Union of Anti-Fascist Romanian Women), in which capacity she traveled to France and Switzerland in 1945.[16] But she quickly became known among Romanians and the foreign press as the Iron Lady of Romania, the omnipotent hand behind Communist demonstrations against the Nicolae Rădescu government in February 1945.[17] During the disturbances Rădescu singled her out when attacking the Communists and branded her and the ethnic-Hungarian Luca "hyenas" and "foreigners without God or country."[18] Rădescu's replacement several weeks later by the Communist-led Groza government (at the insistence of the Soviets) did not change this equation. Pauker continued to work behind the scenes and was not appointed to any government post until November 1946, when she was elected to the Romanian parliament. One year later she was named Romania's Foreign Minister, becoming the first Jew to attain a ministerial post in the country's history, and the first female Foreign Minister in the modern world.[19]

According to a lengthy portrait in *Life* magazine, Pauker was

> the most heavily guarded of all the Romanian Communist hierarchy. Before she became foreign minister callers at her party headquarters on the fashionable Allee Eliza Filipescu were met by three tommy gunners behind an iron gate, three more in the hall, and two on each landing. . . . Ana sped around Bucharest on the front seat of a bulletproof Cadillac, next to a chauffeur from the secret police. She once gave me a lift in the back seat, casually remarking that she preferred the front because shots aimed at a moving car usually hit the rear. Nowadays she sits in the back of a steel-plated Russian Zis, with an extra bodyguard in front and armored Fords before and behind her sedan.

The reporter added that "[t]he non-Communist press was forbidden to criticize her on peril of suspension. One newspaper which so dared was promptly closed by the Soviet censor."[20] This, however, did not prevent a host of rumors about her in the Western press—including mendacious tales of unbridled promiscuity[21] and exaggerated accounts of a penchant for luxury.[22] Exaggerated as well were the many reports of Pauker's preeminence: though initially correct, they generally misconstrued her ongoing and ultimately futile power struggle in the party hierarchy.

When she returned to Romania, Pauker knew little of the party's situation there, for the Comintern had lost all contact with the RCP's interior underground after the Nazi invasion.[23] Officially headed by General Secretary Ștefan Foriș, the RCP both before and during the war had been characterized by continual infighting between the regional organizations and the central command and by increasing friction between Foriș and the Communist cadres in prisons throughout the country.[24] Within the prisons themselves, reportedly ten to twelve factions competed with one another by the end of the war, but the principal group was an alliance of Teohari Georgescu and Iosif Chișinevschi, the leaders of the party organization inside Caransebeș prison, with Gheorghe Gheorghiu-Dej and his followers at the Târgu-Jiu prison camp. (Dej had been a leader of the Caransebeș group, but was transferred to Târgu-Jiu in 1943.)[25] Under interrogation after his arrest in 1953, Georgescu suggested the Dej-Georgescu-Chișinevschi faction bitterly opposed Foriș because of his "unjust working methods," and their suspicion (later found groundless)[26] that he had "provoked" a number of key arrests of important party activists.[27] On April 3, 1944, Foriș announced to his associates that Emil Bodnăraş, a high-ranking Soviet spy who had been released from Caransebeş at the end of 1942 or early 1943, had recently succeeded in reestablishing contact with the Soviet Union "through espionage channels," thanks to the arrival of a certain agent from the USSR.[28] One day later, informing Foriş "that his orders had come from the Soviet Union," Bodnăraş handed him a typed note ordering him to surrender all party materials and placing him under house arrest.[29]

If a Soviet spy agency ordered Foriş's ouster, nothing was known of it at Institute No. 205, the "Ghost Comintern" in Moscow.[30] Interrogated by a party commission in June 1956, Pauker revealed that Georgi Dimitrov, the former General Secretary of the Comintern, ordered her to return to Romania with two radio-transmission specialists and regularly report back to Moscow because they still had no contact with the interior party in Romania (unlike those in the other countries), and had no idea what was going on there. At the same time, Pauker added, Dimitrov instructed her to take over the RCP leadership in Bucharest. "And right then and there I said: 'Comrade Dimitrov, I'm a woman, I haven't been in the country throughout the war, I was in prison [before that], and have no idea how things stand. Ten years have passed, and [leading the party] would be hard for me to do. I'm a woman, a Jew, and an intellectual.'" Instead, Pauker maintained, she proposed to Dimitrov that the new party leader be Gheorghiu-Dej. "I don't know him very well; I met him only for two hours at Caransebeş; but I know that he's a very popular comrade, a railway worker, and a tried and tested man." Dimitrov disagreed. "We've had no information from Romania for four to five years. We don't know anybody [over there], but we know you."[31]

Thus, with Dimitrov's mandate, Pauker promptly took over the RCP from its provisional leaders (General Secretary Constantin Pârvulescu, Iosif Rangheţ, Emil Bodnăraş, and behind them, Gheorghe Gheorghiu-Dej), whom she brashly criticized for ousting the "chosen leadership" of Ştefan Foriş.[32] But she soon found herself in a stalemate with Gheorghiu-Dej, who insisted "in a very unpleasant conversation" that the party wanted him to become general secretary; as a compromise, both agreed to a temporary collective leadership with no general secretary, deferring that choice until later.[33] In reality Pauker served as general secretary through the RCP's national conference in October 1945.[34] Exactly when the Soviets settled on Dej as the RCP leader is not clear, though if one testimonial is correct, Stalin personally did so as early as January 1945.[35] Whatever the case, Pauker herself proposed naming Dej general secretary at a party leadership meeting.[36] Dej would later confirm, "She said: 'Considering the state of cultural backwardness of our people, and the strong prejudices concerning women, they will say: a woman to lead the Communist Party, and a Jewish one at that, who came not long ago from the Soviet Union?' She alone referred to this. 'Thus the most suitable one among us,' she said, 'is Dej.'"[37] When Pauker sent word to Vyacheslav Molotov suggesting Dej's appointment as general secretary at the party's national conference, Molotov's response could not have been clearer: "You're a clever woman" ("*Umnitza*").[38]

Still, Dej was to have plenty of company in the party Secretariat, for appointed as CC secretaries alongside him were Pauker, Vasile Luca, and Teohari Georgescu. A veteran union leader and a prominent member of the party hierarchy since the mid-1920s, Luca had been a deputy of the Supreme Soviet and an officer in the political directorate of the Red Army during the war.[39] He worked for a Soviet espionage agency until his return to Romania in October 1944. (Soon after returning to Romania, Luca was replaced as an espionage agent, at his own request, by Iosif Chișinevschi.)[40] Although she proposed Luca's inclusion in the party leadership, Pauker at that time had little personal sympathy for him, "considered him arrogant and limited of mind, and was unhappy that she [had returned] to Romania with him."[41] Eventually she would closely ally herself to Luca, partly because of Dej's various maneuvers against them and partly because, with time, they adopted increasingly similar views on party policy.[42] For his part, Luca was widely perceived to have been exceedingly servile to Pauker, and always coordinated with her on important issues.[43] In contrast, the personal animosity and political rivalry between Luca and Gheorghiu-Dej was particularly intense, in part because Luca condescendingly considered himself Dej's senior in the party apparat: in prison he referred to Dej as a "protégé" from the past.[44] Before Luca's purge he asserted to an associate that he "had in fact promoted Gheorghiu-Dej, who became a party member much later than he."[45] Apparently this was indeed the case, but it was not something of which Dej appreciated being reminded.[46]

Teohari Georgescu, on the other hand, had been a leader of the Center of the Prisons during the war and was a close ally of Gheorghiu-Dej. He may have been included in the Secretariat, therefore, to maintain parity between Pauker's "Muscovite" and Dej's "interior" factions and, perhaps, to maintain ethnic parity as an ethnic-Romanian. Nevertheless, Georgescu soon fell under Pauker's influence and began to see her "as a

comrade with much more prestige and experience . . . who was incapable of making major mistakes." [47] As he later acknowledged, he began
supporting Pauker's political positions from 1944 to 1948, and their
"fractionalist relations . . . intensified even more" from 1949 on. "[F]or
years," he declared, "especially after 1949, I listened to Ana on innu-
merable occasions, discussing problems with her regarding the decisions
and the line of the Party," and he "joined forces with [her] during that
period on a number of principled matters." [48] He did so, he added, without conferring with the other leaders, for "Ana Pauker's word was
enough for me when resolving problems, and I did not take into account
that many of these matters should have definitely been known about and
decided upon by the party leadership." [49] Georgescu and Pauker's rapidly developing personal friendship further cemented this dynamic.[50]
For her part, Pauker depicted it bluntly: "I did whatever I wanted with
Teohari," she declared, "because I could do that with him." [51] A consensus of those interviewed soundly affirms Georgescu was Pauker's protégé after 1945 and consulted with her on all important matters.[52] This
reportedly continued up until their purge, when Georgescu secretly visited Pauker's home to consult with her.[53]

Pauker's initial predominance in the Secretariat was clear in an October 24, 1945, meeting three days after the party's national conference.
Noting the difficulty Dej would have in handling both his ministerial
and party duties, Luca proposed that "publicly Comrade Gheorghiu-
Dej should be the political secretary, but in practice it should be Comrade Ana." Pauker immediately disagreed: Dej, she insisted, should be
both "nominally and practically the General Secretary," which, she reminded Luca, had already been decided "several months earlier." Still,
she did not explicitly reject Luca's subsequent proposal that "the authority of Comrade Ana, placing her in the role of [Dej's] helper, must
not be diminished." [54] Nor, for that matter, did Georgescu, who, Dej asserted, had fully supported Luca's proposal.[55] Hence Dej, timidly silent
throughout the meeting, reportedly promised to consult with Pauker on
all important matters, while Pauker, after proposing Dej in the first postwar meeting of the Central Committee, made it a point to add, "I'll do
my best to help him." [56] Further, as she later acknowledged, Pauker began to argue after Dej's appointment "that perhaps there's no need for
us to have a General Secretary, just as the Bolshevik Party doesn't have
one. Comrade Stalin is [just] a secretary." [57] Clearly, with or without
Dej's ascent, the "collective leadership" partial to Pauker was meant to
continue.

Gheorghiu-Dej later described the consequence: "Although I was the general secretary, [Pauker] dominated [in the Secretariat] together with Vasile Luca and Teohari Georgescu. This was a permanent faction. . . . [H]ow many times in our meetings would Luca be the first one to speak, as if he was born to do that? He would make a speech for an hour. When the discussion began, Ana would then jump in and say a few words with hocus-pocus, with her great authority. I presided very beautifully: 'Who else wants to speak?' And Teohari would say: 'I agree with Comrade Ana.'"[58]

Although perhaps exaggerated, Dej's account was accurate in that Pauker's policy positions usually prevailed during this period—except, apparently, when the Kremlin leadership directly overruled her. Initially, however, she seemed to have personified the Soviets' political line— echoing, for instance, their disapproval of Ion Antonescu's overthrow on August 23, 1944.[59] Indeed, Lucrețiu Patrașcanu, with whom she clashed on the issue, depicted her at the time as Moscow's principal agent in imposing Soviet rule over Romania.[60] Her record soon became increasingly contradictory, however, and she began to take positions at odds with her Soviet patrons', as well as Gheorghiu-Dej's. This was unmistakable when Pauker, reportedly "out of fear of public opinion," moved to the right of Patrașcanu himself and supported a continued coalition with the National Peasant and National Liberal parties in February 1945, as opposed to the more restrictive grouping that soon comprised the Groza government.[61] (Patrașcanu favored allowing only the National Liberals in the new government.[62]) As Gheorghiu-Dej later revealed, he alone promoted a coalition solely with Gheorghe Tătărăscu, the "formula that was realized on March 6, 1945. First [Pauker and her allies] objected that it was a weak political force, that we needed a strong political body, and it's immoral, that, look, Tătărăscu was . . . interior minister when you sat in prison, and the story of [his quashing the] Tatar Bunar [peasant uprising in Bessarabia in 1924], and all the rest. . . . They didn't agree with me, and we had to go to Moscow." There Stalin sustained Gheorghiu-Dej.[63]

Pauker's position on the matter and, indeed, her postwar positions generally appeared to stem from a realization of the inordinate weakness of the RCP, which could claim only "some 700" members in August 1944.[64] For this reason, she quickly modified her stance on the events on August 23: while characterizing the coup as an act "of rescuing the [Romanian] bourgeoisie," she concluded that it had to be supported nonetheless, given the party's present weaknesses.[65] Finding it "intolerable" that but seven Communists were in Oradea or thirty-two in Botoşani, she pursued "a type of Social Democratic policy" modeled after the French and Italian CPs' mass recruitment campaigns.[66] "My view was that we had to expand the party, to reach the number of 500,000," she later declared.[67] By November, she was insisting that the party open its gates, pressing its local leaders to ease their restrictions on admitting new members and opposing any prior verification of those seeking membership.[68] The spring of 1945 she issued "categorical instructions" to receive new members en masse into the RCP.[69] Moreover, faced with a substantial number of Romanian workers' having formally joined the Iron Guard, Pauker permitted some of them to enter the party under certain circumstances, and did so without consulting Dej or "even Luca or Teohari."[70]

These policies went hand in hand, however, with extensive repression, for which Pauker was unquestionably culpable. As Georgescu revealed to the RCP Central Committee, no fewer than 50,000–70,000 Romanians had been sacked from the government by the end of 1945.[71] That March 7, with tough and strident rhetoric on arresting adversaries, Pauker instructed the party's central *activ* that its "immediate tasks are those of clearing the terrain . . . , that is, purges—but not by leaving people on the street to become active enemies, but by eventually taking them to camps where they'll be sorted out and put to work, and by immediately arresting war criminals."[72] As she confided to leading Romanian Social Democrats on March 28, "[I]f we have anything to reproach Comrade Teohari with [as Interior Minister], it's that he's working too slowly. Because it's not possible that there should not be 50,000 Legionaries arrested by now in Romania."[73] After all, she pointed out, had not France arrested 40,000 Nazi collaborators by then?[74]

But here, too, Pauker soon changed course. By September 1945 she reportedly had resolved to unilaterally dismantle the internment camps without conferring with the party leadership, and had actively "influenced" Georgescu to negotiate a nonaggression pact with Iron Guard leader Nicolae Pătraşcu.[75] Aware that armed detachments of Legionaries were forming throughout the country, and fearful of a protracted rebellion, Pauker and Georgescu offered amnesty to any Iron Guardist who would turn in his weapons, as well as to any found not to have committed serious crimes. As a goodwill gesture they began releasing arrested Legionaries even before their negotiations with Pătraşcu.[76] By August 1945, therefore, the number of people under arrest in the entire country fell to between two and three thousand.[77]

As Pauker later specified, her decision to compromise with the Legionaries was "influenced by the fact that there were more of them, and especially workers, than I'd imagined," which led her into "a kind of panic over what to do with all of them." It also reflected Pauker's emerging attitude on non-Communists generally, favoring inclusion over class conflict in the new order. "I thought," she explained, "that there was a special situation in the country, that it wasn't the October Revolution, but that, in 1944–45 . . . we were going with everyone who was against Hitler." [78] This attitude appeared to continue: Pauker was known to have regularly appointed non-Communist intellectuals, scholars, and cultural figures as Romania's ambassadors when becoming Foreign Minister in 1947; was reported to have opposed the "cleaning out" of "enemy elements" from the Agriculture Ministry upon assuming responsibility for agriculture two years later; and promoted the integration of Romania's rural bourgeoisie (the *chiaburi*) into socialism. [79] Indeed, as her personal secretary Ana Toma revealed, throughout the postwar years Pauker developed

> a relationship with the upper strata of the Romanian bourgeoisie, whom she received whenever they requested it. . . . They would go to her if they had a problem, and Ana wanted to win these people over for the party. . . . Ana also received army generals, even if they weren't party members, if they had problems. She received them, and had discussions with them, regardless of whether she could solve what they requested. . . . She would waste her time at the Foreign Ministry discussing things with them. . . . [Also a] lot of different people, including intellectuals, were coming to her house—for instance, people who had positions in the former regime. These were people who were afraid of being persecuted, and Ana would talk with them in order to convince them politically. She would see them at her home so that she would know what they were thinking, and also so she could influence their opinions; and she would receive them in her home in order to reassure them, to calm their fears. . . . Ana spoke even to people who were in trouble, or about to be tried, or be purged by the party, in order to be informed so that she may help. [80]

Needless to say, the Soviets ultimately overturned most of Pauker's policies, refuting several immediately. Besides Stalin's rejection of her proposed coalition with the historic parties, Andrei Vyshinski in 1945 "vehemently criticized" her and Georgescu's actions on the Iron Guard. [81] (Vyshinski's reproach, however, reportedly did not stop her from pressing her position.) [82] Still, given the lack of coordination within the Communist movement during the early postwar years, [83] it seems that Pauker

had a free hand in most policy issues. For instance, she apparently promoted mass recruitment with no compelling guidance from "the comrades," and did so despite Gheorghiu-Dej's firm objections.[84] Dej also
opposed Pauker's conciliation of the Iron Guard and maintained his fall
1944 view that they should "eradicate the Legionaries like vipers."[85]
Indeed, "on the most important matters," Dej asserted, "and there were
plenty of them, I appeared as a kind of professional oppositionist, because I could not agree with all the issues [she and her allies] were raising."[86] As a prominent party leader later emphasized, Dej and Pauker's
power struggle was intense and permanent from the first moment after
the war, but, at the same time, it reflected genuine policy disputes.[87]

Hence, Stalin's show of support notwithstanding, Gheorghiu-Dej remained a subordinate within the party leadership. "They surrounded
me, they kept me in a pen, they tried to isolate me, and they succeeded,"
Dej declared. "As a matter of fact, they succeeded in maintaining the situation in which the general secretary and the leader was in fact Ana
Pauker. It was not just a coincidence that people would go to Ana. When
they came to me, it was after they had discussed things with her. That
was the rule." Throughout the early postwar years, he insisted, they deliberately reduced him to a "front man."[88]

But Gheorghiu-Dej, whose acumen for political intrigue and behind-
the-scenes maneuvering was beyond the reach of anyone else in the Romanian leadership, was hardly one to accept such an arrangement. In
fact, he had laid the foundation for gaining sole control of the party even
long before leaving the Târgu-Jiu camp. Until 1930, the NKVD utilized
local Communists as its agents, of whom the Romanian authorities arrested and jailed many; in prison, they became close to and dedicated
followers of Gheorghiu-Dej. The most important of them were Emil
Bodnăraş, Pantiuşa Bodnarenko (Gheorghe Pintilie), Sergei Nicolau,
Petre Gonciariuc, Vania Didenco, Iaşa Aleksiev, and Mişa Posteuca,
but they apparently numbered some forty-six in all. Once liberated, they
served as Dej's direct link to Moscow through the NKVD, and they
vouched for him to the Kremlin leaders. In return, Dej granted them
high party positions, and they comprised the base from which he would
launch his bid to monopolize power.[89]

Given that Communist cadres throughout the twenties had maintained connections with both the Comintern and the NKVD, Pauker
seemingly would have had her own ties with Soviet espionage—as
did Luca. But much of the Comintern's liquidation during the Great

Terror put her in an altogether different position. According to Michael Checinski, a former operative in Polish military counterintelligence, the old Comintern militants and former Polish CP members in Poland "were treated with extreme suspicion" by the Soviets after the war, "and were not admitted to local Communist Party organizations."[90] As one scholar observed, after the war Stalin evinced profound mistrust of veteran Cominternists, whom he suspected of maintaining independent plans for their own countries and masking their long-held idealism behind a facade of subservience.[91] This did not bode well for Pauker, a long-standing member of the Comintern hierarchy, whose only real patrons in Moscow were Dimitrov and Manuilsky of the Comintern leadership.[92] Hardly enjoying the Kremlin's good graces as traditionally portrayed, she was actually in a "special situation" in its eyes throughout the war and after because of Marcel Pauker.[93] Although initially sent back to Romania to lead the RCP, she knew the assignment was always intended to be only temporary; and though she maintained close and amicable relations with prominent Soviet officials based in Romania (particularly the Soviet ambassador, Sergei Kavtaradze),[94] she apparently considered her position with the Soviets quite tenuous—even during the immediate postwar years, when she was assumed to have been at the height of her power. Ana Toma recalled that, in late 1944 or early 1945, Pauker was suddenly summoned to Moscow:

> Ana wanted to take her daughter Tania with her. . . . I don't know why Ana wanted her daughter with her, but I assume that she was very much afraid. She didn't know why she was called to Moscow, and she wanted to have Tania by her side just in case. And she took me to take care of her daughter in case anything happened. . . . When we arrived in Moscow, Ana took me aside and said to me, without her daughter hearing, "I want you to go with Tania everywhere. I want you to be with her all the time. I don't want to leave her alone." Ana told Tania to go to museums and other places, and that I should go with her wherever she went. . . . The three of us then went to the Central Committee, which is near the [Bolshoi] theater in Moscow. When we were just across the street, Ana took me aside and said: "Look, I'm going in that door. If I come out and go through the other door, then you can take Tania and go to the museum. But if I don't come out of that door, then go to the hotel, pack up your things, and get away from here as fast as you can." That is just to give you the atmosphere in which she was living. I want you to understand just how frightened she was of Moscow.

Indeed, in Ana Toma's estimation, Pauker's greatest enemy in the postwar period was the Soviet secret police. She asserts that, as Pauker's deputy, she was treated hostilely in 1948 by MGB agent Nikolai Shutov, an adviser in the Soviet embassy, who in fact ordered her to conceal the content of their discussions from Pauker.[95]

Ana Toma's assessment, moreover, was ostensibly corroborated by the actions of Emil Bodnăraş, at the time a leading Romanian agent of Soviet espionage and Gheorghiu-Dej's most important ally.[96] Having organized the party's secret service in the immediate postwar period, Bodnăraş officially supervised the Secret Service of the Council of Ministers (SSI) after the Groza regime's installation.[97] At precisely that time, Pauker revealed, the SSI began spying on her at her home and office, and Bodnăraş dispatched reports to the Soviets on both her and Luca.[98] Once, the Soviet representative to the Allied Control Commission, General I. Susaikov (himself a secret service agent), warned Pauker while intoxicated that "certain organs from Moscow" were reporting unfavorably on her to the Kremlin and demanded to know why she tolerated it.[99] Bodnăraş, added Pauker, was always arguing for replacing her and Luca as party leaders, on the grounds that their opponents were using her Jewish and his Hungarian ethnicity to increase their political advantage.[100]

These moves culminated in the fall of 1945, when Andrei Vyshinski, angry over Pauker's attempt to broaden the Groza government, as well as her position on the Iron Guard, suggested her ouster from the leadership to Dej. Thus began a dramatic episode detailed by Gheorghiu-Dej:

> Vyshinski took me aside and said: "Comrade Dej . . . , how does Ana Pauker help you?" I said, you can see for yourself how she helps me. . . . He then thought a little and said: "Wouldn't it be better perhaps if Ana were removed from here?" You could have understood him to mean either that Ana should be removed from the leadership or removed from Romania. I then told him: "Comrade Vyshinski, such an idea never even crossed my mind, but I'm going to think about it, and reflect on what you said." . . .
>
> Being in Moscow on economic matters . . . , I reminded Vyshinski of our discussion in Bucharest, and he said: "I'm going to talk with Comrade Molotov, and you'll be received by the higher-ups." . . . The next day Ana was summoned. . . . We were at the hotel, and they informed us that Ana had arrived. I thought: Why the devil was she called?
>
> That evening we were called to the Kremlin. Everyone was there—there was Molotov, and Susaikov, who was summoned from [Bucharest]. I thought: What the hell has happened? Of course, I was scared.[101]

The meeting, which also included Soviet ambassador Kavtaradze, took place February 2, 1947; the minutes were found in the Russian archives. After briefly addressing the Romanian elections, Stalin turned to

Gheorghiu-Dej and asked whether there were any divergencies within
the RCP leadership. Dej replied that the only "serious divergence" was
the case of Lucreţiu Patraşcanu, which he proceeded to summarize. But
Stalin pressed on, asking Dej "whether there was any truth to the rumors reaching him that there exists a current in the RCP that wants only
Romanians to be in the party; that is, in concrete terms, that Ana Pauker
and Luca, not being of Romanian nationality, should not hold leadership positions in the party." If that was the case, Stalin emphasized, then
the RCP was being transformed "from a social and class party to a race
party." But Dej denied the existence of any such current, and with that
the matter was dropped.[102] "Ana looked astonished," Dej related. After
the meeting she worriedly asked Dej what Stalin could have been thinking. "She was always asking me what could be on Stalin's mind," Dej
pointedly added. "She was always asking me what will be." [103]

The issue apparently resolved, Pauker immediately returned to Bucharest, while Dej stayed on with the delegation in Moscow.

I think that I was under surveillance there. I was always telling myself what
a stupid thing I did. . . . Some two days later, in the middle of the night, the
phone rang. At the other end of the line was [the official interpreter, Major]
Shkoda. He says . . . : "Gheorghe Afanasievici, get dressed. I'll be over there
in a few minutes." I got dressed, Shkoda came by, and we went to the Kremlin. Stalin was there, Susaikov was there, and Shkoda. I shook hands with
them. Stalin says: "Have a seat." I sat down on a chair and waited.

He says: "You are here before the Central Committee of the C.P.S.U. You
raised the issue of the removal of Ana Pauker and Luca Laszlo [Vasile Luca]."
I said: "I'm surprised that you bring up Vasile Luca. I didn't raise the issue
about him; I raised it about Ana Pauker." And I began to explain to him how
and why. I gave him an extensive explanation there. I referred . . . to the way
the people in the leadership were chosen, to the work methods, to many,
many things related to that, and to the difficulties Ana was making for me,
and how I characterized those difficulties.

He was very inquisitive and became irritated that I had not mentioned one
word about Vyshinski. And then he asked me: "You discussed this and that
with Vyshinski in Bucharest?" I said: "I did." "Why don't you bring it up
here?" I said: "Comrade Stalin, I don't want to hide behind anyone." I told
him how that discussion was held, and the reason it occurred. I told him that
the idea had actually come from Vyshinski. . . . And then Molotov jumped
up with a malicious laugh, and said: "And what if Comrade Vyshinski was
testing you?" . . .

After that Stalin calmed down more and more, and began to speak about
how things should be viewed. He was convinced that I wanted her out because she's a Jew. He gave me the example of Trotsky, and I don't know who

else. At one point, talking about this, giving a kind of lecture, he says: "And if they stand in your way, get rid of them!" . . .

I returned home, and got together with them here, those of us who were in the Secretariat, and I told them in detail how things unfolded— everything, without smoothing things around the edges. . . . The one single thing I did not tell them was that Stalin said "If they stand in your way, get rid of them." [104]

It seems, however, that Stalin was now the one testing Dej. With his suspicions already roused regarding Tito—suspicions that he soon transferred to native, homegrown Communists generally—Stalin apparently was unwilling to give Dej a free hand to monopolize power. He much preferred to divide and rule by encouraging factional infighting in the RCP, as he did in the other "fraternal" parties. Dej was, after all, an enigma of sorts to Stalin, as he was the only satellite leader never connected to the Comintern or directly linked with Moscow.[105] He was, moreover, already under a cloud by the time of the February 2 meeting. As Shkoda informed the Kremlin two days later, Dej ruefully spoke to him about Stalin's angry reaction to a memo he had recently written to Vyshinski. In it, Dej asked the Soviets to reduce the Romanians' reparation payments by allowing them to subtract the amount they had spent to house Soviet troops between July 1945 and February 1947 from their monetary debt and to cover the remainder with Romanian goods. Stalin promptly rejected the request, remarking, "The Hungarians and the Austrians would never have made such a joke." Shkoda reported that "Dej told me that not only did he make a mistake, but he did a very foolish thing, because it placed him in an unpleasant situation, and infuriated people like Stalin and Molotov." [106]

Perhaps inevitably, then, Bodnăraş, who was also instrumental in eliminating Foriş and purging Patraşcanu,[107] now targeted Gheorghiu-Dej. On June 10, 1947, Susaikov forwarded to Mikhail Suslov an informative note from Bodnăraş so scathingly critical of Dej that Susaikov had to temper its conclusions in his accompanying report. "A series of facts," Bodnăraş suggested, "leads one to conclude that, on the issue of maintaining an economic relationship with the Anglo-Americans, Gheorghiu-Dej has diverged in a significant way from the Soviet representatives in Romania, whom he rarely meets with, and some of whom he even ignores." Following the return of Dej's economic delegation to Moscow at the beginning of the year, Dej and his associates at the Ministry of National Economy (Ion Gheorghe Maurer, Gheorghe

Gaston Marin, and Simion Zeiger) began negotiations with American and British representatives on importing wheat to Romania. The Anglo-Americans' apparent readiness to accommodate Romania, Bodnăraş asserted, led to a change of heart in Gheorghiu-Dej, who now favored increasing economic ties with them beyond the previously set "clearly defined limits" of cooperation. That position, added Bodnăraş, resulted in a conflict between Dej and Pauker, Luca, and Bodnăraş himself, who wanted to assure that Dej did not "go further than necessary in his relations with the Anglo-Americans." It also was a consequence of Dej's being demonstrably influenced by Maurer, whom Bodnăraş described as a dangerous element, insufficiently loyal to the Soviet Union. To prove Dej and Maurer's hostility to Soviet interests, Bodnăraş listed eight points—including Dej's claim that the presence of Soviet troops was further harming Romania's economy, and his criticism of the workings of the SOVROMs (the joint Soviet-Romanian companies). Bodnăraş concluded, "These facts should be understood as a very serious sign. Because we have to be concerned here with a certain weakening of Dej from the correct political line, and because it was the beginning of a very dangerous inclination toward the Anglo-Americans, which makes . . . radical measures possible." [108]

These alarming charges, however, had no immediate repercussions. This was perhaps because Susaikov's report drew a sharp distinction between Dej and Maurer and disclosed that Pauker, Luca, and Georgescu favored countering Maurer's undue influence by placing him in the diplomatic service; or perhaps because the report suggested the conflict in the leadership was not about Dej's policies but his unwillingness to discuss those policies with the other leaders; or perhaps because neither Pauker nor Luca accused Dej of any anti-Sovietism in their discussions with V. I. Lesakov, the Soviet representative dispatched to Bucharest in the late summer of 1947, and he thus could not confirm any such charges.[109] But a year later, another faux pas landed Gheorghiu-Dej in trouble. When Tito declined Stalin's invitation to attend the June 1948 Cominform conference, Dej proposed that the other Cominform countries issue their own invitation. He contended he had first discussed the idea with Ana Pauker, who hesitantly agreed. But when he made his proposal at the Cominform, Andrei Zhdanov sternly contradicted him and immediately informed Stalin by phone. "Stalin said," Gheorghiu-Dej said of his own situation, "that Dej was deluding himself, and that it's not excluded that others were doing so as well. . . . From that moment on . . . , all kinds of rumors began to circulate [in Romania] against

Dej." [110] It was said, he related, "that Gheorghiu-Dej is a Titoist, that he's under arrest, or even that Gheorghiu-Dej has been shot. . . . Activists from the Central Committee were asking: 'If Gheorghiu-Dej should come around, should we applaud him?' Things had gotten that bad." [111]

The rumors, Georgescu disclosed, had created considerable consternation among the country's railway workers, who were closely identified with Gheorghiu-Dej. [112] When an assembly of those workers from the Bucharest district of Giuleşti convened, they were alarmed to find Iosif Chişinevschi chairing the meeting instead of Dej, who had normally done so. They defiantly began chanting "Gheorghiu-Dej" while Chişinevschi was speaking. Visibly ruffled, Chişinevschi regained his composure and rashly rejoined, "Let's see, if I scream 'Stalin,' whether you'll scream it just as loud as you screamed 'Gheorghiu-Dej!'" When explaining the Cominform resolution against Tito, moreover, Chişinevschi offered implicit analogies between Tito and Dej. Considering this a provocation, Dej demanded that the Politburo formally censure Chişinevschi, with a warning that he was one mistake away from party expulsion. But, while criticizing Chişinevschi, Pauker prevented the censure vote from passing and berated Georgescu for joining Dej in the attack. "Don't you know," she said, "that that's against Moscow?" [113] Recalled Georgescu:

> After the meeting . . . Ana, extremely upset, said to me in a threatening tone: "What? Are you crazy? Don't you know what you're doing? You think you're helping the party and Comrade Gheorghiu[-Dej] this way? No! What you're doing is against the party, and against Comrade Gheorghiu[-Dej]. . . . Comrade Chişinevschi hasn't done anything wrong; but you have. Haven't you learned anything from what happened in Yugoslavia? Why did Tito end up where he ended up? Because those around him acted the way you're acting, and they put on big airs about him, and they lost him." [114]

Here was that fear of the Soviets that Pauker had shown to Ana Toma and had expressed to Dej after their meeting with Stalin. It was a fear, Georgescu added, that was evident also in her response to Dej's plans to procure American industrial equipment one year earlier. "Ana told me in a worried tone: 'What will the Soviets say? They liberated us and we're looking to the Americans. Comrade Gheorghiu[-Dej] is letting himself be pushed by those in his Ministry.'" [115] These anxieties most distinguished her position from Gheorghiu-Dej's on such issues. Pauker did not, for instance, object to the deal with the Americans, but she wanted a concurrent campaign stressing the extent of Soviet assistance to Romania; nor did she oppose Maurer's negotiating for $500 million in American credits to be received by January 1946, but she stipulated that it "had to be prepared" beforehand—that is, couched in gestures reassuring to the Soviets.[116] She expressed no reservations to Dej's approaching the West for grain at the end of 1946.[117] At the same time, except for demanding higher agricultural prices, Pauker sustained Dej and Maurer's economic program of June 1947, which, based on the theories of Eugen Varga, called for assuring a "reasonable profit" for private industrialists. "[I]f we don't give them a profit," she reasoned, "we could scream and yell all we want, but they won't work."[118] In so doing, she opposed Luca's counterproposal for increasing coercive control over industry and moving "decisively in the direction of nationalization."[119]

As Luca would later recount, Pauker reproached him at that time for pushing nationalization and informed him that the Soviets advising her thought it was still too early for Romania to nationalize. She persisted in her position, Luca added, up to the party's sudden adoption of nationalization on Soviet orders in early 1948.[120] Her firm view, he suggested, was that "we're not going to proceed with nationalization for years to come, and that we can lead the country collaborating with the bourgeoisie and keeping a capitalist regime. *Hilferdingism:* an organized capitalist state led by a bourgeois democratic coalition government. Rather this was how Ana Pauker viewed the 'revolutionary' prospects in Romania."[121]

Accordingly, Pauker's acknowledged antagonism to Maurer and others in Dej's entourage was not a product of a leftist condemnation of their policies, as a recent Russian study suggests, but rather an offshoot of her escalating feud with Gheorghiu-Dej.[122] "In the summer of 1947, in September . . . ," Miron Constantinescu reminded her, "you told me that the situation in our Party leadership is no longer going well and can no longer continue, that we have to put an end to this situation, that Comrade Gheorghiu[-Dej] is trying to impose his line on the party, and that this thing cannot be accepted or tolerated by the other members of the leadership."[123] Likewise, Luca testified under interrogation that Pauker told him in 1948 that she could no longer work with Gheorghiu-Dej.[124] After his arrest in 1952, Luca further revealed to his prison cell mate that Pauker had dispatched him to Kavtaradze to confirm Dej's shortcomings and propose that she replace him.[125] Strangely enough, she reportedly did not attempt to remove Dej when he was the apparent subject of a Soviet inquiry beginning in June 1948.[126] Had she not seriously sought Dej's ouster, or was she simply no more successful in attaining Stalin's nod to monopolize power than Dej had been the year before?

Whatever the case, Dej reportedly had mended fences with Stalin by the beginning of 1949.[127] Maurer was swiftly relegated to an obscure and meaningless post (though, to Dej's credit, he did not suffer a more serious fate), while Chişinevschi became one of Dej's closest associates.[128] From that point, Dej seemed to follow a simple strategy: "He played the card of being the most Stalinist of them all." [129] With no personal ideological motivations to speak of, he readily abandoned previous positions and pursued the most extreme Stalinist policies in order to prove himself to Stalin and win approval to take sole control of the party.[130] Indeed, "disgrace" appears to have had the same effect on Dej as it had on Hungarian General Secretary Mátyás Rákosi, who also had once fallen under suspicion: both would ultimately serve Stalin as infamous yes men.[131]

Having once dodged the bullet, Dej immediately set out to destroy Ana Pauker. He bitterly resented Pauker's attempt to make him a figurehead, begrudged her international standing and popularity among Soviet officials while always finding his name misspelled in *Pravda,* and reviled her "motherly," patronizing attitude towards him.[132] Moreover, while Dej commanded the sincere and abiding loyalty of many who were imprisoned with him, he lacked Pauker's charisma and personal charm. "Dej was respected," Sorin Toma observed, "but he couldn't make people love him." In contrast, Pauker

> was loved by many, many people [in the party]. . . . She had a very poetic nature. I don't doubt that she could be very hard, maybe [even] cruel: I don't know concrete cases, but she was very willful; she was used to the struggle, and particularly the struggle for power; and she didn't think that she was in a fairy tale. She was a very strong politician. But she was also very poetic, and she could be very kind and very human. [For this reason,] she was clearly a dangerous rival to Dej.[133]

Bodnăraş made this point himself in March 1961, when he self-critically noted Pauker's eventual effect even on him.

> [T]he entire atmosphere that Ana created around her, surrounded by petit-bourgeois elements at dinner, making her house a kind of meeting place that was open day and night, with dinners and games, influenced . . . my behavior towards her. . . . Things got to the point that even my wife noticed it, and told me several times: "I don't understand, you aren't a sullen person—and the comrades have rightly accepted us—but why do you become so sullen

when we're having dinner and Comrade Gheorghiu-Dej is talking?" She was probably noticing the dissatisfied look on my face that would appear on such occasions. . . . But Ana would shine. . . . And it wasn't easy not to be impressed with the arrogant and very skillful way she charmed and fooled people. Beginning with [the writer Mihail] Sadoveanu and ending with all types of emissaries that criss-crossed the country, all of the cliques were always there. And, while she, on the one hand, went around with her sophisticated, hard to understand formulations, her sister-in-law [Titi Pauker] would, on the other hand, walk around with bottles of cognac and liqueur, and get everyone drunk. Of course, comrades, in that atmosphere, a man with my weak political experience, and with the education of my past, could not have had a firm position [on Ana Pauker]. . . . Ana would present herself to be on a level that exceeded that of any local cadre. She always spoke of Manuilsky and Stalin, and, when you met with a Soviet personality, and also saw the characterizations Kavtaradze would make of Ana . . . , it wasn't easy not to fall under [her] influence.[134]

Not surprisingly, then, Gheorghiu-Dej quickly maneuvered to compromise Pauker and began gathering information that he could later use against her.[135] A wealth of material was available to him once the Soviets imposed Stalinization on the country and began annulling Pauker's policies one after the other. For one, Pauker's line of integrating democratic elements in the socialist system fell by the wayside as early as 1947, when the Soviets demanded the arrest of the historic parties' leaders. Though Pauker made several conciliatory gestures at that time,[136] she admittedly acceded to Soviet "advice" on the matter[137]—which she often remorsefully referred to after her purge. "There was," her son-in-law Dr. Gheorghe Brătescu recalled,

a certain thing that seemed to be an obsession with her, because she spoke about it many times, and that was her attitude against Romanian democratic politicians who were put in jail and in concentration camps. Especially [Gheorghe] Tătărăscu and other fellow travelers. She felt very guilty about the fact that many people who had initially helped the Communist Party were put in jail: Labor Democrats, Social Democrats, National Liberals. She regretted very much her participation in the decision to neutralize them in '47 and '48. . . . She explained that the idea had come from Moscow. The Russians were expecting every day the start of a war between East and West, and claimed that it was very imprudent for potential enemies to be free.[138]

Likewise, Pauker also regretted what she sarcastically described as her "wonderful idea" of arresting all those who had visited the libraries of the American and British embassies.[139] In January 1950 she told the Central Committee that in the previous years "[w]e've shrugged our shoulders and did not see these people as enemies of our government.

The time has passed for handling them with indulgence, thinking that these people are simply myopic."[140] As was often the case in Communist Party politics, Pauker was probably engaging in a self-criticism of sorts for her earlier line's "indulgence." But a consequence of that self-criticism is evident in the lists of arrested "intellectuals," most of whom were high school and college students or elderly pensioners. Pauker later would claim that she proposed imprisoning them for "two or three days, so that they'd get over their desire to go there"; but Securitate records indicate that most received six-month sentences. "It was," she ruefully acknowledged, "an unlawful act, an uncivilized abuse."[141]

Still, Pauker reportedly chose not to compromise when calls were made in 1948 for deporting class and political "enemies" from Romania's urban centers. According to Luca, "Ana Pauker was opposed to any general revolutionary measures against the bourgeoisie and the nationalized and expropriated landlords, as well as against elements in the state apparatus who were compromised as political enemies. She justified her attitude by saying that 'We don't have remote territory like Siberia in the USSR, where we could gather up and isolate these enemies along with their families.'"[142] Her opposition, he added, stalled for a considerable time these "exploitative elements'" deportation from cities and industrial centers.[143] Apparently, her stance was eventually used to compromise her, for these delays were soon the subject of open criticism. A Central Committee resolution alleged that Georgescu had to be "pushed by the party leadership" to take "even one measure" against "the landlords and capitalists" after their properties were expropriated.[144] As Georgescu disclosed, Gheorghiu-Dej had raised the issue of "completely resolving these matters" in 1950, which at that time led to the immediate expulsions of "expropriated capitalists from [certain] cities and industrial centers"—Hunendoara, Reşiţa, Valea Jiului, and Braşov.[145] But the issue, he noted, was not "resolved [until] the spring of 1952," when the purge of the Pauker faction was well under way.[146]

In addition, following Tito's expulsion, the Cominform criticized mass recruitment, and ordered the verification of party members in every bloc country.[147] Both actions contradicted Ana Pauker's earlier stance. She and her allies had bitterly resisted the verification campaign in Romania between 1948 and 1950.[148] "They suggested," Dej later related, "that we, all of us who went through prison and the camps, were sectarians, that we went through a whirlpool of hardship of the underground, and it imprinted on us a certain amount of harshness; it made us rigid, and made us sectarians."[149] Thus, Pauker reportedly

removed Alexandru Drăghici as the party first secretary of Bucharest in
1949, complaining that he was destroying the cadres of the Bucharest
activ.[150] Not coincidentally, therefore, verification would be the staging ground for the first blow against her, a surreptitious dress rehearsal
for the purge two years later. At the fifth plenary of the party's Central
Committee in January 1950, which reviewed the campaign's execution,
Gheorghiu-Dej "beat up" on Miron Constantinescu, who had assisted
Pauker in recruiting new members. "[B]ut I knew that I wasn't attacking Miron," Dej maintained, "but the one who started that [policy], and
I waited for the one who initiated it, who promoted that line, to say"
that she was in fact the guilty one.[151] At the following plenary, however,
Pauker impatiently dismissed the continuing criticism of mass recruit-
ment and suggested that its detractors "were looking for and creating
phantoms. . . . We've already admitted that, in the matter of accepting
new party members, we didn't see things correctly and made mistakes.
At that time, in conditions of a difficult struggle, even with the Red
Army here . . . , we didn't orient ourselves correctly enough, and we said
that, before anything, we have to take the workers and the poor peasants out of the enemy's hands, so that we don't let them go to the
Right. . . . We therefore made a tactical error."[152] Though she may have
then assumed she had defused the matter once and for all, it would ex-
plode in her face in 1952.

The most damaging evidence against Ana Pauker would materialize
after Dej's recovery—from 1949 to 1952, when Stalinism was methodically imposed on Romania. Her factional disputes with Gheorghiu-
Dej, she later related, "accentuated" in these years "because it was
a turning point in the life of [the] Party," with collectivization (initiated in 1949), the rapid industrialization of the first Five-Year Plan
(adopted in 1950), and other Stalinist ventures.[153] She supported, for
instance, Luca's dogged resistance to the increasingly grandiose construction projects of the time,[154] arguing "that we shouldn't spend so
much money, that we should build residential units" instead.[155] On
these grounds, both opposed constructing the Danube–Black Sea Canal,
one of the Soviet bloc's most notorious postwar symbols of Stalinist
repression. Pauker told her family that Stalin himself personally "proposed" the canal in late 1948.[156] Yet Luca sharply criticized the amount
of money wasted on its construction,[157] and Pauker did not shrink from
expressing her own misgivings at certain party meetings.[158] In contrast,
Gheorghiu-Dej, who officially supervised the project, was a passionate promoter of the canal.[159] Consequently, soon after Pauker and

Luca's purge, the construction speeded considerably. Two months following their ouster in May 1952, twenty-five of the canal's administrators were arrested for sabotage; and with Gheorghiu-Dej pressing for a trial as early as possible, two military tribunals fraudulently convicted them in August and September—resulting in several death sentences and long prison terms.[160] This signaled a renewed push for building the canal. While only three kilometers had been completed during the entire three years of construction before Pauker and Luca's purge, no less than four kilometers were completed during the year from then until mid-1953, when the project was abruptly abandoned.[161]

Pauker's opposition to the canal could not but have compromised her in the eyes of Stalin.[162] Her positions on agrarian issues, Stalinist purges, and Jewish emigration, however, proved the most important factors in her undoing.

CHAPTER FOUR

The Agriculture Secretary

Following the RCP's February 1948 merger with the Social Democrats to create the Romanian Workers Party (RWP), Ana Pauker left her position as head of the party's organizational matters and became the RWP's secretary for agriculture. This was clearly one of the Romanian Communists' most vexing and pivotal problems at that time, for the peasants comprised no less than 78 percent of the Romanian population.[1] Why Pauker chose to tackle this issue puzzled even her family, who basically subscribed to Nicolae Ceauşescu's derisive view that "Ana didn't know the first thing about agriculture. . . . It was evident that she couldn't even tell the difference between the wheat and the sickle."[2] For this reason, her family came to believe the appointment was purposely designed to compromise her.[3] Indeed, after her purge, Pauker soon became infamous for having personally promoted the party's most repressive policies against the peasantry during the Stalinist period, in large part due to Gheorghiu-Dej's persistent campaign to blame all past wrongs on the Pauker faction. As Dej declared in 1961:

> Flagrantly violating the party line and the decisions of the party, and subverting the authority of the party leadership, Ana Pauker organized an unprecedented adventurist and provocative action, which gravely undermined the alliance with the working peasantry. On the basis of directives she gave to [Interior Minister] Teohari Georgescu, mass arrests were simultaneously organized throughout the country of peasants accused of not respecting their obligations to the state. Many tens of thousands of peasants, the great ma-

jority of whom were working peasants provocatively labeled as kulaks, were arrested by the security organs, imprisoned and then tried in public trials.[4]

This portrait became the mainstay of historical accounts of Ana Pauker for several decades and continued to be repeated during the post-Communist period.

The historical record, however, does not jibe with the preponderance of charges against Pauker when she was purged, which accused her of "right-wing deviation" and pursuing "peasantist and anti-Leninist" agrarian policies.[5] Nor does it correspond with the testimony of Vasile Luca, who bore the brunt of such charges in 1952. Under interrogation Luca insisted that Pauker had actually "aspired to have agricultural matters placed under her responsibility, because she wanted to handle the socialization of agriculture and . . . always manifested *a populist sentimentalism* towards the peasantry generally." [6]

Pauker's attitude on the peasants just before becoming agriculture secretary bears Luca out. This was on the occasion of the Currency Reform of August 1947, when a serious dispute broke out within the Romanian Communist leadership over proportionate price increases for industrial and agricultural goods. Addressing the Politburo in a series of meetings immediately after the reform, Ion Gheorghe Maurer, then Gheorghiu-Dej's undersecretary of state at the Ministry of Industry and Commerce, explained how the special RCP commission and its Soviet advisers arrived at the reform's particulars. The commission determined that 1938 was the prewar year closest in economic conditions to 1947, although national revenue in 1947 was only 65 percent of that in 1938. After subtracting an additional 15 percent for reparations to the Soviets, only 50 percent of the national revenue in 1938 remained. Hence, the commission concluded that prices should either be twice, or wages and salaries half, those in 1938. For political reasons, it decided to maintain wages and salaries at the same level and double prices instead. Believing that "we're going to have a good crop" that would "create great wealth and a large amount of money in the peasant sector," the commission resolved to tap that wealth for the benefit of the working class, which it was most interested in aiding. The commission thus raised agricultural and food prices 30 percent less than industrial prices (which were doubled), thereby boosting the proletariat's buying power by that amount. In other words, they arrived at ratios of 1:1 for wages and salaries, maintained at the same level as 1938; 1.4:1 for agricultural prices, doubled minus 30 percent; and 2:1 for industrial prices.[7] This was the

standard Stalinist practice of accumulating capital at the peasantry's expense, adopted from the Trotskyist economist E. Preobrazhensky and
wholeheartedly endorsed by the Soviet advisers.[8]

This new policy, however, created immediate economic problems, as
the scissors between industrial and agricultural prices began markedly
opening in favor of industry. The net result was acute dissatisfaction
among the peasantry and a serious provisions crisis in the cities, as the
peasants began withholding their produce. But "[w]e don't have to worry
ourselves about this matter," Maurer suggested, "because the peasant
sector was the one that suffered the least throughout the inflationary period [during the immediate postwar years]," and it could presumably
sustain such losses more easily until the scissors closed.[9] In any case, he
added, the workers adamantly opposed any agricultural price increases,
and the unions were actively pressuring the government to keep food
prices low.[10]

Ana Pauker angrily rejected Maurer's arguments:

> We are cutting the branch we're standing on, and I don't understand, Com-
> rade Maurer, how we could have such policies. . . . The most stupid thing is
> that, while in 1938, a peasant could buy a suit with 70 kilograms of milk, to-
> day he would have to sell 250 kilograms in order to buy that suit; thus it costs
> 4 to 5 times more. Milk is underpriced so many times more. Or are we to be
> indifferent whether or not we have cows? . . . We aren't concerned enough
> with the poor peasantry, who could overthrow us if we don't win them over
> politically and economically. We have to give them the means of lifting them-
> selves up. We have to give them the means to rebuild their lives. We have to
> do this precisely for the working peasantry, which was hit the hardest by the
> famine, so that they can rebuild. . . . The salaried workers are a minority [in
> this country]. The great majority are the peasants, whose buying power we're
> cutting completely.[11]

As to Maurer's point that the workers themselves were blocking government attempts to raise agricultural prices, Pauker countered:

> We have to put the issue this way: . . . We workers, together with the peas-
> ants and with the intellectuals, can strengthen ourselves, but not one against
> the other; only all united. And thus you don't gain anything, worker, when
> you buy things from the peasant with prices that are nothing. Then he won't
> be able to buy goods and you'll end up unemployed. This is the first mat-
> ter that we have to take measures on immediately. . . . It should be demon-
> strated to the workers . . . why it's not in [their] interest that the peasant be
> plundered.[12]

Finally, Pauker conveniently forgot the Stalinist line of exploiting the
peasantry, thus preempting any suggestion that she opposed it. "We

want to become an industrial country," she declared, "but not by destroying the peasants, like the Trotskyists, but by lifting them up and making them one of the principal factors in production and consumption." [13] This was actually the hallmark of Nikolai Bukharin's agrarian policies, supported by Stalin in the mid-1920s [14] but branded "right-wing deviation" at the end of that decade. In Bukharin's view, socialist industrialization depended on "lifting up [the peasants]," as Pauker put it, and encouraging them to accumulate private capital. Expanding trade with the peasantry on the consumer market would then tap that capital, not with a scissors that raised industrial prices while keeping agricultural prices low but by providing products the peasants desired and were sure to buy. [15] Thus Pauker complained in August 1949, "You can't find nails or horseshoes in the countryside. Whether we want to or not, we have to make them. We don't have enough goods, and we have to make them; and we have to distribute the goods we already have. There's a lot of goods we could be making." [16] In January 1950 she cited Lenin, stressing that

> the dictatorship of the proletariat is . . . the alliance between the workers and the working peasants, which is expressed . . . in the trade that is carried out . . . through loyal trade, in which we put before the peasantry to take part in this "loyalty" of ours. The state and the workers will not exploit them, and they will benefit from the workers' labor, and they must give their produce in exchange. And we are indebted to assure the peasantry what it needs. In this relationship, Lenin particularly criticized the proletariat, that it should produce products for the peasantry. We are obligated to do this. [17]

Indeed, Vasile Luca later described Pauker as "the initiator" of the "raising [of agricultural] prices and our giving greater quantities of industrial goods" to the peasantry, parroting Bukharin's line two decades earlier. [18]

Luca was firmly allied with Pauker on this matter (and on agricultural issues generally), often appearing as the policy's most strident proponent in the Romanian Politburo. [19] "The prices of the peasants' products have gotten to the point that there's no longer anything in the market but vegetables," he observed at the Politburo debate on the currency reform. "When the peasant can't buy industrial goods except with prices that are three to four times higher than in 1938, they aren't crazy enough to sell their produce at lower prices. You can imagine what the situation is when the peasant has reached the point of greasing his axle with butter instead of oil. Instead of selling his milk, he's making butter and greasing his axle with it." [20] Echoing Pauker and Bukharin, Luca insisted that by "imposing misery on the peasant, and forcing him to sell his produce

at fixed prices" the party was ultimately compromising the economic reconstruction of the country. "[H]ow do we think the reconstruction and
industrialization of the country is carried out? It is based . . . on the buying power of the masses, of the peasantry. This is how we'll be able to
rebuild the factories and the country." [21] He therefore backed Pauker's
and Bukharin's line of accumulating capital for industrialization solely
by increasing trade with the peasantry. "Accumulation," he insisted, "is
accomplished by selling goods." [22] Providing the peasantry with the industrial products they desired would not only raise capital but also, he
suggested, induce the peasants to sell their produce even at artificially
low state prices. [23] "The appearance of more goods in the villages will
bring about a reduction of prices. These prices are formed on the market. The prices are dictated by supply and demand, not by what we decide here." [24] Hence Luca, with Pauker, rejected state intervention and
favored the spontaneous workings of the open market, calling for unrestricted, decentralized commerce for the private farmer. [25] At the same
time, he and Pauker opposed the party's Stalinist line of overemphasizing heavy industry at the expense of light industry and the production of
consumer goods. [26] The investment outlays for heavy industry in the
Five-Year Plan, he maintained, were "guided by megalomania. . . . Why
are we developing heavy industry? It's to provide for light industry, agriculture, and for the production of goods. The goal is to strengthen the
sector producing consumer goods" in order to increase trade with the
peasantry. [27]

On the other side of the spectrum stood Gheorghiu-Dej. Cautiously
opposing Pauker and Luca at the Politburo debates in the fall of 1947,
he focused on an article on price policy just published in the party daily
Scânteia. Attributed to Ștefan Voicu, the article had in fact been dictated
by Luca to Voicu and Scânteia's editor Sorin Toma: [28]

GHEORGHIU-DEJ: [reading the article] "It's no wonder that the peasants have
                 begun to grease their axles with butter and to give their
                 milk to their pigs." . . . I have complete admiration for the
                 imagination of whoever wrote this article, but to think
                 that the peasant gives milk to the pigs and greases his cart
                 with butter is ridiculous.

LUCA: Even though it's a concrete fact.

GHEORGHIU-DEJ: It's either shameful demagoguery, or he's intentionally ex-
                 aggerating when he says that. It's totally unfounded what's
                 written here. I can't believe in all this hot air. Whoever
                 says that the peasant gives milk to the pigs and greases his

axle with butter is a demagogue. You won't find a single
peasant who does such a thing.[29]

Having failed to prevent Pauker and Luca from overturning the currency
reform price ratios set by his Industry and Commerce Ministry, Dej bitterly noted in September 1948 that "the scissors in some areas . . . has
returned to favor agricultural prices," and clarified his position on the
issue: "We can't speak to our peasantry of a so-called equilibrium between the prices of industrial goods and agricultural produce. . . . We
want to achieve a socialist accumulation at the expense of the capitalist
elements in the countryside: to siphon it off from [them] and put it in the
industrial sector."[30] Or, as he remarked two years later, "Fine, fine,
'the alliance,' but this 'alliance' must bring about a socialist accumulation."[31] Accordingly, Dej called for implementing any measure that
would "absorb the money filling the peasants' pockets," though he decidedly preferred state intervention over market forces.[32] Opposing
Pauker's and Luca's policy allowing free commerce in the countryside,
he insisted on compelling the peasant to sell all his produce "at the price
we want and not the one he wants."[33] This, in his mind, would be
achieved not by the economics of supply and demand, but by the state's
suppression of the Romanian peasant. "The less money they have, the
more they'll feel the need to bring more produce to the market. If we
provide them with a lot of goods while giving them more and more
money, we've done nothing. . . . The lei must become very much in demand. Let the peasant chase after it with his tongue hanging out. It's not
good if he makes money so easily."[34] Nor was it good, he continually
emphasized, for the peasants to remain autonomous. As long as they remain beyond party control, he insisted, any attempt to regulate the
economy would be futile.[35]

Also opposing Pauker and Luca on this matter were the Soviet advisers on the Currency Reform in Romania. Politburo member Miron
Constantinescu recounted a discussion in the home of Interior Minister
Teohari Georgescu just after the 1947 Currency Reform, attended by the
Soviet adviser Zlobin "and others." There, Gheorghiu-Dej fully agreed
"with Ivan Danilovici and Ivan Ivanovici, while, on the other hand, Luca,
Teohari, and [Ana Pauker] considered that the correlation established
between industrial and agricultural prices was not just."[36] That Pauker
and her allies were willing to oppose the Soviet advisers portended a pattern on the agrarian question in the years ahead, as their actions on collectivization, the kulaks, and obligatory collections make clear.

COLLECTIVIZATION

The Romanian Communists initiated an extensive land reform on March 23, 1945, confiscating the land of all Nazi collaborators, "war criminals," and big landowners, while distributing one million hectares (approximately 2.5 million acres) to some 600,000–700,000 poor and middle-sized peasants.[37] This reflected the situation throughout the Soviet bloc, where up to the end of 1948 no farmland was nationalized or collectivized except in Yugoslavia. As Adam Ulam noted, the Communist leaders in the newly established People's Democracies "had hoped to delay [collectivization] as long as possible. Even the most fanatical among them had seen what an ordeal forced collectivization had been for Russia. They hoped, after consolidating political power, to proceed cautiously and gradually with developing farm cooperatives and to be spared the horrors that took place in the Soviet Union between 1929 and 1934."[38] Thus Ana Pauker, who had witnessed forced collectivization firsthand in 1930 while serving on a Lenin School commission to investigate collectivization abuses in the Volgan Republic, probably spoke for the entire Romanian leadership in November 1946 when she replied to a Soviet embassy official's question: "You asked, will there be kolhozes? Our answer is that the government gave land, and issued documents giving the right to use the land, and is not going to raise the issue of creating kolhozes. The peasants will not respond. It is the same as in Russia: in the beginning land was given, and later the peasants organized themselves in kolhozes. We don't have any convincing arguments to counter the peasants' reservations."[39] The party, moreover, incessantly expounded this position in public, as it sought to portray itself as a passionate defender of peasant property rights.[40] This was largely due to the peasantry's widespread and ever-increasing fear of impending collectivization, which emerged as the primary obstacle to consolidating party control in rural areas.[41]

A severe famine that ravaged Romania in 1946 and 1947 complicated the situation and resulted in starvation in some areas of the country, as even the party daily *Scânteia* acknowledged.[42] The magnitude of the crisis, which compelled party leaders to appeal for massive food imports from the West in 1946, reportedly also led some leaders to favor collectivization as a solution.[43] This was perhaps inevitable given the institutional impediments to increasing food production that the 1945 Agrarian Reform built into Romanian agriculture. As in the Soviet Union's land reapportionment of 1917–1918, the Romanian land reform eliminated big landowners and large estates, provided land to a multitude of landless peasants, and saw the number of private farms rise sharply while the average size of peasant holdings dropped just as markedly. In the fall of 1947, farms of 5 hectares or less made up 73 percent of the total farmland in Romania; those of 10 hectares or less, 19 percent.[44] The agricultural landscape was now one of many small, individual farms, with little or no technology. This vast leveling of agriculture did not bode well for increasing production, for small landowners, lacking methods of intensive cultivation, were traditionally subsistence farmers. The larger, more affluent farmers had always provided the bulk of marketable crops: in prerevolutionary Russia, for instance, the landlords and kulaks furnished 71 percent of the marketable grain, while the far more numerous middle and poor peasantry consumed all but 14.7 percent of their own produce. By implementing the Agrarian Reform, therefore, party leaders effectively reduced the production potential of precisely those elements that traditionally provided marketable food supplies, while massively increasing the numbers of subsistence farmers who contributed little to those supplies.[45]

The same dynamic applied to the problem of generating capital for the breakneck industrialization drive soon imposed by the Soviets, which was to be financed by obtaining a "socialist accumulation" from (presumably) increased agricultural surpluses. To assure such a surplus, whether for enhancing the food supply or accumulating capital, the party leaders had to end subsistence farming by consolidating the small landholdings. But doing so within the framework of individual private farms would have required them to allow the more successful, efficient farmers to expand their productive base at the expense of the less successful—that is, surrender to the dynamics of capitalism, and countenance the poorer peasants' renewed capitalist exploitation by their more affluent counterparts.[46] Quoting Lenin, Stalin insisted in 1929 that the very system of individual private farms would inherently lead to such an outcome, "because the peasantry, as long as it remains an individual peasantry carrying on small commodity production, produces capitalists from its midst, and cannot help producing them, constantly and continuously."[47] Lenin's solution was a combination of cooperation, which would gradually wean the peasants from individual private farming, and mechanization, which meanwhile would increase their output—with the operative word being *gradually*.[48] Both the drought-generated food crisis and the Soviet-imposed industrialization plan, however, effectively precluded that approach. "What is the way out?" Stalin rhetorically asked in December 1927. "The way out is to turn the small and scattered peasant farms into large united farms based on cultivation of the land in common, to go over to collective cultivation." [49] In other words, forced collectivization.

Miron Constantinescu seemed to imply precisely that in October 1947 Politburo discussions, noting that the party had won little support during the 1946 elections in the very villages where it carried out the most extensive land reform. The reason, he maintained, lay in the capitalist social structure created by the reform. "We made a whole number of peasants property owners . . . , and the means of production was transferred to a much larger number of individual property owners. . . . Comrade Stalin demonstrated how agriculture based on individual property generates capitalism. . . . The practical political conclusion for us is . . . that we . . . should have as our objective the liquidation of capitalist exploitation in the agricultural sector," which could only mean preventing the consolidation of private farms and ultimately abolishing them altogether. [50]

Ana Pauker quickly refuted not only Constantinescu's, and indeed Stalin's, conclusions, but their underlying premise as well. "Lenin did not say that the peasantry is a generator of capitalism but that the peasantry is divided into [social] categories," adding that the wealthy peasants are the capitalists, not the mass of poor and middle-sized peasants. By leveling Romanian agriculture and eliminating the big landowners, she suggested, they had effectively "removed the capitalists and enabled a whole number of exploited people . . . [to have] the possibility of living without being exploited to the degree they had been before; and, at the same time, they did not become exploiters and thus capitalists." She acknowledged almost as an afterthought that the kulaks (*chiaburi*) were in fact capitalists, but the party's policies had successfully weakened the kulaks and in the process weakened rural capitalism. Hence, "we got closer to our goal of socialism, and not to a capitalist development of the country, but to a socialist one, with this Agrarian Reform. We did not strengthen capitalism, dear Comrade Miron, but instead weakened exploitative capitalism." [51]

All this, of course, was a revision of Lenin's thesis, which Pauker suggested should be approached "dialectically." [52] It was also an earnest affirmation for maintaining individual private farms and a disavowal of the theoretical grounds for immediate collectivization. Two important witnesses confirmed her staunch position on the matter. "The subject was never discussed in large meetings," Ana Toma recalled, "but I know that [Pauker] was against collectivization. . . . She knew the experience of the Soviet Union. . . . She said that, if we want bread, we must leave the peasants alone to work their own plots." [53] Likewise, Iosif Breban, a high-ranking party official who worked closely with Pauker on agricultural issues, affirmed that Pauker consistently opposed collectivization as long as the country was not sufficiently mechanized.[54] This, as Agriculture Minister Vasile Vaida confirmed in 1950, was a long way in coming: "We see when creating collective farms that in the best of cases some 50 to 60 peasant families come to a farm with some 30 carts, a horse and two cows. We're in a very difficult situation with mechanization." [55] Thus, Breban suggested, Pauker saw collectivization as a gradual process that would perhaps take decades, rather than years, to complete.[56] In so doing she sustained Lenin's, and later Bukharin's, positions on the matter.

Pauker did not hesitate to express her reservations to Stalin himself. Liuba Chişinevschi, the wife of Party Secretary Iosif Chişinevschi and herself a member of the Central Committee, revealed that at a 1948 meeting with Pauker, Gheorghiu-Dej, and Iosif Chişinevschi, Stalin asked if the Romanians were collectivizing. "And Ana replied: 'Comrade Stalin, it's a little soon. We have implemented land reform. We have given land to the peasants. We have to let them enjoy the land. And we don't have mechanization. We don't have industry yet. We don't have anything to give them.'" [57] Indeed, Pauker persistently depicted mechanization (and thus industrialization) as a prerequisite to collectivization, even though the Stalinist line suggested just the opposite, that collectivization was the means for acquiring as large an agricultural surplus as possible to finance industrialization.[58] As late as April 1950, nearly two years after the Soviets had imposed collectivization on its satellites, Pauker objected to a draft proposal of the country's first Five-Year Plan (1951–55) precisely because it embodied the Stalinist line. "Things are backwards in this proposal. Can you really speak of . . . the gradual transformation of the small [peasant] producers [to socialism] before developing industry? It's on the basis of socialist industrialization that one can proceed with the replacement of the kulaks and with collectivization, and it's on the basis of collectivization that one can abolish the kulaks. But here we have it backwards. . . . [Y]ou have to first raise the problem of industry . . . and [then] say here that 'this will make proceeding to the socialist transformation of agriculture possible.'" [59] Or as she put it on another occasion, "We're not industrializing for industrialization's sake, but in large part to lift up agriculture." [60]

Supporting Pauker on this point was Vasile Luca, whose views on collectivization were based on his own principled opposition to over-emphasizing heavy industry.[61] Correcting Pauker in 1947 on Lenin's theories on the matter, Luca acknowledged that "private property in it-self leads to the development of capitalism, and that's why we Commu-nists are for changing this situation. . . . But this is a process, and it's not possible to abolish agrarian property before abolishing capitalism. . . . Right now we're not able to [collectivize], except very, very slowly, while at the same time creating the necessary conditions for it."[62] Up through mid-1948 at least, Gheorghiu-Dej's views evidently were not much dif-ferent. Like Luca, he reminded Pauker that "we enlarged the base of individual property . . . , [and] it's just as Lenin and Stalin taught us: It's a germinator, a supply source, for capitalist elements. In every small producer exists the tendency to being a large landowner."[63] Also like Luca, Dej balked at supporting any extensive collectivization at that time, even opposing an apparent grassroots attempt to set up handi-crafts cooperatives in March 1948. "We don't have the economic and political conditions to achieve such things . . . ," he insisted. "The co-operatives should be organized and set up only gradually. . . . Instead [we should be] saying to the small handicraftsmen that they should work and make do, that taxes will be reduced, that they will be given the possibility of making a living from their work, and that they should sell their produce."[64]

These hesitations became quite academic, however, once the Soviets imposed collectivization on the bloc in 1948. The campaign was for-mally launched in Romania at a Central Committee plenary March 3–5, 1949. A series of Politburo meetings on the campaign had been held in February.[65] While nearly all of the leaders urged caution and stressed the campaign's gradual pace, they still had discernible, albeit nuanced, differences. Gheorghiu-Dej, for one, addressed the issue soberly and pru-dently, but emphasized the new line's necessity just the same.[66] Pauker, on the other hand, appeared indignant and twice complained that the plenary's resolution was written "as if we are going to have massive col-lectivization," to which, she clearly implied, she would not be party. Noting the campaign's initially limited scope, she reminded the others that "collectivization is not the biggest objective we have at the present moment," and thus protested that "nothing was said [in the draft] of the millions of peasants who will remain outside [the collectives]."[67]

Perhaps on the basis of such objections, the Politburo's report to the plenary particularly stressed that the party was not proceeding with massive collectivization but would initially concentrate instead on developing trading cooperatives.[68] At the same time, the plenary embraced the principle of "free consent" and acknowledged the need for practical measures to attract the peasants gradually. It thus allowed simple tillage associations *(întovărăşiri)* as a preliminary step for the mass of poor and middle peasants unwilling to enter collective farms, and it called for establishing a limited number of collectives (identical to the Soviet kolhoz) as models with which the party could explain *(muncă de lămurire)* collectivized farming's benefits.[69] To assure their success, the new collectives were granted tax-exempt status and a 20 percent reduction of obligatory collection quotas for their first two years.[70] A model statute of the collective farm was also drafted, specifying that each member must possess three hectares of land, on the assumption that the collectives would require at least that much land from each member if they were to benefit from mechanization and become viable.[71] An Agrarian Commission whose sole task was to organize and oversee these model collectives was established under the leadership of Ana Pauker.[72]

Working with Pauker in the Agrarian Commission were Agriculture Minister Vasile Vaida, veteran party activists Dumitru Petrescu and Pavel Chirtoacă, Deputy Agriculture Ministers Nicolae Ceauşescu and Mircea Gogioiu, and the Soviet adviser Veretenicov.[73] Immediately after the March plenary, the commission dispatched teams to investigate conditions in the villages that had asked to form collective farms, as well as in places recommended by party county committees. Upon analyzing their reports, the commission accepted forty-eight of the best proposals, which were problematic, nonetheless, because they failed to meet some of the basic requirements: most of those asking to enter collectives were poor peasants who had little land of their own, possessed few tools or livestock, and were deeply in debt. Perhaps because of this, the commission resolved to set up the collectives incrementally in groups of five or six at a time, each to comprise between 35 and 420 people, depending on location. The commission also proposed to add a number of conditions not yet clarified in the statute: the collectives' members could maintain a personal plot of between one-quarter and one-half hectare by their homes; they could keep only one cow for personal use, the rest being taken over by the collective; they would have to work at least 100 days per year; and the collective's members could choose to accept landless peasants.[74] In addition, the commission strengthened the wording of the most crucial point in the March plenary's resolution; the stipulation that collectives were to be established "with the peasants' consent" would now be more restrictively phrased, "the peasants shall enter *on their own initiative.*" [75]

Ana Pauker's caution in approving new collectives during the Agrarian Commission's sessions is striking.[76] At a September 1, 1949, meeting Pauker approved only four of twelve proposals to inaugurate collectives the following Sunday. She postponed an additional four proposals until conditions were met, and she rejected the rest outright. She also expressly instructed the commission not to make promises to entice peasants into the collectives and declared that consolidating a collective's land, which would require expropriating those individual peasant farms that fell within the collective's boundaries, "is only possible when the people renounce their land with their own free will in exchange for the land of those entering the collective." [77] Pauker's attitude was similar during the Council of Ministers' September 13 discussion of proposed expropriations in a number of villages in order to build cotton mills: "Pure and simply there are to be no expropriations from poor and middle peasants for several thousand lei, because they're going to drink away the money and afterwards won't have anything to work with. They must receive other land in return. . . . It's great to have a new railway, but it's not at all great to have peasant discontent." [78] Because of this prudence, along with its limited mandate, the Agrarian Commission created only fifty-six collective farms in 1949, with relatively little resistance from the peasants.[79]

Such caution continued in the months that followed. From fall 1949 to spring 1950, there was no predetermined plan for creating new collective farms. Adhering to the statute's revised clause on forming collectives, the Agrarian Commission waited for peasant-initiated requests to come in spontaneously from the countryside.[80] Despite receiving no fewer than 1,000 requests by October 1949 and an additional 350 that winter, the Commission approved only 120 new collectives, which were started in February and March 1950.[81] The cause of so many rejections was ostensibly a lack of proper conditions, particularly, Pauker noted, "extraordinarily low" productivity that ranked "last among the Popular Democratic countries." [82] Once again, mechanization was her primary focus. With Romania facing a considerable tractor shortage, she called for importing them, insisting that without them the collectives and tillage associations would be tenuous at best.[83] In the meantime, however, she kept a tight lid on collectivization.

On January 23–25, 1950, the Fifth Plenary of the RWP Central Committee resolved to replace the Agrarian Commission with an Agrarian

Section of the Central Committee. Entrusted with expanded resources and responsibilities, Ana Pauker would lead it.[84] This hardly seems fortuitous, for the plenary also threw out the statute's revised clause on peasant initiative. This was done after "it was considered," Dumitru Petrescu related without specifying by whom, though the generic wording implies the Soviets, "that the [clause's] formulation was on principle mistaken."[85] The corrected line was enunciated at a meeting with the secretaries of the party county committees on February 20–23, 1950: "[T]he socialist transformation of agriculture does not happen by itself, for that task falls to the party and the proletariat. The initiative to move towards socialism does not belong to the peasants."[86] Accordingly, Petrescu noted in the same generic language, "[I]t was then brought up that the creation of collective farms was to proceed in a more organized manner."[87] Collectivization, seemingly, was to intensify.

Complying with the new line, Pavel Chirtoacă, the chief functionary of the Agrarian Section (which was officially established that spring), began work on a formal plan for setting up new collective farms. Based on the myriad requests they had received, he concluded that the Agrarian Section could reasonably establish 900 collectives in 1950.[88] Pauker promptly rejected the figure as "madness."[89] Refusing to allow Chirtoacă to fix the number of collectives in the plan, Pauker instead suggested asking the county committees to report on the prospects for new collectives in their respective areas.[90] The committees submitted their reports at the end of March and, interestingly enough, proposed Chirtoacă's exact figure—900—for May and June alone.[91] Their proposals, moreover, corresponded with the Soviets' conclusion "that it was possible to create around 1,000 collectives" at that time, a number Gheorghiu-Dej confirmed on June 6.[92] Pauker's protestations notwithstanding, the proposals reflected the figures stipulated in the first Five-Year Plan, then being redacted in close collaboration with the Soviet advisers.[93] One thousand new collectives were to be established by the fall of 1950, in order to meet the plan's projections of socializing no less than 70 percent of Romania's arable land by the end of 1955.[94] Despite this, the Agrarian Section returned the county committees' proposals for reformulation because their numbers *were too inflated*.[95] Consequently, the county committees revised their proposals downward.[96] By June 15 when Pauker left on vacation, the Agrarian Section had set up no more than 168 of the originally proposed 900 collectives.[97]

By June 1950, therefore, the party line's direction was evident, as was Pauker's position in facing it. When Gheorghiu-Dej asserted on June 6 that "[w]e'll probably have to induce more firmness, and a more active pace, in the preparation work of creating collective farms," Pauker remained hesitant and expressed concern about frightening the peasants.[98] One week later she left for the Soviet Black Sea resort of Soci, from where she was soon rushed to the Kremlin hospital in Moscow to undergo emergency surgery for breast cancer.[99] Assigned in her place as party secretary overseeing the Agrarian Section and Agriculture Ministry was Alexandru Moghioroş,[100] a telling choice that perhaps underscored the leadership's intentions better than anything else. In Politburo discussions on collectivization just before the March 1949 CC plenary, Moghioroş was the only one not to give even token lip service to proceeding cautiously or gradually; instead, he condemned the previous "opportunist-conciliatory line" as "non-Leninist, because we can't build socialism without collective farms."[101] Now Moghioroş voiced the most pointed criticism of Pauker's Agrarian Section policies:

> I was talking with 10 to 15 party county secretaries, and, when I asked them why they made so few proposals for establishing collective farms, they indicated that it was because of the resolution of the March [1949] plenary. And they said: . . . [W]e believed that we were acting in the spirit and the letter of the resolution, which says that these collective farms are to be established only where conditions are met, that these collective farms are to be models that will serve as examples for the peasantry, and that we shouldn't proceed with [collectivization] rashly, but rather take our technical capacities, etc., into account. . . . A year has passed since that resolution, and all the comrades know that the number of people signing up is quite large, and they're aware of this timidity that we've had, this timidity that reveals itself by the methods we've employed.[102]

Not surprisingly, Moghioroş made immediate changes upon taking Pauker's place. While Pauker had not met with the Agrarian Section for a full month before leaving, Moghioroş held nightly meetings with the leading officials working on collectivization to review all proposals for new collective farms. He also informed the Agrarian Section that the scaled-down plan for May and June had been "too slow" and had to be accelerated in July and August. To prevent such plan reductions from recurring, the party leadership took the power to reject proposals out of the Agrarian Section functionaries' hands.[103] Before the spring of 1950, the Agrarian Commission in Bucharest alone approved any new collective; however, after the county committees were asked to submit proposals for new collective farms, "it was emphasized," Petrescu cryptically noted, that establishing collectives required the local authorities' active involvement.[104] Consequently, perhaps, Pauker issued a report before her departure suggesting that such local involvement "should be further utilized in our work . . . without the leadership of the CC losing control of the process, for it should follow how work is carried out on a daily basis."[105] Elaborating on Pauker's proviso, Luca insisted that "the approval [of new collective farms] must remain as it was"—the prerogative of the central party leadership.[106] But Gheorghiu-Dej's dismissive response[107] portended the policy change implemented shortly after: the local party committees were given sole responsibility for approving new collective farms, which, they were expressly told, had to conform to the numbers fixed in the plan.[108] Moghioroş's remarks at a meeting with the secretaries of the party county committees on June 15, the day Pauker left Bucharest, were unambiguous:

> Something curious has happened in this country. Some comrades have thought that we were somehow proceeding with collectivization before we had the necessary conditions for it. Those who interpreted the [March 1949 CC] Resolution in this way are profoundly mistaken. . . . It's true that some conditions need to be there, but the conditions have to be created; they don't fall from the sky. We are by no means indifferent to how many collectives will be established this year. . . . To meet [the] proportion [stipulated in the Five-Year Plan], it is essential that we set up 1,000 collective farms [by September]. . . . I think, comrades, that it should be clear to us by now that the number of collectives that you proposed is insufficient, and that you yourselves must come to the conclusion that it's imperative to revise your plan, and to do so immediately.[109]

Perhaps events in one particular county, Trei Scaune, best illustrate what happened next. Of fourteen new collectives proposed for May and June, the county had managed to establish only three by June 11—all with great difficulty. When the county's party secretary, Mihai Nagy, returned from the June 15 meeting in Bucharest, he informed his associates that "he had received instructions" to set up a specified number of collective farms. "What do you expect?" he told them. "We created only 3 collectives when Odorhei has established 24, Cinc 20, and Târgu Mureş 30." Hence, the county party committee hurriedly devised a new plan, adding fifteen collectives to the three already established, and the county's district committees set out to carry out the plan "with any measure, and at any price."[110] This process repeated itself throughout Romania as district committees scrambled to "create" the necessary conditions to form the 1,012 new collectives the county committees had proposed for July and August, and as contests among regions to form the largest number of collectives broke out nationwide.[111] The pressure intensified further in July when party leaders decreed that each collective had to comprise at least thirty-five families and that each of those families must enter with an equal amount of land. This compelled the district committees to enlist ever greater numbers into the collectives, and among other things, led to their placing particular emphasis on enlisting middle peasants.[112] At the same time, the too few Agrarian Section instructors, often avoided by the local authorities, were "put in an impossible situation and could not exercise effective control."[113]

Thus, while coercion was reported only once in 1949 and remained rare in the first half of 1950, it now reached massive proportions for the first time.[114] The militia and Securitate, having "received instructions 'to assist' in the organizing of collective farms," actively participated in registering new members, often at night, in Alba, Arad, Argeş, Cluj, Putna, Tecuci, Dolj, Făgăraş, Gorj, Ilfov, Mehedinţi, Mureş, Sibiu, Târnava Mică, Trei Scaune, Vâlcea and Vlaşca Counties.[115] At times peasants were arrested for refusing to join the collectives; at other times they were called to militia headquarters, arrested, and told they would be released only upon joining a collective farm.[116] Many were summoned to the Popular Councils, where the militia or Securitate beat and tortured them.[117] At least eight peasants were beaten up in every village in Târnava Mică County; peasants were beaten, had their hands tied behind their back, and were hanged from a ceiling in Vâlcea County; a number of the more influential peasants of one Dolj County village were stripped naked and held an entire night in a refrigerated storage room; and in yet another region (not specified in a party document), uncooperative elements were locked in stables and bulls were let loose on them.[118] Resistant middle peasants were rounded up in Trei Scaune and Ilfov Counties and placed in labor battalions, where they were given impossible deadlines and tried on invented charges when they could not meet them.[119] Peasants were summoned in the middle of the night and forced to read *The Problems of Leninism*.[120] In some cases "they were arrested, put in front of a portrait of Stalin, and ordered to bow down and beg him to make them see the importance of the collective farm"— all the while being warned that they had a half an hour to join up, after which they were beaten and placed back before the portrait to start the process anew.[121] Peasants were commonly enticed to join with false promises of clothing, books, food, various goods, money, land, houses, jobs, or exemption from paying taxes or collection quotas.[122] If they refused they often faced threats such as larger collection quotas, expulsion of their children from school, or dismissal from their jobs.[123] In Trei Scaune they were admonished that the land they had acquired in 1945 would all be reconfiscated, and in Ilfov they were informed that they would have to give up their land in exchange for plots clear across the country.[124] Some in Cluj County were given the choice of either paying a 200,000 lei fine and spending ten years in jail or joining a collective farm.[125] Middle peasants in Trei Scaune and Buzău Counties were threatened with being classified as kulaks and treated accordingly if they stayed out.[126] Still others in Cluj, Trei Scaune, and Alba Counties were told, "Either you join the collective farm within 24 hours or pack your bags, because you're going to the [Danube–Black Sea] Canal." [127] Consequently, as one party document estimated, some 30,000 peasant families were forcibly registered in collective farms during summer and fall 1950.[128]

In addition, coercion also began to be employed to consolidate the new collectives' land *(comăsari terenurilor)*. In Ilfov, Făgăraş, Trei Scaune, Dolj, and Arad Counties, the Securitate and militia collected signatures to the statute stipulating land exchanges.[129] As a rule the best land went to the collectives, and in return individual peasants received either poor land, land far from their homes, or no land at all during the consolidation of many collective farms in every region of the country.[130] In the Dolj County village of Bistreţi, 167 poor and middle peasants were forcibly displaced to provide the area's most fertile land to a collective comprising only 38 peasants, who themselves owned less than one hectare of the fertile land; in exchange, the displaced peasants received 263 parcels mostly of swampland or poor-quality land some fifteen to thirty-five kilometers away.[131] In the Vâlcea County village of Măciuca, 900 peasants were displaced to provide land for 50 others entering a collective farm.[132] In another Vâlcea County village, 800 families lost their land to consolidate a collective comprising only 60–70 families.[133] Upon learning that their farms fell within an emerging collective farm, many peasants joined the collective rather than lose their land[134]—but by no means all: as a prominent party official noted, the land consolidations "provoked a genuine uprising in the Romanian countryside" in the summer and fall of 1950.[135]

Indeed, as a result of its resorting to force, the RWP now encountered mass resistance to collectivization for the first time. Though minor resistance did occur in 1949 and the first half of 1950, it was infinitely weaker and only sporadically violent and was mostly limited to spreading rumors and distributing covert manifestos asking villagers not to join the collectives.[136] Or it was more like what occurred in the village of Roşieşti, Fălciu County, where local kulaks paid individuals 6,000 lei a month to masquerade as beggars at various villages and tell the inhabitants they were registered in the local collective farm, where they had nothing to eat; or in Gârbău, Someş County, where a number of kulaks prevented work at a collective farm by having the local priest ring the church bells, summoning the villagers to prayer every day at twelve noon.[137] But in the summer of 1950 an open rebellion erupted throughout Romania.[138] In the Trei Scaune County village of Micfalău, the flashpoint of the revolt, peasants "surrounded the village with scythes, hatchets, and pitchforks for five days," preventing the militia from entering, and trapping several endangered party activists inside.[139] In Măciuca, Vâlcea County, 250 villagers severely beat members of the collective farm, killing one and critically wounding three others; at Pietroasa, Vâlcea County, 300 peasants armed with pitchforks and axes attacked and beat the president of the collective's party organization and many collective farmers; in Măgurele, Ilfov County, a mob of angry farmers murdered the secretary of the local party committee.[140] Arson fires, mostly of forests but increasingly of farms and factories, raged in practically every region of the country.[141]

The revolt was in full swing when Ana Pauker returned to continue her convalescence in Bucharest sometime in August 1950.[142] Her condition was so precarious, however, that she had to go back to Moscow for additional treatment in September.[143] Though she participated in several government and party meetings in October and November, she would not fully resume her duties until December or January.[144] Yet, despite her impaired health, she quickly reasserted her authority over agricultural policy, returning it to the course she had consistently advocated from the beginning, which she laid out with startling candor to the Agrarian Section in April 1951. "We would be naive if we didn't know that the number of peasant small property owners who've been convinced and are ready to struggle to create collective farms is at the present moment anything but very small. . . . How can you think that these people, who are ready to kill each other over a piece of land, people who cry more over losing some cattle than over losing a child, how can you think that these people can suddenly put their cattle and land together, that they can part with their cow and land?" This, noted Pauker, was why the party had initially promoted collectivization by setting an example with a limited number of technically advanced, mechanized collective farms whose success—and *only* their success—would attract the peasants.

Thus mechanization, she again insisted, was a prerequisite to collectivization, for the collectives had to produce a higher yield and a better crop to have any chance of winning over the Romanian peasantry. According to Pauker, the first 176 collectives established in 1949 and early 1950 did, in fact, produce more than individual peasant farms, and thus convinced other peasants to join new collectives.

> But here intervened our mistakes, comrades, our serious mistakes. Instead of continuing on this path, a path that proved to be the best one, a path where things did not go calmly, for even here there was a struggle, but a path where things went more slowly and carefully—instead of this path, we began to use methods of forcefully pressuring the peasants to enter the collective farms. . . . Beginning with last summer we proceeded with actions that are absolutely opposed to the line of our party and absolutely opposed to any serious Communist thought. Only someone irresponsible, only an adventurer, only a person cut off from the masses and from our party, only a person who imagines himself as here today and gone tomorrow can think that it is possible to establish collective farms with people who are forced, and that such collective farms can possibly be viable. What was done last year, of holding contests between regions to see who had more collective farms and reverting to any means to realize the plan, which was not a plan at all but a bureaucratic mess, is absolutely inimical to our party line and cannot produce anything but negative results. Now we'll have to work hard to salvage our alliance with the working peasantry . . . , which could have been avoided had we been guided by this principle of our party, that it is not allowed to put people in collective farms who don't want to go there.[145]

Pauker went on to list the tasks needed to remedy the situation, most of which she had already completed. First, as an internal party report makes clear, she halted the establishment of new collective farms during the fall and winter of 1950–1951, ordering the Agrarian Section to focus solely on reversing injustices and fortifying existing collectives.[146] "Our first concern," Pauker maintained, "must be the existing collectives, of strengthening and transforming them into examples for the individual peasants."[147] Doing so would be daunting, for many of the recently established collectives were barely functioning.[148] A large percentage of the peasants who were forced to join these collectives were in fact salaried workers and functionaries who were unavailable to work the fields.[149] Many other coerced members simply refused to work.[150] Thus only fifty to sixty of the five hundred members of the Filimon Sârbu collective in the village of Sona, Fărăgaş County; only five or six members of the collective in Jupa, Severin County; only 10 percent of the members of the collective in Cragueşti, Severin County; and not a single member of the collective in Odverem, Cluj County, regularly showed up for work.[151] In addition, an increasing number of peasants reverted to tending their previously owned plots, essentially ignoring the existence of the new collectives. This was the case, for instance, in Chirileanca, Mureş County, where eighty-seven of one hundred registered members could not be found in the collective, and sixty-five of them had never once stepped foot there.[152]

Pauker responded with orders allowing all those wishing to leave a collective farm to do so and giving them parcels detached from the collective's land pool.[153] This promptly led to a mass exodus from many collectives: in Leghia, Cluj County, for example, of 120 families registered, 105 asked to leave, including the collective's president and leadership council; in Hida, Sălaj County, of 77 families registered, 50 opted out.[154] Pauker also immediately halted all trials of collective farmers charged with not bringing their land and possessions to the collectives and annulled all previous sentences.[155] This affected large numbers of arrested peasants.[156] Pauker further insisted that the party immediately allocate land to poor and middle peasants never compensated for lost property during previous land consolidations.[157]

In January 1951, Pauker and the Agrarian Section proposed that the Central Committee draw up Circular No. 13, stipulating penalties up to party expulsion and a criminal trial for anyone forcing peasants into collective farms.[158] "Those who acted in this fashion aren't humans," Pauker declared. "And we don't build Communism with such people." [159] The quickly adopted circular also mandated that the party stop selecting only the best and most accessible land when consolidating new collective farms and repealed the requirement that a collective be comprised of a single body of land, thereby reducing land confiscations.[160] At the same time, the authority to approve the establishment and consolidation of new collectives was restored to the Agrarian Section in Bucharest,[161] which in turn had to obtain the party leadership's permission—which Pauker persistently refused.[162] Reducing by one-third the Five-Year Plan's projected pace of collectivization,[163] she suggested to the section's leaders that "there is no need for us to rush with collectivization, for we must have quiet in the country," and stressed that their situation differed from the Soviets' collectivization in the early 1930s.[164] Instead of creating new collective farms, she repeatedly asserted, they should concentrate on strengthening the existing ones.[165] She steadfastly defended that view as late as March 1952, when Alexandru Moghioroş criticized it.[166] Thus, not one new collective farm was created in Romania in 1951. While 62 were officially established that year (as opposed to 971 in 1950), all had been set up and consolidated during summer and fall 1950 but were not yet formally inaugurated.[167] By the beginning of 1952, therefore, Romania claimed the smallest amount of collectivized land of any Soviet satellite.[168]

All of this quickly led to a serious schism within the RWP leadership, with Gheorghiu-Dej heading the opposition to Pauker. Like Pauker, Gheorghiu-Dej had spoken indignantly of the repression of the summer of 1950, angrily blaming the Agrarian Section functionaries:

> What kind of methods was work carried out with? With torture, revolvers, etc. All these methods, which were used everywhere, where do they come from? Were these methods not somehow suggested by you [the Agrarian Section functionaries]? . . . The report refers to the fact that [force] was evident in every county. This means that these methods were put into play somewhere. If it didn't start out from the center, then it started out from another center, because we're not talking about the methods of the leadership here, but what are categorically foreign methods.[169]

Dej's remarks were disingenuous, to say the least, given the policies he himself pushed through in June in compliance with Soviet directives, and given the course of action (or inaction) that he was now to take. During the remaining months of 1950 no measures were taken against those guilty of such abuses, except for sanctioning Putna County's party leaders; "the rest were promoted to better and more important jobs." [170] Hence no penalties for forcing peasants into collective farms were proposed or established until after Pauker returned at the end of 1950—as she critically noted not long after.[171] A similar dynamic was at work in the summer and fall of 1952, when the RWP reverted to massive forced collectivization soon after Pauker's ouster. It also operated in 1961 during the second wave of collectivization, when Dej vociferously lambasted local officials at a party meeting for coercing peasants into collective farms but did nothing to temper the campaign.[172] On the contrary, he connived in Nicolae Ceauşescu's reign of terror that completely collectivized the country the following year, three years ahead of schedule.[173] Dej's use of proxies had been evident during the early fifties as well: while Dej voiced support for Circular No. 13 at a February 1951 Secretariat meeting, his close ally Moghioroş soon began attacking the circular's inhibition of collectivization, which, he observed, had reverted to the previous period's "spontaneity." [174] Suggesting that resolutions like the circular had led party members to mistakenly conclude that the peasants were again to decide whether to collectivize, Moghioroş called for resuming "a tenacious propaganda campaign among the masses for establishing new collective farms."[175]

By 1951, the rift among party leaders on collectivization had become so acute that they had to convene "a special meeting" to clarify their position.[176] That spring Pauker's brother, Zalman Rabinsohn, told a confidante the Politburo had "decided to gather information and data from across the country" in an attempt to resolve "serious divergencies" among certain unnamed members, with some insisting that collectivization could only be done gradually and with the consent of the peasantry, and others that it should be accelerated "even if things have to be forced, [for] without this collectivization, the entire economy is in private hands that are sabotaging the work of the government."[177] The latter position paralleled Gheorghiu-Dej's remarks on several occasions. Despite his moderate realism on the issue before mid-1948, Dej, like Stalin, apparently came to view collectivization as the only way to control the countryside, where the party's hold was traditionally negligible and continually on the decline.[178] For Dej, the crux of the problem was the economic autonomy of individual private farmers, who "could influence the marketplace and determine the course of prices, regardless of what we, with our decrees, our circulars, and our instructions, did."[179] As long as agriculture remained private, Dej concluded, the peasants would use their badly needed produce to dictate their will to the state. "How do you fix prices for eggs or for milk," he demanded, "when the hen is no longer laying eggs and the cow is no longer giving milk? Regulating is practically impossible with this extensive distribution of individual peasant farms. I beg you to try to regulate this individualized economy that is so dispersed!"[180]

At the same time another factor seemingly motivated Dej: he pushed the Stalinist line to gain Stalin's trust.[181] At the 1948 meeting with Stalin described by Liuba Chişinevschi, Dej was said to have controverted Pauker's expressed hesitations and assured Stalin that collectivization would soon be implemented.[182] Given his vulnerable position that year, he probably was afraid to do anything else. Reportedly asked by a friend why he did not oppose collectivization as his conscience evidently dictated, Dej shot back, "They'll eat me alive if I do that!"[183] Likewise, Ion Gheorghe Maurer, confirming Dej's initial objection to collectivization, bellowed with laughter when asked the same question. "I'm amazed you asked such a question," he retorted. "You should only live under Stalin for five minutes and say you're opposed to forced collectivization, and then you'll know!"[184]

That Pauker's ire over the coercion of 1950 was implicitly directed at the Soviet advisers, who persistently pushed for such measures, was hardly lost on the Agrarian Section leadership.[185] Most dared not directly refer to this pressure when discussing the matter, but one high-ranking official in the Agriculture Ministry related, "I was seriously, seriously criticized for . . . pointing out a number of abuses [committed while creating] collective farms. The Soviet comrades said: Comrade Pricop has done away with the class struggle; he doesn't see the difficulties in the other sectors as well, and considers that the difficulties begin and end with the collective farms." [186] True, facing the rebellion in 1950, the Soviet advisers had approved slowing the Five-Year Plan's pace of collectivization and even scolded the Romanians for having "gone over-board" during the summer campaign, and true, it appears that the Soviets permitted a similar repose in 1951 in other satellites as well.[187] But an enormous gulf undoubtedly separated the tactical retreat they envisioned and the complete shutdown Pauker actually carried out; after all, even the reported one-third reduction in the collectivization plan still required establishing hundreds of new collective farms in 1951, a number Pauker did not even attempt to meet. The Soviets' prompt intervention on Gheorghiu-Dej's behalf in counteracting Pauker's policies was quite predictable, and they stepped in on the issue of tillage associations (*întovărăşiri*) almost immediately after her return to the scene.

The associations, the "inferior form" of production cooperative also invoked at the March 1949 plenary, were comprised of loosely organized groups of peasants who continued to own their land, tools, and livestock but commonly worked all or part of their land over a time frame that they themselves determined.[188] Organized and overseen by the state-run Machine and Tractor Stations (MTS), these associations were created voluntarily; indeed, nearly a third of the nation's peasantry was already working in associations a year before the party began the collectivization drive.[189] But since their members were not required to sign any contract or statute, the associations were more often than not strictly a temporary means to jointly rent MTS tractors during the plowing season.[190] Of some 4,600 "MTS-associations" reportedly created by March 1952, all but 615 were seasonal.[191]

After the collectivization fiasco of 1950, Gheorghiu-Dej proposed creating an intermediary association in addition to the collectives and the existing MTS associations. At first he suggested establishing Bulgarian TKZS (the Bulgarian acronym for Labor Cooperative Agricultural Farm) cooperatives but later recommended Soviet TOZ-type (the Russian acronym for Society for Joint Cultivation of Land) associations instead; the essential difference of both from the earlier associations was that as *permanent* cooperatives they could not be dissolved at the whim of the peasants.[192] Only such permanent associations with binding statutes could, as Dej declared, "constitute a step towards the collective farm. According to some information that we have, several TOZ farms have transformed themselves into kolhozes, a quite serious number of them. This goes to prove the notion that it's possible to transform the TOZ into kolhozes." [193] Nonetheless, Pauker rejected Dej's proposal and called for maintaining the status quo. "I thought," she later related, "that we didn't need [the Bulgarian cooperatives or] even the [TOZ] associations, and that we should keep the kolhoz and the hodge-podge [MTS] associations that we already had." [194]

In early 1951, Gheorghiu-Dej and Pauker discussed the dispute with Stalin. Pauker countered Dej's arguments in favor of an intermediary cooperative and suggested that the peasants would leave the collectives in droves if such cooperatives were offered them. But Stalin sustained Dej and ruled that they should set up TOZ-type associations in place of the old ones, exhorting Pauker "not [to] be afraid of the TOZ." [195] Ostensibly submitting to Stalin's "suggestions," Pauker formally acceded to a March 1951 CC resolution to draft a model statute for future TOZ associations yet did little to comply with either command. A draft of the statute was submitted to the Agrarian Section as early as June 21, but neither the statute nor official instructions on establishing TOZ associations were distributed to local party committees until January 1952— and then without Pauker's approval.[196] Pauker later claimed that the Agrarian Section acted slowly on the TOZ because it had continued to concentrate on "correcting the mistakes" of 1950, but several testimonials suggest she was motivated more by a sectarian insistence on establishing only kolhozes.[197] Given her simultaneously freezing the formation of such collectives, the primary issue for Pauker evidently was not choosing this or that cooperative, but creating them with the consent, if not at the initiative, of Romania's peasantry. Though she apparently preferred associations and had previously promoted their establishment, Pauker now seemed to oppose the TOZ because she saw it as a ploy for pushing collectivization forward after the 1950 rebellion and for further eroding endeavors based on the peasants' initiative.[198] Her foot-dragging ultimately proved futile in the face of Soviet intervention: a formal campaign to register peasants in TOZ associations began in the early spring of 1952, and no fewer than 900 TOZs were established in April alone.[199]

The Soviets also overturned Pauker on the question of state farms (GOSTATs). Admitting to have personally questioned state farming's prospects, Pauker implied that she was influenced by "the general theory that the state is a poor manager," which any cursory review of the GOSTATs' record would certainly verify.[200] Of the 327 existing GOSTATs at the beginning of 1952, only about ten could be considered profitable or self-sufficient.[201] Many regularly attributed massive losses to storms, though the weather usually was not the real culprit: no fewer than 600,000 lambs perished in various GOSTATs, for instance, because they were left outside during storms.[202] As Agriculture Minister Vaida observed, "when the peasant knows that the chickens are his, he brings them in the house when it's cold outside"; not so, however, with GOSTAT workers, who once caused the deaths of an undisclosed number of lambs because they simply did not feed them.[203] At the same time, the GOSTATs' huge facilities for housing large numbers of fowl led to catastrophic losses, for they proved to be efficient breeding grounds for animal diseases.[204] Adding the high turnover of underpaid workers, the massive waste, the widespread theft, and the "worrisome levels" of self-consumption,[205] how the GOSTATs racked up astounding deficits from one year to the next (in 1951 totaling 8,807,706,600 lei—88 percent of circulating funds) is easy to see.[206]

That Pauker was unwilling to provoke the peasantry to consolidate these farms, therefore, is not surprising. The Central Committee's March 1949 plenary resolved to establish the GOSTATs on state land reserves and stipulated that they were to be fully consolidated by 1952, which would have required displacing hundreds of thousands of Romanian peasants. But after a "whole series of grave deviations" during consolidations in 1949 (handled not by Pauker's Agrarian Commission, but by another body), the party leadership temporary halted the project, and Pauker refused to allow its resumption when she assumed responsibility for the GOSTATs with the creation of the Agrarian Section in 1950. In response to the repression and resultant rebellion that summer, she informed Agriculture Minister Vaida that "now's not the time" to resume the half-completed GOSTAT consolidations. Though party leaders approved a plan to consolidate 220,000 hectares in 1951 to meet the 1952 deadline, Pauker insisted that current conditions prevented carrying it out. This compelled Vaida to postpone the consolidations another year, leaving the 327 GOSTATs broken into 19,000 separate plots.[207]

In September 1951, however, a special Soviet commission arrived in Romania to help prepare a new Currency Reform.[208] Considering the GOSTATs crucial to that reform's success, the commission promptly demanded their consolidation. "The Soviet comrades . . . ," Pauker recalled, "were at their wit's end. What kind of state farm is this? The first observation the comrades from the Ukraine made was that we should get things in order, and consolidate the farms."[209] Declaring that nothing would get done otherwise, the commission overruled Pauker and sustained Gheorghiu-Dej's proposition to consolidate the GOSTATs at once.[210] Moreover, the commission apparently stripped Pauker of responsibility over the GOSTAT consolidations, for Gheorghiu-Dej personally dealt with the problem once consolidations were back on the agenda.[211] They resumed in February or March 1952, displacing 35,000 people, and were scheduled for completion that summer, with the displacement of an additional 150,000.[212]

Unfortunately, no existing document indicates whether the commission directly intervened to create new collective farms. But it did impose an iron-fisted collections drive that resulted by the end of 1951 in large numbers of peasants requesting to set up collectives to obtain reductions in collection quotas granted to collective farmers.[213] New collectives were therefore organized in the early months of 1952, with no fewer than 320 inaugurated by the May 27–29 CC plenary that purged Pauker.[214] Soon after, Gheorghiu-Dej stepped-up the campaign even further. In September, he informed the Council of Ministers that "the pace of creating collective farms and TOZ associations will be intensified in the future," and returned authority for approving new collectives to local party committees.[215] In the next two months, the "excesses" of 1950 reappeared throughout the country: subordinate bodies were obliged to meet fixed plans; regions again competed in socialist contests, this time to achieve 100 percent collectivization in the shortest time; threats of economic reprisals or "administrative measures" again forced peasants to join collective farms; coerced consolidations forced farmers off their land and moved them against their will to other regions; and mass protests and even full-fledged uprisings again raged in peasant villages nationwide.[216] In response, Gheorghiu-Dej not only failed to invoke Circular No. 13, but abrogated it. At the end of October it was announced that henceforth local authorities themselves would decide whether to prosecute anyone guilty of coercing peasants. "We shouldn't go with the line," Moghioroş declared, "of arresting large numbers of party members and honest activists, who were goaded by others or, for one reason or another, committed a number of deviations. They shouldn't be arrested for any deviation. . . . Arrests should be a last resort, and only against those who are working with the enemy or are under his influence."[217]

All told, the percentage of collectivized land more than doubled, from 3.1 to 7.2, in 1952: 707 new collectives were established that year, and an additional 252 were created in the first months of 1953 before Soviet Prime Minister Georgi Malenkov's New Course took effect.[218] Collectivization then slowed considerably, but after 1956 Gheorghiu-Dej renewed the campaign on a massive scale, concurrent with continual denunciations of Ana Pauker's alleged brutality against the peasantry.[219] Taking advantage of the fact that Pauker's cancer was a strictly kept secret that did not leave the confines of the Politburo,[220] Gheorghiu-Dej could credibly accuse Pauker during her purge of having waged the repression of 1950[221] —a strategy that he would employ regularly from then on and that his protégés perpetuate even today.[222]

KULAKS AND COLLECTIONS

A fundamental aspect of collectivization was the official policy of "restricting" the wealthier strata of the Romanian peasantry, the *chiaburi* (kulaks). As cautious and guarded as the party leaders (save Moghioroş) were on collectivization in their February 1949 Politburo discussions, they were all but unanimous in their harshness regarding the kulaks (with the ironic exception of Interior Minister Teohari Georgescu).[223] Particularly evocative on the issue was Gheorghiu-Dej. Declaring that "the class struggle" against the kulaks was closely linked even to their initial work in creating collective farms, Dej took aim at the party's past policies in that regard. Though all agreed, he asserted, that constructing socialism was "linked with the fight against the kulaks, we've done practically nothing [to carry it out]. The kulaks succeeded in infiltrating the administrative apparatus and our party ranks, as well as using the Agrarian Reform for their own interests. We can't justify this shortcoming in the leadership of our party."[224] Dej repeated his critique of the previous line at the March 3–5, 1949, CC plenary, suggesting the peasant mentality that saw the kulaks simply as "good farmers" had "penetrated even in the ranks of our party. I recall when it was a matter of placing certain elements at the head of various institutions, we thought of putting these 'good farmers,' who were [seen as being] more capable." [225]

This was, in fact, an unstated attack on Ana Pauker, the main proponent of the earlier line. When implementing the Agrarian Reform in March 1945, Pauker called for limiting the confiscation of large estates to those of fifty hectares or larger to promote "class collaboration" and a broad-based alliance of all antifascist elements in the country. "We must obtain the complete isolation of the landlords through the Agrarian Reform," she suggested, "and we must obtain a pacification of the kulaks, who will have 50 hectares, and who will breathe a sigh of relief that the landlord is gone. We need to do this even though [the kulaks] will profit off the backs of the poorer peasants; for we want, in this way, to acquire an ally." [226] She also countenanced the appointment of kulaks in certain positions based on, as Dej alleged, their standing as "good farmers," apparently on her own, and not the party's, initiative. [227] She argued as well for allowing kulaks to rent state-owned agricultural machinery, asserting that the party needed them to produce, and she favored targeting kulaks as customers of consumer cooperatives. [228] She further criticized Prime Minister Petru Groza's Communist-dominated Ploughman's Front for "sectarian tendencies" in not admitting kulaks. [229] As late as 1950 she told the party-run Union of Romanian Democratic Women not to reject kulak women as members of the union's peace movement, for "[kulaks have] children, too." [230] Indeed, Pauker seems to have regarded the kulaks as she reportedly viewed the bourgeoisie as a whole, potentially integrable elements in the emerging socialist order. This is evident in her remarks at an October 1947 Politburo meeting:

PAUKER: What's interesting is something Comrade Zhdanov related [at the first Cominform conference] in Poland. He said that the kulaks are very active and very pro-Soviet in the USSR. During the dekulakization there was great agitation; but now, and during the war, they were the most helpful elements, especially their children. Soviet law stipulates that the children of kulaks are not allowed to enter the army. During the war they engaged in all kinds of falsification and trickery so that they could nevertheless enter the army, and some were killed, and many returned as heroes of the Soviet Union. After the war, on the initiative of the Bolshevik Party, that law that prohibited children of kulaks from entering the army was abolished. They got rid of the point that took social origins into account. . . .

LUCA: But what a mistake it would be if we did the same thing.

PAUKER: The young people are opening our eyes as well.[231]

Pauker's essentially rejecting the concept of an immutable class enemy persisted long after the Soviets had imposed a hard-line stance against the kulaks.[232] Though at times engaging in strident rhetoric following the policy change,[233] she did not translate that rhetoric into action and seldom veered from what seems to have been a principled position on the matter.

Perhaps one reason Pauker could do this was that throughout her tenure Romania had no precise criteria for defining a kulak.[234] Only after the special Soviet commission to oversee the currency reform arrived in the country in September 1951, "a collective of three comrades was formed" to establish the criteria, which they presented to the leadership shortly before Pauker's ouster.[235] Until then, however, the definition was fluid and broadly open to interpretation. Before 1947, some party theorists considered as kulaks all peasants with ten hectares or more of farmland; after 1947, however, the threshold was raised to twenty hectares.[236] At the March 1949 CC plenary, party leaders identified "approximately 168,000 kulaks" among the nation's peasantry (5.5 percent), defining them only as those who exploited hired labor.[237] Various party officials, particularly Luca, soon raised objections to this definition: what were they to do with certain ethnic-Bulgarian peasants, for instance, whose crop necessitated hiring laborers no matter how small their farmland?[238] How were they to treat elderly peasants, who could no longer work their fields themselves?[239] This apparently left the leadership divided on whether to again base the definition strictly on the amount of land one owned or also to take into account the peasants' income. To define the kulaks solely by their land meant their numbers would assuredly fall. For given that kulaks were barred from purchasing more land (a key component in "restricting" them), their children would each inherit only a part of their farms and thus no longer qualify as kulaks.[240] But if revenue were considered, then any successful farmer could be classified a kulak, and the number of potential kulaks would be limited only by the dubious discretion of party arbiters.[241]

Advocating the land-based definition, Pauker reportedly argued that the number of kulaks would naturally decrease during the transition from capitalism to socialism, citing Stalin's earlier writings on the subject. Using this definition, the Popular Councils (regulated by Georgescu)

listed far fewer kulaks in their areas than the March 1949 plenary estimated,[242] which figures released by Luca's Finance Ministry then reflected.[243] Adamantly opposing this, however, was Gheorghiu-Dej:

> At the Finance Ministry it was pointed out that the percentage of kulaks
> is falling. It's no longer 5.5% as our plenary in March 1949 established.
> They're diminishing! I refuse to believe such a thing. I'm convinced that the
> capitalist elements increased in the countryside due to a whole series of fac-
> tors. For three years they didn't pay taxes, middle peasants proceeded to be-
> come kulaks, and we gave them goods at reduced prices. . . . We [therefore]
> shouldn't go with criteria that don't increase the number of kulaks on the
> lists. We should be guided by criteria . . . based on the peasants' revenue.[244]

Luca eventually adopted Dej's outlook,[245] and in the summer of 1951
Stalin sustained Dej on all points.[246] Still Pauker persisted, insisting as
late as mid-December that middle peasants, regardless of income, "have
not become kulaks because *they can't buy land.*"[247]

Pauker's narrow definition of the kulak led to yet another dispute
within the RWP leadership. Upon returning to Bucharest after her cancer surgery, she learned that during the summer of 1950 large numbers
of kulaks in nearly every region of the country had been forced into
collective farms.[248] When the local committees in the various regions
asked what to do with them, Gheorghiu-Dej ordered their immediate
removal.[249] But after learning at an Agrarian Section meeting in March
1951 that middle peasants had been expelled as kulaks from the Mă-
dăraş collective in the Bihor region, Pauker immediately halted the exclusions.[250] Forbidding any expulsions without the Central Committee's
approval, she called for detailed lists with photographs to be drawn
up to ensure that those in question were not actually middle peasants
(based, presumably, on her definition).[251] "We had not established the
principle of who's a kulak," Pauker recalled. "Those from the Agrarian
Section came with a list that had thousands [of names on it], and it
seemed impossible to me that thousands of kulaks could have entered
[the collectives]. In a single region—in Oradea, I think—there were
some 700 in some 15–20 collective farms. It seemed that they were
[throwing people out] arbitrarily."[252] Hence, after receiving the lists on
March 21, Pauker sent no directive to proceed with the exclusions that
Gheorghiu-Dej had "categorically" ordered.[253] Further, she reproached
a leading Agrarian Section official for expelling thirteen alleged kulaks
without her approval.[254] She finally allowed the exclusions only after the
CC plenary convened on September 18, 1951, coincidental with the
Soviet commission's arrival.[255]

Admitting at the May 1952 CC plenary that she delayed ordering the kulaks' expulsion, Pauker remarked that she "didn't see any great danger in a kulak staying in a collective farm."[256] Her policies at the Agrarian Commission in 1949 clearly reflected this. Although the commission expressly prohibited kulaks from entering collective farms, it instructed the local committees to accept all requests submitted by kulaks to join new collectives, contingent on the kulaks' ceasing to exploit others and working their farms themselves, thus leaving the door open for their future admission.[257] The commission meantime essentially allowed them to "dekulakize" themselves by "donating" land to collective farms, which enabled many to be officially reclassified as middle peasants.[258] The practice of accepting kulak "donations" proved important in consolidating the new collective farms, since the collectives, with the bulk of their members being poor peasants with little or no land of their own, continually suffered from land shortages.[259] But it met the immediate disapproval of the Soviet adviser Veretenicov and the firm opposition of Gheorghiu-Dej. "We have to force [the kulaks] to work [the land] themselves," Verentenicov countered.[260] Dej further insisted, "You don't find, neither in the classics of Marxism-Leninism nor anywhere in history, one example of a class self-destructing."[261] The kulaks were making concessions only to further their own interests, as was also the case, Dej pointed out, with the collections, where they were sharing their crops with poor and middle peasants in order to win them as allies. In fact, Dej concluded, "a battle [was] going on for allies between us . . . and the kulaks."[262] These donations, added Dej, were only aiding the kulaks in that battle. Hence, they must be barred from "donating [their] land and thus becoming a benefactor in the eyes of the working peasantry."[263]

Still, Pauker directed the Agrarian Commission to continue accepting the donations—dismissing her Soviet adviser's "advice" and ignoring Gheorghiu-Dej's objections.[264] Even after the Soviets apparently put their foot down and "requested" that donations be halted (most likely at the beginning of 1950), the Agrarian Section continued to accept kulak land.[265] Certain local party officials had decided the kulaks were not donating their land after all, but abandoning it. Though accepting such "renouncements" "was deemed inappropriate," the Agrarian Section repeatedly allowed collective farms to do just that.[266] Only after Pauker's June 15 departure was "class collaboration" abruptly halted.[267] Upon taking Pauker's place, Moghioroş informed the Agrarian Section that henceforth "renouncements from kulaks are not to be accepted, but that guilty kulaks are to be sent to trial and their land confiscated."[268] This was then relayed to the party county secretaries, who were summoned to Bucharest and told that "[i]t's still possible to take land from the kulaks, but not in the form of charity. It can be taken by way of judicial sentences, for sabotage, etc."[269] They could confiscate the property of "one or two of the most hostile kulaks" in every village, taking either all of their land or nothing at all.[270]

Confiscations of kulak property soon commenced throughout the country, but they quickly surpassed the central authorities' established parameters. Local party officials began seizing the land of all kulaks (and often middle peasants as well) whose farms fell within the boundaries of newly constituted collective farms, in some counties totaling more than ten kulaks from every village.[271] The conviction that "we're creating collective farms at the expense of the kulaks" quickly became a slogan of the period, as party activists considered the kulaks fair game.[272] Some were forced to submit requests for renouncing their land, while others were simply thrown out of their houses, with entire families, including small children, dumped on the street without shelter.[273] Apprised of the mass confiscations, the central party leadership did little to halt the terror.[274] On the contrary, it directed the county committees to expel forthwith from their villages all kulaks whose lands they had confiscated.[275] The central leadership further reminded the county committees to find a "legal basis" for all confiscations—that is, to first arrest and try the kulaks.[276] Consequently, the militia and Securitate, prompted by state and party organizations, began staging mass arrests to "clear the area" for future collectives and take possession of the kulaks' property. "Such cases," Georgescu acknowledged, "were not isolated," and had spread rapidly throughout Romania. "In the Bucharest region alone," he noted, "dekulakization was carried out with the arrest of over a hundred kulaks, whose families were expelled to the outskirts of their villages."[277] In Trei Scaune County, authorities resorted to arresting kulaks and taking their holdings whenever a collective farm needed land; in the Cluj region, kulaks were stripped of their property and sent with their families to the Danube–Black Sea Canal; and in Turda and Mureş Counties, the Securitate arrested and summarily shot a number of kulaks.[278] The "legal basis" for these actions often was found after the fact, as large numbers of kulaks were tried and imprisoned on mostly fabricated charges or for such frivolous reasons as not weeding their gardens, tying up their dogs, or clearing their trees of caterpillars.[279] In Ilfov County, the secretary for agrarian affairs, the president of the county tribunal, and the chief prosecutor "devised a plan of how many kulaks to try and how many to sentence," and they pressured judges to speed convictions and imposed predetermined sentences in many cases.[280] Such practices were rampant in the summer of 1950, as kulaks were falsely arrested and tried in every region of the country.[281]

The repression abruptly halted, however, in or shortly before September 1950—that is, soon after Pauker returned to Bucharest from the Kremlin hospital.[282] The party leadership then set up a special commission, comprising teams of Central Committee and Interior and Justice Ministry functionaries, to investigate the abuses. After a month in the field, the commission submitted a report to Pauker, Georgescu, and Moghioroş sometime in October.[283] Based on its findings, the party ordered the immediate release of all kulaks who had been illegally arrested, and reprimanded the Interior Ministry for the terror.[284] Georgescu then took measures to prevent any repetition of the repression, ordering that henceforth "only those elements who are acting in a hostile and antagonistic manner" would be arrested.[285] In addition, the Interior Ministry informed the Agrarian Section in November that the collectives were to return the kulaks' confiscated land and possessions, causing "very serious difficulties" in some regions when collective farmers refused to comply.[286] Critical of the new policy, a leading Agrarian Section functionary raised the issue in a meeting with Pauker, but got no response.[287] Pauker eventually must have decided not to press the issue, for the following spring she declared that the kulaks "are going to have to wait some more" for the problems to be resolved. "Or if they want land somewhere else," she added, "they can go there."[288] Nonetheless, she apparently did not rescind the order to return kulak property.[289]

The available documents do not indicate who specifically promoted this retreat or whether there was a consensus in the leadership to carry it out. Apparently, however, Gheorghiu-Dej was behind Moghioroş's June 1950 call for confiscations. Though he pointedly condemned them as "provocations" after the fact and insisted that orders to confiscate the most hostile kulaks' lands had been issued without his knowledge, he had in fact proposed confiscating kulak holdings in the Central Committee just before the repression began.[290] On the other hand, it was Luca who had advocated—without Dej's approval—expelling "the most dangerous kulak elements" from every village creating a collective farm.[291] Further, while Pauker effectively ignored Luca's proposal[292] and took no action to confiscate kulak land,[293] she, too, had signaled the harder line in a May 1950 report to the leadership.[294]

In any case, Dej probably did not support halting the anti-kulak terror, for he soon attacked the Pauker faction on this very issue. Throughout the purge in 1952, Pauker was berated for being soft on the kulaks, and Georgescu was rebuked for abating the terror.[295] At the same time, both were denounced for ameliorating the obligatory collections drive, which was essentially the reverse of their kulak policies.[296] With three-quarters of the peasantry possessing small, subsistence holdings that did not bring half of them a minimal taxable income, the kulaks were left to fill the bulk of collection quotas.[297] Hence Pauker's position on collections was linked directly to her views on the kulaks.

Up through 1949 the collections comprised mandatory state acquisitions of a percentage of the peasants' crop. In 1950 they were converted into a "tax in kind" that required peasants to hand over quotas without compensation.[298] This coincided with the spring 1950 creation of the Agrarian Section and Pauker's assuming responsibility for the collections along with Moghioroş, who oversaw the newly established State Collections Committee.[299] In May the government adopted a complicated scheme of progressive quotas based entirely on the Soviet system and categorized by type of crop as well as each respective region's level of productivity.[300] Aware of peasant rebellions over collections the year before, party leaders labored to achieve what they considered a fair and workable system.[301] But serious problems with the plan quickly became apparent, with excessively high quotas leaving many peasants scrambling to feed their families. A widow in Sibiu County, for instance, had to come up with 170 kilograms of wheat when she harvested only 167, and a poor peasant in Botoşani County had to hand over 1,000 kilograms when his total output was only 1,200, leaving him 200 kilograms to sustain eight children.[302]

The situation only worsened in the summer of 1950, when authorities began forcing peasants to meet collection quotas.[303] Coinciding with the antikulak campaign, the coercive measures were carried out on Moghioroş's orders once Pauker had left Bucharest.[304] They reflected views Gheorghiu-Dej expressed at a Central Committee plenary several weeks earlier: "[I]n the case that kulaks don't meet their obligations, we should go so far as to confiscate the kulaks' entire surplus."[305] Railing against the party's "sentimental [and] peasantist policies" that allowed free commerce in the countryside, Dej called for "economic measures [that will] make the peasant understand that this friendship and alliance with the working class does not mean skinning the working class. The economic situation of the peasantry this past year is incomparably dif-

ferent, and radically changed, from what it was earlier. Go to the peasant, the so-called peasant. There isn't one peasant that doesn't have so
much poultry, and so many hens and ducks. . . . At this period in time,
our thinking has to be that the peasant must pay up. If he doesn't pay,
immediate sanction!"[306] Complying with the new line, party collectors
began forcibly requisitioning delinquent farmers' personal belongings,
sparking full-scale rebellions of mostly poor and working peasants.[307]

Returning to Bucharest from Moscow in August 1950, Pauker found
the situation clearly untenable, with organized peasant resistance the
norm in a number of important regions, and extensive noncompliance
even among party members and state apparatchiks.[308] Moreover, local
officials reluctant to enforce collections were continually lobbying the
central authorities for substantial reductions.[309] Hence, arguing that
the collection plan was ill-conceived and unrealistically large, Pauker
reduced the quotas for the 1951 harvest, at times without informing
Dej.[310] She also adopted a new line on collections immediately after resuming full duties at the end of 1950, a line that, ironically, she at least
initially devised with Moghioroş. When she unveiled the plan in the Secretariat on January 11, 1951, the situation in the country had only worsened: collections for corn had officially expired December 31, but the
party had managed to collect only 18,000 wagons of 40,000 planned.
The law required that those not in compliance be penalized with higher
quotas (as much as ten times the original amount) and arrested if they
failed to comply by February 1.[311] But Pauker and Moghioroş deleted
the increased quotas from the law and resolved not to arrest any but a
few offenders.[312] With Pauker's backing, Moghioroş declared, "We have
specified that it's not appropriate right now to prosecute people en
masse, though the law allows it, but to . . . select a couple of the [kulak]
leaders or the worst cases in every village and try them, with the people
of the village attending the trial."[313] Not only were sanctions to be less
severe (except for party functionaries, who were to be dismissed if they
remained noncompliant after being "enlightened" on the subject),[314]
but no peasants were to be forced to hand over collection quotas.
Rather, the party was to limit itself solely to "measures of explaining . . .
and convincing the peasants."[315]

Concurring with these measures (other than halting the higher quota
penalties) was Teohari Georgescu: "I'm scared that the [local] party secretaries in their desire to fulfill the plan, will start constraining people.
That's why things have to be led, and not from there."[316] Hence, when
informing Interior Ministry officials of the new collections policy, he

ordered that no one was to be arrested without his approval.[317] "He said," Deputy Interior Minister Marin Jianu related, "that we should arrest one or two kulaks here and there without scaring the others, because we need them to produce."[318] The kulaks should not be disturbed, Georgescu reportedly added, because no one would be left to work the land, essentially echoing Pauker's position on the matter.[319] As Pavel Cristescu, the director general of the Interior Ministry's militia, confirmed to party leaders, both the Interior and Justice Ministries issued orders "not to arrest the kulaks, but to sequester [their produce] while allowing them to remain free. We could not arrest them for failing to hand over their quotas."[320] Consequently, though a large number of Ialomița County's 4,200 kulaks had not met their quotas, not one was arrested for that offense in 1951; nor were any arrested in Teleorman County, though the majority there also had not met their quotas.[321] In those areas where limited prosecutions were carried out, the arrested kulaks were released after issuing formal self-criticisms and acquitted on the proviso that they would give what they owed.[322]

Ana Pauker later clarified this complete rejection of coercion. "I told the collectors that under no circumstances should they start collecting the quotas, because the kulaks would be harmed, [and there'd be] too much pressure on the working peasants."[323] She did so, moreover, because "I thought that the peasants . . . , and especially the kulaks, would gladly come and . . . , out of goodwill, hand over the quotas."[324] Following her lead, the Agrarian Section assumed that the 1951 collection would "happen by itself" and that, given the bumper crop that year, the peasants would not resist handing over their reduced quotas.[325] But when Pauker returned from an extended vacation at the end of September, she learned that collections had fallen seriously behind.[326] At an October 8–9, 1951, meeting, the Agrarian Section learned that while 86.0 percent of the corn crop had been harvested nationwide, only 1.8 percent had been collected; in Buzău County, 97.0 percent of the corn had been harvested, yet not one wagon had been filled; in Iași County, 96.7 percent had been harvested, but only 0.2 percent collected; and in Teleorman County, 97.9 percent had been harvested, but only 7.8 percent collected. Of sunflowers, 100 percent had been harvested in the Bucharest, Buzău, and Severin regions, but only 7.7 percent, 7.8 percent, and 5.0 percent, respectively, had been collected.[327] In all, only 30 percent of planned yearly collections had been obtained by November 1951.[328]

Sounding the alarm on the low collections, the Agrarian Section leadership pressed Pauker to summon the regional party secretaries and the Popular Council presidents to an urgent meeting on the problem. But Pauker insisted that was not necessary and "categorically opposed" calling the meeting.[329] However, as she would later recall, a far more menacing figure also approached her. "The Soviet comrades were here, that group dealing with the [Currency] Reform, and Macarov came to me and said: 'Comrade, you should know that we're making a mess out of the Currency Reform on account of the collections. And you are with the collections, and look how things are going, what percentages have not been collected. . . . You are at a crucial moment. Either you carry out the collections and have a reserve of grain that you'll be able to put into play, or you'll ruin the Currency Reform.'"[330] Exactly when Macarov spoke to Pauker is not clear, but with the collections crisis already evident by early to mid-October, the Soviets probably intervened quickly at that time. Yet Pauker admitted that "it was only at the end of November or the beginning of December that I took measures, when I saw that things had remained bad."[331] She finally relented and convened a meeting with the regional party secretaries December 1. There an official from the Agriculture Ministry revealed that the ministry had sent out letters to 150,000 farmers, warning that legal action would be taken against them if they did not hand over their quotas. Apparently no longer in the mood for tolerance, Moghioroş insisted that "[l]egal action must be taken whenever the law is broken, without considering who is guilty." But Pauker was resolute: "We have to find something to do on the spot," she replied, "but not with prosecutions."[332]

One suggestion was to send the Central Committee to the rural regions to assure the collections' completion, as the Soviet Union had done.[333] But Pauker continued to hesitate: "[The year before] the collections [were conducted by] removing things from people's homes," she explained. "And, out of fear that it would be repeated, I said only at the last moment that the CC members should go."[334] She dispatched them the second week of December, but then abruptly called them back two weeks later, before the collections were completed.[335] "On December 20, 1951," Luca later revealed, "Ana Pauker stopped the collections without fulfilling the plan, saying that everything that was possible to do had been done, and that it was not possible to do anything more." This was, Luca added, Pauker's standard excuse each year for not meeting the collection plan.[336] As Pauker herself self-critically noted, "Again, this liberalism and lack of firmness goes on. We said that if they've been out for two weeks they can now come back, that things will now proceed without them; and afterwards, we had to send them yet again." [337]

With the Soviet advisers insisting this was "an exceptional matter," and others pressing her to heed Macarov's warning, Pauker reconvened the Central Committee members on January 15, 1952. [338] "Even though we raised the issue with alarm on December 1," she told them, "we are doing horribly with the collections, and we have to fulfill the plan! . . . [I]t's an urgent necessity. We absolutely have to fulfill the collection plan." Thus, she was dispatching them to the countryside again, and they were not to return until they fulfilled the plan 100 percent—with a few exceptions granted for those areas where doing so was simply impossible. "However," she added, "where there were natural disasters, and where they have other means, you are to complete the collections [by] confiscating from the kulaks, taking from the middle peasants, and discovering the thieves like those, for instance, in Botoşani and Bârlad. . . . In this way we'll supplement the shortages from the natural disasters." Complaining that "[t]he peasants do whatever they want, and we stand there and follow the law as if it were handed down by God," Pauker now reversed herself on imposing penalties of increased quotas, and called for utilizing "the entire apparatus, including the party, the state, the militia, the prosecutor's office, and the masses of party members" to complete the collections. "You saw what happened in Teleorman: when they got things moving, they got results. 32,000 people, with 7,000 party members leading them, went from house to house. . . . You have to go back to the cotton-growing regions as well (Ialomiţa, Galaţi, Dolj), and that problem is going to have to be dealt with. We had a contract, on the basis of which we gave people advances, clothes, and cloth—and now they're scoffing at us and not giving us the cotton. We have to put them on trial." [339]

However, Pauker was far too late, for the peasants had long since hidden their produce. [340] Thus, in the Iaşi region collections increased by only 1.5 percent through December and the first week of January. The situation was much the same in Arad County. "Because we started the searches very late," one member reported, "we've obtained only very small amounts at some 270 kulak farms that we conducted searches in." [341] Moreover, party activists were sent to every village in the Bârlad (Tutova) region to bolster the teams of peasants collecting quotas there, and two hundred workers were taken out of factories to assist as well; still they could not fulfill the plan. Predictably, confiscations ensued, with houses raided and possessions lifted. This time, however, the Agrarian Section stepped in and ordered the belongings returned on condition that the peasants sign written promises to hand over their quotas within ten days.[342] Pauker cautioned against such "mistakes," and suggested that collections could be done "without taking people's record players."[343] But an unmistakable pattern had emerged, and the familiar dynamic of the periphery's leading the center soon took over.

Before closing the January 15 meeting, Pauker told the departing members:

> No matter how much we want to be peaceful, they won't let us. If we don't do anything, we're a bunch of spineless jellyfish who aren't carrying out our mission of defending and representing the working class. It's not our role to stand there and complain that the kulaks don't want to give us anything. We know how to go around speaking softly, but we also know how to go around with a clenched fist. . . . Thus we find ourselves in a situation, in which we have to conclude that we haven't yet been firm enough on this matter. We've had our doubts. . . . We haven't taken ourselves seriously. We've carried out collections over the past several years, and we've looked the other way. And because of that, the peasants don't take us seriously, either.[344]

Pauker apparently was accusing herself more than anyone else. Having opposed coercing the peasantry, be it with collections or collectivization, and risking a great deal in the process, she must have felt betrayed by its response. But her ultimate betrayers were her own illusions that the peasants would "gladly" hand over crops to collections whose very purpose was to create reserves that the state could throw on the market to drive down prices or that they would "gladly" cooperate with the regime whose very program was to end their existence as private farmers. Having resisted the Stalinist line on agrarian policy, she must have known its implications for what was still an overwhelmingly private agriculture system: by reducing production of consumer goods in its drive to build heavy industry, the party could offer the peasants increasingly less to buy with their money. Without that incentive for the peasants to sell their produce, the party had no way but force to guarantee supply.[345] With her liberal line on collections now seen as bankrupt, and with Stalin making implied threats to the Romanian leadership's "peasantist politics," Pauker had little room for maneuvering. In the end, she was forced to tread the path of party politics and implement the very actions she so adamantly opposed.[346]

When the Central Committee reconvened on February 4, their tales must have sounded painfully familiar. An army of peasants formed collection detachments that went from house to house in every village of the country. Many kulaks had abandoned their farms altogether and fled their regions. The kulaks "don't even exist," one member asserted. "There's someone at home, but they [the heads of the households] have fled. They didn't even cultivate their land." Party collectors therefore reverted to arresting the wives whom the kulaks often left behind. "Prosecuting the wives . . . isn't pleasant," another retorted. "They scream that we should take the land. For three years they've had quotas imposed on them." Confiscations were also rampant, and apparently no longer discouraged. Following the arrest of delinquent farmers, collectors scrambled to recover their losses by taking whatever they could from the offenders' houses. "When we were confiscating," one of them related, "some came and put their children in the carts as well." [347]

As Pauker acknowledged four years later, she suffered "a guilty conscience" over the episode, which over two months resulted in the arrests of some 2,000 kulaks. [348] When trials began, she related, "I thought it was wonderful, for it had been done on that basis in the USSR as well, and the poor peasants were the ones who provided the support in attacking the kulaks. Why . . . provoke the entire peasantry to rise up against us? With their help and solidarity we can remove the grain." [349] It is tempting to see Pauker's actions not only as a compelled response to an escalating crisis but also as a panicked, opportunistic attempt to avoid the purge she must have seen coming. And it is reasonable to wonder whether she would have agreed to carry out the most repressive policies had she not been ousted from the party leadership. But the evidence indicates that her initial capitulation on this matter, just one of a series of cynical compromises throughout her career, was a decision from which she quickly backed away.

Also speaking at the February 4 meeting was Nicolae Ceauşescu, then a candidate member of the Central Committee, who reported to Pauker that he had arrested 300 kulaks in his region. Pauker's response is telling: "Three hundred kulaks arrested. But will they be seed-planting in the spring?" [350] One month later, she would further caution the Agrarian Section: "We should be careful not to suppress the kulaks but to make it possible for them to work the land." [351]

Shortly after, Gheorghiu-Dej raised the issue of the arrested kulaks. Earlier, he had criticized Pauker for not sending the CC members "from the outset" and had called for a mass mobilization to complete the collections "at any price." [352] But, with seed-planting about to commence, Dej now proposed temporarily releasing the kulaks so they could work the fields. "It's not a matter of exonerating those breaking the law," he suggested. "Those who broke the law will and should be prosecuted. . . . This suspended sentence is to be during the agriculture season, which means from the spring until the late fall, and they will return to prison only during the winter months." Pauker timidly added, "If they carry out their obligations, maybe they can also be . . ." But Dej cut her off mid-sentence.[353]

One week later, the Council of Ministers debated whether to arrest peasants who did not honor their state contracts for growing cotton. "You can't arrest thousands of people for sabotage," Pauker insisted. "Arrest only a couple as examples." [354] She thus renounced her emphatically voiced line from the January 15 meeting and reverted to her previous position. This corroborates Luca's testimony that Pauker steadfastly maintained her long-held views until the day she was purged.

> I had a discussion with Ana Pauker in her office in the spring of 1952. . . . I pointed out that our mistaken policy towards the kulaks and the peasantry in general, encouraging their enrichment, . . . led to an increase in capitalist elements in the countryside, to which Ana Pauker responded: "From where? The kulaks are squeezed by the collections so much that they can't even breathe, and they can't hold out." She thus continued to claim that the number of kulak farms was falling, and, when setting the collections plan for meat and milk, together with the Committee of Collections, she again depicted the number of kulak farms as falling when compared to 1951.[355]

Those who purged her accurately described the simple premise of Pauker's views: she "herald[ed] the anti-Stalinist theory of the peaceful integration of kulaks in socialism," and denied that the class struggle intensifies as socialism advances.[356] Speaking before the students of the Zhdanov Party school on April 17, 1952, she offered what was perhaps her final testament on the eve of her ouster: "We should not bring up the cadres in a permanent 'hatred,' but instead the collections, the seed-planting, the socialist competitions, the party schools, the other schools, indeed all work *should permanently proceed—peacefully*." [357]

In contrast, when addressing the question of internal enemy activity in February 1950, Gheorghiu-Dej told the party county secretaries, "We need to work tenaciously in this area, comrades, with deeds, with setting examples, and, if need be, with administrative measures [a euphemism for coercion]. . . . We need to put an end to this putrid liberalism, which has no place among us . . . , because *we can't build socialism peacefully*." [358]

Not surprisingly, no sooner had the ink dried on the documents of the

"Right Deviation" than terror returned with a vengeance in rural regions across Romania. The collections drive again implemented repressive measures to "encourage" registration in collective farms, and set stiffer sanctions for nonpayment of quotas.[359] On July 3, 1952, Gheorghiu-Dej announced the anti-kulak campaign's resumption and ordered the press "to mobilize the working peasant masses to mercilessly fight the kulaks."[360] Within three months, over 100,000 "kulaks" were discovered to have infiltrated the middle peasants' ranks.[361] A whole series of "leftist deviations" were repeated against kulaks or suspected kulaks across the country: some were forced to drink boiling water, with the water poured on those who could not; others were forced to remain standing, or were put up in trees, throughout the night; and kulak women had their heads shaved for not handing over their grain.[362] Accounts of kulaks sentenced for sabotage, diversionist activities, failure to meet collection quotas, or refusal to pay taxes appeared in the Romanian press practically daily.[363] One observer noted, "The R.P.R. propaganda machine, in an obvious effort to terrorize the peasantry, is currently giving great publicity to trials of alleged kulak saboteurs. Day after day, press and radio report with relish the harsh sentences imposed on hapless farmers throughout the country. . . . [T]rials of 'chiabur' [kulak] saboteurs by local 'people's courts' are commonly staged in the nearest available large assembly hall—school auditoriums, theaters, or any other suitable premises being requisitioned for the purpose—and people from all neighboring villages are brought in to attend the proceedings."[364] Altogether, the Romanian press reported no fewer than 8,000 trials of alleged kulaks in the six months following Ana Pauker's purge.[365]

Elaborating on Gheorghiu-Dej's revelations in 1961, Nicolae Ceauşescu reported that a total of "89,000 peasants were arrested in the years 1950–1951–1952, out of whom 37,000 were middle peasants and 7,000 poor peasants."[366] Thus, the 2,000 arrested during the collections Pauker oversaw in early 1952 were but a drop in the bucket; the vast majority of those 89,000 were instead arrested during the waves of terror in the summer of 1950, when Pauker was away in Moscow, and in the summer and fall of 1952, immediately following her purge.[367] The conclusion to be drawn from this and other evidence presented in this chapter is not merely that party historians slandered a certain disgraced leader. Rather, it would seem that Vasile Luca's last written description of that leader, which at first glance appears typically sensationalist, was actually quite accurate. Though it was he who had been most severely accused in this regard, he insisted in his prison memoirs that "[t]he Right Deviation on the peasant problem had really emerged from Ana Pauker." He maintained that Pauker generally avoided writing articles or giving speeches expanding her ideological positions on these issues but would instead encourage him to do so. Often at odds with the Soviet advisers' expressed "suggestions," she had actually originated most of the positions for which he was later blamed.[368] The reason, Luca suggested, was that Ana Pauker — forever since vilified as the bane of the Romanian peasant—had in fact "become the patron of the peasantry" within the party leadership.[369]

CHAPTER FIVE

Party Purges

Just as Pauker was blamed for the terror against the peasants, after her fall she was widely reputed to have instigated a reign of terror within the party. This became the standard line in Romania once Khrushchev initiated de-Stalinization in 1956, and it was particularly stressed at an RWP Central Committee plenary in 1961. Gheorghiu-Dej then asserted that Pauker and her allies sought to duplicate the mass repression taking place throughout the Soviet bloc during Stalin's anti-Tito campaign:

> As a result of orders given by Ana Pauker, the organs of the Ministry of the Interior, which in point of fact were not under the control of the party leadership, began to put party and state cadres under surveillance, to tap telephone conversations, measures from which not even the general secretary of the party's Central Committee was excepted. . . .
>
> [She] exerted pressure in order to remove from responsible jobs and to indict many old party members, especially from among the comrades who had fought Franco's troops in the International Brigades in Spain, from among the comrades who had fought the Hitlerite occupants in France, and from among activists and party members who during the underground period had succeeded in escaping arrest.
>
> I would here recall a discussion which was typical of the methods [she] wanted to establish. In the course of this discussion, at which Iosif Chişinevschi was also present, Ana Pauker asked me: "Should the enemy underestimate us so much as not to have wormed his way into the leadership of our party?" I asked her to explain, to say whether she had seen any signs of the existence of any hostile elements within the party leadership, and whether she was thinking of anyone in particular, to which she replied: "I don't know,

I don't know. Look at what's happening in Bulgaria, Poland, and Albania; should the enemy avoid us, consider us a negligible quantity? What is disquieting is the fact that things are too quiet in Romania." [1]

Again as with the peasants, however, the charges against Pauker during her purge were quite the opposite. Central failures of the "right-wing deviation" attributed to her and her allies were "an absence of militancy" and a lack of "revolutionary vigilance" toward enemies in the party. In a speech to the National Meeting of Miners in June 1952, Gheorghiu-Dej described the Pauker faction's "opportunism" as having been "disguised in the clothes of conciliation, liberalism, and indulgence toward deviationists, and of sentimentalism, lamentation and compassion for those guilty toward the party, the workers' state and the proletariat." [2] Though it was never published in the party press, Pauker was specifically accused of not sufficiently supporting the prosecution of Lucreţiu Patraşcanu, a member of the Politburo (1946) and Central Committee (1945–48), and Justice Minister from 1944 to 1948. [3] She was further attacked for ignoring the many warnings of enemy infiltration within the party leadership. This chapter will consider the veracity of both sets of charges by examining the Patraşcanu case and the repression of Spanish Civil War and French Resistance veterans in Romania.

THE PATRAŞCANU CASE

When the RCP emerged from the underground with Ion Antonescu's overthrow on August 23, 1944, Lucreţiu Patraşcanu emerged as its most prominent and popular leader. The son of noted writer and historian D. D. Patraşcanu, and respected in his own right among Romanian intellectuals, Lucreţiu had been a founding member of the RSCP in the early 1920s and won election as deputy of Parliament in 1931. The party's main contact with King Michael and other political figures before the August 23 coup, and a minister in the Sănătescu government immediately after, Patraşcanu was widely considered the RCP's real leader at the time. [4] It was Patraşcanu's name that was called out at the party's first public rally after the coup, and "Patraşcanu to power" was the slogan chanted at Communist rallies and meetings throughout September and October. [5] But he quickly became the odd man out of the RCP leadership. Both the Dej and Pauker factions snubbed him equally, excluding him from the provisional Secretariat that replaced the Foriş leadership in April 1944 as well as from the five-person Central Committee set up soon after Pauker's arrival in the country. [6]

Pauker's rejection of Patraşcanu fit the conventional wisdom of that period, which placed them on opposite poles of Romanian Communism—she an international revolutionary and long-standing member of the Comintern hierarchy, he a Romanian patriot who placed his Romanian identity over party loyalties.[7] Nevertheless, Patraşcanu "was certain" that he and Pauker "would work together when she came [back] to Romania" in September 1944, based, apparently, on their close friendship since the party's inception over twenty years earlier.[8] He was therefore "surprised and unhappy" when she did not include him in the provisional Central Committee she headed.[9] "Despite always considering her well-intentioned," he concluded that she would never support him, given her close ties to the Soviets.[10] Suspicious of Patraşcanu from the outset,[11] the Soviets initially ordered Pauker not to meet with him when he led a delegation to Moscow to negotiate the armistice in early September.[12] Echoing the Soviets' antipathy toward the views he expressed there, as well as their outrage that he should even take part in such talks, Pauker returned to Bucharest with a partial transcript of the negotiations and remarked to Teohari Georgescu, "What was he doing there? Look at the positions he had."[13] She later confided to her family that she considered Patraşcanu anti-Soviet.[14]

At the same time, Gheorghiu-Dej and some of his supporters in Romanian prisons were quite hostile to Patraşcanu even before the postwar period.[15] That Patraşcanu was arrested six times between 1924 and 1941 but shortly released on every occasion aroused suspicion among many Communists who were sentenced to long prison terms.[16] Also, though Patraşcanu spent eight months in 1943 at the Târgu-Jiu prison camp along with Gheorghiu-Dej and many other RCP activists,[17] he was reportedly offered (but refused) a place not with the other Communists but in a more comfortable section with "bourgeois" politicians, intellectuals, and writers.[18] Soon released yet again, he was mandated to stay at his parents' villa in the mountain resort town of Poiana Ţapului, from where he was periodically allowed to travel to Bucharest.[19] Although the party later established that Patraşcanu's better treatment was solely because "his family of intellectuals were known and appreciated by certain persons with important positions in the state apparatus,"[20] his privileged status did not particularly endear him to Gheorghiu-Dej—nor, for that matter, did his refusal at Târgu-Jiu when Dej asked him to help oust Ştefan Foriş.[21]

Further, Patraşcanu had apparently posed a challenge to Gheorghiu-

Dej's leadership of the Communist cadres at Târgu-Jiu, where he had arrived some two weeks before Dej.[22] Patraşcanu later revealed to his wife, Elena, that from the moment of Dej's arrival he felt Dej regarded his leadership at the camp with a "certain apprehension." He realized he had no choice but to step aside. "But he couldn't do so in such a servile manner," Elena Patraşcanu added. "That's why he thought that everything started over there [at Târgu-Jiu. He said:] 'Maybe I made a mistake. I should have been more servile towards Gheorghiu-Dej, but I can't do such a thing.'"[23] From then on, Patraşcanu sensed a distinct rivalry from Gheorghiu-Dej and clashed with him at the Council of Ministers throughout the postwar period.[24] Threatened by Patraşcanu's stature as a noted intellectual and his popularity among Romanians generally, aware of his openly expressed ambitions to be party leader, and resentful of his continually condescending attitude, Dej undoubtedly saw him as a serious competitor for the party leadership.[25] This was the one thing he would not tolerate.[26] Corneliu Bogdan witnessed this dynamic at a postwar rally where both Dej and Patraşcanu spoke. "Spontaneously everyone began to chant 'Patraşcanu Prime Minister,'" Bogdan related. "And an agitator was immediately sent to say not Patraşcanu, but Gheorghiu-Dej. . . . He was a real danger [to Dej]. The folklore was that Patraşcanu said, pointing at Dej, 'One day that man will kill me.'"[27]

That Emil Bodnăraş promptly targeted Patraşcanu was, therefore, to be expected:

> Immediately after I came back from Moscow—September 1944—I found out . . . that E. B. [Emil Bodnăraş] ordered Comrade [Vania] Didenco to follow me in a car, when I was minister without portfolio. I've never discussed with B. why he did such a thing, but I got the explanation nevertheless from B. himself, who, in a conversation that took place at precisely that time, told [me] to my face that, in two weeks time—the exact amount of time I stayed in Moscow—anyone could become a traitor or a spy. . . . In December 1944, E. B. called me to the C. C., and took out a dossier—my dossier—and asked me a number of things, from which it was clear that I was being closely followed.[28]

In February 1945, moreover, General Anton Raţiu, the commander of the *jandamarie*, told Patraşcanu they had information that a former Gestapo agent was planning an attempt on his life and "that this agent was none other than an instrument of an organization of ours." Patraşcanu suspected Bodnăraş was behind it.[29] He also asserted that Bodnăraş started a number of mendacious rumors that circulated about him throughout this period and believed that the party leadership intentionally placed him in danger's way with orders to speak before a February 24, 1945, rally where shots were fired.[30]

Still, though he was said to have had a particularly bad opinion of Gheorghiu-Dej, and nothing but contempt for Maurer and Bodnăraş, Patraşcanu apparently shared their view that Pauker and Luca's prominence in the leadership was hardly in the party's interests, for "a lack of popularity could not serve the building of socialism."[31] He therefore believed the Kremlin would inevitably support Dej over Pauker and Luca—despite their being, in his judgment, "the exponents of the Soviets one hundred per cent."[32] Hence, in early 1946 he reportedly decided to reach an accommodation with Dej, who in turn wanted Patraşcanu's backing against the Pauker faction. As Patraşcanu revealed to his friend Herbert (Belu) Zilber, he met with Dej, Maurer, and Bodnăraş in February or March 1946, and agreed to collaborate with them from that point on.[33] But the deal would not last the summer: in June, Dej became enraged when Patraşcanu delivered a controversial speech in Cluj without informing him beforehand. "He had broken their agreement," Zilber noted. "He was not loyal to him, and therefore Patraşcanu was an incorrigible enemy."[34]

Patraşcanu's speech attacked Hungarian nationalism in Northern Transylvania, and declared that the government would not grant citizenship to ethnic-Hungarian Transylvanians who had left Romania before August 1940 and returned during the Hungarian occupation.[35] Later, under interrogation, Patraşcanu admitted he had concealed part of the speech from the Central Committee because he feared they would not allow him to use it.[36] He also justified the speech by pointing out that the RCP's reticence on resurgent Hungarian nationalism in the region was perceived as unpatriotic and allowed the National Peasant Party to appear "as the sole defender of Northern Transylvania."[37] In fact, the speech was a tremendous success and led to a wave of new members among students and intellectuals who had previously considered the RCP anti-Romanian.[38] Still, the party leaders criticized the speech three weeks later in a Central Committee plenary and published a statement contradicting Patraşcanu's remarks.[39] Apparently they feared the speech, coming on the eve of the Paris Peace Conference, would add weight to charges of the Hungarian minority's mistreatment at a time when Romania's sovereignty over Transylvania was still in question.

At the Paris Peace Conference (July 29 to October 15, 1946), Patraşcanu told Zilber that his relations with Dej were again seriously strained.[40] Subsequently, Zilber read a secret report that Dej sent from Paris to the party Secretariat. "I have rarely read something more vulgar and more negative," he asserted. "Though it was ostensibly about the Peace Conference, half of the report dealt with what Patraşcanu was doing and what kind of dresses his wife was wearing."[41] In Paris, moreover, Zilber "found out about a campaign being waged against Patraşcanu in Romania" that he attributed to Dej, Maurer, and Bodnăraş. "I had the impression that Maurer had temporarily left [Paris] for Bucharest especially for this."[42] Even more ominous, however, was the Soviets' potential reaction to Patraşcanu's reported activities in Paris, which, if true, probably put him in imminent danger. According to Dumitru G. Danielopol, one of the economists in the Romanian delegation:

> It appears that Patraşcanu was having very close ties with the members of the opposition group, and through them with the Americans who, according to [the former Romanian Foreign Minister Constantin] Vişoianu, were prepared to facilitate Patraşcanu's switch from the Communist Party to a non-Communist anti-Soviet policy, which Patraşcanu was prepared to do. He was—it seems—negotiating [his] departure to the U.S.A. . . . However, Patraşcanu reluctantly gave up this plan, when he saw how weak American resistance to Soviet demands was. He is quoted to have declared something in this vein: "The Americans are crazy. They are giving even more to the Russians than [they] are asking [for] and expecting. If I go to the American side they might even hand me over to the Russians. I prefer to go home."[43]

Further, Danielopol added that Zilber, making similar contacts of his own, privately pleaded with the American and Australian delegations not to abandon Romania to the Soviets, which would lead, he claimed, to Romania's disappearance as a separate nation. How much the Soviets knew of Patraşcanu's and Zilber's actions is uncertain, though Molotov's request during the conference that the Romanian delegation halt all contacts with the Western, and particularly the American and British, delegations—"unless permission for such talks is asked for in advance and granted"—indicates that they were indeed aware.[44] Another indication, no doubt, were the secret service's actions back in Bucharest: they again put both Patraşcanu and his wife under surveillance not long after.[45]

Ironically, Patraşcanu was immediately heartened regarding his party standing upon returning to Bucharest, when Pauker and Georgescu—to both of whom, he later related, he was closest among the party leaders—met him with some fanfare at the airport.[46] His reception was perhaps the most public of a series of reassuring gestures on Pauker's part that revealed, at the very least, a certain ambivalence toward Patrașcanu. Having supported his exclusion from the party leadership in 1944, which Patrașcanu assumed to have been partly due to her personal jealousies of his popularity, Pauker generally concurred with the criticism leveled against him early after the war— brashly affirming in October 1945 that Gheorghiu-Dej "correctly view[ed] Patrașcanu as a foreign body within our party."[47] Nevertheless, she hedged on such criticism and at times skeptically derided those who reproached Patrașcanu.[48] She also reportedly backed his inclusion in the Politburo over Dej's firm objections in late 1945, a quarrel resolved only when Stalin, agreeing the move would boost the party's popularity, ruled in Patrașcanu's favor.[49] At the same time, Pauker demanded a halt to SSI surveillance of Patrașcanu and other party members (herself included) and insisted on punitive measures against Bodnăraș for initiating it.[50] By 1947, moreover, Pauker appeared more protective of Patrașcanu, in September dismissing Dej's complaints that the leadership had never discussed his Justice Ministry's shortcomings and reportedly rejecting Bodnăraș's call for Patrașcanu's arrest for allegedly planning to flee the country.[51] As she hinted to Patrașcanu at that time, Bodnăraș and Interior Minister Georgescu—and, by extension, Pauker herself—held clearly different opinions on such matters. She revealed this during one of "a whole series of discussions and conversations" she privately held with Patrașcanu, "either at her house or at party headquarters," throughout this period—talks Patrașcanu specifically attributed to their "long-standing friendship."[52] Presumably these discussions became more and more frequent as his situation deteriorated and he increasingly panicked. Pauker seemingly tried to ease his fears at the Foreign Ministry in early 1948, just before his downfall. After talking with her for nearly an hour, Patrașcanu left Pauker's office quite agitated—upon which Pauker, trying to reassure him, called out in his conspiratorial name, "Relax, Andrei. Relax."[53]

In the end Patrașcanu's fears were right on target. According to Charlotte Gruia, a top official of the party's Control Commission, in December 1947 Stalin ordered the Politburo to link Patrașcanu with the arrested leaders of the historical parties.[54] By the end of February, at the First Congress of the RWP, Georgescu accused him of having "fallen under the influence of the bourgeoisie," and he was summarily dropped from the Central Committee. Soon after he was ousted from the Justice Ministry.[55] A June 1948 resolution of the following CC plenary formalized his disgrace, officially denouncing him as "the bearer of the ideol-

ogy and interests of the bourgeoisie" within the party ranks and a promoter of "nationalist-chauvinist policies" and "counter-revolutionary
theories inspired by . . . the class enemy."[56] By then, however, he had already disappeared.

Delivering the closing speech at the February 1948 Congress, Pauker
appeared to abandon Pătrăşcanu when, without mentioning names, she
declared, "There are no fetishes in our party. No one can live on his past
merits." But, at the same time, she pointedly hinted that a self-criticism,
which he had refused to offer after his speech in Cluj, would satisfy
her.[57] Likewise, when the Politburo reproached Pătrăşcanu two days
earlier, Pauker sternly scolded him for having long pursued a different
line than the party's, one that "overestimated the strength of the bourgeoisie, and underestimated the strength of the working class." But, as
in the Congress, she criticized only his political mistakes, while ignoring
the far more serious charge of treason in attempting to flee the country.
She mentioned the latter only in a backhanded threat that Bodnăraş
should be thrown out of the party if he could not prove his allegations
of Pătrăşcanu's escape plans—which, up to then, he had not done.[58]
Apparently Pauker's position at this meeting reflected her stand generally on the case: while supporting sanctioning and demoting Pătrăşcanu
for his apparent political deviations, she resisted any attempt to broaden
the indictment to include criminal charges.[59] Accordingly, Ana Toma
reported, Pauker steadfastly opposed Pătrăşcanu's arrest:

> Ana gave me a dossier, which was Pătrăşcanu's memoirs . . . , and in writing
> them he tried to prove his innocence. He was making a defense for himself.
> Ana gave me the dossier when he was arrested . . . , and said to keep it in a
> secret place until she asked for it. She said she would probably need it later,
> though at the time she didn't know what would happen to Pătrăşcanu. . . . I
> don't know what he wrote, but I know that she was against his prosecution.
> She was disappointed and disillusioned with what happened to him. . . . She
> admitted to me that she was upset. . . . She didn't talk about it, except [to say]
> that he got involved in things that he shouldn't have.[60]

Though she could not prevent his arrest and tried unsuccessfully to obtain his release soon afterward,[61] the tortuous trail of Pătrăşcanu's investigation reveals that Pauker used her influence to ensure an honest inquiry and refused to agree to a trial based on fabricated evidence.

According to the 1968 RCP report on the case, Pătrăşcanu was
detained on April 28, 1948, "[o]n the basis of a deposition given by
Gheorghe Gheorghiu-Dej," and investigated by a party commission
composed of Teohari Georgescu, Iosif Rangheţ, Alexandru Drăghici,

and, in some instances, Gheorghiu-Dej himself.[62] This resulted directly, Georgescu asserted, from Dej's again raising the treason charges immediately after the February Congress. Dej assigned Georgescu to formally criticize Patrașcanu at the Congress, but afterward criticized him for doing so insufficiently—perhaps because Georgescu, too, limited his criticism as well to Patrașcanu's political errors. Dej promptly pressed for investigating Patrașcanu's alleged plans to flee the country.[63] At one point, Patrașcanu revealed, Dej took out of his briefcase the declarations of two informers and gave them to Georgescu, "telling him which passages to read and which not to read. I was convinced that those documents came from the SS[I], and that Teo[hari] didn't even know about them."[64] Based on those declarations, the Secretariat voted not to formally arrest Patrașcanu but to hold him in a party house where he would be treated more humanely.[65] Drăghici later disclosed that he and Dej personally took Patrașcanu to a secret house of investigation belonging to the party's secret service in the town of Baneasa, close to Bucharest, where the just-formed commission interrogated him.[66] He stubbornly denied everything, however, until one of the informers, his friend Nicolae Betea, eventually confronted him. Beginning in the summer of 1947, Betea on several occasions had urged Patrașcanu to flee, which was an apparent SSI provocation. The next day, Patrașcanu asked to meet with Georgescu alone:[67] "He was completely shattered and cried all the time," Georgescu recalled, and he admitted for the first time that he had accepted Betea's proposals—though he did so, he insisted, only to get rid of him.[68] Georgescu instructed him to write it all down and promised he would be freed the following day.[69] A short time later, the Secretariat informed him that his "self-criticism had been taken into consideration" and that the inquiry was to end. "I was sure," Patrașcanu asserted, "that the Secretariat had decided to release me."[70] But, while the commission was indeed disbanded, Patrașcanu was not released; instead, a warrant for his arrest was formally issued on August 24, accusing him of being an agent of the bourgeoisie and the English espionage services and ordering him interned at the Jilava penitentiary.[71] Yet he was not sent to Jilava. Instead, after Patrașcanu declared a hunger strike to protest his continued detention, Georgescu apprised him that he and his wife would be allowed to live together in a resort of their own choosing. At their request, both were sent to the lakeside village of Snagov.[72] Clearly, two forces were working against each other within the RWP leadership, one promoting Patrașcanu's prosecution, the other endeavoring to mitigate it.

It was probably no coincidence that Patrașcanu was permitted to stay at Snagov precisely when Dej himself was under suspicion or that he was abruptly removed from the resort in January 1949, around the time Dej reportedly regained Stalin's trust.[73] Not surprisingly, Georgescu was specifically attacked after his purge for having personally placed Patrașcanu in Snagov.[74] Drăghici maintained that Georgescu was convinced the commission had no case against Patrașcanu throughout the inquiry at Baneasa, and had, Dej suspected, privately counseled Patrașcanu not to confess to anything there of which he was not actually guilty.[75] Under interrogation, Patrașcanu disclosed that at Baneasa he told Georgescu his situation would have been altogether different if Georgescu had sole control of his inquiry. Georgescu told him "not to have the slightest worry, that the whole investigation will be objective, and that 'the working class would never forgive us if anyone touches a single hair on your head.'" Nevertheless, Patrașcanu added, "My deep personal opinion was that my situation did not depend at that time on Teohari Georgescu."[76]

Accordingly, once Patrașcanu was brought back to Bucharest from his Snagov exile, his inquiry was immediately intensified. When the inquiry, which had formally remained within the party, failed to prove any criminal activity, Gheorghiu-Dej personally ordered its transfer to the SSI.[77] This, no doubt, also resulted from the Soviets' pushing the process forward. Significantly, its October 1949 timing coincided with László Rajk's trial in Budapest, which began September 16. At the trial, one of Rajk's codefendants, Lazar Brankov, testified that Patrașcanu "wanted to carry out Tito's plans in Romania" of creating a federation of Western-oriented "bourgeois democratic states" in the Balkans.[78] Soon afterward, L. Baranov, the deputy chief of the Foreign Section of the Soviet Central Committee, made an official visit to Bucharest. Complaining that Patrașcanu was being held under house arrest in some party villa, Baranov insisted to Pauker and Luca that "he has to be isolated" (presumably, that is, confined in a prison cell), and they promised to take appropriate action.[79] At the convening of the third Cominform conference in November, Gheorghiu-Dej delivered a major address formally identifying Patrașcanu as an American and British agent together with Rajk, Tito, and Traicho Kostov of Bulgaria.[80] "The report," Khrushchev noted, "was prepared in Moscow by Yudin, Suslov, and Malenkov."[81] Its message to the Romanians was only too obvious: it "directed the investigative organs toward the fabrication of evidence that would, by any means, confirm these accusations."[82] As Eugen Szabo, a high-ranking officer in the Interior Ministry during Patrașcanu's subsequent trial, confirmed, throughout this period the Soviets pressed intensely for Patrașcanu's trial as a "Romanian Rajk."[83]

Yet while the Soviets unilaterally achieved what the RWP could not accomplish after seventeen months of inquiry—that is, uncover Patrașcanu's "guilt" in conspiring with Tito and the Anglo-American spy agencies—the Romanian press at first barely mentioned it. Though *Scânteia* did carry a TASS-transmitted transcript of the Rajk trial that included the reference to Patrașcanu, it did not repeat the accusation against him in any of its numerous articles and commentaries on the trial.[84] Zamfir Brumaru, the Romanian party journalist sent to Budapest to cover the proceedings, subsequently revealed that he was ordered not to mention Patrașcanu in his daily reports of the trial.[85] Indeed, throughout the fall of 1949, at a time when speeches and articles calling for increasing vigilance against party enemies appeared in *Scânteia* almost daily, Patrașcanu's name rarely appeared in print, and the press consistently ignored the Soviet-inspired charge linking him with Tito.[86]

Nevertheless, the pendulum would soon swing in the opposite direction. Emerging from the Cominform conference as a prominent spokesman of the Soviet line, Gheorghiu-Dej pressed for its compliance within the Romanian Party leadership: in December 1949, Charlotte Gruia revealed, he ordered the Control Commission "to prepare the trial of Patrașcanu."[87] The text of Dej's Cominform speech denouncing Patrașcanu as an imperialist agent was released for publication on December 6.[88] Gheorghiu-Dej's address to the party *activ* followed two days later. Referring to the Rajk and Kostov trials, Dej declared, "We must not consider that such phenomena, such manifestations, and such enemy elements are found only in the other Popular Democratic countries. Such monsters can be found in our ranks and in our Popular Republic as well. They must and will be discovered and completely destroyed by the party without hesitation."[89]

Similar rhetoric characterized the published resolution of the RWP's Fifth CC plenary the following month. While praising Gheorghiu-Dej for heading a "struggle against the traitors infiltrated into the Party leadership" during the Second World War, it called for "the strengthening of vigilance" that would lead to the "discovery and extermination of imperialist agents and agents of the class enemy" within party ranks—such as Lucrețiu Patrașcanu, "unmasked" by the party as an "agent of the bourgeoisie and imperialism."[90] Significantly, this reference to Patrașcanu had not been in the resolution when the Secretariat approved it several days earlier but was added to the text that was read to the plenary[91]—the version subsequently appearing in the party press.[92]

These developments coincided with the arrests of Remus Koffler and thirty-five others in December 1949 and January 1950.[93] Detained on Dej's orders,[94] Koffler had been a member of the Central Committee during the war and headed the party's Central Financial Commission 1937–1944—in which capacity he solicited donations for the financially strapped RCP from prominent industrialist Alexandru Ştefănescu. Known for his Anglophile and anti-Nazi views, and closely connected to English capital, Ştefănescu provided the RCP through Koffler's Central Financial Commission information received via two-way radio from the English command in Cairo in 1943 and 1944. Though the party leadership at the time saw and sanctioned these activities as legitimate transactions between allies, both Koffler and Ştefănescu were now accused of espionage and arbitrarily linked to Patraşcanu to provide the missing proof of his ties to British intelligence.[95]

Hence the familiar Stalinist frame-up became increasingly evident during the SSI's investigation of Patraşcanu. Though as early as February 1948 he confided to friends his deep depression and fears for the future, and even discussed suicide with Ana Pauker, Patraşcanu apparently continued to hope that his "comrades" would not abandon him.[96] Shortly before the party detained him, he reportedly wrote to the leadership pleading for his life and expressing the desire to write a history of the party if allowed to survive.[97] While under investigation at Baneasa, he drafted a letter imploring the Secretariat, "as comrades among whom are some that I started my activities in the party with, to judge with objective facts and weigh without preconceived notions the material brought to discussions, and to not make a decision that would result not only in my moral, but also my physical, destruction."[98] But by the time he was handed to the SSI, he apparently had few illusions as to what awaited him. The day after the SSI began its inquiry, Patraşcanu attempted suicide by cutting the veins of his arms with a razor blade and then breaking the blade into pieces and swallowing them to hide the identity of the person who gave him the razor. Once he had recovered, he was moved to the headquarters of the SSI's Directorate of Investigations to be kept under closer guard while the inquiry proceeded. Despite receiving "preferential treatment" there and never being subjected to physical coercion, he soon tried again to kill himself by taking an overdose of sleeping pills.[99]

Ten days later, at the end of March 1950, Patraşcanu's interrogations suddenly halted, and in May the SSI inquiry formally disbanded.[100] The case was then transferred to the Interior Ministry, where it was immediately suspended for some six months while the ministry's officers reviewed the facts.[101] At the same time, the party press immediately halted all references to Patrașcanu as "an agent of the bourgeoisie and imperialism," which had begun to appear regularly after the January 1950 Central Committee plenary.[102] A scaling back of the accusation against Patrașcanu followed in the resolution of the CC plenary of July 1950, which referred to "the case of Patrașcanu and other traitors in the service of the bourgeoisie" and conspicuously omitted the far more serious charge linking Patrașcanu with Western imperialism.[103] Apparently a significant retreat, and not just a change of venue, occurred in the spring of 1950, and evidence suggests it was the work of Ana Pauker and her allies in opposition to Gheorghiu-Dej.

For one, while Dej maintained close ties with Soviet agents heading the Securitate in the Interior Ministry,[104] he considered the SSI his own turf and a service that he could personally utilize.[105] Hence, his control of the inquiry could have diminished only with its transfer to the Interior Ministry, headed as it was by Pauker's ally and protégé Teohari Georgescu. In addition, Securitate chief Gheorghe Pintilie testified in 1967 that, despite the active interest of several Soviet advisers assigned to the case after supervising purge trials in other bloc countries, as well as that of a top official in the Soviet embassy who regularly reported the inquiry's progress to his superiors in Moscow, the investigation was suspended for review when transferred to the Interior Ministry because "some comrades in the party leadership" argued in meetings he attended "that it was not possible that a connection of an enemy nature existed among" Patrașcanu and the other detainees. In so doing, they most likely overruled Gheorghiu-Dej, whom Pintilie confirmed ardently and persistently promoted Patrașcanu's prosecution.[106] Subsequently Pintilie would reveal to Cristina Boico what he was too diplomatic to report publicly, that Ana Pauker was among those unnamed comrades who opposed the inquiry.[107] Likewise, Harry Brauner, one of Patrașcanu's associates arrested in early 1950, told his friend Victor Bîrlădeanu that "during the time of the Kostov trial in Bulgaria [December 1949], Gheorghiu-Dej wanted to put Patrașcanu on trial. But it wasn't possible, because certain members of the Politburo were against it, among them Ana Pauker."[108] On this point Ana Toma was quite categorical: Ana Pauker, she insisted, consistently opposed all attempts to prosecute Patrașcanu on arbitrary or fabricated charges.[109]

Thus by mid-1950 Pauker was in an excellent position to shape the course of the Patraşcanu inquiry, which apparently was made contingent on the Interior Ministry's determining a factual basis that plainly did not exist. As the 1968 RCP report makes clear, "there did not exist even one document, nor one piece of testimony, from which it could be established that [Patraşcanu] was an agent of the Anglo-American spy agencies" when Gheorghiu-Dej denounced him at the Cominform in November 1949, and so far not a single confession implicating Patraşcanu as an imperialist agent was obtained from the large number of people who had since been arrested.[110] Much of the case particularly depended on Remus Koffler's testimony, but Koffler continued to deny any wrongdoing on his or Patraşcanu's part during his first eight months of detention. On August 16, 1950, however, while Pauker was sidelined after her cancer surgery, "someone from the Central Committee" surreptitiously approached Koffler and persuaded him "in the interests of the Party" to change his testimony and declare that he, Patraşcanu, Ştefănescu, Ştefan Foriş, and others conspired during the war to destroy the RCP in the service of Antonescu's Siguranţă and English espionage. This was the "smoking gun" on which future inquiries in the case would ultimately be based, and it was the "proof" to which Gheorghiu-Dej referred in a major address in May 1951, lauding "the unmasking of Patraşcanu, who—as has been proved—was long connected to enemy agents."[111]

Dej's proclamation ignored the facts that Koffler had long since retracted his August declaration and that the Patraşcanu inquiry, resumed in the Interior Ministry in February 1951, had quickly stalled due to the detainee's defiance.[112] This was perhaps inevitable given that Georgescu had prohibited the use of physical force—even though the ministry's chief Soviet adviser, Alexandr Mihailovich Sakharovskii, had demanded that the inquiry do everything necessary to establish the accused's guilt and had attacked interrogators for not obtaining "appropriate" answers to his dictated questions.[113] Gheorghiu-Dej, as well, pressured Georgescu to advance the inquiry. Accompanying him to Patraşcanu's cell at one point that year, Dej was overheard exhorting Georgescu, "Are you convinced? Even now you tell me he's innocent."[114] Likewise, when Georgescu informed him that there was no proof of a Patraşcanu-Siguranţă connection, which Dej had ordered him to certify, Dej countered that Patraşcanu's contacts were actually outside the country "on the international stage, like the Gestapo."[115] Seeking a basis for this scenario, Dej then further escalated the case, ordering the arrest of one Emil Calmanovici.[116]

An engineer by profession who had donated to the party an entire fortune he had made in construction in the 1930s,[117] Calmanovici had served as Koffler's assistant at the party's Financial Commission and was the primary conduit through whom Ştefănescu relayed information to the RCP from the British command in Cairo.[118] Detained on May 26, 1951,[119] Calmanovici was compelled to admit having arranged imaginary meetings between Patraşcanu and Ştefănescu during the war, and thus provided the still elusive "proof" of an Anglo-American nexus.[120] Ana Pauker, who thought highly of Calmanovici and appreciated his generosity to the party, reportedly met with his family after his arrest and attempted to intervene for him within the party leadership.[121] Doing so as well was Calmanovici's brother-in-law, Mirel Costea, a top official in the Central Committee's Verification Section. An exceptionally amicable idealist and one of the more popular figures in the party hierarchy, Costea became despondent over Calmanovici's arrest and quickly despaired of obtaining his release. Bemoaning to family members that "we'll never see him again," Costea shot himself a week after Calmanovici's arrest.[122] His suicide sent shock waves through the party's upper ranks[123]—including, presumably, both Georgescu, who was reported to have been a close friend of Costea's,[124] and Pauker, who ordered that Costea's widow was to retain all party privileges despite the suicide. (The order was rescinded immediately after Pauker's purge.)[125] Perhaps no more than a straw in the wind, Costea's death may have been a turning point in the Patraşcanu case, as Georgescu halted the inquiry not long after.

"In 1951," Georgescu recounted, "I took everything in connection with Patraşcanu, and I reached the conclusion—not only me, but also those I was working with [including Pintilie and the head of the ministry's Directorate of Investigations, Mişu Dulgheru][126]—that we don't have any basis to try him. . . . I was convinced that we had absolutely nothing."[127] This was, more precisely, sometime in June or July 1951, for Belu Zilber (one of Patraşcanu's "co-conspirators") was informed on August 1 "that the investigation is terminated, that [his] innocence is completely proved, and that Patraşcanu's trial will not take place" because of a lack of evidence.[128] This occurred while the Soviet advisers in the Interior Ministry were away on vacation. On returning, they angrily vetoed releasing any prisoners, blocked the completion of a final report on the inquiry's findings, and confiscated the ministry's documents on the case.[129] Soon afterward, the Kremlin expressed its displeasure, publishing in *Pravda* Gheorghiu-Dej's lengthy article again linking Patraş-canu with Tito and American espionage.[130] There would be no tabling of Patraşcanu's inquiry, the article clearly suggested, signaling a renewed Soviet push for Patraşcanu's trial.

At this crucial juncture, Pauker's own position must have been critical. For, given the Soviet reaction, it is doubtful that Georgescu would have acted without first conferring with other leaders or that the Soviets would not have protested to the party leadership immediately afterward. Publicly, at least, Pauker had always avoided denouncing Patraş-canu, despite official Cominform or Soviet statements to the contrary; indeed, not one of her speeches or articles published between 1949 and 1951 even mentions his name.[131] Just as she held considerable sway over Georgescu, she apparently did so over Pintilie as well.[132] Her exact position in the Politburo, however, is difficult to determine. For, with the exception of the Russian archives' account of the February 1948 Politburo meeting, no record exists of any Politburo or Secretariat debate on Patraşcanu's case, as the transcripts of all such meetings were summarily destroyed on Dej's orders.[133] Still, the testimony of a number of important witnesses, as well as the documented, though never published, charges against Pauker during her purge, all paint a fairly clear picture: denounced by the Central Committee (along with Luca) for maintaining "a conciliatory attitude towards Patraşcanu,"[134] Pauker was condemned with Georgescu for refusing to support his continuing inquiry.[135] She was portrayed at the plenary as the invisible hand guiding Georgescu, who in turn was seen as Pauker's "servant" in an ongoing quest to undermine Dej.[136] The Soviet adviser Sakharovskii also attacked both, ordering a memorandum drawn up to accuse Pauker and Georgescu of having "sabotaged and postponed investigations" in the Patraşcanu case.[137]

Thus what Patraşcanu had "naively" hoped for actually occurred: *against Soviet wishes,* Georgescu halted Patraşcanu's inquiry in the summer of 1951, with Pauker's backing. With their ouster, however, and with Alexandru Drăghici's ascent as Interior Minister, the Soviets took complete control of the case, seemingly for the first time since Patraşcanu's arrest over four years earlier. This increased "coordination" was illustrated, Mihai Burcă noted, by Sakharovskii's conspicuously moving his desk next to Drăghici's immediately after Drăghici became Interior Minister, though "it was not that way when Teohari [Georgescu] was in charge."[138] One of Drăghici's first acts as minister, in conjunction with

Sakharovskii, was to transfer the Patraşcanu inquiry from the ministry's Directorate of Investigations to a specially created investigative group headed by Lt. Col. Ioan Şoluţiu and his Soviet adviser Ţiganov, directly subordinate to Drăghici.[139] At the same time, he replaced some 800 Interior Ministry officials in both the militia and the Securitate with people who had no experience in police matters but were willing to do whatever the party and the Soviets demanded.[140] One of those removed was the chief of the Directorate of Investigations, Mişu Dulgheru, whose conclusions on the lack of proof in the case were the same as Georgescu's. Consequently, not long after Georgescu was purged, Dulgheru was arrested and accused of espionage.[141]

These special investigators' testimony clearly states that *for the first time* since the Patraşcanu inquiry began they were ordered in the summer of 1952 "to use all means and procedures of moral and physical force to obtain appropriate proof that Lucreţiu Patraşcanu had been an agent of the Siguranţă and an Anglo-American spy."[142] They were candidly told that the investigation was no longer to be conducted "normally" but was now to involve physical coercion, because "Patraşcanu's trial must take place *at any price,* and the top leaders of the Party were convinced of the guilt of all those arrested in the Patraşcanu case."[143] They were informed further that they were to consider Koffler's August 1950 declaration authentic despite his subsequent retraction. And they were instructed to do everything necessary to obtain confessions from the other detainees that would confirm Koffler's declaration.[144] Hence Patraşcanu's friend Lena Constante reports that her interrogator was replaced immediately after Teohari Georgescu's portrait was removed from the interrogation room at the time of his purge. When her interrogations resumed two months later, she was tortured for the first time since her arrest in 1950.[145] "When she was let go screaming," Securitate Lt. Col. Mircea Anghel related, "I noticed a large bundle of hair from her head torn out by [her interrogator Teodor] Micle and thrown on the floor. Also, I saw when Micle tore out, beginning from the ears, more than a third of the white hair of Koffler. As a matter of fact, this was a method often used by Micle in other interrogations."[146] Likewise, Emil Calmanovici revealed in a letter from prison that he was tortured only after the investigation resumed in September 1952.[147] Anghel witnessed this as well: "he was stripped naked and beaten until he was bloody by the former chief of arrests, Lt. Maj. Dinu, known for his talents in this domain. . . . After approximately two hours of torture,

I saw Calmanovici being brought in. . . . barely able to stand. He was with torn clothes and full of blood and screamed as he held his jaw."[148] Belu Zilber reported that in September 1952 he, too, was beaten for the first time since his arrest in February 1948.[149] He learned why a few months later when the chief investigator, Ioan Şoltuţiu, pressured him to confess, declaring, "Mr. Zilber, your defenders don't exist any longer. The party is now in safe hands."[150]

In an investigation sustained and personally supervised by Gheorghiu-Dej, these new methods "uncovered" evidence against Patraşcanu for the first time at the end of 1952.[151] Deputy Interior Minister Mihai Burcă, himself purged from the ministry in the fall of 1952, recalls that Dej told him "that with the placing of Drăghici in the Ministry of Interior, he now has a very tough hand there. He boasted to me that he was pleased about that."[152] Moreover, Grigore Râpeanu, one of Patraşcanu's four prosecutors, revealed that Dej read every declaration and document in the Patraşcanu file, drew arrows to or underlined passages for special emphasis, and issued instructions on what points to pursue; all together, Belu Zilber pointed out, "The Patraşcanu file contained 50,000 pages!" [153] Dej undeniably was following Soviet orders, given their consistent pressure in the case and its escalating simultaneous with Soviet-inspired purges throughout the bloc.[154] Indeed, evidence suggests that at the beginning of 1953 the Soviets were preparing a Slansky-type trial in Romania that would have combined the Patraşcanu prosecution with that of Pauker, Luca, and Georgescu.[155] However, despite then Politburo member Gheorghe Apostol's testimony to the contrary, Soviet pressure for Patraşcanu's trial appears to have effectively ended with Stalin's death in March 1953.[156] Henceforth the Soviets evidently showed no interest in the matter and gave Dej a free hand in its pursuit.[157] This was the conclusion of a clear consensus of those interviewed, including Simion Bughici, Pauker's replacement as Foreign Minister, who inferred that the Soviets no longer targeted national Communists after a number of Soviet officials in 1953 told him that "[w]e were wrong about Tito"; Interior Minister Alexandru Drăghici, who revealed to Eduard Mezincescu that the files of Patraşcanu's 1954 trial were put at the disposal of the Soviet advisers at the Interior Ministry but were returned with a notation that the Soviet government was no longer interested in the case; Belu Zilber, who asserted to his close friend Henri Wald that the Soviets were completely indifferent at the time of Patraşcanu's (and Zilber's) trial; and Eugen Szabo, who witnessed this indifference firsthand as an Interior

Ministry officer.[158] Moreover, Miron Constantinescu revealed that he was dispatched to Moscow with Patraşcanu's dossier in 1954 to receive the Soviets' endorsement of the trial, but Malenkov told him, "It's your business" *(Vashe delo)*.[159] Gheorghiu-Dej keenly saw that with thawing Soviet politics Patraşcanu posed an even greater threat to him.[160] Thus, he convened Patraşcanu's trial after the Soviets' incessant badgering had ended but, ironically, had been unable to do so for four years when Soviet pressure was unrelenting. This appears to have been due fundamentally to the Pauker faction's resistance.

The trial took place April 6–13, 1954, almost six years to the day after Patraşcanu's arrest.[161] Patraşcanu's continued defiance forced Gheorghiu-Dej, who closely monitored the proceedings through telephone lines directly linking the courtroom with his office, to scrap his plans of an open trial and settle for secret proceedings.[162] This, despite Patraşcanu's condition having deteriorated to the extent that he appeared at the trial with one leg amputated.[163] On the last day of the trial

> Patraşcanu was permitted to say the last word. He rose up with difficulty from the defendant's bench, but when he was seen standing, he straightened himself like an arrow. "Assassins!" Patraşcanu screamed with the voice of a tenor, pointing with his forefinger at the president of the Tribunal, then in turn, to every people's prosecutor. "History will put you here, in this box! You and also your supporters, you servants!" Patraşcanu's speech was interrupted by security officers who rushed at him. "Assassins!" he was able to scream once more as he was removed from the hall.[164]

Patraşcanu was sentenced to death and executed the night of April 16–17 at Jilava penitentiary.[165] "He was shot as he stood in his cell, with his back to the door," Charlotte Gruia revealed. "[T]hey shot him in the back of his head through the spy hole."[166] The shooting signified Dej's reply to Patraşcanu's last-minute promise to stay out of politics if Dej would spare his life.[167] Also executed was Remus Koffler, who retracted his August 1950 declaration one final time during the trial.[168] (In fact, Jaques Berman was the only defendant who did not retract his previous admissions at the trial.)[169] Zilber, Calmanovici, and Ştefănescu received life sentences; Brauner, Constante, Berman, and others were given sentences ranging between twelve and fifteen years of hard labor.[170] Nearly all were kept in prison under horrible conditions, including solitary confinement, until 1964, long after amnesties were granted elsewhere in the Soviet sphere. The only one not to survive imprisonment was Emil Calmanovici, who declared a hunger strike to affirm his innocence and died after forty-five days in 1956.[171]

THE "VETERANS"

As in the Patraşcanu case, the Romanian leaders were increasingly pressured after the Rajk trial in September 1949 to purge the veterans of the Spanish Civil War (the "Spaniards") and the French Resistance in Romania, whom the Soviets' anti-Tito campaign had targeted. Internal documents on the trial from Budapest explicitly pointed to Romanian coconspirators in the affair and called for their prosecution.[172] The Hungarian leader, Mátyás Rákosi, informed the Romanians a month after Rajk's arrest that he had received information from the Soviets that everyone who fought in Spain and France was an American agent.[173] Immediately after the trial he forwarded to them a list of names including Politburo member Gheorghe Vasilichi, a veteran of the French Resistance, and reportedly every prominent Spaniard in Romania.[174] Soon afterward, in a state visit to Bucharest, Klement Voroshilov revealed that Soviet intelligence had "uncovered" Rajk's treachery and passed the evidence on to the Hungarians. Sorin Toma, who served as an interpreter during the visit, recalls that Voroshilov's message to the Romanians was unmistakable: the Rajk prosecution was a Soviet initiative, and should therefore be duplicated in Romania.[175]

Purges of Spanish Civil War and French Resistance veterans soon commenced throughout the bloc and were important in the mass repression that preceded and accompanied the Kostov and Slansky trials in Bulgaria and Czechoslovakia.[176] The terror also reached Poland and East Germany: in November 1949, Polish party leader Boleslaw Bierut publicly identified veterans of the Dombrowski Brigade, the Polish fighting unit in Spain, as fascist spies.[177] Henceforth, in both Poland and East Germany, the Spanish veterans were connected with "the American agent" Noel Field and treated accordingly.[178]

This same scenario began to unfold in Romania. In the summer of 1949, party cadres chief Iosif Ranghet was dispatched to Budapest to speak with László Rajk in prison regarding possible Romanian coconspirators, but apparently Rajk refused to implicate anyone.[179] After Rajk's trial, Ranghet returned to Budapest seeking clarification of Rákosi's list of suspected Romanian veterans, but again could not substantiate anything.[180] He then headed a special party commission formed in December to investigate the Spaniards,[181] who were summoned for "a very tough, very strict, and serious interrogation."[182] The commission could find nothing conclusive. At one point, Gheorghiu-Dej revealed, Nikolai Shutov, the MGB agent at the Soviet embassy, approached him on the matter. "He came to me very official-like, standing at attention. 'Comrade Dej, you know that I'm an intelligence officer of the Soviet Union. I have been authorized by my superiors to ask you to assist us in determining the situation of some Central Committee members in the party leadership, about whom my superiors know very little.'" According to Gheorghiu-Dej, he responded rather unenthusiastically to the request, upon which Shutov remarked, "Since you're so busy, please tell Comrade Ana to deal with it."[183] Pauker was then entrusted with overseeing Iosif Rangheţ's commission and "took out a whole number of dossiers" of suspected party officials.[184] In the meantime, certain Spaniards, such as Valter Roman, the army's chief of staff, were taken out of their sensitive posts and placed in less important positions,[185] and Vasilichi was barred from Politburo meetings while his investigation proceeded.[186]

Still, the mass arrests and dismissals that raged elsewhere in the bloc did not take place in Romania, and the party commission did not "discover" false evidence to implicate the Spaniards. Moreover, the Romanian party press did not repeat accusations against the Spaniards made at the Rajk trial.[187] Nor did RWP leaders refer to them in published speeches regarding the trial. As one scholar noted, the trial led to intense Cominform pressure on the satellites to strengthen their vigilance against enemies within their ranks, and "[s]earching for them turned into perhaps the greatest preoccupation of both party and security authorities."[188] While their speeches clearly reflected this heightened militancy, the Romanian leaders spoke only vaguely of abstract infiltrated enemies and consistently failed to mention the Spaniards and the French Resistance veterans.[189] Indeed, throughout 1950 and 1951 no accusations against the veterans appeared even in *Scânteia*'s most militant writings, with the sole exception of a *For a Lasting Peace, for a People's Democracy* article reprinted on Soviet orders.[190] In fact, such accusations were censored from the Romanian translation of Czechoslovak President Klement Gottwald's landmark speech on the issue.[191]

By 1951 those Spaniards who had been removed from their posts were promoted once again to leading government positions, despite the Soviets' unremitting pressure on the Romanian leadership to purge them.[192] Much of this pressure apparently came via the Hungarians,[193] who continually criticized the RWP leaders' lackadaisical approach and offered them prepared material to advance their inquiry.[194] Victor Vezendean, the deputy chief of the Foreign Section of the Central Committee, experienced this firsthand in a meeting with Rákosi during an official visit to Budapest in the summer of 1950:

> After I explained the reason for my visit, Rákosi asks: "Tell me, Comrade Victor. Why is it so quiet over there in Romania? . . . What is this silence?" I acted as if I didn't understand what he meant. So he explained to me: " . . . Look, in every party there are traitors. There were in ours, and there were in Bulgaria, where they tried Kostov. There are also traitors in Czechoslovakia, and I told Gottwald, 'Gottwald, be careful.' So there must be traitors in your party as well. You have to look for them." [195]

Despite such warnings, Spanish veteran Mihai Burcă was appointed Deputy Interior Minister at the end of 1950; Bazil Şerban, a veteran of both Spain and the French Resistance, was placed in an important Foreign Ministry post at the end of 1950 or in the first half of 1951; Mihai Florescu, also a Spaniard and French Resistance veteran, who returned from France via Yugoslavia, was appointed Deputy Minister for Metallurgy and Chemical Industries in February 1951; and Valter Roman was appointed Minister of Posts and Telecommunications soon after.[196]

Hence, as with the Patrașcanu case, Romania's leaders lagged sorely behind the other satellites' in repressing "Titoist" agents. But, unlike the Patrașcanu case, during this period Gheorghiu-Dej evidently did not adopt his customary Stalinist line on this issue. Although he reportedly distrusted the Spanish and French Resistance veterans, as he did the party's old guard generally, and considered many of them Pauker's partisans,[197] he did not press for purging them in 1950 and 1951 when it was certainly in his power to unilaterally do so; on the contrary, he made no attempt to arrest them and he personally promoted and protected such veterans as Gheorghe Gaston Marin and Mihai Florescu.[198] In addition, the *Scânteia* articles that Dej most likely initiated, such as those denouncing Patrașcanu as an enemy agent, conspicuously did not mention the veterans. The Spaniards' leader in Romania, Petre Borilă, confirmed to former Trade Minister Mircea Oprișan Dej's essential neutrality regarding the veterans: having no ideological commitment to the Soviet campaign against them, Dej did not hinder Borilă's (and others') efforts to impede it.[199]

For her part, Ana Pauker was known to have sympathized with the Spaniards,[200] many of whom (such as Borilă and Valter Roman) had served under her in the Soviet Union during the war.[201] One veteran, Sergiu Sevcenko, pointed out that the Spaniards had considered Pauker a patron as far back as the mid-1930s, when as general secretary of the

International Committee of the Red Aid (MOPR), she placed assisting the Spanish Republic at the very top of her agenda and, following her arrest, issued declarations from prison calling for party members to volunteer in Spain.[202] Another veteran, Carol Neumann, noted that he always approached Pauker on matters concerning the Spaniards during the postwar period, because she was the party leader most sympathetic to them.[203]

Nevertheless, some veterans assumed that Pauker abandoned them once the Soviets initiated the anti-Tito campaign, if only because she was universally seen as the Soviets' mouthpiece in the country. In Mihai Florescu's words, "that explains everything."[204] Pauker herself appeared to confirm their suspicions when she defensively maintained under arrest in 1953 that she became "preoccupied with and convinced [of the notion] that it's not possible that the enemy did not have someone here as well, just as they had someone in the leadership of other Popular Democratic countries."[205] Georgescu later claimed she made similar remarks to him, but he described them as "transparent allusions" to certain adversaries in the party leadership, not the veterans.[206] (Several sources suggest that she was actually referring to Gheorghiu-Dej.)[207] Likewise, Pauker acknowledged lamenting that "things are too quiet in Romania," as Dej quoted her.[208] But she implied that she was posturing in response to Dej's own September 1951 assertions in *Pravda* that "undiscovered enemies" had infiltrated the Romanian leadership, which was actually an implicit attack on her.[209] Clearly vulnerable for her liberal line on recruiting and verifying the cadres, Pauker no doubt openly feared, as she habitually did, Stalin's potential response. After all, her visceral terror of him could only have intensified when she personally learned the circumstances surrounding Stalin's "unmasking" of the Bulgarian leader Traicho Kostov in 1949, "how he took his glasses off and said to him that 'You're not looking in the right direction,' and . . . how after returning home he was immediately arrested."[210] Perhaps predictably, then, Pauker was extremely careful always to appear ever-vigilant, and reportedly favored thorough investigations of even the party's top brass to verify Soviet claims of enemy infiltration.[211]

Hence, when Shutov approached her on the need for inquiries, Pauker readily provided the personal dossiers of certain members of the party leadership:

> I gave him the dossiers I got from [Alexandru R]ogojinschi [of the Verification Section of the Central Committee], and I didn't even look at them. There was also a dossier on me from the Interior Ministry among them. . . . I

handed them over just as they came, bound together, without looking at the dossier on me, or the other ones. This thing shouldn't have been done. The party leadership should have been notified. Maybe I should have said something, maybe not. I didn't say anything; and I did things that way for some time.[212]

She complied with the Soviets, she explicitly added, because

[i]f a Soviet official told me something, it was the gospel for me. That's how I was brought up. . . . I'm telling you that things got to the point that anything Soviet was considered wonderful. If they had told me that the USSR needed it, I would have done it. A mistake, no doubt, but I would have done it. . . . [I]f they had told me to throw myself into the fire, I would have done it.[213]

The evidence, however, suggests that, as with Patraşcanu, Pauker did not follow Soviet plans to frame the veterans. Archival sources corroborate the testimony of Gheorghe Gaston Marin, a French Resistance veteran and protégé of Gheorghiu-Dej, that Pauker favored an authentic inquiry to find genuine agents but opposed purging innocent people.[214] This, of course, assured her ultimate defection from the Soviets' campaign, based as it was on fabricated charges, and it appears that she eventually took action to stop the campaign in Romania, going so far as to attack its primary players. Gheorghe Pintilie revealed in a 1956 declaration, "After [the Rangheţ] commission functioned for a time, Teohari Georgescu informed me with much discretion that the commission must immediately cease all activity, because there were serious suspicions regarding Iosif Rangheţ's honesty, and there were certain unclear issues concerning his party activities." Likewise, Pintilie added, Pauker herself told him she considered Rangheţ "very suspect."[215] As a result, the commission was promptly disbanded, but Rangheţ was never purged—suggesting that Pauker's actual target was not Rangheţ personally, but his commission. Indeed, once the commission halted its inquiry into the veterans, it was never reformulated under a new leadership but remained suspended up through Pauker's ouster.

Similarly, Pauker unsuccessfully attempted in 1951 to remove Alexandru Moghioroş from his position as the party's organizational secretary.[216] In that capacity he supervised the Central Committee's Verification Section, which, along with the party's Control Commission, continued to investigate certain individuals (such as Vasilichi) after the Rangheţ commission disbanded.[217] Pauker had in fact assisted Moghioroş at the Verification Section and oversaw work at the Control Commission until her bout with cancer in June 1950; perhaps tellingly, she did not resume helping him upon resuming her duties at the end of the year.[218] During her purge Control Commission chief Constantin Pârvulescu addressed her apparent disdain for the extended inquiries, suggesting that Pauker

> put us in a difficult situation many times when it came to resolving various cases. She [displayed] a lack of consistency towards opportunist elements who had no business being in the party. Many times she would not help us resolve a problem in a correct manner; and I think that the question of this conciliatory attitude is a problem that Comrade Ana must condemn with complete seriousness, because she pursued a sentimental line based on personal relations, and not on principle.[219]

This apparently reflected the fact that, as Spaniard Carol Neumann firmly emphasized, Pauker "continued to esteem" and "defended" the veterans after the Stalinist campaign against them had begun.[220] Even after 1949, Ana Toma insisted, Pauker "consistently" made herself available to the veterans in her office, and "would ask me to help them, to resolve various problems, private problems, that they had."[221] It is a fair assumption, therefore, that the issue was eventually used to compromise her.

Seemingly seconding Pauker's call for an honest inquiry was Teohari Georgescu. "Regarding the fate of a man," he later asserted, "I always went with the line of seeking the truth. [But] I wouldn't be sincere if I said that I wasn't influenced when others said 'What, are you stupid? Do you think that they're not working here as well?'" His failure in "discovering enemies," Georgescu added, "put [him] in a difficult position in 1951," and Shutov personally castigated him for not initiating arrests.[222] His protection of a number of Spaniards in his ministry, moreover, led to a clash between himself and then Deputy Interior Minister Alexandru Drăghici in March 1952. Echoing a reproach from the ministry's chief Soviet adviser, Alexandr Sakharovskii, Drăghici called for the dismissal of Deputy Interior Minister Mihai Burcă from the ministry's border guards, along with several of his associates—General Mihail (Bibi) Boico, General Iacov Bulan, and Colonel Andrei (Bondi) Roman—all of whom except Bulan were Spanish veterans.[223] Denouncing them as a "clique of opportunists," Drăghici harshly rebuked the group for not removing certain elements from the border region next to Yugoslavia, resulting in a recent rash of defections. But Georgescu defended the group (some of whom had broken down crying at the meeting), contending they were "essential figures" in the ministry's hierarchy.[224] Two months later, he was condemned for his position at the Central Committee plenary.[225] "You've lost a sense of vigilance," Gheorghiu-Dej sternly berated him. "You've become lazy. There are more counter-revolutionary elements in this country than there are in Czechoslovakia and Hungary."[226]

This theme was fully developed at the May 1952 CC plenary. "Neither Teohari nor Ana . . . ," Petre Borilă declared, "was concerned that the enemy is working, that the imperialists couldn't be ignoring us, that there's sabotage and espionage going on. . . . And we won't even talk about Luca."[227] Pursuing the point further was Miron Constantinescu: "Regarding revolutionary vigilance," he observed, "Comrade Gheorghiu-Dej said in September last year [1951]: 'It would be a dangerous illusion to think that there are not still undiscovered enemies in our Party. . . . [And t]here is no doubt that foreign elements will try in the future to infiltrate into the ranks of our Party.' . . . Comrade Ana and Comrade Teohari, you were warned where these deviations would lead to, and where these anti-party manifestations would lead to, but you didn't heed those warnings."[228] Such claims were expressed to the public as well, as when a January 1953 Scânteia editorial attacked "the opportunists [that is, the Pauker faction, accused of a right-wing 'opportunist' deviation] who sought to deceive the heroic masses, contending that our country and our party are an exception where the attempts of American-British imperialism at infiltrating their paid agents are concerned."[229] As unpublished party documents repeatedly noted, Pauker publicly affirmed shortly before her purge that "[w]e have many enemies outside the country. But there are relatively few inside the country, and they are weak. They've been cast aside and they've been beaten."[230] This contradicted Stalin's doctrine that enemy activity intensified as socialism advanced, which became sacrosanct in bloc politics from mid-1948 on, and which Dej's Pravda piece explicitly emphasized.[231]

Toward the close of the May 1952 plenary, the deputy chief of the Control Commission, Dumitru Coliu, made the following declaration:

[I]n 1946–1947, Comrade Dumitru Petrescu, the current Finance Minister, showed me evidence . . . of the existence of certain groups that were engaging in acts of undermining the authority of Comrade Gheorghiu-Dej. He maintained that Valter Roman, at that time a general in the army, had frequent meetings with Boico (Bibi), presently a general in the Interior Ministry, and Colonel Dr. Brill and other Jewish comrades, and they often met with one another and spoke against Comrade Gheorghiu-Dej, how he is incapable of leading the party, and how Ana is much smarter, and that she's actually the party leader. Comrade Petrescu indicated . . . that Valter Roman expressed objections to an article of Comrade Gheorghiu-Dej's that appeared in Scânteia. . . . Comrade Petrescu told me that he handed over the material to the party's Control Commission, and that he also informed Comrade Teohari and others. . . . I'm of the opinion that it should be investigated how Valter Roman got to be the head of the Ministry of Posts.[232]

That Coliu chose to describe the Spaniards Roman, Boico, and Brill as "Jewish comrades" underscored Gaston Marin's point that it was often difficult to determine whether Spaniards were targeted at this time because they were Spaniards or because they were Jews.[233] (At least two-thirds of the Spaniards, and perhaps as many as four-fifths of them, were Jews.)[234] It was also an ominous harbinger of things to come—for, with Pauker now out of the picture, the "quiet in Romania" was to quickly evaporate.

Hence, in the fall of 1952, only a few months following Pauker's purge, systematic repression of the Spanish Civil War and French Resistance veterans began in Romania for the first time.[235] Another investigative body in the party Control Commission now began a new inquiry into the veterans, conducting an entirely new series of interrogations.[236] This coincided with the Slansky trial in Prague (November 1952), from where internal documents specifically identifying Romanian coconspirators arrived in Romania, as they had from Budapest during the Rajk trial.[237] But, unlike after the Rajk trial, the party press now issued an uncensored reprint of Klement Gottwald's 1951 speech accusing the veterans of being enemy agents.[238] This was but one public manifestation, contended the Control Commission's Charlotte Gruia and the Interior Ministry's Mihai Burcă, of secret preparations to stage a Slansky trial in Romania. "All the interrogations," claimed Burcă, "pointed to that intention."[239]

Indeed, Charlotte Gruia, a veteran of the French Resistance, was in a unique position to witness events not only as a member of the party's Control Commission but also as its potential victim. "It started in October or November [1952]. . . . All the veterans of Spain and the French Resistance were under investigation. . . . [My husband and I] were under surveillance day and night by the Securitate at that time." This was, she insisted, the first time this had happened to them.[240] Moreover, Deputy Interior Minister Mihai Burcă and his associates Mihail (Bibi) Boico and Andrei (Bondi) Roman were promptly purged from the Interior Ministry.[241] "It was in '52," Burcă related. "I was thrown out of my job then. I was in a desperate situation, and even contemplated suicide right here in this house." Asked if he had ever been in danger of losing his position before, he replied "Not until the Right Deviation."[242] Purged as well from the Interior Ministry were the Spaniards Ianoş Birtaş (head of the Securitate's first directorate), Mihail Patriciu (Braşov's Securitate chief), and Andre Micu (chief of political cadres).[243] Spanish veteran Sanda Sauvard also reported being "kicked out of my position in 1952. I was in a research laboratory, and was told that I was an agent, and kicked out. . . . I never had trouble before that."[244] Other purged Spaniards included Carol Neumann and Ionel Munteanu, both arrested in December 1952, and Dr. Shuli Brill, whom Coliu specifically mentioned at the May plenary and who was expelled from the party and interrogated over an extended period.[245] French Resistance veterans in trouble included S. Marinescu, who was dismissed as director of the Băiţa mines, and Yvonne Florescu (the wife of Mihai Florescu), who was intensely interrogated in October 1952.[246] They and quite a few others were repressed when Pavel Cristescu, a Spanish veteran, reportedly brought a document to the Control Commission contending that all those who returned to Romania from Spain or France via Yugoslavia were engaged in espionage[247]—though Spaniards who spent the war years in Moscow, such as Andrei Roman and Dr. Brill, were targeted as well.[248] Perhaps the most notorious victims of this repression were Gheorghe Vasilichi and Valter Roman. Though Dej seemingly cleared him immediately after the May plenary, Vasilichi was again threatened in the fall of 1952, reportedly after he refused to dismiss Spanish and French Resistance veterans from the Union of Production Cooperatives, which he then headed.[249] Similarly, Valter Roman was abruptly removed as Minister of Posts and Telecommunications in December 1952; placed under house arrest; subjected to daily interrogations at the Control Commission, where he was accused of being an enemy agent in Spain; and targeted as a likely candidate to appear in a Romanian Slansky trial.[250]

Preparations for such a trial, however, were canceled after Stalin's death in March 1953, which suggests the Soviets and not Gheorghiu-Dej had initiated them.[251] Unlike the party leadership before Pauker's ouster, however, Dej apparently did not risk his position to protect the veterans during the mass repression that followed it. Rather, he did not hesitate to use the matter for his own political advantage. Although Soviet plans for prosecuting the veterans ended with Stalin's death,[252] their repression, though no longer as virulent and systematic as during Stalin's last months, by no means halted in Romania. Uncertain of his own position with the thaw in Soviet politics and suspicious of the loyalty of the party's old guard, Dej maintained an atmosphere of fear and intimidation in Romania in order to ward off any attempts to replace him.[253] Hence, Valter Roman was sanctioned with a "vote of censure

with a warning" in May 1954 for his "repeated anti-party manifestations," and he was not formally rehabilitated until 1956.[254] Dr. Shuli
Brill's exclusion from the party lasted until the latter part of 1954.[255]
Gheorghe Gaston Marin, though a close associate of Dej, did not get
back his party card until 1955.[256] And Spaniard Jean Coler remained
under surveillance until 1957.[257] Furthermore, the Control Commission
continued to investigate the veterans more than two years after Stalin's
death, accusing the Spaniards of being "Beria's agents" soon after Lavrenti Beria's fall in June 1953.[258] In June or July 1955, the commission's
dossiers were transferred for the first time to the Interior Ministry,
where Securitate officer Eugen Szabo investigated them. According to
Szabo, Gheorghiu-Dej wanted to prosecute Spanish veterans at that
time: "Dej told me that I must find some people among them who are
spies. . . . I have no doubt that Dej wanted trials when he gave me the
dossiers." Szabo specified that Dej called him into his office three times
to report on his progress, adding that he did not consult the Soviet
advisers on the matter. He did manage, however, to drag out the inquiry, which he was still conducting when Khrushchev delivered his
Secret Speech at the Twentieth Soviet Party Congress in February 1956.
Soon after, Dej abandoned the investigation and began publicly accusing Pauker of seeking the veterans' demise.[259] That summer, she was
again called to the Control Commission and pressured to confess her
guilt in their repression.[260]

Hence, the evidence corroborates the initial accusation against Pauker
in 1952 and invalidates the subsequent charges against her. It also sup-
ports the claim of a former high-ranking party official from Transylvania, in a manuscript smuggled to the West, that Dej brought to Stalin's
attention a certain fact that he hoped would justify purging Pauker.
She and her allies, Dej informed Stalin, had "prevented a Rajk trial in
Romania."[261] This indeed appears to have been a major factor in her
downfall.

Figure 1. Romania, 1944–51.

Figure 2. Ana Pauker, 1913. Courtesy of Tatiana Brătescu
and Gheorghe Brătescu.

Figure 3. Ana Pauker with her daughter Tatiana, ca. 1928–29. Courtesy of Tatiana Brătescu and Gheorghe Brătescu.

Figure 4. Marcel Pauker at Magtitogorsk, USSR, ca. 1931–32. Courtesy of Tatiana Brătescu and Gheorghe Brătescu.

Figure 5. Ana Pauker speaking at her trial, Craiova, Romania, 1936. Courtesy of Soviet Archive, Moscow.

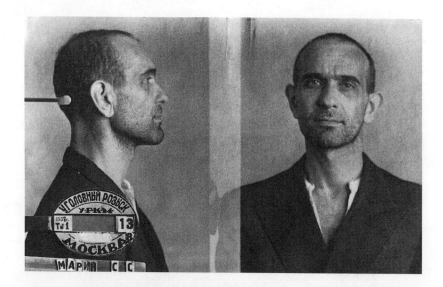

Figure 6. Marcel Pauker in a Soviet prison after his arrest in Moscow in March 1938. Courtesy of Tatiana Brătescu and Gheorghe Brătescu.

Figure 7. Ana Pauker in prison, 1938. Courtesy of Tatiana Brătescu and Gheorghe Brătescu.

Figure 8. Hersh Rabinsohn, Ana Pauker's father. Sketched by G. Löwendal, 1943. Courtesy of Tatiana Brătescu and Gheorghe Brătescu.

Figure 9. Lucreţiu Patraşcanu (left) and Teohari Georgescu, May 1, 1946. Courtesy of Tatiana Brătescu and Gheorghe Brătescu.

Figure 10. Gheorghe Gheorghiu-Dej, 1946. Courtesy of Tatiana Brătescu and Gheorghe Brătescu.

Figure 11. Ana Pauker receiving a foreign delegation, November 1947.
Courtesy of ROMPRES.

Figure 12. Ana Pauker, official portrait, 1948. Courtesy of
Tatiana Brătescu and Gheorghe Brătescu.

Figure 13. Prime Minister Petru Groza (third from left) and Ana Pauker
(second from left) at a rally honoring the just-deceased Georgi Dimitrov,
July 1949. Courtesy of ROMPRES.

Figure 14. Ana Pauker at the Palace of the Republic, May 9, 1948. Courtesy of
Tatiana Brătescu and Gheorghe Brătescu.

Figure 15. Ana Pauker presenting a decoration at the Palace of the Republic, May 9, 1948. Courtesy of ROMPRES.

Figure 16. Ana Pauker speaking at a cultural delegation, May 1948. Courtesy of ROMPRES.

Figure 17. Ana Pauker at the opening of the Congress of the Union of Young Workers. Pauker greets a delegation of children, March 3, 1949. Courtesy of ROMPRES.

Figure 18. Rally held in
Bucharest's Victory Square,
celebrating the International
Day of Women, March 1950.
Pictured (from left to right)
are Petru Groza, C. I. Parhon,
Gheorghe Gheorghiu-Dej,
Ana Pauker, Vasile Luca,
L. Radaceanu, and Iosif
Chişinevschi. Courtesy of
ROMPRES.

Figure 19. Propaganda
cartoon against kulaks,
December 1950. Private
collection of the author.

Figure 20. From left to right: Gheorghe Gheorghiu-Dej, Ana Pauker, Vasile Luca, and Teohari Georgescu at a meeting of the Great National Assembly, April 5–7, 1951. The meeting was held to launch an appeal for a peace treaty. Courtesy of ROMPRES.

Jewish Emigration

A third issue surrounding Ana Pauker's purge was Jewish emigration to Israel (or *aliya*) from Romania—an enigma of sorts throughout Pauker's tenure. With the largest postwar Jewish community in the Soviet bloc except for the USSR, Romania tolerated, if not facilitated, both legal and illegal emigration up through 1947,[1] in compliance with a general Soviet policy in that regard.[2] But during 1948 and 1949, when other Soviet satellites continued allowing substantial emigration to the newly born state of Israel, Romania shut its gates to all but a trickle of Jewish emigrants. Then suddenly, it dramatically reversed itself in 1950 and 1951, and permitted a massive emigration of roughly 100,000 Romanian Jews, precisely when all other Soviet satellites began to clamp down on emigration in line with Stalin's escalating anti-Semitic campaign.[3]

These puzzling shifts in emigration policy preoccupied the Zionist organizations and the Israeli government, for Romania was central in their efforts to bring Jewish immigrants to Israel. A relatively high number of Romanian Jews had survived the Second World War—some 353,000 souls, or roughly 50 percent of the prewar population.[4] They had been universally blacklisted from the country's economy and emerged from the war with large numbers completely impoverished and economically dispossessed. According to one source, the latter comprised 45 percent of Romanian Jewry, about 150,000 people;[5] a similar number suffered from hunger and needed basic clothing. Romanian authorities estimated that in mid-1946 no fewer than 40,000—two-thirds—of the Jewish children in the country, and 100,000 Romanian Jews generally, needed financial assistance just to survive. The overall figure rose over 30 percent in the next two years.[6]

But the Communist-led regime, installed in March 1945, provided little such assistance. RCP activists openly debated this issue at an October 1945 meeting, where a leader of the newly created Jewish Democratic Committee (JDC), which represented the Communist Party in the Jewish community, candidly criticized the party's negligence. "[W]e are very, you can even say, disturbed," he declared. "Jews in this country can't get a job. We asked the General Confederation of Labor that Jews be employed in production wherever places are available. . . . And what was the Confederation's response? That all the jobs are taken, and that another group of repatriates, that is, those who were former prisoners [of war] . . . , are now returning [to Romania], and *they* have to be given jobs. And you see, once again the Romanian Jews are pushed aside. . . . Thousands and thousands of Jews don't have any means of existence."[7] A Jewish veteran party activist raised similar concerns at a meeting several months later: "There has been an under-appreciation of the Jews in and within the Party," she suggested. "[In Moldavia] the Jews were hit the hardest, and they haven't received one thing in return. OK, so we gave them freedom. But the mass of widows over there are dying of starvation and aren't receiving any help whatsoever. The only assistance is coming from the Americans, from the Joint [Distribution Committee]."[8] This failure to aid the Jews seems to have been a by-product of the party's attempt to appeal to ethnic-Romanians. Determined to portray itself as patriotic and not to alienate the ethnic-Romanians, it delayed for years the trials of leading Romanian fascists and hesitated to return confiscated Jewish property.[9]

It is not surprising, then, that more than 100,000 Romanian Jews had applied to emigrate by the beginning of 1945.[10] But the British authorities severely restricted legal immigration to Palestine *(Aliya Alef)*, granting a yearly quota of only 3,500 entry visas to Palestine for all of Romanian Jewry.[11] Likewise, the British naval blockade also precluded illegal sea transports *(Aliya Bet)*. While one or two shiploads of emigrants reportedly left the Danubian port of Giurgiu soon after August 1944, no other transports took place for two years thereafter.[12] Therefore, beginning in 1945, Romanian Jews emigrated almost exclusively across the western border with Hungary and Yugoslavia (dubbed *Aliya Gimel*), and proceeded to Austria under the auspices of Zionist organizations and the Joint Distribution Committee—all with the Romanian authorities' tacit cooperation. On orders of the Interior Ministry, the Romanian police and border guards permitted Jews to group at certain points within the frontier zone and even withdrew at night from border crossing sites.[13] This complied with a general Soviet policy at the time that promoted illegal Jewish immigration to Palestine, primarily to undermine the British Mandate there and the British presence in the Middle East generally.[14]

Initially, most emigrants were the economically ruined and the survivors of concentration camps.[15] Most Romanian Jews, it seems, at first adopted a tentative wait-and-see attitude, while a considerable number, particularly among the young, pinned their hopes on the emerging new order. Few were inclined, apparently, to heed the myriad warnings from Soviet Jews in the Red Army and the NKVD regarding Stalinist anti-Semitism, that Romanian Jewry would be jumping from the frying pan into the fire under Soviet rule.[16] After all, they reasoned, had not the Soviets rescued them from certain death under the Nazis? "Forgotten," Jacob Talmon noted, "was the Nazi-Soviet pact of 1939 which unleashed the horrible war, and forgotten was the fact that after all Soviet Russia had taken up arms when invaded and not in defense of the Jews or other persecuted peoples. The world had come to such a pass that not killing Jews and allowing them to breathe the fresh air freely was considered a tremendous altruistic deed." [17]

By 1947, however, most Jews' willingness to remain in Romania had all but evaporated, in part because of their continued economic decline. Romania's deteriorating economy hurt the Jewish middle class and the more affluent elements, and the regime's Currency Reform of August 1947 hit them particularly hard. The reform had devastated the economy's private sector and by the spring of 1948 had left no less than 40 percent of the Jewish community without a livelihood.[18] Coinciding with a severe famine in 1946 and 1947 that resulted in starvation in Moldavia, where a large number of Jews resided, this led to the departure of tens of thousands over the western border, appropriately dubbed "the hunger flight." [19]

A rising tide of anti-Semitism in Romania, caused in part by their conspicuous presence in the Communist Party hierarchy, further compelled Jews to emigrate.[20] While they by no means predominated at the top of the party leadership (the Politburo and Secretariat), Jews did comprise a large number of Central Committee and regional party apparatchiks. Likewise, while they comprised no more than 10 percent of the Securitate in 1949, their proportionally greater presence in its leadership left the impression, or was exploited by anti-Semites to create the impression, that Jews predominated within the secret police.[21] Hence, a 1946 police report in the Moldavian city of Piatra Neamţ revealed widespread anger among non-Jewish party members over "Jews occupying all the responsible posts" in the city.[22]

Even the country's ethnic-Romanian Prime Minister Petru Groza displayed such acrimony in a meeting with Emil Bodnăraş, with the expressed purpose of transmitting his concerns to Stalin. The Americans and the British, Groza asserted, had tried without success to play various cards in Romania.

> Now the Americans are playing the Jewish card. And it's not at all difficult to play that card, in a country with 400,000 Jews, and with several tens of thousands of them infiltrated in our state, economic, political, and cultural apparatus. . . . It's all full of Jews. Everywhere you look, there are Jews. How can you expect the Jews [working, for instance, in the State Planning Commission] to carry out an honest and decent day's work . . . [when they've] been placed in posts planning [the daily functioning of] the very factories and commercial enterprises that were expropriated from them? The Zionists are perfect candidates for being a fifth column [in this country].[23]

Petru Groza's attitude adds credence to the conventional wisdom that the party and government leaders who promoted unrestricted Jewish emigration from Romania were precisely those who, like Groza, resented the considerable Jewish presence within the government and party elite. Thus it was ethnic-Romanians in the "interior faction" of the Romanian Workers Party, led by Gheorghiu-Dej, who supposedly favored such emigration as a means of cultivating popular support by providing badly needed jobs and housing for ethnic-Romanians in the place of Jewish "competitors" in highly coveted posts. At the same time, they reasoned, mass emigration would rid the country of unassimilated, "unproductive" Jews who presumably would not have easily integrated into the new society then being created.

On the other hand, the conventional wisdom posited, the opponents of mass Jewish emigration were high-ranking Jewish Communists, especially those in the "Muscovite" or "exterior" faction headed by Ana Pauker, who fervently believed in assimilation as the answer to the Jewish Question and who also considered the very notion of Jews being either "unassimilable" or "over-represented" in important positions as threatening their personal prospects within the party hierarchy.[24] But the evidence suggests that precisely the opposite was true. While the party leadership indeed diverged on Jewish emigration, the issue of contention was not "Jewish predominance" or "unassimilated" or "unproductive" Jews, but the mounting emigration of modern, assimilated Jews practicing vitally important professions within the Romanian economy. Petru Groza notwithstanding, it was the ethnic-Romanian Gheorghiu-Dej and others allied to him who pushed for denying exit visas to these Jewish professionals, while Ana Pauker adamantly opposed any such restrictions.

What was to be a protracted conflict within the Romanian leadership started at the end of 1947, with the first policy change on Jewish emigration, apparently in response to the Jewish emigrants' rapidly escalating numbers. With professional and middle-class Jews now opting to leave the country on an unprecedented scale, the resulting "brain drain" led the leadership to reconsider and rescind the open gates policy: they closed the western border, thus precluding all illegal emigration;[25] they allowed no legal emigration, and throughout the first half of 1948 held no negotiations on the matter; and in June they began repressive measures against Zionist organizations.[26] In March 1948 the government also issued for the first time secret, never-published criteria restricting Jewish emigration from Romania. Lt. Col. Laurian Zamfir, the chief of the Office of Foreigners and Passport Control (DCSP) within the General Police Command of the Interior Ministry, revealed under interrogation in 1953 that the criteria were issued in a report prepared by his predecessor, Ervin Voiculescu, that formally prohibited Jews who were skilled workers (handicraftsmen or *meseriaşi*), doctors, or engineers from emigrating—with an exception made for those Jews from the towns of Siret and Tereblecea in Northern Bukovina's Rădăuți County who had been repatriated from the USSR in 1945–1946. These criteria, he added, were to last until February 1950.[27]

Ana Pauker never mentioned the new criteria in her July 1948 meetings with Israeli envoy Mordechai Namir, who requested that 5,000 people of draftable age be allowed to emigrate each month to participate in Israel's war with the Arab League. Nonetheless, Namir had the firm impression that his request had generated some controversy among the party leadership, though Pauker personally assured him of her support on the matter and seemed genuinely pleased eleven days later to inform him the government had approved the quota.[28] As Namir later related to the Romanian Zionist Melania Iancu, Pauker declared that she personally agreed to the emigration and added that they could even fix a precise monthly figure, with a total of approximately 40,000–50,000 people. Namir thus left the meeting convinced, Iancu asserted, that the emigration would soon begin.[29]

Although the agreement did not technically violate the emigration criteria, it fell apart even before Namir could report it to the Israeli government. Within days, the RWP unilaterally lowered the number of monthly emigrants from 5,000 to 3,000, and postponed implementing the agreement until September.[30] And though Pauker reportedly assured Namir that the Zionist emissary Moshe Agami (Auerbach) could handle the emigration,[31] the government now decreed that Communists alone were to organize it. This sudden reversal, which Namir thought had entirely surprised an indignant Pauker,[32] most likely resulted from a Soviet volte-face on Israel and aliya soon after the Jewish state's creation. Until then, the Soviets favored temporary, selective emigration as a means of military aid to the Jewish community in Palestine in its war of independence with the British-backed Arab League. With Israel's victory over the Arabs, Soviet interest in continued emigration evaporated.[33] Not surprisingly, the RWP did not even come close to meeting its self-imposed reduced monthly quota of emigrants, but now "categorically opposed" Jewish emigration, as both Gheorghiu-Dej and Miron Constantinescu pointedly affirmed at an October 1948 Politburo meeting. "It is a right," Gheorghiu-Dej added, "but not one that we support, especially as there is an organization across the border that is working on facilitating emigration . . . and is helping non-Jewish, enemy elements to emigrate." Pauker conspicuously refrained from condemning Jewish emigration at this meeting. Instead, she reminded the others that Jews had been an oppressed population in Romania and read them Lenin's observations on the need for treating such oppressed peoples "with particular sensitivity." In addition, she emphasized that "while we allow the nationalities the right of self-determination up to secession," which was the doctrinal basis for permitting emigration, Lenin's thesis on the national question combating "Bundists and exclusivists" nonetheless mandated them to try "to convince the [Jewish] population that secession is not in their interest."[34] This dialectical approach would be the hallmark of the mass emigration a year and a half later.

Pauker's hesitance vis-à-vis the new line was evident despite the Soviet Union's launching a violent "anti-Zionist" campaign in the fall of 1948. The offensive ultimately led to the wholesale arrest of the entire Soviet-Jewish elite—including, to Pauker's distress, Molotov's wife, Polina Zhemchuzhina, who had reportedly become Pauker's warm friend over the years.[35] These events were immediately reflected in Romania. Police repression against the Zionist movement began in November, and by the end of the year security forces had shut down the offices of Zionist organizations and clubs across the country. Moreover, propaganda attacks on Zionism and Jewish nationalism intensified, culminating in a Politburo resolution in December condemning "Zionism in all its forms [as] a nationalist, reactionary political movement of the Jewish bourgeoisie." [36] Pauker reportedly opposed the resolution and unsuccessfully argued against making it public. [37] At the same time, she continued to promote Jewish emigration, albeit now limited to building Israeli Communism. At precisely this time, the leadership launched a campaign to recruit *Communist* immigrants to Israel. The party held special courses in Marxism-Leninism for the prospective emigrants, whose "mission" was to help fight the class war in Israel. The party also held meetings where they expressly told Jewish members that moving there was their duty as Communists. [38] The result was the perplexing spectacle of two ships leaving for Israel with 3,600 Jewish Communists and leftist sympathizers in December 1948 and January 1949, just as the government was closing Zionist facilities throughout the country. [39]

This "Red Aliya," as it was dubbed, in the end brought the Israeli CP few new members: most of the immigrants renounced Communism upon arriving in Israel. [40] Acknowledging this in April 1953, Pauker took personal responsibility for the emigration and admitted that she initiated it. [41] High-ranking JDC functionaries confirmed her position on the matter, [42] as did Shmuel Mikunis, the general secretary of the Israeli CP. According to Mikunis, Pauker personally had him travel 700 kilometers to address Jewish audiences about Israel and sit for a week in the offices of the JDC to answer questions from potential immigrants during a visit to Romania in 1949. [43] In contrast, when Mikunis asked to see Gheorghiu-Dej in 1950, he was refused because he had once been a Zionist. [44]

Mikunis's stay in Romania is interesting also because in meetings with Vasile Luca during that 1949 visit he asked the Romanians to give exit visas not only to "progressives" emigrating to Israel, but to "progressive *technicians, doctors and dentists*" as well. [45] In addition to solidifying Israeli Communism, Mikunis's emphasis on Communist emigration also may have been a roundabout way of circumventing the restrictive criteria. Indeed, Teohari Georgescu admitted under interrogation to doing precisely that by issuing exit visas to Jews barred from emigrating during this period—"at the request of Ana Pauker." [46] The March 1948 criteria had two loopholes: Jews from the restricted categories could leave if Interior Minister Georgescu decreed them "special cases" and granted special permission; and those who could not practice their profession because of illness could leave once they obtained a medical certificate from a specially formed commission at the Health Ministry. This latter provision led a number of Jews to offer bribes to commission members for false certificates. When the DCSP discovered this, Chief Laurian Zamfir proposed no longer issuing medical certificates and called for the offending doctors' arrest. According to Zamfir, Georgescu rejected the proposal and ordered him not to arrest any of the doctors.[47]

Pauker and Georgescu's reputed violations notwithstanding, the number of emigrants from Romania remained small. With the exception of the Red Aliya, the RPR disallowed all group departures to Israel throughout 1948 and only approved Jewish emigration case by case.[48] Consequently, the Israeli government, which had agreed to the Communist immigration after receiving assurances that Romania would later allow some 4,000–5,000 Zionist activists to leave,[49] began pressing the RWP leadership for expanded emigration. This reportedly included an offer to pay a large sum in exchange for the mass emigration of Romanian Jewry, which the RPR leaders rejected on the grounds that it was tantamount to "a slave trade."[50] Assuming that negotiations on the matter would continue through the Romanian Foreign Ministry and, thus, Ana Pauker, the Israelis selected Romanian Jewish painter Reuven Rubin as their first ambassador to Romania precisely because he and she had been on friendly terms during their early adulthood. Having given Rubin the specific mission of resolving the emigration problem, the Israelis hoped that his and Pauker's earlier friendship would facilitate a satisfactory resolution.[51] But, despite the daily spectacle of large numbers of Jews lining up outside the Interior Ministry to seek permission to leave the country, and despite Rubin's persistent pressure on Pauker to ease emigration, such a resolution appeared increasingly unlikely.[52] The resultant tensions exploded one tumultuous week in February 1949, when the country's Zionist organizations staged three massive demonstrations in Bucharest to protest the government's emigration policies.[53]

Predictably, Romanian authorities responded swiftly to this unprecedented open dissent. On February 18, one day after the largest demonstration, in which 20,000 Jews participated, the regime arrested three Israeli emissaries *(shlichim)* and began investigating them for espionage.[54] On March 2, the Interior Ministry ordered Romania's Zionist leaders immediately to dissolve the Zionist parties and youth organizations, shut down their institutions and training camps, and halt all activity in the country.[55] As a direct reprisal to the protests, the government proceeded to restrict aliya even further, allowing only sixteen Jews to leave the country during February, and roughly 100 to leave each month thereafter through November 1949—40 percent of whom were not even Romanian citizens.[56]

The cutbacks certainly made it appear that the demonstrations had backfired on their organizers. But the RWP leadership actually intended the retaliation to be only temporary, and the intense pressure ultimately induced them to open emigration. This was evident as early as February 18, when the Secretariat addressed the issue of the demonstrations. Pauker, supported by Georgescu, cautiously maintained her dialectical approach to Jewish emigration. "We have 350,000 Jews, among whom 300,000 are agitated," she asserted, ranging from deportees from Transnistria who had yet to be resettled, to those angry over losing businesses to government confiscation. "We are not concerned with a population that emigrates out of poverty, as was the case with Romanians who emigrated to America, but with a psychosis that's been created by certain factors. [Hence I agree] that those who are doing the agitating be called in and spoken to in their capacity as Romanian citizens, and warned that they should respect our laws." Adding that the genuine desire to emigrate existed among the country's Jews, Pauker then proposed first allowing the elderly and those with children in Israel to emigrate, while simultaneously conducting an extensive propaganda campaign *(muncă de lămurire)* elucidating the party's position on emigration. "After things calm down," she concluded, "we should start letting them go." [57]

Both Luca and Gheorghiu-Dej took a noticeably harder line on the demonstrations' organizers, with Dej proclaiming that the leaders of the Zionist organizations "should be summoned and treated like leaders of fascist organizations. We should tell them that this is the first and last time they're being called in, and several of those who organized the demonstration should be held responsible." Indeed, both he and Luca strongly emphasized at the meeting that "the Zionist organizations must be," as Luca put it, "disbanded as enemies of the Republic and treated as such," while Pauker failed to even mention dissolving the local Zionist groups.[58] According to Georgescu's testimony, as well as the plan of the indictment against Pauker compiled soon after her ouster, she had in fact opposed their dissolution, arguing that it would lead to an international campaign against Romania.[59] Their contrasting attitudes on this issue would resurface one month later, when Pauker personally ordered the release and expulsion of the three Israeli emissaries, along with four other emissaries arrested in December 1948, despite the determination of Dej, Luca, and a majority of the Secretariat to try them for espionage.[60]

On the other hand, while Luca objected at the meeting to allowing mass departures to Israel (an objection he apparently renounced later that year), Dej took a step back from his "categorical" opposition to Jewish emigration. "[W]e should not adopt a rigid line," he suggested, "and we should examine the matter on a case by case basis. We have to take into account a sentiment among the Jewish population that's connected to their suffering during the war. We should set a date for those agitating for emigration to leave. And we should not forcibly hold on to those who don't want in any way to remain here, and we should let them go."[61]

The minutes of an August 31, 1949, Secretariat meeting reveal what prompted Dej's reconsideration. Noting that the matter had been raised and discussed at an earlier session, Teohari Georgescu called on the secretaries to specify in precise terms the party line on Jewish emigration and proposed issuing passports to all those who were determined to emigrate to Israel. First to respond was Pauker, who quickly agreed. "We can't hold on to people by force," she succinctly declared, prompting Dej's equally pointed reply: "I agree. I've come to the conclusion that if we allow them to go, there is going to be less emigration to Palestine. I've read some of the letters: it makes you want to cry reading about the misery over there."[62]

Hence the RWP Secretariat had reached a consensus of sorts to allow increased Jewish emigration.[63] The party leaders' decision was discussed at a November 29 meeting in the Interior Ministry attended by Deputy Interior Minister Gheorghe Pintilie, DCSP chief Laurian Zamfir, SSI chief Sergei Nicolau, and Ana Toma, Pauker's assistant at the Foreign Ministry. They were informed that the party leadership had resolved in principle to expand the criteria for Jewish emigration, though it continued to oppose the emigration of technicians and all others whose departure would disrupt Romania's economy, and it reserved the right to take any action that would prevent such disruptions.[64] Those attending were to propose a means of expanding the criteria without impairing production, which they promptly communicated to party headquarters.[65] Their proposals led to the passage on February 20, 1950, of new criteria expanding the March 1948 rules. In addition to the previous medical loophole, those in the three proscribed categories (skilled workers, doctors, and engineers) could now leave if they were at least sixty years old, or at least fifty years old if they had family members in Israel.[66] While the changes did not formally take effect until February 20, emigration expanded unmistakably immediately after the November 29 meeting. A synthesis prepared by the DCSP at the end of 1949 revealed that, while only 400–500 Jews had been allowed to emigrate between January and September–October 1949, the number had increased to some 3,000–4,000 by the end of the year.[67] A JDC report confirms this: the pace of departures jumped from 100 to between 500 and 600 a month in the last part of 1949 and increased further to roughly 2,500 per month at the beginning of 1950—with a total of 15,500 people leaving for Israel between November 1949 and April 1950, when the gates suddenly sprang completely open.[68]

On March 31, 1950, the Interior Ministry leadership met to discuss the party's decision to issue 10,000–12,000 exit visas per month beginning in April 1950, as well as to abrogate the criteria that had become effective only several weeks earlier, on February 20. In its place, the RWP adopted a third set of criteria approving "the departure of *all applicants* for emigration to Israel . . . , with the exception of those with a negative record at the Securitate, those being sought by the police, or those in the course of being tried for crimes or theft."[69] Thus the party leadership officially overturned its policy forbidding Jews with vitally needed professions from emigrating. Soon afterward, Georgescu ordered a substantial reduction in the number of certificates required of those applying for exit visas and directed the militia to issue new, simplified application forms to any Jews wishing to leave for Israel.[70] The militia performed the directive with discernibly exceptional vigor.[71] Both actions were reportedly carried out with Ana Pauker's backing[72] and were devised to help facilitate a mass emigration expected to reach several tens of thousands by June or July.[73] The numbers rapidly exceeded all expectations, as from January 1 to June 1, 1950, some 47,000 people received exit visas, 37,000 of them in April and May alone.[74] The JDC files plainly reveal the extent of the exodus, which took the Israeli government completely by surprise.[75] In Suceava, 2,000 of a Jewish population of 2,900, applied to emigrate; in Sighet, 1,600 of 1,800 applied; in Craiova, 70 percent of the Jewish population applied; in Botoşani, 70–90 percent; in Constanţa, 80 percent; and the city of Arad's entire Jewish population was reported to be leaving.[76] In all, no fewer than 220,000 Romanian Jews applied for emigration visas within two weeks in the spring of 1950.[77]

Needless to say, Gheorghiu-Dej must have quickly realized he had badly miscalculated when predicting an imminent decline in Jewish emigration. Believing that only the Jewish "bourgeoisie" would ultimately opt to leave the country,[78] he was reportedly shocked and bewildered by the mounting exodus and promptly acted to reimpose restrictions.[79] His subsequent stance was revealed at the May 1952 Central Committee plenary that purged Pauker, Luca, and Georgescu. Responding to a reference by Miron Constantinescu regarding *"the principled position* [that Georgescu] and Comrade Ana have in the problem of the Zionists and emigration to Israel," Georgescu declared: "It's true that our letting them go was raised at a meeting, and that *later Comrade Gheorghiu [-Dej] said that we should stop."* Confirming this, Pauker reminded the others that there had been a "common position" on Jewish emigration within the party leadership, but that *"Comrade G. Dej raised the issue that only the elderly should leave."* [80] Neither Dej nor anyone else attending the plenary disputed either remark.

As a number of Interior Ministry directives indicate, the party leadership initiated the move to retract unrestricted emigration during several meetings in May 1950. Unfortunately, the transcripts of these meetings are missing from the collection of Politburo and Secretariat documents presently housed in Romania's National Archives, perhaps because the meetings were not protocoled, or perhaps (as was the fate of many documents from this period) because the transcripts were subsequently destroyed.[81] But, in addition to the disclosures at the May 1952 CC plenary, there is the testimony of Teohari Georgescu, both under interrogation in prison as well as after his release in 1956. Though this testimony is inherently suspect, the party commission that rehabilitated Georgescu and a significant number of witnesses corroborate it on this matter.[82] Existing Politburo and Secretariat transcripts further prove the accuracy of its account of earlier events, as also holds true for the testimony of Zamfir and other Interior Ministry officers. According to Georgescu, Gheorghiu-Dej, on learning of the massive and perpetually mounting number of emigration applicants, pressed for renewed restrictions in a meeting of the Secretariat[83] that other documents reveal to have taken place on May 12, 1950.[84] The Secretariat apparently overruled Dej and maintained Pauker's dialectical approach to Jewish emigration: it issued a decree detailing precisely how the party organs should "enlighten" the Jewish population on the evils of Zionism and the futility of aliya. At the same time it stipulated that all those insistent on leaving would still be allowed to do so, and it even mandated finding additional ships to facilitate their more rapid emigration.[85] This last point clearly suggested the hand of Ana Pauker, who, Zamfir reported, attempted to locate additional ships to transport emigrants to Israel and had her assistant, Ana Toma, conduct unsuccessful negotiations on the matter with representatives of the Polish and Bulgarian governments.[86]

One week later Dej would raise the issue again, but this time at the Politburo, where he was more assured of a majority.[87] There Pauker "firmly asserted," Georgescu related, "that [they] should issue passports to anyone who wanted to leave for Israel, [and] had no reason to prevent a mass emigration."[88] The Politburo rebuffed her and issued new restrictions spelled out at a May 20 meeting of the Interior Ministry leadership: while the massive number of emigration applicants before May 15 would be allowed to leave in June and July, new applications beginning May 29 would be restricted to "the elderly, nonprofessionals, private functionaries, small food sellers and small handicraftsmen," with all technicians and employees of the state apparatus and state enterprises prohibited from leaving.[89] Because many immediately left their jobs to meet the new criteria, however, the Politburo soon met again to revise the criteria yet one more time.[90] As a May 31 Interior Ministry meeting disclosed, all exit visas issued before May 15 were now rescinded for anyone who had worked in the state apparatus (ministries, heavy industrial enterprises, or the more important light industrial enterprises), and exit visas would henceforth be denied to all those in the free professions (for instance, doctors, pharmacists, and technicians) up to age sixty-five, as well as skilled workers and functionaries working in the state apparatus or in state enterprises of any kind, up to age fifty.[91]

The Politburo's sharp reversal on Jewish emigration predated by only several weeks the first wave of arrests of Zionist leaders on July 10[92] and was but the first step in a continual process of restricting aliya from then on. On November 9, 1950, also reportedly on Gheorghiu-Dej's initiative, the leadership barred all those who had been privy to state secrets in the past, all those in the military service, and all medical students in the third year or later from leaving the country.[93] It also raised the age threshold from fifty to sixty for accountants, plumbers, electricians, and builders.[94] Restrictions widened further in February 1951, when all students attending technical schools, including those studying medicine, pharmaceuticals, mechanics, and architecture, were also denied exit visas.[95] Sometime around October 1951, the party leadership decided to accept no new emigration applications and to stop issuing passports to those who had already applied, while also stipulating that the emigration of those with previously issued passports would continue only six more months.[96] Thus in April 1952 Jewish emigration from Romania completely halted and would remain a dead issue for six years.[97]

This piecemeal proscription of Jewish emigration was carried out over the continued objections of Ana Pauker, who evidently attempted to counteract it. She was, for instance, reportedly behind Georgescu's immediate maneuvers to sidestep the May 1950 criteria.[98] Directly after their passage, Georgescu ordered Deputy Interior Minister Marin Jianu to modify the prohibitions and allow those falling in the restricted categories to leave at any age if they were ill, thus reopening the medical loophole.[99] On June 7, Georgescu ordered Zamfir to unilaterally remove skilled workers and handicraftsmen from the restricted categories as well, which, Zamfir suggested, "effectively rescinded the proposal to revoke the exit permits, as the great majority were skilled workers and handicraftsmen." [100] In addition, Pauker pushed Georgescu to speed the departures in 1951 and the beginning of 1952, complaining in a 1951 Secretariat meeting that they not only were going extremely slowly but were being delayed.[101] Through most of 1951 some 50,000–60,000 Jews had received exit visas and were waiting to leave the country, and their numbers had jumped to 100,000 when the party decided to end aliya.[102] Therefore, acknowledged Georgescu, he unilaterally acted to expedite the emigration of all those who had received their passports,[103] and he did so at Pauker's insistence on accelerating aliya at this eleventh hour.[104] For example, Pauker again suggested using foreign ships to complete the emigration more rapidly.[105] This, however, again proved unworkable. Hence Georgescu, also on Pauker's suggestion, at a certain point in 1951 reduced from seven to five days the voyage time of the sole vessel taking emigrants to Israel, the SS *Transylvania,* and took action to double the ship's transport capacity (from 1,500 to 3,000 passengers).[106] Miron Constantinescu critically noted another such measure, when he later lambasted Georgescu for "the militia's posters [being] put on every street, and . . . the militia going from house to house to mobilize the Jewish population to leave," *after* the party had resolved to put an end to Jewish emigration.[107] As a result, no fewer than 50,000 Jews left for Israel in 1951, a number almost as large as the mass exodus in 1950 before the reimposition of restrictive criteria.[108] Another 4,000 departed in the first months of 1952.

Hence the evidence suggests that Pauker and Georgescu indeed had a "principled position on Jewish emigration," having been backed by Luca on this issue from late 1949 on.[109] It was but a short step from this, however, to inflated charges of Pauker's fostering a "nationalist attitude on Jewish emigration to Israel," as the official plan of Pauker's inquiry suggested;[110] or of her serving as "an agent . . . for international Zionism and other groups,"[111] as alleged after her arrest on February 18, 1953, but dropped with Stalin's death only two weeks later. Though the Romanian press never made it public, Pauker's promotion of unrestricted Jewish emigration would remain a centerpiece of the case against her. As the final report of the party commission investigating Pauker concluded, the two most important components of Pauker's "counterrevolutionary line" were her opening the party's gates to Legionaries and other "enemy elements" in 1945 and her position on Zionism and Israel. On the latter issue, the report added, "she [was] particularly distinguished by the role she played in pushing the Jewish population to mass emigrate and on the occasion of those 7 Zionist spies [the Israeli emissaries whom she freed]."[112] The report, issued in April 1954, after all plans for a trumped-up show trial had been abandoned, was at least on this point not far from the truth.

But does the fact that, as the evidence now indicates, the Soviets orchestrated Pauker's purge and inquiry and ultimately focused it on her pro-aliya policies necessarily suggest that such policies had violated the Kremlin's directives?[113] Initially this does not appear to have been the case. As Pauker's brother, Zalman Rabinsohn, informed Romanian Zionist leader Marcu Cohin, Pauker revealed that the Soviets had decided on principle to let the satellites administer Jewish emigration based on their own needs and passed a resolution to that effect at the Cominform.[114] Moreover, given the various bloc countries' divergent policies on emigration, and given the Arab world's failure to respond to Soviet goodwill gestures up through 1953, the Soviets' hands-off attitude on Jewish emigration from its satellites seems to have lasted through most of this period.[115] An unmistakable change can be discerned in 1951, however, as anti-Semitic purges escalated throughout the Soviet sphere: that year, aliya was effectively terminated in every Soviet satellite, including Poland—which until then had consistently allowed unrestricted Jewish emigration —with the sole exception of Romania.[116] It was perhaps no accident, then, that the decision to halt aliya in October 1951 coincided with the arrival in Romania of a special Soviet commission that imposed a number of substantive policies on the RWP leadership[117] and began the process that would culminate in Pauker's, Luca's, and Georgescu's removal. Indeed, according to at least one veteran RWP activist, it was candidly revealed at high-level meetings he attended "that the Soviets did not agree on principle" with the mass emigration of Romanian Jewry in 1950–1951.[118]

A final question remains: Why would so steeled and tested a Stalinist as Ana Pauker continue to support mass emigration if Moscow opposed it? One possible reason, Ana Toma suggested, was that Pauker, who had openly expressed esteem for Golda Meir, was personally committed to Israel's creation (though she presciently predicted danger if the Palestinians were not also given a state).[119] Another factor, seemingly, was the effect on Pauker of the upsurge of popular and state anti-Semitism in the Soviet Union during and after the Second World War.[120] As one scholar noted, this anti-Semitism "brought . . . Jewish awareness to [Jewish Communists] hitherto untouched by it. Expressions of doubt and renewed connections to their Jewishness occurred in even the most assimilated." [121] Indeed, Pauker's family, with whom she candidly discussed Stalin's hatred of Jews, believed she was deeply affected by the wartime anti-Semitism in the USSR and that she decided emigration was the Jews' only option once Stalin launched his postwar anti-Semitic campaign.[122]

The late Chief Rabbi Moses Rosen provided a third possible explanation for Pauker's attitudes on Jewish emigration. Ana Pauker, Rosen asserted, though "an honest [and] believing Communist," was in fact "a *marrano*" [a "secret Jew" who had converted to Christianity in Spain but surreptitiously continued to practice Judaism], who "after Auschwitz . . . had another look" at her own identity as a Jew and at the Jewish Question generally.[123] Her father and brother apparently shared this opinion, confiding to a friend their belief that she "continued to have a connection with Jews and Judaism in her heart." [124] Although subjective motivations of this sort can rarely be verified, two incidental details perhaps provide a glimmer of insight. Pauker's brother, Zalman Rabinsohn, who emigrated to Palestine in 1944, revealed that in a letter persuading him to return to Romania, she referred to the Holocaust and asked, "After all that has happened, how many of us are left?" [125] Moreover, after reading *The Diary of Anne Frank* and earnestly recommending it to her family, Pauker attended the stage version with her daughter in the late 1950s and openly cried during the performance.[126] This so astonished some in the audience that news of it quickly spread among Jewish circles in Bucharest.[127]

People were astonished, of course, because of Pauker's widely reputed hostility, or at least indifference, to Jews and her Jewish origins during the postwar period. This most likely resulted from her persistent avoidance of all things Jewish during her years in power, an apparent reaction to the highly contentious issue of her Jewishness throughout that period.[128] Clandestine oppositionist manifestos emphasizing the number of Jews in the Romanian Communist leadership, for instance, always mentioned her name first, along with those such as Luca's and Georgescu's, who were falsely depicted as Jews.[129] Dej and others used this fact in arguing for her ouster. Pauker's sensitivity to the issue was evident in her stated reason for seeking her brother's return to Romania: she was worried, she claimed, that "that part of the population that is most anti-Semitic would say that we have a person in the party leadership . . . who has a brother in enemy territory, and look how the kikes are."[130] In an interview with an American journalist in 1946, she justified the regime's press restrictions by suggesting that "[w]e have madmen here capable of inciting people to pogroms and other unspeakable crimes if we give them half the chance."[131] British diplomats in Bucharest at the time agreed with this assessment, reporting that anti-Semitism had escalated to the extent that Romanians tended "to look upon Jews as traitors *who should be exterminated at the first opportunity.*"[132] Not surprisingly, Pauker was careful never to do anything that underscored her Jewish origins.

Still, her public aloofness masked an altogether different attitude—one that was remarkably unique for a Stalinist leader. Under interrogation, Vasile Luca suggested

> Ana was the one who introduced her own personal anti-party line on the Jewish problem, involving me in this area as well. As early as 1945–1946, she mapped out an anti-Marxist line on the Jewish problem, and sought to resolve it not from the proletarian internationalist perspective, but as a problem that had to be distinguished from others, considering it as a problem of the entire Jewry. She viewed Jewry in its totality without class distinctions, and felt that it was the party's duty to protect all Jews, thus also the Jewish bourgeoisie and the Zionist organizations, and compensate them for the suffering they endured under the Antonescu dictatorship. She endorsed the thesis of Jewish emigration from the very beginning.[133]

Although this presumably could be typical Stalinist hyperbole as part of an attempt to frame Pauker as a Zionist agent, remarks that she made in the Politburo suggest otherwise.

In October 1948, Pauker took issue with the position of Dej, Luca, Constantinescu, and others that the Jewish Question should be viewed solely from the perspective of the class struggle and that a segment of Romanian Jewry were exploiters: "She does not agree with the observation that the Jewish population lived a life of ease, and pointed out that the Jewish petit bourgeoisie was always in a difficult situation, having been opposed by the bourgeoisie. The Jewish population *in its entirety* was oppressed and suffered at the hands of not only the ruling strata, but of the workers, infected with anti-Semitism, as well."[134] She made these remarks, moreover, two months after Ilya Ehrenburg's article denying the notion of Jewish unity appeared in *Pravda,* and after the Soviets launched their bloc-wide "anti-Zionist" campaign.

Her position no doubt reflected how she regarded her own Jewishness, as well as its open expression by those around her. "It's very important to know," her son-in-law Dr. Gheorghe Brătescu asserted, "that Ana, in comparison with other Jewish Communists, never rejected her Jewish origins." He knew this, he added, "[f]rom everything she said and did. She never once expressed a negative thing about Jews or Judaism, as Marx had done."[135] Concurring with this was Cristina Boico, a high-ranking official in the Foreign Ministry. "Generally Ana's attitude toward the Jews," Boico suggested, "was extremely positive."[136] Carol Lustig, her administrative director at the ministry, personally witnessed her tolerance on the issue. A Transylvanian Jew from Satu Mare who lost nearly his entire family in the Holocaust, Lustig married after the war and fathered a baby boy in 1948. "And what did I do?" he related. "I gave [my son] a *Brit Milah* [Jewish religious circumcision]. Nobody knew about it." Two months later he and his family stayed with Pauker at a villa in the resort town of Snagov. At one point, Pauker walked into the room when Lustig's wife, Eva, was changing the baby's diapers, and saw that he had been circumcised. Recalls Eva Lustig:

> Ana asked, "What's this? In 1948 you're still doing this?" And I told her that I'm still a Jew, and I want my son to be a Jew, and that, even if I didn't want it, he would still be a Jew. She just looked at me and didn't say anything, and I thought that we were going to have to look for a new job. She left the room. I started to breast-feed the baby. Five minutes later she came back to give me a glass of milk, as if nothing happened. Later she said in front of a group of people: "Look at this woman. She's half your age and look at the education she's giving her children, and how well she takes care of them. You should learn from her." And she gave me a kiss.

No one at that time circumcised their boys, Lustig emphasized, "not even the 'lowest' Jews" in the party apparat. "But she accepted it, even from the administrative director of her Foreign Ministry."[137]

Such an attitude was also evident in Pauker's close and respectful relations with her Orthodox Jewish parents and brother throughout her

years in the Communist Party. Pauker's daughter Tatiana Brătescu recalled that during the war years in the Soviet Union Pauker spoke often
and with great affection of her own mother, Sarah Rabinsohn. Soon after the end of the war, Sarah Rabinsohn died:

> When [Ana Pauker] was assisting in her mother's funeral, she cut her cloth-
> ing. There was a custom to cut your coat, and she let them cut it, without
> protesting that it was her best coat. I was there and wondered why she was
> cutting her clothing, and she explained very kindly that there is a law and it
> must be respected. She respected traditional Jewish customs for her parents'
> sake, out of respect for her parents and the lives they led. But she didn't re-
> spect those customs for herself.[138]

Pauker's father, Hersh Rabinsohn, who was known in the Bucharest
Jewish community for his crusty and strong-willed personality, had created an uproar in 1938 when, at the age of seventy-five, he beat up a
gang of anti-Semitic youths with his cane after they threatened him in a
streetcar.[139] Ten years later in Israel he gave an interview to *Time* magazine, recalling a visit with his daughter in 1946: "Zvi [Rabinsohn's Hebrew name] came to Ana," *Time* reported, "asking for help for a group
of Rumanian Jews. She received him amicably on a Saturday afternoon.
Coffee and cake was brought in. Old Zvi exploded: 'How dare you offer
me hot coffee on a Sabbath! Have you gone mad?' Ana, trying to calm
her father, led him to the kitchen and showed him the electric percolator. She explained that, since no one needed to strike a match, no religious law was being violated, but he called the percolator a wicked machine and stormed out."[140] The thought of one of the world's most
prominent Communists feverishly trying to convince her father that
she did not break the Sabbath may seem incongruous, but it nonetheless corresponds with the testimony of those who knew him. Israel Levanon, a close friend of both Hersh and Zalman Rabinsohn, contends
that Pauker and her father "had an excellent relationship, up until the
end. . . . He loved her very much, and she appreciated him a great
deal. . . . She was very fond of her father. She had a great respect for
him, for everything he did." According to Levanon, Hersh Rabinsohn
was more or less an outcast in the religious Jewish community throughout the war, on account of his daughter. The synagogues did not want
anything to do with him, for fear that the Antonescu regime would accuse them of having Communist connections. The only exception was
Rabbi Yitzchak Friedman's congregation from the town of Buhuşi. When
Zalman Rabinsohn returned to Romania in 1949,

[T]he first question [Ana] asked him was "How is the Rebbe from Buhuşi?" You know why? Because she knew that the only one who stayed close to her father in those difficult days was the Rebbe from Buhuşi. And not only that. At that time there was a severe food shortage. And on *Tu B'shvat* [a Jewish holiday commemorating the harvest], Ana called Zalman and said to him: "Today's *Tu B'shvat*. Take this package of *Tu B'shvat* fruit for the Rebbe of Buhuşi." There weren't any fruit in Bucharest at that time. She gave him oranges, almonds, and all kinds of fruit. And Zalman gave that package to the Rebbe of Buhuşi—a gift from Ana Pauker.[141]

When Hersh Rabinsohn informed Pauker in 1947 that he wanted to emigrate to Palestine, she contacted Romanian Zionist leader Kiva Orenstein, whom she had known since her Hebrew teaching days, and asked him to secretly arrange her father's emigration.[142] In August 1947 she dispatched Ana Toma to escort him to the port of Constanţa and assure his safe passage with the captain of the SS *Transylvania*.[143] Rabinsohn traveled under an assumed name as the husband of a woman he had never met before and from whom he parted company upon embarking in Palestine.[144] Pauker planned the trip with the assistance of Georgescu and Pintilie in the Interior Ministry, but without informing the other party leaders.[145] And she surreptitiously sent her father monthly support payments via a Romanian firm in Israel until his death in 1951.[146]

In December 1947, Pauker sternly rebuffed an American protest of Romania's allowing two ships loaded with immigrants to leave for Palestine in defiance of the British blockade. "After [meeting the Zionist agent Joseph Klarman] Madame Pauker told the American ambassador that there was no point in his intervention. The departure of Romanian citizens was an 'internal affair,' and there was nothing 'illegal' about it, as the American ambassador had intimated. These people were returning to what they considered their homeland."[147] As Hersh Rabinsohn's immigration remained a secret until Israel's independence the following year, the ambassador had no idea that Ana Pauker was actually talking about her own father.

CHAPTER SEVEN

"The Empress's Brother"

Yet another enigma in the story of Jewish emigration and the "Zionist question" is the mysterious return of Ana Pauker's brother, Zalman (Solomon) Rabinsohn, to Romania in 1949. Unlike Ana's sister, Bella, who followed Pauker into the Communist Party, Zalman remained an Orthodox Jew throughout his lifetime. Five years Pauker's junior, he attended various Jewish religious schools in Moldavia as a child and served as a rabbi in his grandparents' village of Codăeşti in the early 1920s; thereafter, he worked as a primary and high school Hebrew teacher and a Jewish school administrator in Bucharest.[1] A member of the Poalei Mizrachi religious Zionist movement, he emigrated to Palestine with his wife, Dina, and daughters, Tzipora and Leia, in May 1944, joining his son, Yechiel, whom he had sent there at the beginning of the war.[2]

Soon after Pauker arrived in Bucharest from the Soviet Union, she wrote to her brother, asking why he had left Romania and adding that she eagerly awaited his return. Zalman replied that he had no intention of leaving Palestine.[3] During the next two years, she regularly sent greetings in her parents' letters to him and reportedly told subordinates "that [Zalman] and his family is to be helped financially in order to tempt them to come back to Romania."[4] She sought his return, she later claimed, "out of panic that questions would be put to him and then published," and "that there would be consequences should the imperialists and their agents put him on the radio in the case of war"—consequences that included, she feared, a potential anti-Semitic backlash in Romania.[5]

If this were the case, why she felt the need to bring back her taciturn and tight-lipped brother, who consistently refused all interviews, while allowing her loquacious father to leave, is an open question.[6] The contradiction suggests, perhaps, that her real reasons lay elsewhere. Zalman told friends in Israel that Pauker pressured him to return simply because she missed him.[7] By all accounts they loved each other a great deal and had not seen each other since 1936, when he visited her in prison.[8] Pauker herself appeared to hint at this in interrogations after her purge. "I have only one brother in the world," she told her inquisitors in 1956, repeating sentiments she expressed to them three years earlier.[9] "He was," she had then declared, "the only one I had left from my family."[10] Perhaps tellingly, she crossed out the statement when proofreading the interrogation's transcript—reluctant, it seems, to reveal anything overly personal.[11]

In 1946, Zalman decided to travel to Romania to see his parents and family. After failing to obtain a visa through connections with Romanian Zionists in Palestine, he wrote to Ana (via Marcel Pauker's sister Titi) expressing his wishes to visit the country.[12] Ana, however, apparently pressed him to return permanently. According to Ana Toma, "When her brother requested to temporarily come to Romania to visit her, she did not agree, but told the [Romanian] chargé d'affaires in Israel . . . to convince him to come back permanently."[13] Yet, when Hersh Rabinsohn arrived in Palestine in August 1947, he brought a visa for Zalman to visit Romania. Zalman did not use it.[14] This time, it appears, it was he who refused, reportedly due to a dispute with Ana over the burial of their younger sister, Bella.[15]

Bella Rabinsohn had been in poor health since returning from the Soviet Union after the war and suffered from a number of ailments, including obesity, before dying of tuberculosis on March 12, 1946.[16] When Zalman learned of her death and burial at a party sanitarium, he immediately demanded that she be reburied at the Jewish cemetery in Bucharest.[17] Pauker at first evaded the issue, but when Zalman broke relations with her over the matter, she relented and had Bella moved to the Jewish cemetery on November 12, 1947.[18] Upon receiving the body, the cemetery summoned an astonished Chief Rabbi Moses Rosen, who "could not understand why . . . Ana would want a rabbi there."[19] He described the incident in his memoirs:

> Ana Pauker arrived at the "Filantropia" cemetery, where [Bella] was to be reburied, but she stayed at the entrance of the cemetery, and called for David

Schiffer, the president of the *Sacra Hevra Kadisha* society. She told him that there was to be no religious ceremony whatsoever, and Schiffer obsequiously complied. He came over to me, as I was several steps away, and transmitted her order. My answer was: "In that case, she should take the remains somewhere else. There's no way to do it in this cemetery without a religious service." Horrified by my response, Schiffer replied: "Fine, Mr. Chief Rabbi, but look who you're dealing with." But I refused to budge. Ana noticed Schiffer's desperate demeanor, and came over and asked what the problem was. I told her: "Pardon me, Mrs. Minister, but this is a religious cemetery, which has its own rules. We don't force anyone to come here, but whoever does come must respect those rules. Otherwise, we would be transforming the character of the cemetery, and defaming the memory of those buried here under those rules." Her gaze bore into me with her angry eyes, and she asked me: "What do you want, then?" I answered: "I'm prepared to keep the service to a minimum. For instance, I won't lead the service, and I won't give a sermon. That isn't important. But what is absolutely necessary is the *Kaddish* mourner's prayer and *Eil Malei Rahamim.*" (She knew full well what those prayers were.) And Ana gave her consent.[20]

With that, the service commenced. Rosen recalled,

> We then began carrying the coffin, and it was very heavy. The people carrying the coffin had such a hard time that they kept stopping. It is a Jewish custom to stop seven times, and Ana knew that. She said to someone: "*Tovarăşa* Ana says not to stop." And I said back: "Tell her they aren't stopping for religious reasons, but because the coffin is so heavy!"[21]

Rosen recalled that Pauker went over to him after the ceremony, excused herself, and respectfully tried to explain her behavior to him. Her mother was religious, she told Rosen, and she had no problem with having a religious ceremony for her; but her sister had been an atheist, and that is why she objected.[22]

Having acceded to Zalman's wishes, Pauker reportedly now asked him to come to visit her.[23] Although he consented, he did not leave for Romania until November 1949, precisely when Jewish emigration was at a standstill. His acquaintances' in Bucharest overall impression was that he had hardly come just to see his sister. As one rabbi told him soon after his arrival, he was very happy that Zalman had come to Romania "on such an important mission."[24] But Zalman persistently denied any such thing. After his arrest in 1953, he rather fancifully claimed that, before his departure, he received (through the Romanian embassy) a message from several unnamed RWP Central Committee members asking him to return with his family to Romania in protest against a recent attack on Pauker by Israeli Prime Minister David Ben-Gurion. He came, he said, only to explain to those members why he could not leave Israel. Naturally, his interrogators did not believe him.[25]

As she would later acknowledge, Pauker personally arranged Zalman's trip without the party leadership's approval.[26] An official of the Romanian consulate accompanied him to the Israeli port of Haifa, where he was permitted to board the SS *Transylvania* without a ticket. Arriving in Romania on November 20, he was met at the port of Constanţa by a civilian he did not know, given several thousand lei, and driven to the train station. As he approached Bucharest, a soldier from the militia of the Interior Ministry greeted him and took him straight to Pauker's residence.[27] Under interrogation, Zalman described what happened next:

> My sister met me in the hall of her house, and, after inquiring how my trip was, asked me: "Well, have you come home? Where you've lived all your life, and where your mother and sister are buried?" And "where there's a new way of life?" I replied that I didn't understand; there's going to be a new life there as well, that is, in Israel. She asked me why, if I'm aware of this new way of life, won't I live where she does. I asked her: Why don't the Jews have a right to a country and a life of their own just like any other people? She asked me, if I really have sympathy for Communism, why am I not a Communist? I told her that it's an important issue for me, about which I need to clear something up. Can I be a Communist and religious?—adding that I don't accept that religion hinders the class conflict in any way. I see religion as something superior, not as superstition, but as something above science, and that religion has a precept that Communism only strives for: "You should love your neighbor as you love yourself." The first of the Ten Commandments says: "I am God, your God who took you out of Egypt and out of slavery." Thus the first commandment is against slavery. You tell me that religion is a deception that blinds the masses, but the prophets said that a time will come when the people will turn the swords into ploughshares. I read in a newspaper in Israel what a Soviet scholar said about using atomic energy for peaceful purposes. What that Soviet scholar said was said two thousand years ago by the prophets.
> Ana did not agree with me, and she told me that you can't be both a Communist and religious.[28]

At their first meeting, Pauker insisted that Zalman remain in Romania and bring his family back from Israel.[29] But, he related, he insisted "that I would never decide to come back indefinitely to the RPR with my family, because I'm determined to live in Israel. . . . In the days that followed . . . , I talked constantly with Ana Pauker, with her trying to convince me to come back and resettle in the RPR, and my affirming that I will not renounce Israel."[30] Pauker also had both Ana Toma and Liuba Chișinevschi try to convince her brother, to no avail.[31] At one point, Vasile Luca asked Pauker "if her brother was going to stay in the country, and she answered that he was returning to Palestine. I then told Ana," Luca recounted, "that it isn't good to have relatives in capitalist countries, and asked why doesn't she influence her brother to remain in the country. She replied that she can't influence him."[32]

The first few months, Zalman stayed at Pauker's residence, where he met many of her colleagues in the party leadership.[33] "Zalman's presence was very fascinating for us," Pauker's daughter, Marie, recalled, "because he was from another world."[34]

"It was always a problem with Zalman," Tatiana added, "because he was very religious. It was always difficult to prepare food for him. He always had to eat canned sardines because he wouldn't eat nonkosher food. He always kept his head covered. . . . When he came home he took off his hat and put on his *kippah* when he sat at the table."[35]

"He didn't participate very much in the family life," continued Marie. "He was much more isolated. He would come for dinner and then he would go back to his room or to town. . . . In the beginning we didn't like him very much, but later we discovered that he was a very special person, very cultivated, and very educated."[36] Soon Pauker's children began with amusement, if not affection, to call him "Uncle Sam."[37]

Several weeks after his arrival, Zalman came home one evening to find his wife, Dina, and daughter, Leia, waiting for him. It was a total surprise, he later asserted, for Pauker had brought them to Romania without his knowledge.[38] After living at Pauker's house for two months, Zalman's family were "moved into a specially established house, [with] good material conditions," in the hope of convincing them to remain in the country.[39] Now Zalman informed Pauker he had decided to remain in Romania one year, though he would not allow his wife and daughter to stay. (They returned to Israel in the summer of 1950.)[40] In one of their talks, Pauker suggested that he would not receive an exit visa when the year was over, and that is precisely what happened.[41] At the end of 1950, he began to approach her about returning to Israel, but he got nowhere with her.[42] Perhaps, with talk of war continually on the increase and her conflict with Dej escalating over collectivization and other matters, she feared his leaving would be used against her; or perhaps, with her prognosis of surviving her cancer still uncertain, her reasons for detaining him were far more personal. Whatever the case, she refused to even consider his leaving through most of 1951.[43]

Consequently, Rabinsohn revealed that

[w]hen, in April 1951, I got a telegram from Israel that my father is ill, Ana again told me I couldn't leave. Some time later, I received a letter that my daughter is sick, but once again Ana would not help me leave. She was busy, and we weren't seeing each other, especially now that we weren't living together. So I then wrote a letter to Ana, to which I attached a request to "the ministers to whom approval of my leaving depends." . . . I wrote Ana that, with the sending of this letter, I was hereby declaring a hunger strike until I received a positive answer.[44]

He was soon forced to halt the hunger strike, however, when it aggravated an ulcer, requiring emergency surgery only two days later. Although Pauker personally took him to the hospital, she would see less and less of him during this period. Still, she apparently relented several months later. After getting no answer during the summer (while Pauker was mostly away on vacation), in mid-October Zalman was finally promised permission to leave in three months (January 1952). In the interim, he received word that his daughter's condition (a nervous disorder) had continued to deteriorate, and he decided she should be treated in Bucharest. Tragically, therefore, he postponed his departure, and his wife and daughter returned to Romania.[45] When Ana Pauker fell five months later, all three of them found themselves trapped in the country. After the police arrested Zalman in February 1953, his daughter reportedly attempted suicide by throwing herself out of a second-story window.[46]

As influential as Pauker apparently was in pressuring Zalman to stay in Romania, she was by no means alone. Shlomo Leibovici, a former functionary of the Israeli Foreign Ministry and personal friend of Zalman Rabinsohn, revealed that "someone quite senior in the Israeli government" approached Zalman shortly before he left for Romania and asked him to intervene with his sister on Jewish emigration.[47] Likewise, Dina Rabinsohn was summoned to the Israeli Foreign Ministry just before she left and told that her husband should use his status as Pauker's brother to personally work on the emigration problem.[48] In March 1950, moreover, only days before the Romanian regime opened the floodgates to mass aliya, the Israeli embassy in Bucharest asked Zalman to intervene with Pauker on expanding the criteria for Jewish emigrants (further proving it was totally unaware of the impending breakthrough).[49] Though he may have briefly appeared superfluous, with open emigration in the spring of 1950, the embassy persistently pressured him to stay in the country when the tide again turned that summer.[50] With the renewed restrictions on Jewish emigration and the arrest of the Romanian Zionist movement's leaders soon after, the Israelis relied increasingly on Zalman—dubbed "the empress's brother" by David Ben-Gurion[51]—as a go-between to press Ana Pauker on Jewish and Zionist issues.

Rabinsohn's actions in Romania bear this out. From the outset, he "used every opportunity and every occasion" to intervene with his sister, and appealed to her "countless times . . . for allowing free emigration . . . , particularly for Zionist leaders."[52] Beginning in December 1949, he exhorted her to let Zionists, especially religious Zionists, emigrate, arguing that religious Jews and Zionists should be allowed to leave since they were not well-regarded in Romania.[53] That month he asked her to talk to the Soviets about aliya when she left for Moscow to celebrate Stalin's seventieth birthday;[54] he told her of meeting many Jews on a trip to Moldavia who complained of their difficulties in applying to emigrate;[55] and he spoke to her on behalf of family members and acquaintances, as well as former students from her Hebrew-teaching days, who wanted to leave.[56] He also intervened on other issues such as supplying Jewish prisoners with matzo over Passover, allowing a group of Transylvanian Jews to start their own collective farm, or creating Jewish community centers.[57] Though he personally warned the Israeli embassy that its government's criticism of the RWP was angering Romania's leaders and harming the Zionists and emigration—a warning based on information from Ana Pauker[58]—Zalman generally kept a low profile and avoided Zionist leaders throughout the first half of 1950. He did meet "one or two Zionists" during that period, a Romanian Zionist related, "but he had such a bizarre attitude that people would not try to meet with him anymore."[59] "Nobody knew, and he didn't tell anybody, why he came, how long he was staying, or what he was doing," a prominent rabbi added. "If someone asked him, he wouldn't answer."[60] But that summer his reticence would suddenly end.

The turning point seemingly was July 10, 1950, when the regime began arresting the former leaders of the Romanian Zionist movement.[61] From then on, Zalman willingly accepted direct appeals for his intervention and actively sought the Zionists' release.[62] Immediately after the arrests, Rabbi Yitzchak Friedman and the prominent Zionist A. L. Zissu asked him to intervene. When he told them Ana Pauker was out of the country, they asked him to approach Iosif Chişinevschi, whom he had met on several occasions at Pauker's residence. He was granted an audience with Chişinevschi the following day:

> Receiving me, [Chişinevschi] said that, if I had a personal problem, he'd be
> ready to help. I then told him that Zionists had been arrested despite the
> fact that they're no longer active, and it's clear that they're being persecuted
> simply for their ideas, at a time when . . . [Andrei] Gromyko supported the
> creation of the State of Israel. I took a Zionist brochure out of my pocket,
> which I personally had for some time (it was mine), and I began to read a pas-
> sage from Gromyko's speech at the U.N. Iosif Chişinevschi abruptly inter-
> rupted me, being very angry, and asked me: "And why are you coming to me
> with this? I am an internationalist, and the fate of the Arabs pains me. Anti-
> Semitism no longer exists here in the RPR, and the proof of that is that Jews
> are even ministers here. And besides, if there is evidence of espionage, it's a
> government matter. How dare you come to me." I answered: "I'm also a
> Zionist, and I should be arrested as well."[63]

That evening, he reported the details of the meeting to Zissu. The situation was very serious, he warned him, and warranted the Israeli government's immediate intervention.[64] Zalman instructed Dina, who was
leaving for Israel, to communicate the same message to Israeli Foreign
Minister Moshe Sharett.[65]

When Pauker returned to Bucharest in August, Zalman asked her to
inquire into the condition of the imprisoned Zionists and, based on her
information, reported that they were healthy and had adequate clothing
and medicine.[66] He also warned her that their arrest had dangerous implications for Romanian Jewry, for their prosecution as spies would provoke an anti-Semitic backlash in the country. "I'm a Zionist, too," he
clamored. "They aren't any more guilty than I am, and I'm no cleaner
than they are."[67] Pauker responded that "the guilty Zionists would be
punished. . . . [T]hey weren't being arrested for their ideas or for their
activities in the past," she insisted, "but for offenses committed after the
Zionist organizations had dissolved themselves."[68] But Zalman continued to push:

> I talked with Ana about the arrested Zionists on other occasions as well, try-
> ing to win her over and create goodwill for them. I told her that I'd swear on
> the memory of our mother and our brother whom Ana loved very much, and
> that I'd swear on the lives of her and my children, for the arrested Zionists.
> She told me to leave her children out of it. She started to leave, but I blocked
> her way. She then [again] said to me that the guilty ones will be put on trial.[69]

Zalman apparently took this to mean, or Pauker later elaborated to suggest, that only those truly guilty would be prosecuted, for he proceeded

to assure his contacts "that there was no chance that a trial would be held on imaginary facts" and even predicted that no trial would take place.[70]

In mid-August 1950, Zalman began meeting Romanian Zionist Marcu Cohin every week at Rabbi Friedman's residence. He had known Cohin since the early 1920s, and apparently trusted him the most among his Zionist contacts. The meetings with Cohin, who was then closely connected to the Israeli embassy, would be a centerpiece in the case against Rabinsohn—though exactly what Zalman imparted to Cohin is unclear, as both were undoubtedly constrained during their prison interrogations. What seems certain, however, is that, at Cohin's prodding, Zalman "insistently intervened" with Pauker and Georgescu against convening a trial of the arrested Zionists and for allowing emigration. He even suggested arguments to use before the party leadership—that an anti-Zionist trial would escalate anti-Semitism in Romania, as non-Jewish Romanians would equate the Zionist defendants with all Jews, and that restricting Jewish emigration was causing discontent in Israel and increasing international strife.[71] Further, he began offering specific proposals to end the crisis.

Thus, in January 1951, Zalman proposed allowing three or four rabbis to emigrate. They would then form a delegation to the United States and ask affluent Jews to lobby the American government to permit Israel to proclaim its neutrality. This presumably would lead to improved relations with the RPR and the Zionists' release.[72] About that time, learning that the United States had prevented Switzerland from selling imported American goods to the Soviet bloc, he proposed to Pauker that Marcu Cohin be allowed to emigrate to Israel. There, he would arrange with the Israeli government and American Jews to send a quantity of badly needed American goods to Romania through Israel in exchange for the arrested Zionists' release and permission to emigrate. When Pauker refused (Cohin was in fact arrested in May 1951),[73] Zalman suggested to Cohin that Israel take the first step and send an initial transport as a goodwill gesture before asking for anything in return.[74] In March 1951, Rabinsohn again proposed funneling banned American goods to Romania through Israel.[75] Israeli ambassador Ehud Avriel was informed of the plan, as well as of Pauker's refusal.[76]

Still, as Zalman later affirmed, Pauker never prevented him from requesting assistance for Zionism.[77] Though she occasionally agreed to Zalman's appeals (as in January 1950, when she intervened to assure the transfer of a prominent rabbi's remains to Israel), she usually made no promises and at times categorically refused to intervene.[78] Nevertheless, Zalman asserted, he "always saw" that what he asked for was subsequently granted.[79] For instance, when he asked Pauker to allow Israel Leivetman, the former secretary of Poalei Mizrachi, to emigrate, she refused, but Leivetman soon received a visa.[80] Or when he asked that Rabbi Friedman be given an exit visa, she said nothing, but Friedman was soon allowed to leave.[81] Or when he told her that Zionist Kiva Orenstein was sick in prison and needed streptomycin, she did not respond, but Orenstein promptly received the medicine.[82] And though she repeatedly clashed with Zalman over the arrested Zionists, she ultimately did as he requested: "As long as she was part of the government," Zalman concluded, "[Ana Pauker] prevented the trial of the Zionists from taking place. And she helped others to leave the country."[83]

Although additional arrests took place in May and September 1951 and continued unabated throughout the winter of 1951–1952, and though Georgescu revealed to Zalman in November 1951 that the Zionists would soon be tried, the trial never materialized.[84] As Cohin later testified under interrogation, Zalman informed him that Pauker and her allies had convinced a majority of the Politburo to oppose the trial, in defiance of a faction led by Chişinevschi. Pauker apparently did so, moreover, with Zalman's argument that a trial would harm all Jews, universally tainting them with espionage.[85]

With Pauker out of the picture, the situation would change dramatically. In the summer of 1953 and the spring of 1954, many imprisoned Zionists were tried, convicted of being "imperialist agents," and sentenced to lengthy prison terms. "Secret trials reached such numbers," one observer remarked, "as to constitute a mass terror. . . . The roster [of the accused] reads like a who's who in Romanian Jewry."[86] Hence, their prosecution took place not during the anti-Semitic madness of Stalin's last months but during Soviet politics' post-Stalin thaw.[87] As with the Patraşcanu case, Dej and Chişinevschi apparently staged these trials independent of the new Soviet leaders, who had restored fairly normal relations with Israel immediately after Stalin's death.[88] Also as with the Patraşcanu case, no such trials took place as long as Pauker remained in power, despite apparent Soviet pressure to convene them. The police interrogators, therefore, apparently were not at all facetious when they told their Zionist prisoners after Pauker's purge, "You don't have Aunt Ana to protect you anymore."[89]

Hence, as Zalman Rabinsohn himself acknowledged, he apparently was not responsible for Pauker's favoring the Zionists and Jewish emigration, for she had formulated those positions well before he returned to Romania.[90] Nonetheless he probably influenced her decision to block an anti-Zionist show trial. For her part, Pauker at the very least gave her brother information on the imprisoned Zionists' condition. As Rabbi Yitzchak Friedman subsequently confirmed to an Israeli journalist, "[T]he people concerned were grateful to her for securing the information she got, which Rabinsohn relayed each day to [him]."[91] How much more she confided in her brother we do not yet know, for the only evidence now available on the matter is questionable prison interrogations. But if, as Cohin claimed, Rabinsohn did in fact speak to him about the problems emigration posed for the Romanian economy or about the Soviet position on Jewish emigration or about the party leadership's divergencies over collectivization, Rabinsohn almost certainly got that information from his sister.[92] True or not, this deduction would become crucial in the planned prosecution of Ana Pauker.

CHAPTER EIGHT

The Purge

Upon patching things up with Stalin at the beginning of 1949, Gheorghiu-Dej emerged as the RWP leadership's predominant force. The verification campaign of 1948–1950 vastly strengthened his position, for the policy of increasing worker representation among party members "made it possible for Dej to build up his personal power base, to place his own men in key positions, and step by step gain control over the whole apparatus." [1] This was doubly true with the appointment to the Secretariat of Alexandru Moghioroş, who assumed Pauker's role of overseeing organizational matters inside the party and was made responsible for verifying the cadres. [2] Dej therefore solidified his standing through the classic Stalinist technique of assuring social mobility to new party members who owed their rise solely to him, while gradually eroding the position of the party's old guard—many, if not most, of whom were inclined to support Ana Pauker. [3]

Hence, Gheorghiu-Dej promptly set out to rid himself of the Pauker faction. Stalin's remark to Dej in February 1947 that he should remove Pauker if she ever hindered him was probably a ruse or an empty gesture, particularly once the conflict with Tito started. But Pauker's subsequent positions gave Dej the ammunition he needed for her ouster—though the matter by no means remained a simple policy dispute: "she needed," he later related, "to be completely unmasked, so it would be clear for all the CC members, because she had a lot of them fooled." [4] Whether Stalin instructed Dej to "unmask" Pauker in ways other than exposing her "deviationist" policies, many of which were undoubtedly popular among the party cadres, or whether Dej felt it necessary to do so to transform Stalin's earlier insinuations into outright support is not known. Whatever the reason, beginning in 1949, Dej actively sought "evidence" that would compromise Pauker and her allies as party enemies, and Pauker's cancer made doing so much easier. As her family would later recall, Pauker was "in very bad physical and psychological condition" when she returned to her duties in late 1950, and "was completely handicapped by the psychological shock of the cancer. She had lost her strength to fight." [5] Pauker herself asserted, "I was preoccupied with the fact that I was soon going to die, that I didn't have much time." [6] In such a state, Pauker could not counter Dej's immediate moves to isolate her in the leadership, let alone block any attempts to discredit her. [7]

Pauker's purge was strategically structured to begin with an attack on Vasile Luca, compromising both Pauker and Georgescu through their close association with him. Focusing on Luca, despite Pauker's having initiated many of the transgressions of which he stood accused, was quite logical. Whereas many in the party hierarchy genuinely loved and idolized Pauker, they widely disliked Luca, though esteeming him for certain attributes. [8] Suffering from a pronounced nervous condition that apparently stemmed from advanced syphilis, [9] Luca was noted for an abusive temper that led to many a conflict within the party and government, and his ouster was, as one colleague put it, "a relief to everybody." [10] Further, while Pauker was highly disciplined and forever measured when debating policy issues, Luca was quite the opposite and was easily provoked to say things that could later be used against him. Dej reportedly made a practice of goading him to make regrettable statements. [11] Most significantly, Luca openly opposed certain policies that favored the Soviets. Indeed, Radu Mănescu, the deputy chief of the March 1952 party commission investigating Luca's Finance Ministry, was left with the firm impression upon concluding the inquiry *"that Luca had quite anti-Soviet ideas and always contradicted the Soviet positions."* [12] Luca acknowledged, for instance, that he opposed fulfilling Romania's reparation commitments to the Soviets, which led to a heated conflict between himself and Gheorghiu-Dej [13]—a conflict that apparently also centered on a controversy surrounding CASBI.

An acronym for *Casa de administrare și supraveghere a bunurilor inamice* (the "government body dealing with enemy-owned properties"), CASBI came into being immediately after the September 1944 armistice convention, which mandated Romania's handing over all German and Italian properties to Soviet authorities.[14] An enormous number of such properties were taken over, inventoried, and administered by CASBI staff: as Luca revealed in January 1946, most of the country's factories had "entered into CASBI" and consequently had "been left almost abandoned."[15] By mid-1948 all clearly defined enemy property had long been relinquished to the Soviet Union, yet CASBI officials continued to search deeper for hidden properties, increasing resentment among Romanians.[16] Critical of this state of affairs, Luca pressed to disband CASBI: "Complaining that it was giving everything to the Russians," he instructed his assistants to replace CASBI with another commission in the Finance Ministry.[17] This new body, the Commission to Liquidate CASBI, settled all outstanding cases within a year, and CASBI was formally dissolved in the spring of 1950.[18] Assuring a subordinate that the Secretariat had sanctioned the move, Luca specifically cited Pauker's support[19]—which she acknowledged herself soon after her purge.[20] Numerous officials, reportedly affiliated with Dej, opposed curtailing CASBI,[21] and the party's Economic Control Commission began an immediate inquiry of all those working on the problem in the Finance Ministry. Accused of anti-Soviet activity, Luca's associates were investigated over several months before the matter was suddenly dropped in fall or winter 1950.[22] A year and a half later the charges reappeared with a vengeance.[23]

At the time of CASBI's dissolution, the Central Committee was also extensively investigating Luca's deputy, Alexandru Iacob. A party member since 1931, and part of the underground RCP leadership in Cluj during the war,[24] Iacob fell under intense suspicion after a police informer betrayed the leadership to the Hungarian DEF in 1941; he was the only one not arrested. Thus, the party verification committee refused him as a party member in 1948.[25] Miron Constantinescu denounced him as a "provocateur" at the Council of Ministers, and Gheorghiu-Dej declared him suspect.[26] But Luca, who had repeatedly received anonymous letters accusing Iacob and other associates of spying, persistently defended him.[27] Supporting Luca was Ana Pauker, who reportedly had appointed Iacob party secretary of Cluj in 1945 despite the suspicions against him and had demurred from the incessant demands for his removal from the Finance Ministry.[28] In 1949, party cadres chief Iosif Ranghet began to investigate Iacob.[29] When Ranghet visited László Rajk in his jail cell in September, Iacob was no doubt on his list of suspects, along with the

Spaniards. The case was next handed over to Ioan Vinţe of the party Control Commission and then to Victor Vezendean, deputy chief of the Foreign Section of the Central Committee (which was under Iosif Chişinevschi). After an exhaustive search, Vezendean reported that he "could find not one person who would tell me that Iacob was a pro-vocateur." In July 1950 Gheorghiu-Dej and Chişinevschi dispatched Vezendean to Budapest to thoroughly check the DEF files.[30] When Vezendean returned to Romania, a demonstrably eager Moghioroş and Ceauşescu received him. "When I walked in," he related, "Moghioroş said, 'Victor, we've been waiting for you like we were waiting for God!'"[31] He had found nothing in Budapest, however, and they gave the case to another functionary, Ladislau Adi Laci.[32] Ultimately the inquiry landed in the lap of Alexandru Keleti, the head of the Securitate in Cluj. Alexandru Drăghici summoned Keleti to Central Committee headquar-ters in Bucharest and informed him "that he was to be responsible, and his life depended on it, to bring out Alexandru Iacob as a spy, that he was in the service of the Hungarians."[33] Keleti apparently did not dis-appoint them.[34]

The case against Iacob was important in undermining Luca and, by extension, Ana Pauker. Nevertheless, the key to Pauker's downfall evi-dently was the anti-Semitic campaign rapidly escalating throughout the bloc. The open anti-Semitism in the USSR from 1948 on quickly spilled into the Soviet satellites. Throughout the bloc the offensive against "bour-geois nationalism," imposed by the Kremlin in response to Tito's defi-ance, "was accompanied by an official anti-Jewish, anti-Zionist and anti-Israel campaign."[35] By 1951, however, Soviet-imposed purges shifted from eradicating homegrown "Titoists" to diverting nationalist senti-ment against Jews and thus attaining a modicum of support for the Communist regimes.[36] That January, Stalin convened the bloc countries' defense ministers and "announced that the Americans must be swept out of Europe before their increasing military and political power could be consolidated."[37] The satellites, Stalin demanded, must now con-tribute more to the Soviets' defense and must immediately militarize their economies.[38] Hence, Hilary Minc, a member of the Polish Polit-buro, told a subordinate that "we have to be prepared for the worst; a world war can break out within a year, at most in two years time; we're re-programming our economy for arms."[39] And hence, Miron Constan-tinescu informed the Council of Ministers that the proportions of heavy and light industry in Romania were to be further altered in favor of the former, "because of the intervention of the problems of defense."[40] Not surprisingly, then, as the *Manchester Guardian* reported, Romania's "financial and economic position . . . reached the edge of disaster [in 1951]. Discontent is rife and growing. [In that] year, for the first time, open strikes broke out in industrial centers."[41] Ana Pauker's purge, therefore, provided a badly needed scapegoat at a time of mounting deprivation and economic crisis.

Signs of "anti-Zionism" in the case being constructed against both Pauker and Luca emerged as early as 1949 and 1950, when arrested Romanian Zionists were pressured to implicate them. Their interrogators drilled them about Pauker's meetings with Mordechai Namir in July 1948 (What did Ana Pauker discuss with Namir? What bribe did she get from him?), and repeatedly questioned them about Luca's trip to Palestine in 1947.[42] In addition, Luca was branded a Zionist via his Jewish wife, Elisabeta Luca (née Birnbaum), a member of the old guard, a veteran of the Spanish Civil War, and for a time Pauker's wartime secretary in Moscow.[43] In the summer of 1949, Elisabeta Luca's first husband, Avram Weissman, was arrested in the Soviet Moldavian city of Cernăuți and interrogated about her past. Depicting her as a "fervent Zionist" throughout the 1930s, Weissman maintained that Elisabeta engaged in "Zionist propaganda" upon returning from Palestine with Vasile Luca in 1947, telling those around her "that all Jews should leave for their homeland Israel." What was more, added Weissman, "Vasile Luca expressed the same opinion."[44] At one point, Pauker revealed, Dej told her of suspicions against Luca in connection with his Palestine visit but dropped the matter when she insisted on telling Luca.[45]

Dej also began to gather evidence against Pauker's relatives for alleged espionage, which would be crucial to the charges against her. Interrogating French Press Agency reporter Israel Pinhas in July 1950, the Securitate identified an espionage "network" linked to Emil Pauker, Marcel Pauker's uncle, who relayed to Pinhas information he received "directly from the house of Ana Pauker."[46] The "secrets" Pinhas obtained were mundane details of Ana Pauker's whereabouts, such as news that she was to travel to Sofia to attend Georgi Dimitrov's funeral or that she had spent the weekend in the resort town of Sinaia or that she returned after spending several days at the Danube Conference in Belgrade.[47] When the Securitate informed Pauker and Georgescu of Pinhas's revelations, Georgescu, "under Ana's influence, . . . sought to kill the whole affair, saying to [Gheorghe Pintilie]: 'What's the big deal you discovered, that it was said that Ana left for Moscow?' And on Ana's part, there wasn't the slightest concern." [48] The issue nonetheless reemerged with full force during the purge. Emil Pauker was arrested in 1953 and charged with espionage, as was Ana Pauker's brother, Zalman Rabinsohn—accused of spying for Israel.

This scenario was tailor-made to fit Stalin's increasingly delusional suspicions of Jewish women. As Arkady Vaksberg recently observed, by this time Stalin seemed obsessed with the notion that Western imperialism "used international Zionism and the Jewish wives of major Soviet figures" to discover secrets of his personal life—specifically, his wife's suicide, the details of which her close women friends knew well, particularly Molotov's wife, Polina Zhemchuzhina, who was arrested in January 1949. Accordingly:

> Bronislava Solomonovna Poskrebysheva, the wife of . . . [Stalin's] private secretary, was arrested. So was Esfir Khruleva (née Gorelik), the wife of Army General Andrei Khrulek, who commanded the rear in the war and played a significant role in Russia's victory. They arrested . . . Revekka Levina, corresponding member of the Academy of Sciences, a famous economist. The list goes on. Each one of them . . . was accused of the same thing—informing the Zionists, and through them the American intelligence services, about the personal life of the unnamed head of the Soviet government. [49]

Not only Pauker's Jewishness, therefore, but also her gender predisposed Stalin to think the worst of her. [50]

Indeed, one charge during Pauker's purge was that she had created "a petit-bourgeois, conciliatory atmosphere at the Foreign Ministry, which was particularly connected to the groups of women there." [51] Having filled many of the leading posts in the ministry with women, Pauker was now vulnerable for having fostered what was widely regarded as the "Women's Foreign Ministry" in Romania.

Hence, Dej could choose from a panoply of issues—both genuine and invented—when he and Iosif Chişinevschi met with Stalin in late August 1951 and won approval to purge the Pauker faction. [52] Dej reported to the Politburo that his discussion with Stalin dealt solely with the country's economic crisis and conveyed Stalin's "advice" on the matter: Stalin defined "the principal source of our mistakes," Dej related, "as '*Krestianskaia politika*,' '*Nemarxistikaia politika*,' an assessment that our policies are peasantist, non-Marxist policies." [53] The key issue, Stalin apparently observed, was trade with the peasantry. [54]

The party's "peasantist policies," Dej emphasized, began with the Politburo debates following the first Currency Reform in 1947, when "some among us" had railed against the proposed price ratios for industrial and agricultural products, and when, soon after, they pushed through a tax cut for industrial goods sent to the countryside.[55] From that point, agricultural prices soared, effectively tripling from 1947 to 1951.[56] Luca persistently attributed this to a shortage of goods for the peasantry, a consequence of the party's overemphasizing heavy industry. Reducing the price of industrial goods that were in high demand and short supply, Luca maintained, "enabled the peasantry to buy up everything that appeared in the cooperatives and state stores. When goods arrived at the cooperatives, they disappeared immediately," having been scooped up by those working there or in the Popular Councils. With no other goods available, the peasant had no incentive to lower the price of his produce; nor did he have "the slightest interest to bring his produce to market or to produce more."[57] Even after Luca raised the prices of industrial products earmarked for the peasantry in 1950 the problem remained.[58] As long as there was a shortage of goods to buy, he concluded, the peasants would continue to sit on their produce.[59] Providing more consumer goods was impossible, however, given the Soviet-imposed increase in emphasis on military expenditures.

Stalin's solution, offered to Gheorghiu-Dej during their meeting, was a second Currency Reform, which amounted to nothing less than the confiscation of the peasants' savings.[60] He promptly dispatched a group of special advisers to Bucharest to help plan it and carry it out.[61] Gheorghiu-Dej had in fact proposed such a solution in the winter of 1950–1951.[62] At the beginning of February 1951, the party leadership resolved that Pauker should discuss the issue with Stalin during a planned trip to Moscow, but as she later admitted, she avoided doing so.[63] This was probably because Pauker most consistently promoted the "peasantist, non-Marxist policies" to which Stalin had pointed. As Luca would later testify, she firmly opposed his efforts to raise taxes on the peasantry, asserting in numerous discussions in 1948 and 1949 "that the peasantry is oppressed by taxes," and insisting on levying the smallest possible tax on them. When Luca persisted, she pushed through a resolution criticizing him for "robbing the peasantry" and forced him to annul all fines for nonpayment of taxes, rescind all obligatory sanctions, and accept tax payments in intervals over an extended time.[64] Likewise, Pauker "was the initiator—under the pretext that we have to encourage the peasantry to harvest industrial produce—of the raising of [agricultural] prices, and our giving [them] greater quantities of industrial goods and cotton."[65]

Yet Luca was first to be purged for the peasantist deviation. He seems to have brought it on himself, when soon after the Soviet advisers' arrival, he dared to openly oppose Stalin's Currency Reform—claiming it did not deal with the root of the problem, the shortage of consumer goods.[66] Dej quickly criticized him for this within the party leadership, and the Soviet advisers shunned him while writing a January 28, 1952, report on the economy and the implementation of the Currency Reform.[67] Instead, the advisers worked closely with Miron Constantinescu, who presented the completed report to the Politburo on February 19. It constituted an attack on Luca's associates in the Finance Ministry and the National Bank and accused them of enemy activity and sabotage. Despite the Soviets' clear involvement, Pauker tried to downplay the report and opposed its reading at the meeting.[68] The Politburo quickly overruled her, however, and embarked on a weeklong debate on the matter.[69] At the outset Dej offered reassurance that "[w]e're not crazy enough to lump Luca together" with his subordinates. But by the end of the week, Luca had been summarily dismissed from the Finance Ministry. When Moghioroş called for his ouster and others began to express approval, Luca grasped his chest and fainted.[70] He was taken home in an ambulance and watched by a doctor the entire night.[71]

On February 29, the report was presented at a plenary of the Central Committee, for the first time openly blaming Luca for the peasantist, right deviation.[72] Pauker formally criticized Luca at the meeting, but during a break in the proceedings, she promised, "I'm not going to let them throw you out." [73] Attempting to limit his punishment to a party sanction and dismissal as Finance Minister, she urged retaining him in the party leadership—not only because she shared many of his positions, but in part because she believed his ouster had long been surreptitiously sought and in part because she knew, given their common thinking, "that Luca's unmasking would itself lead to my unmasking." [74] Hence, she "did everything that was possible" to avoid such a "catastrophe," worrying to Dej that Luca would kill himself and asserting his removal would cause trouble in Transylvania.[75] She admonished the Politburo that "[w]e shouldn't wake up and find that we, too, discovered an enemy among us, as was the case in Czechoslovakia and Hungary." [76] And she tried—unsuccessfully—to obtain Soviet ambassador Kavtaradze's assistance, apparently arguing that the measures against Luca went too far.[77]

One outcome of the CC plenary was a special commission to investigate the Finance Ministry and National Bank.[78] Another was a

"Closed Letter" to every party member disclosing the details of Luca's dismissal.[79] Pauker and Georgescu both objected to the letter, which they believed unfairly blamed Luca for decisions the entire leadership had made. Meeting Georgescu in her office, Pauker affirmed that such severe criticism would surely lead to Luca's expulsion from the Central Committee, and they agreed to express their objections to the Politburo.[80] When the Politburo met later that day (March 13), Georgescu—with Pauker's backing—criticized the Closed Letter. As a result, both Georgescu and Pauker were attacked for the first time.[81]

While Pauker and Georgescu conferred in her office, Luca, "who not for a moment recognized his mistakes, and disagreed with the criticism leveled against him," entered "in a state of panic, declaring that the Closed Letter meant his destruction, and how was he to go on living?" The two pledged to support him and suggested he personally appeal to Gheorghiu-Dej.[82] At the following plenary, all three were denounced for this "fractionalist" rendezvous in Pauker's office.[83] The irony of their being assailed for "fractionalism" by the very people who had secretly plotted their ouster was perhaps too ludicrous to have gone unnoticed, but it comprised a key element in the purge.

Indeed, by the time of the March 13 meeting, the formal accusation against Pauker, Luca, and Georgescu had already been written. At the end of February or the beginning of March, a group of Russian-speaking party activists were held in seclusion for four days and nights in Moghioroş's office, where they were handed the resolution of the May 27–29 CC Plenary to translate into Russian, one page at a time.[84] The document was probably drafted by Constantinescu and Chişinev-schi, in close collaboration with a number of Soviet officials, particularly Mark Borisovich Mitin, then editor in chief of the Cominform journal, *For a Lasting Peace, for a People's Democracy,* and a close adviser to Gheorghiu-Dej.[85] The documents were then typed at Chişinevschi's Foreign Section of the Central Committee and sent directly to MGB agent Nikolai Shutov at the Soviet embassy.[86] Shutov, in turn, regularly transmitted the Kremlin's directives to Chişinevschi.[87]

Soviet pressure in the case was evident throughout this period. "The advisers had a fit," for instance, when it was proposed at one point that Aurel Vijoli, the head of the National Bank, be allowed to present his side of the story to the Politburo, and they insisted "that he had no business being there." [88] Together with Constantinescu, the advisers, who "had sabers in their teeth for Vijoli," then handed Pauker incriminating material that she forwarded to Georgescu—material that included a list

with Vijoli's and other economists' names on it.[89] Constantinescu revealed that prior to the plenary the Soviets had proposed sending the
Closed Letter to party members.[90] And Moghioroş informed the commission created at the plenary to investigate Luca and his associates that
the advisers were convinced of the guilt of all those under inquiry.[91]
Once the case was transferred to the Interior Ministry, the Soviets took
complete control. "The entire plan of the investigation, including the
questions, were translated into Russian, and their execution was followed by the advisers. The questions put at the beginning of the investigation . . . were formulated by them."[92]

Further pressure came from Stalin personally. In April, Dej flew to
Moscow with Constantinescu, Chişinevschi, and Gheorghe Apostol,
and, as he later recalled, was received by an angry Stalin:

> When I reported there what we had done and what difficulties we had, and
> that we removed V. Luca from his position as Finance Minister, and that
> there was a commission that was investigating, things did not end there. . . .
> It was then that, laughing, they, I don't remember who among them, said:
> "Look, they threw out Luca from his post as Finance Minister but left him
> in the Politburo." And they asked us whether it was more important to be Fi-
> nance Minister than it was to be a member of the Politburo. They called me
> a conciliator, saying that I defended Ana Pauker. . . . Then Stalin began:
> "What kind of proletarian are you?" Molotov started up that I had velvety
> hands, that I was a refined, delicate man. They asked us whether we knew
> whom Luca met with when he went hunting. . . . "You hear that?" [Stalin] said.
> "They're bringing him into line over there. He in fact committed treason, he
> deserted, instead of staying and working as Finance Minister." Afterwards I
> told him: "Comrade Stalin, we will examine everything, we have a commis-
> sion." And he attacked me: "What are you going to examine? Of course we
> will examine everything. We have to know everything, we have to examine
> everything well, to establish what their guilt consists of."[93]

According to Apostol, Dej and the others were awakened at 2:00 A.M.
and summoned to eat dinner with Stalin. They found Molotov, Beria,
and Anastas Mikoyan at the table. At a certain moment, "Stalin asked
Dej: 'Dej, how many times did I tell you to get rid of Ana Pauker, and
you didn't understand me?' Dej didn't answer. 'If I were in your place, I
would have shot her in the head a long time ago. . . . I was convinced
that only proletarian blood flowed through your veins, but [I now see
that] it's petit-bourgeois blood.'" At that point, continued Apostol,
Miron Constantinescu imprudently offered, "Comrade Stalin, Comrade
Dej is somewhat sentimental." Back at the hotel, Dej rewarded Constantinescu's faux pas: "Miroane," he told him, "you're assigned to

shoot Ana Pauker in the head." Constantinescu "started to cry," Apostol related. "And he cried all the way from Moscow to Bucharest." [94]

As Pauker would later tell it, both she and Georgescu became panic-stricken when the criticism of Luca's handling of the Currency Reform began,[95] and were "terrified" upon discovering the severity of the Closed Letter.[96] But she calmed down when Luca was allowed to remain in the party leadership pending the commission's findings, and she chose, in effect, to ignore the developments unfolding around her.[97] Once she noticed Dej and Constantinescu writing materials unknown to her, and she asked Leonte Răutu what they were doing.[98] Another time, she discovered that Dej and Chişinevschi had secretly left for Moscow and had ordered her deputy, Ana Toma, to arrange the trip without Pauker's knowing.[99] Yet another time, an unnamed colleague informed Pauker that Vasile Vaida had begun making declarations against her and warned, "You're standing at the edge of the knife. I heard that they're going to accuse you of a Right-wing Deviation. . . . Be aware!" Pauker refused to believe it. "[I]n my arrogance," she recalled, "I said: 'But why would they accuse me? For what?'"[100] Evidently, she preferred to believe several Soviet officials' pledges sometime in May that they knew her far too well to believe she was in any way guilty.[101]

Likewise, Georgescu, who had resisted an appeal from Dej to abandon Pauker,[102] first realized his precarious situation when he began to be avoided "even on matters of the Interior Ministry" after the March 13 meeting. "For example, when the matter of arresting Vijoli and the others was raised, I wasn't called, and Pintilie was. And he was given a list of people to arrest. Thus, from March on I was pushed aside."[103] But he, too, apparently began to relax as things appeared to normalize not long after. He later wrote in his personal notes, "I considered everything to have been resolved after the March 13 meeting."[104]

When the commission presented its report to the Politburo on May 26, Luca declared the findings "make me out to be a counter-revolutionary. I'll be arrested, tried, and shot!"[105] Georgescu's notes concisely describe his own and Pauker's reactions: "The surprise of the accusations."[106] The Politburo branded them "conciliators" of Luca, accused them of "right-wing deviations" of their own, and harshly attacked them in an almost moblike atmosphere. Now Dej even intimated the espionage charge against Pauker:

GHEORGHIU-DEJ: How do you explain that, with only ten people [in the Politburo], our discussions are becoming known on the outside? How do you explain that? From where are the imperialist radio stations and newspapers from the capitalist countries [learning about] the critical situation that Teohari was put in with the Currency Reform? . . . It was discussed, and Teohari was very severely criticized, only at the March 13 meeting. How did the imperialist radio stations know about that? And April 30 was referred to. And in a newspaper in Israel. . . . How did they know? Ten people were [at that meeting]. Please explain it to me. How far is this leaking going to go?

PAUKER: And you think that this thing is coming from me?

GHEORGHIU-DEJ: I'm asking a question: From where? How? I'm not saying anything about anyone. I'm simply raising the issue: From where? If not even in this restricted body of ten people who know each other, if not even here we can say our opinion, without finding out that the radio is talking about these things several days later, where will we end up?

PAUKER: It's extremely serious if suspicions fall on one of us.

GHEORGHIU-DEJ: How can you not have suspicions? . . . And it's always been the same story here. There were decisions made at the CC, for example, regarding Jewish emigration. How did the Jewish population know about that, when it was decided at levels so high up? . . .

PAUKER: I spoke about these things to no one, absolutely no one. I ask that you believe that.[107]

The following day, the Central Committee convened to discuss the commission's findings. One of its members, Sorin Toma, revealed that the plenary "was prepared in a factional . . . or fractionalist manner. . . . [A]t four o'clock, the plenum was supposed to begin; we were called to come at *three o'clock*. We were summoned to another building close to the Central Committee." Meeting them were Moghioroş and Chişinevschi, who explained in detail the new charges, "which astounded everyone," and told the members what was expected of them. The group then proceeded to the Central Committee building completely prepared—unbeknown to Pauker, Luca, and Georgescu.[108]

There, the questions for Pauker were ready at hand. "Who was responsible for the policy of not taking timely measures in the collections and acquisitions? . . . What led you to think that the collection plan is too big? . . . Were not the serious deviations . . . committed at the Agriculture Ministry . . . completely rooted in Comrade Ana's positions? . . . What was the reason that, after the mistakes committed in the creation of collective farms, we did not occupy ourselves at all in creating new collectives? . . . Did you ever contest the role of Comrade Gheorghiu [-Dej] as general secretary and as party leader? . . . Did Comrade Ana ever raise . . . the question of abolishing the position of general secretary? . . . When and with whom did Comrade Ana discuss the party's position towards the Legionaries? . . . By what authority did Comrade Ana intervene to free the group of 7 Zionists, and for whom did she do so? . . . Did Comrade Ana make any promises to the representative of the State of Israel to free those 7 [Zionist] emissaries? . . . Was there any connection between the freeing of these American spies and the principled position [Georgescu] and Comrade Ana have on the problem of the Zionists and emigration to Israel?" [109]

Along with the charges of a lack of "revolutionary vigilance" regarding Patraşcanu and other party "enemies," Pauker was further denounced at the plenary for failing to condemn her husband when she was in prison in 1938.[110] Party inquisitors continually referred to this topic, accusing her of allying herself with the Luximin faction in 1930; of leaving the residence provided for her upon her arrival in Bucharest in September 1944 and moving into the house of Marcel Pauker's parents (which, her daughter Tatiana firmly asserted, never happened); and habitually manifesting "a hesitating, conciliatory attitude" toward her husband after he "was unmasked by the party as a Trotskyist traitor and an enemy of the working class." [111]

Several days after the plenary, at the side of Tatiana, who had just had her second child, Pauker could not help but endlessly ramble about her revolutionary past and indignantly cite her service to the cause.[112] But, aware that the purge "had been prepared many years beforehand," her tack was one of stoic discipline and compliant self-criticism.[113] The few instances when she did defend herself were to no avail. She reminded her attackers that the repression during the collectivization drive in the summer of 1950 was waged precisely when she was out of the country, but this did not prevent them from also charging her with "left-wing deviationism" for forcing peasants into collectives.[114] In the end, she submissively admitted to "unprincipled, un-party-like, opportunistic and accommodating" behavior, and denounced her own "arrogance" for not recognizing her mistakes.[115] She also abandoned Luca in the hope of saving what she could of her own position, and declared that she "absolutely agreed" that his actions were "counterrevolutionary" and "inimical to the party and state." [116] The plenary unanimously voted to expel her from the Secretariat and Politburo but allowed her to remain in the Foreign Ministry and the Orgbureau because of her self-critical stance. They removed Georgescu from both the Interior Ministry and the party leadership but not from the Central Committee, and they expelled Luca from all party positions and sent him to the Control Commission for further inquiry.[117]

Two weeks later, the party organization of the Foreign Ministry met to discuss the plenary's decision. Attending the meeting were the ministry's leading cadres, who proceeded to attack Deputy Foreign Minister Ana Toma in Pauker's place. "[T]hey respected and loved her too much," Ana Toma recalled. "So they hurt me, and they criticized me. . . . Nobody dared to say anything against Ana [Pauker], only me."[118] A rather harsh and vigilant personality, Toma was an easy target for her subordinates.[119] But perhaps another reason for their vitriol was that she reportedly served as Chişinevschi's agent against Pauker, which may have been apparent to those working close to her.[120] The discussion, chaired by Constantin Pârvulescu, was reconvened several days later by Chişinevschi himself, who criticized the staff for failing to denounce the right person. "Some comrades have demanded Ana Toma's head," he exclaimed. "The Politburo is not willing to [let you have it]."[121] He dismissed all the directors, deputy directors, and political officers and ordered them to wait at home for further instructions.[122] Naturally, they expected to be arrested at any moment, particularly several from Cluj who had fallen under intense suspicion.[123] But in the end, only one among them was arrested: Egon Balaş, the head of the Directorate of Economic Affairs, who was closely connected to Iacob.[124]

In June, Kavtaradze invited Pauker to attend the inauguration of a club for Soviet citizens in Romania. Amazed, no doubt, at Kavtaradze's temerity, she at first declined but relented when he insisted that she was overreacting.[125] This was to be the last invitation Kavtaradze would issue as ambassador: Moscow recalled him a short time later and replaced him with Anatoli Lavrentiev.[126] The Soviet ambassador to Yugoslavia during the break with Tito, Lavrentiev served as Deputy Foreign Minister in Moscow until he was appointed ambassador to Czechoslovakia on November 15, 1951, just before former Czechoslovak General Secretary Rudolf Slansky's November 28 arrest.[127] Lavrentiev's arrival in Prague was reportedly a factor in Slansky's demise.[128] His transfer to Bucharest hardly boded well for Pauker and her allies.

On June 23, suggesting that "we don't need women in the hierarchy" of the Foreign Ministry, Chişinevschi told the Politburo that Pauker should be immediately replaced as Foreign Minister, asserting that foreign dignitaries and ministry personnel were too embarrassed to do business with her. Dej promptly agreed: "We thought that she could remain Foreign Minister. But look at this unpleasant situation. It's not only a matter of the emotional state that she's in, which could not be otherwise. . . . There are very delicate problems." [129] Soon to follow was their decision to retire her from the Orgbureau and place her in an obscure post dealing with local Popular Councils. [130] They also demanded a written self-criticism on her past activities and then objected to what she submitted as containing "only generalities. They [then] gave me questions," Pauker related, "to which I answered at length—questions that also comprised the [future] accusations and fabrications. . . . There was another series of questions that I answered. That was in the summer of 1952. The summer went by, ten months also went by, without any answer . . . , without . . . once being called in and spoken to." [131] In the interim, she and her close relatives were put under surveillance, while a criminal case was being methodically built against her. [132]

The first step in that process was the arrest of some one hundred Finance Ministry and National Bank officials—practically every high-level official from both institutions—in the spring of 1952. [133] This was done without a shred of evidence. The arrests caught Interior Ministry officers completely by surprise, for they had not been prepared beforehand and had nothing on the detainees. [134] When the interrogators asked on what basis they should begin the inquiry, "[t]hey were told by the Soviet advisers and [Alexandru] Drăghici: 'Read the plenary resolution.'" [135] They also eventually received the special party commission's report but found it contained only "mistaken conclusions based on erroneous facts and exaggerations." [136] The interrogators' task, the Soviet advisers insisted, was to obtain declarations proving those conclusions. The Soviets at times reproached the officers for determining that the resolutions "did not correspond with the truth," and demanded that they take an "activist, combative" stance "with a sense of responsibility" to further a case that "was in the superior interests of the party." [137]

Particularly important, of course, was the inquiry of Alexandru Iacob. Gheorghiu-Dej gave him a chance to save himself at the end of 1951, Iacob later confided, in overtures that he should turn against Luca. But Iacob refused. [138] His arrest came March 27, 1952, when Central Committee officials picked him up and took him straight to the Securitate. At the beginning, Iacob recalled, the inquiry was conducted "in relatively civilized conditions," though he persistently denied all charges. [139] After approximately one month, however, he clearly saw that his interroga-

tors sought to establish his guilt rather than the truth. The beatings began August 1, 1952. First his interrogator conducted them, then his interrogator's superior, and finally four officers, who took turns in pairs
applying the blows. They interrogated him day and night, and continuously deprived him of sleep.[140] During one interrogation, the investigator was suddenly called from the room and inadvertently left on the desk
a piece of a razor blade with which he was sharpening a pencil. "At that
moment," an officer reported, "Alexandru Iacob got up and locked the
door—which could not be opened from the outside—went to the interrogation table, took the razor blade, and tried to kill himself by cutting
his throat. Colonel Enoiu broke down the door and grabbed the razor
from his hand. Hearing the commotion, I ran into the room, and saw
Colonel Enoiu hitting Alexandru Iacob's face." [141] Covered in blood, his
throat wound not serious enough to kill him, Iacob was promptly beaten
and manacled.[142] Eventually, he began to confess following each beating, but always retracted his admissions immediately afterward. Iacob's
defiance continued throughout the inquiry and through his (and Luca's)
trial in October 1954.[143] He was held in solitary confinement eleven and
a half years, probably as a result.[144]

Two weeks after Iacob's first beating, Vasile Luca was arrested.
Though the May plenary formally decreed that the party's Control Commission would investigate him, that body never conducted an inquiry. It
was decided instead, his wife, Elisabeta, maintained, to move them into
another house and keep them there to await a decision of the Central
Committee.[145] At one point Luca spoke on the phone with Gheorghiu-
Dej, who told him to relax and assured him that nothing would happen
to him.[146] But, on August 14, 1952, an unnamed person from the Central Committee paid an unexpected visit and told Elisabeta that he was
taking Luca to work at a state farm.[147] Luca left with the official and
never came back. Three days later, three security officers arrived to
search the house—and to arrest Elisabeta Luca.[148]

During the first two to three months of Luca's detention, his interrogator was Lieutenant Colonel Francisc Butyka, who had been brought
into the Interior Ministry to head the inquiry.[149] As Butyka later related,
Luca "was very impulsive from the beginning. He would always ask
why he was arrested," and insisted that he should have been investigated within the party.[150] He was, Butyka emphasized, never beaten or
denied medical treatment for his heart condition and was given special
food and allowed to sleep regular hours.[151] But the officer failed to
mention anything about Luca's nervous disorder—reportedly due to

advanced syphilis—which required, his doctor Sandu Liblich revealed to Dr. Gheorghe Brătescu, daily injections to control.[152] Butyka evidently denied Luca this treatment, for his interrogation transcripts during the first few months of imprisonment reveal a man who was highly confused and at times quite incoherent.[153] Not surprisingly, he "would frequently break down crying," Butyka recounted, "and lash out with insults." After six weeks of interrogation, Luca one day began sobbing and admitted he had once been a Siguranţa agent. When Butyka reported this to the party leadership, "there was jubilation all around."[154]

Henceforth, Luca was "an unrecognizably exhausted, morally defeated man," who "mechanically repeated, without the slightest opposition, all the details" of his Siguranţa ties[155]—even though, as an RCP commission later concluded, he had never worked for the Siguranţa.[156] His "confession," therefore, probably resulted from his impaired state and the authorities' promise to pardon him. An officer working on the case revealed that, once Luca broke down and confessed, "he was no longer nervous"[157]—suggesting that he was only then given his injections. That same officer maintained "Luca was convinced that he would not be tried. He was told that the party leadership requested that he shed some light on certain issues" and led to believe he would be released if he complied.[158] Alexandru Iacob confirmed this, having discussed the issue with Luca himself in a car transporting them from Râmnicu Sărat to Aiud prison in 1962.[159] Whatever Luca's reason, his confession was the sole piece of evidence obtained in his inquiry and became the basis for the attack against Pauker and Georgescu. Those heading the investigation believed that the "fractionalist group formed by Ana, Luca, and Teohari was actually formed during the [interwar] period, and that . . . all their activities after August 23, 1944, were based on their earlier connections before the war."[160]

Shaping the inquiry even more, however, was the escalating anti-Semitic campaign in the Soviet Union, which "reached new heights in 1952." Jews were dismissed en masse for alleged "cosmopolitan tendencies" or signs of "bourgeois nationalism," and Jewish doctors and scientists were accused of "subversion against Soviet science" or of mysterious, undisclosed conspiracies.[161] In January, the prosecution of the former leaders of the Jewish Anti-Fascist Committee resumed after being temporarily stalled by MGB chief Victor Abakumov (leading to his arrest in 1951). Fifteen of them were secretly tried March 5, and all but one (Professor Lina Shtern) were executed on August 12, 1952.[162] In November the campaign intensified with the show trial of Rudolf Slansky and thirteen others in Prague. This spectacle attempted "to show that the ties inherent in a person's Jewish origin were strong enough to transform even a Communist veteran such as Slansky into a traitor to the Communist cause." [163] Indeed, the trial's message was that all Jews were "predisposed by birth, character or education to become instruments of American espionage." [164] It additionally demonstrated that opposing anti-Semitism was tantamount to treason, for Slansky admitted to shielding his crimes behind the fight against anti-Semitism. This endangered any Communist who publicly opposed anti-Semitism.[165] Finally, the trial accused "a whole generation of Jews . . . of murder, treason, espionage, sabotage and other terrible crimes which were all allegedly committed within the framework of a world-wide Jewish conspiracy"—a conspiracy that specifically and conspicuously listed Ana Pauker with David Ben-Gurion and Moshe Sharett of Israel, Moshe Pijade of Yugoslavia, and Henry Morgenthau of the United States, as Slansky's accomplices.[166] To implicate Pauker with the Prague defendants, the Czechoslovak authorities intensely interrogated Mordechai Oren, an Israeli emissary imprisoned during the Slansky prosecution, on her supposed links with Zionism and Israel.[167]

Two days after the Slansky trial, the "Kiev Affair" was widely publicized in the USSR, reportedly leading to the arrest and trial of large numbers of Jews for economic crimes in the Ukraine.[168] Soon after, with *Pravda*'s announcement of the Doctors' Plot on January 13, 1953, anti-Semitic hysteria raged unchecked through the country. Thousands of Jewish doctors and specialists were expelled as a "prophylactic measure" from medical schools and hospitals, with many institutions losing half their staffs. Forthcoming books by Jews were canceled and medicines developed by Jewish scientists banned. Increasing numbers of patients, fearing they would be poisoned, refused treatment by Jewish doctors not yet drummed out of hospitals and clinics.[169]

The Soviet satellites, including Romania, duplicated the anti-Semitic campaign, though without the Soviet Union's popular hysteria.[170] The conventional wisdom generally resisted linking Pauker's downfall with an overall anti-Semitic purge, as another Jew, Simion Bughici, replaced her in the Foreign Ministry and Jews such as Iosif Chişinevschi and Leonte Răutu retained their prominence within the party hierarchy.[171] Nevertheless, a JDC report documented that, beginning in July 1952, "the heads of some enterprises and institutions . . . fired Jewish salaried workers en masse . . . [for having] nonproletarian pasts." [172] Also, on July 11, 1952, a Federation of Jewish Communities memo called for the immediate dismissal of any federation employee "who did not give up on emigration to capitalist Israel within 24 hours"—a condition mandated in other institutions as well.[173] Jews working in the state and party apparatus were increasingly distrusted and became particularly vulnerable in conspicuous, well-defined posts.[174] Hence, in late 1952 the State Control Commission's vice president, Mihail Gavriliuc, ordered sector chief David Rotman not to "create a synagogue" by hiring Jews. When Rotman refused the order, he was removed from his position, expelled from the party, and nearly arrested.[175] Likewise, both Ghizella Vass and Victor Vezendean were ousted from the Foreign Section of the Central Committee in January 1953 as a direct result of the Doctors' Plot. Given events in the Soviet Union, Vezendean recalled, "they had to do something against the Jews here as well. They couldn't have so many Jews in key positions. . . . A lot of Jews were thrown out in January 1953, and Chişinevschi explained that there were too many Jews at the top."[176]

Pauker's purge further signaled an intensified "anti-cosmopolitan" campaign, primarily against Jewish intellectuals. On May 15, 1952, coinciding with "a wave of university purges" throughout the country,[177] the Section of Propaganda of the Central Committee attacked Professor of Art History Radu Bogdan for "cosmopolitanism and objectivism" in his lectures, as well as Professor E. Schileru for "acting on various occasions like a cosmopolite" at the Plenary of the Union of Plastic Artists of the RPR.[178] Two weeks later, Radu Lupan, editor in chief of the Literature Publishing House and head of the foreign department of the journal Contemporanul, was purged for displaying "cosmopolitan leanings" in his work. Prior to the Right Deviation, Lupan recalled, he was criticized for "cosmopolitanism" and for insufficiently radical writings but was nevertheless tolerated at his posts. This was, he added, typical of the party's handling of intellectuals until then. The day after the Romanian press announced Pauker's ouster, however, he found himself suddenly unemployed. "I went to the Central Committee and asked them why. . . . And they said 'There is no explanation [we] can give you. It is a fact. From now on you are not allowed to write in your name, and you are thrown out of all your jobs.' I was turned out on the street. At exactly that time, that very month, my wife gave birth. . . . My wife was working as a kind of clerk at the Foreign Ministry at that time, and she was told to divorce me."[179] The formal announcement of the Doctors' Plot in Scânteia, which pointedly denounced "cosmopolitans without country or people" in its lead editorial, clearly linked the "anti-cosmopolitan" and anti-Semitic campaigns.[180] This was the first appearance in Romania of such phraseology, closely resembling the Soviet Union's references to Jews as "rootless" or "homeless cosmopolitans," as opposed to "cosmopolitans" generally.[181] The phrase was repeated at least twice during this period.[182]

Further, the reporting of the Slansky trial in Romania began to publicly link Pauker to these developments. Immediately following the proceedings, Radio Bucharest reportedly announced the preparation of a major trial against subversive elements in Romania and indicated that the featured defendant might be Pauker.[183] "We also have criminals among us," Radio Bucharest declared, "Zionist agents and agents of international Jewish capital. We shall expose them, and it is our duty to exterminate them."[184] The ever expanding inquiry clearly reflected this—at first particularly in the interrogations of Elisabeta Luca, who, being a Spaniard, a Muscovite, and a Jew with a Zionist past, seemed the prototypical Prague trial defendant. She was almost immediately questioned about her "criminal activities" in Spain and later about her time at the Perpignan internment camp in France and as Pauker's secretary in the Soviet Union during the war.[185] From December on, however, her interrogations increasingly focused on linking the non-Jew Vasile Luca to Zionism and Israel, in close collaboration with Ana Pauker.[186] Concurrently, several Interior Ministry officers were arrested and, beginning in January 1953, intensely queried on Pauker and Georgescu's promotion of mass Jewish emigration.[187]

The stage was set for Pauker's and Georgescu's arrests on February 18, 1953.[188] Pauker was taken away blindfolded while officers began a thorough search of her house, confiscating books and family photos and even opening the wooden floor in search of hidden items.[189] Her arrest was carried out unknown to the Politburo, to whose members Gheorghiu-Dej presented a *fait accompli* the following day. Only then did they retroactively rubber-stamp the action.[190] Though allowed to sleep during the day,[191] Pauker "was interrogated night after night, with few exceptions, in order to increase the pressure. Every night . . . ," she recalled, "[there were] interrogations with all kinds of indecencies, which was a regular occurrence. They told me, 'Stop denying your crimes. Admit your crimes . . . ,' with all the abuse that one can level at a person—insults and derision, without the slightest basis. It was all based on suspicions."[192] At the time of her arrest her investigators had absolutely no evidence against her,[193] there being "only one declaration in my file. I was told, in addition to other evidence that they had, [this declaration] proved that I'm a spy. I was accused of being Truman's agent, and that I was resisting because I wanted Truman to erect a monument for me." [194] She was also continually pressed to reveal why she became an agent:

[A]nd that's the question that's asked in all the trials. You wonder how Slansky got to the place of doing that thing and why Kostov or Tito did what they did. The same question was put to me: Why or for what reason did I enter at I don't know what time the service of certain foreign countries. . . . And that I had been an agent for a long time. . . . And that already a long time ago I conspired with Luca based on this fact, and that Luca as well was a Siguranţă agent, and that I conspired with him and came to this country. . . . [T]hat was the reception I got from the [prison] inquiry.[195]

But her interrogators could not get a confession. When they first told her, "Luca is an agent, and you're an agent just like he is," she could not keep from laughing.[196]

And then they began to deceive me "that there were also other agents of the imperialists, and, if they told the truth, they got 12 years and others only 10 years, instead of being shot," and that it was in my interest to tell them all that they wanted, and that "[w]e're no longer the old type [of interrogators]. We have experience. We know, and we'll find out, and we have dates and facts, and we know certain things, and we know everything, but you just have to confirm it to us, and nothing else." [197]

When Pauker refused to do so, the interrogators apparently resorted to a "mild" form of torture.[198] Still she did not confess.

One issue upon which Pauker was pressured to expand was the matter Gheorghiu-Dej raised at the Politburo just before the May plenary: secrets' being divulged to "the enemy" [199] (the United States) through its principal agent, "International Zionism." [200] Her primary conduit for this activity was allegedly her brother, Zalman Rabinsohn, who was arrested the same day as Pauker, February 18.[201] Under interrogation, Rabinsohn at first stubbornly denied the accusations and immediately began a "speech strike," refusing to answer all questions when he was charged of being a Siguranţă and Gestapo agent during the war.[202] He also repeatedly insisted that he had returned to Romania in 1949 on his own initiative and was not on an official mission of the Israeli government.[203] In time, however, he admitted to apprising the Israeli embassy in Bucharest in July 1950 (through Zionist leader A. L. Zissu), and Israeli Foreign Minister Moshe Sharett (via his wife, Dina Rabinsohn), on the state of the arrested Romanian Zionist leaders after having discussed the matter personally with Iosif Chişinevschi.[204] After persistent interrogations, he eventually "confessed" to regularly reporting to the Israeli

embassy through a number of go-betweens, often disclosing "state secrets" he had learned in private discussions with Ana Pauker.[205]

With confession in hand, the inquiry formally branded Rabinsohn an
"agent informator . . . [of] the Israeli government."[206] Noting that Romanian Zionists had regularly dubbed him "the telephone to the Cominform," the inquiry concluded that he became the Zionists' primary
means of communication with Pauker after their formal dissolution, and
thus "also served as the principal channel through which the imperialists would influence the affairs of the RWP and even the Informative Bureau of the Communist and Workers' Parties [the Cominform]."[207]

To bolster its case, the inquiry made much of Rabinsohn's apparently engaging in the universal practice of seeking *protectzia* (privileges
through insider contacts) in Israel, allegedly for his work in Romania.
Thus Rabinsohn was pressed to acknowledge instructing his wife, Dina,
to ask the Israeli Foreign Ministry for a house when she returned to
Israel in July 1950, as well as seeking arrangements for his son to receive
free room and board at the dormitory of the Haifa Polytechnic.[208] Soon
after her return, Rabinsohn maintained, a Foreign Ministry representative approached her with assurances that the ministry was at her disposal,
should her family need any assistance.[209] She was then given a house,
with all expenses paid, over the seven months she stayed in Jerusalem
with their daughter Leia, who was receiving treatment there for her
nervous disorder.[210] This was, Rabinsohn ultimately "confirmed," in exchange for his providing "secret information" to the Israeli embassy,
and was, as he understood it, a sign that he should continue his activities in Bucharest.[211] Upon learning he had decided to return to Israel in
April 1951, Rabinsohn added, the Israeli government offered his wife
yet another house on condition that he stay in Romania.[212] Supposedly
Rabinsohn specified that he wanted a house either in Haifa or Jerusalem
in return, and his family was given one free of charge in July 1952.[213]

With that, the inquiry had all it needed to establish that Ana Pauker's
brother was a paid Israeli spy. In the end, Rabinsohn "confessed" that
his agenda was, on the one hand, to provide information and assistance
to the Israeli authorities, "and, on the other hand, to obtain compensation, which I thought I deserved for the activity I was doing."[214] Or, as
he succinctly put it on another occasion, "I didn't engage in espionage
for money. Rather, I got money because I engaged in espionage."[215] Of
course, without corroborating evidence, Rabinsohn's statements are
hardly acceptable at face value, for he was certainly under duress during
interrogation.[216] Indeed, another source disputes his confession's only

presently verifiable detail—that he received financial payments from the Israeli embassy from June 1952 until his arrest the following February.[217] Rabinsohn told his interrogators that Chief Rabbi Moses Rosen personally delivered the payments each month, but Rosen suggests otherwise. Rosen revealed in his memoirs that, during a two-month period, he did in fact receive money to relay to the Rabinsohns from one David Faibiş, "probably the Israeli embassy." But this was for Rabinsohn's desperate wife and child *after* Rabinsohn's arrest, not before.[218] Evidently, this was a typical attempt on the inquiry's part to embellish Rabinsohn's role in this affair, which, as two of his confidants emphatically insisted, was infinitely simpler: having returned to Romania simply to visit his sister, he thought he could influence her on Jewish emigration and, later, the imprisoned Zionist leaders. After the leaders' arrests he began regularly conferring with several local Zionists, but he was far too naive to be involved in anything more elaborate.[219]

One venture upon which Rabinsohn did embark, however, and which the prison inquiry underscored, was the drafting of a letter in March or April 1951 to Israeli Foreign Minister Moshe Sharett, with the formal stipulation that it also be shown to Israeli Prime Minister David Ben-Gurion. Signed by Chief Rabbi Moses Rosen, Rabbi Yitzchak Friedman, and Rabbi Zisse Portugal and delivered to the Israeli embassy, the letter protested Israel's siding with the West on the Korean conflict and suggested that action clearly endangered the Jews inside the Soviet bloc, whom it likened to being under house arrest. That Israel should immediately improve its relations with the RPR and declare its neutrality in the case of war, the letter emphasized, was a fundamental interest of Romanian Jewry. After his arrest, Rabinsohn was forced to confess to criminal activities in connection to the letter, and Rabbi Rosen and others were also interrogated about it at that time.[220] According to Rosen, the letter was to be included in the indictment of a Romanian "Slansky trial."[221] "They had it all prepared: jail, the case against me, a big show trial . . . ," he declared. "For six months I lived like this, ready for the knock on the door during the night."[222] In fact, a synthesis of Rabinsohn's inquiry officially recommended Rosen's arrest, but its reason for doing so was actually his allegedly forwarding the Israeli embassy's payments.[223]

Rabinsohn, Rosen, and those connected to them were apparently slated for roles—though secondary —in an upcoming show trial, their sole purpose being to link the chief defendant, Ana Pauker, to Zionism and Israel. Hence, Rabinsohn confessed that Pauker was aware of, yet took no action to prevent, his assistance to Zionists and the Israeli embassy. On the contrary, she often aided and furnished him with information, which constituted, he ultimately admitted, "treason" against the RPR.[224] The documents in the cases of Pauker and her "co-conspirators" contain a series of similar charges against her: she supported "the subversive and espionage activities of the Israeli Legation and of the Zionists in the country";[225] she made secret commitments to the Israeli embassy, by unilaterally freeing the seven Israeli emissaries;[226] she exhibited a "nationalist attitude on the emigration of Jews to Israel, the dissolution of the Zionist organizations, the various collaborationist endeavors with those organizations, [and] the acceptance of Zionists in the party";[227] she advocated including left-wing Zionists in both the JDC and the National Democratic Front;[228] she sanctioned the postwar activities of the Joint Distribution Committee in Romania;[229] and she pursued "harmful cadre policies" in the party that gave preference to "petit-bourgeois," "sectarian," and "careerist" elements (in a word, Jews).[230]

The indictment further maintained that Pauker's non-Jewish allies, Luca and Georgescu, actively assisted her in promoting pro-Zionist policies. While it connected Luca to the Zionists through his wife, Elisabeta, and his position as the CC secretary responsible for national minorities,[231] it branded Georgescu as Pauker's accomplice in superseding the party's emigration restrictions and freeing the seven Zionist emissaries.[232] This appears to confirm the former Securitate chief Ion Mihai Pacepa's claim that Stalin directly imposed the anti-Zionist motif paramount in their prosecution, ordering his security services "'to get rid of the kikes' from the leadership of the [RWP] through their executions as Western spies."[233]

Although no Jew in the leadership was immune to Stalin's apparent dictum, a number appear as likely codefendants in Pauker, Luca, and Georgescu's trial. First were Elisabeta Luca and several other Spanish Civil War veterans, among them Valter Roman, dismissed as Minister of Posts and Telecommunications and investigated by a special commission in December 1952, and identified as Pauker's protégé in Moscow during the war and her loyal supporter during her years in power; Mihail (Bibi) Boico and Dr. Shuli Brill, accused with Roman at the May 1952 CC plenary of secretly favoring Pauker as party leader over Gheorghiu-Dej; Mihail Patriciu, mistakenly believed to be half-Jewish and closely associated with Luca and Iacob; and Carol Neuman, arrested in December 1952, ostensibly in connection with the Pătrăşcanu inquiry.[234] Second, in addition to Iacob, were Zoltan Eidlitz, Alexandru Nistor,

and many other Jews in Luca's entourage—including Egon Balaş, chief
of the Economic Directorate of Pauker's Foreign Ministry. Third were
Patraşcanu's "co-conspirator" Emil Calmanovici, who was actually arrested for Zionist espionage and interrogated on his links with Pauker
in March 1953; and the Interior Ministry's Mişu Dulgheru, whose inquiry, tainted with anti-Semitism from the outset, emphasized his alleged protection of Calmanovici and charged him with sabotaging the
prosecution of arrested Zionists.[235] Calmanovici's and Dulgheru's cases
were but two among a number of details suggesting that the Pauker and
Patraşcanu inquiries were to converge into one show trial[236]—as happened in the Prague Trial, where the Jewish "Zionist" Rudolf Slansky
was tried with the Slovak "bourgeois nationalist" Vladimir (Vlado)
Clementis.[237] Fourth was the Bessarabian Jew Samoilov (Samuel), a
colonel in the Political Directorate of the Red Army, who was closely associated with Pauker and Luca both during and after the war and who
had recruited Luca into the Soviet secret service in 1940.[238] Samoilov
was now depicted as actually having been recruited by Luca into the
Romanian Siguranţă and arrested by the Soviets for espionage.[239] Last
was Dr. Sandu Liblich, a member of the RCP's old guard and the personal physician of Luca and other party leaders, who was arrested in
February 1953 as a Zionist spy with links to the Joint Distribution
Committee—apparently a Romanian version of the Doctors' Plot in
Moscow.[240] Indeed, Pacepa revealed that he was personally assigned to
find "proof," using material sent by Stalin, that would directly implicate
Pauker and her allies in the "Zionist" conspiracy of the Soviet Doctors'
Plot, and he further suggested that the trial of the "Right Deviationists"
was to coincide with that of the arrested Kremlin doctors.[241]

Reportedly scheduled to convene March 18, 1953,[242] the Doctors'
Trial in Moscow was apparently to lead to the following scenario:

> Act One, sentencing after full confessions; Act Two, execution by hanging (it
> is said that this execution would have taken place in Red Square, in Moscow,
> as in days of yore); Act Three, pogroms throughout the country; Act Four,
> Jewish personalities from the world of culture would turn to Stalin, asking
> that he protect the Jews from pogroms and give them permission to leave the
> big cities and go back to the land; Act Five, mass deportation of Jews, "at
> their own request," to the country's eastern territories.[243]

In early 1953 the MVD publishing house printed and readied for distribution one million copies of "Why Jews Must Be Resettled from the Industrial Regions of the Country," a pamphlet by Dmitry Chesnokov, a
highly placed police official.[244] Ready as well in the eastern regions by

the end of 1952 or the beginning of 1953 were thousands of shabby, temporary barracks for the deported Jews—"two kilometers long [with] ramshackle walls [that] were one board thick with plenty of knotholes. Leaky roofs, knocked-out windows. Inside were rows of double bunks." The barracks were so shoddy that they were later declared unfit for storing grain.[245]

What seemed an impending Holocaust of Soviet Jewry likely would have spread throughout the satellite countries as well: camps were planned for "cosmopolites" in Mazuria, Poland, and an anti-Semitic show trial in Bucharest could have led to similar consequences.[246] Everything abruptly halted, however, with Stalin's death on March 4. The Doctors' Trial was canceled, and the long-awaited trial of Ana Pauker never began. Like the arrested doctors in Moscow, she was suddenly released from prison in late March—her investigation by the Securitate terminated after approximately one month.[247] Miron Constantinescu recounted, "After Stalin's death, immediately after, Molotov began to intervene for letting Ana out of prison, and [his interventions] occurred, categorically, three times. The fact that she was freed is due to Molotov's pressure on Gheorghiu-Dej."[248] Molotov's wife, Polina Zhemchuzhina, released from prison herself immediately following Stalin's death, reportedly demanded his intervention.[249] Pauker was much luckier than her brother, who spent two and half years in prison before being expelled to Israel; than Teohari Georgescu, who was jailed for just over three years; than Vasile Luca, whose death sentence at his October 1954 trial was commuted to life imprisonment, and who died at Aiud prison in 1963, reportedly after going insane.[250] She had, indeed, escaped Slansky's fate by the skin of her teeth—as she personally discovered soon after leaving prison. At a party house on the outskirts of Bucharest where she was held the first three weeks of April, Alexandru Moghioroş informed her of Stalin's death. When she burst into tears, Moghioroş quipped: "Don't cry. If Stalin were still alive, you'd be dead."[251]

Epilogue

Upon being released from Malmezon prison in late March 1953, Ana Pauker was held under arrest an additional month at a party house in Otopeni, near Bucharest. She could have no contact with outsiders, except several party leaders who occasionally questioned her, and was forced to sleep in the same bed with the woman guarding her.[1] In an April 18 telephone conversation with Alexandru Moghioroş, she expressed the desire to go the countryside to work as a teacher, but Moghioroş was noncommittal.[2] Two days later, she was placed under a loose form of house arrest in Bucharest, being allowed to leave the house but always guarded by her chauffeur and housekeeper—both, of course, Securitate agents.[3] A special party commission, meanwhile, took up where Pauker's prison interrogators had left off and began their own formal investigation.[4] Whereas Pauker was submissive and self-critical for seven months following her purge, and was, her family reported, "extremely upset, troubled, depressed and disoriented" throughout that period, her demeanor changed completely once she was arrested.[5] Henceforth she stubbornly defended herself and persistently issued firm denials, and continued to do so with the party commission.[6] The commission's report to the Politburo at the beginning of 1954 proposed expelling Pauker from the party and pursuing her inquiry further through a "state agency." On May 11 the Politburo accepted the report but, on Alexandru Drăghici's insistence, appended the following point to its conclusions: "The American, English and Israeli espionage agencies, learned of party and state secrets through the intermediary of Pauker's relatives—Emil Pauker, Rabinsohn and other suspicious elements—who visited her." [7] Though Moghioroş had assured Pauker that the espionage charge was no longer valid,[8] the majority of the Politburo apparently thought otherwise.

Nevertheless, the commission's punishments were never implemented. On the contrary, authorities ended Pauker's house arrest in February 1954 and allowed her to reside with her daughter Tatiana and son Vlad, Tatiana's husband, Dr. Gheorghe Brătescu, and the Brătescus' three children.[9] In September, she was given a post at the Editura Politică publishing house, editing socioeconomic texts (but not the Marxist-Leninist classics, it was expressly stipulated) and translating French and German works, for a salary of 1,500 lei a month.[10] This relative leniency likely resulted from the "persistent interest" of prominent Communists in Moscow and elsewhere. "Whenever I met with [Klement] Voroshilov," Emil Bodnăraş recalled, "no matter what we were discussing, we would invariably end up on Ana Pauker. There was still an interest in her among certain people over there. Not all the Soviets over there were convinced that Ana was an agent who did not belong in the Communist Party." [11]

In April 1954, Pauker was reportedly offered "a certain degree" of rehabilitation if she would testify against Lucreţiu Patraşcanu, but she adamantly declined. Years later, one of Patraşcanu's defense attorneys would report her as retorting, "I'm in no hurry to receive your rehabilitation. History will rehabilitate me." [12]

The following year, Zalman Rabinsohn revealed, Pauker asked for a meeting with Gheorghiu-Dej and demanded that he release her brother from prison. "You of all people should know," Zalman Rabinsohn quoted her as saying, "that my brother is not guilty of any anti-government activities! Why, then, has he been jailed?" Not long after, in the summer of 1955, Rabinsohn was released and expelled to Israel.[13] If true, Rabinsohn must have heard the story from Pauker herself before his departure.[14]

Then, in February 1956, Khrushchev attacked Stalin in his "Secret Speech" to the Twentieth Congress of the Soviet CP in Moscow. Not long afterward, the Romanian Party leadership began a systematic campaign to blame all Stalinist manifestations in the country on the Pauker faction. Soon she was to read the first allegations in the press that she had tried (among other things) to liquidate the Spanish Civil War veterans. "One of the reasons she suffered so much [after her purge],"

Gheorghe Brătescu related, "was that she couldn't understand how they could say such a thing. She had no opportunity to defend herself." [15]

That June, moreover, party investigators again hauled Pauker in and put her through a second round of questioning, this time focusing more on her supposed "left-wing deviations." She was even more defiant than she had been three years earlier and indignantly renounced her previous admissions as "self-flagellation." "And I'm not going to do it anymore," she declared, for she lived only in the hope that the truth one day would be known. She was fully aware, she asserted, that she had been slated "to be brought out as a Rajk or a Kostov, . . . perhaps in the spirit of Slansky," but was spared that fate after "a couple of things had changed" in Moscow soon after Stalin's death, "just like with the Jewish doctors, who had been arrested. But that didn't prevent," she bitterly added, "my brother spending three years in jail for nothing!" [16] Her pent-up anger and frustration appear to have suddenly come to the fore. "You take a person," she bellowed, "you arrest him, you call him an agent, you [subject him to] methods that, in all my life, with all the prisons and Siguranţă stations, I'd never encountered . . . , you throw mud at him, you jeer at him, you throw his kids out of their houses, you take his books, and you don't even say 'I'm sorry,' as any person would if he stepped on someone's foot. You couldn't care less!" [17] When the commission suggested that she had been a Soviet informer during her years in power, Pauker again exploded. "I didn't inform on people like Bodnăraş did, sending reports to the NKVD," she shot back, so infuriated that her interlocutors had to appeal to her to calm down. [18] Perhaps the irony of the moment was too much for her, for a perusal of the Russian archives reveals that Alexandru Moghioroş, the head of the commission, was in fact one of the more active informers in the Romanian leadership. [19]

During these sessions the commission assured Pauker that she was still a party member (though she had not paid any dues since her arrest) and, in one of the meetings, again referred to her as "comrade." [20] With a cloud hanging over Gheorghiu-Dej with Khrushchev's de-Stalinization campaign, these seem faint signs of her possible rehabilitation. Pauker herself apparently thought so several years later. In 1959 she asked Dr. Gheorghe Brătescu whether he thought a certain professor would make a good public health minister. "It was," Brătescu recalled, "a very difficult period for Gheorghiu-Dej, who was fighting with Khrushchev and making contacts with China. So this was how I found out that she was thinking, perhaps, of forming a new government. It's a family secret." [21]

In the end, however, she would remain an ostracized pariah until her death. Other than relatives, only four persons dared visit her after the purge: Maria (Băbica) Andreescu, an old Romanian worker who had befriended her in prison; Bernard Teiter, a professor of pharmacology; Livia Ardeleanu, a Jewish pensioner and longtime Communist sympathizer; and Radu Olteanu, a lawyer who defended Communists between the wars and who was jailed for homosexuality in 1949.[22] (Maria Sârbu also visited Pauker once when she was hospitalized in 1959.)[23] The hordes of adoring "comrades," including the women imprisoned with her in Dumbrăveni, now seemed to shrug off any thought of her. Sârbu later recalled that during her visit Pauker expressed how much this upset her.[24] Given Pauker's perennial craving for approval and admiration, this easily might have been so.[25] But surely no one better understood the mandates of party discipline and the harsh penalties for any deviator. She herself had told her close friend Liuba Chişinevschi to stay away after her fall, insisting that Chişinevschi should think of her children.[26]

For the party apparat, attacking and forsaking *tovarăşa* Ana, who had long been the object of so much affection, became a test of loyalty — yet another "painful sacrifice" expected of the professional revolutionary. But at least once their discipline momentarily faltered. In 1955 or 1956, Pauker accompanied her family to a performance at the city's opera house. Though the hall was full of her former friends and colleagues, she did not exchange a word with any of them. But after the performance, as Pauker began to leave the building, the crowd of party functionaries spontaneously formed two lines and silently stood almost at attention as Pauker passed.[27]

In the summer or fall of 1958, Pauker again fell ill, suffering from what at first seemed a toxic condition. When she began to deteriorate in the spring of 1959, it was suggested that she be hospitalized. She refused to check into Elias Hospital, where party officials were normally cared for, going instead to an ordinary clinic run by her doctor. There it was determined that she had a severe recurrence of cancer, too advanced for any effective treatment. Released one month later, she went with her youngest daughter, Marie (Maşa), to a party villa in the mountains. Soon after her return to Bucharest, a letter arrived from the Soviet Union. Fully three years earlier, her son and daughter had written to the Presidium of the Supreme Soviet requesting information on their father's fate. The Soviets' official answer finally came by way of the Romanian Red

Cross: Marcel Pauker, the letter informed them, died August 16, 1938, adding no other information was available. A distraught Ana Pauker immediately took to bed and remained bed-ridden until her death nine months later.[28]

Though rumors abounded that she had visited a dying Marcel in a Siberian gulag[29] or that she secretly went to his unmarked grave in a Moscow cemetery just before returning to Bucharest,[30] Ana Pauker apparently had done exactly as Varia Manuilsky advised and refrained from inquiring into her husband's whereabouts. Upon arriving in Romania, she evasively assured Marcel's parents that he was still alive,[31] but confided to his sister Titi that he was probably dead.[32] When her father asked about Marcel, she told him never to bring up the subject again, and she avoided it even with her children.[33] Soon after the war, party activist Mihai Alexandru told friends he thought he had seen Marcel Pauker marching in a Communist Party parade during a recent trip to Paris; Iosif Chişinevschi promptly asked him to write down every detail of what he had seen. He had the firm impression, he later related, that the request had actually come from Ana Pauker.[34] As her anguished response in 1959 indicated to her family, and remarkable as it may seem, she apparently never knew for sure what had happened to Marcel and irrationally continued to hope that he would one day appear.[35]

The cancer having spread to her heart and lungs, Pauker suffered considerably before dying of cardiac arrest on June 3, 1960.[36] The New York Times reported her death some two weeks later, but the Romanian press ignored it completely.[37] Attending her cremation along with her family were the four friends who had continued to visit her and, ironically enough, Gheorghe Cristescu, her old nemesis from the 1920s— long since expelled from the Communist Party and free, therefore, to follow his conscience. None of her former protégés and admirers within the party dared turn up. A representative of an antifascist fighters organization did appear with a speech in hand, but her family would not allow him to read it. When the director of the crematorium asked whether they wanted The Internationale played, as was customary for party officials, the family declined and had him play Beethoven's Third Symphony instead.[38]

Immediately after her death, her nearby neighbors suddenly vanished and new families promptly replaced them —plainly indicating that the former had all been Securitate agents.[39] Pauker's grandson Michel

(Mircea) Birnbaum recalled when she and her family had moved into that house:

> There were no lights on the street. And just before they moved in, the city put a street light right in front of the house. It was the only light on the whole street. In Bucharest street lights were broken very often, and it would take months before they were replaced. But every time this light was broken by children playing football or something, within two hours and six minutes it was changed immediately. When Ana died, the light was broken, and they never replaced it. And [her son-in-law Dr. Gheorghe Brătescu] said: "Well, now she's really dead." [40]

Subsequently, her family learned that Gheorghiu-Dej had thrown a party upon hearing the news.[41]

A family member recently confessed that he painfully regretted *The Internationale*'s not being played at Pauker's cremation, for he realized that it reflected the family's estrangement from Communism more than her own. In truth, while Ana Pauker welcomed Khrushchev's reforms and seemed more in her element with de-Stalinization, even speaking of returning to Marx while conspicuously ignoring Lenin, she remained to the end a devoted and unrepentant Communist. When her daughter Tatiana bought her a diary for one of her birthdays and suggestively dedicated it "to the memories," Pauker firmly told her, "I'll never write." [42] Evidently her memories—like everything else in her life—belonged to the party, which she was determined never to harm or betray. Though she began to criticize specific mistakes and shortcomings, she never expressed any doubt over the totality.[43] As she affirmed to Marie in 1956 or 1957, "You'll see. The people may not be the best, but the ideology will triumph." [44]

This was, no doubt, but one of a long line of rationalizations she employed to avoid drawing the ultimate conclusions—as did so many others of her generation. An axiom of party life during Pauker's time was that Communists regularly suffered bouts of deep disillusionment— "recurrent crises," as Arthur Koestler described them, "comparable to the periods of temptation and doubt in the case of religious believers. . . . I know of one or more such crises in the life of nearly every comrade who has been near to me." [45] But, in the end, few deserted—not even those like Wolfgang Leonhard who lost close family to the Terror or like Stephen Staszewski who were themselves sent to the gulags.[46] This was because, Koestler observed, believing in Communism had two permanent dimensions: attraction to the potential of a just social order and rejection of the existing one. Every time a Communist he knew would begin to falter, "it was some repellent aspect of capitalist society which put him back again on the road." [47] The degeneration under Stalinism may have revolted them, but the injustices of capitalism revolted them even more. As Manes Sperber put it, "[W]hat was going on in the capitalistic world at that time was like a provocation that grew more intolerable every day. . . . The hope that I had despite everything for the land of the October Revolution was not fed by a utopian superstition but by a contemptuous antipathy to a social order that had . . . caused a world war, the most insane carnage in history, and was now determined to safeguard its continued existence at the price of world-wide misery." [48]

Added to this was the Communists' strong revulsion to Social Democracy (forever fed by party propaganda), which convinced many that they had no choice as socialists but to remain in the party: "What else was there to do?" a Polish Communist rhetorically asked. "Return to capitalism? To the 'Whites' who were responsible for all the backwardness?" [49] The Great Depression, which "confirmed to so many non-Marxists the bankruptcy of capitalism," only sharpened this perceived polarization, and the rise of Nazism and the growing threat of fascism throughout Europe compounded it. [50] As Georg Lukacs saw it, "The crucial task of the time being—the destruction of Hitler—could not be expected from the West, but only from the Soviet Union. And Stalin was the only existing anti-Hitler force." [51] The Nazi-Soviet pact may have dispelled such illusions for some Communists, but for most it did so only briefly. For the Nazi invasion of the Soviet Union enabled them to cast aside all doubts and toil against what they certainly considered a greater evil. [52] Their seemingly miraculous victory vindicated Stalin in the eyes of many. They could now dismiss Trotsky's critique of a "degenerate bureaucracy" (how could such a bureaucracy defeat Hitler?) and applaud the Nazi-Soviet pact as a tactical wonder. [53] Even the Terror could now be said actually to have strengthened the Soviets: as Molotov later put it, "Thanks to 1937 there was no fifth column in our country during the war." [54]

The Soviet victory, moreover, suddenly transformed the despair and hopelessness of the Great Terror and early war years into sheer euphoria. As one scholar observed, "one very often finds that terrible misery co-exists with utopian longings. The more terrible the destruction, the greater the hopes for the future." [55] When Pauker and the bulk of Romanian Communists sat in prison in the 1930s, never in their wildest dreams did they imagine that they would be ruling the country so soon. Suddenly they had the power to "create the realities" that had inspired

Pauker's generation two decades earlier. They could plausibly deny the all-too-obvious fact that their power was merely a by-product of Soviet occupation by pointing out that the horrors and bloodshed of the war created a widespread longing in the region for significant social (though not political) change.[56] The agrarian reforms they instituted immediately after the war addressed such longings and reinforced the illusion that the party had somehow earned a mandate from the populace at large. Such illusions were perhaps a natural corollary to the moment's euphoria —the belief that everything could now be made anew, just as the Bolsheviks had believed after the First World War.

At the same time, the victory fulfilled the hope that Communism would spread beyond the Soviet Union's borders and put a long-desired end to the Russian stranglehold on the movement, which was widely blamed for all the barbarities of the previous years. Or at the very least it might break the USSR's two-decade-old isolation and enable it finally to transcend its autocratic and sinister nature. Such hope stemmed from a long tradition of wishful thinking among Communists that a "kinder and gentler" Bolshevism was just around the corner. As Ignazio Silone pointed out, those of his generation in the 1920s always cherished the illusion of ultimate democratization once the regime was consolidated, the economy strengthened, and the attacks from abroad halted.[57] Likewise, in the early and mid-1930s, many Communists in the Soviet Union hoped industrialization would increase the population's standard of living enough that Stalin would no longer feel threatened by a return to democracy, at least within the party.[58] Others rationalized that, despite Stalin's horrible distortions and crimes, the USSR nonetheless had public ownership and a collectivist economy; hence, socialism could be saved once Stalin was gone.[59] During the war Communists fervently believed, "almost to the point of monomania," that defeating the Nazis was the solution to everything and would "bring about a Golden Age of Communist democracy."[60] As Pauker affirmed to her family in 1956, her faith in the party remained despite Stalin's crimes because she firmly believed things would change for the better after the war.[61]

Such expectations were widespread among Communists after the Second World War. Many assumed that in their countries they would be allowed to do things differently than the Soviets "had been forced to do" in their own, and they spoke of creating new socialist models based on their particular cultures.[62] "The Muscovites who came home from Moscow," the former Hungarian Communist Bela Szász recalled, "told us other Communists that they hoped it would not be in our country like it was in Moscow. . . . It was not only my expectation, but the expectation of even the most Stalinist leaders." [63] All were convinced, Sorin Toma asserted, that Popular Democracy was a unique form of socialism, "something entirely new that arose during the war when Social Democrats and Communists were allies. And until 1948 we all thought in this manner." [64] The lack of coordination within the movement during the first years after the war also bolstered these sentiments, as did the initial fleeting liberalism imbuing Kremlin postwar policy.[65] Such hopes were rooted in the

> conviction that conditions in Russia were what they were not because of any fault in our system, but because of the backwardness of the Russian people. In Germany, in Austria or France, the Revolution would take an entirely different form. There was a saying among German Communists in Russia that could only be pronounced in a whisper: *"Wir werden es besser machen"*— "we shall know better." In other words, every Communist who had lived in the Soviet Union for some length of time, returned to his country as a Titoist at heart. It was this conviction that "we shall know better" that kept my faith alive.[66]

For many Communists, therefore, the doctrine was not the problem; the unfortunate circumstance that a still-primitive Russia was first to attempt Communism transformed a glorious liberation philosophy into a tool of brutal despotism. "It is the Russian distortion that has brought Communism into disrepute—hence: peel off the Russian accretion and you have Communism in its unblemished state, ready to be applied in Western Europe." [67]

Another factor was many Communists' strong sense of entitlement after long years in prison or the underground. Such feelings had certainly animated Pauker's actions after the war, both in her yen for the good life and the perks of office and in her selfish, narcissistic family behavior. Expressing regret to her two older children that she had not been able to watch them grow up, she evidently had no intention of allowing that to happen a third time. In 1945 she forcibly removed her youngest daughter, Marie, from Aurore Thorez, her surrogate mother in Paris— the only mother she had known until then. Having assured Marie that she could go back to visit Aurore every summer, Pauker would break her promise only one year later. "[F]rom the second year on," Marie related, "she cut off all relations with my family in France" on the dubious pretext that Aurore's refusal to grant Maurice Thorez a divorce had hurt the PCF politically or that "Aurore had become 'too bourgeois' because she owned a hotel. . . . Aurore wanted to come to Romania to visit me, but my mother cut off all ties with her." [68] Pauker behaved similarly toward her brother, Zalman Rabinsohn. Having coaxed and cajoled him to return to Romania, she would not let him leave when he decided to go back to Israel— not even to attend their dying father or to be with his distraught daughter. Granted, other elements discouraged Rabinsohn from leaving Romania at that time, but they did not exonerate Pauker's rigidity throughout most of 1951, when she ostensibly held her brother hostage.

This was, indeed, characteristic of many Communists who had "paid their dues" (and then some) during the harsh and bitter years of the underground. "We must not forget," one observer pointed out,

> that the Communists who moved into the Ministerial armchairs . . . after the war were no parliamentary politicians returning cheerfully to office after a brief spell in opposition. They were mostly men and women who, for twenty-five years and more, had patiently endured every form of persecution and hardship in the service of their faith. Whatever can be said against these men, their personal courage and loyalty to their ideals are beyond question. . . . All of them had lived for a generation in a world of forged passports and secret frontier-crossings, passwords and police spies, backroom meetings and prison "interrogations." . . . What emerges from this is, first, the inevitability of personal hates and squabbles (inseparable indeed from any form of refugee politics); and, second, the tremendous impact which the sudden enjoyment of power and luxury in their own native lands must have made. . . . The remarkable thing is not that many of them, like Szakasits in Hungary or Ana Pauker in Rumania, were weakened by these temptations, but that any at all found the inner strength to resist.[69]

Hence, once she attained power, Pauker had every motivation to close her eyes to anything troubling her conscience and to go on subverting herself to the collective whole. As the dream of a more humane Communism evaporated, she undoubtedly reverted to what Koestler described as the "private and secret philosophy . . . of every single educated Communist . . . , whose purpose is not to explain the facts, but to explain them away. It does not matter by what name one calls this mental process—double-think, controlled schizophrenia, myth addiction, or semantic perversion; what matters is the psychological pattern. Without it the portrait of the [Communist] would not be comprehensible." [70] Some readily brushed off any crime or outrage as the party's temporary lack of "consciousness"—a consciousness that Lenin predicted was sure to develop under socialism.[71] Others rationalized that no one could improve or influence the party from the outside but only from the inside.

Continuing to sacrifice by remaining a disciplined soldier within the
movement was the only possible way to effect change.[72] Still others reasoned that things would only get worse if they abandoned the fold: "our
whole leadership," the Polish Communist leader Jakub Berman insisted,
"would be got rid of and blasted to hell, naturally, and the people who
would come after us would be terrible, so terrible it's better not to think
about it."[73] Or as Dorothy Healy, encouraged by disillusioned comrades
in the American CP to make the break in 1958, willfully put it, "I'm not
going to let those bastards have the Party."[74]

Perhaps the most crucial element in this equation was fear. On the
one hand, there was the ever present fear of the Soviets—particularly
among the "Muscovites," those who, like Pauker, returned to their
countries after extended exiles in the USSR. As two former Hungarian
Stalinists observed, the

> leitmotif [of their lives] was fear. A Muscovite's life was never safe, wherever
> he went—and least of all in the Soviet Union. He knew that neither his age
> nor his long Party membership would protect him. He knew that he did not
> even have to commit a mistake in order to be relieved of his job, or be ar-
> rested and tried. To him, nothing was impossible. After all he had seen it all
> in the Soviet Union. His smile, his loyalty, and his zeal served but one pur-
> pose: to survive.[75]

But even more paralyzing, evidently, was the "fear of losing yourself. . . . Of finding yourself deprived of any perspective of the future.
The collapse of everything, of your whole world."[76] For many, such a
collapse would invariably result if they were suddenly removed from
their community of activists. One of the Communist underground's most
important dimensions was its basis in the cell, the closed and intimate
grouping of like-minded people powerfully bonded by their opposition
to, and oppression by, the outside world.[77] "The Party became family,
school, church, barracks; the world that lay beyond it was to be destroyed and built anew. The psychological mechanism whereby each
single militant becomes progressively identified with the collective organization is the same as that used in certain religious orders and military colleges, with almost identical results."[78] This was, Stephen Staszewski declared, the primary reason why he remained a committed
Communist after spending seven years in the gulag. "This kind of tie between combatants," he emphasized, "plays no trifling role in a person's
life."[79] Indeed, a number of Communists confided to one scholar "that
their original impulse to join the communist movement was strongly

colored by *a religious kind of need to belong* and to have a philosophi-
cal certainty at [their] beck and call." [80] Aleksander Wat often observed
this dynamic among his former comrades:

> Back in 1937, the time of the Moscow trials, when I spoke with some quite
> important communists, friends of mine, I would ask them, "So is everything
> clear to you now?" And they would answer, "Yes, it is, but we can't walk
> away from it. That's our entire youth." Communism proved how incredibly
> hard it is to walk away from one's youth when that youth was some sort of
> high point, a period of unselfishness, a beautiful way of life. All those old
> communists had come to communism by different routes, but they all had
> come to it through idealism, great unselfishness. [81]

Added to this was a simple point made by one of Pauker's old Comintern
friends upon hearing Tatiana Brătescu's reasons for rejecting Communism: "Well, I can't admit that myself," she told her, "because it would
mean that I would have to admit that my whole life had been a waste." [82]

So, too, with Ana Pauker—even after the purge, the invented charges,
and the incessant obloquy. She did not, Dr. Gheorghe Brătescu observed,
have time to arrive at the fundamental conclusions that later would dis-
illusion many. "Those conclusions had begun to be made after the war;
but nothing had really crystallized until the late sixties, when everything
became clear. The Soviet conflict with China inside the Bloc was a significant event in this process." [83] Hence, while acknowledging the extent
of Stalin's depravity to her family, she would never talk ill of the Romanian Party leadership to them, in part because she feared that doing
so would turn her family away from Communism.[84] Solzhenitsyn de-
picts a strikingly similar incident:

> Here's the sort of people they were. A letter from her fifteen-year-old daugh-
> ter came to Yelizaveta Tsvetkova in the Kazan Prison for long-term prison-
> ers: "Mama! Tell me, write to me—are you guilty or not? I hope you weren't
> guilty, because then I won't join the Komsomol, and I won't forgive them be-
> cause of you. But if you are guilty—I won't write you any more and will hate
> you." And the mother was stricken by remorse in her damp gravelike cell
> with its dim little lamp: How could her daughter live without the Komsomol?
> How could she be permitted to hate Soviet power? Better that she should hate
> me. And she wrote: "I am guilty. . . . Enter the Komsomol!" [85]

But, then again, if one word encapsulated Pauker's psychology, it
would have to be *duplicity*.[86] This included the interminable self-delu-
sions—that the constant twists and turns of party policy were somehow
based on scientific method; that uprooting the social structure would
somehow alter human nature; that the cheers and accolades somehow

reflected the Romanian people's true feelings; or that Marcel Pauker had somehow survived Stalin's bloodletting. More important, it included deliberately deceiving those below her. In how many speeches, how many rallies, how many private meetings had she used her vast persuasive talents to trick a weary and dubious populace on the merits of that "beloved leader and teacher," the glorious Comrade Stalin? True, she thought she could pursue her own policy favoring peaceful integration over class warfare; and true, the Soviets imposed the repression that followed during an increasingly heightened war scare. But, like all party leaders of that time, Ana Pauker cannot escape moral responsibility—and condemnation—either for her continual complicity in Stalinism or for her pivotal role in imposing Communism on a helpless, though resistant, Romania.

Clearly, the Stalinization of the Romanian regime left Pauker highly vulnerable for her earlier, now discredited policies, and in a panic to salvage her position, she often made the necessary cynical compromises. Perhaps the only moral course at that point would have been to step down and refuse to participate. If one account is correct, Pauker actually entertained thoughts of taking such a step but feared its potential consequences. Her brother reportedly told a Zionist leader that sometime after his arrival in November 1949 she had confided to him, "she'd like to retire, but is scared that she'd be shot." [87] On the other hand, her bout with cancer presumably enabled her to plead physical incapacity and thus avoid the charge of "treason" likely awaiting any Communist leader who voluntarily resigned. But she evidently chose a different tack. Ana Toma recalls that

> when [Ana Pauker] was purged, they told me, among other things, to take down her pictures from the [Foreign] Ministry. I didn't know what was going on, because Ana didn't tell me anything. I was just told one day to take down the pictures, and I refused. . . . When I refused to remove the pictures, Ana called me to her office and said "Let them take the pictures." And she added: "What? I'm not a fractionalist? I *am* a fractionalist." It was as if she stated a fact. [88]

Party doctrine defined "fractionalism" as sustaining one's personal opinions or principles in opposition to the party line. Ana Pauker certainly engaged in fractionalism in opposition not only to Gheorghiu-Dej's policies, but to the Soviets' as well. No other Stalinist leader save Tito has been shown to have resisted the Soviet-imposed line as she did—whether on collectivization, the fight against the kulaks and the urban bourgeoisie, the prosecution of Lucreţiu Patraşcanu, the purge of the

Spanish Civil War and French Resistance veterans, the dimensions of the
Five-Year Plan, the staging of a show trial of Romanian Zionists, or the
facilitation of mass Jewish emigration. While Pauker's personal line immediately after the war was paradigmatic of a general trend in the bloc
to pursue independent roads to socialism, the same cannot be said of
her actions *after* "high Stalinism's" implementation, from 1948 on.[89]
Though many bloc leaders certainly maneuvered on various aspects of
Stalinist policy during that period,[90] Pauker's defiance—no matter how
flawed or deficient it may have been—was qualitatively different.

Hence, the accusation of "right-wing deviationism" against Pauker
and her allies, though obviously political hyperbole, was nonetheless true,[91] and hardly the arbitrary charge that scholars have long believed masked what was solely a power struggle between Pauker and
Gheorghiu-Dej. The concomitant charge of "left-wing deviationism,"
however, a mainstay of historical accounts of Pauker for nearly four
decades, was indeed false. Though Pauker's purge soon assumed a decidedly trumped-up "anti-Zionist" character much like the Slansky prosecution in Prague (also contradicting conventional wisdom on her fall),
the fact remains that her ouster resulted in part from a genuine policy
dispute, with the "Cominternist" Ana Pauker often promoting policies
at odds with the Kremlin's, while the "native" Communist Gheorghiu-
Dej faithfully executed the Stalinist line.

These findings challenge a long-standing truism that during this period the "Muscovites" (those Communists who spent the Second World
War inside the Soviet Union) were the Soviets' most reliable and servile
tools for implementing Stalinism in the People's Democracies. The case
of Ana Pauker, long considered the classic Muscovite, begs the question
of whether the traumas of the Great Terror and the war years in the
USSR created some Communists' determination not to repeat the Soviet example in their own countries. Given the apparent singularity of
Pauker's actions, however, any conclusions on the matter should be
drawn with prudence.

No easy explanations account for Pauker's behavior. Her brush with
death from breast cancer, and the prolonged uncertainty of her recovery, may have freed her from the paralyzing fear of the Soviets. Though
this was probably a factor, Pauker had begun blocking Patrașcanu's
prosecution, had disbanded the commission investigating the Spaniards,
had pushed for unrestricted Jewish emigration, and had refused to establish a fixed and inflated number of collectives, all before her cancer
diagnosis in June 1950. Or Pauker arrogantly may have felt immune to

any sanction for her policies, given her prominence in the movement. This, too, probably holds a grain of truth, but one contradicted by her always being frightfully aware of her vulnerability as the wife of Marcel Pauker and knowing from the outset that, as a woman and a Jew, her initial selection as party leader would be only temporary.[92] Further, as a woman, she was never included in Stalin's late-night dinners with party leaders, which were strictly male-only affairs, and, perhaps consequently, never had nearly as close a relationship to Stalin as did Dej.[93] As neither explanation fully suffices, Pauker's bouts of resistance must have been vestiges of courage that few Communist leaders could muster.

Indeed, Pauker's defiance was all the more remarkable in that it garnered no political benefit. Keenly aware of the rules of Stalinist power politics, she must have known that maintaining her positions would assure defeat in her escalating power struggle with Gheorghiu-Dej. Whereas Patraşcanu, for instance, consciously sought to increase his popularity as a political strategy in his struggle with other leaders, Pauker—as both a woman and a Jew—had no such option.[94] No matter how liberal or tolerant or patriotic she became, Romanians would react to her precisely as indignant peasants had reacted to Jewish revolutionaries who "went to the people" in nineteenth-century Russia: *"But you're a Jew."*[95] That Pauker never articulated her "peasantist" policies in public speeches (not even in the early postwar years) suggests that she instinctively understood this.

Further, Pauker's lack of political legitimacy goes a long way in explaining her postwar attempts at creating a genuine popular base for party rule, as it does her decision to disqualify herself as general secretary and her preference for a broad coalition with Romanian democrats. Such positions evoked prominent Jews' similar moves in the Russian revolutionary movement several decades earlier. The Mensheviks in 1917, for instance, persistently refrained from taking sole control of the government despite the workers' demands that they do so, instead continuing to seek coalitions with the "bourgeois" parties. A possible explanation for this, Israel Getzler maintained, is that, having been primarily Jewish (and Georgian) urban intellectuals, the Menshevik leaders "simply lack[ed] the confidence" to govern on their own in a country with widespread anti-Semitic and anti-foreign sentiments. "Here," Getzler suggests, "there are significant straws in the wind: it was, *e.g.,* precisely because he was a Jew that [Fiodor] Dan refused to become a minister in the first coalition government and sent M. I. Skoblelev instead."[96] Likewise, Leon Trotsky refused to become the Minister of

Interior, and Lev Kamenev the president of the Soviet Union, for that very reason.[97] These Jews seemingly felt that placing Russians in their stead would help legitimate the revolutionary government. Certainly, Pauker was no different in this regard.

Most significantly, Pauker's lack of legitimacy underscored her position's inherent futility, and Communism's failure to transcend traditional gender-based restrictions or solve the Jewish Question. It was in response to her own marginality, her own perpetual "otherness," that Pauker embraced revolutionary internationalism early in the century. How much her gender actually influenced her decision is a matter of speculation, as a study of this phenomenon still awaits its scholar. Clearly, however, like the vast majority of Jews who entered the RCP between the wars, Pauker became a Communist not only as a member of an oppressed class, but also—indeed, particularly—as a member of a persecuted national minority. Thus, only Jews (and, to a lesser extent, Hungarians) were attracted to the RCP's antagonism toward Romanian nationalism, for only they were victimized by it. To them, Communism represented the sole means of both waging class warfare and ending national oppression by eradicating nationalism entirely. It represented their "entrance ticket" into Romanian society, and it appeared to fulfill that promise immediately after the war. Indeed, Romanian Jews' readiness to fill vacated government and civil service positions seemingly was crucial in consolidating the revolutionary regime in postwar Romania—just as Lenin had credited it with being in Russia two decades earlier.[98] But, as in the Soviet Union during the 1920s,[99] the Jews' sudden and conspicuous presence in the new regime created mass resentment among ethnic-Romanians. Having till now been barred from government posts and from a whole series of important professions, Jews suddenly appeared in prominent positions for the first time, and ethnic-Romanians widely considered them a Trojan horse bolstering the Soviet-sponsored regime—the true power behind the Communist throne.

The extent of such sentiment, and the party's sensitivity to it, is apparent in Vasile Luca's remark at a party meeting in October 1945:

> If we think dialectically, then we shouldn't complain that, in our actual situation, we have a political line of sorts not to advance Jews in the leadership of party organizations. And every Jewish Communist has to understand this . . . , because what a disaster we had in Moldavia. The party was made up only of Jews, the various organizations, the police and the administrative apparatus were all Jewish. And then people began asking: "What's going on

here? Is this a Jewish state or a Romanian state?" And this is continuing to go on in lots of places.[100]

As a result, Jews in the party and state apparatus were ordered en masse to change their names, and a systematic process of "Romaniazation" began. Though Stalin's death evidently circumvented the mass Jewish purge apparently in the offing during Pauker's fall, it was, alas, only a postponement: nearly all the Jews in the old guard were unceremoniously replaced in 1958–1960.[101] What happened to them, and to Jews in other Communist states, was, Talmon concluded, "[t]he last, and perhaps the most bewildering, illustration of [a] recurrent pattern [in Jewish history], the passage from the status of indispensable pioneer to that of a usurping parasite."[102] Or as Rosa Luxemburg once remarked, quoting a Polish proverb: "To the Jews for help—and when it's over, away with you, Jews."[103] In the end, the Communist regime reverted to nationalism and diversionist anti-Semitism to win popular support. While purged Jewish party veterans were permitted to live a comfortable retirement in privileged conditions, the bulk of Romanian Jewry found itself increasingly marginalized, at times persecuted, and unable to integrate into Romanian society. The "revolution as emancipation" proved a dismal failure.

Ana Pauker's "Jewish agenda"—and Romanian Jewish Communists' generally—seemed much like the sentiments of Jews in the *Narodnaia Volia* in nineteenth-century Russia. As Erich Haberer observed, these cosmopolitan socialists sought a universalist solution to the Jewish Question, one solely within the context of international revolution; however, at the same time, "on many occasions [these revolutionary] Jews were quite explicit in their concern for things Jewish and in linking their revolutionary dedication with Jewish aspirations."[104] Ana Pauker's consistent stance on mass aliya, her unique position on the Jewish Question, her tolerance of Jewish tradition, and her remarkable relationship with her Orthodox Jewish family all corroborate Haberer's thesis. Here was a Jewish Communist who did not fit the widely accepted prototype of "non-Jewish Jew" in the Communist movement. A convinced internationalist who had long since discarded a strictly Jewish identity, she neither evinced the stereotypical Jewish revolutionary's self-loathing nor shrank from promoting policies benefiting Romanian Jewry.

Zalman Rabinsohn once revealed to the Romanian Zionist leader Marcu Cohin that "Ana Pauker was troubled by the attack Ben-Gurion made on her [in 1949], saying to Rabinsohn that she's being depicted in such a false light when it's claimed that she's an adversary of Zionism; and, with the position she occupies, she can't speak out. Nevertheless, [she added,] history will set things right and reestablish the truth." [105]

The same can surely be said of Pauker's record with the Romanian people. Long the party propagandists' scapegoat as the source of all the horrors of the Stalinist period, Ana Pauker continues to be vilified in post-Communist Romania as the party leader most culpable for the postwar years' repression. But the truth is that this perpetually contradictory figure, though a Stalinist herself, and one who played a key role in imposing Communism on Romania, paradoxically presented an alternative to the rigid, harsh Stalinism that soon emblemized Romanian party life and left a hidden legacy as a persistent patron of Romania's peasantry within the Communist hierarchy. The fall of Ana Pauker was a significant step in a process that precluded any reformist leadership from prevailing in Romania (unlike Hungary, Poland, and Czechoslovakia) and fated its citizens to endure the extreme hardships that would culminate in the Ceaușescu regime. If for no other reason, Romanians would do well to take a second look at this enigmatic leader from their past.

Biographical Notes

(limited to the period under review)

Alexandru, Mihai	member of the party old guard; Deputy Minister of Commerce during the period under review
Alterescu, Sara	member of the old guard; jailed with Pauker in the late 1930s
Apostol, Gheorghe	president of the General Confederation of Labor, 1944–53; appointed member of the Central Committee in 1945, and member of the Politburo in 1948; a member of the party commission that investigated Ana Pauker, 1953–54 and 1956
Bălănescu, Mircea	an assistant to Ştefan Foriş in the late thirties; was head of the party press from 1940 to 1943; later held various positions and became Romania's ambassador to China, East Germany, France, and elsewhere
Balaş, Egon	an associate of Alexandru Iacob in the Cluj party organization during the immediate postwar period; appointed chief of the Directorate of Economic Affairs in Pauker's Foreign Ministry in 1948; arrested in August 1952; released in 1954
Barbu, Cora	sister of Emil Calmanovici
Belu, Nicolae	member of the old guard; editor in chief of *România liberă* during the period under review

Beria, Lavrenti   prominent Kremlin leader, 1938–53; arrested in
                                      June 1953; executed in December 1953

Berman, Jaques   construction engineer; arrested in 1952 in con-
                                      nection with the Patraşcanu case; appeared as a
                                      codefendant at Patraşcanu's trial in April 1954

Birnbaum, Marie   Pauker's third child

Birnbaum, Michel   Pauker's grandson

Bîrlădeanu, Alexandru   Deputy Minister of Exterior Commerce 1948–
                                      53; Minister of Exterior Commerce 1953–55

Bîrlădeanu, Victor   journalist in the cultural section of *Scânteia* dur-
                                      ing the period under review

Bodnăraş, Emil   officer in the Royal Romanian Army 1928–32;
                                      deserted to the Soviet Union in 1933; returned
                                      to Romania several years later, and arrested; re-
                                      leased from Caransebeş prison in late 1943 or
                                      early 1944; active in toppling Ştefan Foriş in
                                      April 1944; a member of the troika leading the
                                      RCP (with Contstantin Pârvulescu and Iosif
                                      Rangheţ) from April to September 1944; head
                                      of the party's "Patriotic Guard" in 1944; ap-
                                      pointed member of the Central Committee in
                                      1945; subsecretary of state, and president of the
                                      Council of Ministers 1946–47; head of the Se-
                                      cret Service of the Council of Ministers (SSI)
                                      1944–47; believed to be the resident Soviet
                                      agent in Romania 1944–48; appointed Minis-
                                      ter of National Defense in 1947; appointed
                                      member of the Politburo in 1948

Bogdan, Corneliu   member of the Communist youth organization
                                      during the war, officially joining the party in
                                      1941; served as the director of the cabinet of
                                      Pauker's Foreign Ministry from December 1948
                                      to the end of 1949; subsequently served for
                                      many years as Romania's ambassador to the
                                      United States

Bogdan, Radu   professor of art history; attacked by the Section
                                      of Propaganda of the Central Committee on
                                      March 15, 1952, for "cosmopolitanism and
                                      objectivism" in his lectures

Boico, Cristina   veteran of the French Resistance; director in the
                                      Ministry of Information from 1945 to 1947;
                                      press-attaché of the Romanian embassy in Bel-
                                      grade from 1947 to 1948; chief of the Cultural

Directorate in the Romanian Foreign Ministry
from 1948 to 1952; dismissed from the Foreign
Ministry in June 1952

Boico, Mihail Bibi   veteran of the Spanish Civil War; general in the
Interior Ministry; dismissed from the ministry
in the fall of 1952

Borilă, Ecaterina   member of the old guard; wife of Petre Borilă

Borilă, Petre   veteran of the Spanish Civil War; spent war years
in USSR; headed the Tudor Vladimirescu divi-
sion in 1943–44; head of the Bucharest Party
organization 1944–47; became member of the
Central Committee in 1948; chief of the political directorate of the Romanian army 1948–50;
Minister of Construction in 1950; chairman of
the State Control Commission in 1951; member
of the Organizational Bureau 1950–53; appointed member of the Politburo in May 1952;
served in the special party commission investigating Ana Pauker 1953–54, and again in 1956

Brătescu, Gheorghe, Dr.   Pauker's son-in-law; medical doctor; historian
of medicine; served in the Foreign Ministry in
1948; was counselor (vice-ambassador) of the
Romanian embassy in Moscow 1949–52

Brătescu, Tatiana   Pauker's eldest daughter, professor of Russian,
with whom Pauker resided after her purge

Brâncu, Zina   member of the old guard; imprisoned with Ana
Pauker in the late 1930s; spent war years in the
USSR; appointed member of the Directorate of
Propaganda and Agitation of the Central Com-
mittee in 1949; appointed deputy chief of the
Section of the Leading Organizations of the
Central Committee in 1950

Breban, Iosif   deputy chief of the Agrarian Section of the Central Committee during the period under review

Brill, Janetta   member of the old guard; wife of the Spaniard
Dr. Shuli Brill

Brucan, Silviu   assistant chief editor of *Scânteia* during the
period under review

Bughici, Simion   member of the old guard; ambassador to
Moscow 1949–52; appointed candidate mem-
ber of the Central Committee in 1949; full
member of the Central Committee in 1950;
Foreign Minister 1952–56

Burcă, Mihai	veteran of the Spanish Civil War; appointed Deputy Interior Minister in late 1950; dismissed from the ministry in the fall of 1952
Butyka, Francisc	chief officer of the Luca inquiry in the Interior Ministry
Calmanovici, Emil	assistant to Remus Koffler at the party's Financial Commission during the late 1930s and the war years; director general of the Ministry of Construction during the postwar period; arrested on May 26, 1951; tried in the Patraşcanu trial in April 1954; died in prison in 1956
Călin, Vera	worked as a messenger to Lucreţiu Patraşcanu in 1943–44; professor of comparative literature at the University of Bucharest until her emigration in 1976
Ceauşescu, Nicolae	appointed candidate member of the Central Committee in 1948; full member in 1952; appointed Deputy Minister of Agriculture in 1949; appointed secretary of the CC in 1948; member of the Agrarian Commission under Ana Pauker in 1949–50; member of the Organizational Bureau 1950–53; appointed candidate member of the Politburo in 1954; full member of the Politburo in 1955
Chirtoacă, Pavel	chief functionary of the Agrarian Section of the Central Committee 1950–52
Chişinevschi, Iosif	appointed member of the Central Committee in 1945 and of the Politburo in 1948; appointed member of the Secretariat, and vice-president of the Council of Ministers in 1950; member of the Organizational Bureau in 1950; head of Agitprop; oversaw the Foreign Section of the Central Committee beginning in 1950
Chişinevschi, Liuba	member of the old guard; imprisoned with Pauker in the late 1930s; appointed member of the Central Committee in 1945; appointed vice-president of the General Confederation of Labor in 1944
Clementis, Vladimir	member of the Czechoslovak CP since 1924; Foreign Minister of Czechoslovakia, 1948–51; arrested in 1951; tried and executed, November–December 1952
Coler, Jean	veteran of the Spanish Civil War; member of the

Directorate of Cadres of the Central Committee
1945–50

Coliu, Dumitru   spent war years in the Soviet Union; returned to
                                    Romania with the Tudor Vladimirescu division;
                                    appointed member of the Central Committee in
                                    1948; appointed deputy head of the party Con-
                                    trol Commission in 1948

Constante, Lena   painter; personal friend of Lucrețiu Patrașcanu;
                                    briefly arrested in connection to Patrașcanu in
                                    1948; rearrested in January 1950; tried in Pa-
                                    trașcanu's trial in 1954; imprisoned until 1956

Constantinescu, Miron   member of the Central Committee and Polit-
                                    buro 1945–57; director of Scânteia 1947–49;
                                    president of the State Planning Commission
                                    1949–55; member of the Organizational Bureau
                                    1950–53

Coposu, Corneliu   personal secretary of Iuliu Maniu 1937–40; as-
                                    sistant general secretary of the National Peasant
                                    Party 1944–47; arrested in 1947; released in
                                    1964; opposition leader after 1989

Costea, Mirel   brother-in-law of Emil Calmanovici; a member
                                    of the Patriotic Guards in 1944; a top official
                                    (chief of secret documents) in the Section of
                                    Cadres of the Central Committee 1945–51;
                                    committed suicide in June 1951

Cristescu, Gheorghe   leader of the Romanian Social Democratic Party
                                    after W.W.I.; headed the faction that affiliated
                                    with the Comintern in 1921; general secretary
                                    of the RSCP and RCP, 1922–24; expelled from
                                    the party in 1926

Danielopol, Dumitru G.   economist; member of the National Liberal
                                    Party; member of the Romanian delegation at
                                    the Paris Peace Conference in 1946

Diamantshtein, Ella   secretary of Ana Pauker in her office at party
                                    headquarters, 1944–47

Dragan (Kajesco), Vilma   member of the old guard; jailed with Pauker in
                                    the late 1930s; member of the party Control
                                    Commission during the postwar period

Drăghici, Alexandru   member of the Central Committee beginning in
                                    1948; first secretary of the Bucharest party or-
                                    ganization in 1949; appointed Deputy Interior
                                    Minister in 1951, and full minister in May 1952

Dulgheru, Mihai (Mişu)	member of the party's Patriotic Guard in 1944; appointed member of the Organizational Directorate of the Central Committee in 1949; chief of the Directorate of Investigation of the Interior Ministry 1950–52; arrested in November 1952
Dumitrescu, Liuba	member of the old guard; jailed with Pauker in the late 1930s
Eidlitz, Zoltan	member of the old guard; chief of staff of Luca's Finance Ministry 1948–52; arrested in 1952; released in 1954
Einhorn, Wilhelm	veteran of the Spanish Civil War; deputy chief of the Securitate in Cluj during immediate postwar period; appointed chief of staff of Securitate chief Gheorghe Pintilie in late 1940s; high-ranking officer in the secret police throughout the 1950s
Felix, Ida	RCP member since 1924; member of the party Control Commission 1945–50; director of cadres at the Foreign Ministry 1950–52
Filipescu, Gheorghe	chief of the Directorate of Investigations of the SSI
Finkelştein, Uşer	veteran of the Spanish Civil War
Florescu, Mihai	veteran of the Spanish Civil War; general secretary of the Arts and Information Agency in 1948; chief of the army's political department in 1949; Deputy Minister of Metallurgy and Chemical Industries 1951–53; appointed Minister of Chemical Industry in January 1953
Foriş, Ştefan	general secretary of the RCP 1936–44; forcibly removed from the leadership on April 4, 1944; worked in the party newspaper *România liberă* April–May 1944; twice arrested and twice released in 1944–45; rearrested on July 9, 1945; executed in the summer of 1946
Gaston Marin, Gheorghe	veteran of the French Resistance; personal secretary to Gheorghiu-Dej during the immediate postwar period; Minister of Electrical Energy and Electronic Industries during the period under review; elected to the Central Committee in 1960; appointed president of State Planning Commission in 1962; was also vice-president of the Council of Ministers until 1965

Georgescu, Teohari

member of the Secretariat, Politburo, and Central Committee of the RCP (RWP) 1945–52; subsecretary of state (for administration) of the Interior Ministry 1944–45; Minister of Interior 1945–54; purged with Ana Pauker in 1952; arrested on February 18, 1953; released on March 19, 1956; worked as a director of a printing firm thereafter; died in 1976

Gheorghiu-Dej, Gheorghe

a participant in the Grivița railroad strike in 1933; imprisoned from 1933 to 1944; Minister of Communications 1944–45; general secretary of the RCP (RWP) 1945–65; Minister of National Economy 1946–47; Minister of Industry and Commerce, 1947–48; died in 1965

Giladi, David

a functionary in the Israeli embassy in Bucharest in 1949–50

Goldstücker, Eduard

member of the Czechoslovak CP since 1933; worked in the Czechoslovak Foreign Ministry in Prague, 1945–47; Czechoslovak embassy in London, 1947–49; ambassador to Israel, 1949–51; ambassador to Sweden, 1951; arrested in 1951; sentenced to life imprisonment as a "Jewish bourgeois nationalist" in May 1953; released at the end of 1955

Gottwald, Klement

member of the Czechoslovak CP since 1925; elected president of Czechoslovakia in June 1948; died on March 14, 1953

Groza, Petru

head of the "Ploughmen's Front"; Prime Minister 1945–52; president of the Presidium of the Great National Assembly 1952–58; died in 1958

Gruia, Charlotte

veteran of the French Resistance; a high-ranking official in party's Control Commission from 1949 to 1966; led the section in the Control Commission investigating the Spanish and French Resistance veterans during the period under review

Iacob, Adam (Feuerştein)

member of the old guard of the RCP

Iacob, Alexandru

member of the old guard; head of the RCP organization in Cluj after the war; appointed Deputy Finance Minister in 1948; arrested in March 1952; tried with Vasile Luca in November 1954; released in 1964

Jianu, Marin   Deputy Interior Minister 1945–52; purged
                                  from the ministry in May 1952; arrested in Feb-
                                  ruary 1953; released in 1956

Kavtaradze, Sergei   Soviet ambassador to Romania, 1945–52

Koffler, Remus   member of the Central Committee of the RCP
                                  during the war years; head of the party's Finan-
                                  cial Commission in late 1930s and during war
                                  years; dismissed from all party functions in
                                  1945; arrested in December 1949; tried in the
                                  Patrașcanu trial in April 1954; executed on
                                  April 16–17, 1954

Köblös, Elek   participated in the founding of the RSCP in
                                  1921; elected to the Central Committee in
                                  1922; General Secretary of the RCP, 1924–28;
                                  emigrated to the Soviet Union in 1928; arrested
                                  soon afterward as a Trotskyist, but released
                                  several months later; worked in an airplane fac-
                                  tory until 1937, when he was liquidated in the
                                  Great Terror

Kuller, Harry   veteran member of the Romanian Zionist move-
                                  ment; historian and scholar

Lavrentiev, Anatoli   Soviet ambassador to Yugoslavia, 1945–48;
                                  Deputy Foreign Minister of the USSR, 1948–51;
                                  Soviet ambassador to Czechoslovakia, Novem-
                                  ber 1951–June 1952; Soviet ambassador to
                                  Romania beginning in June 1952

Leibovici, Shlomo   veteran member of the Romanian Zionist move-
                                  ment; was subsequently an official in the Israeli
                                  Foreign Ministry

Levanon, Israel   veteran member of the Romanian religious
                                  Zionist movement; personal friend of Hersh and
                                  Zalman Rabinsohn; emigrated to Israel in 1950

Luca, Elisabeta   veteran of the Spanish Civil War; married Vasile
                                  Luca during W.W.II; arrested in August 1952
                                  and kept in solitary confinement for twenty-
                                  seven months; released in 1954; worked in a
                                  factory until Luca's rehabilitation in 1968

Luca, Vasile   regional RCP secretary of Brașov, 1924–29;
                                  elected president of the United Unions in Roma-
                                  nia in 1929; demoted in 1930 for his participa-
                                  tion in the fractionalist struggle (in the Luximin
                                  faction) in 1930; elected regional RCP secretary
                                  of Iași in 1932; imprisoned from 1933 to 1939;

appointed officer in the political directorate of
the Red Army and a member of the Supreme
Soviet during the war; member of the Secretariat, Politburo, and Central Committee of the
RCP (RWP) 1945–52; Minister of Finance
1947–52; purged with Ana Pauker in 1952;
arrested on August 14, 1952; tried in October 1954 and sentenced to death; sentence
commuted to life imprisonment; died in prison
in 1963; officially rehabilitated in 1968

Lupan, Radu

editor in chief of the Literature Publishing
House and chief of the foreign department of
the journal *Contemporanul* 1948–52; dismissed from both positions for "cosmopolitanism" in June 1952

Lustig, Carol

administrative director of the Foreign Ministry,
1948–52; dismissed from the Foreign Ministry
in June 1952; emigrated to Israel in the early
1960s

Manea, Tudor

a leading official of the Counter-Espionage
Directorate of the SSI, 1948–50

Maurer, Ion Gheorghe

lawyer; served as chief defense attorney in
Pauker's 1936 trial; appointed member of the
Politburo and Central Committee of the RCP
(RWP) in 1945; undersecretary of state at the
Ministry of Industry and Commerce, 1945–48;
Deputy Minister of Exterior Commerce in Oc-
tober 1948; demoted to the post of chairman of
the Association for the Dissemination of Science
and Culture in early 1949; appointed Foreign
Minister, and returned to the party leadership,
in 1956

Mănescu, Radu

member of the old guard; director of the Press
Publishing Office; appointed member of the Directorate of Propaganda and Agitation of the
Central Committee in 1949; appointed Deputy
Minister of Finance in March 1952; served as
deputy chief of the special party commission
investigating Luca's Finance Ministry and the
National Bank after the February 29–March 1,
1952, CC plenary

Mezincescu, Eduard

member of the old guard; one of the leaders of
the Red Aid (MOPR) organization in Romania
during W.W.II. Deputy Minister in Pauker's For-

eign Ministry in 1948; Minister of Arts from 1949 to 1952; later entered diplomatic corps

Micu, Andre
veteran of the Spanish Civil War; chief of political cadres in the Interior Ministry during the postwar period; ousted from the Interior Ministry after Pauker and Georgescu's purge

Mihail, David
veteran of the Spanish Civil War; an officer in the SSI until 1950

Moghioroş, Alexandru
arrested with Ana Pauker in 1935; sentenced to ten years' imprisonment in 1936; released in 1944; elected to the Central Committee of the RCP in 1945; appointed as full member to the Politburo in 1948; oversaw organizational matters in the RWP, and supervised the Section of Cadres (renamed the Verification Section) of the Central Committee, beginning in 1949; appointed member of the Secretariat in 1950; president of the State Collections Committee 1950–51; replaced Ana Pauker as CC secretary overseeing the Agrarian Section of the Central Committee in the summer of 1950; member of the Organizational Bureau 1950–53; head of the party commission that investigated Ana Pauker, 1953–54 and 1956

Molotov, Vyacheslav
a prominent Soviet party and government leader until 1957

Neumann, Carol
member of the old guard; veteran of the Spanish Civil War; arrested in December 1952; released in September 1953

Nicholschi, Alexandru
high-ranking officer in the Interior Ministry

Nistor, Alexandru
associate of Alexandru Iacob in the Cluj party organization after the war; appointed as a director in Luca's Finance Ministry in 1948; a member of the Committee to Liquidate CASBI (1948–50); arrested in May 1952; released in 1954

Olaru, Tudor
member of the old guard; leading journalist of *Scânteia* during the period under review

Oprişan, Mircea
vice-president of the State Planning Commission from 1950 to 1954; Minister of Trade in 1954–55

Patraşcanu, Lucreţiu
founding member of the RSCP in the early 1920s; official delegate to the 4th Comintern Congress in 1922; elected deputy of Parliament

in 1931; representative of the RCP in the Comintern in Moscow 1933–34; appointed secretary of state, and minister without portfolio in August 1944; member of the Romanian delegation at the armistice negotiations in Moscow in September 1944; appointed Minister of Justice in November 1944; member of the Central Committee of the RCP 1945–48; member of the Politburo 1946–47; dismissed from the Central Committee in February 1948; dismissed from the Justice Ministry in March 1948; arrested on April 20, 1948; tried in April 1954; executed on April 16–17, 1954

Patriciu, Mihail

member of the old guard; veteran of the Spanish Civil War and the French Resistance; Securitate chief in Cluj and Braşov 1945–52; purged in the fall of 1952; worked as an ordinary factory worker until mid-1953; subsequently appointed director of the Reşiţa metal works

Pauker, Emil

uncle of Marcel Pauker

Pauker, Titi

sister of Marcel Pauker

Pătraşcu, Nicolae

a leader of the Iron Guard; conducted negotiations with Teohari Georgescu in 1945

Pârvulescu, Constantin

founding member of the RSCP in the early 1920s; a member of the troika leading the RCP (with Iosif Rangheţ and Emil Bodnăraş) from April to September 1944; elected member of the Central Committee of the RCP in October 1945; chairman of the party Control Commission 1945–61; a member of the party commission that investigated Ana Pauker, 1953–54 and 1956

Petrescu, Dumitru

member of the old guard; head of the Organizational Directorate of the Central Committee in 1948; candidate member of the Central Committee 1948–50; full member beginning in 1950; member of the Agrarian Commission under Ana Pauker 1949–50; chief of the Organizational Section of the Central Committee 1950–51; president of the State Provisions Committee 1951–52; appointed Minister of Finance in March 1952

Pintilie, Gheorghe

(aka Pantiuşa Bodnarenko) believed to be longest-standing Soviet agent in the RCP during

the interwar and postwar period; headed the
party's Secret Service 1944–48; elected to the
Central Committee of the RWP in 1948; appointed Deputy Interior Minister in 1949;
headed the Securitate in the Interior Ministry; a
member of the party commission investigating
the Spanish Civil War veterans in 1950

Popper, Armand

an assistant of Lucreţiu Patraşcanu in the early
postwar period; director of the "Cartea Rusa"
publishing house in the 1950s; later entered
academia

Rangheţ, Iosef

a member of the troika leading the RCP (with
Contstantin Pârvulescu and Emil Bodnăraş)
from April to September 1944; member of the
Central Committee of the RCP (RWP) 1945–
52; chief of party cadres 1945–48; head of the
external section of the SSI 1949–50; head of
the special party commission investigating the
Spanish Civil War veterans in 1950; died in
1952

Rădescu, Nicolae

Prime Minister of Romania, December 1944–
March 1945

Răutu, Leonte

member of the old guard; member of the Central Committee 1945–72; member of the Organizational Bureau 1950–53; appointed chief of
the Section of Propaganda and Agitation of the
Central Committee in 1950

Rogojinschi, Alexandru

member of the old guard; appointed chief of the
Directorate of Cadres of the Central Committee
in 1949, and chief of the Verification Section of
the Central Committee in 1950

Roman, Valter

veteran of the Spanish Civil War; spent the war
years in the Soviet Union working under Ana
Pauker; chief of the Directorate of Propaganda
in the Inspector General of the Army, 1945–48;
the army chief of staff, 1948–50; deputy chairman of the Association for the Dissemination
of Science and Culture, 1950–51; appointed
Minister of Posts and Telecommunications in
April 1951; dismissed as minister in December
1952; placed under house arrest, and investigated by the Control Commission, in the early
months of 1953; appointed to a low-level post
in the Agriculture Ministry in 1953; sanctioned

	with a "vote of censure with a warning" in May 1954
Rosen, Moses	chief rabbi of Romania, 1949–94
Rotman, David	member of the old guard; chief of a section of the State Control Commission until his dismissal and expulsion from the party in January 1953
Sakharovskii, Alexandr Mihailovich	chief Soviet adviser to the Interior Ministry during period under review
Sauvard, Sanda	veteran of the Spanish Civil War; purged in the fall of 1952
Sârbu, Maria	member of the old guard; imprisoned with Pauker in the late 1930s; worked as a director in Pauker's Foreign Ministry from 1948 to 1952
Sencovici, Alexandru	a member of the RCP Secretariat throughout the 1930s; Deputy Minister of Labor and Minister of Light Industry during the postwar period
Sevcenko, Sergiu	veteran of the Spanish Civil War; an official in the RCP trade unions during the immediate postwar period; an officer in the Interior Ministry in 1947; a high-ranking officer in the Romanian army thereafter
Shutov, Nikolai	an adviser in the Soviet embassy, a leading MGB agent in Romania
Slansky, Rudolf	member of the Czechoslovak CP since 1921; general secretary of the Czechoslovak CP 1945–51; demoted to deputy vice premier, 1951; arrested in November 1951; tried and executed in late November–December 1952
Szabo, Eugen	an official in the Central Committee apparatus 1948–52; a leading officer in the Interior Ministry in the 1950s
Şafran, Alexandre	chief rabbi of Romania, 1940–47
Şerer, David	member of the Central Committee of the Jewish Democratic Committee, 1945–53
Şiperco, Alexandru	member of the old guard; editor in chief of *Editura politică,* the party publishing house, in the 1960s; later became Romania's official representative to the International Olympic Committee
Tătărăscu, Gheorghe	prominent politician of the National Liberal Party; held various positions, including Prime Minister and Interior Minister, during the inter-

war period; led the National Liberal "dissi-
dents" who formed a coalition with the ruling
Communists in 1945; Foreign Minister 1945–
47; arrested in 1948

Tismăneanu, Hermina
veteran of the Spanish Civil War; medical
doctor; worked in the office of Alexandru
Moghioroş in early 1952; served in a special
group of party members translating the documents of the May 1952 CC plenary into Russian

Toma, Ana
member of the old guard; Pauker's personal
secretary after W.W.II; Deputy Foreign Minister
from 1950 to 1952; appointed Deputy Minister
in the Foreign Trade and Interior Trade Ministries after Pauker's purge

Toma, Sorin
member of the old guard; member of the Central Committee 1949–60; member of the Organizational Bureau 1950–53; chief editor of
Scânteia 1949–60

Tudorache, Elena
joined the RCP in 1927; was a regional party
secretary in Bukovina in 1935 and in Bucharest
in 1936; member of the Central Committee
1945–48; chief of the Organizational Directorate of the Central Committee in 1949; chief
of the Section of Light Industry of the Central
Committee from 1948 to 1952

Vaida, Vasile
member of the old guard; Minister of Agriculture, 1948–52

Vasilichi, Gheorghe
leader of the Grivița railroad strike in 1933; a
veteran of the French Resistance during W.W.II,
appointed to the Politburo and Central Committee of the RCP (RWP) in 1945; Minister of
National Education 1946–49; Minister of Min-
ing and Petroleum 1949–51; dismissed from the
ministry, and appointed head Union of Production Cooperatives, in April 1951; dismissed
from the Politburo in May 1952

Vass, Ghizela
member of the old guard; candidate member of
the Central Committee 1945–52; full member
beginning in 1952; chief of the Foreign Section
of the Central Committee 1950–53; a member
of the party commission investigating the Spanish Civil War veterans in 1950

Veretenicov
(first name unknown) chief Soviet adviser to the
Agrarian Section of the Central Committee

Vezendean, Victor   deputy chief of the Foreign Section of the Central Committee 1950–53; appointed deputy mayor of Bucharest in 1953

Vijoli, Aurel   head of the National Bank of Romania 1948–52; purged in March 1952; arrested in May 1952; imprisoned until 1956

Vinţe, Ioan   candidate member of the Central Committee of the RWP 1948–55; Minister of Food Industry 1948–50; Chief of the Organizational Section of the Central Committee 1950–52; appointed Deputy Minister of the Interior in May 1952; a member of the party commission that investigated Ana Pauker, 1953–54 and 1956

Wald, Henri   professor (retired) of logic at the University of Bucharest

Zaharescu, Barbu   member of the old guard; leading party economist; appointed to the Directorate of Propaganda and Agitation of the Central Committee in 1949

Zaharescu, Vladimir   member of the Party Historical Commission; investigated the Patraşcanu case in 1966–68

Zaharia, Ilie   member of the old guard; appointed head of the party press in 1943; general secretary of the Ministry of Industry and Commerce, 1945–48; a leading functionary at the State Planning Commission, 1948–53

Zeiger, Simion   member of the old guard; imprisoned with Gheorghiu-Dej in the late 1930s and early 1940s; a leading figure in the State Planning Commission prior to his dismissal in 1950

Zetkin, Clara   prominent socialist and Communist in Germany; worked in the Comintern in the 1920s, leading the Red Aid (MOPR)

Zhdanov, Andrei   member of the Politburo of the CPSU; died in August 1948

Zhemchuzhina, Polina   joined the Bolsheviks in 1918; married Vyacheslav Molotov in 1921; appointed deputy people's commissar of the food industry, November 1937; appointed people's commissar of the food industry, January 1939; elected candidate member of the Central Committee of the CPSU, 1939; appointed head of Chief Administration of the Textile-Haberdashery Industry of the People's Commissariat of Light Industry, November 1939; dismissed "due to poor health" on May 10, 1948; arrested on January 21, 1949, and exiled to Kustanaí region of Kazakhstan; ordered returned to Moscow by Joseph Stalin, charged with "Jewish nationalism," and interrogated in connection to the Doctors' Plot; released on March 10, 1953, the day after Stalin's funeral

Zilber, Herbert (Belu)   economist; friend of Lucreţiu Patraşcanu; arrested in February 1948; tried in Patraşcanu's trial in April 1954; imprisoned until 1964

Notes

INTRODUCTION

1. "A Girl Who Hated Cream Puffs," *Time,* September 20, 1948, p. 31; Hal Lehrman, "Ana Pauker," *Life,* January 3, 1949, p. 73.

2. The diplomat was Moredechai Namir; Informative note, June 13, 1953, Archive of the Romanian Information Service (ASRI), Fond P, Dosar 40009, Vol. 50, pp. 340–341. David Krivine, "Who Was Ana Pauker?" *Jerusalem Post Magazine,* December 26, 1975, p. 9.

3. *Rumanian National Committee Bulletin,* no. 42, July 1952, p. 7; Gordon Shephard, *Russia's Danubian Empire* (London, 1954), pp. 53, 56.

4. For example, Pauker is nowhere to be found in Rosalind Miles, *The Women's History of the World* (London, 1988); or in Bonnie S. Anderson and Judith P. Zinnser, *A History of Their Own: Woman in Europe from Pre-History to the Present* (New York, 1988); or in Sondra Henry and Emily Taitz, *Written Out of History: A Hidden Legacy of Jewish Women Revealed through Their Writings and Letters* (New York, 1978).

5. Isaac Deutscher, *The Non-Jewish Jew and Other Essays* (Oxford, 1968), pp. 25–41.

6. *New York Herald Tribune,* November 1, 1949; Raphael Vago, "Jews in the Communist Regime, 1944–1948," in Benjamin Pinkus, ed., *Yahadut Mizrach Europa ben Sho'ah li-tekumah, 1944–1948* [Eastern European Jewry from the Holocaust to Redemption, 1944–1948] (Sde Boker, Israel, 1987), p. 143.

7. Ion Gheorghe Maurer, interview, in Lavinia Betea, *Maurer şi lumea de ieri, mărturii despre stalinizarea româniei* [Maurer and Yesterday's World, Testimony on the Stalinization of Romania] (Arad, 1995), p. 119; Silviu Brucan, interview by author, November 25, 1993; Anton Raţiu, *Cumplita odisee a grupului Lucreţiu Pătrăşcanu* [The Terrible Odyssey of the Lucreţiu Patraşcanu Group], vol. 2 (Bucharest, 1996), pp. 80–84.

8. A recent study on postwar Romania described Pauker as a "radical 'Muscovite'" and one of "the most overt Stalinists" in the party leadership (Elizabeth W.

Hazard, *Cold War Crucible: United States Foreign Policy and the Conflict in Romania, 1943–1953* [Boulder, 1996], pp. 90, 235). Based on this image, scholars have generally dismissed the authenticity of the charges of "right-wing deviationism" leveled against Pauker when she was purged in 1952, contending that her downfall was solely the result of a power struggle within the party leadership (see, e.g., Vladimir Tismaneanu, "The Tragicomedy of Romanian Communism," *East European Politics and Societies* 3, no. 2 [Spring 1989], p. 362; Michael Shafir, *Romania, Politics, Economics and Society* [Boulder, 1985], pp. 45–46; Stephen Fischer-Galati, *The New Rumania: From People's Democracy to Socialist Republic* [Cambridge, Mass., 1967], p. 39). At least one scholar, moreover, more readily accepted the revised, opposite charge of leftist adventurism made against Pauker after 1956 (Robert R. King, *History of the Romanian Communist Party* [Stanford, 1980], p. 92).

9. Robert Conquest, *The Great Terror* (New York, 1968), p. 582; A. Vaksberg, *Hotel Lux* (Paris, 1993), p. 262; Shephard, *Russia's Danubian Empire*, p. 54 n. 1.

10. J. L. Talmon, *The Myth of the Nation and the Vision of Revolution* (London, 1981), p. 169.

11. Jaff Schatz, *The Generation: The Rise and Fall of the Jewish Communists of Poland* (Berkeley and Los Angeles, 1991), pp. 11–19.

12. Sorin Toma interview, August 25, 1989; Ilie Zaharia interview, March 25, 1989; Jean Coler interview, August 31, 1989; Ida Felix interview, December 24, 1993; Radu Mănescu interview, August 28, 1989; Mircea Oprişan interview, September 4, 1985; Adam Iacob (Feurştein) interview, June 25, 1991; and Victor Vezendean interview, November 30, 1990 (see biographical note for brief biographies of those interviewed).

13. Michael Shafir, *Romania, Politics, Economics and Society*, p. 25; Wilhelm Einhorn interview, August 4, 1989; Ilie Zaharia and Victor Vezendean interviews; Transcript of a Meeting with the Central Activ of the Romanian Communist Party, April 25–27, 1945, National Archives of Romania, Fond CC al PCR—Cancelarie, Dosar 53/1945, p. 14; Transcript of a Meeting [of RCP Leaders] on June 26, 1945, National Archives of Romania, Fond CC al PCR—Cancelarie, Dosar 53/1945, p. 12.

14. Stephen Fischer-Galati, "Fascism, Communism, and the Jewish Question in Romania," in Bela Vago and George L. Mosse, eds., *Jews and Non-Jews in Eastern Europe, 1918–1945* (New York and Toronto, 1974), pp. 172–173.

15. Zvi Y. Gitelman, *Jewish Nationality and Soviet Politics: The Jewish Sections of the C.P.S.U., 1917–1930* (Princeton, 1972), pp. 115–116.

16. Transcript of a Meeting of the Politburo of the RCP, December 21, 1945, National Archives of Romania, Fond CC al PCR—Cancelarie, Dosar 122/1945, p. 11.

17. Solomon M. Schwarz, "The New Anti-Semitism of the Soviet Union," *Commentary*, January 1950, p. 40.

18. Talmon, *The Myth of the Nation*, pp. 184–185; Paula E. Hyman, *The Jews of Modern France* (Berkeley and Los Angeles, 1998), pp. 95–98; Shmuel Ettinger, "The Origins of Modern Anti-Semitism," *Dispersion and Unity* 9 (1969), pp. 32–34; Eugen Weber, "Jews, Antisemitism, and the Origins of the Holocaust," *Historical Reflections* 5, no. 1 (Summer 1978), p. 10.

19. Talmon, *The Myth of the Nation*, pp. 179–180.

20. Ibid., p. 181; Shmuel Ettinger, "The Origins of Modern Anti-Semitism," pp. 31–32; M. J. Rosman, *The Lord's Jews: Magnate-Jewish Relations in the Polish-Lithuanian Commonwealth during the Eighteenth Century* (Cambridge, Mass., 1990); Stanislav Andreski, "An Economic Interpretation of Antisemitism in Eastern Europe," *Jewish Journal of Sociology* 5, no. 2 (December 1963), pp. 206–209;

Werner J. Cahnman, "Socio-Economic Causes of Antisemitism," *Social Problems* 5, no. 1 (July 1957), pp. 25–26.

21. Bernard Weinryb, "The Economic and Social Background of Modern Anti-semitism," in Koppel S. Pinson, ed., *Essays on Antisemitism* (New York, 1942), pp. 145–166.

22. An earlier "Romaniazation" campaign in the party during the 1930s was mostly an effort to recruit ethnic-Romanians, and rarely involved replacing or purging ethnic minorities.

23. Jacob Katz, *From Prejudice to Destruction: Anti-Semitism, 1700–1933* (Cambridge, Mass., 1980), pp. 23–47, 159–160; Shmuel Ettinger, "The Modern Period," in H. H. Ben-Sasson, ed., *A History of the Jewish People* (Cambridge, Mass., 1976), p. 805; Shmuel Ettinger, "The Young Hegelians: A Source of Modern Anti-Semitism?" *Jerusalem Quarterly* 28 (Summer 1983), pp. 73–82; Edmund Silberner, "German Social Democracy and the Jewish Problem Prior to World War I," *Historica Judaica* 15, part 1 (April 1953), pp. 4–14.

24. Ibid., pp. 7–9; Robert Wistrich, *Socialism and the Jews: The Dilemmas of Assimilation in Germany and Austria-Hungary* (East Brunswick, N.J., 1982), p. 48; Jacob B. Agus, *Jewish Identity in an Age of Ideologies* (New York, 1978), pp. 172–173; Abraham Ascher, *Pavel Axelrod and the Development of Marxism* (Cambridge, Mass., 1972), pp. 69–78; Eric Goldhagen, "The Ethnic Consciousness of Early Russian Jewish Socialists," *Judaism* 23 (1974), pp. 490–494; Jonathan Frankel, *Prophecy and Politics: Socialism, Nationalism and the Russian Jews, 1862–1917* (Cambridge, 1981), pp. 98–99; Werner T. Angress, *Stillborn Revolution: The Communist Bid for Power in Germany, 1921–1923* (Princeton, 1963), pp. 314–377; Martin Jay, "Anti-Semitism and the Weimar Left," *Midstream,* January 1974, p. 47.

25. Erich Haberer, *Jews and Revolution in Nineteenth-Century Russia* (Cambridge, 1995), p. 261.

26. Cited in Talmon, *The Myth of the Nation,* p. 218.

27. Zygmunt Bauman, *Modernity and Ambivalence* (Oxford, 1991), p. 112.

28. Aviva Cantor, *Jewish Women/Jewish Men: The Legacy of Patriarchy in Jewish Life* (New York, 1995), pp. 157–158.

29. Bauman, *Modernity and Ambivalence,* pp. 67–68, 71; Zygmunt Bauman, "The Literary Afterlife of Polish Jewry," *Polin: A Journal of Polish-Jewish Studies* 7 (1992), p. 280.

30. Zygmunt Bauman, "Exit Visas and Entry Tickets: Paradoxes of Jewish Assimilation," *Telos,* no. 75 (Spring 1988), pp. 51–52; Bauman, *Modernity and Ambivalence,* p. 112.

31. Sander L. Gilman, *Jewish Self-Hatred* (Baltimore and London, 1986), pp. 2–3; Cantor, *Jewish Women/Jewish Men,* p. 158.

32. Bauman, "Exit Visas and Entry Tickets: Paradoxes of Jewish Assimilation," pp. 52–53.

33. Hannah Arendt, *The Origins of Totalitarianism* (Cleveland and New York, 1958), pp. 79–88.

34. Bauman, *Modernity and Ambivalence,* pp. 119–120.

35. Oscar Handlin, "Prejudice and Capitalist Exploitation: Does Economics Explain Racism?" *Commentary,* July 1948, p. 84.

36. Talmon, *The Myth of the Nation,* pp. 170, 181.

37. Jonathan Frankel, "Assimilation and the Jews in Nineteenth-Century Europe: Towards a New Historiography?" in Jonathan Frankel and Steven J. Zipperstein, eds., *Assimilation and Community: The Jews in Nineteenth-Century Europe* (Cambridge, 1992), p. 5.

38. Ibid., pp. 16–23.

39. Tony Judt, "Why the Cold War Worked," *New York Review of Books,* October 9, 1997, p. 39.

40. A number of witnesses expressed this to the author.

41. Wilhelm Einhorn interview.

42. Report of the Party Commission Established to Clarify the Situation of Lucreţiu Patraşcanu, Submitted to the Party Leadership on June 29, 1968, Executive Archive of the Central Committee of the RCP, pp. 43–44.

43. "Questionnaire," October 12, 1956, Ana Pauker Inquiry File, Executive Archive of the Central Committee of the RCP, pp. 715–718.

44. Robert Conquest, "The Somber Monster," *New York Review of Books,* June 8, 1995, pp. 10–11.

CHAPTER 1

1. Declaration of Bella Rabinsohn, Russian Center for the Preservation and Study of Documents of Most Recent History (RTsKhIDNI), Fond 495, Opis 255, Dossier 4 (I), p. 45, side 1; Tatiana and Gheorghe Brătescu interview, November 11, 1990.

2. Liviu Rotman, "Mental and Cultural Structures of Romanian Jews at the Turn of the Century," *Shvut: Jewish Problems in Eastern Europe* 16 (1993), p. 152; Avram Rosen, "The Contribution of the Jews to the Industrial Development and Modernization of Romania, 1900–1938: The Case of Bucharest," *Shvut: Jewish Problems in Eastern Europe* 16 (1993), p. 235.

3. Israel Bar-Avi, *O istorie a evreilor români* [A History of the Romanian Jews], vol. 3 (Jerusalem, 1966), p. 12.

4. Ibid., p. 12; Victor Eskenasy, "Moses Gaster and His Memoirs—the Path to Zionism," *Shvut: Jewish Problems in Eastern Europe* 16 (1993), pp. 166, 169.

5. Rotman, "Mental and Cultural Structures of Romanian Jews," p. 153; Autobiographical Statement of Ana Pauker, March 5, 1930, Russian Center for the Preservation and Study of Documents of Most Recent History (RTsKhIDNI), Fond 495, Opis 255, Dossier 4 (I), p. 26.

6. Ibid; Marius Mircu, *Ana Pauker şi alţii* [Ana Pauker and the Others] (Bat Yam, Israel, 1989), p. 27; Moses Rosen, *Primejdii, incercări, miracole* [Dangers, Tests, and Miracles] (Bucharest, 1991), p. 115. This is the Romanian version of Rosen's memoirs, which is slightly different than the English text.

7. Ibid., p. 116; Mircu, *Ana Pauker şi alţii,* p. 27.

8. Declaration of Bella Rabinsohn, p. 45, side 1.

9. Ibid.

10. Mircu, *Ana Pauker şi alţii,* pp. 27–28.

11. Declaration of Bella Rabinsohn, p. 45, sides 1–2; Bar-Avi, *O istorie a evreilor români,* p. 12.

12. Autobiographical Statement of Ana Pauker, March 5, 1930, p. 26; Ana Pauker's Application for a Party Card of CPSU, 15 June 1944, Russian Center for the Preservation and Study of Documents of Most Recent History (RTsKhIDNI), Fond 495, Opis 255, Dossier 4 (I); Declaration of Bella Rabinsohn, p. 45, side 2.

13. Declaration of Bella Rabinsohn, pp. 44; 45, side 2. Beck was one of three leaders of the Central Committee of Israelite Schools in the capital, which coordinated the activities of all the Jewish schools in Bucharest (Bar-Avi, *O istorie a evreilor români,* p. 13).

14. Bar-Avi, *O istorie a evreilor români,* p. 12.

15. Autobiographical Statement of Ana Pauker, March 5, 1930, p. 26; Ana Pauker's Application for a Party Card of CPSU, 15 June 1944; Declaration of Bella Rabinsohn, pp. 44.

16. Shaul Stampfer, "Gender Differentiation and Education of the Jewish Woman in Nineteenth-Century Eastern Europe," *Polin: A Journal of Polish-Jewish Studies* 7 (1992), pp. 61–87.

17. I. C. Butnaru, *The Silent Holocaust: Romania and Its Jews* (New York, 1992), p. 22.

18. *The Jewish Encyclopedia,* vol. 10 (New York and London, 1901–1906), pp. 515, 517.

19. Michael Stanislawski, introduction to Emil Dorian, *The Quality of Witness: A Romanian Diary, 1937–1944,* edited by Marguerite Dorian (Philadelphia, 1982), p. xxv; Keith Hitchins, *Rumania, 1966–1947* (Oxford, 1994), pp. 164–165.

20. Uniunea Evreilor Pământeni [Union of Native Jews], *Petiția evreilor pământeni adresată corpurilor legiuitoare. Cuvântul evreilor pământeni* [The Petition of the Native Jews Addressed to the Legislative Body. The View of the Native Jews] (Bucharest, 1990); cited (with a slightly different translation) by Jean Ancel, "The Image of the Jew in the View of Romanian Anti-Semitic Movements: Continuity and Change," *Shvut: Jewish Problems in Eastern Europe* 16 (1993), pp. 39–40.

21. Eugen Weber, "Romania," in Hans Rogger and Eugen Weber, eds., *The European Right* (Berkeley and Los Angeles, 1966), p. 505; Leon Volovici, *Nationalist Ideology and Antisemitism: The Case of Romanian Intellectuals in the 1930s* (Oxford, 1991), p. 4.

22. *The Universal Jewish Encyclopedia,* vol. 9, p. 252; *The Jewish Encyclopedia,* p. 513.

23. Butnaru, *The Silent Holocaust,* p. 1; Radu Ioanid, *The Sword of the Archangel: Fascist Ideology in Romania* (Boulder and New York, 1990), pp. 29–30; William O. Oldson, *A Providential Anti-Semitism: Nationalism and Polity in Nineteenth-Century Romania* (Philadelphia, 1991), p. 156; Ancel, "The Image of the Jew," pp. 41–42.

24. *The Jewish Encyclopedia,* pp. 513–514; Butnaru, *The Silent Holocaust,* p. 10.

25. Emil Cioran, *Schimbarea la față a României* (Bucharest, 1937), pp. 127–128; cited in Volovici, *Nationalist Ideology and Antisemitism,* p. 96. Hașdeu's quote is cited in Weber, "Romania," p. 505. On the Greeks in Romania, see Weber, "Romania," p. 501; on Romania's fear of foreigners, see Volovici, *Nationalist Ideology and Antisemitism,* p. 4. Also see Stephen Fischer-Galati, "Romanian Nationalism," in Peter F. Sugar and Ivo J. Lederer, eds., *Nationalism in Eastern Europe* (Seattle and London, 1969), p. 374; Ioanid, op. cit., pp. 29–30; on European nationalism, see Peter F. Sugar, "Roots of Eastern European Nationalism," in *Nationalism in Eastern Europe,* pp. 34–44.

26. Nicolas Spulber, *The State and Economic Development in Eastern Europe* (New York, 1966), pp. 92–93, 108–109; Weber, "Romania," pp. 501–502, 505; *The Universal Jewish Encyclopedia,* p. 250.

27. Spulber, *The State and Economic Development,* pp. 108–109.

28. Nicolas Sylvain, "Rumania," in Peter Meyer, ed., *The Jews in the Soviet Satellites* (Syracuse, 1953), p. 495; Zeev Shlomo Arnon, *Ha-Yahas la-Yehudim shel ha-mimshal veha-tsibur be-Romanyah, ba-me'ah ha-19 (1812–1917)* [Attitudes and Relations to the Jews of the Public and Administration in Rumania during the 19th Century (1812–1917)], Ph.D. dissertation, Hebrew University, May 1986, p. vi; Butnaru, *The Silent Holocaust,* p. 8; Spulber, *The State and Economic Development,*

p. 99; *The Universal Jewish Encyclopedia,* p. 250; Barbara Jelavich, *History of the Balkans,* vol. 2 of *Twentieth Century* (Cambridge and New York, 1983), p. 26.

29. Spulber, *The State and Economic Development,* p. 99.

30. On trade contacts, see Spulber, *The State and Economic Development,* pp. 100, 102, and David Vital, *The Origins of Zionism* (Oxford, 1975), p. 89; on Bukovinian industry, Eugen Weber, "The Men of the Archangel," in George L. Mosse, ed., *International Fascism: New Thoughts and New Approaches* (London, 1979), p. 331; on urban Jews' acculturation, Stanislawski, introduction to *The Quality of Witness,* p. xxvi.

31. Ezra Mendelsohn, *The Jews of East Central Europe between the World Wars* (Bloomington, Ind., 1983), p. 180.

32. Raphael Vago, "The Traditions of Antisemitism in Romania," *Patterns of Prejudice* 27, no. 1 (1993), pp. 108–111; Ancel, "The Image of the Jew," p. 45; Volovici, *Nationalist Ideology and Antisemitism,* p. 17.

33. The quote is from T. W. Ryker, *The Making of Roumania* (London, 1931), p. 5, cited in *The Universal Jewish Encyclopedia,* pp. 248–249; on the importance of the peasant question, see Stephen Fischer-Galati, "Jew and Peasant in Interwar Romania," *Nationalities Papers* 16, no. 2 (Fall 1988), p. 201, and Volovici, *Nationalist Ideology and Antisemitism,* p. 7; on peasant land holdings, Henry L. Roberts, *Rumania: Political Problems of an Agrarian State* (New Haven, 1951), pp. 12–15, Spulber, *The State and Economic Development,* p. 94, and Hitchins, *Rumania,* p. 167.

34. On Jewish occupations, see Weber, "The Men of the Archangel," p. 331; *The Universal Jewish Encyclopedia,* p. 250; Arnon, *Ha-Yahas la-Yehudim,* p. vii; Bar-Avi, *O istorie a evreilor români,* p. 42; Spulber, *The State and Economic Development,* p. 103. On their role in transforming the economy, see Arnon, *Ha-Yahas la-Yehudim,* p. vii, and Spulber, *The State and Economic Development,* pp. 138–139; on their role as scapegoats, Fischer-Galati, "Romanian Nationalism," p. 386; Oldson, *A Providential Anti-Semitism,* p. 156; Volovici, *Nationalist Ideology and Antisemitism,* pp. 7–8.

35. The quote is from Butnaru, *The Silent Holocaust,* p. 2. On obstacles to reform, see *The Universal Jewish Encyclopedia,* p. 250; on broken promises, Arnon, *Ha-Yahas la-Yehudim,* p. 59; on the boyars, Trond Gilberg, "The Multiple Legacies of History: Romania in the Year 1990," in Joseph Held, ed., *The Columbia History of Eastern Europe* (New York, 1992), pp. 278–279. On the overthrow of Prince Alexandru Ion Cuza, see Fischer-Galati, "Romanian Nationalism," p. 385; *The Universal Jewish Encyclopedia,* p. 254; Arnon, *Ha-Yahas la-Yehudim,* p. viii; Lloyd A. Cohen, "The Jewish Question during the Period of the Romanian National Renaissance and the Unification of the Two Principalities of Moldavia and Wallachia, 1848–1866," in Stephen Fischer-Galati, Radu R. Florescu, and George R. Ursul, eds., *Romania between East and West: Historical Essays in Memory of Constantin C. Giurescu* (Boulder and New York, 1982), p. 212. On the regulations against the peasants, see Arnon, *Ha-Yahas la-Yehudim,* pp. vii–ix, and Ettinger, "The Modern Period," in Ben Sasson, ed., *A History of Jewish People,* p. 822.

36. Arnon, *Ha-Yahas la-Yehudim,* pp. ix, 60.

37. Mitchell Cohen, *The Wager of Lucien Goldmann: Tragedy, Dialectics, and a Hidden God* (Princeton, 1994), p. 20.

38. Roberts, *Rumania,* pp. 18–19.

39. Volovici, *Nationalist Ideology and Antisemitism,* pp. 7, 10, 29; Ancel, "The Image of the Jew," pp. 42–43.

40. Bar-Avi, *O istorie a evreilor români,* p. 43.

41. Brătianu circular to Moldavian prefects, undated, in *British and Foreign State Papers 1867–1868*, 58, p. 887; cited in Fredrick Kellogg, *The Road to Romanian Independence* (West Lafayette, Ind., 1995), p. 49; *The Universal Jewish Encyclopedia*, p. 256.

42. *The Universal Jewish Encyclopedia*, pp. 252.

43. Ibid., pp. 256–257; Arnon, *Ha-Yahas la-Yehudim*, p. 61.

44. *The Universal Jewish Encyclopedia*, p. 256; Arnon, *Ha-Yahas la-Yehudim*, p. 60.

45. *The Universal Jewish Encyclopedia*, p. 256.

46. Bar-Avi, *O istorie a evreilor români*, p. 43.

47. On the revolt, see Phillip G. Eidelberg, *The Great Rumanian Peasant Revolt of 1907* (Leiden, 1974).

48. Roberts, *Rumania*, p. 14.

49. Of 1,102 *arendaşi* operating in Moldavia in 1902, 556 were Romanians, 440 were Jews, and 106 were Greeks and Armenians. Arnon, *Ha-Yahas la-Yehudim*, p. 63.

50. Bar-Avi, *O istorie a evreilor români*, p. 82.

51. V. Popovici et. al., eds., *Dezvoltarea economiei Moldovei între anii 1848 şi 1864* [Economic Development of Moldavia between 1848 and 1864], Academia R.P.R. (Bucharest, 1963), pp. 41, 55; Dan Berindei, "Aspecte ale problemei agrare în ţara ramânească la începutul domniei lui Cuza vodă" [Aspects of the Agrarian Problem in the Romanian Countryside at the Beginning of the Reign of Prince Cuza], in Gh. Haupt and Gh. Gheorghescu-Buzău, eds., *Studii şi materiale de istorie modernă* [Studies and Materials of Modern History], 1957, vol. 1, pp. 167 ff.; both studies cited in Spulber, *The State and Economic Development*, pp. 101–102.

52. On agricultural prices, see E. J. Hobsbawm, *The Age of Empire, 1875–1914* (New York, 1989), pp. 36–37; on peasant exploitation, Spulber, *The State and Economic Development*, p. 94; on blaming middlemen, Roberts, *Rumania*, pp. 14–15; on land ownership and leasing, Butnaru, *The Silent Holocaust*, pp. 20–21.

53. Bar-Avi, *O istorie a evreilor români*, pp. 41, 48, 73.

54. Ibid., p. 98; Butnaru, *The Silent Holocaust*, pp. 27–28; Roberts, *Rumania*, pp. 16, 21; Hitchins, *Rumania*, p. 177.

55. Butnaru, *The Silent Holocaust*, p. 28; Bar-Avi, *O istorie a evreilor români*, p. 98.

56. Fischer-Galati, "Romanian Nationalism," p. 389.

57. Bar-Avi, *O istorie a evreilor români*, p. 82.

58. Ibid., pp. 44–47.

59. The quote is from Butnaru, *The Silent Holocaust*, pp. 17–18, 28. On middle-class anti-Semitism, see Spulber, *The State and Economic Development*, pp. 109–110, and Vago, "The Traditions of Antisemitism," pp. 108–111; on the population explosion, Roberts, *Rumania*, pp. 13–14, and Hitchins, *Rumania*, pp. 155–156; on the prevalence of Yiddish, Weber, "The Men of the Archangel," p. 331.

60. Carol Iancu, *Les Juifs en Roumanie, 1866–1919, de l'exclusion à l'émancipation* (Aix-en-Provence, 1978), p. 259; cited in Arnon, *Ha-Yahas la-Yehudim*, p. 73.

61. Arnon, *Ha-Yahas la-Yehudim*, p. ix.

62. *The Jewish Encyclopedia*, vol. 10 (New York and London, 1901–1906), pp. 516–517; on the March 16, 1902, law, also see Zeev Shlomo Arnon, *Ha-Yahas la-Yehudim*, p. ix.

63. Bar-Avi, *O istorie a evreilor români*, p. 7.

64. Arnon, *Ha-Yahas la-Yehudim*, pp. ix–x.

65. Kellogg, *The Road to Romanian Independence*, pp. 50, 52–53; Ettinger,

"The Modern Period," in Ben Sasson, ed., *A History of Jewish People,* pp. 822–823; *The Jewish Encyclopedia,* p. 514; *The Universal Jewish Encyclopedia,* p. 256; Arnon, *Ha-Yahas la-Yehudim,* p. x.

66. Oldson, *A Providential Anti-Semitism,* pp. 154–155.

67. Judd Teller, *Scapegoat of Revolution* (New York, 1954), pp. 164–165.

68. Ana Pauker's Application for a Party Card of CPSU, 15 June 1944; Autobiographical Statement of Ana Pauker, March 5, 1930, p. 1.

69. Paula E. Hyman, *Gender and Assimilation in Modern Jewish History: The Roles and Representation of Women* (Seattle and London, 1995), pp. 52–53, 55–57, 66–67.

70. Stampfer, "Gender Differentiation and Education of the Jewish Woman," pp. 81–82.

71. Declaration of Bella Rabinsohn, p. 44.

72. Hyman, *Gender and Assimilation,* pp. 52–53.

73. Lothar Kahn, "The Ugly Jew and the Cry for Normalcy: Jewish Self-Criticism at the Turn of the Century," *Judaism* 32, no. 2 (Spring 1983), p. 153.

74. Declaration of Bella Rabinsohn, p. 44.

75. Gustav Freytag, *Debit and Credit* (New York, 1990); George L. Mosse, "The Image of the Jew in German Popular Culture: Felix Dahn and Gustav Freytag," *Leo Baeck Institute Yearbook* (London, 1957), pp. 222–223, 226.

76. The year of her becoming a socialist is from the Autobiographical Statement of Ana Pauker, March 5, 1930, p. 26.

77. Jack Jacobs, *On Socialists and "the Jewish Question" after Marx* (New York and London, 1992), p. 5; Bruno Frei, "Marxist Interpretations of the Jewish Question," *The Wiener Library Bulletin,* n.s., 28, no. 35/36 (1975), p. 2; Walter Laqueur, *A History of Zionism* (New York, 1976), p. 417.

78. Enzo Traverso, *The Marxists and the Jewish Question: The History of a Debate, 1843–1943,* translated by Bernard Gibbons (Atlantic Highlands, N.J., 1994), p. 83.

79. Karl Kautsky, "Das Judentum," *Die Neue Zeit* 8 (1890), p. 28; cited in Traverso, *The Marxists and the Jewish Question,* p. 83.

80. Laqueur, *A History of Zionism,* p. 418; Traverso, *The Marxists and the Jewish Question,* p. 83.

81. Frei, "Marxist Interpretations," p. 2.

82. Traverso, *The Marxists and the Jewish Question,* pp. 83.

83. Laqueur, *A History of Zionism,* p. 420.

84. Karl Kautsky, *Rasse und Judentum* (Stuttgart, 1921), p. 108; cited in Traverso, *The Marxists and the Jewish Question,* p. 86.

85. On the Jews' economic role and ability to survive, see David Ruben, "Marxism and the Jewish Question," *The Socialist Register* (1982), pp. 205–237. On the same topic, also see Toni Oelsner, "The Place of the Jews in Economic History as Viewed by German Scholars," *Leo Baeck Institute Yearbook* (1962), pp. 183–212; Toni Oelsner, "Wilhelm Roscher's Theory of the Economic and Social Position of the Jews in the Middle Ages: A Critical Examination," *Yivo Annual* 1958–1959, pp. 176–195; Miriam Beard, "Anti-Semitism: Product of Economic Myths," in Isacque Graebner and Stewart Henderson Britt, eds., *Jews in a Gentile World: The Problem of Anti-Semitism* (New York, 1942), pp. 352–401; Werner J. Cahnman, "Role and Significance of the Jewish Artisan Class," *Jewish Journal of Sociology* 7, no. 2 (December 1965), pp. 207–220; and Robert A. Pois, "An Essay on the Jewish Problem in Marxist Historiography," *East European Quarterly* 11, no. 2 (1977), pp. 234–246.

86. Jacobs, *On Socialists and "the Jewish Question,"* pp. 5–33; Mosse, "The Image of the Jew in German Popular Culture," pp. 233–234.

87. Paul R. Mendes-Flohr, "The Throes of Assimilation: Self-Hatred and the Jewish Revolutionary," *European Judaism* 12, no. 1 (Spring 1978), p. 34. Mendes-Flohr cautions, however, that self-hatred "should be emphatically distinguished from anti-Semitism proper. The thin and not always so clear line between self-hatred and anti-Semitism is suggested by the adage, so typical of the modern Jew's ironic self-awareness, 'an antisemite hates the Jews more than necessary'" (ibid.).

88. On Pauker's involvement in the hostel, see Declaration of Bella Rabinsohn, p. 43, side 2; Israeli painter (and ambassador to Romania, 1949–51) Reuven Rubin, who was one of the hostel's organizers, revealed that Pauker worked as a waitress at the hostel in 1917–1918 (Reuven Rubin, *My Life My Art* [New York, 1969], p. 218). On her part in the defense units, see Autobiographical Statement of Ana Pauker, March 5, 1930, p. 1; according to her sister, these were Jewish workers' self-defense units organized by Barbu Eftimiu (Declaration of Bella Rabinsohn, p. 43, side 2). On her association with Jewish intellectuals, see Cristina Boico interview, September 16, 1989.

89. Interrogation of Ana Pauker, March 11, 1953, Ana Pauker Inquiry File, Executive Archive of the Central Committee of the RCP, p. 5.

90. Autobiography of Marcel Pauker, November 1937, in *Lichidarea lui Marcel Pauker, o anchetă stalinistă (1937–1938)* [The Liquidation of Marcel Pauker: A Stalinist Inquiry, 1937–1938], G. Brătescu, trans. (Bucharest, 1995), pp. 19, 21, 29, 31.

CHAPTER 2

1. Interrogation of Ana Pauker, March 11, 1953, Ana Pauker Inquiry File, Executive Archive of the Central Committee of the R.C.P., p. 1.

2. Steinberg's recruitment of Rabinsohn was revealed by her brother Zalman (Solomon) Rabinsohn to his prison cell mate in 1953 and confirmed to *Time* magazine in 1949 by one of Pauker's close childhood friends, then living in Israel (Report of Solomon Rabinsohn's cell mate, July 5, 1953, Archive of the Romanian Information Service [ASRI], Fond P, Dosar 40009, Vol. 50, p. 386; "A Girl Who Hated Cream Puffs," p. 32). Also see Hal Lehrman, "Ana Pauker," p. 73.

3. *The Universal Jewish Encyclopedia,* p. 258.

4. Hyman, *Gender and Assimilation in Modern Jewish History: The Roles and Representation of Women,* p. 78.

5. Ezra Mendelsohn, *Class Struggle in the Pale: The Formative Years of the Jewish Workers' Movement in Czarist Russia* (Cambridge, 1970), pp. 196–199 n. 13.

6. Jonathan Frankel, *Prophecy and Politics—Socialism, Nationalism and the Russian Jews, 1862–1917* (Cambridge, 1981), pp. 178–185.

7. Interrogation of Ana Pauker, March 11, 1953, Ana Pauker Inquiry File, Executive Archive of the Central Committee of the R.C.P., p. 1.

8. Declaration of Bella Rabinsohn, p. 44.

9. Autobiography of Ana Pauker, March 5, 1930, p. 26; Interrogation of Ana Pauker, March 11, 1953, Ana Pauker Inquiry File, Executive Archive of the Central Committee of the R.C.P., p. 1.

10. Autobiography of Ana Pauker, March 5, 1930, p. 26; Declaration of Bella Rabinsohn, p. 43, side 2; Ana Pauker's Application for a Party Card of CPSU, June 15, 1944.

11. Interrogation of Ana Pauker, March 11, 1953, Ana Pauker Inquiry File, Executive Archive of the Central Committee of the R.C.P., pp. 1–2.

12. Iancu, *Les Juifs en Roumanie,* p. 277.

13. Lucien Karchmar, "Communism in Romania 1918-1921," in Ivo Banac, ed., *The Effects of WWI: The Class War after the Great War. The Rise of Communist Parties in East Central Europe, 1918–1921* (New York, 1983), pp. 129–130.

14. Spulber, *The State and Economic Development,* p. 105.

15. Roberts, *Rumania,* p. 245.

16. Ibid., pp. 245–246; Interrogation of Ana Pauker, March 11, 1953, Ana Pauker Inquiry File, Executive Archive of the Central Committee of the R.C.P., p. 2.

17. On the strikes in general and the radicals' predominance in Bucharest, see Karchmar, "Communism in Romania," pp. 134, 158, 159, 162. On the radical's involvement in the strikes, see also the Interrogation of Ana Pauker, March 11, 1953, Ana Pauker Inquiry File, Executive Archive of the Central Committee of the R.C.P., p. 2. The quote is from Karchmar.

18. Autobiography of Ana Pauker, March 5, 1930, Ana Pauker Inquiry File, Executive Archive of the Central Committee of the Romanian Communist Party, p. 26; Interrogation of Ana Pauker, March 11, 1953, Ana Pauker Inquiry File, Executive Archive of the Central Committee of the R.C.P., p. 2; Declaration of Bella Rabinsohn, p. 43, side 2.

19. Autobiography of Ana Pauker, March 5, 1930, Ana Pauker Inquiry File, Executive Archive of the Central Committee of the R.C.P., p. 26; Interrogation of Ana Pauker, March 11, 1953, Ana Pauker Inquiry File, Executive Archive of the Central Committee of the R.C.P., p. 6; Declaration of Bella Rabinsohn, p. 43, side 2.

20. Tatiana and Gheorghe Brătescu interview.

21. Autobiography of Ana Pauker, March 5, 1930, p. 26.

22. Autobiography of Marcel Pauker, p. 34.

23. Ibid., pp. 19–20, 25, 67–68, 73, 78, 83, 88, 101, 135, 144, 147, 158 n.1; Marin C. Stănescu, *Moscova, Cominternul, filiera comunistă bacanică şi România (1919–1944)* [Moscow, the Comintern, the Balkan Communist Channel and Romania (1919–1944)] (Bucharest, 1994), pp. 25–26, and Ghita Ionescu, *Communism in Romania* (London, 1964), p. 21.

24. Interrogation of Ana Pauker, March 11, 1953, Ana Pauker Inquiry File, Executive Archive of the Central Committee of the R.C.P., p. 2; "The Rise and Fall of Ana Pauker," *News behind the Iron Curtain,* July 1952, p. 16.

25. Direcţia Poliţiei şi Siguranţei Generale, Brigada III-a, Agent Nr. 33, Nr. 4760, Dosar 2143, February 28, 1921, p. 100 (the report was found in the still-closed Romanian Workers' Party file of Ana Pauker's inquiry); Interrogation of Ana Pauker, March 11, 1953, Ana Pauker Inquiry File, Executive Archive of the Central Committee of the R.C.P., p. 2.

26. Declaration of Bella Rabinsohn, p. 43, side 2.

27. Interrogation of Ana Pauker, March 11, 1953, Ana Pauker Inquiry File, Executive Archive of the Central Committee of the R.C.P., p. 3; Declaration of Bella Rabinsohn, p. 43, side 2.

28. Tatiana and Gheorghe Brătescu interview; Interrogation of Ana Pauker, March 11, 1953, Ana Pauker Inquiry File, Executive Archive of the Central Committee of the R.C.P., p. 3; Interrogation of Solomon Rabinsohn, February 25, 1953, ASRI, Fond P, Dosar 40009, Vol. 60, p. 16. The author has been unable to determine the name of the dead brother, as neither Pauker nor her other brother, Solomon (Zalman) Rabinsohn, mentioned his name when speaking of him during their interrogations, and Pauker failed to do so as well in discussions with family members. Rabinsohn did, however, specify to his friend Israel Levanon that his family had been

greatly traumatized by the suicide, and had mourned his brother for a long time (Israel Levanon interview, July 30, 1989).

29. Interrogation of Ana Pauker, March 11, 1953, Ana Pauker Inquiry File, Executive Archive of the Central Committee of the R.C.P., pp. 3, 5; Declaration of Bella Rabinsohn, p. 43, side 2.

30. Autobiography of Marcel Pauker, pp. 40–41; Autobiography of Ana Pauker, March 5, 1930, p. 26.

31. Karchmar, "Communism in Romania," p. 163.

32. Autobiography of Marcel Pauker, p. 40; Stănescu, *Moscova, Cominternul, filiera comunistă balcanică și România (1919–1944)*, p. 20.

33. Ibid., p. 100. Also see the NKVD chronology of Marcel Pauker's party career, February 2, 1938, *Lichidarea lui Marcel Pauker, o anchetă stalinistă, 1937–1938*, p. 238.

34. While Ana Pauker called this fifteen-member body "The Council of the Country" in her March 5, 1930, autobiography, Marin C. Stănescu refers to it as the "General Council" in his study (*Moscova, Cominternul, filiera comunistă balcanică și România [1919–1944]*, p. 100).

35. Ibid., p. 25.

36. Autobiography of Ana Pauker, March 5, 1930, pp. 25–26; Interrogation of Ana Pauker, March 11, 1953, p. 3.

37. Ștefan Voicu, "Cui dăm votul și încrederea noastră. Lucrețiu Patrașcanu—un cărutrar și organizator al luptei pentru democrație, cultură și progres," *Scânteia*, no. 674, November 10, 1946; cited in Victor Frunza, *Istoria stalinismului în România* [The History of Stalinism in Romania] (Bucharest, 1990), pp. 148–149; Autobiography of Marcel Pauker, p. 47.

38. Autobiography of Ana Pauker, March 5, 1930, p. 25; Autobiography of Marcel Pauker, p. 64.

39. Autobiography of Ana Pauker, March 5, 1930, p. 25; Interrogation of Ana Pauker, March 11, 1953, Ana Pauker Inquiry File, Executive Archive of the Central Committee of the R.C.P., p. 3.

40. Autobiography of Ana Pauker, March 5, 1930, p. 25; Autobiography of Marcel Pauker, p. 65.

41. Autobiography of Ana Pauker, March 5, 1930, p. 25; Interrogation of Ana Pauker, March 11, 1953, Ana Pauker Inquiry File, Executive Archive of the Central Committee of the R.C.P., p. 3.

42. Interrogation of Ana Pauker, March 11, 1953, Ana Pauker Inquiry File, Executive Archive of the Central Committee of the R.C.P., pp. 3–4; Autobiography of Ana Pauker, March 5, 1930, p. 24.

43. Autobiography of Marcel Pauker, pp. 50, 60, 124 n. 57; Tatiana and Gheorghe Brătescu interview.

44. Letter of Marcel Pauker, January 19, 1923, pp. 3–4. The letter, originally found in his Siguranță file, is now in the still-closed Ana Pauker Inquiry File, Executive Archive of the Central Committee of the R.C.P.

45. Autobiography of Marcel Pauker, p. 60.

46. Ignazio Silone, in Richard Crossman, ed., *The God That Failed* (New York, 1950), p. 88.

47. George Lichtheim, "Social Democracy and Communism: 1918–1968," *Studies in Comparative Communism* 3, no. 1 (January 1970), p. 5; Manes Sperber, *The Unheeded Warning* (New York, 1991), pp. 163–164.

48. According to Marcel Pauker's account, even Romanian socialist "leaders,

who just the previous year had harshly attacked the Soviets, were now transformed to being on their side both body and soul" (the Autobiography of Marcel Pauker, p. 33).

49. Milorad M. Drachkovitch and Branko Lazitch, "The Communist International," in Milorad M. Drachkovitch, ed., *The Revolutionary Internationals, 1864–1943* (Stanford, 1966), p. 161.

50. Aleksander Wat, *My Century: The Odyssey of a Polish Intellectual* (New York, 1988), pp. 54–55; Benjamin Gitlow, *The Whole of Their Lives* (New York, 1948), pp. 3–4.

51. Wat, *My Century*, pp. 4–5; Bertram D. Wolfe, "Marxism and the Russian Revolution," in Milorad M. Drachkovitch, ed., *Fifty Years of Communism in Russia* (London, 1968), p. 29, and Franz Borkenau, *World Communism: A History of the Communist International* (Ann Arbor, 1962), p. 44; Sperber, *The Unheeded Warning*, p. 164.

52. Drachkovitch and Lazitch, "The Communist International," p. 161.

53. Neil McInnes, "The Labor Movement," in *The Impact of the Russian Revolution, 1917–1967* (London, 1967), p. 42.

54. Drachkovitch and Lazitch, "The Communist International," pp. 166–167, 175.

55. Adam Ulam, "Titoism," in Milorad M. Drachkovitch, ed., *Marxism in the Modern World* (Stanford, 1965), p. 139.

56. Jules Monnerot, *Sociology and Psychology of Communism* (Boston, 1953), p. 54.

57. "Comintern Reminiscences: Interview with an Insider," *Survey*, no. 32 (April–June 1960), p. 110; this anonymous "insider" had been "active in the communist movement in a number of countries" and subsequently "worked in the Executive Committee of the Communist International (ECCI) in Moscow." Silone, in *The God That Failed*, p. 61.

58. Tatiana and Gheorghe Brătescu interview.

59. Autobiography of Marcel Pauker, pp. 42–43; and Stănescu, *Moscova, Cominternul*, pp. 21, 100–101; Michael Bruchis, "The Jews in the Revolutionary Underground of Bessarabia and Their Fate after Its Annexation by the Soviet Union," in his *Nations-Nationalities-People* (New York, 1984), p.161.

60. "[I]n general," Marcel Pauker acknowledged, "I did not do *anything* without conferring with the Bulgarian delegation" of the Communist Balkan Federation (Autobiography of Marcel Pauker, pp. 42–43, 60, 68).

61. Ibid., pp. 42–43; A. Esaulenco, "K voprosu ob organizatsionykh sviaziakh mezhdu kommunisticheskimi gruppami Rumynii i bol'shevikami Bessarabii, 1918–1922 gody," in *Vekovaia druzhba. Materialy nauchnoi sessii Instituta istorii Moldavskogo filiala AN SSSR*, 27–29 noiambria 1958g (Kishinev, 1961), p. 395; I. Copanschi, *Obshchestvo bessarabtsev v SSSR i Soiuzy bessarabskikh emigrantov, 1924–1940* (Kishinev, 1978), pp. 12–14; cited in Bruchis, "The Jews in the Revolutionary Underground," p. 161. Also see Autobiography of Marcel Pauker, pp. 136–137.

62. Bruchis, "The Jews in the Revolutionary Underground," p. 161; Patrașcanu, then head of the country's communist youth organization (until he left Romania in 1923), allowed Pauker to use the organization's weekly *Tineretul socialist* as his propaganda mouthpiece until Pauker became the editor of *Socialismul* (Autobiography of Marcel Pauker, pp. 43, 66, 74, 138). Headed by Ion Mihalache, Dr. Nicolae Lupu, the Bessarabian philosopher Constantin Stere, and the economist Virgil Madgearu, the Peasant Party had at that time not yet merged with Iuliu Maniu's

National Party of Transylvania, and, according to Marcel Pauker's account, still stressed a program of class struggle (ibid., p. 66; Roberts, *Rumania,* p. 250). In calling for a united front, Marcel Pauker was clearly to the right of the Comintern line adopted in December 1921 mandating that Communist parties collaborate with socialists in united fronts in all countries. Not surprisingly, Bukharin vetoed Pauker's proposal in November 1923 as "right-wing opportunism." However, after the intervention of "the Bulgarian comrades," the Comintern agreed to a united front with the Peasant Party, but the Peasant Party leadership rejected the idea (ibid., pp. 67, 71); Gunther Nollau, *International Communism and World Revolution: History and Methods* (London, 1961), pp. 75–76.

63. Autobiography of Marcel Pauker, pp. 60, 138. Cristescu opposed a united front with the Peasant Party because it would reduce the Communists to a minority in the unions; ibid., p. 60; Autobiography of Ana Pauker, March 5, 1930, p. 25.

64. Autobiography of Marcel Pauker, pp. 48, 50, 66–67, 140; the NKVD chronology of Marcel Pauker's party career, February 2, 1938, in *Lichidarea lui Marcel Pauker: o anchetă stalinistă, 1937–1938,* p. 238.

65. Autobiography of Marcel Pauker, pp. 71, 73, 75, 77.

66. Autobiography of Ana Pauker, March 5, 1930, p. 25.

67. Ibid., pp. 22–24; Autobiography of Marcel Pauker, p. 82.

68. Ana Pauker's Written Self-Criticism to the Politburo, September 22, 1952, Ana Pauker Inquiry File, Executive Archive of the Central Committee of the R.C.P.

69. Autobiography of Ana Pauker, March 5, 1930, p. 22.

70. Letter of Ana Pauker to the Central Committee of the Romanian Communist Party, October 27, 1928, Russian Center for the Preservation and Study of Documents of Most Recent History (RTsKhIDNI), Fond 495, Opis 255, Dossier 4 (I), p. 17; Ana Pauker's Written Self-Criticism to the Politburo, September 22, 1952; Autobiography of Ana Pauker, March 5, 1930, p. 22; Letter of Ana Pauker to the Central Committee of the Romanian Communist Party, October 27, 1928, p. 17.

71. Autobiography of Marcel Pauker, p. 82.

72. Sandor Korosi-Krizsan reports that the Romanian Party leaders who traveled to Moscow to confer with the Comintern in November 1923 "took Trotsky's side, although we did not agree with all his political views. We found Stalin's tactics revolting, and at the same time could not understand why Trotsky did not use the same methods" (Sandor Korosi-Krizsan, "Rumania and the Comintern," *East Europe,* no. 12 [1966], p. 15). The Romanian leaders were Korosi-Krizsan, Gheorghe Cristescu, Alexandru Dobrogeanu-Gherea, Heinrich Sternberg, and Marcel Pauker; they were joined in Moscow by Ecaterina Arbore (N.C. Stănescu, N. Popescu, "P.C.R. și Congresele Internaționalei a III-a," *Anale de istorie,* nr. 5, 1975; cited in Frunza, *Istoria Stalinismului,* pp. 39–40.

73. Robert C. Tucker, *Stalin as Revolutionary, 1879–1929: A Study in History and Personality* (New York, 1973), pp. 368–420; Moshe Lewin, *The Making of the Soviet System: Essays in the Social History of Interwar Russia* (New York, 1985), pp. 25–27; Sheila Fitzpatrick, ed., *Cultural Revolution in Russia, 1928–1931* (Bloomington, Ind., 1984).

74. Autobiography of Ana Pauker, March 5, 1930, p. 22; Autobiography of Marcel Pauker, p. 86; Two letters dated January 13 and January 30, 1928, written by Zetkin on Pauker's behalf are in Ana Pauker's Comintern file, Russian Center for the Preservation and Study of Documents of Most Recent History (RTsKhIDNI), Fond 495, Opis 255, Dossier 4 (I), pp. 7–8; Branko Lazitch, in collaboration with Milorad M. Drachkovitch, *Biographical Dictionary of the Comintern,* rev. ed. (Stanford, 1986), p. 527; Interrogation of Ana Pauker, March 11, 1953, p. 4.

75. Autobiography of Ana Pauker, March 5, 1930, pp. 21–22; Letter of Ana Pauker to the Central Committee of the Romanian Communist Party, October 27, 1928, p. 17.

76. Hersh Mendel, *Memoirs of a Jewish Revolutionary* (London, 1989), p. 256.

77. Autobiography of Ana Pauker, March 5, 1930, p. 21; Aino Kuusinen, *Before and after Stalin: A Personal Account of Soviet Russia from the 1920s to the 1930s*, Paul Stevenson, trans. (London, 1974), pp. 52–53; Gitlow, *The Whole of Their Lives,* pp. 243, 247.

78. Gitlow, *The Whole of Their Lives,* p. 243; Ana Pauker's Written Self-Criticism to the Politburo, September 22, 1952, Ana Pauker Inquiry File, Executive Archive of the Central Committee of the R.C.P.

79. Ibid.; Autobiography of Ana Pauker, March 5, 1930, p. 21; Eugen Iacobovici, *Memorii,* Institute of Historical and Socio-Political Studies Next to the C.C. of the R.C.P. (Bucharest, 1968), cited in Mircu, *Ana Pauker și alții,* p. 68.

80. Ana Pauker's Written Self-Criticism to the Politburo, September 22, 1952, Ana Pauker Inquiry File, Executive Archive of the Central Committee of the R.C.P.; Autobiography of Ana Pauker, March 5, 1930, p. 21; Gitlow, *The Whole of Their Lives,* p. 246.

81. Ana Pauker's Written Self-Criticism to the Politburo, September 22, 1952, Ana Pauker Inquiry File, Executive Archive of the Central Committee of the R.C.P.; Branko Lazitch, "Two Instruments of Control by the Comintern," in Milorad M Drachkovitch, ed., *The Comintern: Historical Highlights* (Stanford, 1966), p. 61.

82. Tatiana and Gheorghe Brătescu interview; Declaration of Valter Roman, October 12, 1956, Ana Pauker Inquiry File, Executive Archive of the Central Committee of the R.C.P., p. 4; Declaration of Zina Brâncu, n.d., Ana Pauker Inquiry File, Executive Archive of the Central Committee of the R.C.P., p. 4; "Comintern Reminiscences, Interview with an Insider," p. 111; *Biographical Dictionary of the Comintern,* p. 296; Lazitch, "Two Instruments of Control by the Comintern," p. 51.

83. Ernst Fischer, *An Opposing Man: The Autobiography of a Romantic Revolutionary* (New York, 1974), pp. 296–297.

84. "Comintern Reminiscences, Interview with an Insider," p. 114.

85. Ana Pauker's Written Self-Criticism to the Politburo, September 22, 1952.

86. Philippe Robrieux, *Histoire interieure du parti communiste,* vol. 4 (Paris, 1980), p. 248. Also see Annie Kriegel and Stéphane Courtois, *Eugen Fried, le grand secret du PCF* (Paris, 1997).

87. Roza Elbert, a former RCP activist, gave birth to a baby boy (named Iakov) fathered by Marcel Pauker in February 1931 (*Lichidarea lui Marcel Pauker: o anchetă stalinistă, 1937–1938,* pp. 212 n. 4, 239 n. 1; Tatiana and Gheorghe Brătescu interview).

88. *Lichidarea lui Marcel Pauker: o anchetă stalinistă,* p. 221; "The Rise and Fall of Ana Pauker," July 1952, p. 16; Krivine, "Who Was Ana Pauker?" p. 9; Lehrman, "Ana Pauker," p. 73; Tatiana and Gheorghe Brătescu interview; Marie Birnbaum (Pauker and Fried's daughter) interview, November 11, 1990.

89. On Pauker's time in Moscow, see *Biographical Dictionary of the Comintern,* p. 354; for examples of vague and erroneous documents, see Ana Pauker's Application for a Party Card of CPSU, June 15, 1944; Ana Pauker's Written Self-Criticism to the Politburo, September 22, 1952, Ana Pauker Inquiry File, Executive Archive of the Central Committee of the R.C.P.; Interrogation of Ana Pauker, February 19, 1953, Ana Pauker Inquiry File, Executive Archive of the Central Committee of the R.C.P., p. 1; on her return to Romania, see "O convorbire cu Ana Pauker," *Liber-*

tatea, no. 56, October 22, 1944, cited by Frunza, *Istoria stalinismului,* p. 102; Mircu, *Ana Pauker și alții,* pp. 73, 74; Report Regarding the Results of the Inquiry of Ana Pauker, January 20, 1954, Ana Pauker Inquiry File, Executive Archive of the Central Committee of the R.C.P., p. 2; Fernando Claudin, *The Communist Movement: From Comintern to Cominform* (Middlesex, England, 1975), pp. 174–175; Borkenau, *World Communism,* pp. 388–395; Ionescu, *Communism in Romania,* p. 50; Autobiography of Marcel Pauker, p. 107.

90. Minutes of an Interrogation of Ana Pauker at the Council of War, July 25, 1935, Dossier No. 12413–146 (31), pp. 2–3.

91. The other defendants were Șmil Marcovici, Dimitrie Ganev (a leading Bulgarian Communist after the war, and for a time Bulgaria's ambassador to Romania), Alexandru Drăghici (the future Interior Minister), Alexandru Moghioroș (a future secretary of the party's Central Committee), Estera Radoșovețchi (Stela Moghioroș), Liuba Chișinevschi (future secretary of the Central Council of Syndicates), Andor Bernat (the future secretary of the Union of Communist Youth), Ladislau Ady (the future deputy interior minister), Emanoil Kaufman, Vilma Kajesco, Donca Simo, Samuel Krug, Iancs Herbach, Ernest Schoen, Ștefan Naghy, Leizar Grimberg, Ștefan Csaszar, and Ana Csaszar.

92. Vilma Dragan (Kajesco) interview (one of Pauker's codefendants at the trial), July 13, 1991; Mircu, *Ana Pauker și alții,* pp. 82–85.

93. Vilma Dragan (Kajesco) interview; Maria Sârbu interview, December 7, 1990.

94. Mircu, *Ana Pauker și alții,* pp. 89–90.

95. Vilma Dragan (Kajesco) interview.

96. Mircu, *Ana Pauker și alții,* p. 86.

97. Bela Vago, *The Shadow of the Swastika: The Rise of Fascism and Anti-Semitism in the Danubian Basin, 1936–39* (London, 1975), p. 58.

98. Eugen Weber, *Varieties of Fascism* (New York, 1964), p. 102. Also see Hitchins, *Rumania,* pp. 418–419. On the LANC's ties with Hitler, see Eugen Weber, "Romania," in Hans Rogger and Eugen Weber, eds., *The European Right,* p. 553.

99. Bela Vago, *The Shadow of the Swastika,* p. 25.

100. For details of this period, see Hugh Seton-Watson, *Eastern Europe Between the Wars 1918–1941* (New York, 1967), p. 209; Francisco Veiga, *Istoria gărzii de fier 1919–1941* [The History of the Iron Guard, 1919–1941] (Bucharest, 1993), p. 228; and Bela Vago, *The Shadow of the Swastika,* pp. 21–45, 58–59.

101. On the effects of Pauker's trial, see Ioanid, *The Sword of the Archangel,* pp. 105–108, and Bela Vago, *The Shadow of the Swastika,* p. 58. On the Iron Guard, see Weber, *Varieties of Fascism,* p. 102. The quote is from Weber, "Romania," p. 551; also see Bela Vago, *The Shadow of the Swastika,* pp. 39–40. On Antonescu's junta, see Raul Hilberg, *The Destruction of the European Jews* (New York, 1973), pp. 488–497; Lya Benjamin, ed., *Legislația antievreiască, Evreii din România între anii 1940–1944* [Anti-Jewish Legislation: The Jews in Romania, 1940–1944], vol. 1 (Bucharest, 1993), pp. xci–xciii; Ioanid, *The Sword of the Archangel,* pp. 202–234.

102. Vilma Dragan (Kajesco) interview, Mircu, *Ana Pauker și alții,* p. 104.

103. Sara Alterescu interview, February 28, 1994; Vilma Dragan (Kajesco) interview; Maria Sârbu interview; Mircu, *Ana Pauker și alții,* p. 104.

104. Vilma (Kajesco) Dragan interview.

105. Ibid.

106. Ibid.; Sara Alterescu interview.

107. Transcript of an Interrogation of Ana Pauker by a Party Commission of the

R.W.P., June 18, 1956, Ana Pauker Inquiry File, Executive Archive of the Central Committee of the R.C.P., p. 11; Maria Sârbu interview; Mircu, *Ana Pauker și alții*, p. 109.

108. Vilma (Kajesco) Dragan interview; Tatiana and Gheorghe Brătescu interview; Sara Alterescu interview.

109. Vladimir Tismaneanu, "The Ambiguity of Romanian Communism," *Telos* no. 60 (Summer 1984), p. 68. Ion Mihalache confirmed under interrogation that the Soviets expressly requested Ana Pauker in any prisoner exchange with Romania (Interrogation of Ion Mihalache, June 12, 1953, Ana Pauker Inquiry File, Executive Archive of the Central Committee of the R.C.P., p. 3).

110. Milovan Djilas, *Wartime* (New York, 1977), p. 357.

111. Sara Alterescu interview.

112. Ibid.; Ernst Fischer, *An Opposing Man*, p. 297; *Lichidarea lui Marcel Pauker: o anchetă stalinistă, 1937–1938*, pp. 272–273; Tatiana and Gheorghe Brătescu interview.

113. Branko Lazitch, "Stalin's Massacre of the Foreign Communist Leaders," in Milorad M. Drachkovitch, ed., *The Comintern: Historical Highlights*, pp. 139–174; Alfred Burmeister (the alias for the Polish communist Wanda Pampuch-Bronska), *Dissolution and Aftermath of the Comintern: Experiences and Observations, 1937–1947* (New York, 1955), pp. 1–14.

114. Lazitch, "Stalin's Massacre of the Foreign Communist Leaders," pp. 147–151; Isaac Deutscher, "The Tragedy of the Polish Communist Party," in Tamara Deutscher, ed., *Marxism in Our Time* (San Francisco, 1971), pp. 150–160.

115. Franz Borkenau, *European Communism* (London, 1951), p. 227; Lazitch, "Stalin's Massacre of the Foreign Communist Leaders," pp. 151–163; Joseph Berger, *Nothing but the Truth* (New York, 1971).

116. Margarete Buber-Neumann, *Under Two Dictators* (London, 1949).

117. Of roughly 6,000 Spanish veterans who arrived in the Soviet Union immediately after the Republican defeat (among whom were 2,000 children), only 1,500 were reported to be alive in 1948. As for the Austrian veterans, they were "almost without exception" arrested and sent to Siberia (Robert Conquest, *The Great Terror: A Reassessment* [Oxford, 1990], p. 411).

118. Alexander Weissberg, *The Accused* (New York, 1951), p. 513.

119. Robrieux, *Histoire interieure du parti communiste*, pp. 248–249.

120. Cristina Boico interview. Boico was present when Pauker discussed the matter with Thorez.

121. A recently published biography of Fried demonstrates that he was in fact shot by the Gestapo (Annie Kriegel, Stéphane Courtois, *Eugen Fried*); Robrieux, *Histoire interieure du parti communiste*, pp. 248–249; *Biographical Dictionary of the Comintern*, p. 125.

122. Lazitch, "Stalin's Massacre of the Foreign Communist Leaders," p. 141; Borkenau, *European Communism*, p. 283.

123. On the rumors' origins, see Mircu, *Ana Pauker și alții*, p. 108; the accusation against Pauker was recently repeated by A. Vaksberg, *Hotel Lux* (Paris, 1993), p. 262, and by Ion Mihai Pacepa, *Moiștenirea kremlinului* [The Kremlin's Legacy] (Bucharest, 1993), p. 83. Perhaps the worst example of the vitriolic attacks on Pauker in today's Romania is the account of former Securitate official Ion Boian: "Ana knew Stalin. I was told that she was even intimate with him. As a matter of fact, the incident when she and her husband were called to the Kremlin is well known. Stalin asked her: 'How do we punish deviationists?' And she replied: 'We shoot them.' So Stalin then took out a pistol from his desk drawer and gave it to her. Ana shot Mar-

cel Pauker—her husband with whom she had two children!!" (Ion Boian, interviewed by Dumitru Mitel Popescu, in "Libertate cu dreptate," the weekly supplement of *Astra,* March 14, 1990, p. 3); the quote is from Drachkovitch and Lazitch, "The Communist International," p. 193.

124. Ignazio Silone, *Emergency Exit* (London, 1969), p. 47.

125. Interrogation of Ana Pauker, March 1, 1953, Ana Pauker Inquiry File, Executive Archive of the Central Committee of the R.C.P., p. 1.

126. Wat, *My Century,* p. 17.

127. Victor Serge, *Memoirs of a Revolutionary, 1901–1941,* translated and edited by Peter Sedgwick (London, 1963), p. 177.

128. V. I. Lenin, "The Tasks of the Youth Leagues," speech delivered at the Third All Russian Young Communist League, October 2, 1920, in his *Selected Works,* vol. 2 (London, 1947), pp. 669–670.

129. Autobiography of Ana Pauker, March 5, 1930, p. 22.

130. Wat, *My Century,* p. 37.

131. Maxime Rodinson, *Cult, Ghetto and State: The Persistence of the Jewish Question* (London, 1983), p. 28; Howard Fast, *The Naked God: The Writer and the Communist Party* (New York, 1957), p. 89.

132. Boris Bazhanov, interviewed by George R. Urban, *Stalinism* (London, 1982), pp. 21–22; Eduard Goldstücker, interviewed by George R. Urban, *Communist Reformation* (London, 1979), pp. 38–39.

133. "'A Writer Not a Hero': An Interview with Julian Stryjkowski," translated by Ursula Phillips, *East European Jewish Affairs* 25, no. 1 (Summer 1995), p. 87; Wat, *My Century,* p. 21; Serge, *Memoirs of a Revolutionary,* pp. 134–135; Fischer, *An Opposing Man,* p. 288.

134. Mendel, *Memoirs of a Jewish Revolutionary,* pp. 268–269.

135. Lewin, "Society, State and Ideology," in Fitzpatrick, ed., *Cultural Revolution in Russia,* p. 38.

136. Ibid.

137. Goldstücker, in *Communist Reformation,* p. 38.

138. Hermina Tismăneanu interview, May 20, 1988; letter of Ana Pauker to the Central Committee of the Romanian Communist Party, October 27, 1928, p. 16; Wolfgang Leonhard, *Child of the Revolution* (Chicago, 1958), pp. 102, 104, 106, 234, 235 (though belonging to a later time, Leonhard's experiences also apply to the Lenin School's practices during Pauker's tenure, as Koestler's similar experiences in 1931 demonstrate); Arthur Koestler, *The Invisible Writing: An Autobiography* (Boston, 1954), pp. 25–26.

139. Leonhard, *Child of the Revolution,* pp. 251, 254, 265–266; Koestler, *The Invisible Writing,* pp. 26–27.

140. Alfred Burmeister, *Dissolution and Aftermath of the Comintern,* p. 16; Leonhard, *Child of the Revolution,* p. 186.

141. Mendel, *Memoirs of a Jewish Revolutionary,* pp. 259–261; Gitlow, *The Whole of Their Lives,* pp. 181–182; Interrogation of Ana Pauker, February 19, 1953, pp. 2–4; and Interrogation of Vasile Luca, February 11, 1953, ASRI, Fond P, Dosar 40005, Vol. 4, pp. 421–422.

142. On the turmoil and disenchantment, see Koestler, *The Invisible Writing,* p. 68, and Wat, *My Century,* p. 84; the quotes are from Ypsilon [pseud.], *Pattern for World Revolution* (Chicago, 1947), pp. 231, 234–235, 238.

143. Gitlow, *The Whole of Their Lives,* pp. 181–182; Jacob H. Rubin, *I Live to Tell: The Russian Adventures of an American Socialist* (New York, 1934), p. 271.

144. Autobiography of Ana Pauker, March 5, 1930, p. 88; Alexandru Sencovici

interview, December 29, 1993; Marcel Pauker personally spoke of his difficulties to Alexandru Sencovici, when both were members of the RCP Secretariat in 1934. Also see *Lichidarea lui Marcel Pauker: o anchetă stalinistă, 1937–1938*, pp. 132–133, n. 119, 302–306.

145. Tatiana and Gheorghe Brătescu interview; Autobiography of Marcel Pauker, p. 15.

146. Milovan Djilas, *Rise and Fall* (San Diego, 1985), p. 103.

147. Angelica Balabanoff, *Impressions of Lenin* (Ann Arbor, 1968), pp. 28–29; Gitlow, *The Whole of Their Lives*, p. 4; Mendel, *Memoirs of a Jewish Revolutionary*, p. 269.

148. Autobiography of Ana Pauker, March 5, 1930, p. 26; the Comintern presumably asked Pauker's younger sister Bella Rabinsohn to write a declaration of her own on Pauker's childhood, from which they were able to ascertain the intentional lapses in Pauker's autobiography; both documents were placed in Pauker's Comintern file; Maria Sârbu interview; Declaration of Natala Corotcova-Scurtu, October 22, 1956, Ana Pauker Inquiry File, Executive Archive of the Central Committee of the R.C.P., p. 2.

149. Declaration of Elvira Gaisinschi, n.d., Ana Pauker Inquiry File, Executive Archive of the Central Committee of the R.C.P., p. 1.

150. Bruchis, "The Jews in the Revolutionary Underground," p. 167.

151. Memoir of Vasile Luca, November 5, 1954, ASRI, Fond P, Dosar 40005, Vol. 126, p. 22; Stănescu, *Moscova, Cominternul*, pp. 106, 111.

152. Autobiography of Marcel Pauker, p. 89. Nollau, *International Communism and World Revolution*, pp. 107–108.

153. Autobiography of Marcel Pauker, p. 89.

154. Ibid., pp. 94–95; Interrogation of Ana Pauker, February 19, 1953, Ana Pauker Inquiry File, Executive Archive of the Central Committee of the R.C.P., p. 2.

155. Declaration of Dumitru Chelerman, ASRI, Fond P, Dosar 40005, Vol. 127, p. 48. Chelerman, then head of the RCP organization of Chişinau, attended the Politburo meeting in question. A notation on the document indicates that his declaration was made "after March 4, 1931" (ibid., p. 33).

156. Autobiography of Marcel Pauker, pp. 94–95, 158 n. 3.

157. Ibid., p. 97, 147–148; Interrogation of Vasile Luca, February 13, 1954, ASRI, Fond P, Dosar 40005, Vol. 2, pp. 31–32; Stănescu, *Moscova, Cominternul*, p. 111; Declaration of Dumitru Chelerman, ASRI, Fond P, Dosar 40005, Vol. 127, pp. 51–52.

158. Autobiography of Marcel Pauker, p. 98.

159. Ibid., pp. 87, 153; Memoir of Vasile Luca, November 5, 1954, ASRI, Fond P, Dosar 40005, Vol. 126, pp. 20–22, 42–43.

160. Interrogation of Vasile Luca, February 13, 1954, ASRI, Fond P, Dosar 40005, Vol. 2, pp. 30–31; Autobiography of Marcel Pauker, pp. 88, 99, 147, 158 n. 2; Stănescu, *Moscova, Cominternul*, p. 106.

161. Interrogation of Vasile Luca, February 13, 1954, ASRI, Fond P, Dosar 40005, Vol. 2, p. 28.

162. Autobiography of Marcel Pauker, p. 97.

163. Ibid., pp. 99, 147.

164. *Lichidarea lui Marcel Pauker: o anchetă stalinistă, 1937–1938*, pp. 130 n. 101, 132–133 n. 119.

165. The document, dated September 22, 1932, is in Ana Pauker's Comintern file, pp. 36–37; Manuilsky's remark is cited in the Declaration of Zina Brâncu, p. 4.

166. "Note Concerning Ana Pauker," March 4, 1940, Ana Pauker's Comintern

file, p. 149 (reprinted in *Lichidarea lui Marcel Pauker: o anchetă stalinistă, 1937–1938*, pp. 269–270); Sara Alterescu interview; the response is in Ana Pauker's Comintern file, p. 151 (reprinted in *Lichidarea lui Marcel Pauker: o anchetă stalinistă, 1937–1938*, pp. 270–271). On Ana Pauker's acquaintance with Rakovsky and his ambassadorship to France, see Declaration of Bella Rabinsohn, p. 43; *Biographical Dictionary of the Comintern*, p. 384; Conquest, *The Great Terror*, p. 360.

167. "Ana Pauker," July 3, 1940, Ana Pauker's Comintern file, p. 250 (reprinted in *Lichidarea lui Marcel Pauker: o anchetă stalinistă, 1937–1938*, pp. 271–272). According to Elvira Gaisinschi, the material was not presented to the larger collective for a full year. Sara Alterescu, however, contends that the delay was only "a matter of months" (Declaration of Elvira Gaisinschi, Ana Pauker Inquiry File, Executive Archive of the Central Committee of the R.C.P., pp. 1–2; Sara Alterescu interview). Declaration of Zina Brâncu, Ana Pauker Inquiry File, Executive Archive of the Central Committee of the R.C.P., p. 3.

168. Ana Pauker's Written Self-Criticism to the Politburo, September 22, 1952; Pauker's confession to Patrașcanu is documented in the memorandum of Col. Ioan Șoltuțiu to Interior Minister Alexandru Drăghici and General Secretary Gheorghe Gheorghiu-Dej, November 7, 1952, ASRI, Fond P, Dosar 40002, Vol. 16, p. 4; Alexandru Sencovici interview.

169. "Ana Pauker," July 3, 1940, Ana Pauker's Comintern file, p. 250; Declaration of Elvira Gaisinschi, Ana Pauker Inquiry File, Executive Archive of the Central Committee of the R.C.P., p. 2.

170. Ana Toma interview, November 16, 1990.

CHAPTER 3

1. Tatiana and Gheorghe Brătescu interview.
2. Hermina Tismăneanu interview.
3. Frunza, *Istoria stalinismului*, p. 103; Vladimir Tismaneanu, "Ceaușescu's Socialism," *Problems of Communism* 34, no. 1 (January–February 1985), p. 54.
4. Enrique Castro Delgado, *Mi Fe Se Perdio en Moscu* (Barcelona, 1964), p. 78.
5. Tatiana and Gheorghe Brătescu interview.
6. Hermina Tismăneanu interview.
7. Declaration of Natalia Scurtu, Ana Pauker Inquiry File, Executive Archive of the Central Committee of the R.C.P., pp. 4–5. On Pauker's listlessness, also see the Declaration of Valter Roman, October 15, 1956, Ana Pauker Inquiry File, Executive Archive of the Central Committee of the R.C.P., p. 1.
8. Interrogation of Ana Pauker, Ministry of Interior Affairs, February 25, 1953, Ana Pauker Inquiry File, Executive Archive of the Central Committee of the R.C.P., pp. 1–2.
9. Declaration of Natalia Scurtu, Ana Pauker Inquiry File, Executive Archive of the Central Committee of the R.C.P., p. 4.
10. Interrogation of Ana Pauker, Ministry of Interior Affairs, February 25, 1953, Ana Pauker Inquiry File, Executive Archive of the Central Committee of the R.C.P., p. 1; Interrogation of Vasile Luca, April 10, 1953, ASRI, Fond P, Dosar 40005, Vol. 4, p. 527.
11. Mircea Suciu and Mircea Chirițoiu, "Ana Pauker: Repere pentru o biografie neretușată" [Ana Pauker: Landmarks of a Real Biography], *Dosarele istoriei* 2, no. 8 (13) (1997), p. 7.
12. Declaration of Natalia Scurtu, Ana Pauker Inquiry File, Executive Archive of the Central Committee of the R.C.P., p. 5.

13. Interrogation of Ana Pauker, Ministry of Interior Affairs, February 25, 1953, Ana Pauker Inquiry File, Executive Archive of the Central Committee of the R.C.P., p. 1; Transcript of an Interrogation of Ana Pauker by a Party Commission of the R.W.P., June 18, 1956, Ana Pauker Inquiry File, Executive Archive of the Central Committee of the R.C.P., p. 21.

14. Declaration of Zina Brâncu, p. 6.

15. Interrogation of Ana Pauker, Ministry of Interior Affairs, February 25, 1953, Ana Pauker Inquiry File, Executive Archive of the Central Committee of the R.C.P., p. 5.

16. Lehrman, "Ana Pauker," p. 74; "The Rise and Fall of Ana Pauker," p. 18; "Ana Pauker," *Current Biography,* 1948, p. 494.

17. Ibid.

18. Ionescu, *Communism in Romania,* pp. 105–106.

19. "In New Romania," *Survey Reports,* June 15, 1953, p. 20; Lehrman, "Ana Pauker," p. 74. Lehrman described Pauker's ascent to the ministry thus: "The evening before she became [foreign] Minister all the ministry personnel were loaded into police vans as they came out the front door and were carted away to be searched for incriminating documents. Next morning when those not still in jail returned to work, they found their offices bolted. Ana called all hands and demanded their keys to their files, safes and cashboxes. The Ministry stayed shut for 5 days while her inspectors went through the place. The first day it reopened . . . Ana fired 165 of its 500 career officials, including 12 'permanent' functionaries of the ministerial rank, 10 counselors and 36 consuls. . . . The same clean-up transpired abroad. A general order summoning 160 ranking diplomats to come home and meet their new chief brought only 25 takers. The rest quit" (Lehrman, "Ana Pauker," p. 75).

20. Ibid., pp. 74–75.

21. Describing Pauker as an "aging nymphomaniac," Gordon Shephard maintained that "Romanian prisoners-of-war used to refer to the '[Tudor] Vladimirescu' division as 'The Love Brigade,' owing to Ana Pauker's romantic principle of selecting her officers" (Shephard, *Russia's Danubian Empire,* pp. 56–57). Likewise, Pauker was often said to have had an ongoing affair with her handsome, younger bodyguard, ex-actor Ion Victor Vojen, who was reportedly the former Iron Guard envoy to Mussolini's government (Lehrman, "Ana Pauker," p. 76; "The Rise and Fall of Ana Pauker," p. 18). However, every interviewee whom I asked about these accounts adamantly disputed both.

22. Pauker was reported to have procured three homes in Bucharest, including a mansion confiscated from Prince Calimachi (among which she supposedly moved back and forth for security); two villas in the lakeside resort of Snagov and on the Black Sea coast; and two cottages in the mountain resorts of Bușteni and Predeal ("The Rise and Fall of Ana Pauker," p. 19; Lehrman, "Ana Pauker," p. 76; Shephard, *Russia's Danubian Empire,* p. 55). But the reports were untrue: Pauker resided in one house in Bucharest; the rest were party houses reserved for vacationing officials (*Rumanian National Committee Bulletin* no. 34, January 1952, p. 26; Ella Diamantshtein interview, August 28, 1989; Ana Toma, Sorin Toma, Tatiana and Gheorghe Brătescu interviews).

23. Transcript of an Interrogation of Ana Pauker by a Party Commission of the R.W.P., June 18, 1956, Ana Pauker Inquiry File, Executive Archive of the Central Committee of the R.C.P., p. 13.

24. Declaration of Remus Koffler, undated, ASRI, Fond P, Dosar 40002, Vol. 51, pp. 378–398; Declaration of Nicolae Petrea, October 21, 1951, ASRI, Fond P, Dosar

40002, Vol. 73, pp. 127–130; Declaration of Victoria Sârbu, November 2, 1950, ASRI, Fond P, Dosar 40002, Vol. 58, pp. 55–68.

25. Radu Mănescu interview.

26. Report of the Special R.C.P. Commission on the Case of Ştefan Foriş, March 11, 1968, Executive Archive of the Central Committee of the R.C.P., pp. 1–11.

27. Interrogation of Teohari Georgescu, May 18, 1953, ASRI, Fond P, Dosar 40009, Vol. 1, pp. 231–232.

28. Declaration of Remus Koffler, undated, ASRI, Fond P, Dosar 40002, Vol. 48, p. 85; Declaration of Nicolae Petrea, p. 126.

29. Declaration of Victoria Sârbu, February 7, 1950, ASRI, Fond P, Dosar 40002, Vol. 54, p. 18. Bodnăraş also told this to Central Committee member Nicolae Petrea, asserting that the agent "from the Soviet Union . . . agrees with the changes being made in the party" (Declaration of Nicolae Petrea, p. 126).

30. Pauker revealed that certain "Soviet comrades" had asked her why Foriş had been removed from the leadership, suggesting that they were completely in the dark over his removal (Conversation of Ana Pauker and Two Party Leaders at a Party House in Otopeni, April 8, 1953, ASRI, Fond P, Dosar 40009, Vol. 68, p. 229).

31. Interrogation of Ana Pauker by a Party Commission of the R.W.P., June 18, 1956, Ana Pauker Inquiry File, Executive Archive of the Central Committee of the R.C.P., pp. 7–8, 13.

32. Transcript of a Meeting of the Politburo of the R.W.P., November 29, 1961, Executive Archive of the Central Committee of the R.C.P., p. 18; Speech of Gheorghe Gheorghiu-Dej, Transcript of the Plenary of the Central Committee of the R.W.P., December 5, 1961, Executive Archive of the Central Committee of the R.C.P., pp. 92–93.

33. Tatiana and Gheorghe Brătescu interview.

34. Transcript of an Interrogation of Ana Pauker by a Party Commission of the R.W.P., June 18, 1956, Ana Pauker Inquiry File, Executive Archive of the Central Committee of the R.C.P., p. 16; Declaration of Lucreţiu Patraşcanu, November 2, 1949, ASRI, Fond P, Dosar 40002, Vol. 1, p. 56; Memoir of Vasile Luca, November 5, 1954, ASRI, Fond P, Dosar 40005, Vol. 126, p. 45; Ana Toma and Tatiana and Gheorghe Brătescu interviews.

35. Silviu Brucan, Generaţia irosită [The Wasted Generation] (Bucharest, 1992), pp. 58–61.

36. Transcript of an Interrogation of Ana Pauker by a Party Commission of the R.W.P., July 6, 1956, Ana Pauker Inquiry File, Executive Archive of the Central Committee of the R.C.P., p. 7.

37. Transcript of a Meeting of the Politburo of the R.W.P., November 29, 1961, Executive Archive of the Central Committee of the R.C.P., p. 19.

38. Interrogation of Ana Pauker by a Party Commission of the R.W.P., June 18, 1956, Ana Pauker Inquiry File, Executive Archive of the Central Committee of the R.C.P., pp. 7–8.

39. Interrogation of Vasile Luca, March 13, 1954, ASRI, Fond P, Dosar 40005, Vol. 2, p. 97.

40. Memoir of Vasile Luca, February 15, 1957, pp. 7–8. Luca made the request when he was appointed general secretary of the National Democratic Front in late 1944 (ibid.).

41. On her proposing Luca's inclusion, see Interrogation of Ana Pauker, February 25, 1953, Ana Pauker Inquiry File, Executive Archive of the Central Committee of the R.C.P., p. 5; on her lack of sympathy for him, see Transcript of an Interroga-

tion of Ana Pauker by a Party Commission of the R.W.P., June 18, 1956, Ana Pauker Inquiry File, Executive Archive of the Central Committee of the R.C.P., pp. 4, 20–21; quote is from the declaration of Zina Brâncu, Ana Pauker Inquiry File, Executive Archive of the Central Committee of the R.C.P., p. 6.

42. Self-Criticism of Ana Pauker to the Politburo of the R.W.P., September 22, 1952, Ana Pauker Inquiry File, Executive Archive of the Central Committee of the R.C.P.; Transcript of an Interrogation of Ana Pauker by a Party Commission of the R.W.P., July 29, 1953, Ana Pauker Inquiry File, Executive Archive of the Central Committee of the R.C.P., p. 7; Interrogation of Ana Pauker by a Party Commission of the R.W.P., June 12, 1953, Ana Pauker Inquiry File, Executive Archive of the Central Committee of the R.C.P., pp. 71–72, 84; Transcript of an Interrogation of Ana Pauker by a Party Commission of the R.W.P., June 18, 1956, Ana Pauker Inquiry File, Executive Archive of the Central Committee of the R.C.P., p. 9.

43. On Luca's servility, see L. Clejan, Explanatory Meeting of the Right Deviation with Diplomats, June 21 and 23, 1952, National Archives of Romania, Fond CC al PCR—Cancelarie, Dosar 55/1952, p. 43; Ana Toma interview; Declaration of Ana Toma, "Excerpts of Declarations of Some Comrades," November 5, 1956, Ana Pauker Inquiry File, Executive Archive of the Central Committee of the R.C.P., p. 4; on his coordinating with Pauker see Declaration of Zoltan Eidlitz, National Archives of Romania, Fond 1, Dosar 40005, Vol. 111, pp. 119, 123; Alexandru Nistor interview, January 22, 1994.

44. Synthesis of Reports, Ministry of Interior Affairs, Văcăreşti Prison, Bureau D, No. 00385, May 21, 1955, ASRI, Fond P, Dosar 40005, Vol. 154, p. 17.

45. Declaration of Zoltan Eidlitz, July 10, 1953, ASRI, Fond P, Dosar 40005, Vol. 111, p. 48.

46. Sorin Toma interview.

47. Answers of Teohari Georgescu to Questions of the Party Control Commission, September 15, 1952, ASRI, Fond P, Dosar 40009, Vol. 32, p. 209.

48. Declaration of Teohari Georgescu, April 26, 1956, Ana Pauker Inquiry File, Executive Archive of the Central Committee of the R.C.P., pp. 8, 11–12, 14, 18.

49. Interrogation of Teohari Georgescu, July 1, 1955, ASRI, Fond P, Dosar 40009, Vol. 4, p. 223.

50. Tatiana and Gheorghe Brătescu, Ana Toma, Sorin Toma, Jean Coler, Ida Felix, and Cristina Boico interviews; Mihail Patriciu interview, March 12, 1994; Elena Tudorache interview, December 10, 1990; Tudor Olaru interview, July 13, 1991; Mihai Alexandru interview, July 11, 1991.

51. Transcript of an Interrogation of Ana Pauker by a Party Commission of the R.W.P., July 29, 1953, Ana Pauker Inquiry File, Executive Archive of the Central Committee of the R.C.P., p. 34.

52. Simion Bughici interview, July 11, 1991; Gheorghe Gaston Marin interview, July 27, 1991; Sergiu Sevcenko interview, December 10, 1990; Ana Toma, Gheorghe and Tatiana Brătescu, Cristina Boico, Alexandru Şiperco, Tudor Manea, Sorin Toma, Radu Mănescu, Alexandru Sencovici, Elena Tudorache, Tudor Olaru, Jean Coler, and Mihai Alexandru interviews.

53. Ana Toma interview.

54. Transcript of a Meeting of the Secretariat of the R.C.P., October 24, 1945, Ana Pauker Inquiry File, Executive Archive of the Central Committee of the R.C.P., pp. 2–3.

55. Transcript of a Meeting of the Politburo of the R.W.P., November 29, 1961, Executive Archive of the Central Committee of the R.C.P., p. 19.

56. Radu Mănescu learned this from Iosif Chişinevschi, who witnessed Dej's

declaration (Radu Mănescu interview); on Pauker's pledge of support, see Elena Tudorache interview.

57. Transcript of the Plenary Meeting of the Central Committee, May 27–29, 1952, National Archives of Romania, Fond CC al PCR—Cancelarie, Dosar 41/1952, p. 88.

58. Transcript of a Meeting of the Politburo of the R.W.P., November 29, 1961, Executive Archive of the Central Committee of the R.C.P., p. 13; Transcript of a Meeting of the Politburo of the R.W.P., June 21, 1952, National Archives of Romania, Fond CC al PCR—Cancelarie, Dosar 54/1952, p. 9.

59. When he traveled to Moscow in early September 1944 as head of the Romanian delegation to sign the armistice agreement with the Soviets, and after twice meeting with Pauker there, Lucrețiu Patrașcanu informed his wife, Elena, that the Soviets appeared to have been "caught unawares" and were "shocked by August 23rd." Pauker's personal position reflected this: "Ana did not like it that we carried out this August 23rd [coup]," Patrașcanu imparted, "and she would have preferred for them to have come, and for [us Communists] to have implemented August 23rd ourselves" (Transcript of the Declaration Given by Elena Patrașcanu before the R.C.P. Commission, October 25, 1967, ASRI, Fond P, Dosar 40002, Vol. 202, p. 205). Also see the Interrogation of Elena Patrașcanu, March 9, 1950, ASRI, Fond P, Dosar 40002, Vol. 87, pp. 44–45. This is also confirmed by Belu Zilber, whom Patrașcanu told much the same thing, and by Ana Toma and Nicolae Belu, who discussed the matter on separate occasions with Pauker herself (Interrogation of Herbert [Belu] Zilber, February 23, 1950, ASRI, Fond P, Dosar 40002, Vol. 38, p. 126; Declaration of Ana Toma, October 12, 1956, Ana Pauker Inquiry File, Executive Archive of the Central Committee of the R.C.P., pp. 1–2; Nicolae Belu interview, January 26, 1994).

60. On Patrașcanu's clash with Pauker, see Silviu Brucan, *The Wasted Generation: Memoirs of the Romanian Journey from Capitalism to Socialism and Back* (Boulder, Colo., 1993), p. 39; on his depiction of her, see Declaration of Elena Patrașcanu, March 9, 1950, ASRI, Fond P, Dosar 40002, Vol. 87, p. 59.

61. The quote is from the declaration of Anton Alexandrescu, in "New Pieces in the 'Ana Pauker Dossier,'" *Magazin istoric* 26, no. 10 (307) (October 1992), p. 26. On Pauker's move to the right, see the speech of Gheorghe Gheorghiu-Dej, Transcript of the Plenary of the Central Committee of the R.W.P., December 5, 1961, pp. 103–105; Transcript of a Meeting of the Central Activ of the R.C.P., April 26, 1945, National Archives of Romania, Fond 1, Dosar 16/1945, p. 13; Declaration of Vasile Luca, Transcript of a Meeting of the Council of the National Democratic Front, March 5, 1945, Central Archive of the Party Historical Institute Adjacent to the Central Committee of the R.C.P., Fond 80, Dosar 16, pp. 169–170; Declaration of Anton Alexandrescu, p. 26. Moreover, according to a July 22, 1945, secret telegram to the U.S. secretary of state from foreign service officer Roy M. Melbourne in Bucharest, Pauker continued to pursue a broad-based coalition by attempting to convince the National Peasant leader Dr. Nicolae Lupu to enter, with the wing of the National Peasant Party loyal to him, into a new coalition government (Telegram No. 871.00/7–2245, Division of Central Services [Telegraph Section], Office of European Affairs, Department of State, published in *Cotidianul,* Historical Supplement ["Arhiva"] 3, no. 3 [24], March 25, 1994, p. 4).

62. Declaration of Lucrețiu Patrașcanu, November 18, 1949, ASRI, Fond P, Dosar 40002, Vol. 1, pp. 107–108.

63. Speech of Gheorghe Gheorghiu-Dej, Transcript of the Plenary of the Central Committee of the R.W.P., December 5, 1961, Executive Archive of the Central Committee of the R.C.P., pp. 103–105. Transcripts of National Democratic Front meet-

ings on February 16 and 26, 1945, confirm Dej's position (Central Archive of the Party Historical Institute Adjacent to the Central Committee of the R.C.P., Fond 80, Dosar 16, pp. 8, 11; Transcript of a Meeting of the National Democratic Front, February 26, 1945, National Archives of Romania, Fond CC al PCR—Cancelarie, Dosar 11/1945, p. 5).

64. Remarks of Ana Pauker, Transcript of a Meeting of the R.C.P. Leadership, June 26, 1945, National Archives of Romania, Fond CC al PCR—Cancelarie, Dosar 53/1945, p. 12.

65. Meeting with the Communist Ministers of the Government, April 23, 1945, National Archives of Romania, Fond 1, Dosar 15/1945, pp. 1–2.

66. Answers Given by Ana Pauker to Questions Put by the Party Commission of the C.C. of the R.W.P., June 20, 1953, Ana Pauker Inquiry File, Executive Archive of the Central Committee of the R.C.P., pp. 1, 7–8; Transcript of an Interrogation of Ana Pauker by a Party Commission of the R.W.P., June 12, 1953, Ana Pauker Inquiry File, Executive Archive of the Central Committee of the R.C.P., p. 6; Self-Criticism of Ana Pauker to the Politburo of the R.W.P., September 22, 1952, Ana Pauker Inquiry File, Executive Archive of the Central Committee of the R.C.P.

67. Transcript of an Interrogation of Ana Pauker by a Party Commission of the R.W.P., June 12, 1953, Ana Pauker Inquiry File, Executive Archive of the Central Committee of the R.C.P., p. 34.

68. Answers Given by Ana Pauker to Questions Put by the Party Commission of the C.C. of the R.W.P., June 20, 1953, Ana Pauker Inquiry File, Executive Archive of the Central Committee of the R.C.P., p. 8; Self-Criticism of Ana Pauker to the Politburo of the R.W.P., September 22, 1952, Ana Pauker Inquiry File, Executive Archive of the Central Committee of the R.C.P.; Report Regarding the Findings of the Inquiry of Ana Pauker, January 20, 1954, Ana Pauker Inquiry File, Executive Archive of the Central Committee of the R.C.P., p. 5.

69. Transcript of an Interrogation of Ana Pauker by a Party Commission of the R.W.P., June 12, 1953, Ana Pauker Inquiry File, Executive Archive of the Central Committee of the R.C.P., p. 10.

70. Self-Criticism of Ana Pauker to the Politburo of the R.W.P., September 22, 1952, Ana Pauker Inquiry File, Executive Archive of the Central Committee of the R.C.P.; Transcript of the Plenary of the Central Committee, May 27–29, 1952, National Archives of Romania, Fond CC al PCR—Cancelarie, Dosar 41/1952, p. 88.

71. Transcript of a Plenary Meeting of the Central Committee of the R.C.P., January 25–28, 1946, National Archives of Romania, Fond 1, Dosar 1/1946, p. 317.

72. Transcript of a Meeting with the Central Activ of the R.C.P., March 7, 1945, National Archives of Romania, Fond CC al PCR—Cancelarie, Dosar 14/1945, p. 4. Pauker's tough posturing was also evident two weeks later during a Politburo discussion of a serious shortage of medical doctors in the countryside. Concurring with Ion Gheorghe Maurer's proposal that "the plethora of doctors" doing nothing in urban hospitals should be sent forthwith to the provinces, Pauker caustically added, "If they don't go there, they should go to the front, godammit!" (Transcript of a Meeting of the Politburo of the R.W.P., March 26, 1945, National Archives of Romania, Fond CC al PCR—Cancelarie, Dosar 20/1945, p. 14).

73. Transcript of a Meeting of the United Workers' Front, March 28, 1945, National Archives of Romania, Fond CC al PCR—Cancelarie, Dosar 22/1945, p. 25.

74. Transcript of a Meeting with the Communist Ministers, April 2, 1945, National Archives of Romania, Fond CC al PCR—Cancelarie, Dosar 24/1945, p. 6.

75. On dismantling the internment camps, see Declaration of Teohari Georgescu, April 26, 1956, Ana Pauker Inquiry File, Executive Archive of the Central Commit-

tee of the R.C.P., pp. 4–6; Interrogation of Teohari Georgescu, June 20, 1955, ASRI, Fond P, Dosar 40009, Vol. 4, p. 183. On the Iron Guard pact, see Interrogation of Ana Pauker, Ministry of Interior Affairs, March 4, 1953, Ana Pauker Inquiry File, Executive Archive of the Central Committee of the R.C.P., p. 2.

76. Transcript of the Plenary of the Central Committee of the R.W.P., May 27–29, 1952, National Archives of Romania, Fond CC al PCR—Cancelarie, Dosar 41/1952, pp. 61–63; Resolution Regarding the Activities of Comrade Teohari Georgescu in the Leadership of the Interior Ministry, Plenary of the C. C. of May 26–27, 1952, National Archives of Romania, Fond CC al PCR—Cancelarie, Dosar 41/1952, p. 170; Interrogation of Teohari Georgescu, March 1, 1955, ASRI, Fond P, Dosar 40009, Vol. 3, pp. 458–459; Interrogation of Teohari Georgescu, March 9, 1955, ASRI, Fond P, Dosar 40009, Vol. 3, pp. 474–477; "Synthesis on the Findings of the Inquiry of the Former Minister of Interior Affairs, Teohari Georgescu," September 14, 1955, ASRI, Fond P, Dosar 40009, Vol. 21, p. 146.

77. Declaration of Teohari Georgescu, Transcript of a Meeting of the United Workers' Front, August 21, 1945, National Archives of Romania, Fond CC al PCR—Cancelarie, Dosar 71/1945, p. 22.

78. Transcript of an Interrogation of Ana Pauker by a Party Commission of the R.W.P., June 12, 1953, Ana Pauker Inquiry File, Executive Archive of the Central Committee of the R.C.P., pp. 53, 63.

79. On Pauker's ambassadorial appointments, see Tudor Olaru interview, July 13, 1991; Corneliu Bogdan interview, August 8, 1989; Ana Toma interview; Tatiana and Gheorghe Brătescu interview. On her opposition to eliminating opponents, see Transcript of the Plenary of the Central Committee of the R.W.P., May 27–29, 1952, National Archives of Romania, Fond CC al PCR—Cancelarie, Dosar 41/1952, p. 87; National Archives of Romania, Fond 1, Dosar 748/1952, pp. 24, 56; National Archives of Romania, Fond 1, Dosar 748/1952, p. 56.

80. Ana Toma interview. A number of veteran R.C.P. activists who worked in the Central Committee apparat at the time confirm this: Tudor Manea interview, July 11, 1991; Ida Felix, Elena Tudorache, Tudor Olaru, Sara Alterescu, and Jean Coler interviews. Pauker's attitude was evident in her August 16, 1946, remarks at a party conference of the Bucharest region: "The employers and factory owners have to understand that it's in their own interest, and in the interest of the homeland, for them to come with all they have to the great battle to rebuild the country. There are industrialists, and there are businessmen, and there are bankers who have proved, and continue to prove, their love for the country, and come with their capital, their expertise, and their enthusiasm for rebuilding the country" (Report Regarding the Findings of the Inquiry of Ana Pauker, January 20, 1954, Ana Pauker Inquiry File, Executive Archive of the Central Committee of the R.C.P., p. 9).

81. Transcript of a Meeting of the Politburo of the R.W.P., November 29, 1961, Executive Archive of the Central Committee of the R.C.P., p. 13; Declaration of Teohari Georgescu, June 9, 1956, Ana Pauker Inquiry File, Executive Archive of the Central Committee of the R.C.P., p. 7.

82. Declaration of Teohari Georgescu, June 9, 1956, Ana Pauker Inquiry File, Executive Archive of the Central Committee of the R.C.P., p. 7.

83. Vladislav Zubok and Constantine Pleshakov, *Inside the Kremlin's Cold War: From Stalin to Khrushchev* (Cambridge, MA, 1996), pp. 120, 129; John Lewis Gaddis, *We Now Know: Rethinking the Cold War* (Oxford, 1997), pp. 40–41.

84. Transcript of the Plenary of the Central Committee of the R.W.P., May 27–29, 1952, National Archives of Romania, Fond CC al PCR—Cancelarie, Dosar 41/1952, p. 78; Transcript of an Interrogation of Ana Pauker by a Party Commission

of the R.W.P., June 12, 1953, Ana Pauker Inquiry File, Executive Archive of the Central Committee of the R.C.P., pp. 15–16.

85. Transcript of an Interrogation of Ana Pauker by a Party Commission of the R.W.P., June 12, 1953, Ana Pauker Inquiry File, Executive Archive of the Central Committee of the R.C.P., p. 27; Transcript of the Plenary of the Central Committee of the R.W.P., May 27–29, 1952, National Archives of Romania, Fond CC al PCR—Cancelarie, Dosar 41/1952, pp. 61–62.

86. Transcript of a Meeting of the Politburo of the R.W.P., November 29, 1961, Executive Archive of the Central Committee of the R.C.P., p. 13.

87. Leonte Răutu interview, August 22, 1993. Sorin Toma interviewed Răutu for the author.

88. Transcript of a Meeting of the Politburo of the R.W.P., November 29, 1961, Executive Archive of the Central Committee of the R.C.P., pp. 13, 20.

89. Alexandru Şiperco, Sorin Toma, Gheorghe Gaston Marin, Ilie Zaharia, Mihai Alexandru, and Radu Mănescu interviews.

90. Michael Checinski, *Poland: Communism, Nationalism, Anti-Semitism* (New York, 1982), pp. 47–48.

91. William O. McCagg, Jr., *Stalin Embattled* (Detroit, 1977), pp. 42–44.

92. Tatiana and Gheorghe Brătescu interview; Ana Toma interview.

93. Tatiana and Gheorghe Brătescu interview.

94. On Pauker's leading the R.C.P., see Ana Toma interview. On her relations with Soviet officials, see Ana Toma, ibid., and Tatiana and Gheorghe Brătescu interview.

95. Ana Toma interview.

96. Conversation of Ana Pauker and Two Party Leaders at the Party House in Otopeni, April 8, 1953, ASRI, Fond P, Dosar 40009, Vol. 68, p. 229; Transcript of a Meeting of the Politburo of the R.W.P., March 13–14, 1961, Executive Archive of the Central Committee of the R.C.P., p. 163. Also see Dennis Deletant, "New Light on Gheorghiu-Dej's Struggle for Dominance in the Romanian Communist Party," *The Slavonic and East European Review* 73, no. 4 (October 1995), pp. 673–674.

97. Eduard Mezincescu and Alexandru Şiperco interviews.

98. Conversation of Ana Pauker and Two Party Leaders at the Party House in Otopeni, April 8, 1953, ASRI, Fond P, Dosar 40009, Vol. 68, p. 229.

99. Transcript of an Interrogation of Ana Pauker by a Party Commission of the R.W.P., June 18, 1956, Ana Pauker Inquiry File, Executive Archive of the Central Committee of the R.C.P., p. 25.

100. Conversation of Ana Pauker and Two Party Leaders at the Party House in Otopeni, April 8, 1953, ASRI, Fond P, Dosar 40009, Vol. 68, p. 229.

101. Transcript of a Meeting of the Politburo of the R.W.P., November 29, 1961, Executive Archive of the Central Committee of the R.C.P., pp. 10, 12–13.

102. "Note Regarding the Conversation of I. V. Stalin with Gh. Gheorghiu-Dej and A. Pauker on the Situation within the R.C.P., and the State of Affairs in Romania in Connection to the Peace Treaty," No. 191, February 2, 1947, 9:00 P.M., AP RF.F.45, op. 1, d. 361, l. 62–66, in Galina P. Muraschko, Albina F. Noskowa, and Tatjana W. Wolokitina, eds., *Vostochnaia Evropa v dokumentakh arkhivov: 1944–1953* [Eastern Europe in the Documents of the Russian Archives, 1944–1953], vol. 1 (Moscow, 1997), pp. 564–565.

103. Transcript of a Meeting of the Politburo of the R.W.P., November 29, 1961, Executive Archive of the Central Committee of the R.C.P., p. 14.

104. Ibid., pp. 14–16.

105. Eduard Mezincescu and Alexandru Şiperco interviews.

106. "Information of the Interpreter and Major of the Soviet Army Shkoda Re-

garding a Conversation with Gh. Gheorghiu-Dej and his Meeting with I. V. Stalin," No. 192, February 4, 1947, A VP RF, f.0125, op. 35, p. 136, d. 12, l. 15–16, in G. P. Muraschko et al., eds., *Vostochnaia Evropa v dokumentakh arkhivov,* pp. 568–570. Muraschko notes that Gheorghiu-Dej's memo is also in the Russian archives: A VP RF, f. 0125, op. 35, p. 136, d. 11, l. 15–16, 18–20, 22–23 (ibid., p. 569).

107. The mysterious and contradictory circumstances of Foriş's demise remain unclear and were disputed by the parties involved. Immediately after his removal as general secretary on April 4, 1944, the provisional R.C.P. leadership permitted Foriş to work on the party newspaper *România liberă.* One month later, without any explanation, he was abruptly isolated and kept under permanent guard. He was ordered on several occasions to furnish detailed reports and participate in lengthy discussions on his wartime activities and was accused of being a criminal and a party enemy. But on August 26 the party leaders suddenly reversed themselves. They began allowing him to take walks in the city, though only accompanied, and Bodnăraş informed him that they did not consider him a Siguranţă agent. Then, in the second half of September, soon after Pauker's arrival, Foriş was formally arrested by Bodnăraş himself and several other party activists and was imprisoned at the headquarters of the R.C.P.'s Patriotic Guard, which Bodnăraş formally headed. However, although his wife, Victoria Sârbu, was informed that proof of his guilt was now established, Foriş was suddenly released on December 24, and was told by Bodnăraş on January 6, 1945, that he had been found innocent and was to be appointed the "Agit-Prop" chief of the Cluj region. Delaying his departure to Cluj for several weeks, Foriş at that time wrote a detailed memoir on his wartime positions that reportedly accused Gheorghiu-Dej's group of anti-Sovietism and national chauvinism, and he apparently forwarded it to the Soviets. On March 23, 1945, he was again arrested, this time by the Communist-controlled Siguranţă, on the suspicion of having written a manifesto against the R.C.P. leadership. His wife, then nine months pregnant, was ordered by the Central Committee to divorce him. Imprisoned inside the Interior Ministry, Foriş immediately declared a hunger strike and was freed after twenty days, when the charges could not be verified. Nevertheless, on July 9, 1945, the Soviet agent Gheorghe Pintilie (Pantiuşa Bodnarenko) arrested him yet again on the direct orders of Gheorghiu-Dej. Pauker revealed to her family that Dej and Bodnăraş at that time declared to the other party leaders that they had irrefutable proof that Foriş had been a Siguranţă agent during the war; based on their claim, the entire leadership voted for his re-arrest. The delegates of the R.C.P. National Conference in October 1945 were informed that Foriş was indeed found to be a traitor. After being held for one year, he was executed by Pintilie in the summer of 1946 by being struck with an iron bar and was buried in a makeshift common grave with two other bodies in the basement of the party house in which he was held. After his arrest in 1953, Teohari Georgescu declared that the execution had been ordered by all four CC secretaries—though he later admitted to a party commission that he had made false declarations on Foriş's assassination and other issues in order to garner the support of Gheorghiu-Dej. His 1953 declaration, moreover, was contradicted by Pauker, who claimed to her family that Foriş's 1946 execution was carried out on orders of Dej and Bodnăraş, without the party Secretariat's knowledge or approval. When Pauker protested the execution after the fact, Dej and Bodnăraş defended it, insisting that putting Foriş on trial would have been impossible. Pauker's account was confirmed by Ana Toma, whose source of information was her late husband, Gheorghe Pintilie, who arrested Foriş and executed him. Finally, Maria Sârbu, the sister of Foriş's wife, Victoria (who lingered in jail for fifteen years), reports that when she visited Pauker in the hospital in 1959, Pauker expressed her disgust regarding Foriş's

murder and affirmed his innocence. R.C.P. Commission Report on Ştefan Foriş, March 11, 1968, pp. 2–3; Letter of Ştefan Foriş to the Central Committee of the R.C.P., June 24, 1944, ASRI, Fond P, Dosar 40002, Vol. 56, p. 1; Letter of Victoria Sârbu to the Central Committee of the R.C.P., undated, ASRI, Fond P, Dosar 40002, Vol. 56, p. 124; Declaration of Victoria Sârbu, February 7, 1950, ASRI, Fond P, Dosar 40002, Vol. 54, pp. 20–21; Declaration of Victoria Sârbu, undated, ASRI, Fond P, Dosar 40002, Vol. 56, p. 124; Declaration of Remus Koffler, undated, ASRI, Fond P, Dosar 40002, Vol. 45, pp. 64, 119; "Note Regarding the Arrest and Inquiry of Teohari Georgescu," R.C.P. Commission, April 14, 1968, Executive Archive of the Central Committee of the R.C.P., p. 3; Egon Balaş, *Will to Freedom: A Perilous Journey through Fascism and Communism* (Syracuse, N.Y., 2000), p. 164; Tatiana and Gheorghe Brătescu, Tudor Olaru, Ana Toma, and Maria Sârbu interviews.

108. Galina P. Muraschko, Albina F. Noskowa, and Tatjana W. Wolokitina, "Das Zentralkomitee der WKP(b) und das Ende der 'nationalen Wege zum Sozialismus,'" *Jahrbuch für historische Kommunismus-forschung*, 1994 (Akademie Verlag) pp. 15–17.

109. Ibid., pp. 17–19.

110. Declaration of Gheorghe Gheorghiu-Dej, Transcript of a Meeting of the Politburo of the R.W.P., December 7, 1961, Executive Archive of the Central Committee of the R.C.P., p. 12.

111. Transcript of a Meeting of the Politburo of the R.W.P., November 29, 1961, Executive Archive of the Central Committee of the R.C.P., p. 25. Confirming Dej's account is a recently published synopsis of a July 13, 1948, Politburo meeting, where the rumors were discussed in detail (Ioan Scurtu, "PMR şi 'criza iugoslavă'" [The R.W.P. and "the Yugoslav Crisis"], *Dosarele istoriei*, no. 3 (19), 1998, p. 37.

112. Declaration of Teohari Georgescu, May 23, 1956, Ana Pauker Inquiry File, Executive Archive of the Central Committee of the R.C.P., p. 5.

113. Transcript of a Meeting of the Politburo of the R.W.P., November 29, 1961, Executive Archive of the Central Committee of the R.C.P., pp. 26, 29–30; Scurtu, "PMR şi 'criza iugoslavă,'" pp. 35–41. Chişinevschi was a high-ranking Soviet agent, regularly referred to as "Beria's man" in the Romanian Politburo (ibid., p. 30; Memoir of Vasile Luca, February 15, 1957, pp. 7–8; Radu Mănescu, Elena Tudorache, Alexandru Şiperco, Hermina Tismăneanu, Eduard Mezincescu, Tudor Olaru, and Cristina Boico interviews; Charlotte Gruia interview, July 15, 1991).

114. Declaration of Teohari Georgescu, May 23, 1956, Ana Pauker Inquiry File, Executive Archive of the Central Committee of the R.C.P., p. 7.

115. Ibid., p. 3. Gheorghe Pintilie also reported Pauker's continual concern over "what the Soviets will say" (Declaration of Gheorghe Pintilie, June 10, 1956, Ana Pauker Inquiry File, Executive Archive of the Central Committee of the R.C.P., p. 5).

116. Transcript of a Meeting of the Politburo of the R.W.P., December 21, 1945, National Archives of Romania, Fond CC al PCR—Cancelarie, Dosar 122/1945, p. 29.

117. Transcript of a Meeting of the Politburo of the R.W.P., September 23, 1946, National Archives of Romania, Fond CC al PCR—Cancelarie, Dosar 49/1946, pp. 15–19.

118. Transcript of a Meeting of the Politburo of the R.C.P., September 11, 1947, National Archives of Romania, Fond CC al PCR—Cancelarie, Dosar 28/1947, pp. 1–7; Transcript of a Meeting of the Politburo of the R.C.P., September 12, 1947, National Archives of Romania, Fond CC al PCR—Cancelarie, Dosar 28/1947, pp. 25, 41.

119. Transcript of a Meeting of the Politburo of the R.C.P., September 12, 1947, National Archives of Romania, Fond CC al PCR—Cancelarie, Dosar 28/1947, pp. 14–16.

120. On the Soviet orders, see Sorin Toma interview.

121. Memoir of Vasile Luca, November 5, 1954, ASRI, Fond P, Dosar 40005, Vol. 126, pp. 47–48.

122. Pauker admitted that she "didn't have complete confidence in Maurer and Zeiger" in 1947 (Answers of Ana Pauker to Questions of the Party Commission of the R.W.P., June 12, 1953, Ana Pauker Inquiry File, Executive Archive of the Central Committee of the R.C.P., p. 87); the Russian study mistakenly linked Pauker to an attack on Dej and Maurer's economic program, and to a call for nationalizing Romanian industry, by her longtime close associate in the Comintern apparat, Bulgarian diplomat Demiter Ganev (T. V. Volokitina, G. P. Muraschko, and A. F. Noskova, *Narodnaia demokratiia, mif ili realnost? Obshchestvenno-politicheskie protessy v Vostochnoi Evrope, 1944–1948* [Popular Democracy, Myth or Reality? Sociopolitical Processes in Eastern Europe, 1944–1948] [Moscow, 1993] pp. 180–181); as Dej suggested, he was the target when Pauker accused Maurer, erroneously, of opposing the SOVROM's creation (Transcript of a Meeting of the Politburo of the R.W.P., December 7, 1961, Executive Archive of the Central Committee of the R.C.P., p. 11).

123. Transcript of a Meeting of the Politburo of the R.W.P., May 26, 1952, National Archives of Romania, Fond CC al PCR—Cancelarie, Dosar 40/1952, p. 77.

124. Interrogation of Vasile Luca, February 11, 1954, ASRI, Fond P, Dosar 40005, Vol. 2, p. 10.

125. Synthesis, May 1–15, 1955, Ministry of Internal Affairs, Văcărești Penitentiary, ASRI, Fond P, Dosar 40005, Vol. 154, p. 18.

126. Teohari Georgescu and Iosif and Liuba Chişinevschi (the latter having worked in the Party Control Commission) revealed to Alexandru Şiperco that Gheorghiu-Dej was under investigation by the Soviets beginning in June 1948, though he was not demoted or isolated in any way. This was also confirmed by Charlotte Gruia, another official in the Party Control Commission: "People who were called to the commission of inquiry (during the verification of party members that began in 1948) later talked among themselves about what they were asked, and they spoke about how the questions got closer and closer to Gheorghiu-Dej." According to Georgescu and the Chişinevschis, however, neither Pauker, Luca, nor Georgescu attempted to take advantage of the inquiry to topple Dej (Alexander Şiperco and Charlotte Gruia interviews).

127. Alexandru Şiperco interview.

128. Maurer, who was listed as the Deputy Minister of Industry as late as June 1948, was named the chairman of the Association for the Dissemination of Science and Culture soon afterward (*The Romanian Press Review*, annex, June 3, 1948; *The Romanian Press Review*, no. 561, November 3, 1949; Ion Gheorghe Maurer interview, July 12, 1991). On Dej and Chişinevschi, see Transcript of a Meeting of the Politburo of the R.W.P., November 29, 1961, Executive Archive of the Central Committee of the R.C.P., p. 31.

129. Sorin Toma interview.

130. Alexandru Şiperco interview.

131. On Rákosi, see RtskhIDNI, f. 575, op. I, d. 94; l. 90, 92–94, cited in Leonid Gibianskii, "The Last Conference of the Cominform," in Giuliamo Procacci, ed., *The Cominform: Minutes of the Three Conferences, 1947/1948/1949* (Milan, 1994), p. 657.

132. Tatiana and Gheorghe Brătescu interview; Mihai Alexandru interview; Luiza Năvodaru interview, August 17, 1993.

133. Sorin Toma interview.

134. Transcript of a Meeting of the Politburo of the R.W.P., March 12–14, 1961, Executive Archive of the Central Committee of the R.C.P., pp. 162–163. Teohari Georgescu made the same point: "In the period of 1948–1952, Ana created family relations and received at her home both foreigners who came on visits to the country, as well as diplomats of [popular] democratic countries. In discussions, Ana told me that she does this despite the leadership having pronounced its opposition to it. . . . " (Declaration of Teohari Georgescu, April 26, 1956, Ana Pauker Inquiry File, Executive Archive of the Central Committee of the R.C.P., p. 17.)

135. After placing, for instance, the veteran party activist Dumitru Petrescu as head of the Organizational Section of the Central Committee, Gheorghiu-Dej started soliciting useful information from him on Pauker and her allies (Transcript of the Discussion of Comrade Dumitru Petrescu with the R.C.P. Commission, November 2, 1967, ASRI, Fond P, Dosar 40002, Vol. 203, p. 328).

136. A leader of the National Peasant Party, Corneliu Coposu, learned in prison from the economist Herbert (Belu) Zilber that Pauker expressed her opposition to the Soviet-imposed arrest of Coposu and the National Peasants' Ghiţa Pop at a meeting he attended in 1947 (Corneliu Coposu interview, January 6, 1994; Corneliu Coposu, *Dialoguri,* with Vartan Arachelian [Bucharest, 1993], pp. 66–67). Similarly, Ion Cârja, the secretary general of the Association of Writers in Transylvania who was jailed for anti-Communist activities between 1949 and 1964, contends that imprisoned members of Patraşcanu's entourage told him that Pauker intervened on behalf of Iuliu Maniu in 1947 by writing a letter to General Alexandru Petrescu, the presiding judge at Maniu's trial, asking for leniency in Maniu's sentencing (Ion Cârja, *Canalul Morţii* [The Canal of Death] [Bucharest, 1993], p. 173). In addition, Camil Dumetrescu, a high-ranking National Peasant activist who worked in the codes department of the Foreign Ministry before his arrest in March 1947, reported that "Ana Pauker was the only person in the Communist leadership who informed my parents that I was healthy" while in prison (Interview of Camil Dumetrescu, *Cotidianul,* anul 2, no. 156 [321], August 12, 1992, p. 4).

137. Transcript of an Interrogation of Ana Pauker by a Party Commission of the R.W.P., June 18, 1956, Ana Pauker Inquiry File, Executive Archive of the Central Committee of the R.C.P., p. 37; Tatiana and Gheorghe Brătescu interview. Lucreţiu Patraşcanu reportedly revealed to his friend Herbert (Belu) Zilber that Pauker told him at the time "that some 2,000 people have to be arrested so that we can do what we want!" (Declaration of Herbert Zilber, February 5, 1952, ASRI, Fond P, Dosar 40002, Vol. 39, p. 106).

138. Gheorghe Brătescu interview.

139. Transcript of an Interrogation of Ana Pauker by a Party Commission of the R.W.P., June 18, 1956, Ana Pauker Inquiry File, Executive Archive of the Central Committee of the R.C.P., p. 37.

140. Transcript of a Plenary Meeting of the Central Committee of the R.W.P., January 23–24, 1950, National Archives of Romania, Fond CC al PCR—Cancelarie, Dosar 7/1950, Vol. 2, p. 213.

141. Transcript of an Interrogation of Ana Pauker by a Party Commission of the R.W.P., June 18, 1956, Ana Pauker Inquiry File, Executive Archive of the Central Committee of the R.C.P., p. 37; ASRI, Fond P, Dosar 4121, Table Nr. 9.

142. Memoir of Vasile Luca, November 5, 1954, ASRI, Fond P, Dosar 40005,

Vol. 126, p. 56. Ana Toma and Wilhelm Einhorn made a similar point (Ana Toma and Wilhelm Einhorn interviews).

143. Interrogation of Vasile Luca, February 22, 1954, ASRI, Fond P, Dosar 40005, Vol. 2, p. 57.

144. Resolution Regarding the Activities of Comrade Teohari Georgescu in the Leadership of the Interior Ministry, Plenary of the C.C. of May 26–27, 1952, National Archives of Romania, Fond CC al PCR—Cancelarie, Dosar 41/1952, pp. 170, 173–174; Transcript of a Meeting of the Politburo, March 13, 1952, National Archives of Romania, Fond CC al PCR—Cancelarie, Dosar 19/1952, p. 68.

145. Answers of Teohari Georgescu to Questions of the Party Control Commission, September 15, 1952, ASRI, Fond P, Dosar 40009, Vol. 32, pp. 213–214.

146. Answers of Teohari Georgescu to Questions of the Party Control Commission, September 15, 1952, ASRI, Fond P, Dosar 40009, Vol. 32, pp. 213–214.

147. The Cominform's criticism of mass recruitment was revealed in a Central Committee plenary in May 1950 (Transcript of a Plenary Meeting of the Central Committee of the R.W.P., May 15–17, 1950, National Archives of Romania, Fond CC al PCR—Cancelarie, Dosar 32/1950, p. 124). Simion Zeiger discusses the Cominform's order to verify party members in "Certain Aspects of the Policies of the Party and State Leadership in Romania towards the Jewish Population in the First Years after Taking Power," unpublished manuscript, p. 1.

148. According to Dej, the Pauker faction opposed the resolutions calling for verification passed at the First Congress of the Romanian Workers' Party (R.W.P.) in February 1948 (Speech of Gheorghe Gheorghiu-Dej, Transcript of the Plenary of the Central Committee of the R.W.P., December 5, 1961, Executive Archive of the Central Committee of the R.C.P., p. 116). Pauker and Luca's opposition to expelling large numbers of party members through verification was evident at an October 1948 Secretariat meeting and appeared to have led to a compromise on the criteria for expulsions (Transcript of a Meeting of the Secretariat of the R.W.P., October 4, 1948, National Archives of Romania, Fond CC al PCR—Cancelarie, Dosar 38/1952, pp. 1–10). Moreover, Pauker and Georgescu were criticized during their purge for hindering the work of the verification commission (Transcript of the Plenary of the Central Committee of the R.W.P., May 27–29, 1952, National Archives of Romania, Fond CC al PCR—Cancelarie, Dosar 41/1952, p. 16; Resolution Regarding the Activities of Comrade Teohari Georgescu in the Leadership of the Interior Ministry, Plenary of the C.C. of May 26–27, 1952, National Archives of Romania, Fond CC al PCR—Cancelarie, Dosar 41/1952, p. 171).

149. Speech of Gheorghe Gheorghiu-Dej, Transcript of the Plenary of the Central Committee of the R.W.P., December 5, 1961, Executive Archive of the Central Committee of the R.C.P., p. 116.

150. Interrogation of Teohari Georgescu, July 4, 1955, ASRI, Fond P, Dosar 40009, Vol. 4, p. 235.

151. Transcript of a Meeting of the Politburo of the R.W.P., June 21, 1952, National Archives of Romania, Fond CC al PCR—Cancelarie, Dosar 54/1952, pp. 7–8.

152. Transcript of a Plenary Meeting of the Central Committee of the R.W.P., May 15–17, 1950, National Archives of Romania, Fond CC al PCR—Cancelarie, Dosar 32/1950, pp. 122, 124, 127.

153. Transcript of an Interrogation of Ana Pauker by a Party Commission of the R.W.P., June 12, 1953, Ana Pauker Inquiry File, Executive Archive of the Central Committee of the R.C.P., p. 82.

154. As Finance Minister, Luca persistently opposed inefficient or unprofitable

investments, and thus repeatedly clashed with Miron Constantinescu, the head of
the state planning commission, as well as Gheorghiu-Dej (Transcript of a Meeting
of the Secretariat of the R.W.P., September 12, 1949, National Archives of Romania,
Fond CC al PCR—Cancelarie, Dosar 77/1949, pp. 6–7; Transcript of a Meeting of
the Secretariat of the R.W.P., September 27, 1949, National Archives of Romania,
Fond CC al PCR—Cancelarie, Dosar 83/1949, pp. 5–15; Interrogation of Teohari
Georgescu, June 12, 1953, ASRI, Fond P, Dosar 40009, Vol. 1, p. 317; Declaration
of Teohari Georgescu, May 23, 1956, Ana Pauker Inquiry File, Executive Archive of
the Central Committee of the R.C.P., p. 10; Declaration of Zoltan Eidlitz, undated,
ASRI, Fond P, Dosar 40005, Vol. 111, pp. 64–66; Alexandru Nistor interview;
Nicolae Belu interview). Luca also halted the financing of badly administered projects, including those of the Soviet-Romanian joint construction company. At his behest, his deputy Alexandru Iacob blocked funds for the SOVROM's projects, causing many construction sites to stop work entirely. Soviet Deputy Minister Iatrov later
complained to the party leadership, asserting that such a thing had never happened
in the Soviet Union; a joint Soviet-Romanian commission and the Romanian Investment Bank were later criticized for the move (Declaration of Zoltan Eidlitz, undated,
ASRI, Fond P, Dosar 40005, Vol., 111, p. 74).

   155. Transcript of an Interrogation of Ana Pauker by a Party Commission of the
R.W.P., June 18, 1956, Ana Pauker Inquiry File, Executive Archive of the Central
Committee of the R.C.P., p. 21; Transcript of a Meeting of the Secretariat of the
R.W.P., September 27, 1949, National Archives of Romania, Fond CC al PCR—
Cancelarie, Dosar 83/1949, p. 8.

   156. Tatiana and Gheorghe Brătescu interview.

   157. Transcript of a Meeting of the Secretariat of the R.W.P., October 10, 1949,
National Archives of Romania, Fond CC al PCR—Cancelarie, Dosar 92/1949,
pp. 6–7; Transcript of a Meeting of the Council of Ministers, March 31, 1950, National Archives of Romania, Fond Consiliul de Miniştri—Cabinetul, Dosar 3/1950,
p. 10; Transcript of the Plenary of the Central Committee of the R.W.P., May 27–29,
1952, National Archives of Romania, Fond CC al PCR—Cancelarie, Dosar 41/1952,
pp. 8–9; Interrogation of Ioan Weisz by a Party Commission, May 15, 1952, National Archives of Romania, Fond 1, Dosar 30/1952, pp. 7–8, 10; Interrogation of
Zoltan Eidlitz, May 23, 1953, ASRI, Fond P, Dosar 40005, Vol. 112, p. 14; Declaration of Vasile Modoran, August 14, 1952, ASRI, Fond P, Dosar 40005, Vol. 93,
p. 113; Elisabeta Luca interview, July 8, 1991; Alexandru Nistor and Nicolae Belu
interviews.

   158. Elena Tudorache personally witnessed Pauker express her opposition to the
canal at an administrative meeting of the Central Committee in 1949: "[S]he said,"
Tudorache revealed, "that she did not agree to such exaggerated investments of not
only money, but especially cement, for the Canal. . . . [S]he said that people, and peasants, didn't have enough cement and other materials to build their houses. It's a sheer
waste to devote millions of tons of cement to build the Canal" (Elena Tudorache interview; confirmed by Alexandru Nistor, interview). Pauker's dislike of the project is
apparent in remarks to the Secretariat in September 1949: "We're a small country,"
she declared, "which has just emerged from the war, and we're in the process of rebuilding. Despite this, we've embarked on a project that no capitalist country would
dare to embark on in the situation that we're in. . . . [T]he Soviet Union . . . has done
it, but she did not do so in the period of transition to socialism. And here we are, a
country that is now in transition to socialism, a tiny country, building a canal. Not
even our bourgeoisie, in the best of times, could have done such a thing. It's an ex-
traordinary venture. It's a venture that won't pay for itself for years and years to

come" (Transcript of a Meeting of the Secretariat of the R.W.P., September 22, 1949, National Archives of Romania, Fond CC al PCR—Cancelarie, Dosar 81/1949, p. 18).

159. On Dej's supervising the project, see Declaration of Zoltan Eidlitz, undated, ASRI, Fond P, Dosar 40005, Vol. 111, p. 75; Interrogation of Zoltan Eidlitz, May 23, 1953, ASRI, Fond P, Dosar 40005, Vol. 112, p. 14; Alexandru Nistor interview. On his promoting it, see Mihai Alexandru interview; Transcript of a Meeting of the Council of Ministers, May 17, 1951, National Archives of Romania, Fond Consiliul de Miniştri—Cabinetul, Dosar 3/1951, p. 5. The leader of the Romanian economic agency in Moscow during the late 1940s also confirms Dej's attitude. That leader recalls that Gheorghiu-Dej's bounding enthusiasm about the canal after his meetings with Stalin in 1948 gave the impression that the idea was Dej's own. The official, who has requested anonymity, was interviewed on July 1, 1991.

160. Note Regarding Certain Problems Resulting from the Study of the Dossiers of the Two Trials of the Danube–Black Sea Canal, undated, Executive Archive of the Central Committee of the R.C.P., pp. 1–6. The arrests were initially ordered in March 1952 but did not occur until after Georgescu was purged from the Interior Ministry in May (ibid., p. 3).

161. George H. Bossy, "Transportation and Communications," in Stephen Fischer-Galati, ed., Romania (New York, 1957), pp. 340–341.

162. Whether Pauker also opposed the canal because it used slave labor is unclear. After her purge, lawyer Radu Olteanu, who had been arrested in 1949 for homosexuality and sent to the canal, visited her regularly. Pauker's son-in-law, Dr. Gheorghe Brătescu, recalls that Olteanu "spoke to Ana about what was happening at the Canal. *She didn't know?* No. She only knew what was officially said, that it was a reeducation camp for bourgeois personalities. In my opinion, she didn't want to know what was going on there. *How did she react to what Olteanu said?* She was horrified." (Dr. Gheorghe Brătescu interview.)

CHAPTER 4

1. Hugh Seton-Watson, *The East European Revolution* (New York, 1962), p. 13 n. 1. This figure applied to the 1930s.

2. Transcript of the Plenary Meeting of the Central Committee of the R.W.P., November 30–December 5, 1961, Executive Archive of the Central Committee of the R.C.P., p. 218.

3. Tatiana and Gheorghe Brătescu interview.

4. Transcript of the Plenary Meeting of the Central Committee of the R.W.P., November 30–December 5, 1961, Executive Archive of the Central Committee of the R.C.P., p. 126.

5. National Archives of Romania, Fond 1, Dosar 73/1952, p. 56.

6. Interrogation of Vasile Luca, February 22, 1954, ASRI, Fond P, Dosar 40005, Vol. 2, p. 57 [emphasis added]. Teohari Georgescu also asserted that Pauker had requested responsibility for agriculture (Declaration of Teohari Georgescu, April 26, 1956, Ana Pauker Inquiry File, Executive Archive of the Central Committee of the R.C.P., p. 13).

7. Transcript of a Meeting of the Politburo of the R.C.P., October 4, 1947, National Archives of Romania, Fond CC al PCR—Cancelarie, Dosar 33/1947, pp. 27–28.

8. R. W. Davies, *The Socialist Offensive: The Collectivization of Soviet Agriculture, 1929–1930* (Cambridge, Mass., 1980), p. 32; Transcript of a Meeting of the

Politburo of the R.C.P., September 12, 1947, National Archives of Romania, Fond CC al PCR—Cancelarie, Dosar 28/1947, p. 31.

9. Ibid., p. 8.

10. Ibid., pp. 30, 33–34.

11. Ibid., pp. 27–28.

12. Ibid., pp. 27–28, 45.

13. Ibid., p. 25.

14. J. Stalin, *Collected Works,* Vol. 7, 1947, pp. 286–287 (November 1926), pp. 122–129 (April 1926), pp. 315–316, 339–340 (December 1925); cited in Davies, *The Socialist Offensive,* pp. 31–32.

15. Stephen F. Cohen, *Bukharin and the Bolshevik Revolution: A Political Biography, 1888–1938,* rev. ed. (Oxford, 1980), pp. 175–176, 178.

16. Transcript of a Meeting of the Secretariat of the R.W.P., August 31, 1949, Fond CC al PCR—Cancelarie, Dosar 74/1949, p. 5.

17. Transcript of a Meeting of the Secretariat of the R.W.P., January 2, 1950, Fond CC al PCR—Cancelarie, Dosar 1/1950, pp. 8–9.

18. Memoir of Vasile Luca, November 5, 1954, ASRI, Fond P, Dosar 40005, Vol. 126, p. 56.

19. Interrogation of Vasile Luca, February 11, 1954, ASRI, Fond P, Dosar 40005, Vol. 2, p. 8; Self-Criticism of Ana Pauker to the Politburo of the R.W.P., September 22, 1952, Executive Archive of the Central Committee of the R.C.P.; Written Statement of Ana Toma, November 5, 1956, Executive Archive of the Central Committee of the R.C.P., p. 4; Written Declaration of Zoltan Eidlitz, ASRI, Fond P, Dosar 40005, Vol. 111, pp. 119, 123; Alexandru Nistor interview.

20. Transcript of a Meeting of the Politburo of the R.C.P., October 3, 1947, National Archives of Romania, Fond CC al PCR—Cancelarie, Dosar 32/1947, p. 47.

21. Transcript of a Meeting of the Politburo of the R.C.P., September 12, 1947, National Archives of Romania, Fond CC al PCR—Cancelarie, Dosar 28/1947, p. 13.

22. Transcript of a Meeting of the Council of Ministers, December 18, 1951, National Archives of Romania, Fond Consiliul de Miniştri—Cabinetul, Dosar 9/1951, p. 129.

23. Transcript of a Meeting of the Council of Ministers, June 20, 1951, National Archives of Romania, Fond Consiliul de Miniştri—Cabinetul, Dosar 4/1951, p. 9.

24. Transcript of a Meeting of the Council of Ministers, October 16, 1951, National Archives of Romania, Fond Consiliul de Miniştri—Cabinetul, Dosar 8/1951, p. 46.

25. On Luca's position see the Transcript of a Meeting of the Politburo of the R.W.P., September 1, 1950, Fond CC al PCR—Cancelarie, Dosar 54/1950, pp. 1–8, 14–18; Transcript of a Plenary Meeting of the Central Committee of the R.W.P., May 15–17, 1950, National Archives of Romania, Fond CC al PCR—Cancelarie, Dosar 32/1950, p. 216; Transcript of a Meeting of the Council of Ministers, June 18, 1951, National Archives of Romania, Fond Consiliul de Miniştri—Cabinetul, Dosar 4/1951, pp. 2–7; Transcript of a Meeting of the Politburo of the R.W.P., March 13, 1952, National Archives of Romania, Fond CC al PCR—Cancelarie, Dosar 19/1952, p. 56; Transcript of a Party Commission Interrogation of Interior Commerce Minister Vasile Malinschi, June 9 and June 21, 1952, National Archives of Romania, Fond 1, Dosar 254/1952, pp. 170, 211, 218–219. On Pauker's position see the Transcript of a Meeting of the Secretariat of the R.W.P., January 2, 1950, Fond CC al PCR—Cancelarie, Dosar 1/1950, pp. 8–9; Transcript of the Plenary Meeting of

the Central Committee of the R.W.P., February 29–March 1, 1952, National Archives of Romania, Fond CC al PCR—Cancelarie, Dosar 13/1952, p. 119.

26. Transcript of a Meeting of the Secretariat of the R.W.P., April 13, 1950, National Archives of Romania, Fond CC al PCR—Cancelarie, Dosar 27/1950, pp. 8–9; Transcript of a Meeting of the Politburo, September 1,1950, Fond CC al PCR—Cancelarie, Dosar 54/1950, p. 3; Transcript of a Meeting of the Council of Ministers, December 18, 1951, National Archives of Romania, Fond Consiliul de Miniştri—Cabinetul, Dosar 9/1951, pp. 130–132; National Archives of Romania, Fond 1, Dosar 19/1952, p. 14; Fond 1, Dosar 563/1952, pp. 25–37.

27. Transcript of a Meeting of the Secretariat of the R.W.P., April 13, 1950, National Archives of Romania, Fond CC al PCR—Cancelarie, Dosar 27/1950, pp. 9–10.

28. Personal correspondence of Sorin Toma to the author, January 30, 1993.

29. Transcript of a Meeting of the Politburo of the R.C.P., October 4, 1947, National Archives of Romania, Fond CC al PCR—Cancelarie, Dosar 33/1947, p. 25.

30. On Gheorghiu-Dej's failure to prevent Pauker and Luca from overturning the Industry and Commerce Ministry's price ratios, see National Archives of Romania, Fond 1, Dosar 711/1952, p. 83. The quote is from Transcript of a Meeting of the Council of Ministers, September 30, 1948, National Archives of Romania, Fond Consiliul de Miniştri—Cabinetul, Dosar 9/1948, pp. 79, 81.

31. Transcript of a Meeting of the Council of Ministers, September 19, 1950, National Archives of Romania, Fond Consiliul de Miniştri—Cabinetul, Dosar 9/1950, p. 15.

32. Transcript of a Meeting of the Council of Ministers, September 29, 1950, National Archives of Romania, Fond Consiliul de Miniştri—Cabinetul, Dosar 9/1950, p. 30.

33. Extracts from a Meeting of the Ministerial Commission, March 10, 1948, National Archives of Romania, Fond CC al PCR—Cancelarie, Dosar 5/1948, p. 6; Transcript of a Meeting of the Council of Ministers, September 29, 1950, National Archives of Romania, Fond Consiliul de Miniştri—Cabinetul, Dosar 9/1950, p. 30; Transcript of a Meeting of the Politburo, March 13, 1952, National Archives of Romania, Fond CC al PCR—Cancelarie, Dosar 19/1952, p. 56. The quote is from the Transcript of a Meeting of the Council of Ministers, September 19, 1950, National Archives of Romania, Fond Consiliul de Miniştri—Cabinetul, Dosar 9/1950, p. 20.

34. Transcript of a Meeting of the Council of Ministers, September 29, 1950, National Archives of Romania, Fond Consiliul de Miniştri—Cabinetul, Dosar 9/1950, pp. 30–32.

35. Transcript of a Meeting of the Politburo of the R.C.P., October 4, 1947, National Archives of Romania, Fond CC al PCR—Cancelarie, Dosar 33/1947, p. 21; Transcript of a Meeting of the Council of Ministers, September 30, 1948, National Archives of Romania, Fond Consiliul de Miniştri—Cabinetul, Dosar 9/1948, p. 28; Transcript of the Plenary Meeting of the Central Committee, February 29–March 1, 1952, National Archives of Romania, Fond CC al PCR—Cancelarie, Dosar 13/1952, pp. 118–119.

36. Transcript of a Meeting of the Politburo of the R.W.P., May 26, 1952, Fond CC al PCR—Cancelarie, Dosar 40/1952, p. 77.

37. Ionescu, *Communism in Romania,* pp. 110–111; J. Montias, *Economic Development in Communist Rumania* (Cambridge, Mass., 1967), p. 89. Transcript of a Meeting of the Politburo of the R.C.P., October 4, 1947, National Archives of Romania, Fond CC al PCR—Cancelarie, Dosar 33/1947, p. 9.

38. Adam Ulam, *Stalin: The Man and His Era* (New York, 1973), p. 669.

39. On Pauker's involvement in the Lenin School commission, see Self-Criticism of Ana Pauker to the Politburo of the R.W.P., September 22, 1952, Ana Pauker Inquiry File, Executive Archive of the Central Committee of the R.C.P. The quote is from the Archive of the Russian Foreign Ministry, Fond 0125, Op. 34, Doc. 16, p. 131, l. 119–120; cited in Volokitina, Muraschko, and Noskova, *Narodnaia demokratiia, mif ili realnost?* p. 174.

40. Regional Committee of the R.W.P., Iaşi, State Archives of Iaşi, Fond 1, Dosar 46/1945, p. 4; cited in Gheorghe Onişoru, "Propaganda and Counterpropaganda: The Matter of Kolhozes (1944–1949)," in *Instraurarea comunismulni—între rezistenţă şi represiune* (The Installation of Communism—Between Resistance and Repression), Papers Presented at the Conference of Sighetu Marmaţiei (June 9–11, 1995), Analele Sighet II (Bucharest, 1995), p. 36.

41. Ibid., pp. 38–40; Transcript of a Meeting of the Secretariat of the R.C.P., December 19, 1945, National Archives of Romania, Fond CC al PCR—Cancelarie, Dosar 121/1945, p. 4.

42. *Scânteia*, February 23, 1948, p. 1. At a meeting of the Central Committee Teohari Georgescu described the drought and resultant famine, which primarily affected Moldavia and southeastern Transylvania: "The privations have become indescribable in the regions ravaged by famine. There are families with many children who have not seen a single strand of wheat or a piece of corn in ten days. They've seen nothing but weeds, which they're now gathering up to eat. The death rate as a result of eating such things has risen and is climbing continuously" (Transcript of a Meeting of the [Enlarged] Central Committee of the R.C.P., August 31, 1946, p. 112).

43. The severity of the crises is discernible in a comparison of grain production in 1939 and 1946. In 1939 the country produced 1,224,000 wagons of grain, including 445,000 wagons of wheat; 605,000 of corn; 83,000 of rice; 49,000 of oats; and 43,000 of rye. In 1946, those figures were reduced to a total production of 251,000 wagons, including 132,000 wagons of wheat; 77,000 of corn; 17,000 of rice; 20,000 of oats; and 5,000 of rye (*The History of the Romanian Communist Party*, Documentary Synthesis, The Institute of Historical and Social-Political Study Next to the Central Committee of the P.C.R., chapter 6, August 1944–December 1947, p. 974). On the appeals for Western imports, see the Transcript of a Meeting of the Politburo of the R.C.P., September 23, 1946, National Archives of Romania, Fond CC al PCR—Cancelarie, Dosar 49/1946, pp. 15–19. On collectivization as a solution, see Ana Toma interview; Ida Felix interview, June 25, 1991.

44. Transcript of a Meeting of the Politburo of the R.C.P., October 4, 1947, National Archives of Romania, Fond CC al PCR—Cancelarie, Dosar 33/1947, p. 9.

45. Alec Nove, *An Economic History of the USSR*, rev. ed. (London, 1976), pp. 107–110, 124; Robert Lee Wolff, *The Balkans in Our Time* (Cambridge, Mass., 1974), pp. 161–165.

46. Nove, *An Economic History of the USSR*, p. 109.

47. Joseph V. Stalin, *Selected Works* (Davis, Calif., 1971), p. 259.

48. Moshe Lewin, *Russian Peasants and Soviet Power: A Study of Collectivization* (New York and London, 1968), p. 94; Nove, *An Economic History of the USSR*, p. 109.

49. Stalin's Speech to the Fifteenth C.P.S.U. Congress, December 3, 1927; cited in Nove, *An Economic History of the USSR*, p. 148.

50. Transcript of a Meeting of the Politburo of the R.C.P., October 4, 1947,

National Archives of Romania, Fond CC al PCR—Cancelarie, Dosar 33/1947, pp. 9–10.

51. Transcript of a Meeting of the Politburo of the R.C.P., October 3, 1947, National Archives of Romania, Fond CC al PCR—Cancelarie, Dosar 32/1947, p. 64; Transcript of a Meeting of the Politburo of the R.C.P., October 4, 1947, National Archives of Romania, Fond CC al PCR—Cancelarie, Dosar 33/1947, pp. 17–18.

52. Transcript of a Meeting of the Politburo of the R.C.P., October 4, 1947, National Archives of Romania, Fond CC al PCR—Cancelarie, Dosar 33/1947, p. 17.

53. Ana Toma interview.

54. Iosif Breban interview, March 16, 1994. Pauker's opposition to collectivization was also confirmed by Elena Tudorache, a member of the Central Committee from 1944 to 1948, and Victor Vezendean, who worked closely with Gheorghiu-Dej and Iosif Chişinevschi in the party Secretariat from 1950 to 1953 (Elena Tudorache interview, December 10, 1990; Victor Vezendean interview).

55. Transcript of a Meeting of the Council of Ministers, July 20, 1950, National Archives of Romania, Fond Consiliul de Miniştri—Cabinetul, Dosar 7/1950, p. 28.

56. Iosif Breban interview.

57. Liuba Chişinevschi revealed this to Cristina Boico. Her source was, of course, her husband Iosif, who was at the meeting and was "absolutely astonished" by Pauker's answer (Cristina Boico interview, September 16, 1989).

58. As Nove asserted, "no one doubts that the motive (or the principal motive) of collectivization was to mobilize a larger agricultural surplus" (Alec Nove, "Stalin and Stalinism: Some Introductory Thoughts," in Nove, ed., The Stalin Phenomenon [New York, 1992], p. 35).

59. Transcript of a Meeting of the Secretariat of the R.W.P., April 13, 1950, National Archives of Romania, Fond CC al PCR—Cancelarie, Dosar 27/1950, p. 5.

60. Transcript of a Meeting of the Secretariat of the R.W.P., September 21, 1949, National Archives of Romania, Fond CC al PCR—Cancelarie, Dosar 80/1949, p. 11.

61. Transcript of a Meeting of the Secretariat of the R.W.P., April 13, 1950, National Archives of Romania, Fond CC al PCR—Cancelarie, Dosar 27/1950, pp. 8–9.

62. Transcript of a Meeting of the Politburo of the R.C.P., October 4, 1947, National Archives of Romania, Fond CC al PCR—Cancelarie, Dosar 33/1947, pp. 16–17.

63. Transcript of a Meeting of the Politburo of the R.C.P., October 4, 1947, National Archives of Romania, Fond CC al PCR—Cancelarie, Dosar 33/1947, p. 20.

64. Extracts from a Meeting of the Ministerial Commission, March 10, 1948, National Archives of Romania, Fond CC al PCR—Cancelarie, Dosar 5/1948, 1–4.

65. Transcripts of Meetings of the Politburo of the R.W.P., February 15, 16, and 17, 1949, National Archives of Romania, Fond CC al PCR—Cancelarie, Dosar 15/1949, pp. 2–25.

66. Transcript of a Meeting of the Politburo of the R.W.P., February 17, 1949, National Archives of Romania, Fond CC al PCR—Cancelarie, Dosar 15/1949, pp. 22–23.

67. Transcript of a Meeting of the Politburo of the R.W.P., February 15, 1949, National Archives of Romania, Fond CC al PCR—Cancelarie, Dosar 15/1949, pp. 5–6.

68. Transcript of the Plenary of the Central Committee of the R.W.P., March 3–5, 1949, National Archives of Romania, Fond CC al PCR—Cancelarie, Dosar 21/1949, p. 63.

69. *Hotărîrea plenarei a Comitetului Central al P.M.R., 3–5 martie, 1949* [The Resolution of the Plenary Meeting of the Central Committee of the R.W.P., March 3–5, 1949] (Bucharest, 1949), pp. 11–13, 15, 19, 23, 29; Summary of the Transcript of the Plenary Meeting of the C.C. of the R.W.P., March 3–5, 1949, National Archives of Romania, Fond CC al PCR—Cancelarie, Dosar 21/1949, p. 63; David A. Kideckel, "The Socialist Transformation of Agriculture in a Romanian Commune, 1945–62," *American Ethnologist* 9, no. 2 (May 1982), p. 324.

70. Gheorghe Surpat, ed., *România în anii socialismului 1948–1978* [Romania in the Years of Socialism, 1948–1878] (Bucharest, 1980), p. 89.

71. National Archives of Romania, Fond 1, Dosar 755/1952, pp. 1–2.

72. National Archives of Romania, Fond 1, Dosar 75/1952, pp. 49, 106.

73. National Archives of Romania, Fond CC al PCR—Cancelarie, Dosar 59/1950, p. 7.

74. Transcript of a Meeting of the Secretariat of the R.W.P., May 31, 1949, National Archives of Romania, Fond CC al PCR—Cancelarie, Dosar 55/1949, pp. 6–8; Transcript of a Meeting of the Politburo of the R.W.P., July 21, 1949, National Archives of Romania, Fond CC al PCR—Cancelarie, Dosar 57/1949, p. 7.

75. Statement of Pavel Chirtoacă, Transcript of a Meeting of the Agrarian Section of the Central Committee of the R.W.P., June 18, 1952, National Archives of Romania, Fond 1, Dosar 748/1952, p. 10 [emphasis added].

76. National Archives of Romania, Fond 1, Dosar 268/1949, pp. 1–22; Fond 1, Dosar 270/1949, pp. 1–7; Fond 1, Dosar 272/1949, pp. 1–4; Fond 1, Dosar 275/1949, pp. 1–4.

77. Transcript of a Meeting of the Agrarian Commission of the R.W.P., September 1, 1949, National Archives of Romania, Fond 1, Dosar 270/1949, pp. 1–7.

78. Transcript of a Meeting of the Council of Ministers, September 13, 1950, National Archives of Romania, Fond Consiliul de Miniştri—Cabinetul, Dosar 8/1949, pp. 62–63.

79. National Archives of Romania, Fond 1, Dosar 755/1952, p. 3; National Archives of Romania, Fond 1, Dosar 206/1950, pp. 130–131.

80. Transcript of a Meeting of the Secretariat of the R.W.P., October 10, 1950, National Archives of Romania, Fond CC al PCR—Cancelarie, Dosar 59/1950, p. 7.

81. The figure of 1,000 requests is from the Transcript of a Meeting of the Politburo of the R.W.P., October 4, 1949, National Archives of Romania, Fond CC al PCR—Cancelarie, Dosar 89/1949, p. 14; Transcript of a Meeting of the Agrarian Commission, August 16, 1949, National Archives of Romania, Fond 1, Dosar 268/1949, p. 14. The figure of 350 requests is from the Transcript of a Meeting of the Secretariat of the R.W.P., October 10, 1950, National Archives of Romania, Fond CC al PCR—Cancelarie, Dosar 59/1950, p. 11. The figure of 120 approved requests is from the National Archives of Romania, Fond CC al PCR—Cancelarie, Dosar 41/1950, p. 36; National Archives of Romania, Fond 1, Dosar 74/1952, p. 284.

82. Transcript of a Meeting of the Politburo of the R.W.P., October 4, 1949, National Archives of Romania, Fond CC al PCR—Cancelarie, Dosar 89/1949, p. 14.

83. Ibid., pp. 14–15.

84. National Archives of Romania, Fond 1, Dosar 75/1952, pp. 49, 106.

85. Transcript of a Meeting of the Secretariat of the R.W.P., October 10, 1950, National Archives of Romania, Fond CC al PCR—Cancelarie, Dosar 59/1950, p. 8.

86. Transcript of a Meeting with the Secretaries of the Party County Committees, February 20–23, 1950, Fond CC al PCR—Cancelarie, Dosar 11/1950, pp. 29–30.

87. Transcript of a Meeting of the Secretariat of the R.W.P., October 10, 1950, National Archives of Romania, Fond CC al PCR—Cancelarie, Dosar 59/1950, p. 8.

88. Ibid., pp. 7–8.

89. Answers Given by Ana Pauker to Questions Asked by the Party Commission of the C.C. of the R.W.P. (extracts), June 12, 1953, Ana Pauker Inquiry File, Executive Archive of the Central Committee of the R.C.P., p. 6.

90. Transcript of a Meeting of the Secretariat of the R.W.P., October 10, 1950, National Archives of Romania, Fond CC al PCR—Cancelarie, Dosar 59/1950, p. 12; Transcript of an Interrogation of Ana Pauker by a Party Commission of the C.C. of the R.W.P., June 12, 1953, Ana Pauker Inquiry File, Executive Archive of the Central Committee of the R.C.P., p. 64.

91. Transcript of a Meeting of the Organizational Bureau of the R.W.P., May 24, 1950, National Archives of Romania, Fond CC al PCR—Cancelarie, Dosar 41/1950, p. 29; Transcript of a Meeting of the Secretariat of the R.W.P., October 10, 1950, National Archives of Romania, Fond CC al PCR—Cancelarie, Dosar 59/1950, p. 8; Report on the Activities of the Agrarian Section of the Central Committee of the R.W.P. from its Establishment to the Present, National Archives of Romania, Fond 1, Dosar 755/1952, p. 4.

92. On the Soviets' conclusion, see the Transcript of a Meeting of the Secretariat of the R.W.P., October 10, 1950, National Archives of Romania, Fond CC al PCR—Cancelarie, Dosar 59/1950, p. 8. Petrescu, who is quoted here, typically did not mention the Soviets by name. But Ana Pauker later revealed that this increased plan had in fact been made up by "the comrades," a euphemism for the Soviets (Transcript of the Plenary of the Central Committee of the R.W.P., May 27–28, 1952, National Archives of Romania, Fond CC al PCR—Cancelarie, Dosar 41/1952, p. 72). For Dej's confirmation, see the Transcript of a Meeting of the Organizational Bureau of the R.W.P., June 6, 1950, National Archives of Romania, Fond CC al PCR—Cancelarie, Dosar 41/1950, p. 24.

93. Transcript of a Meeting of the Politburo of the R.W.P., April 13, 1950, National Archives of Romania, Fond CC al PCR—Cancelarie, Dosar 27/1950, p. 2.

94. Transcript of the Plenary of the Central Committee of the R.W.P., May 15–17, 1950, National Archives of Romania, Fond CC al PCR—Cancelarie, Dosar 32/1950, p. 169; Transcript of a Meeting of the Secretariat of the R.W.P., June 15, 1950, National Archives of Romania, Fond CC al PCR—Cancelarie, Dosar 43/1950, p. 13.

95. Transcript of a Meeting of the Secretariat of the R.W.P., October 10, 1950, National Archives of Romania, Fond CC al PCR—Cancelarie, Dosar 59/1950, p. 8.

96. Mihai Nagy, former secretary of Trei Scaune County, in a Meeting with the Party Leadership, October 11, 1950, National Archives of Romania, Fond CC al PCR—Cancelarie, Dosar 59/1950, pp. 18, 25.

97. Statistics in archival documents reveal that 51 collective farms were established in May and 194 in June, but they do not specify how many of the 194 were created by June 15. While *Scânteia* normally reported the number of collective farms inaugurated each Sunday, it failed to provide precise figures for two of the four weeks in June. Still, it is possible to adduce from the numbers *Scânteia* did publish that a maximum of 117 collectives were created between June 1 and June 15; this, added to the 51 set up in May, totals 168 (National Archives of Romania, Fond 1, Dosar 74/1952, p. 284; Fond 1, Dosar 755/1952, p. 4; Transcript of a Meeting of the Secretariat of the R.W.P., October 10, 1950, National Archives of Romania, Fond CC al PCR—Cancelarie, Dosar 59/1950, p. 8; *Scânteia,* no. 1,752, June 6, 1950, p. 3;

Scânteia, no. 1,758, June 13, 1950, p. 3; *Scânteia,* no. 1,764, June 20, 1950, p. 2; *Scânteia,* no. 1,770, June 27, 1950, p. 1).

98. Transcript of a Meeting of the Organizational Bureau of the R.W.P., June 6, 1950, Fond CC al PCR—Cancelarie, Dosar 41/1950, pp. 25–26.

99. Tatiana Brătescu, "Ana Pauker: ulteme ani" [Ana Pauker: The Last Years], *Cotidianul,* Historical Supplement 4, no. 10 (42) (October 27, 1995), p. 4; Tatiana and Gheorghe Brătescu interview. Confirmation of Pauker's hospitalization in Moscow has been found in the Russian archives (G. P. Muraschko, et. al., eds., *Vostochnaia Evropa v dokumentakh arkhivov,* vol. 2 [1998], p. 424).

100. Transcript of a Meeting of the Secretariat of the R.W.P., October 10, 1950, National Archives of Romania, Fond CC al PCR—Cancelarie, Dosar 59/1950, p. 9.

101. Transcript of a Meeting of the Politburo of the R.W.P., February 17, 1949, Fond CC al PCR—Cancelarie, Dosar 15/1949, pp. 16–17.

102. Transcript of a Meeting of the Organizational Bureau of the R.W.P., June 6, 1950, Fond CC al PCR—Cancelarie, Dosar 41/1950, pp. 21–22.

103. Transcript of a Meeting of the Secretariat of the R.W.P., October 10, 1950, National Archives of Romania, Fond CC al PCR—Cancelarie, Dosar 59/1950, pp. 8–10, 12.

104. Ibid., p. 9.

105. Transcript of a Meeting of the Organizational Bureau of the R.W.P., May 24, 1950, National Archives of Romania, Fond CC al PCR—Cancelarie, Dosar 41/1950, p. 30.

106. Transcript of a Meeting of the Organizational Bureau of the R.W.P., June 6, 1950, Fond CC al PCR—Cancelarie, Dosar 41/1950, p. 21.

107. Ignoring Luca's assertion, Gheorghiu-Dej immediately countered, "The basis for organizing collective farms is narrow. [Otherwise] the party organizations themselves won't have a growing sense of responsibility for creating collective farms." This followed Gheorghiu-Dej's announcement that "we're going to have to involve the [local] party organizations in order to develop the largest possible initiative [in the collectivization drive], and should not limit this to be entrusted to some commission" (ibid.).

108. Transcript of a Meeting of the Secretariat of the R.W.P., October 10, 1950, National Archives of Romania, Fond CC al PCR—Cancelarie, Dosar 59/1950, pp. 7, 9.

109. Transcript of a Meeting with the Secretaries of the Party County Committees and the Instructors of the Central Committee, June 15, 1950, National Archives of Romania, Fond CC al PCR—Cancelarie, Dosar 44/1950, pp. 28, 30, 32.

110. Statements of Nagy Mihai and Toth Geza at a Meeting with the R.W.P. Party Leadership, October 11, 1950, National Archives of Romania, Fond CC al PCR—Cancelarie, Dosar 59/1950, p. 38.

111. On collectivization in general at this time, see Report Regarding the Work of Organizing Collective Agricultural Farms from the Summer of 1949 to September 1950, National Archives of Romania, Fond CC al PCR—Cancelarie, Dosar 59/1950, p. 79; National Archives of Romania, Fond 1, Dosar 755/1952, p. 5. On the contests, see the National Archives of Romania, Fond 1, Dosar 755/1952, p. 6.

112. National Archives of Romania, Fond CC al PCR—Cancelarie, Dosar 59/1950, pp. 78–79.

113. On the instructors' numbers, see the National Archives of Romania, Fond CC al PCR—Cancelarie, Dosar 59/1950, p. 36; Fond 1, Dosar 748/1952, p. 41; Fond 1, Dosar 755/1952, pp. 5, 9. On the local authorities' avoiding them, see National Archives of Romania, Fond CC al PCR—Cancelarie, Dosar 59/1950, p. 79.

The quote is from the National Archives of Romania, Fond 1, Dosar 755/1952, pp. 8–9.

114. National Archives of Romania, Fond CC al PCR—Cancelarie, Dosar 42/1950, pp. 13–20; Fond CC al PCR—Cancelarie, Dosar 59/1950, pp. 64, 72–75; Fond 1, Dosar 755/1952, pp. 3–6. Coercion was widespread in the consolidation of the state farms (GOSTATs) in 1949, but this was not handled by the Agrarian Commission and was a separate venture from the collectivization campaign (National Archives of Romania, Fond 1, Dosar 75/1952, pp. 223, 352–353).

115. National Archives of Romania, Fond CC al PCR—Cancelarie, Dosar 59/1950, pp. 35, 73, 81; Fond CC al PCR—Cancelarie, Dosar 42/1950, p. 17; Fond 1, Dosar 75/1952, pp. 192–196; Fond 1, Dosar 59/1951, pp. 5–6; Fond 1, Dosar 206/1950, pp. 40, 43.

116. National Archives of Romania, Fond 1, Dosar 75/1952, pp. 192–196, 246; Fond 1, Dosar 755/1952, p. 6.

117. National Archives of Romania, Fond CC al PCR—Cancelarie, Dosar 59/1950, pp. 35, 73; Fond 1, Dosar 755/1952, p. 6; Fond 1, Dosar 206/1950, p. 43.

118. National Archives of Romania, Fond CC al PCR—Cancelarie, Dosar 59/1950, p. 37; National Archives of Romania, Fond 1, Dosar 59/1951, p. 6; Fond 1, Dosar 69/1951, p. 83; Minutes of the Interrogation of Teohari Georgescu, December 17, 1955, ASRI, Fond P, Dosar 40009, Vol. 4, p. 426; National Archives of Romania, Fond CC al PCR—Cancelarie, Dosar 10/1952, p. 26.

119. National Archives of Romania, Fond CC al PCR—Cancelarie, Dosar 59/1950, p. 74; Fond 1, Dosar 755/1952, p. 6.

120. National Archives of Romania, Fond 1, Dosar 748/1952, p. 10; Fond 1, Dosar 59/1951, p. 6.

121. National Archives of Romania, Fond 1, Dosar 75/1952, p. 244.

122. National Archives of Romania, Fond 1, Dosar 75/1952, p. 245; Fond 1, Dosar 59/1951, p. 10; Fond 1, Dosar 93/1951, p. 2.

123. National Archives of Romania, Fond 1, Dosar 755/1952, p. 6; National Archives of Romania, Fond 1, Dosar 75/1952, p. 194; National Archives of Romania, Fond CC al PCR—Cancelarie, Dosar 59/1950, pp. 22, 42–43; National Archives of Romania, Fond CC al PCR—Cancelarie, Dosar 59/1950, p. 75; Fond 1, Dosar 75/1952, p. 194; Dosar 755/1952, p. 6.

124. National Archives of Romania, Fond CC al PCR—Cancelarie, Dosar 59/1950, p. 45; Fond 1, Dosar 59/1951, p. 9.

125. National Archives of Romania, Fond 1, Dosar 51/1951, p. 11.

126. National Archives of Romania, Fond CC al PCR—Cancelarie, Dosar 59/1950, pp. 35, 74; Fond 1, Dosar 75/1952, p. 193.

127. National Archives of Romania, Fond CC al PCR—Cancelarie, Dosar 23/1951, p. 1; Fond 1, Dosar 93/1951, p. 2; Fond CC al PCR—Cancelarie, Dosar 59/1950, p. 34; Fond CC al PCR—Cancelarie, Dosar 23/1951, p. 1. The quotation was attributed to the secretary of the Provisional Committee of the village of Cistei in Alba County.

128. National Archives of Romania, Fond 1, Dosar 73/1952, p. 130.

129. National Archives of Romania, Fond CC al PCR—Cancelarie, Dosar 59/1950, p. 6; Fond 1, Dosar 75/1952, pp. 192–196.

130. National Archives of Romania, Fond CC al PCR—Cancelarie, Dosar 59/1950, p. 74; Fond CC al PCR—Cancelarie, Dosar 42/1950, p. 18; Fond 1, Dosar 218/1951, pp. 53–54, 89; Fond 1, Dosar 207/1950, pp. 110–120; Fond 1, Dosar 59/1951, p. 7.

131. National Archives of Romania, Fond 1, Dosar 77/1951, pp. 27–29.

132. National Archives of Romania, Fond 1, Dosar 59/1951, p. 7.

133. National Archives of Romania, Fond 1, Dosar 75/1952, p. 248.

134. National Archives of Romania, Fond CC al PCR—Cancelarie, Dosar 59/1950, p. 32.

135. National Archives of Romania, Fond 1, Dosar 75/1952, p. 281.

136. National Archives of Romania, Fond 1, Dosar 206/1950, p. 136. There was considerable violent resistance on the peasants' part prior to this period, as Pauker observed at the Fifth CC plenary in January 1950: "There isn't a week . . . that goes by when an activist of ours isn't attacked, beaten, and sometimes killed [in the countryside]." Before the summer of 1950, however, such violence was in response to mandatory collection quotas and the consolidation of the state farms (GOSTATs) but not to the creation of collective farms (Transcript of the Fifth Plenary of the R.W.P. Central Committee, January 23–25, 1950, National Archives of Romania, Fond CC al PCR—Cancelarie, Dosar, 7/1950, p. 215; ASRI, Dosar 4638, pp. 35–39, 46–56, 80–90; Fond 1, Dosar 75/1952, pp. 352–353).

137. Report on the Results of the Work in Organizing Collective Farms, June 6, 1950, Fond CC al PCR—Cancelarie, Dosar 41/1950, p. 49.

138. Report Regarding the Work of Organizing Collective Agricultural Farms from the Summer of 1949 to September 1950, National Archives of Romania, Fond CC al PCR—Cancelarie, Dosar 59/1950, p. 77.

139. National Archives of Romania, Fond CC al PCR—Cancelarie, Dosar 59/1950, p. 54. The rebellion at Micfalău was led by a woman, a widow with eight children (ibid., p. 57). After the authorities finally succeeded in apparently restoring calm, the villagers proceeded to work their old individual plots, ignoring the consolidations that had just been implemented (Transcript of a Meeting of the Secretariat, October 10, 1950, National Archives of Romania, Fond CC al PCR—Cancelarie, Dosar 59/1950, p. 16).

140. National Archives of Romania, Fond 1, Dosar 206/1950, pp. 132, 134–135. The revolt was particularly violent in Ilfov County, which incorporates Bucharest. In the village of Gruia, for example, a group of women peasants ripped the clothes off and beat up a mechanic of the newly established collective farm. When a number of party activists arrived to investigate, their car was immediately surrounded by a mob of 300 men and women, and they were dragged away, severely beaten, and held hostage in two separate houses—while approximately 1,000 people blockaded the Provisional Committee headquarters, imprisoning the functionaries and militia men inside. Moreover, in the village of Drăgoiești, a mob of 500 villagers, armed with scythes, hoes, and pitchforks, surrounded and disarmed a group of militia soldiers and Securitate agents in the process of arresting kulak "instigators" and then seriously beat them, critically wounding two militia men and torturing a Securitate sergeant. The villagers then proceeded to ransack the local Securitate headquarters, destroying the phone lines (Bulletin, Ministry of Interior Affairs, July 10, 1950, ASRI, Fond D, Dosar 4640, pp. 162–164).

141. Bulletin, Ministry of Interior Affairs, July 10, 1950, ASRI, Fond D, Dosar 4640, p. 165; National Archives of Romania, Fond 1, Dosar 206/1950, pp. 44–47.

142. Tatiana Brătescu recalled that Pauker returned to attend the August 23 commemoration festivities in Bucharest, but Scânteia reported her at an event in the Romanian capital on August 10 (Tatiana Brătescu, "Ana Pauker: The Last Years," p. 4; Scânteia, no. 1,809, August 11, 1950, p. 1; G. P. Muraschko, et al., eds., Vostochnaia Evropa v dokumentakh arkhivov, vol. 2, p. 424).

143. Tatiana and Gheorghe Brătescu interview.

144. Transcript of the Plenary Meeting of the Central Committee of the R.W.P., October 26, 1950, National Archives of Romania, Fond CC al PCR—Cancelarie, Dosar 62/1950, p. 1; Transcript of a Meeting of the Council of Ministers, October 27, 1950, National Archives of Romania, Fond Consiliul de Miniștri—Cabinetul, Dosar 10/1950, p. 1; Transcript of a Meeting of the Agrarian Section of the C.C. Regarding the Reception of Soviet Kolhoz Delegates, November 1, 1950, National Archives of Romania, Fond CC al PCR—Cancelarie, Dosar 63/1950, p. 1; Transcript of a Meeting of the Secretariat, November 16, 1950, National Archives of Romania, Fond CC al PCR—Cancelarie, Dosar 65/1950, p.1; Transcript of a Meeting of the Organizational Bureau of the R.W.P., October 10, 1950, National Archives of Romania, Fond CC al PCR—Cancelarie, Dosar 66/1950, p. 1; Transcript of an Interrogation of Ana Pauker by a Party Commission of the C.C. of the R.W.P., June 12, 1953, Ana Pauker Inquiry File, Executive Archive of the Central Committee of the R.C.P., p. 64; Transcript of an Interrogation of Ana Pauker by a Party Commission of the C.C. of the R.W.P., June 18, 1956, Ana Pauker Inquiry File, Executive Archive of the Central Committee of the R.C.P., p. 10.

145. Declaration of Ana Pauker, Transcript of a Meeting of the Agrarian Section of the Central Committee of the R.W.P., April 28, 1951, National Archives of Romania, Fond 1, Dosar 218/1951, pp. 111–113.

146. Report on the Activities of the Agrarian Section of the Central Committee of the R.W.P. from its Establishment to the Present, National Archives of Romania, Fond 1, Dosar 755/1952, p. 4. This was also maintained in an unpublished party document on Pauker's purge (National Archives of Romania, Fond 1, Dosar 73/1952, pp. 127–128). Both Pavel Chirtoacă and Iosif Breban also made this assertion in 1952, and Breban again confirmed it in his 1994 interview (Transcript of a Meeting of the Agrarian Section of the Central Committee of the R.W.P., June 12, 1952, National Archives of Romania, Fond 1, Dosar 748/1952, pp. 11, 38; Transcript of an Interrogation of Pavel Chirtoacă by a Party Commission, May 29, 1952, National Archives of Romania, Fond 1, Dosar 75/1952, pp. 83–84; Iosif Breban interview).

147. National Archives of Romania, Fond 1, Dosar 218/1951, p. 117.

148. National Archives of Romania, Fond 1, Dosar 748/1952, p. 1.

149. National Archives of Romania, Fond CC al PCR—Cancelarie, Dosar 42/1950, p. 18; Fond CC al PCR—Cancelarie, Dosar 59/1950, p. 75; Fond 1, Dosar 59/1951, p. 10.

150. Bulletins of the Ministry of Interior Affairs, August 27, 1951, September 26, 1951, ASRI, Fond D, Dosar 9404, Vol. 1, pp. 38, 41, 121–122; Report, Ministry of Interior Affairs, undated, ASRI, Fond D, Dosar 4638, pp. 199–200; National Archives of Romania, Fond CC al PCR—Cancelarie, Dosar 59/1951, pp. 3, 24.

151. Report, Ministry of Interior Affairs, September 14, 1951, ASRI, Fond D, Dosar 9404, Vol. 1, p. 78; Bulletin, Ministry of Interior Affairs, August 27, 1951, ASRI, Fond D, Dosar 9404, Vol. 1, pp. 136, 139; Report, Ministry of Interior Affairs, undated, ASRI, Fond D, Dosar 4638, p. 200; Bulletins of the Ministry of Interior Affairs, July 19, 1951, August 27, 1951, September 14, 1951, and September 26, 1951, ASRI, Fond D, Dosar 9404, Vol. 1, pp. 25, 33–34, 42, 49, 52, 55–56, 176.

152. Report, Ministry of Interior Affairs, undated, ASRI, Fond D, Dosar 4638, p. 199; National Archives of Romania, Fond 1, Dosar 51/1951, p. 10; Fond 1, Dosar 748/1952, p. 41; National Archives of Romania, Fond 1, Dosar 75/1952, p. 65.

153. National Archives of Romania, Fond 1, Dosar 755/1952, p. 10; Fond 1, Dosar 748/1952, p. 3. Pauker dispatched the Control Commission's Charlotte Gruia during this period to investigate problems at a new collective farm in the Cluj region.

When informed by Gruia that many members who had been forced to join were now demanding to leave the collective, Pauker ordered that they be immediately given back their land (Charlotte Gruia interview, July 15, 1991).

154. National Archives of Romania, Fond 1, Dosar 93/1951, pp. 1–37; Dosar 51/1951, pp. 9–10.

155. National Archives of Romania, Fond 1, Dosar 755/1952, p. 10.

156. National Archives of Romania, Fond 1, Dosar 743/1952, p. 74; Dosar 207/1950, pp. 4, 7–8; Dosar 218/1951, p. 41; undated report, Ministry of Interior Affairs, ASRI, Fond D, Dosar 4638, pp. 199–200; Fond 1, Dosar 748/1952, p. 41.

157. National Archives of Romania, Fond 1, Dosar 69/1951, p. 89.

158. National Archives of Romania, Fond 1, Dosar 755/1952, pp. 9–10; Dosar 748/1952, p. 4. It appears that Dumitru Petrescu was himself penalized for the repression of 1950: his involvement in the collectivization campaign was effectively terminated with his removal as head of the Organizational Section of the Central Committee and appointment as president of the State Provisions Committee in 1951 (Transcript of a Discussion of Comrade Dumitru Petrescu with the R.C.P. Commission, November 2, 1967, ASRI, Fond P, Dosar 40002, Vol. 203, p. 328).

159. National Archives of Romania, Fond 1, Dosar 218/1951, p. 115.

160. The Circular was discussed at a Central Committee meeting March 5 (Transcript of a Meeting of the Central Committee of the R.W.P., March 5, 1951, National Archives of Romania, Fond 1, Dosar 59/1951, pp. 21–22); National Archives of Romania, Fond 1, Dosar 755/1952, p. 10.

161. The county party secretaries were informed of this at a meeting on February 9, 1951 (National Archives of Romania, Fond CC al PCR—Cancelarie, Dosar 10/1951, p. 30).

162. National Archives of Romania, Fond 1, Dosar 748/1952, p. 4; Transcript of an Interrogation of Vasile Luca, February 19, 1953, ASRI, Fond P, Dosar 40005, Vol. 4, p. 452.

163. Agriculture Minister Vasile Vaida reported that Pauker informed him that the ministry should work toward achieving 40 percent collectivization by the end of the Five-Year Plan, and not 60 percent (or, more precisely, 62 percent) as stipulated in June 1950 (Transcript of an Interrogation of Vasile Vaida by a Party Commission, May 29, 1952, National Archives of Romania, Fond 1, Dosar 75/1952, p. 306). Hence, Miron Constantinescu informed the Central Committee in December 1950 that the party leadership had replaced the precise projections initially set in the Five-Year Plan with the mere phrase that "the socialist sector must predominate" by the end of 1955 (Transcript of the Plenary of the Central Committee of the R.W.P., December 12–13, 1950, National Archives of Romania, Fond CC al PCR—Cancelarie, Dosar 69/1950, p. 24).

164. National Archives of Romania, Fond 1, Dosar 75/1952, pp. 62, 87; Dosar 748/1952, p. 4; Dosar 73/1952, pp. 37, 127–128.

165. National Archives of Romania, Fond 1, Dosar 218/1951, p. 117; Dosar 75/1952, pp. 72, 235, 306–307.

166. Transcript of a Meeting of the Agrarian Section of the Central Committee, March 12, 1952, National Archives of Romania, Fond 1, Dosar 28/1952, p. 30.

167. National Archives of Romania, Fond 1, Dosar 755/1952, p. 11; Dosar 74/1952, p. 284.

168. National Archives of Romania, Fond 1, Dosar 28/1952, p. 31. Romania had 300,000 hectares (3.1 percent of total farmland) collectivized by the begin-

ning of 1952, as compared with Poland (645,000) and Hungary (865,000), and way below Czechoslovakia and Bulgaria, which already had 19 and 47.5 percent of their farmland collectivized respectively (Edmund O. Stillman, "The Collectivization of Bulgarian Agriculture," Ernest Koenig, "Collectivization in Czechoslovakia and Poland," Nicolas Spulber, "Collectivization in Hungary and Romania," in Irwin T. Sanders, ed., *Collectivization of Agriculture in Eastern Europe* [Lexington, Ky., 1957], pp. 70, 105, 145, 147).

169. Transcript of a Meeting of the Secretariat, October 10, 1950, National Archives of Romania, Fond CC al PCR—Cancelarie, Dosar 59/1950, p. 6.

170. Report on the Activities of the Agrarian Section of the Central Committee of the R.W.P. from its Establishment to the Present, National Archives of Romania, Fond 1, Dosar 755/1952, p. 7.

171. Transcripts of the Agrarian Section of the Central Committee, April 28, 1951, National Archives of Romania, Fond 1, Dosar 218/1951, p. 113.

172. Dumitru Popescu, *Am fost și cioplitor de himere* (Bucharest, 1994), p. 90.

173. When then Politburo member Leonte Răutu complained to Dej of Ceaușescu's oppressive measures, Dej ordered Răutu to "leave him alone" (Leonte Răutu interview).

174. For Dej's remarks, see Transcript of a Meeting of the Secretariat, February 10, 1951, National Archives of Romania, Fond CC al PCR—Cancelarie, Dosar 9/1950, p. 4. For Moghioroș's, see Transcript of a Meeting of the Agrarian Section of the C.C., March 1, 1951, National Archives of Romania, Fond 1, Dosar 58/1951, p. 63, and Transcript of a Meeting of the Secretariat, February 10, 1951, National Archives of Romania, Fond CC al PCR—Cancelarie, Dosar 9/1950, p. 14.

175. Transcript of a Meeting of the Agrarian Section of the C.C., March 1, 1951, National Archives of Romania, Fond 1, Dosar 58/1951, pp. 63–64.

176. Vasile Luca disclosed this to his chief of staff at the Finance Ministry, Zoltan Eidlitz (Declaration of Zoltan Eidlitz, ASRI, Fond P, Dosar 40005, Vol. 111, p. 61).

177. Minutes of the Interrogation of Marcu Cohin, March 19, 1953, ASRI, Fond P, Dosar 40009, Vol. 62, p. 265b.

178. In the early 1950s, Gheorghiu-Dej reportedly expressed his true opinions on collectivization to an old friend, sarcastically quipping, "And so it didn't work for them [the Soviets], and it *will* work here" (Edward Mezincescu interview). On Stalin's position, see Nove, *An Economic History of the USSR,* pp. 158–159.

179. Transcript of the Plenary of the Central Committee of the R.W.P., February 29–March 1, 1952, National Archives of Romania, Fond CC al PCR—Cancelarie, Dosar 13/1952, pp. 118–119. Similar remarks by Dej appear in the Transcript of a Meeting of the Politburo of the R.C.P., October 3, 1947, National Archives of Romania, Fond CC al PCR—Cancelarie, Dosar 32/1947, p. 21.

180. Transcript of a Meeting of the Council of Ministers, September 30, 1948, National Archives of Romania, Fond Consiliul de Miniștri—Cabinetul, Dosar 9/1948, p. 28.

181. Sorin Toma, Edward Mezincescu, Charlotte Gruia, and Iosif Breban interviews.

182. Cristina Boico interview.

183. Eduard Mezincescu interview (see note 178).

184. Ion Gheorghe Maurer interview.

185. Iosif Breban interview.

186. National Archives of Romania, Fond 1, Dosar 75/1952, p. 119.

187. Transcript of an Interrogation of Vasile Vaida by a Party Commission,

May 29, 1952, National Archives of Romania, Fond 1, Dosar 75/1952, p. 347. (Also see note 163.)

188. Nove, *An Economic History of the USSR,* p. 150; Spulber, in Sanders, ed., *Collectivization of Agriculture in Eastern Europe,* p. 144.

189. National Archives of Romania, Fond 1, Dosar 75/1952, pp. 101, 234, 259; Fond 1, Dosar 743/1952, p. 76. Transcript of the Plenary of the Central Committee of the R.W.P., March 3–5, 1949, National Archives of Romania, Fond CC al PCR—Cancelarie, Dosar 21/1949, p. 63.

190. National Archives of Romania, Fond 1, Dosar 75/1952, pp. 101, 259; Dosar 743/1952, p. 76; Dosar 754/1952, p. 57.

191. National Archives of Romania, Fond 1, Dosar 28/1952, pp. 2, 16.

192. Transcript of a Meeting of the Politburo, May 26, 1952, National Archives of Romania, Fond CC al PCR—Cancelarie, Dosar 40/1952, pp. 77, 83; Fond 1, Dosar 748/1952, p. 2; Declaration of Teohari Georgescu, May 18, 1956, p. 13; Sorin Toma, personal communication to the author.

193. Transcript of a Meeting of the Politburo, March 10, 1952, National Archives of Romania, Fond CC al PCR—Cancelarie, Dosar 17/1952, p. 22.

194. Transcript of a Meeting of the Politburo, May 26, 1952, National Archives of Romania, Fond CC al PCR—Cancelarie, Dosar 40/1952, p. 85.

195. Ibid., p. 84.

196. Ibid.; National Archives of Romania, Fond 1, Dosar 73/1952, p. 51; Fond 1, Dosar 748/1952, pp. 5, 36.

197. For Pauker's explanation, see National Archives of Romania, Fond 1, Dosar 28/1952, p. 30. For the testimonials, see Brucan, *The Wasted Generation,* pp. 49–50; Alexandru Moghioroş, "Speech of Comrade Alexandru Moghioroş to the Plenary Meeting of the C.C. of the R.W.P., November 30–December 5, 1961," *Scânteia,* no. 5380, December 16, 1961, p. 3; interview with Alexandru Bîrladeanu, *Totuşi Iubirea* 2, no. 6 (23) (February 1991), p. 9; no. 7 (24) (February 1991), p. 8.

198. Pauker declared her preference for associations on various occasions in the presence of Elena Tudorache, Radu Mănescu, and Iosif Breban (Elena Tudorache, Radu Mănescu, and Iosif Breban interviews). Pauker told the Politburo that she gave every MTS written instructions to do its utmost to facilitate the creation of MTS associations. "And we criticized them when there was reason to, that they weren't creating enough associations like they were supposed to" (Transcript of a Meeting of the Politburo, March 10, 1952, National Archives of Romania, Fond CC al PCR—Cancelarie, Dosar 17/1952, p. 14).

199. National Archives of Romania, Fond 1, Dosar 73/1952, p. 58.

200. Transcript of the Plenary of the Central Committee of the R.W.P., May 27–29, 1952, National Archives of Romania, Fond CC al PCR—Cancelarie, Dosar 41/1952, p. 85.

201. National Archives of Romania, Fond 1, Dosar 748/1952, p. 33.

202. National Archives of Romania, Fond 1, Dosar 75/1952, p. 343.

203. Ibid., p. 344.

204. Ibid., p. 345; Transcript of a Meeting of the Council of Ministers, March 27 1951, National Archives of Romania, Fond Consiliul de Miniştri—Cabinetul, Dosar 2/1951, p. 44.

205. National Archives of Romania, Fond 1, Dosar 75/1952, pp. 261, 351.

206. The figures for 1951 are from the National Archives of Romania, Fond 1, Dosar 73/1952, p. 10.

207. National Archives of Romania, Fond 1, Dosar 75/1952, pp. 42–43, 75, 281, 301, 306, 347, 352–353.

208. Transcript of a Meeting of the Politburo, February 20, 1952, National Archives of Romania, Fond CC al PCR—Cancelarie, Dosar 11/1952, p. 94.

209. Transcript of a Meeting of the Council of Ministers, February 11, 1952, National Archives of Romania, Fond Consiliul de Miniştri—Cabinetul, Dosar 2/1952, p. 101.

210. National Archives of Romania, Fond 1, Dosar 75/1952, p. 75.

211. Ibid., p. 347.

212. Ibid., p. 115.

213. National Archives of Romania, Fond 1, Dosar 28/1952, p. 19; Fond 1, Dosar 741/1952, pp. 2, 5.

214. National Archives of Romania, Fond 1, Dosar 748/1952, p. 3.

215. Transcript of a Meeting of the Council of Ministers, September 1, 1952, National Archives of Romania, Fond Consiliul de Miniştri—Cabinetul, Dosar 9/1952, pp. 29–30.

216. National Archives of Romania, Fond 1, Dosar 754/1952, pp. 55–57.

217. Transcript of a Party Meeting on October 30–31, 1952, National Archives of Romania, Fond CC al PCR—Cancelarie, Dosar 96/1952, pp. 9, 13.

218. Spulber, in Sanders, ed., *Collectivization of Agriculture in Eastern Europe,* p. 147.

219. Michael Shafir, *Romania, Politics, Economics and Society,* p. 46; Vladimir Tismaneanu, "The Ambiguity of Romanian Communism," *Telos* 60 (Summer 1984), pp. 71–72. Thereafter, Dej began to garner "evidence" of Pauker's "leftist adventurist line in agriculture," such as a December 17, 1955, declaration by the imprisoned Teohari Georgescu attributing the repression of the forced collectivization in the summer of 1950 solely to Ana Pauker—"without the knowledge or approval of the Party leadership" (Interrogation of Teohari Georgescu, December 17, 1955, ASRI, Fond P, Dosar 40009, Vol. 4, pp. 425–429). Five days later, Dej would repeat much of this to the Second RWP Congress, which constituted a turning point in revising the charge against Pauker from a right-wing to left-wing deviation (Ionescu, p. 200).

220. Tatiana Brătescu revealed that Pauker's illness was kept so secret that, after her return from Moscow, she was not treated by doctors normally assigned to care for the party leaders but by her son-in-law, Dr. Gheorghe Brătescu, who had only recently completed medical school and was not practicing medicine at that time (Tatiana Brătescu, "Ana Pauker: The Last Years," p. 4; Sorin Toma, Simion Bughici, and Eduard Mezincescu interviews).

221. "Pentru continua intărire a Partidului" [For Continually Strengthening the Party], *Scânteia* (June 3, 1952), p. 1; reprinted in *Rezoluţii şi Hotărîri ale Comitetului Central al Partidului Muncitoresc Român* [Resolutions and Decrees of the Central Committee of the Romanian Workers' Party], vol. 2, 1951–1953 (Bucharest, 1954), pp. 199–200.

222. One example is the post-1989 testimony of Alexandru Bîrlădeanu, who suggested that Pauker was the proponent of forced collectivization in Romania and that Stalin criticized her in January 1952(!) for pushing collectivization too hard. "Dej was for a slow pace, and for encouraging primary forms of associations and so on. Ana, who had come from Moscow and who was out of touch with Romanian life, wanted everything to take place quickly. . . . The dispute went so far as to reach Moscow, and both presented themselves to Stalin for arbitration. Stalin asked her: 'Why are you hurrying? We had to go fast because we were alone in the world and were threatened by the entire capitalist world.' Stalin completely backed Dej and was of the opinion that the pace of collectivization should be slowed down" (Interview with Alexandru Bîrlădeanu, *Totuşi iubirea* 2, no. 6 [23] [February 1991], p. 9, and

no. 7 [24] [February 1991], p. 8). This is, one suspects, an embellished account of
Pauker and Dej's meeting with Stalin at the beginning of 1951, when Stalin supported Dej on establishing TOZ associations.

223. Transcript of a Meeting of the Politburo, February 15, 1949, National Archives of Romania, Fond CC al PCR—Cancelarie, Dosar 15/1949, pp. 8–9.

224. Transcript of a Meeting of the Politburo of the R.W.P., February 16–17,
1949, National Archives of Romania, Fond CC al PCR—Cancelarie, Dosar 15/1949,
pp. 13, 22.

225. Transcript of the Plenary of the Central Committee of the R.W.P., March 3–
5, 1949, National Archives of Romania, Fond CC al PCR—Cancelarie, Dosar 21/
1949, p. 81.

226. Transcript of a Meeting with the Central Activ of the R.W.P., April 26–27,
1945, National Archives of Romania, Fond 1, Dosar 16/1945, p. 86.

227. Transcript of an Interrogation of Ana Pauker by a R.W.P. Commission,
June 12, 1953, Ana Pauker Inquiry File, Executive Archive of the Central Committee of the R.C.P., pp. 55, 59.

228. On allowing kulaks to rent agricultural machinery, see ibid., p. 69. On tar-
geting them as customers, see Report Regarding the Findings of the Inquiry of Ana
Pauker, January 20, 1954, Ana Pauker Inquiry File, Executive Archive of the Central
Committee of the R.C.P., p. 8.

229. Pauker expressed this at a party conference on propaganda on January 28,
1945 (Transcript of an Interrogation of Ana Pauker by a R.W.P. Commission,
June 12, 1953, Ana Pauker Inquiry File, Executive Archive of the Central Committee of the R.C.P., p. 35).

230. Transcript of the Plenary of the Central Committee of the R.W.P., May 27–
29, 1952, National Archives of Romania, Fond CC al PCR—Cancelarie, Dosar
41/1952, p. 25; Transcript of an Interrogation of Ana Pauker by a R.W.P. Commission, June 12, 1953, Ana Pauker Inquiry File, Executive Archive of the Central Committee of the R.C.P., p. 57; Interrogation of Elisabeta Luca, March 5, 1953, ASRI,
Fond P, Dosar 40005, Vol. 13, p. 287.

231. Transcript of a Meeting of the Politburo of the R.C.P., October 4, 1947, National Archives of Romania, Fond CC al PCR—Cancelarie, Dosar 33/1947, p. 18.

232. This began as early as November 1946, when Stalin criticized the Romanian leadership for not drawing class distinctions when handling the peasants and
for failing to "mobilize the [working] peasantry against . . . rural capitalism." It culminated at the Second Cominform Conference in June 1948, when the Soviets reproached the bloc countries for taking neither the agrarian "class struggle" nor the
"danger" of the kulaks seriously (Russian Center of the Conservation and Study of
Records for Modern History [RTsKhIDNI], f. 575, op. 1, d. 50, l. 15, 28; cited by
Silvio Pons, "The Twilight of the Cominform," in *The Cominform: Minutes of the
Three Conferences 1947/1948/1949*, p. 487).

233. "[W]e have to take as much as possible from [the kulak], with high taxes
and coercive measures," Pauker asserted in November 1948. "[W]e should take the
kulak wherever he is," she added in February 1949, "and put him someplace where
the land is of less quality" (Transcript of a Meeting of the Politburo of the R.W.P.,
November 11, 1948, National Archives of Romania, Fond CC al PCR—Cancelarie,
Dosar 55/1948, p. 7; Transcript of a Meeting of the Politburo of the R.W.P., February 16, 1949, National Archives of Romania, Fond CC al PCR—Cancelarie, Dosar
15/1949, p. 12).

234. Transcript of an Interrogation of Ana Pauker by a R.W.P. Commission,
June 12, 1953, Ana Pauker Inquiry File, Executive Archive of the Central Commit-

tee of the R.C.P., p. 54; Transcript of a Meeting of the Organizational Bureau of the R.W.P., April 21, 1951, Fond CC al PCR—Cancelarie, Dosar 32/1952, p. 29.

235. Transcript of a Meeting of the Council of Ministers, December 18, 1951, National Archives of Romania, Fond Consiliul de Miniştri—Cabinetul, Dosar 9/1951, p. 124; Transcript of a Meeting of the Organizational Bureau of the R.W.P., April 21, 1952, National Archives of Romania, Fond CC al PCR—Cancelarie, Dosar 32/1952, pp. 29–32.

236. Ionescu, *Communism in Romania*, p. 188.

237. National Archives of Romania, Fond 1, Dosar 589/1952, p. 15; Ionescu, *Communism in Romania*, p. 189.

238. Speech of Vasile Luca to the Secretaries on Economic Problems of the Party Regional Committees, January 9, 1951, ASRI, Fond P, Dosar 40005, Vol. 145, pp. 16–17; Speech of Vasile Luca at a Meeting with the First Secretaries of the Regional Committees [and others], October 7, 1950, National Archives of Romania, Fond 1, Dosar 176/1950, pp. 131–132.

239. Transcript of a Meeting of the Organizational Bureau of the R.W.P., April 21, 1952, National Archives of Romania, Fond CC al PCR—Cancelarie, Dosar 32/1952, p. 30.

240. Transcript of a Meeting of the Secretariat of the R.W.P., October 4, 1948, National Archives of Romania, Fond CC al PCR—Cancelarie, Dosar 38/1948, p. 2.

241. Addressing the arbitrary nature of identifying kulaks, Luca complained of discovering cases of "poor peasants who didn't make 12,000 lei a year" (the minimum taxable income) being classified as kulaks. "Or things would happen this way: The wife of some 'kulak' says something against the kolhoz, the Securitate intervenes, and they arrest her kulak husband. He has 15 oxes, 9 children, has worked his entire life, and doesn't even own a jacket. [But] some sectarian elements have put forward that all those with 5 oxes or more must be considered kulaks" (Transcript of a Meeting of the Organizational Bureau of the R.W.P., June 6, 1950, National Archives of Romania, Fond CC al PCR—Cancelarie, Dosar 41/1950, p. 20).

242. Memoir of Vasile Luca, November 5, 1954, ASRI, Fond P, Dosar 40005, Vol. 126, pp. 54–55; Interrogation of Vasile Luca, February 11, 1954, ASRI, Fond P, Dosar 40005, Vol. 2, p. 8.

243. The number of individual kulak farms officially estimated by the Finance Ministry was 68,594 in 1949, 64,780 in 1950, and 48,133 in 1951 (National Archives of Romania, Fond 1, Dosar 562/1952, p. 35).

244. Transcript of a Meeting of the Council of Ministers, September 29, 1950, National Archives of Romania, Fond Consiliul de Miniştri—Cabinetul, Dosar 9/1950, p. 28, 39–40.

245. Luca initially objected to considering revenue in defining kulaks and suggested that the party must give the peasants the incentive of benefiting from doing good work. Instead, he complained, "when someone works his land well like he's supposed to, and has a bigger crop, you make him a kulak." By the beginning of 1951, however, Luca began to reconsider his position; affirming that the financial situation of the peasantry had "fundamentally changed" for the better, he concluded that the criteria for defining social classes should no longer be based on land (Speech of Vasile Luca at a Meeting with the First Secretaries of the Regional Committees [and others], October 7, 1950, National Archives of Romania, Fond 1, Dosar 176/1950, p. 139; Transcript of a Meeting of the Secretariat of the R.W.P., February 10, 1951, National Archives of Romania, Fond CC al PCR—Cancelarie, Dosar 9/1951, p. 11).

246. Transcript of a Meeting of the Politburo of the R.W.P., February 19, 1952,

National Archives of Romania, Fond CC al PCR—Cancelarie, Dosar 11/1952, p. 66; Transcript of a Meeting of the Politburo of the R.W.P., February 21, 1952, National Archives of Romania, Fond CC al PCR—Cancelarie, Dosar 11/1952, pp. 107, 110.

247. Transcript of a Meeting of the Council of Ministers, December 18, 1951, National Archives of Romania, Fond Consiliul de Miniştri—Cabinetul, Dosar 9/1951, p. 128 [emphasis added].

248. Transcript of the Plenary of the Central Committee of the R.W.P., May 27–29, 1952, National Archives of Romania, Fond CC al PCR—Cancelarie, Dosar 41/1952, p. 72; Fond 1, Dosar 75/1952, p. 244.

249. Transcript of the Plenary of the Central Committee of the R.W.P., May 27–29, 1952, National Archives of Romania, Fond CC al PCR—Cancelarie, Dosar 41/1952, p. 72; Transcript of a Meeting of the Secretariat of the R.W.P., October 10, 1950, National Archives of Romania, Fond CC al PCR—Cancelarie, Dosar 59/1950, pp. 16–17.

250. Transcript of the Plenary of the Central Committee of the R.W.P., May 27–29, 1952, National Archives of Romania, Fond CC al PCR—Cancelarie, Dosar 41/1952, pp. 72–73; National Archives of Romania, Fond 1, Dosar 748/1952, p. 2.

251. National Archives of Romania, Fond 1, Dosar 75/1952, p. 16; Fond 1, Dosar 69/1951, p. 96.

252. Transcript of an Interrogation of Ana Pauker by a R.W.P. Commission, June 12, 1953, Ana Pauker Inquiry File, Executive Archive of the Central Committee of the R.C.P., pp. 54–55.

253. Transcript of the Plenary of the Central Committee of the R.W.P., May 27–29, 1952, National Archives of Romania, Fond CC al PCR—Cancelarie, Dosar 41/1952, pp. 72–73; Transcript of a Meeting of the Secretariat of the R.W.P., October 10, 1950, National Archives of Romania, Fond CC al PCR—Cancelarie, Dosar 59/1950, p. 17; National Archives of Romania, Fond 1, Dosar 748/1952, pp. 2, 30; Fond 1, Dosar 75/1952, p. 16.

254. Party Commission Interrogation of Iosif Breban, May 31, 1952, National Archives of Romania, Fond 1, Dosar 75/1952, p. 61; Iosif Breban interview.

255. National Archives of Romania, Fond 1, Dosar 748/1952, p. 2.

256. Transcript of the Plenary of the Central Committee of the R.W.P., May 27–29, 1952, National Archives of Romania, Fond CC al PCR—Cancelarie, Dosar 41/1952, p. 73.

257. This was contingent on the kulaks' ceasing to exploit others and working their farms themselves (National Archives of Romania, Fond 1, Dosar 748/1952, pp. 10, 38, 62; Fond 1, Dosar 73/1952, p. 19).

258. National Archives of Romania, Fond 1, Dosar 755/1952, pp. 1–2; National Archives of Romania, Fond 1, Dosar 73/1952, p. 129; Fond 1, Dosar 711/1952, p. 18. On attempts of "self-dekulakization" in the Soviet Union, see Lynne Viola, *Peasant Rebels under Stalin* (New York and Oxford, 1996), pp. 67–99.

259. National Archives of Romania, Fond CC al PCR—Cancelarie, Dosar 59/1950, pp. 12–13; Fond 1, Dosar 755/1952, pp. 1–2.

260. Transcript of a Meeting of the Agrarian Commission, September 29, 1949, National Archives of Romania, Fond CC al PCR—Cancelarie, Dosar 87/1949, p. 1.

261. Transcript of the Plenary of the Central Committee of the R.W.P., February 29–March 1, 1952, National Archives of Romania, Fond CC al PCR—Cancelarie, Dosar 13/1952, p. 117.

262. Transcript of a Meeting with the Secretaries of the Party County Committees, February 20–23, 1950, National Archives of Romania, Fond CC al PCR—Cancelarie, Dosar 11/1950, pp. 184–185.

263. Transcript of a Meeting of the Organizational Bureau of the R.W.P., June 6, 1950, National Archives of Romania, Fond CC al PCR—Cancelarie, Dosar 41/1950, p. 25.

264. Transcript of the Plenary of the Central Committee of the R.W.P., May 27–29, 1952, National Archives of Romania, Fond CC al PCR—Cancelarie, Dosar 41/1952, p. 72.

265. On the Soviet mandate, see the Transcript of a Meeting of the Secretariat of the R.W.P., October 10, 1950, National Archives of Romania, Fond CC al PCR—Cancelarie, Dosar 59/1950, p. 9. On the Agrarian Section's continued resistance, see the Transcript of a Meeting of the Agrarian Section of the Central Committee, June 12, 1952, National Archives of Romania, Fond 1, Dosar 748/1952, p. 41.

266. Transcript of a Meeting of the Secretariat, October 10, 1950, National Archives of Romania, Fond CC al PCR—Cancelarie, Dosar 59/1950, pp. 9, 13.

267. National Archives of Romania, Fond 1, Dosar 75/1952, p. 90.

268. Statement of Agrarian Section functionary Elisa Mihalca, Transcript of a Meeting of the Agrarian Section of the Central Committee, June 12, 1952, National Archives of Romania, Fond 1, Dosar 748/1952, p. 41. Agriculture Minister Vaida also confirmed that the confiscations of kulaks began in June only after Moghioroş began meeting with the leadership of the Agrarian Section and the Agriculture Ministry (Transcript of a Meeting of the Secretariat of the R.W.P., October 10, 1950, National Archives of Romania, Fond CC al PCR—Cancelarie, Dosar 59/1950, p. 10).

269. Transcript of a Meeting with the Secretaries of the Party County Committees and the Instructors of the Central Committee, June 15, 1950, National Archives of Romania, Fond CC al PCR—Cancelarie, Dosar 44/1950, p. 20.

270. National Archives of Romania, Fond CC al PCR—Cancelarie, Dosar 59/1950, pp. 78–79.

271. Ibid.; Transcript of a Meeting of the Secretariat of the R.W.P., October 10, 1950, National Archives of Romania, Fond CC al PCR—Cancelarie, Dosar 59/1950, p. 9.

272. National Archives of Romania, Fond 1, Dosar 75/1952, pp. 119–120.

273. National Archives of Romania, Fond 1, Dosar 743/1952, p. 73; Fond CC al PCR—Cancelarie, Dosar 59/1950, pp. 10, 75.

274. National Archives of Romania, Fond CC al PCR—Cancelarie, Dosar 59/1950, p. 79.

275. Transcript of a Meeting of the Secretariat of the R.W.P., October 10, 1950, National Archives of Romania, Fond CC al PCR—Cancelarie, Dosar 59/1950, p. 10.

276. Ibid., pp. 9, 37; National Archives of Romania, Fond 1, Dosar 743/1952, p. 16.

277. Written Answers of Teohari Georgescu to Questions Submitted by a Party Commission, September 15, 1952, ASRI, Fond P, Dosar 40009, Vol. 32, p. 213. Georgescu was probably understating the situation there, for Dumitru Petrescu revealed to the party leadership that no fewer than fifty peasants were put on trial as "speculators" and had their land confiscated on a single day in Ilfov County (Transcript of a Meeting of the Secretariat of the R.W.P., October 10, 1950, National Archives of Romania, Fond CC al PCR—Cancelarie, Dosar 59/1950, p. 10).

278. National Archives of Romania, Fond CC al PCR—Cancelarie, Dosar 59/1950, p. 33; Fond 1, Dosar 207/1950, pp. 128–137; Fond 1, Dosar 75/1952, pp. 192–196; Report Regarding the Shooting of the Kulaks Iosif Trifa, Traian Pom, and Ioan Andreşel in the Village of Bistra, in Turda County, August 22, 1950, ASRI, Dosar 4638, pp. 163–171.

279. National Archives of Romania, Fond 1, Dosar 743/1952, p. 73; National

Archives of Romania, Fond CC al PCR—Cancelarie, Dosar 59/1950, pp. 11, 75; National Archives of Romania, Fond CC al PCR—Cancelarie, Dosar 59/1950, p. 81; Fond CC al PCR—Cancelarie, Dosar 10/1951, p. 28; Fond 1, Dosar 207/1950, pp. 128–137; Fond 1, Dosar 748/1952, p. 41; Fond 1, Dosar 755/1952, p. 7; National Archives of Romania, Fond CC al PCR—Cancelarie, Dosar 59/1950, p. 3.

280. National Archives of Romania, Fond CC al PCR—Cancelarie, Dosar 59/1950, pp. 2, 78–79.

281. National Archives of Romania, Fond 1, Dosar 207/1950, pp. 128–137.

282. Statement of Elisa Mihalca, Transcript of a Meeting of the Agrarian Section of the Central Committee, June 12, 1952, National Archives of Romania, Fond 1, Dosar 748/1952, p. 40. Georgescu confirmed, "The party intervened and demanded that the party line be applied" (Written Answers of Teohari Georgescu to Questions Submitted by a Party Commission, September 15, 1952, ASRI, Fond P, Dosar 40009, Vol. 32, p. 213).

283. Statement of Elisa Mihalca, Transcript of a Meeting of the Agrarian Section of the Central Committee, June 12, 1952, National Archives of Romania, Fond 1, Dosar 748/1952, pp. 40–41.

284. Statement of Pavel Chirtoacă, Transcript of a Meeting of the Agrarian Section of the Central Committee, March 1, 1951, National Archives of Romania, Fond 1, Dosar 58/1951, p. 61.

285. Written Answers of Teohari Georgescu to Questions Submitted by a Party Commission, September 15, 1952, ASRI, Fond P, Dosar 40009, Vol. 32, pp. 213–214.

286. Statement of Elisa Mihalca, Transcript of a Meeting of the Agrarian Section of the Central Committee, June 12, 1952, National Archives of Romania, Fond 1, Dosar 748/1952, pp. 40–41; Statement of Pavel Chirtoacă, Transcript of a Meeting of the Agrarian Section of the Central Committee, March 1, 1951, National Archives of Romania, Fond 1, Dosar 58/1951, p. 61.

287. Statement of Elisa Mihalca, Transcript of a Meeting of the Agrarian Section of the Central Committee, June 12, 1952, National Archives of Romania, Fond 1, Dosar 748/1952, p. 41.

288. Transcript of a Meeting of the Secretaries for Agrarian Problems with the Regional First Secretaries of the R.W.P., May 29, 1951, National Archives of Romania, Fond 1, Dosar 69/1951, p. 89.

289. At Vaida's urging, however, Pauker did sign a resolution on the specific case of kulaks expelled from collective farms. It stipulated that those "for whom it was not possible to restore their land in their respective regions should be moved with their entire families to new villages in the region of Ialomiţa" and given land there (National Archives of Romania, Fond 1, Dosar 749/1952, p. 5).

290. On Dej's denials, see the Transcript of a Meeting of the Secretariat of the R.W.P., October 10, 1950, National Archives of Romania, Fond CC al PCR—Cancelarie, Dosar 59/1950, p. 6. His earlier proposal to confiscate kulak lands is in the Transcript of a Plenary Meeting of the Central Committee of the R.W.P., May 15–17, 1950, National Archives of Romania, Fond CC al PCR—Cancelarie, Dosar 32/1950, p. 226.

291. Transcript of a Meeting of the Organizational Bureau of the R.W.P., June 6, 1950, National Archives of Romania, Fond CC al PCR—Cancelarie, Dosar 41/1950, pp. 20–21.

292. As Luca himself later noted, the party leadership made no decision on his proposals following the June 6 meeting. At that meeting, moreover, Pauker's stated

interpretation of the "struggle against the kulaks" was merely that of union organizing of poor peasants working for the kulaks (Transcript of a Meeting of the Secretariat of the R.W.P., October 10, 1950, National Archives of Romania, Fond CC al
PCR—Cancelarie, Dosar 59/1950, p. 9; Transcript of a Meeting of the Organizational Bureau of the R.W.P., June 6, 1950, National Archives of Romania, Fond CC
al PCR—Cancelarie, Dosar 41/1950, pp. 9–10, 23).

293. Agriculture Minister Vaida revealed that confiscations began to be raised
only after Pauker departed, in the mid-June 1950 meetings called by Moghioroş to
review proposals for new collective farms. In so doing, he pointedly corrected Dumitru Petrescu, who alleged that Pauker had approved the "dekulakization" of the
most prominent kulaks—an allegation, moreover, that does not correspond with the
chronology garnered from the documents (Transcript of a Meeting of the Secretariat
of the RWP, October 10, 1950, National Archives of Romania, Fond CC al PCR—
Cancelarie, Dosar 59/1950, pp. 9–10).

294. Report of Ana Pauker to the Organizational Bureau of the R.W.P., May 24,
1950, National Archives of Romania, Fond CC al PCR—Cancelarie, Dosar 41/
1950, p. 34.

295. National Archives of Romania, Fond 1, Dosar 73/1952, pp. 22–24, 37;
Report on the Results of the Investigation of Ana Pauker, June 6, 1953, ASRI, Fond
P, Dosar 40005, Vol. 173, p. 156; Transcript of the Plenary of the Central Commit-
tee of the R.W.P., May 27–29, 1952, National Archives of Romania, Fond CC al
PCR—Cancelarie, Dosar 41/1952, pp. 97–98; Resolution of the C.C. Plenary of
May 26–27, 1952 on the Activities of Comrade Teohari Georgescu in the Interior
Ministry Leadership, Fond CC al PCR—Cancelarie, Dosar 41/1952, pp. 173–174;
Scânteia, June 28, 1952, p. 3.

296. National Archives of Romania, Fond 1, Dosar 73/1952, pp. 24, 56; Fond
CC al PCR—Cancelarie, Dosar 41/1952, p. 173; Transcript of the Plenary of the
Central Committee of the R.W.P., May 27–29, 1952, National Archives of Romania, Fond CC al PCR—Cancelarie, Dosar 41/1952, pp. 21, 73, 85; Resolution Regarding the Activities of Comrade Teohari Georgescu in the Leadership of the Interior Ministry, Plenary of the C.C. of May 26–27, 1952, National Archives of
Romania, Fond CC al PCR—Cancelarie, Dosar 41/1952, p. 173.

297. Transcript of a Meeting of the Politburo of the R.W.P., May 26, 1952, National Archives of Romania, Fond CC al PCR—Cancelarie, Dosar 40/1952, p. 64;
Fond 1, Dosar 562/1952, p. 18; Spulber, in Sanders, ed., Collectivization of Agriculture in Eastern Europe, p. 143.

298. National Archives of Romania, Fond 1, Dosar 743/1952, p. 21.

299. National Archives of Romania, Fond 1, Dosar 755/1952, p. 15; Fond 1,
Dosar 743/1952, p. 21; Transcript of a Meeting of the Council of Ministers, October 14, 1949, National Archives of Romania, Fond Consiliul de Miniştri—Cabinetul, Dosar 9/1949, pp. 65–66.

300. Transcript of a Meeting of the Secretariat of the R.W.P., January 2, 1950,
National Archives of Romania, Fond CC al PCR—Cancelarie, Dosar 1/1950, pp. 5–
12; Transcript of a Meeting of the Council of Ministers, February 17, 1950, National
Archives of Romania, Fond Consiliul de Miniştri—Cabinetul, Dosar 2/1950,
pp. 39–50; Transcript of a Meeting of the Council of Ministers, May 22, 1950, National Archives of Romania, Fond Consiliul de Miniştri—Cabinetul, Dosar 5/1950,
pp. 28–49.

301. Rebellions over collections were reported in July–August 1949 in Arad and
Bihor Counties, with large numbers of peasants arrested in both regions (ASRI, Fond
D, Dosar 4638, pp. 19, 66–67); Transcript of a Meeting of the Council of Ministers,

May 22, 1950, National Archives of Romania, Fond Consiliul de Miniştri—Cabinetul, Dosar 5/1950, pp. 28–49.

302. Information Report, July 22, 1950, National Archives of Romania, Fond 1, Dosar 205/1950, pp. 117, 119.

303. Transcript of a Meeting of the Politburo of the R.W.P., May 26, 1952, National Archives of Romania, Fond CC al PCR—Cancelarie, Dosar 40/1952, p. 87; "The Directives of the Central Committee of the R.W.P. Regarding the Elections to Leading Party Organs," March 12, 1951, in *Rezoluţii şi Hotârîri ale Comitetului Central al Partidului Mucitoresc Român* [Resolutions and Decrees of the Central Committee of the Romanian Workers Party], vol. 2, p. 47.

304. Sorin Toma interview. Vasile Luca confirmed to his prison cell mate in 1955 that the person "who gave the order" to forcibly take collection quotas from the peasants was at that time still in the party leadership (Informative Note, April 26–27, 1955, Ministry of Internal Affairs, Văcăreşti Penitentiary, Bureau D, ASRI, Fond P, Dosar 40005, Vol. 154, p. 21).

305. Transcript of a Plenary Meeting of the Central Committee of the R.W.P., May 15–17, 1950, National Archives of Romania, Fond CC al PCR, Dosar 32/1950, p. 226.

306. Transcript of a Meeting of the Council of Ministers, September 19, 1950, National Archives of Romania, Fond Consiliul de Miniştri—Cabinetul, Dosar 9/1950, pp. 14–15; Transcript of a Meeting of the Council of Ministers, September 29, 1950, National Archives of Romania, Fond Consiliul de Miniştri—Cabinetul, Dosar 9/1950, pp. 27–28.

307. Transcript of a Meeting of the Politburo of the R.W.P., May 26, 1952, National Archives of Romania, Fond CC al PCR—Cancelarie, Dosar 40/1952, p. 87; Transcript of an Interrogation of Ana Pauker by a R.W.P. Commission, June 12, 1953, Ana Pauker Inquiry File, Executive Archive of the Central Committee of the R.C.P., p. 65; The Committee for the Investigation of Abuses and for Petitions, Dosar 5578/1992; ASRI, Dosar 4640, pp. 154–159; both cited in Octavian Roske, *Dosarul Colectivizării Agriculturii în România, 1949–1962* [The Dossier of the Collectivization of Agriculture in Romania, 1949–1962] (Bucharest, 1992), pp. 33–34.

308. Transcript of a Meeting of the Secretariat of the R.W.P., January 11, 1951, National Archives of Romania, Fond CC al PCR—Cancelarie, Dosar 3/1951, p. 3; Transcript of a Meeting with the First Secretaries of the Regional Party Committees, February 9, 1951, National Archives of Romania, Fond CC al PCR—Cancelarie, Dosar 10/1951, pp. 3–4; Transcript of a Meeting of the Secretariat of the R.W.P., January 11, 1951, National Archives of Romania, Fond CC al PCR—Cancelarie, Dosar 3/1951, p. 3.

309. Representatives of the Central Committee reported that regional party leaders were hesitating to enforce the collections in their respective areas. "Secretaries of Popular Councils . . . are standing firm in the position that they can't do a thing," one of them related. "In one village . . . one of them said: 'What do you want? Haven't you taken enough from the peasants?'" In Ialomiţa County, moreover, the local party officials resisted imposing increased quotas as penalties for noncompliance. They told the Central Committee representatives that they could not do the math to figure out the increases and had to be threatened by those representatives before they would impose them (Transcript of a Meeting with Representatives of the Central Committee and Council of Ministers, February 4, 1952, National Archives of Romania, Fond CC al PCR—Cancelarie, Dosar 6/1952, pp. 6, 13); National Archives of Romania, Fond 1, Dosar 75/1952, p. 91.

310. C.C. Transcript of the Plenary of the Central Committee of the R.W.P., May 27–29, 1952, National Archives of Romania, Fond CC al PCR—Cancelarie, Dosar 41/1952, pp. 83, 92; Transcript of a Meeting of the Politburo of the R.W.P., February 26, 1952, National Archives of Romania, Fond CC al PCR—Cancelarie, Dosar 12/1952, p. 22; Report of the Party and State Commission on the Activities of the Ministry of Food Industries, National Archives of Romania, Fond 1, Dosar 150/1952, pp. 4–5; Statement of Iosif Breban, Transcript of a Meeting of the Agrarian Section of the Central Committee, June 12, 1952, National Archives of Romania, Fond 1, Dosar 748/1952, p. 36.

311. Transcript of a Meeting with Representatives of the Central Committee and Council of Ministers, February 4, 1952, National Archives of Romania, Fond CC al PCR—Cancelarie, Dosar 6/1952, p. 6; Transcript of a Meeting of the Secretariat of the R.W.P., January 11, 1951, National Archives of Romania, Fond CC al PCR—Cancelarie, Dosar 3/1951, pp. 3, 5.

312. Ibid., pp. 5, 10; Statement of Ana Pauker, Transcript of a Meeting with Representatives of the R.W.P. Central Committee and the Government on the Problem of the Collections, January 15, 1952, National Archives of Romania, Fond CC al PCR—Cancelarie, Dosar 3/1952, p. 10.

313. Transcript of a Meeting of the Secretariat of the R.W.P., January 11, 1951, National Archives of Romania, Fond CC al PCR—Cancelarie, Dosar 3/1951, pp. 4–5, 10.

314. Ibid., pp. 4, 9–10.

315. Ibid., p. 5.

316. Ibid., pp. 10–11.

317. Interrogation of Marin Jianu, June 11, 1953, ASRI, Fond P, Dosar 40009, Vol. 14, pp. 71–72.

318. Interrogation of Marin Jianu, February 21, 1953, ASRI, Fond P, Dosar 40009, Vol. 26, p. 13.

319. Interrogation of Marin Jianu, March 10, 1953, ASRI, Fond P, Dosar 40009, Vol. 26, p. 90; for Pauker's position, see Transcript of a Meeting of the Agrarian Section of the Central Committee, March 12, 1952, National Archives of Romania, Fond 1, Dosar 28/1952, p. 38.

320. Transcript of a Meeting with the Regional Party Secretaries, December 1, 1951, National Archives of Romania, Fond 1, Dosar 99/1951, p. 9.

321. National Archives of Romania, Fond 1, Dosar 99/1951, pp. 7–8.

322. Interrogation of Marin Jianu, June 11, 1953, ASRI, Fond P, Dosar 40009, Vol. 14, p. 72.

323. Transcript of a Meeting of the Politburo of the R.W.P., May 26, 1952, National Archives of Romania, Fond CC al PCR—Cancelarie, Dosar 40/1952, p. 87.

324. Transcript of the Plenary of the Central Committee of the R.W.P., May 27–29, 1952, National Archives of Romania, Fond CC al PCR—Cancelarie, Dosar 41/1952, pp. 73, 85.

325. National Archives of Romania, Fond 1, Dosar 743/1952, p. 18; Fond 1, Dosar 748/1952, p. 8; Fond 1, Dosar 75/1952, p. 84.

326. Transcript of an Interrogation of Ana Pauker by a Party Commission of the R.W.P., June 12, 1953, Ana Pauker Inquiry File, Executive Archive of the Central Committee of the R.C.P., p. 65.

327. National Archives of Romania, Fond 1, Dosar 219/1951, p. 141.

328. National Archives of Romania, Fond 1, Dosar 73/1952, p. 129. To make

matters worse, in many locations peasants who brought their quotas to state collectors were actually turned away with their carts full because of a lack of storage space
(National Archives of Romania, Fond 1, Dosar 99/1951, p. 9).

329. Transcript of an Interrogation of Iosif Breban by an R.W.P. Commission,
May 31, 1952, National Archives of Romania, Fond 1, Dosar 75/1952, pp. 59–60;
Declaration of Francisc Ţapoş, May 31, 1952, National Archives of Romania, Fond
1, Dosar 75/1952, p. 14.

330. Transcript of an Interrogation of Ana Pauker by a Party Commission of the
R.W.P., June 18, 1956, Ana Pauker Inquiry File, Executive Archive of the Central
Committee of the R.C.P., p. 36.

331. Transcript of an Interrogation of Ana Pauker by a Party Commission of the
C.C. of the R.W.P., June 12, 1953, Ana Pauker Inquiry File, Executive Archive of the
Central Committee of the R.C.P., p. 65.

332. Transcript of a Meeting with the Regional Party Secretaries, December 1,
1951, National Archives of Romania, Fond 1, Dosar 99/1951, pp. 3–4, 12.

333. Transcript of an Interrogation of Ana Pauker by a R.W.P. Commission,
June 18, 1956, Ana Pauker Inquiry File, Executive Archive of the Central Committee of the R.C.P., p. 37

334. Transcript of an Interrogation of Ana Pauker by an R.W.P. Commission,
June 12, 1953, Ana Pauker Inquiry File, Executive Archive of the Central Committee of the R.C.P., p. 65.

335. Transcript of a Meeting of the Politburo of the R.W.P., February 26, 1952,
National Archives of Romania, Fond CC al PCR—Cancelarie, Dosar 12/1952, p. 22.

336. Interrogation of Vasile Luca, February 19, 1953, ASRI, Fond P, Dosar
40005, Vol. 4, p. 453.

337. Transcript of a Meeting of the Politburo of the R.W.P., February 26, 1952,
National Archives of Romania, Fond CC al PCR—Cancelarie, Dosar 12/1952, p. 22.

338. Transcript of an Interrogation of Ana Pauker by an R.W.P. Commission,
June 18, 1956, Ana Pauker Inquiry File, Executive Archive of the Central Committee of the R.C.P., pp. 36–37.

339. Transcript of a Meeting with Representatives of the R.W.P. Central Committee and the Government on the Problem of the Collections, January 15, 1952,
National Archives of Romania, Fond CC al PCR—Cancelarie, Dosar 3/1952, pp. 2,
7, 12.

340. Transcript of a Meeting of the Politburo of the R.W.P., February 26, 1952,
National Archives of Romania, Fond CC al PCR—Cancelarie, Dosar 12/1952, p. 22.

341. Transcript of a Meeting with Representatives of the R.W.P. Central Committee and the Government on the Problem of the Collections, January 15, 1952, National Archives of Romania, Fond CC al PCR—Cancelarie, Dosar 3/1952, p. 8.

342. National Archives of Romania, Fond 1, Dosar 741/1952, p. 35.

343. Transcript of a Meeting with Representatives of the R.W.P. Central Committee and the Government on the Problem of the Collections, January 15, 1952, National Archives of Romania, Fond CC al PCR—Cancelarie, Dosar 3/1952, p. 12.

344. Ibid., pp. 10–11.

345. Pauker showed an understanding of this as late as December 1951: "Throw
cement, tile, and brick on the market," she insisted, "and all the grain you want will
emerge" (Transcript of a Meeting of the Council of Ministers, December 10, 1951,
National Archives of Romania, Fond Consiliul de Miniştri—Cabinetul, Dosar 9/
1951, p. 67).

346. According to Nicolae Belu, Pauker was delegated to lead the anti-kulak

campaign as a form of self-criticism for not having previously taken appropriate measures against the kulaks (Nicolae Belu interview, January 25, 1994).

347. Transcript of a Meeting with Representatives of the Central Committee and Council of Ministers, February 4, 1952, National Archives of Romania, Fond CC al PCR—Cancelarie, Dosar 6/1952, pp. 7–9, 18.

348. Transcript of an Interrogation of Ana Pauker by a Party Commission of the C.C. of the R.W.P., June 18, 1956, Ana Pauker Inquiry File, Executive Archive of the Central Committee of the R.C.P., p. 36; Written Answers of Teohari Georgescu to Questions Submitted by a Party Commission, September 15, 1952, ASRI, Fond P, Dosar 40009, Vol. 32, p. 214.

349. Transcript of an Interrogation of Ana Pauker by a Party Commission of the C.C. of the R.W.P., June 18, 1956, Ana Pauker Inquiry File, Executive Archive of the Central Committee of the R.C.P., p. 36.

350. Transcript of a Meeting with Representatives of the Central Committee and Council of Ministers, February 4, 1952, National Archives of Romania, Fond CC al PCR—Cancelarie, Dosar 6/1952, p. 11.

351. Transcript of a Meeting of the Agrarian Section of the Central Committee, March 12, 1952, National Archives of Romania, Fond 1, Dosar 28/1952, p. 38.

352. Transcript of a Meeting of the Politburo of the R.W.P., February 21, 1952, National Archives of Romania, Fond CC al PCR—Cancelarie, Dosar 11/1952, pp. 115–116, 121–122.

353. Transcript of a Meeting of the Politburo of the R.W.P., March 14, 1952, National Archives of Romania, Fond CC al PCR—Cancelarie, Dosar 20/1952, pp. 29–30.

354. Transcript of a Meeting of the Council of Ministers, March 20, 1952, National Archives of Romania, Fond Consiliul de Miniştri—Cabinetul, Dosar 3/1952, p. 131.

355. Memoir of Vasile Luca, November 5, 1954, ASRI, Fond P, Dosar 40005, Vol. 126, p. 56.

356. National Archives of Romania, Fond 1, Dosar 73/1952, pp. 23–24, 107–108, 128–129.

357. "Choosing, Developing and Distributing the Cadres—a Lecture Delivered by Ana Pauker to the Zhdanov Party School on April 17, 1952," National Archives of Romania, Fond 1, Dosar 74/1952, p. 249 [emphasis added].

358. Transcript of a Meeting with Secretaries of the Party County Committees, February 20–23, 1950, National Archives of Romania, Fond CC al PCR—Cancelarie, Dosar 11/1950, pp. 191–192 [emphasis added].

359. Transcript of a Party Meeting, October 30, 1952, National Archives of Romania, Fond CC al PCR—Cancelarie, Dosar 96/1952, p. 7. The more severe penalties were ratified on June 18, 1952 (Octavian Roske, "Colectivizarea agriculturii în România, 1949–1962" [The Collectivization of Agriculture in Romania, 1949–1962], Arhivele Totalitarismului 1, no. 3 [1993], p. 160).

360. Ibid.

361. This was reported in a Central Committee document dated August 31, 1952 (National Archives of Romania, Fond 1, Dosar 646/1952, p. 14).

362. Transcript of a Party Meeting, October 30, 1952, National Archives of Romania, Fond CC al PCR—Cancelarie, Dosar 96/1952, p. 7.

363. News from behind the Iron Curtain 1, no. 10 (October 1952), p. 3.

364. Rumanian National Committee Bulletin, no. 44, November 1952, p. 10.

365. As estimated by the Swiss (Basel) newspaper National-Zeitung of Janu-

ary 14, 1953. Cited in the *Rumanian National Committee Bulletin*, no. 47, February 1953, p. 9.

366. Transcript of the Plenary Meeting of the Central Committee of the R.W.P., November 30–December 5, 1961, Executive Archive of the Central Committee of the R.C.P., p. 218.

367. Dej essentially acknowledged this in November 1952, when he called for less repressive methods in handling the issue, noting that the country's prisons had been filled to capacity with arrested peasants after Pauker's ouster (Transcript of a Meeting of the Politburo of the R.W.P., November 19, 1952, National Archives of Romania, Fond CC al PCR—Cancelarie, Dosar 107/1952, pp. 7–13).

368. Memoir of Vasile Luca, November 5, 1954, ASRI, Dosar 40005, Vol. 126, pp. 5, 51. During her purge, party documents accused Pauker of "disregarding Soviet experience and the assistance given by Soviet advisers . . . , and not taking measures that put their advice into practice." As Agriculture Minister Vasile Vaida subsequently acknowledged, "we had quite serious arguments" with the Soviet advisers while Pauker was responsible for agriculture (National Archives of Romania, Fond 1, Dosar 73/1952, p. 21; Fond 1, Dosar 75/1952, p. 325).

369. Memoir of Vasile Luca, November 5, 1954, ASRI, Fond P, Dosar 40005, Vol. 126, p. 51.

CHAPTER 5

1. Gheorghe Gheorghiu-Dej, Report to the Plenary Meeting of the C.C. of the R.W.P., November 30–December 5, 1961, *Agerpres Information Bulletin*, no. 22–23, December 10, 1961, pp. 15–16.

2. Speech of Gheorghe Gheorghiu-Dej to the National Meeting of Miners on June 27–28, 1952, reprinted in *Scânteia*, July 2, 1952, pp. 2–3.

3. Patraşcanu himself used this spelling, as opposed to Pătrăşcanu; thus, all citations will use the former.

4. Declaration of Harry Brauner, February 24, 1950, ASRI, Fond P, Dosar 40002, Vol. 60, p. 130; Mircea Bălănescu interview, July 16, 1991; Corneliu Bogdan, Radu Mănescu, and Ilie Zaharia interviews.

5. Radu Mănescu interview; Ionescu, *Communism in Romania*, p. 95.

6. Declaration of Lucreţiu Patraşcanu, June 10, 1948, ASRI, Fond P, Dosar 40002, Vol. 10, p. 431; Declaration of Lucreţiu Patraşcanu, November 2, 1949, ASRI, Fond P, Dosar 40002, Vol. 1, p. 55; Declaration of Lucreţiu Patraşcanu, December 9, 1949, ASRI, Fond P, Dosar 40002, Vol. 1, p. 165.

7. The National Liberal Party's leader C. I. C. Brătianu revealed in a meeting at the Council of Ministers that, when he first made contact with Patraşcanu, the latter assured him, "Mr. Brătianu, before anything we are Romanians. We should work with a common goal, because on this line we are no different from you" (Transcript of the Council of Ministers' Session on September 16, 1944, Former Central Archive of the Party Historical Institute Adjacent to the Central Committee of the R.C.P., Fond 103, Dosar 8,468, Archive of the Academy of Sciences of Romania, pp. 1–77).

8. Declaration of Lucreţiu Patraşcanu, December 9, 1949, ASRI, Fond P, Dosar 40002, Vol. 1, p. 165; Declaration of Lucreţiu Patraşcanu, undated, ASRI, Fond P, Dosar 40002, Vol. 1, p. 27.

9. Declaration of Lucreţiu Patraşcanu, December 9, 1949, ASRI, Fond P, Dosar 40002, Vol. 1, p. 165.

10. Declaration of Elena Patraşcanu, March 9, 1950, ASRI, Fond P, Dosar 40002, Vol. 87, p. 50.

11. Patraşcanu apparently came close to being liquidated in Moscow during the initial wave of arrests that followed Sergei Kirov's assassination. Serving as the RCP's official representative to the Comintern from the fall of 1933 to the spring of 1934, he was unable to leave Moscow at the end of that period and clashed with officials in the Comintern who opposed his return to Romania (Report of the Party Commission Established to Clarify the Situation of Lucreţiu Patraşcanu, Submitted to the Party Leadership on June 29, 1968, pp. 27–28). According to one unconfirmed account, Patraşcanu was married at the time to a Russian Communist whose father was an important figure in the Comintern apparat and who warned him of his imminent arrest if he did not leave the country. Subsequently she was arrested and executed (Alexandru Şiperco interview).

12. Tatiana and Gheorghe Brătescu interview. Patraşcanu personally told Nicolae Belu in 1945 that he thought that the Soviets hated him (Nicolae Belu interview).

13. Transcript of the Declaration Given by Teohari Georgescu to the R.C.P. Commission, October 23, 1967, ASRI, Fond P, Dosar 40002, Vol. 203, p. 295.

14. Tatiana and Gheorghe Brătescu interview. For examples of Patraşcanu's criticism of the Soviet Union, see Declaration of Lena Constante, April 22, 1950, ASRI, Fond P, Dosar 40002, Vol. 65, p. 187; Declaration of Herbert Zilber, November 13, 1950, ASRI, Fond P, Dosar 40002, Vol. 38, p. 359; Declaration of Harry Brauner, February 24, 1950, ASRI, Fond P, Dosar 40002, Vol. 60, pp. 130–131.

15. Statement of Gheorghe Pintilie to the R.C.P. Commission, October 19, 1967, ASRI, Fond P, Dosar 40002, Vol. 203, p. 276.

16. Report of the Party Commission Established to Clarify the Situation of Lucreţiu Patraşcanu, Submitted to the Party Leadership on June 29, 1968, Executive Archive of the Central Committee of the R.C.P., pp. 9–11.

17. Ibid., p. 10.

18. Tudor Olaru interview.

19. "Report of the Party Commission Established to Clarify the Situation of Lucreţiu Patraşcanu." This portion of the report was published in *Cuvîntul,* September 1–7, 1992, p. 9.

20. Ibid.

21. Transcript of the Plenary Meeting of the Central Committee of the R.C.P., October 22, 1945, Executive Archive of the Central Committee of the R.C.P., No. 850/1945, p. 23.

22. Interrogation of Leoveanu Şerban, September 8, 1953, ASRI, Fond P, Dosar 40002, Vol. 15, p. 129–130; Ion Gheorghe Maurer interview.

23. Transcript of the Declaration Given by Elena Patraşcanu before the R.C.P. Commission, October 25, 1967, ASRI, Fond P, Dosar 40002, Vol. 202, p. 207.

24. Declaration of Elena Patraşcanu, March 9, 1950, ASRI, Fond P, Dosar 40002, Vol. 87, p. 50. Corneliu Coposu witnessed this both before and after meetings of the Council of Ministers in the immediate postwar period (Corneliu Coposu interview).

25. On Patraşcanu's popularity, see the Declaration of Harry Brauner, February 24, 1950, ASRI, Fond P, Dosar 40002, Vol. 60, p. 132. On his leadership ambitions, see Silviu Brucan interview. On his condescension to Dej, see Declaration of Herbert (Belu) Zilber, February 22, 1950, ASRI, Fond P, Dosar 40002, Vol. 38, p. 136; Transcript of a Declaration Given by Nicolae Betea before the R.C.P. Commission, October 23, 1967, ASRI, Fond P, Dosar 40002, Vol. 202, p. 237.

26. Silviu Brucan interview; "Suspicious and vengeful by nature, Dej could not stand anyone contesting his imagined merits and his abilities as a leader, or anyone having intellectual prestige if they were not under his shadow" (Herbert [Belu]

Zilber, *Actor în procesul Pătrăşcanu, Prima versiune a memoriilor lui Belu Zilber* [Actor in the Patraşcanu Trial: The First Version of Belu Zilber's Memoirs], edited by G. Brătescu [Bucharest, 1997], p. 195). Dej reportedly clashed for this reason at Târgu-Jiu with a number of intellectuals, including Grigore Preoteasa, Atanase Joja, and Ilie Cristea (Gheorghe Brătescu interview).

27. Corneliu Bogdan interview, August 8, 1989. Also see the statement of Gheorge Pintilie to the R.C.P. Commission, October 19, 1967, ASRI, Fond P, Dosar 40002, Vol. 203, p. 268.

28. Declaration of Lucreţiu Patraşcanu, undated [1949], ASRI, Fond P, Dosar 40002, Vol. 1, p. 23.

29. Declaration of Lucreţiu Patraşcanu, November 12, 1949, ASRI, Fond P, Dosar 40002, Vol. 1, p. 90.

30. Declaration of Lucreţiu Patraşcanu, undated, ASRI, Fond P, Dosar 40002, Vol. 1, pp. 23–24; Declaration of Elena Patraşcanu, March 9, 1950, ASRI, Fond P, Dosar 40002, Vol. 87, p. 50.

31. For Patraşcanu's opinion of Dej, Maurer, and Bodnăraş, see the Declaration of Herbert Zilber, February 23, 1950, ASRI, Fond P, Dosar 40002, Vol. 38, p. 130; Declaration of Herbert Zilber, November 13, 1950, ASRI, Fond P, Dosar 40002, Vol. 38, p.323. For his views of Pauker and Luca, see the Transcript of the Declaration Given by Elena Patraşcanu before the R.C.P. Commission, October 25, 1967, ASRI, Fond P, Dosar 40002, Vol. 202, p. 207.

32. Ibid., pp. 206–207.

33. Declaration of Herbert Zilber, February 23, 1950, ASRI, Fond P, Dosar 40002, Vol. 38, p. 133; Zilber, *Actor în procesul Pătrăşcanu,* pp. 197–198.

34. Ibid., p. 198.

35. Lucreţiu Patraşcanu, "No Compromise on the Question of Transylvania," *Scânteia,* June 14, 1946, pp. 1, 3.

36. From the documents of the R.C.P. Commission, *Magazin istoric,* November 1991, p. 41.

37. "The Report of the Party Commission Established to Clarify the Situation of Lucreţiu Patraşcanu," *Cuvîntul,* no. 42 (142), October 20–26, 1992, p. 6.

38. This was indicated by a high-ranking party official in Cluj, who has requested anonymity.

39. Gheorghe Gheorghiu-Dej, "The Position of the Romanian Communist Party Towards Chauvinism and Revisionism," *Scânteia,* July 8, 1946, p. 3. Officially Gheorghiu-Dej authored the statement, but Pauker and Luca actually dictated it to *Scânteia's* editor, Sorin Toma (Sorin Toma interview).

40. Declaration of Herbert Zilber, February 22, 1950, ASRI, Fond P, Dosar 40002, Vol. 38, p. 134.

41. Zilber, *Actor în procesul Pătrăşcanu,* pp. 195–196. Lena Constante confirmed that Gheorghiu-Dej reproached Patraşcanu for the "petit-bourgeois mentality" of his wife, Elena, who, Dej asserted, pushed Patraşcanu into making mistakes (Declaration of Lena Constante, March 6, 1950, ASRI, Fond P, Dosar 40002, Vol. 64, p. 208).

42. Declaration of Herbert Zilber, February 22, 1950, ASRI, Fond P, Dosar 40002, Vol. 38, p. 134.

43. Dumitru G. Danielopol, "Romania at the Peace Conference, Paris 1946," unfinished manuscript in the archives of the Hoover Institution on War, Revolution and Peace, Stanford. The author thanks Professor Florin Constantiniu for kindly making this available.

44. Ibid.

45. ASRI, Fond P, Dosar 40002, Vol. 10, pp. 272–370; Transcript of the Declaration of Comrade Alexandru Nicolschi Before the R.C.P. Commission, October 31, 1967, Archive of the Executive Committee of the C.C. of the R.C.P., No. 264/ 18.02.1972, Vol. 21, p. 135.

46. On Patraşcanu's relationship with Pauker and Georgescu, see the Declaration of Lucreţiu Patraşcanu, November 18, 1949, ASRI, Fond P, Dosar 40002, Vol. 1, p. 113. On his return to Bucharest, see the Declaration of Herbert Zilber, February 22, 1950, ASRI, Fond P, Dosar 40002, Vol. 38, p. 134.

47. Declaration of Lucreţiu Patraşcanu, November 2, 1949, ASRI, Fond P, Dosar 40002, Vol. 1, pp. 55–56; Minutes of a Meeting of the Secretariat of the R.C.P., October 24, 1945, p. 3.

48. Transcript of the Plenary Meeting of the Central Committee of the R.C.P., October 22, 1945, Executive Archive of the C.C. of the R.W.P., no. 850/1945, pp. 3, 5–6, 13, 24; Minutes of a Meeting of the Secretariat of the R.C.P., October 24, 1945, p. 3.

49. Declaration of Dumitru Petrescu to the R.C.P. Commission, November 2, 1967, quoted in *Magazin istoric* 26, no. 3 (300) (March 1992), p. 38.

50. Declaration of Teohari Georgescu, June 9, 1956, Ana Pauker Inquiry File, Executive Archive of the Central Committee of the R.C.P., p. 5.

51. Pauker's sister-in-law, Titi Pauker, who was on intimate terms with Patraşcanu, revealed to her friend Armand Popper in late 1946 or 1947 that Pauker protected Patraşcanu at that time (Armand Popper interview, December 6, 1990. Confirmed by Ida Felix, interview); Transcript of a Meeting of the Politburo of the R.C.P., September 9, 1947, National Archives of Romania, Fond CC al PCR—Cancelarie, Dosar 27/1947, p. 41; Andrei Şerbulescu (Belu Zilber), *Monarhia de drept dialectic* (Bucharest, 1991), pp. 69–70.

52. Interrogation of Lucreţiu Patraşcanu, November 1, 1952, ASRI, Fond P, Dosar 40002, Vol. 2, p. 441.

53. Gheorghe Brătescu interview.

54. Charlotte Gruia interview. Confirming that the Soviets ordered Patraşcanu's arrest is Eugen Szabo of the Interior Ministry, interview, July 24, 1991.

55. Report of the Party Commission Established to Clarify the Situation of Lucreţiu Patraşcanu, Submitted to the Party Leadership on June 29, 1968, p. 3; Speech of Teohari Georgescu at the First R.W.P. Congress, February 21–23, 1948, *România liberă*, February 25, 1948, pp. 3–4.

56. The Resolution of the Second Plenary of the R.W.P., June 10–11, 1948, *Scânteia*, June 21, 1948, pp. 1, 3.

57. On Patraşcanu's refusal to offer a self-criticism, see "The Report of the Party Commission Established to Clarify the Situation of Lucreţiu Patraşcanu," *Cuvîntul*, no. 43 (143), October 20–26, 1992, p. 6. On Pauker's intimations, see *Cuvânt de încheiere de Congresul Partidului Muncitoresc Român din 21–23 februarie 1948* [Ana Pauker's Concluding Speech at the First R.W.P. Congress, February 23, 1948], Editura R.W.P. (Bucharest, 1948), pp. 7–8.

58. Notes of Iosif Chişinevschi of the Politburo Meeting of February 19, 1948, published by Tatiana Pokivailova, "Tragica greşeală a lui Lucreţiu Patraşcanu" [The Tragic Mistake of Lucreţiu Patraşcanu], *Magazin istoric* 30, no. 9 (354), p. 44; Declaration of Lucreţiu Patraşcanu, March 20, 1948, ASRI, Fond P, Dosar 40002, Vol. 10, p. 428.

59. Ana Toma, Sorin Toma, Charlotte Gruia, Elena Tudorache, Cristina Boico, Iosif Breban, and Alexandru Şiperco interviews.

60. Ana Toma interview.

61. Elena Tudorache interview.

62. Report of the Party Commission Established to Clarify the Situation of Lucrețiu Patrașcanu, Submitted to the Party Leadership on June 29, 1968, Executive Archive of the Central Committee of the R.C.P., p. 3.

63. Transcript of the Declaration Given by Teohari Georgescu to the R.C.P. Commission, October 23, 1967, ASRI, Fond P, Dosar 40002, Vol. 203, pp. 297, 308.

64. Declaration of Lucrețiu Patrașcanu, undated, ASRI, Fond P, Dosar 40002, Vol. 1, p. 25.

65. Transcript of the Declaration Given by Teohari Georgescu to the R.C.P. Commission, October 23, 1967, ASRI, Fond P, Dosar 40002, Vol. 203, p. 298.

66. Eduard Mezincescu, "Detenție fără mandat de arestare" [Detention without an Arrest Warrant], Magazin istoric 26, no. 6 (303) (June 1992), p. 57.

67. Interrogation of Lucretiu Patrașcanu, November 1, 1952, ASRI, Fond P, Dosar 40002, Vol. 2, p. 439.

68. Transcript of the Declaration Given by Teohari Georgescu to the R.C.P. Commission, October 23, 1967, ASRI, Fond P, Dosar 40002, Vol. 203, p. 298.

69. Interrogation of Lucrețiu Patrașcanu, November 1, 1952, ASRI, Fond P, Dosar 40002, Vol. 2, pp. 439–440; Memorandum of Ioan Șoltuțiu, November 7, 1952, ASRI, Fond P, Dosar 40002, Vol. 16, p. 4.

70. Declaration of Lucretiu Patrașcanu, undated, ASRI, Fond P, Dosar 40002, Vol. 1, p. 26.

71. For the text of the warrant, see Magazin istoric 25, no. 7 (292) (July 1991), p. 62.

72. Interrogation of Lucretiu Patrașcanu, November 1, 1952, ASRI, Fond P, Dosar 40002, Vol. 2, p. 440.

73. Eduard Mezincescu, "Procedural Gap or . . . Socialist Legality?" Magazin istoric 26, no. 7 (304) (July 1992), p. 33.

74. Memorandum of Ioan Șoltuțiu, November 7, 1952, ASRI, Fond P, Dosar 40002, Vol. 16, p. 3.

75. Eduard Mezincescu, "Detention without an Arrest Warrant," p. 58; Transcript of a Discussion with Alexandru Drăghici, April 20, 1968, Executive Archive of the Central Committee of the R.C.P., No. 264/18.02.1972, Vol. 7, p. 8.

76. Interrogation of Lucretiu Patrașcanu, November 1, 1952, ASRI, Fond P, Dosar 40002, Vol. 2, p. 440.

77. Report of the Party Commission Established to Clarify the Situation of Lucrețiu Patrașcanu, Submitted to the Party Leadership on June 29, 1968, Executive Archive of the Central Committee of the R.C.P., pp. 3–4; Report Regarding the Findings of Investigations Made in the Patrașcanu Case During the Period of October 1949–May 1949, ASRI, Fond P, Dosar 40002, Vol. 12, p. 364; Statement of Former S.S.I. Director General Sergei Nicolau to the R.C.P. Commission (March 9, 1967); quoted in Magazin istoric 25, no. 12 (297) (December 1991), p. 71.

78. George Hodos, Show Trials (New York, 1987), p. 63.

79. Tatiana A. Pokivailova, "Tragica greșeală a lui Lucrețiu Patrașcanu," p. 44.

80. Gheorghe Gheorghiu-Dej, "Partidul Comunist din Iugoslavia în mâinile unor asasini și spioni" [The Communist Party in Yugoslavia in the Hands of Assassins and Spies], in Gh. Gheorghiu-Dej, Articole și Cuvântări, p. 402. For English excerpts of the speech, see Fernando Claudin, The Communist Movement: From Comintern to Cominform (Middlesex, England, 1975), p. 524.

81. Khrushchev Remembers: The Glasnost Tapes, translated and edited by Jerrold L. Schecter with Vyacheslav V. Luchkov (Boston, 1990), p. 103.

82. "Decision of the Central Committee of the R.C.P. Concerning the Rehabilitation of Some Party Activists," reprinted in *Scânteia,* April 26, 1968, p. 1.

83. Eugen Szabo interview.

84. *Scânteia,* September 20, 1949, p. 6. See *Scânteia's* lead articles "The Failure of the Imperialist Plans in the People's Democracies," September 22, 1949, pp. 1, 6, and "The Organizers of Anti-Soviet Conspiracies from Belgrade and Their Imperialist Masters Take a Powerful Blow," October 1, p. 1, as well as a *Scânteia* lead editorial on the trial, "The Camouflage of the Titoist Conspirators Has Been Shattered," October 4, 1949, p. 1. Likewise, while the September 20, 1949, *România liberă* printed the Tass transcript of the Rajk trial that included Brankov's statement on Patrașcanu (p. 7), it did not repeat the charge in its September 23 editorial, "The Trial in Budapest: A Defeat for Imperialist Conspiracies against the Popular Democratic Countries" (p. 3). Patrașcanu's name also did not appear in accounts of the trial in *Viața sindicală* or *Universal* (see reprints in the *Romanian Press Review,* September 14, 1949, pp. 5–6). A conspicuous exception, however, is Eduard Mezincescu's brief reference to Patrașcanu's alleged support of Tito in an article entitled "The Trial in Budapest: A New Blow Given to the Imperialist Camp," in the party's theoretical journal *Lupta de clasă* 5, no. 4 (October 1949), p. 98.

85. Alexandru Șiperco interview. See Brumaru's comments on Brankov in *Scânteia,* September 20, 1949, p. 6, and September 21, 1949, p. 4.

86. Both *Scânteia's* lead editorial on October 1 and Teohari Georgescu's speech reported in the September 27 *România liberă* do mention Patrașcanu, but only in terms of the June 1948 CC plenary's condemning Patrașcanu's "nationalist and bourgeois deviation," not the Rajk trial's official, updated line of "Titoist co-conspirator" (*Scânteia,* October 1, 1949, p. 1; *România liberă,* September 27, 1949, pp. 1, 5).

87. Charlotte Gruia interview.

88. *Scânteia,* December 6, 1949, p. 3.

89. Gheorghe Gheorghiu-Dej, "Lupta pentru pace, sarcină centrală a partidului nostru. Expunere în fața activului de partid" [The Struggle for Peace, a Central Task of Our Party: Explanations before the Party Activ], December 8, 1949, *Scânteia,* December 14, 1949, p. 3; reprinted in *Gh. Gheorghiu-Dej, Articole Și Cuvântări,* p. 428.

90. "Hotărîrea plenarei a V-a a Partidului Muncitoresc Român din 23–24 ianuarie, 1950, asupra sarcinilor Partidului în domeniul muncii organizatorice" [Decision of the Fifth Plenary of the Central Committee of the Romanian Workers' Party, on January 23–24, 1950, Regarding the Party Tasks in the Domain of Organizational Work], *Lupta de clasă,* February 1950, pp. 5, 14.

91. Transcript of a Meeting of the Secretariat of the R.W.P., January 17, 1950, National Archives of Romania, Fond CC al PCR—Cancelarie, Dosar 5/1950. Nor did two archival versions of the resolution mention Patrașcanu (National Archives of Romania, Fond CC al PCR—Cancelarie, Dosar 7/1950, Vol. 1, pp. 114–136; National Archives of Romania Fond CC al PCR—Cancelarie, Dosar 7/1950, Vol. 2, p. 22). Alexandru Moghioroș read the text to the plenary.

92. Probably because of the discrepant versions, *Scânteia* did not repeat the Central Committee's condemnation of Patrașcanu in its January 25, 1950, lead article on the plenary (p. 1), or in its February 2, 1950, lead editorial on the plenary (p. 1). The condemnation finally appeared, however, when *Scânteia* published the full text of the resolution on February 10, 1950 (pp. 1–2).

93. "The Report of the Party Commission Established to Clarify the Situation of Lucrețiu Patrașcanu," *Cuvîntul,* no. 36 (136), September 8–14, 1992, p. 6; *Magazin istoric,* September 1991, p. 48.

94. Report of the Party Commission Established to Clarify the Situation of Lucreţiu Patraşcanu, Submitted to the Party Leadership on June 29, 1968, Executive Archive of the Central Committee of the R.C.P., p. 53.

95. "The Report of the Party Commission Established to Clarify the Situation of Lucreţiu Patraşcanu," *Cuvîntul*, no. 37 (137), Septêmber 15–21, 1992, p. 6. Stefănescu was arrested in 1948.

96. "The Report of the Party Commission Established to Clarify the Situation of Lucreţiu Patraşcanu," *Cuvîntul*, no. 45 (145), November 10–16, 1992, p. 6; Declaration of Lucreţiu Patraşcanu, April 3, 1950, ASRI, Fond P, Dosar 40002, Vol. 1, p. 324.

97. Alexandru Sencovici interview.

98. "The Report of the Party Commission Established to Clarify the Situation of Lucreţiu Patraşcanu" *Cuvîntul*, September 1–7, 1992, p. 8.

99. Interrogation of Lucreţiu Patraşcanu, November 4, 1952, ASRI, Fond P, Dosar 40002, Vol. 16, p. 30; Statement of Petre Gonciariuc to the R.C.P. Commission (July 3, 1967), *Magazin istoric* 26, no. 1 (298) (January 1992), p. 87; Statement of Former S.S.I. Director General Sergei Nicolau to the R.C.P. Commission, in *Magazin istoric*, p. 71; Eduard Mezincescu, "Procedural Gap or . . . Socialist Legality?" pp. 35–36.

100. Interrogation of Lucreţiu Patraşcanu, November 4, 1952, ASRI, Fond P, Dosar 40002, Vol. 16, p. 30; Statement of Petre Gonciariuc to the R.C.P. Commission, in *Magazin istoric*, p. 87; "Report Regarding the Findings of Investigations Made in the Patraşcanu Case During the Period of October 1949–May 1950," ASRI, Fond P, Dosar 40002, Vol. 12, p. 365; "General Synthesis of the 'Patraşcanu' Problem," April 1952, ASRI, Fond P, Dosar 40002, Vol. 12, p. 3.

101. Statement of Gheorghe Pintilie to the R.C.P. Commission, October 19, 1967, ASRI, Fond P, Dosar 40002, Vol. 203, p. 264; "Report Regarding the Findings of Investigations Made in the Patraşcanu Case During the Period of October 1949–May 1950," ASRI, Fond P, Dosar 40002, Vol. 12, p. 365.

102. Those articles referring to Patraşcanu as an imperialist agent include Tudor Olaru, "Five Years of Struggle and Victory under the Leadership of the Party," *Scânteia*, February 24, 1950, p. 5; Tudor Olaru, "Aspects of the Struggle for Thwarting the Imperialist Conspiracy against Romania," *Scânteia*, March 3, 1950, p. 3; and A. Grigorescu, "We Must Increase and Organize Revolutionary Vigilance of the Masses," *Scânteia*, April 12, 1950, p. 3. In addition, *România liberă* published Eduard Mezincescu's speech condemning the "servants of imperialism, and the agents and spies of the type like Tito, Rajk, Traicho Costov, and Patraşcanu" (March 1, 1950, p. 1), as well as Miron Constantinescu's address declaring, "As early as 1946–47, our Party publicly unmasked and stigmatized the nationalist conspiracies attempted by Patraşcanu and his accomplices in the service of Anglo-American imperialism and the Romanian bourgeoisie and landowners" (April 4, 1950, p. 2). Compare these with *Scânteia's* articles beginning in late April, none of which mention either Patraşcanu or the accusation against him. For example, see Tudor Olaru, "Under the Cover of Information Officers," April 29, 1950, p. 2; Grigore Preoteasa, "A Day Proclaimed for National Independence," May 9, 1950, p. 3; Silviu Brucan, "Fieldmarshal Tito: An Active Agent of 'Total Diplomacy,'" June 7, 1950, p. 3; or the unsigned "Fascist Warmongers in Belgrade Show Their True Colors," May 25, 1950, p. 3.

103. The text of the resolution was published in *România liberă,* July 21, 1950, p. 3.

104. Mihai Burcă interview, July 5, 1991; Tudor Manea, Alexandru Şiperco, Alexandru Sencovici, Radu Mănescu, and Sorin Toma interviews.

105. The SSI's director general, Sergei Nicolau, confirmed that Dej was its superior party connection (Statement of Sergei Nicolau, in *Magazin istoric*, p. 71). Also confirming this are the Remarks of Emil Bodnăraş, Transcript of a Meeting of the Politburo of the R.W.P., March 12–14, 1961, Executive Archive of the Central Committee of the R.C.P., p. 165. Further corroboration was provided by Gheorghe Gaston Marin, Sergiu Sevcenko, Jean Coler, Radu Mănescu, Mircea Oprişan, Alexandru Şiperco, Eduard Mezincescu, Cristina Boico, Tudor Manea, Mihai Burcă, Tudor Olaru, and Sorin Toma (interviews).

106. Statement of Gheorghe Pintilie to the R.C.P. Commission, October 19, 1967, ASRI, Fond P, Dosar 40002, Vol. 203, pp. 264–265.

107. Cristina Boico interview.

108. Victor Bîrlădeanu interview, December 8, 1990.

109. Ana Toma interview.

110. "The Report of the Party Commission Established to Clarify the Situation of Lucreţiu Patraşcanu," *Cuvîntul*, September 8–14, 1992, p. 6.

111. "The Report of the Party Commission Established to Clarify the Situation of Lucreţiu Patraşcanu," *Cuvîntul*, September 8–14, 1992, p. 6, and September 15–21, 1992, p. 6; Gheorghe Gheorghiu-Dej, "Thirty Years of Struggle of the Party under the Banner of Lenin and Stalin," Report Presented on May 8, 1951, to a Gathering Honoring the 30th Anniversary of the R.C.P., *Scânteia*, May 11, 1951, p. 1; reprinted in *Gh. Gheorghiu-Dej, Articles and Speeches*, p. 538.

112. Declaration of Victor Vînătoru, April 19, 1968, ASRI, Fond P, Dosar 40002, Vol. 203, p. 44; "The Report of the Party Commission Established to Clarify the Situation of Lucreţiu Patraşcanu," *Cuvîntul*, September 8–14, 1992, p. 6, and September 15–21, 1992, p. 6; "General Synthesis of the 'Patraşcanu' Problem," April 1952, ASRI, Fond P, Dosar 40002, Vol. 12, p. 4; Transcript of the Declaration Given by Teohari Georgescu to the R.C.P. Commission, October 23, 1967, ASRI, Fond P, Dosar 40002, Vol. 203, p. 300; Declaration of Teohari Georgescu, Transcript of a Discussion with Alexandru Drăghici, April 20, 1968, Executive Archive of the Central Committee of the R.C.P., No. 264/18.02.1972, Vol. 7, p. 13; Declaration of Mişu Dulgheru, April 24, 1967, ASRI, Fond P, Dosar 40002, Vol. 203, p. 63; Declaration of Nicolae Dumitrescu, September 15, 1967, ASRI, Fond P, Dosar 40002, Vol. 203, p. 182.

113. On the prohibition of physical force, see the Transcript of the Declaration Given by Teohari Georgescu to the R.C.P. Commission, October 23, 1967, ASRI, Fond P, Dosar 40002, Vol. 203, pp. 299, 303. On Sakharovskii, see the Declaration of Mişu Dulgheru, April 27, 1967, ASRI, Fond P, Dosar 40002, Vol. 203, p. 71; Declaration of Nicolae Dumitrescu, September 15, 1967, ASRI, Fond P, Dosar 40002, Vol. 203, pp. 182–183.

114. Declaration of Gheorghe Filipescu, July 7, 1967, ASRI, Fond P, Dosar 40002, Vol. 203, p. 92.

115. Report of the Party Commission Established to Clarify the Situation of Lucreţiu Patraşcanu, Submitted to the Party Leadership on June 29, 1968, Executive Archive of the Central Committee of the R.C.P., p. 50; Transcript of the Declaration Given by Teohari Georgescu to the R.C.P. Commission, October 23, 1967, ASRI, Fond P, Dosar 40002, Vol. 203, p. 300.

116. Report of the Party Commission Established to Clarify the Situation of Lucreţiu Patraşcanu, Submitted to the Party Leadership on June 29, 1968, Executive Archive of the Central Committee of the R.C.P., p. 53; Interrogation of Mişu Dulgheru, May 12, 1954, ASRI, Fond P, Dosar 40007, Vol. 2, p. 413.

117. Cora Barbu interview, December 8, 1990; Radu Mănescu interview. Also

see the statement of Gheorghe Pintilie to the R.C.P. Commission, October 19, 1967, ASRI, Fond P, Dosar 40002, Vol. 203, p. 270.

118. "The Report of the Party Commission Established to Clarify the Situation of Lucreţiu Patraşcanu," *Cuvîntul*, September 15–21, 1992, p. 6.

119. Report Regarding Emil Calmanovici, ASRI, Fond P, Dosar 40007, Vol. 5, p. 145.

120. Interrogation of Mişu Dulgheru, May 6, 1953, ASRI, Fond P, Dosar 40007, Vol. 2, p. 209.

121. Ana Toma interview. Cora Barbu confirms Pauker's approval of Calmanovici (interview).

122. Costea left two suicide notes, one to the party and one to his wife. To his wife he wrote that he feared he would be arrested as well, given his high position in the party apparat. Expecting that his wife's arrest would soon follow, as it often did in Stalinist purges, he feared that his children would be left as orphans and sent to a children's home. Thus he decided to preempt her arrest by killing himself (Cora Barbu interview).

123. Charlotte Gruia confirmed the general reaction, reporting that immediately after Costea's suicide a distraught Alexandru Moghioroş summoned her and asked her about the circumstances leading to the death (Charlotte Gruia interview).

124. On Georgescu's friendship with Costea, see Jean Coler interview.

125. Cora Barbu interview.

126. Declaration of Mişu Dulgheru, April 27, 1967, ASRI, Fond P, Dosar 40002, Vol. 203, p. 71.

127. Declaration of Teohari Georgescu, Transcript of a Discussion with Alexandru Drăghici, April 20, 1968, Executive Archive of the Central Committee of the R.C.P., No. 264/18.02.1972, Vol. 7, pp. 9, 13. This is confirmed by Lt. Col. Ioan Şoltuţiu, who subsequently took over the Patraşcanu case. According to his testimony, the Interior Ministry inquiry (under Georgescu) concluded that Patraşcanu was guilty only of mistakes vis-à-vis the party line, but not of criminal acts (Declaration of Lt. Col. Ioan Şoltuţiu to the R.C.P. Commission, *Magazin istoric*, December 1991, p. 74); also see "The Report of the Party Commission Established to Clarify the Situation of Lucreţiu Patraşcanu," *Cuvîntul*, September 15–21, 1992, p. 6.

128. Zilber, *Monarhia de drept dialectic*, pp. 74–75. Similarly, on July 31, 1951, an Interior Ministry general asked Lena Constante, arrested in January 1950, whether an earlier confession she made in desperation was actually true and did not react negatively when she proceeded to retract it. It was her impression that the inquiry had reached an impasse after failing to prove the charges against Patraşcanu. Moreover, the interrogations of Emil Calmanovici suddenly stopped also at the end of July, as he reported in a statement made in prison to party officials: "After two months of investigation," he wrote, "I was held without anyone saying a word to me" (Lena Constante, *The Silent Escape, Three Thousand Days in Romanian Prisons* [Berkeley and Los Angeles, 1995], pp. 82, 88; "The Report of the Party Commission Established to Clarify the Situation of Lucreţiu Patraşcanu," *Cuvîntul*, September 15–21, 1992, p. 6).

129. Declaration of Nicolae Dumitrescu, September 15, 1967, ASRI, Fond P, Dosar 40002, Vol. 203, pp. 185–186.

130. Gheorghe Gheorghiu-Dej, "The People's Revolutionary Vigilance," *Pravda*, no. 247 (12.084), September 4, 1951; reprinted in *Scânteia*, September 6, 1951, p. 2.

131. See Ana Pauker, "Traitors of Socialism," initially published in *For a Lasting Peace, for a People's Democracy*, no. 13 (40), and reprinted in *Scânteia*, July 6, 1949, p. 5; the lead editorial written by Ana Pauker on the fifth anniversary of Au-

gust 23, *Scânteia,* August 21, 1949, p. 1; Ana Pauker's address to a party meeting in Giuleşti, *Scânteia,* October 6, 1949, p. 1; a speech to a women's conference on December 16, 1949, at the State Opera Hall in celebration of Stalin's seventieth birthday, *Scânteia,* December 18, 1949, pp. 1, 3; "At the 70th Anniversary of the Birth of Comrade Stalin," in *Lupta de clasa,* seria V-a, no. 6, December 1949, pp. 23–30; a speech honoring International Women's Day, *Scânteia,* March 9, 1950, pp. 1, 3; "March 6, 1945," *Izvetzia,* March 7, 1950, and reprinted in *Scânteia,* March 14, 1950, p. 3; "International Solidarity of the Supporters of Peace Is Indivisible," *For a Lasting Peace, for a People's Democracy,* no. 17(77), reprinted in *Scânteia,* no. 1725, May 4, 1950, p. 3; a speech to the Congress of Anti-Fascist Women, *Scânteia,* June 15, 1950, pp. 1, 3; Pauker's election address, *Scânteia,* December 1, 1950, pp. 3, 4; A. Pauker, "International Solidarity of the Supporters of Peace Is Indivisible," *For a Lasting Peace, for a People's Democracy,* no. 17(77), reprinted in *Scânteia,* May 4, 1950, p. 3; "Six Years Since the Liberation of Romania," *For a Lasting Peace, for a People's Democracy,* no. 33 (93), August 18, 1950; and "Ana Pauker's Address in Honor of the Thirty-Fourth Anniversary of the October Revolution," *Scânteia,* November 7, 1951, pp. 1, 3.

132. Declaration of Teohari Georgescu, May 23, 1956, Ana Pauker Inquiry File, Executive Archive of the Central Committee of the R.C.P., pp. 7–8; Declaration of Gheorghe Pintilie, June 10, 1956, Ana Pauker Inquiry File, Executive Archive of the Central Committee of the R.C.P., p. 4.

133. Report of the Party Commission Established to Clarify the Situation of Lucreţu Patraşcanu, Submitted to the Party Leadership on June 29, 1968, Executive Archive of the Central Committee of the R.C.P., pp. 43–44.

134. Remarks of R.C.P. Commission Chief Gheorghe Stoica, Transcript of the Discussion of Comrade Dumitru Petrescu with the R.C.P. Commission, November 2, 1967, ASRI, Fond P, Dosar 40002, Vol. 203, p. 324. Stoica, however, omitted this detail from his commission's report on the Patraşcanu case.

135. Sorin Toma, Elena Tudorache, Simion Bughici, and Leonte Răutu interviews.

136. Declaration of Miron Constantinescu, Transcript of the Plenary of the Central Committee of the R.W.P., May 27–29, 1952, National Archives of Romania, Fond CC al PCR—Cancelarie, Dosar 41/1952, pp. 126–127.

137. Transcript of the Declaration Given by Ioan Şoltuţiu Before the R.C.P. Commission, October 20, 1967, ASRI, Fond P, Dosar 40002, Vol. 203, p. 152. The memo, written by Ioan Şoltuţiu on November 7, 1952, is found in the ASRI Archive, Fond P, Dosar 40002, Vol. 16, pp. 2–16. Also see Robert Levy, "From the Secret Archives: New Revelations on the Purge of Lucreţiu Patraşcanu," *Sfera politicii,* no. 29–30 (July–August 1995), pp. 39–45.

138. Mihai Burcă interview.

139. "The Report of the Party Commission Established to Clarify the Situation of Lucreţiu Patraşcanu," *Cuvîntul,* September 15–21, 1992, p. 6; Statement of Securitate Major Victor Vînatoru to the R.C.P. Commission (May 12, 1967), *Magazin istoric,* December 1991, p. 72.

140. Vladimir Zaharescu interview, July 10 1989; Mihai Burcă interview.

141. Declaration of Mişu Dulgheru, April 24, 1967, ASRI, Fond P, Dosar 40002, Vol. 203, pp. 67, 71; "Report Regarding the Findings of the Inquiry [of] Mişu Dulgheru . . . ," August 16, 1954, ASRI, Fond P, Dosar 40007, Vol. 12, pp. 12–16; Charlotte Gruia interview.

142. "The Report of the Party Commission Established to Clarify the Situation of Lucreţiu Patraşcanu," *Cuvîntul,* September 1–7, 1992, p. 8.

143. Statement of Securitate Major Victor Vønatoru, *Magazin istoric,* p. 72.

144. "The Report of the Party Commission Established to Clarify the Situation of Lucreţiu Patraşcanu," *Cuvîntul,* September 8–14, 1992, p. 6.

145. Lena Constante, *The Silent Escape,* pp. 95–96.

146. Statement of Securitate Lt. Colonel Mircea Anghel to the R.C.P. Commission, April 28, 1967, in *Magazin istoric,* December 1991, p. 73. Anghel was removed from the investigation in January 1953 at his own request.

147. "The Report of the Party Commission Established to Clarify the Situation of Lucreţiu Patraşcanu," *Cuvîntul,* September 15–21, 1992, p. 6.

148. Statement of Securitate Lt. Colonel Mircea Anghel, p. 73.

149. Zilber, *Monarhia de drept dialectic,* pp. 77–79, 182.

150. Ibid., p. 84.

151. "Decision of the Central Committee of the R.C.P. Concerning the Rehabilitation of Some Party Activists," p. 1.

152. Mihai Burcă interview.

153. Statement of the prosecutor Grigore Râpeanu to the R.C.P. Commission (December 25, 1967), *Magazin istoric,* January 1992, p. 88; Ştefan Popescu, whose source was Gogu Popescu, a high-ranking officer in the Interior Ministry, confirms this (Ştefan Popescu interview, July 22, 1991); Zilber, *Monarhia de drept dialectic,* p. 94. Gheorghiu-Dej's preoccupation with the Patraşcanu case was confirmed by his chief of staff, Paul Svetcu, in discussions with Alexandru Şiperco (Şiperco interview).

154. See John A. Armstrong, *The Politics of Totalitarianism* (New York, 1961), pp. 226–237; Francios Fejtö, *History of the People's Democracies* (New York, 1971), pp. 2–10; Roy A. Medvedev, *Let History Judge: The Origins and Consequences of Stalinism* (New York, 1971), pp. 476–477; George Hodos, *Show Trials,* pp. 113–164.

155. See chapter 8.

156. Apostol asserted recently that Soviet agent Gheorghe Pintilie had Patraşcanu executed with the knowledge of neither Drăghici nor Gheorghiu-Dej after Dej let it be known that he intended to commute Patraşcanu's death sentence to life imprisonment and later to cut the sentence further (Interview with Gheorghe Apostol, *Totuşi iubirea* 2, no. 18 [35] [May 1991], p. 9). Alexandru Şiperco, Mihai Florescu, and Professor Nicolae Marcu also insist that the Soviets continued to pressure for Patraşcanu's trial after Stalin's death (Alexander Şiperco interview; Mihai Florescu interview, July 12, 1991; Nicolae Marcu interview, July 10, 1991).

157. In stark contrast to the statements of the investigators in the case to the R.C.P. Commission, which all emphasized the Soviet advisers' dominance during the investigation, the declarations of the prosecutor Grigore Râpeanu and the judge Ilie Moisescu, who began working on the case in November or December 1953, mention no involvement of Soviet advisers in preparing the trial (Statement of Ilie Moisescu to the R.C.P. Commission [April 24, 1967], *Magazin istoric,* January 1992, pp. 89–90; statement of Grigore Râpeanu, in *Magazin istoric,* p. 88).

158. Simion Bughici, Eduard Mezincescu, Henri Wald, and Eugen Szabo interviews. Also confirmed by Charlotte Gruia, Gheorghe Gaston Marin, Sorin Toma, Mircea Oprişan, Ilie Zaharia, Radu Mănescu, Corneliu Bogdan, Elena Tudorache, Cristina Boico, Ştefan Popescu, Jean Coler, Silviu Brucan, and Mihai Alexandru (interviews).

159. Constantinescu revealed this at the Central Committee session in 1968 that presented the report on Patraşcanu's prosecution (Tudor Olaru interview). Moreover, Constantinescu personally related this to Ilie Zaharia, telling him that he brought the file of both Patraşcanu and Luca on a trip to Moscow to coordinate economic strategy with the Soviets (Ilie Zaharia interview).

160. Patraşcanu was put on trial at a time when the Soviets were promoting national Communists in the leadership of the bloc countries, particularly those, like himself, who were untainted by Stalinism (Vladimir Tismaneanu, "Ceauşescu's Socialism," p. 57; Vladimir Tismaneanu, "Ambiguity of Romanian Communism," p. 74 n. 11; Michael Shafir, Romania, Politics, Economics and Society, p. 43; Report of the Party Commission Established to Clarify the Situation of Lucreţiu Patraşcanu, Submitted to the Party Leadership on June 29, 1968, Executive Archive of the Central Committee of the R.C.P., p. 55).

161. "The Report of the Party Commission Established to Clarify the Situation of Lucreţiu Patraşcanu," Cuvîntul, September 1–7, 1992, p. 9.

162. On Patraşcanu's defiance, see Mircea Oprişan and Eduard Mezincescu interviews. On the telephone lines, see Charlotte Gruia, Sorin Toma, and Alexandru Şiperco interviews.

163. "The Report of the Party Commission Established to Clarify the Situation of Lucreţiu Patraşcanu," Cuvîntul, September 8–14, 1992, p. 6; Victor Frunza, Istoria stalinismului, p. 409. This is confirmed by Vera Călin, interview, September 18, 1990.

164. Ion Mihai Pacepa, Moştenirea kremlinului [The Kremlin's Legacy] (Bucharest, 1993), p. 125. Pacepa's account includes considerable errors and falsehoods. Consequently, it is cited only in those instances when he provides direct, first-hand testimony (Pacepa, pp. 83, 86–87, 95–96); Tatiana and Gheorghe Brătescu interview.

165. "The Report of the Party Commission Established to Clarify the Situation of Lucreţiu Patraşcanu," Cuvîntul, September 1–7, 1992, p. 9.

166. Charlotte Gruia interview. This was confirmed by Alexandru Sencovici and Mircea Oprişan (interviews).

167. Transcript of the Declaration Given by Comrade Miron Constantinescu Before the R.C.P. Commission, March 13, 1968, Executive Archive of the Central Committee of the R.C.P., No. 264/18.02.1972, Vol. 21, pp. 151–152.

168. "The Report of the Party Commission Established to Clarify the Situation of Lucreţiu Patraşcanu," Cuvîntul, September 15–21, 1992, p. 6.

169. Report of the Party Commission Established to Clarify the Situation of Lucreţiu Patraşcanu, Submitted to the Party Leadership on June 29, 1968, Executive Archive of the Central Committee of the R.C.P., p. 18.

170. Ionescu, Communism in Romania, pp. 155–156.

171. Report of the Party Commission Established to Clarify the Situation of Lucreţiu Patraşcanu, Submitted to the Party Leadership on June 29, 1968, Executive Archive of the Central Committee of the R.C.P., pp. 42–43; Cora Barbu interview. Afterward his wife was given a shirt on which he had written, with his own blood, "I am innocent" (Radu Mănescu interview).

172. Transcript of the Declaration Given by Teohari Georgescu to the R.C.P. Commission, October 23, 1967, ASRI, Fond P, Dosar 40002, Vol. 203, p. 299; Charlotte Gruia interview.

173. Gheorghe Gaston Marin interview. That Rákosi twisted Dej's arm on this matter was confirmed by Teohari Georgescu (Transcript of the Declaration Given by Teohari Georgescu to the R.C.P. Commission, October 23, 1967, ASRI, Fond P, Dosar 40002, Vol. 203, p. 299). It appears, however, that at the time of the Rajk trial only a section of the veterans of the International Brigades in Spain was threatened—those who had spent the years of World War II in Western Europe, primarily France. Tito had recruited Yugoslav Spaniards quite heavily in the French internment camps after the Republican collapse to serve as officers in his partisan army and thus was

not connected to those veterans who went directly to Moscow from Spain and spent the war years in the USSR. In fact, the latter group, under Ernö Gero, was actually favored in Hungary (John A. Armstrong, *The Politics of Totalitarianism,* pp. 216–217). But it seems that eventually all the Spanish veterans became suspect. Writes the Czech Spanish veteran Artur London of his imprisonment in 1951, "It became more and more obvious that the interrogations were being aimed against the former volunteers in the International Brigades, and that there was a basic prejudice against all the veterans, who were considered, *without exception,* as spies and dangerous elements. . . . *This attitude covered all the members of the Brigades; no one was spared"* (Artur London, *The Confession* [New York, 1970], pp. 82–83; emphasis added).

174. On Vasilichi, see the Transcript of a Meeting of the Politburo of the R.W.P., May 29, 1952, National Archives of Romania, Fond CC al PCR—Cancelarie, Dosar 44/1952, p. 5; Transcript of the Declaration Given by Teohari Georgescu to the R.C.P. Commission, October 23, 1967, ASRI, Fond P, Dosar 40002, Vol. 203, p. 299. On the list in general, see Mihai Burcă interview.

175. Sorin Toma interview.

176. Spanish Civil War veterans were repressed in Bulgaria despite the fact that they were not mentioned in the Kostov trial of December 1949 (see Nissan Oren, *Revolution Administered, Agrarianism and Communism in Bulgaria* [Baltimore, 1973], p. 58; Nissan Oren, *Bulgarian Communism: The Road to Power* [New York, 1971], pp. 133–38). On their fate in Czechoslovakia see Karel Kaplan, *Report on the Murder of the General Secretary* (Columbus, Ohio, 1990), pp. 38–73. The French Resistance veterans were targeted as part of a larger group known as "Westerners," who were all those who spent the war years in the West. According to Michael Checinski, the secret police of every country in the Soviet sphere considered all Spaniards and Westerners as potential spies (Michael Checinski, *Poland: Communism, Nationalism, Anti-Semitism,* p. 78).

177. Bierut made his accusation at a Central Committee plenum November 11–13, 1949 (cited by Ygael Gluckstein, *Stalin's Satellites in Europe* [London, 1952], p. 283).

178. Checinski, *Poland: Communism, Nationalism, Anti-Semitism,* p. 78. Also see Kaplan, *Report on the Murder of the General Secretary,* p. 49.

179. Victor Vezendean, then deputy director of the Foreign Section of the Central Committee, read secret files documenting the meeting (Vezendean interview).

180. Mihai Burcă interview.

181. Ranghet's assistants in the commission were Gheorghe Pintilie and Ghizela Vass (Jean Coler, Charlotte Gruia, Mihai Burcă, Wilhelm Einhorn, Mihai Florescu, Cristina Boico, Hermina Tismăneanu, and Gheorghe Gaston Marin interviews).

182. Cristina Boico interview; according to Wilhelm Einhorn, the commission was "working very hard" to establish the veterans' guilt (Einhorn interview).

183. Transcript of a Meeting of the Politburo of the R.W.P., November 29, 1961, pp. 22–23. Pauker confirmed this (Transcript of an Interrogation of Ana Pauker by a Party Commission of the R.W.P., June 18, 1956, Ana Pauker Inquiry File, Executive Archive of the Central Committee of the R.C.P., pp. 26–27).

184. Declaration of Gheorghe Pintilie, June 10, 1956, Ana Pauker Inquiry File, Executive Archive of the Central Committee of the R.C.P., p. 12; Declaration of Gheorghe Gheorghiu-Dej, Transcript of a Meeting of the Politburo of the R.W.P., November 29, 1961, Executive Archive of the Central Committee of the R.C.P., p. 23.

185. Roman was placed in the inconsequential post of vice-chairman (under Ion Gheorghe Maurer) of the Association for the Dissemination of Science and Culture, which he held until the spring of the following year (Ion Gheorghe Maurer,

Sorin Toma, and Tudor Olaru interviews). (Roman later confided to Vladimir Za-harescu that he considered his demotion an act of the party leadership's protection, effectively hiding him from the Soviets by placing him in his new post. Had Roman not been removed as chief of staff, fellow Spanish veteran Jean Coler suggested, "the Russians would have taken him to *their* jails" [Vladimir Zaharescu and Jean Coler interviews].)

186. Declaration of Gheorghe Vasilichi, Transcript of the Plenary of the Central Committee of the R.W.P., March 25, 1956, pp. 104, 107.

187. For example, an unsigned editorial in *Scânteia* of September 29, 1949, states, "The Budapest trial . . . proved the nature of [Rajk's espionage] ties, and showed that they date from the time of World War II." But it never once mentions the Spaniards' being recruited in French internment camps by Rajk or Tito, as was emphasized at the trial (reprinted in the *Romanian Press Review*, September 29, 1949, p. 6).

188. Kaplan, *Report on the Murder of the General Secretary*, p. 74.

189. See, for example, Ana Pauker's speech at a party meeting in Giuleşti on October 6, 1949, Iosif Chişinevschi's speech at the Bucharest Street-Car Co. on November 2, and Gheorghiu-Dej's address at the Aro Theatre on November 6 (*Scânteia*, October 6, 1949; *Romanian Press Review*, November 3, 1949, p. 3; *Scânteia*, November 7, 1949).

190. Dolores Ibarruri, "Tito and His Bandits: Treacherous Enemies of the Spanish People," *For a Lasting Peace, for a People's Democracy*, no. 5 (65), reprinted in *Scânteia*, February 5, 1950, p. 3. *Scânteia* was mandated by the Soviets to automatically reprint all articles on Tito (as well as all editorials) published in *For a Lasting Peace, for a People's Democracy*, the official journal of the Cominform (Sorin Toma interview).

191. Gottwald's actual speech is quoted in Artur London, *The Confession*, p. 90; the censored reprint is in *Scânteia*, February 27, 1951, p. 4.

192. Persistent Soviet pressure on the Romanian leadership is confirmed by Mihai Florescu, Gheorghe Gaston Marin, and Alexandru Şiperco (interviews).

193. Transcript of the Declaration Given by Teohari Georgescu to the R.C.P. Commission, October 23, 1967, ASRI, Fond P, Dosar 40002, Vol. 203, p. 299. Hungarian pressure on the Czech party is described in detail by Karel Kaplan, *Report on the Murder of the General Secretary*, pp. 42–52. Also see George Hodos, *Show Trials*, pp. 77–78.

194. Wilhelm Einhorn interview.

195. Victor Vezendean interview.

196. *Romanian Press Review*, July 1, 1952; *Rumanian National Committee Bulletin*, no. 24, March 1, 1951, p. 1; *Rumanian National Committee Bulletin*, no. 26, May 1, 1951, p. 24; Egon Balaş, *Will to Freedom*, pp. 235–236; Egon Balaş, personal communication to the author.

197. Jean Coler, Cristina Boico, Charlotte Gruia, Eugen Szabo, and Sergiu Sevcenko interviews; Andre Micu (Adolf Klein) interview, April 14, 1994.

198. Gheorghe Gaston Marin and Mihai Florescu interviews.

199. Mircea Oprişan interview.

200. Ana Toma, Carol Neumann, Mihai Florescu, Cristina Boico, Gheorghe Gaston Marin, Elisabeta Luca, Elena Tudorache, Sergiu Sevcenko, Jean Coler, Sorin Toma, Janetta Brill, and Charlotte Gruia interviews.

201. Victor Frunza, *Istoria stalinismului*, p. 103; Vladimir Tismaneanu, "Ceauşescu's Socialism," p. 54; both Tudor Manea and Charlotte Gruia witnessed Borilă's devotion to Pauker firsthand, and Roman's allegiance to her is confirmed by Gheorghe Gaston Marin and Janetta Brill (interviews).

202. Sergiu Sevcenko interview. Barbu Zaharescu, who worked in the Red Aid until 1937, confirms that Pauker was its general secretary (Barbu Zaharescu interview, December 7, 1990). Also confirmed by Elena Tudorache, interview.

203. Carol Neumann interview.

204. Mihai Florescu interview. The Spaniards Mihai Burcă and Hermina Tismăneanu shared this view (Mihai Burcă and Hermina Tismăneanu interviews).

205. Conversation of Ana Pauker and Two Party Leaders at a Party House in Otopeni, April 8, 1953, ASRI, Fond P, Dosar 40009, Vol. 68, p. 228.

206. Declaration of Teohari Georgescu, April 26, 1956, Ana Pauker Inquiry File, Executive Archive of the Central Committee of the R.C.P., p. 14; Declaration of Teohari Georgescu, May 23, 1956, Ana Pauker Inquiry File, Executive Archive of the Central Committee of the R.C.P., pp. 10–11.

207. Alexandru Șiperco drew this conclusion from discussions with Alexandru Moghioroș, the Control Commission's Liuba Chișinevschi and Ioan Vințe, and Teohari Georgescu himself; leading Control Commission officials also revealed it to Charlotte Gruia (Alexandru Șiperco and Charlotte Gruia interviews).

208. Gheorghe Gheorghiu-Dej, "Report of the Delegation of the Rumanian Workers' Party to the 22nd Congress of the C.P.S.U. at the Plenary Meeting of the C.C. of the R.W.P., November 30–December 5, 1961," p. 16. Significantly, Dej wrote of Pauker's "too quiet in Romania" remark in the margin of a document concerning her inquiry in the fall of 1952—long before he responded to Khrushchev's de-Stalinization campaign by blaming Stalinist repression on the Pauker faction ("Plan with the Principal Points for Orientating the Ana Pauker Inquiry," Ana Pauker Inquiry File, Executive Archive of the Central Committee of the R.C.P., p. 1).

209. Transcript of an Interrogation of Ana Pauker by a Party Commission of the R.W.P., June 18, 1956, Ana Pauker Inquiry File, Executive Archive of the Central Committee of the R.C.P., pp. 34–35; Transcript of an Interrogation of Ana Pauker by a Party Commission of the R.W.P., July 6, 1956, Ana Pauker Inquiry File, Executive Archive of the Central Committee of the R.C.P., p. 35. Gheorghiu-Dej declared in *Pravda*, "The penetration of enemy agents in our party leadership is explained by the fact that during the war and immediately afterwards our vigilance was weak, and the solid familiarity of the condition of the cadres did not constitute a serious preoccupation" (Gheorghe Gheorghiu-Dej, "The People's Revolutionary Vigilance," *Pravda*, no. 247 [12.084], September 4, 1951, reprinted in *Scânteia*, September 6, 1951, p. 2).

210. Remarks of Gheorghe Gheorghiu-Dej, Transcript of a Meeting of the Politburo of the R.W.P., November 29, 1961, p. 21.

211. Alexandru Moghioroș and Ioan Vințe told Alexandru Șiperco that Pauker, who oversaw the verification of potential Titoists at the Control Commission, instructed the commission to "look higher" in its investigations. The Control Commission's Charlotte Gruia and Ida Felix confirmed this (Alexandru Șiperco, Charlotte Gruia, and Ida Felix interviews).

212. Transcript of an Interrogation of Ana Pauker by a Party Commission of the R.W.P., June 18, 1956, Ana Pauker Inquiry File, Executive Archive of the Central Committee of the R.C.P., p. 27. Rogojinschi was the chief of the Verification Section beginning in 1950 (The Decree on the Organizing of the Sections of the C.C. and the Naming of the Sections' Chiefs, undated, National Archives of Romania, Fond CC al PCR—Cancelarie, Dosar 15/1950, p. 5; personal information of Vladimir Tismaneanu).

213. Transcript of an Interrogation of Ana Pauker by a Party Commission of the R.W.P., June 18, 1956, Ana Pauker Inquiry File, Executive Archive of the Central Committee of the R.C.P., pp. 27, 34; Transcript of an Interrogation of Ana Pauker by a Party Commission of the R.W.P., July 6, 1956, Ana Pauker Inquiry File, Executive Archive of the Central Committee of the R.C.P., p. 9.

214. Gheorghe Gaston Marin interview. This was also asserted by Alexandru Şiperco, who, based on his discussions with Teohari Georgescu, Alexandru Moghioroş, and others, concluded that Pauker favored such vigorous verification in order to more effectively answer the Soviet advisers' massive pressure on her, essentially enabling her to claim, "We looked hard, but found nothing" (Alexandru Şiperco interview).

215. Declaration of Gheorghe Pintilie, June 10, 1956, Ana Pauker Inquiry File, Executive Archive of the Central Committee of the R.C.P., pp. 12–13. Gheorghiu-Dej confirmed Pauker's targeting of Rangheţ (Transcript of a Meeting of the Politburo of the R.W.P., March 12–14, 1961, Executive Archive of the Central Committee of the R.C.P., p. 164).

216. Transcript of a Meeting of the Politburo of the R.W.P., May 26, 1952, National Archives of Romania, Fond CC al PCR—Cancelarie, Dosar 40/1952, p. 103; Interrogation of Teohari Georgescu, July 4, 1955, ASRI, Fond P, Dosar 40009, Vol. 4, p. 237; Declaration of Teohari Georgescu, April 26, 1956, Ana Pauker Inquiry File, Executive Archive of the Central Committee of the R.C.P., p. 17.

217. Transcript of a Meeting of the Politburo of the R.W.P., May 29, 1952, National Archives of Romania, Fond CC al PCR—Cancelarie, Dosar 44/1952, p. 2. Hence it was Moghioroş who instructed activists working in verification committees on eliminating party members who were "class aliens" in 1951 (Transcript of a Meeting regarding the C.C.'s Instructions on the Elimination of Party Members Who Were Class Aliens, August 27, 1951, National Archives of Romania, Fond 1, Dosar 88/1951, p. 1).

218. Interrogation of Ana Pauker by a Party Commission of the R.W.P., June 12, 1953, Ana Pauker Inquiry File, Executive Archive of the Central Committee of the R.C.P., p. 64.

219. Transcript of the Plenary of the Central Committee of the R.W.P., May 27–29, 1952, National Archives of Romania, Fond CC al PCR—Cancelarie, Dosar 41/1952, p. 16.

220. Carol Neumann interview.

221. Ana Toma interview.

222. Transcript of the Declaration Given by Teohari Georgescu to the R.C.P. Commission, October 23, 1967, ASRI, Fond P, Dosar 40002, Vol. 203, pp. 301, 306. Georgescu revealed being castigated to Alexandru Şiperco (Şiperco interview); Georgescu's refusal to arbitrarily arrest Spanish and French Resistance veterans was confirmed by Mihai Florescu, Charlotte Gruia, Jean Coler, Andre Micu (Adolf Klein), and Mihai Burcă (interviews).

223. Remarks of Teohari Georgescu, Transcript of a Discussion with Alexandru Drăghici, April 20, 1968, Executive Archive of the Central Committee of the R.C.P., No. 264/18.02.1972, Vol. 7, pp. 15–16; Interrogation of Marin Jianu, April 3, 1953, ASRI, Fond P, Dosar 40009, Vol. 14, pp. 43–44; Cristina Boico interview.

224. Remarks of Teohari Georgescu, Transcript of a Discussion with Alexandru Drăghici, April 20, 1968, Executive Archive of the Central Committee of the R.C.P., No. 264/18.02.1972, Vol. 7, pp. 15–16; Remarks of Alexandru Drăghici, Transcript of a Discussion with Alexandru Drăghici, April 20, 1968, Executive Archive

of the Central Committee of the R.C.P., No. 264/18.02.1972, Vol. 7, pp. 16–17;
Interrogation of Marin Jianu, April 3, 1953, ASRI, Fond P, Dosar 40009, Vol. 14,
pp. 43–44.

225. Transcript of the Plenary of the Central Committee of the R.W.P., May 27–
29, 1952, National Archives of Romania, Fond CC al PCR—Cancelarie, Dosar
41/1952, p. 123.

226. Transcript of a Meeting of the Politburo of the R.W.P., May 26, 1952,
National Archives of Romania, Fond CC al PCR—Cancelarie, Dosar 40/1952,
p. 36.

227. Declaration of Petre Borilă, Transcript of the Plenary of the Central Committee of the R.W.P., May 27–29, 1952, National Archives of Romania, Fond CC al
PCR—Cancelarie, Dosar 41/1952, pp. 120–121.

228. Declaration of Miron Constantinescu, Transcript of the Plenary of the Central Committee of the R.W.P., May 27–29, 1952, National Archives of Romania,
Fond CC al PCR—Cancelarie, Dosar 41/1952, p. 127. Another excerpt of Dej's September 1951 article in *Pravda,* "The People's Revolutionary Vigilance in the Struggle
for Socialism," was read to the regional party leadership during Pauker's purge: "It
would be a dangerous illusion for us to think that there have remained undiscovered
enemies in our party. Given that we are the government party and the leading force
within the regime of Popular Democracy, there is no doubt that foreign elements will
attempt in the future as well to infiltrate within the ranks of our party, and particularly within the leadership" (Explanatory Remarks of Iosif Chişinevschi Regarding
the May 27–29, 1952 C.C. Plenary at a Meeting of First Secretaries of the Party Regional Committees and the Party Activ of the Central Committee, June 5, 1952, National Archives of Romania, Fond 1, Dosar 19/1952, p. 17).

229. "The All-Conquering Strength of the Ideas of Leninism," *Scânteia,* January 23, 1953, p. 1.

230. National Archives of Romania, Fond 1, Dosar 73/1952, pp. 23–24, 107–
108, 128–129; "Choosing, Developing and Distributing the Cadres: A Lecture
Delivered by Ana Pauker to the Zhdanov Party School on April 17, 1952," National
Archives of Romania, Fond 1, Dosar 74/1952, pp. 225–226.

231. Kaplan, *Report on the Murder of the General Secretary,* p. 74; Gheorghe
Gheorghiu-Dej, "The People's Revolutionary Vigilance," p. 2.

232. Transcript of the Plenary of the Central Committee of the R.W.P., May 27–
29, 1952, National Archives of Romania, Fond CC al PCR—Cancelarie, Dosar
41/1952, p. 151.

233. Gheorghe Gaston Marin interview.

234. The Spanish veteran Wilhelm Einhorn asserted that two-thirds of the Spaniards were Jews. His fellow veteran David Mihail, however, suggested that "300 out
of 400 were Jews," while the Spaniards Jean Coler and Andre Micu estimated close
to 80 percent were Jews (Wilhelm Einhorn, Jean Coler, and Andre Micu interviews;
David Mihail interview, July 19, 1991).

235. Charlotte Gruia, Mihai Burcă, Carol Neumann, Gheorghe Gaston Marin,
Elena Tudorache, Sergiu Sevcenko, Elisabeta Luca, Alexandru Şiperco, Armand Pop-
per, Ana Toma, Tudor Olaru, Andrei Micu, and Cristina Boico interviews; Ecaterina
Borilă interview, July 17, 1991; Uşer Finkelştein interview, September 11, 1993;
Janetta Brill interview, June 28, 1991; Josef Bujes interview, September 12, 1990.

236. Headed by Elvira Gaisinsky, the new commission included Ronea Gheorghiu
and Sorica Clejan (Charlotte Gruia, Alexandru Şiperco, and Jean Coler interviews).

237. Charlotte Gruia interview.

238. Charlotte Gruia and Mihai Burcă interviews. Spanish veteran Carol Neu-

mann also notes that a brochure commemorating the Spanish Civil War, written by Valter Roman and published in early 1952, was suddenly overshadowed later in the year by another publishing house's brochure that conspicuously denigrated the Spaniards (Carol Neumann interview).

239. Charlotte Gruia and Mihai Burcă interviews. This is also confirmed by Mihai Alexandru, whom high party officials told of such preparations (Mihai Alexandru interview). In addition, Ronea Gheorghiu of the Control Commission and several Interior Ministry officers were sent to Czechoslovakia to observe the Slansky trial and confer with Czech security officials (Elena Tudorache and Hermina Tismaneănu interviews).

240. Charlotte Gruia interview. Gruia's husband, who was accused of being a spy in September 1952, was also a French Resistance veteran (ibid.).

241. Mihai Burcă, Cristina Boico, Jean Coler, Janetta Brill, and Charlotte Gruia interviews.

242. Mihai Burcă interview.

243. Transcript of the Declaration of Comrade Alexandru Nicolschi Before the R.C.P. Commission, October 31, 1967, Executive Archive of the Central Committee of the R.C.P., No. 264/18.02.1972, Vol. 21, p. 135.

244. Sanda Sauvard interview, December 9, 1990.

245. Carol Neumann interview; Janetta Brill interview.

246. Charlotte Gruia and Mihai Florescu interviews. Gruia asserts that Mihai Florescu was also under suspicion at this time, though he was not demoted or interrogated. In fact, Ronea Gheorghiu ordered her not to speak with Florescu after Gheorghiu had observed the Slansky trial in late November 1952.

247. Charlotte Gruia interview.

248. Hermina Tismăneanu, a Spaniard who spent the war years in Moscow, noted that the period of the Slansky trial (late fall 1952) was the first time she personally felt threatened (Hermina Tismăneanu interview).

249. On Vasilichi's being cleared, see the Transcript of a Meeting of the Politburo of the R.W.P., May 29, 1952, National Archives of Romania, Fond CC al PCR— Cancelarie, Dosar 44/1952, pp. 5–6. On his renewed danger, see Sanda Sauvard, Charlotte Gruia, Gheorghe Gaston Marin, Mihai Florescu, David Rotman, and Janetta Brill interviews. On his refusal to dismiss Spanish and French Resistance veterans, see Charlotte Gruia and Gheorghe Gaston Marin interviews; both Gaston Marin and Gruia add that Vasilichi also refused to purge Jews from the cooperative.

250. On Roman's removal, see Note on the Inquiry of Valter Roman, May 7, 1954, Directorate of Affairs of the C.C. of the R.W.P., No. 486/3.Vol. 954, Executive of the R.C.P., pp. 1–3; Cristina Boico, Sorin Toma, Gheorghe Gaston-Marin, Jean Coler, Tudor Olaru, and Janetta Brill interviews. On his house arrest, see Charlotte Gruia and Tudor Olaru interviews. Roman personally related to Jean Coler that his interrogations focused on the fact that he had been captured by enemy forces in Spain but had managed to escape. When interrogated by Elvira Gaisinsky of the Control Commission, Roman was accused of having been freed by Franco's forces in order to conduct espionage for them (Jean Coler interview). On his being targeted to appear in a Slansky trial, see Vladimir Tismaneanu, "The Tragicomedy of Romanian Communism," p. 356 n. 62.

251. An indication of this was a wave of repression against Spanish Civil War veterans at the same time in Poland, resulting in the arrest of Deputy Defense Minister Waclaw Komar in early 1953 (Jakub Berman's interview in Teresa Toranska, *Them: Stalin's Political Puppets* [New York, 1987], pp. 331–332, 371; Ernst Halperin, *The Triumphant Heretic* [London, 1957], p. 249).

252. Simion Bughici interview. The plan's being dropped apparently was communicated in a November 1953 article by Dolores Ibarruri in the Soviet historical review *Questions of History* and later distributed in the languages of the satellites in a pamphlet entitled "The National Revolutionary War of the Spanish People, 1936– 1939." The article made no mention of anyone recruited as enemy agents either in Spain or in the French internment camps and was clearly a retraction of the charges in Ibarruri's 1950 *For a Lasting Peace* article cited above (Ernst Halperin, *The Triumphant Heretic*, p. 249). Regarding Soviet efforts to influence the satellites to rehabilitate the victims of the anti-Tito campaign in 1954 and 1955, see Wolfgang Leonhard, *The Kremlin since Stalin* (New York, 1962), pp. 100–119.

253. Cristina Boico, Jean Coler, Sorin Toma, Radu Mănescu, and Eugen Szabo (interviews) all contend that Gheorghiu-Dej was very apprehensive of the old guard and did not feel he could rely on their support.

254. One such manifestation was Roman's writing a letter to Gheorghiu-Dej after being ousted as Minister of Posts and Telecommunications, which had, he wrote, "led him to desperation" and caused him to "lose his reason for living" (Note of Inquiry of Valter Roman, May 7, 1954, Direction of Affairs of the C.C. of the R.W.P., No. 486/3.Vol. 954, Executive Archive of the Central Committee of the R.C.P., pp. 1–3). On Roman's rehabilitation, see Sorin Toma interview.

255. Janetta Brill interview.

256. Gheorghe Gaston Marin interview.

257. Jean Coler interview.

258. Gheorghe Gaston Marin and Alexandru Şiperco interviews; Alexandru Şiperco, Charlotte Gruia, and Andre Micu interviews.

259. Eugen Szabo interview; also see the Gruia and Coler interviews.

260. Transcript of an Interrogation of Ana Pauker by a Party Commission of the R.W.P., June 18, 1956, Ana Pauker Inquiry File, Executive Archive of the Central Committee of the R.C.P., pp. 26–27; Transcript of an Interrogation of Ana Pauker by a Party Commission of the R.W.P., July 6, 1956, Ana Pauker Inquiry File, Executive Archive of the Central Committee of the R.C.P., pp. 6, 21. A list of questions given to her at that time, some dealing with her supposed desire for purges within the party, was published in *Dosarele istoriei* 2, no. 8(13) (1997), pp. 57–60.

261. Gyorgy Lazar (pen name), "Memorandum," in *Witness to Cultural Genocide: First-Hand Reports on Rumania's Minority Policies Today* (New York, 1979), pp. 96–97. The full Hungarian text originally appeared in the émigré periodical *Irodalmi Ujsag* (Paris), March–April 1977.

CHAPTER 6

1. Declaration of Melania Iancu, January 16, 1953, ASRI, Fond P, Dosar 40005, Vol. 160, pp. 121–125; Interrogation of Theodor Loewenstein (Lavi), January 20, 1953, ASRI, Fond P, Dosar 40009, Vol. 54, p. 41; Interrogation of Lt. Col. Laurian Zamfir, January 17, 1953, ASRI, Fond P, Dosar 40,009, Vol. 14, p. 201(b), p. 203.

2. Ya'acov Ro'i, *Soviet Decision Making in Practice: The U.S.S.R. and Israel, 1947–1954* (New Brunswick, 1980), pp. 26–28, 33.

3. For details of the campaign, see Gennadi Kostyrchenko, *Out of the Red Shadows: Anti-Semitism in Stalin's Russia* (Amherst, N.Y., 1995); Arkady Vaksberg, *Stalin against the Jews* (New York, 1994); Yehoshua A. Gilboa, *The Black Years of Soviet Jewry* (Boston, 1971), pp. 149–186; Benjamin Pinkus, *The Soviet Government and the Jews* (London, 1984), pp. 195–196, 507 n. 13; Peter Meyer, ed., *The Jews in the Soviet Satellites* (Syracuse, 1953); Yakov Rapoport, *The Doctors' Plot of*

1953 (Cambridge, Mass., 1991); Shimon Redlich, *Propaganda and Nationalism in Wartime Russia: The Jewish Antifascist Committee in the U.S.S.R., 1941–1948* (Boulder, 1982), pp. 167–170; and Ya'acov Ro'i, *Soviet Decision Making in Practice,* pp. 313–326.

4. Liviu Rotman, "Romanian Jewry: The First Decade after the Holocaust," in Randolph L. Braham, ed., *The Tragedy of Romanian Jewry* (New York, 1994), pp. 287–288.

5. Sylvain, "Rumania," in Meyer, ed., *The Jews in the Soviet Satellites,* p. 519.

6. Ibid.; Jean Ancel, *Yahadut Romanyah ben 23.8.1944 le-ven 30.12.1947* [Rumanian Jewry, August 23, 1944–December 30, 1947], doctoral thesis, Hebrew University (Jerusalem, 1979), p. 287.

7. Transcript of a Meeting with Leading Activists of the Mass Organizations, October 5, 1945, National Archives of Romania, Fond CC al PCR—Cancelarie, Dosar 86/1945, pp. 13–14.

8. Transcript of a Meeting of Leading Activists of the Mass Organizations, February 23, 1946, National Archives of Romania, Fond CC al PCR—Cancelarie, Dosar 18/1946, pp. 27–28.

9. Jean Ancel, "*She'erit Hapletah* in Romania during the Transition Period to a Communist Regime, August 1944–December 1947," in Yisrael Gutman and Avital Saf, eds., *She'erit Hapletah, 1944–1948: Rehabilitation and Political Struggle,* Proceedings of the Sixth Yad Vashem International Historical Conference (Jerusalem, 1990), pp. 151–155.

10. Arieh J. Kochavi, "British Diplomats and the Jews in Poland, Romania and Hungary during the Communist Takeovers," *East European Quarterly* 29, no. 4 (Winter 1995), p. 449; Sylvain, "Rumania," p. 530.

11. Ancel, "*She'erit Hapletah* in Romania," p. xxix.

12. Declaration of Melania Iancu, ASRI, Fond P, Dosar 40005, Vol. 160, pp. 121–125.

13. Ibid.; Interrogation of Lt. Col. Laurian Zamfir, September 28, 1955, ASRI, Fond P, Dosar 40009, Vol. 14, p. 239; Interrogation of Lt. Col. Laurian Zamfir, January 17, 1953, ASRI, Fond P, Dosar 40,009, Vol. 14, p. 201.

14. Jakub Berman, interviewed by Teresa Toranska, *Them: Stalin's Political Puppets,* p. 317. Ya'acov Ro'i claims that, in addition to this, the Soviets hoped to weaken the Western alliance by cooperating with the U. S. against the British on this matter, appeal to the American Jewish community and its allies on the American political scene, and stimulate radical national liberation movements within the Arab world ("Soviet Policies and Attitudes toward Israel, 1948–1978: An Overview," *Soviet Jewish Affairs* 11, no. 2 [1981], p. 36).

15. Sylvain, "Rumania," p. 530.

16. David Șerer interview, July 22, 1991; Gheorghe Rojha interview, July 16, 1991; Carol Lustig interview, September 8, 1989; Harry Kuller interview, January 11, 1994; Alexandru Nistor, Ida Felix, Eugen Szabo, Ilie Zaharia, Radu Mănescu, Elena Tudorache, Mircea Oprișan, and Simion Bughici interviews.

17. Talmon, *Israel among the Nations,* p. 78.

18. Sylvain, "Rumania," pp. 519, 541; National Archives of Romania, Fond 37, Dosar 10, p. 212; Harry Kuller interview.

19. Ancel, "*She'erit Hapletah* in Romania," p. xxix.

20. On the growing anti-Semitism, see Documents of the Jewish Democratic Committee, National Archives of Romania, Fond 37, Dosar 23, p. 7; Dosar 18, pp. 187, 217; Kochavi, "British Diplomats and the Jews in Poland, Romania and Hungary," pp. 450–451, 455.

21. The 10 percent figure is from Marius Oprea, "Pagini din 'copilăria' Securității române" [Pages from the "Childhood" of the Romanian Securitate], *Dosarele istoriei*, no. 5, 1996, p. 36.

22. Ioan Scurtu, ed., *România, viața politică în documente 1946* [Romania: Political Life in Documents, 1946] (Bucharest, 1996), p. 292.

23. "Meeting of Bodnăraș and Groza," June 23, 1949, Executive Archive of the Central Committee of the R.C.P., pp. 5–6.

24. Liviu Rotman, for instance, subscribes to the conventional wisdom in his otherwise excellent "Romanian Jewry: The First Decade after the Holocaust," in Randolph L. Braham, ed., *The Tragedy of Romanian Jewry* (New York, 1994), p. 321.

25. Interrogation of Teohari Georgescu, January 13, 1954, ASRI, Fond P, Dosar 40,009, Vol. 2, p. 115; Interrogation of Lt. Col. Laurian Zamfir, September 28, 1955, ASRI, Fond P, Dosar 40,009, Vol. 14, p. 239 (side b).

26. *Yahadut Romanyah bi-tekumat Yisrael* [Rumanian Jewry during the Revival of Israel], vol. 2, *Prisoners of Zion* (Tel Aviv, 1994), pp. 44–45.

27. Interrogation of Lt. Col. Laurian Zamfir, January 17, 1953, ASRI, Fond P, Dosar 40009, Vol. 26, pp. 236, 238.

28. Mordechai Namir, *Shelihut be-Moskvah* [Mission to Moscow] (Tel Aviv, 1971), pp. 28–29.

29. Declaration of Melania Iancu, January 16, 1953, ASRI, Fond P, Dosar 40005, Vol. 160, p. 133. Perhaps based on these meetings, Israeli Foreign Minister Moshe Sharett wrote to Chaim Weizmann in July 1948 that, in his opinion, Pauker "is not connected to the wild anti-Zionist category" among the Romanian Party elite (Raphael Vago, "The Traditions of Antisemitism in Romania," pp. 145–146).

30. *Yahadut Romanyah bi-tekumat Yisrael*, pp. 45–46.

31. David Krivine, "Who Was Ana Pauker?" p. 9.

32. Namir (then known also as Mordechai Nemirowsky) revealed to Pauker's brother, Zalman Rabinsohn, that he met again with Pauker to officially protest the agreement's abrogation and was left with the impression that the new line caught her angrily off-guard (ASRI, Fond P, Dosar 40009, Vol. 50, p. 340).

33. Ya'acov Ro'i, *Soviet Decision Making in Practice*, pp. 143–144, 418.

34. Minutes of the Meeting of the Politburo of the Central Committee of the R.W.P., October 24, 1948, National Archive of Romania, Fond CC al PCR—Cancelarie, Dosar 50/1948, pp. 1–8.

35. On the anti-Zionist campaign, see Gennadi Kostyrchenko, *Out of the Red Shadows*, pp. 30–247; Pinkus, *The Soviet Government and the Jews*, pp. 195–196, 509 n. 19; Ro'i, *Soviet Decision Making in Practice*, pp. 316, 326; Redlich, *Propaganda and Nationalism in Wartime Russia*, pp. 167–170; Ilya Ehrenburg, *Post-War Years* (New York, 1967), p. 125; Chimen Abramsky, "The Rise and Fall of Soviet Yiddish Literature," *Soviet Jewish Affairs* 12, no. 3 (1982), p. 36; Roy A. Medvedev, *On Stalin and Stalinism* (Oxford and New York, 1979), p. 146. On Polina Zhemchuzhina's arrest, see Kostyrchenko, *Out of the Red Shadows*, pp. 119–123; on Pauker's distress and friendship with Zhemchuzhina, see Ana Toma interview.

36. Sylvain, "Rumania," pp. 535–539.

37. Pauker's brother, Zalman Rabinsohn, informed Romanian Zionist leader Marcu Cohin that Pauker had confided her opposition to him (Interrogation of Marcu Cohin, March 19, 1953, ASRI, Fond P, Dosar 40009, Vol. 62, p. 266). Pauker suggested that publicly "lumping all Zionists together in the same pot" would only result in the party's losing the support of the workers in Israel, while consolidating

those forces opposing Romania (Minutes of the Meeting of the Politburo of the Central Committee of the R.W.P., November 15, 1948, National Archives of Romania, Fond CC al PCR—Cancelarie, Dosar 55/1948, pp. 1–7).

38. Historian Liviu Rotman confirmed the existence of these indoctrination courses, on which he found documents in the archives of the Romanian labor unions (Liviu Rotman interview, August 1, 1989); also see Liviu Rotman, "Romanian Jewry: The First Decade after the Holocaust," p. 315. Elena Tudorache interview; Elena Vrancea interview, December 26, 1991; Eugen Szabo and Victor Vezendean interviews; Ya'acov Ro'i, *Soviet Decision Making in Practice*, p. 146.

39. *Yahadut Romanyah bi-tekumat Yisrael*, p. 46.

40. The joke was that the only thing that turned red as a result of this immigration was the Black Sea, with all of the red party cards the immigrants threw overboard immediately after their departure (Liviu Rotman interview).

41. Declaration of Ana Pauker, April 20, 1953, Ana Pauker Inquiry File, Executive Archive of the Central Committee of the R.C.P., p. 1.

42. David Şerer and Gheorghe Rojha interviews.

43. David Krivine, "Who Was Ana Pauker?" p. 9.

44. Gheorghiu-Dej and Iosif Chişinevschi instead dispatched Victor Vezendean (deputy chief of the Foreign Section of the Central Committee) to meet with Mikunis, and told Vezendean why they refused to meet with him (Victor Vezendean interview).

45. Interrogation of Vasile Luca, February 6, 1953, ASRI, Fond P, Dosar 40005, Vol. 4, p. 413 [emphasis added].

46. "Report Concerning the Results of the Investigation in the Case of Former Interior Minister Teohari Georgescu," November 11, 1955, ASRI, Fond P, Dosar 40009, Vol. 21, p. 204.

47. Interrogation of Lt. Col. Laurian Zamfir, January 17, 1953, ASRI, Fond P, Dosar 40009, Vol. 26, pp. 236, 238, 250–251.

48. Report, Ministry of Internal Affairs, ASRI, Fond P, Dosar 40009, Vol. 54, p. 41.

49. *Yahadut Romanyah bi-tekumat Yisrael*, p. 46.

50. Israeli emissary Moshe Agami spoke of these negotiations to Zoltan Eiglitz, Luca's chief of staff in the Finance Ministry, in November or December 1948. Eiglitz in turn discussed the matter with Luca, who told him why the Romanians rejected the Israeli offer (Interrogation of Zoltan Eiglitz, May 29, 1953, ASRI, Fond P, Dosar 40005, Vol. 8, pp. 178–179).

51. Prominent Zionist Theodor Loewenstein (Lavi) testified under interrogation in January 1953 that Rubin revealed this to officials at the Israeli embassy in Bucharest (Report on the Testimony of Theodor Leowenstein, undated, ASRI, Fond P, Dosar 40009, Vol. 54, pp. 44–45).

52. On the lines outside the ministry, see the Interrogation of Marin Jianu, March, 5, 1953, ASRI, Fond P, Dosar 40009, Vol. 26, pp. 82–83; David Giladi interview, July 29, 1989. On Rubin's pressuring Pauker, see the Memoir of Vasile Luca, November 5, 1954, ASRI, Fond P, Dosar 40005, Vol. 125, p. 63; E. Vered, *Minimum*, no. 4, July 1987, cited by Marius Mircu, *Ana Pauker şi alţii*, p. 174.

53. *Yahadut Romanyah bi-tekumat Yisrael*, p. 49.

54. Memorandum, Ministry of the Interior, January 30, 1954, ASRI, Fond P, Dosar 40009, Vol. 22, p. 203.

55. Interrogation of Marin Jianu, March 5, 1953, ASRI, Fond P, Dosar 40009, Vol. 26, p. 82.

56. Documents of the Jewish Democratic Committee, Archives of the Central Committee of the R.W.P., National Archives of Romania, Fond 37, Dosar 18, p. 131; Sylvain, "Rumania," p. 556 n. 16.

57. Minutes of the Meeting of the Secretariat of the Central Committee of the R.W.P., February 18, 1949, National Archives of Romania, Fond CC al PCR—Cancelarie, Dosar 16/1949, pp. 14–15.

58. Ibid., pp. 13–16. Pauker did, however, join the other secretaries in voting to ban the American-based Organization for Education Resources and Technical Training (ORT) and the Joint Distribution Committee from the country (ibid.).

59. Declaration of Teohari Georgescu, June 9, 1956, Ana Pauker Inquiry File, Executive Archive of the Central Committee of the R.C.P., p. 6; "Plan with the Principal Points for Orientating the Ana Pauker Inquiry," Chapter VI, Point 8, Ana Pauker Inquiry File, Executive Archive of the Central Committee of the R.C.P.

60. Pauker admitted to unilaterally intervening to free the seven emissaries while Dej was away on vacation (Transcript of an Interrogation of Ana Pauker by an R.W.P. Party Commission, July 29, 1953, Ana Pauker Inquiry File, Executive Archive of the Central Committee of the R.C.P., pp. 17–28; also see Teohari Georgescu's Written Answers to Questions Posed to Him by the Party Control Commission, September 15, 1952, ASRI, Fond P, Dosar 40009, Vol. 32, p. 220, sides a and b; and the Interrogation of Vasile Luca, February 6, 1953, ASRI, Fond P, Dosar 40005, Vol. 4, p. 414). At a meeting of the Secretariat on March 22, 1949, Pauker proposed immediately expelling the emissaries without trying them, arguing that a trial would spark an international campaign against the RPR. The Secretariat, however, voted for a trial, at both Luca's and Gheorghiu-Dej's behest (Minutes of the Meeting of the Secretariat of the Central Committee of the R.W.P., March 22, 1949, National Archives of Romania, Fond CC al PCR—Cancelarie, Dosar 25/1949, p. 14).

61. On Luca's shifting positions, see the Minutes of the Meeting of the Secretariat of the Central Committee of the R.W.P., February 18, 1949, National Archives of Romania, Fond CC al PCR—Cancelarie, Dosar 16/1949, p. 13, and the Interrogation of Vasile Luca, February 14, 1953, ASRI, Fond P, Dosar 40005, Vol. 4, p. 435. The quote is from the Minutes of the Meeting of the Secretariat of the Central Committee of the R.W.P., February 18, 1949, National Archives of Romania, Fond CC al PCR—Cancelarie, Dosar 16/1949, p. 16.

62. Minutes of the Meeting of the Secretariat of the Central Committee of the R.W.P., August 31, 1949, National Archives of Romania, Fond CC al PCR—Cancelarie, Dosar 74/1949, p. 9.

63. Declaration of Teohari Georgescu, April 27, 1956, Ana Pauker Inquiry File, Executive Archive of the Central Committee of the R.C.P., p. 1.

64. Protocol, Ministry of Internal Affairs, November 29, 1949, ASRI, Fond D, Dosar 10089, pp. 204–205. The author thanks Mr. Marius Oprea for kindly making this document available to him.

65. Interrogation of Lt. Col. Laurian Zamfir, January 22, 1953, ASRI, Fond P, Dosar 40009, Vol. 26, pp. 239–240; Interrogations of Marin Jianu, May 13, 1953, and August 10, 1955, ASRI, Fond P, Dosar 40009, Vol. 14, p. 63, 193.

66. Interrogation of Lt. Col. Laurian Zamfir, January 22, 1953, ASRI, Fond P, Dosar 40009, Vol. 26, p. 241.

67. Interrogation of Lt. Col. Laurian Zamfir, January 29, 1953, and Interrogation of Major Octav Holban [Zamfir's deputy at the DCSP], January 30, 1953, ASRI, Fond P, Dosar 40009, Vol. 26, pp. 263, 286.

68. Documents of the Jewish Democratic Committee, National Archives of Romania, Fond 37, Dosar 18, p. 131.

69. Protocol, Ministry of Internal Affairs, March 31, 1950, ASRI, Fond D, Dosar 10090, pp. 207–208 [emphasis added]. (The author thanks Mr. Marius Oprea for kindly making this document available to him.) This was communicated in a March 23 memo to the Central Committee of the JDC declaring that anyone could leave for Israel "regardless of age and social position" (Documents of the Jewish Democratic Committee, National Archives of Romania, Fond 37, Dosar 18, p. 119).

70. On the reduction in certificates, see the Interrogation of Lt. Col. Laurian Zamfir, January 17, 1953, ASRI, Fond P, Dosar 40,009, Vol. 14, p. 201 (b), pp. 270–271; Documents of the Jewish Democratic Committee, Archives of the Central Committee of the R.W.P., National Archives of Romania, Fond 37, Dosar 18, p. 131. On the simplified application forms, see the Interrogation of Teohari Georgescu, January 13, 1954, ASRI, Fond P, Dosar 40009, Vol. 2, p. 115; Declaration of Teohari Georgescu, April 27, 1956, Ana Pauker Inquiry File, Executive Archive of the Central Committee of the R.C.P., p. 1.

71. A report found in the archives noted that in the village of Beiuş, Bihor County, for example, the number of people applying to emigrate jumped from ten to eighty-five after the militia went "from house to house" to publicize the simplified application procedures for obtaining exit visas. In the village of Târgu Ocna, Bacău County, there was an apparent flood of applications after the militia announced that "if the Jewish population does not apply within two hours, it would no longer be allowed to apply." In addition, a report of a JDC activist bitterly complained that, in the town of Bistriţa, the militia was "going to Jewish households encouraging the people to apply for passports." When Zamfir pointed out the inherent contradiction of both the militia's actions and the Interior Ministry's policy of issuing passports to any prospective Jewish emigrant while the JDC was conducting a massive propaganda campaign against such emigration, Deputy Interior Minister Gheorghe Pintilie responded that the party had decided on "a dialectical resolution" to Jewish emigration, seeking to convince Romanian Jewry to stay in the country, while at the same time "letting those whom it has not convinced leave. It's the same situation with recruiting people to work in the collective farms." Apparently those eager to leave even included JDC activists: a report analyzing the JDC's work revealed cases of activists sent to "enlighten" people who had received exit permits, "and, instead of working to convince them, they told the people in the neighborhood that they're also leaving for Israel" (National Archives of Romania, Fond 1, Dosar 232/1950, p. 36; Rotman, "Romanian Jewry," p. 321; Interrogation of Lt. Col. Laurian Zamfir, January 17, 1953, ASRI, Fond P, Dosar 40009, Vol. 14, pp. 274–275; "A Short History of the Activities of the Jewish Democratic Committee since Its Establishment," undated, National Archives of Romania, Fond 37, Dosar 10, p. 214).

72. Jianu and Zamfir confirmed Pauker's "complete agreement" with Georgescu's actions in easing emigration (Interrogation of Marin Jianu, February 24, 1953, ASRI, Fond P, Dosar 40009, Vol. 14, p. 4; Interrogation of Marin Jianu, February 25, 1953, ASRI, Fond P, Dosar 40009, Vol. 26, p. 34; Interrogation of Marin Jianu, May 13, 1953, ASRI, Fond P, Dosar 40009, Vol. 14, p. 62; Interrogation of Lt. Col. Laurian Zamfir, January 17, 1953, ASRI, Fond P, Dosar 40009, Vol. 14, pp. 204b, 270–271; Interrogation of Lt. Col. Laurian Zamfir, January 29, 1953, ASRI, Fond P, Dosar 40009, Vol. 26, p. 263).

73. Interrogation of Major Octav Holban [Zamfir's assistant at the DCSP], January 30, 1953, ASRI, Fond P, Dosar 40009, Vol. 26, p. 288.

74. Interrogation of Lt. Col. Laurian Zamfir, January 17, 1953, ASRI, Fond P, Dosar 40009, Vol. 14, pp. 270–271.

75. Report on the Testimony of Theodor Leowenstein, undated, ASRI, Fond P, Dosar 40009, Vol. 54, pp. 41–42.

76. Documents of the Jewish Democratic Committee, National Archives of Romania, Fond 37, Dosar 18, pp. 124, 166, 170, 174, 200, 205; National Archives of Romania, Fond 1, Dosar 232/1950, p. 29.

77. Interrogation of Lt. Col. Laurian Zamfir, January 17, 1953, ASRI, Fond P, Dosar 40009, Vol. 14, p. 271. Georgescu reported that over 100,000 applications were filed at the Interior Ministry by May 1950. Given, however, that the applications also requested visas for the spouses and children of each respective applicant, one easily arrives at Zamfir's figure of 220,000 (Interrogation of Teohari Georgescu, January 13, 1954, ASRI, Fond P, Dosar 40009, Vol. 2, pp. 115–116; Declaration of Teohari Georgescu, April 27, 1956, Ana Pauker Inquiry File, Executive Archive of the Central Committee of the R.C.P., pp. 1–2).

78. Minutes of the Meeting of the Secretariat of the Central Committee of the R.W.P., August 31, 1949, National Archives of Romania, Fond CC al PCR—Cancelarie, Dosar 74/1949, p. 9.

79. Constantin Pârvulescu, the chief of the Party Control Commission, revealed to his deputy Charlotte Gruia that Gheorghiu-Dej discussed the matter with him and asked, "Where are all these people going? Why are they leaving?" He was, related Pârvulescu, "very astonished" and "very unhappy" that so many wanted to emigrate. Simion Bughici, Dej's Foreign Minister (1952–1956), and Mircea Oprişan, his Minister of Internal Commerce (1954–1955), both confirm his reaction (Charlotte Gruia, Simion Bughici, and Mircea Oprişan interviews).

80. Transcript of the Plenary of the Central Committee of the R.W.P., May 26–27, 1952, National Archives of Romania, Fond CC al PCR—Cancelarie, Dosar 41/1952, pp. 65, 91.

81. As already noted, the special party commission investigating the Patraşcanu case in 1967–68 revealed that Alexandru Drăghici destroyed certain documents concerning the Patraşcanu inquiry on Gheorghiu-Dej's orders. The meetings presently in question may have dealt also with Patraşcanu's case, as the party Secretariat suspended his investigation for review precisely in May 1950. The documents thus could have been destroyed for that reason ("The Report of the Party Commission Assigned to Clarify the Case of Lucreţiu Patraşcanu," May 3, 1968, Executive Archive of the Central Committee of the R.C.P., pp. 43–44).

82. Note Regarding the Arrest and Inquiry of Teohari Georgescu, April 14, 1968, Executive Archive of the Central Committee of the R.C.P., p. 2.

83. Interrogation of Teohari Georgescu, January 13, 1954, ASRI, Fond P, Dosar 40009, Vol. 2, pp. 115–116. Vasile Luca confirms this in an interrogation on February 14, 1953, ASRI, Fond P, Dosar 40005, Vol. 4, p. 436.

84. Decision of the Secretariat of the Central Committee of the R.W.P., May 12, 1950, ASRI, Fond D, Dosar 9916, pp. 19–20; Minutes of a Meeting with the Secretaries of the Party County Committees and Instructors of the Central Committee of the R.W.P., June 15, 1950, National Archives of Romania, Fond CC al PCR—Cancelarie, Dosar 44/1950, p. 44.

85. Decision of the Secretariat of the Central Committee of the R.W.P., May 12, 1950, ASRI, Fond D, Dosar 9916, pp. 19–20.

86. Interrogation of Laurian Zamfir, January 17, 1953, ASRI, Fond P, Dosar 40009, Vol. 14, pp. 270–271.

87. Declaration of Teohari Georgescu, April 27, 1956, Ana Pauker Inquiry File, Executive Archive of the Central Committee of the R.C.P., pp. 1–2.

88. Ibid.

89. Protocol, Ministry of Interior Affairs, May 20, 1950, ASRI, Fond D, Dosar 10090, p. 325.

90. Declaration of Teohari Georgescu, April 27, 1956, Ana Pauker Inquiry File, Executive Archive of the Central Committee of the R.C.P., pp. 1–2.

91. Protocol, Ministry of Interior Affairs, May 31, 1950, ASRI, Fond D, Dosar 10090, pp. 342–343.

92. Declaration of Melania Iancu, January 16, 1953, ASRI, Fond P, Dosar 40005, Vol. 160, p. 133.

93. Georgescu revealed that Dej intervened twice in 1950 to impose restrictions on Jewish emigration (Interrogation of Teohari Georgescu, January 13, 1954, ASRI, Fond P, Dosar 40009, Vol. 2, p. 116).

94. Interrogation of Lt. Col. Laurian Zamfir, January 29, 1953, ASRI, Fond P, Dosar 40009, Vol. 26, p. 275.

95. Ibid., p. 276; Interrogation of Marin Jianu, August 10, 1955, ASRI, Fond P, Dosar 40009, Vol. 14, p. 192. The restrictions are reflected in a JDC report dated May 26, 1951, which stated that in the recent period, many applications to leave were refused—especially those from the productive elements ("technicians, engineers, accountants, doctors, dentists and others") (National Archives of Romania, Fond 37, Dosar 28, p. 218).

96. Interrogation of Teohari Georgescu, January 13, 1954, ASRI, Fond P, Dosar 40009, Vol. 2, p. 116; Transcript of the Plenary of the Central Committee of the R.W.P., May 26–27, 1952, National Archives of Romania, Fond CC al PCR—Cancelarie, Dosar 41/1952, p. 62.

97. Interrogation of Lt. Col. Laurian Zamfir, January 29, 1953, ASRI, Fond P, Dosar 40009, Vol. 26, p. 276.

98. Ibid.; "Report Concerning the Results of the Investigation in the Case of Former Interior Minister Teohari Georgescu," March 19, 1956, ASRI, Fond P, Dosar 40009, Vol. 1, p. 27.

99. Interrogation of Marin Jianu, January 29, 1953, ASRI, Fond P, Dosar 40009, Vol. 26, pp. 272–273.

100. Interrogation of Lt. Col. Laurian Zamfir, January 29, 1953, ASRI, Fond P, Dosar 40009, Vol. 26, p. 273.

101. Interrogation of Teohari Georgescu, January 13, 1954, ASRI, Fond P, Dosar 40009, Vol. 2, p. 116; Declaration of Teohari Georgescu, April 27, 1956, Ana Pauker Inquiry File, Executive Archive of the Central Committee of the R.C.P., p. 2.

102. Interrogation of Teohari Georgescu, January 13, 1954, ASRI, Fond P, Dosar 40009, Vol. 2, p. 116; Transcript of the Plenary of the Central Committee of the R.W.P., May 26–27, 1952, National Archives of Romania, Fond CC al PCR—Cancelarie, Dosar 41/1952, p. 62.

103. Declaration of Teohari Georgescu, April 26, 1956, Ana Pauker Inquiry File, Executive Archive of the Central Committee of the R.C.P., p. 15; Declaration of Teohari Georgescu, April 27, 1956, Ana Pauker Inquiry File, Executive Archive of the Central Committee of the R.C.P., p. 2. Pauker's brother, Zalman Rabinsohn, revealed to the Romanian Zionist Marcu Cohin that Georgescu assigned a large number of functionaries to the Interior Ministry's passport division in order to accelerate departures and ordered the militia in the provinces to move things forward by using special couriers to avoid delays. He agreed as well to meet with anyone soliciting an audience with him to discuss the status of their applications—either receiving them personally or ordering Marin Jianu to do so. Georgescu also ordered Jianu to resolve

the last unresolved dossiers and accepted schedules from the Israeli embassy to better synchronize the departures (Interrogation of Marcu Cohin, April 20, 1953, ASRI, Fond P, Dosar 40009, Vol. 62, p. 268).

104. Declaration of Teohari Georgescu, April 26, 1956, Ana Pauker Inquiry File, Executive Archive of the Central Committee of the R.C.P., p. 15.

105. Declaration of Teohari Georgescu, April 27, 1956, Ana Pauker Inquiry File, Executive Archive of the Central Committee of the R.C.P., p. 2.

106. "Report Concerning the Results of the Investigation in the Case of Former Interior Minister Teohari Georgescu," November 11, 1955, ASRI, Fond P, Dosar 40009, Vol. 21, p. 204.

107. Transcript of the Plenary of the Central Committee of the R.W.P., May 26–27, 1952, National Archives of Romania, Fond CC al PCR—Cancelarie, Dosar 41/1952, p. 65.

108. "Report Regarding Marin Jianu, Former Deputy Minister of the Ministry of Internal Affairs," February 17, 1953, ASRI, Fond P, Dosar 40009, Vol. 26, p. 430; *Immigration to Israel: 1948–1972,* Central Bureau of Statistics, Ministry of Immigrant Absorption, Jewish Agency of Aliya and Absorption Department, Special Series No. 489 (Jerusalem, 1975), p. 4. (The Israeli Ministry of Immigrant Absorption's 1951 total was roughly 10,000 less than the Romanian government's figure.)

109. Pauker's persistent promotion of unrestricted aliya was confirmed by Ana Toma, Carol Lustig, Cristina Boico, Iosif Breban, Elena Tudorache, Charlotte Gruia, Mircea Oprişan, David Şerer, Gheorghe Rojha (interviews), and Chief Rabbi Moses Rosen (Moses Rosen interview, August 7, 1989). Pauker's brother, Zalman Rabinsohn, also confirmed it to Romanian Zionist Marcu Cohin, as well as under interrogation and in conversations with his prison cell mate (Interrogation of Marcu Cohin, March 19, 1953, ASRI, Fond P, Dosar 40009, Vol. 62, p. 266; Interrogation of Solomon [Zalman] Rabinsohn, March 26, 1953, ASRI, Fond P, Dosar 40009, Vol. 60, p. 54; Note, May 8, 1953, ASRI, Fond P, Dosar 40009, Vol. 60, p. 206). Moreover, Emil Pauker, the brother of Pauker's father-in-law, reported to Israeli ambassador Ehud Avriel (Rubin's successor) that Pauker favored Jewish emigration ("Report Regarding the Results of the Inquiry of Ana Pauker," June 6, 1953, ASRI, Fond P, Dosar 40009, Vol. 45, p. 12). Also see the declaration of Teohari Georgescu, April 27, 1956, Ana Pauker Inquiry File, Executive Archive of the Central Committee of the R.C.P., pp. 1–2; Memoir of Vasile Luca, November 5, 1954, ASRI, Fond P, Dosar 40005, Vol. 126, p. 63; Interrogation of Laurian Zamfir, January 17, 1953, ASRI, Fond P, Dosar 40009, Vol. 14, p. 201(b), pp. 270–271; Interrogation of Laurian Zamfir, January 29, 1953, ASRI, Fond P, Dosar 40009, Vol. 26, p. 263; Interrogation of Marin Jianu, February 22, 1953, ASRI, Fond P, Dosar 40009, Vol. 14, p. 34; Interrogation of Marin Jianu, February 24, 1953, ASRI, Fond P, Dosar 40009, Vol. 14, p. 4; Interrogation of Marin Jianu, May 13, 1953, ASRI, Fond P, Dosar 40009, Vol. 14, p. 62. The party commission that investigated his case in 1967–68 confirmed Georgescu's position (Note Regarding the Arrest and Inquiry of Teohari Georgescu, April 14, 1968, Executive Archive of the Central Committee of the R.C.P., p. 2). On Luca's backing, see the Interrogation of Vasile Luca, February 14, 1953, ASRI, Fond P, Dosar 40005, Vol. 4, p. 435.

110. "Plan with the Principal Points for Orientating the Ana Pauker Inquiry," Chapter VI, Point 8, undated, made available to the author by the Archives of the National Defense Ministry.

111. As confirmed by Emil Bodnăraş in a March 1961 Politburo meeting (Transcript of the Politburo of the C.C. of the R.W.P., March 13–14, 1961, Executive Archive of the Central Committee of the R.W.P., p. 166).

112. "Report Regarding the Investigation of Ana Pauker," April 5, 1954, Ana Pauker Inquiry File, Executive Archive of the Central Committee of the R.C.P., pp. 185–186.

113. See chapter 8.

114. Interrogation of Marcu Cohin, April 20, 1953, ASRI, Fond P, Dosar 40009, Vol. 62, pp. 267(b)–268.

115. Ya'acov Ro'i, "Soviet Policies and Attitudes toward Israel, 1948–1978: An Overview," pp. 35–45.

116. The multicolumn list below shows Jewish immigration to Israel from Poland, Hungary, and Romania from 1948 to 1952. Compare Poland's emigration totals in 1951–1952 with those of 1948–1950 and contrast them with the numbers from Romania. Compare also the wide difference throughout this period between Romania and Hungary, the only other Soviet satellite with a large Jewish population. (From *Immigration to Israel: 1948–1972*, p. 4.)

	1948	*1949*	*1950*	*1951*	*1952*
Poland	28,788	47,384	26,587	3,655	778
Hungary	3,463	6,844	2,732	1,285	239
Romania	17,678	13,602	46,442	40,228	3,663

117. National Archives of Romania, Fond 1, Dosar 75/1952, p. 75; Transcript of a Meeting of the Politburo, February 20, 1952, National Archives of Romania, Fond CC al PCR—Cancelarie, Dosar 11/1952, p. 94; Transcript of an Interrogation of Ana Pauker by a Party Commission of the C.C. of the R.W.P., June 18, 1956, p. 36.

118. Iosif Breban interview.

119. Ana Toma interview. A possible indication of Pauker's attitude was her surprise appearance with Georgescu and Luca at an Israeli embassy reception celebrating Israel's first anniversary in May 1949. In contrast, no one from Gheorghiu-Dej's faction appeared at the reception (David Giladi, "In Bucharest: Ana Pauker at Israel's Independence Day Party," *Ma'ariv*, April 15, 1975, p. 25; David Giladi interview).

120. Kostyrchenko, *Out of the Red Shadows*, pp. 14–27; Soloman Schwarz, *Jews in the Soviet Union*, pp. 303–304, 327, 346–348; Benjamin Pinkus, *The Jews of the Soviet Union* (Cambridge, 1988), pp. 138–140; Yehoshua A. Gilboa, *The Black Years of Soviet Jewry*, pp. 7–10; Zvi Y. Gitelman, *Anti-Semitism in the U.S.S.R.: Sources, Types, Consequences* (New York, 1974), p. 17; Alfred A. Skerpan, "Aspects of Soviet Antisemitism," *Antioch Review* 12, no. 3 (September 1952), p. 312; Mendel Mann, quoted by Gerard Israel in *The Jews in Russia* (New York, 1975), pp. 184–185; Salo W. Baron, *The Russian Jew under Tsars and Soviets* (New York, 1964), pp. 257–261.

121. Ya'acov Ro'i, *Soviet Decision Making in Practice*, p. 345. Also see Joel Cang, *The Silent Millions* (New York, 1969), p. 84.

122. Tatiana and Gheorghe Brătescu interview.

123. Chief Rabbi Moses Rosen interview.

124. Israel Levanon interview.

125. Rabinsohn revealed this to Shlomo Leibovici, whom the author interviewed August 4, 1989.

126. Tatiana Brătescu interview.

127. Vladimir Zaharescu interview.

128. In a three-hour interview with the American journalist Hal Lehrman in 1946, Pauker agreed to discuss any issue except one: the Jewish Question. Moreover,

when Pauker "paid a state visit to a neighboring country, and a newspaper wrote . . . a character sketch saying that she came of 'bourgeois' Jewish stock," she reportedly "complained personally to the Prime Minister, and demanded that the man who wrote the study be punished on the ground that it was a needless irrelevance to discuss a person's background." Former Chief Rabbi Alexandre Şafran confirmed such sensitivity on Pauker's part, relating an occasion during the early postwar period when a receiving line of government ministers and party leaders met him at a reception in the Soviet embassy. "We shook hands, and they greeted me with respect," he noted. "Ana Pauker was the sole exception. She was standing in the middle of the row, and when she saw me approaching the Prime Minister and the other ministers, she stepped out of the line and turned aside for a moment in order not to greet me. She just sought to demonstrate that she, the Communist, did not want to have anything to do with the chief rabbi and Jewry; and that she had less in common with him than even the other members of the government" (Hal Lehrman, "Hungary-Rumania: Crime and Punishment, Pages from a Correspondent's Notebook," *Commentary,* October 1946, p. 333; John Gunther, *Behind the Curtain* [New York, 1948], p. 124; Şafran, *Resisting the Storm: Romania, 1940–1947, Memoirs,* edited and annotated by Jean Ancel [Jerusalem, 1987], p. 161).

129. One manifesto found in the archives erroneously includes Luca and Georgescu in the list of Jewish leaders who, it suggested, "have shot, tortured and imprisoned the best Romanians in the name of class conflict and the fight against racial hatred, and have removed Romanians from institutions, enterprises, colleges and offices, and replaced them with Jews" (Bulletin, June 1948, ASRI, Fond D, Dosar 1599, p. 374). Georgescu's depiction as a Jew whose original name was Baruch Tescovici is common in post-Communist Romania, and historian Gheorghe Buzatu has given it "scholarly" sanction. In his recent study of documents in the Soviet archives on Romania, Buzatu fails to cite any source when listing Baruch Tescovici as Teohari Georgescu's "real name"—and for good reason: Georgescu's Securitate file nowhere mentions any such name or Georgescu's supposed Jewish origins (in stark contrast with the files on Ana Pauker and Georgescu's deputy Mişu Dulgheru)—despite the inquiry's clear anti-Semitic motif, beginning as it did in conjunction with the Doctors' Plot in Moscow (Gheorghe Buzatu, *Românii în Arhivele Kremlinului* [The Romanians in the Kremlin Archives] [Bucharest, 1996], p. 148 n. 90).

130. Transcript of an Interrogation of Ana Pauker by a Party Commission of the R.W.P., June 12, 1953, Ana Pauker Inquiry File, Executive Archive of the Central Committee of the R.C.P., p. 70.

131. Lehrman, "Hungary-Rumania: Crime and Punishment, Pages from a Correspondent's Notebook," p. 333.

132. Kochavi, "British Diplomats and the Jews in Poland, Romania and Hungary," p. 455 [emphasis added].

133. Interrogation of Vasile Luca, February 22, 1954, ASRI, Dosar 40005, Vol. 2, p. 54.

134. Minutes of the Meeting of the Politburo of the R.W.P., October 26, 1948, National Archives of Romania, Fond CC al PCR—Cancelarie, Dosar 50/1948, p. 4 [emphasis added].

135. Gheorghe Brătescu interview.

136. Cristina Boico interview.

137. Carol and Eva Lustig interview, September 8, 1989.

138. Tatiana Brătescu interview.

139. Israel Levanon interview.

140. "A Girl Who Hated Cream Puffs," *Time,* September 20, 1948, p. 34.

141. Israel Levanon interview. A report detailing Pauker's inquiry confirmed that she "sent greetings via Rabinsohn to Rabbi Friedman" ("Report Regarding the Findings of the Inquiry of Ana Pauker, Former Secretary of the C.C. of the R.W.P. and Minister of Foreign Affairs," June 6, 1953, ASRI, Fond P, Dosar 40005, Vol. 173, p. 159).

142. "Report Regarding the Findings of the Inquiry of Ana Pauker, Former Secretary of the C.C. of the R.W.P. and Minister of Foreign Affairs," June 6, 1953, ASRI, Fond P, Dosar 40005, Vol. 173, p. 157.

143. Ana Toma interview; Declaration of Ana Toma, October 12, 1956, Ana Pauker Inquiry File, Executive Archive of the Central Committee of the R.C.P., p. 3.

144. Interrogation of Solomon Rabinsohn, March 3, 1953, ASRI, Fond P, Dosar 40009, Vol. 60, p. 25.

145. Declaration of Gheorghe Pintilie, June 10, 1956, Ana Pauker Inquiry File, Executive Archive of the Central Committee of the R.C.P., p. 14. Interrogation of Vasile Luca, February 22, 1954, ASRI, Fond P, Dosar 40005, Vol. 2, p. 55.

146. Interrogation of Solomon Rabinsohn, March 3, 1953, ASRI, Fond P, Dosar 40009, Vol. 60, p. 29; Review of the Findings of the Investigation of Ana Pauker, June 6, 1953, ASRI, Fond P, Dosar 40005, Vol. 173, p. 158.

147. Ehud Avriel, *Open the Gates! A Personal Story of "Illegal" Immigration to Israel* (New York, 1975), p. 340.

CHAPTER 7

1. Interrogation of Solomon Rabinsohn, February 24, 1953, ASRI, Fond P, Dosar 40009, Vol. 60, p. 11; Interrogation of Solomon Rabinsohn, May 29, 1953, ASRI, Fond P, Dosar 40009, Vol. 60, p. 120.

2. Interrogation of Solomon Rabinsohn, February 20, 1953, ASRI, Fond P, Dosar 40009, Vol. 60, pp. 7–8; Interrogation of Solomon Rabinsohn, March 3, 1953, ASRI, Fond P, Dosar 40009, Vol. 60, pp. 21–23, 26.

3. Interrogation of Solomon Rabinsohn, March 26, 1953, ASRI, Fond P, Dosar 40009, Vol. 60, p. 51.

4. Ibid., p. 52; Synthesis of the Findings of the Inquiry of Solomon Rabinsohn, undated, ASRI, Fond P, Dosar 40009, Vol. 54, p. 60; Declaration of Ana Toma, October 12, 1956, Ana Pauker Inquiry File, Executive Archive of the Central Committee of the R.C.P., p. 3.

5. Answers given by Ana Pauker to questions put before her by an R.W.P. Commission, June 20, 1953, Ana Pauker Inquiry File, Executive Archive of the Central Committee of the R.C.P., p. 15; Transcript of an Interrogation of Ana Pauker by a Party Commission of the R.W.P., June 12, 1953, Ana Pauker Inquiry File, Executive Archive of the Central Committee of the R.C.P., p. 70.

6. This had indeed occurred to the Securitate chief Gheorghe Pintilie. (Declaration of Gheorghe Pintilie, June 10, 1956, Ana Pauker Inquiry File, Executive Archive of the Central Committee of the R.C.P., p. 14.)

7. Shlomo Leibovici and Israel Levanon interviews.

8. Ibid.; Tatiana and Gheorghe Brătescu, Marie Birnbaum, Yisrael Gutman, and Moses Rosen interviews; Interrogation of Solomon Rabinsohn, May 29, 1953, ASRI, Fond P, Dosar 40009, Vol. 60, p. 121.

9. Transcript of an Interrogation of Ana Pauker by a Party Commission of the R.W.P., July 6, 1956, Ana Pauker Inquiry File, Executive Archive of the Central Committee of the R.C.P., pp. 36–37.

10. Transcript of an Interrogation of Ana Pauker by a Party Commission of the

R.W.P., June 12, 1953, Ana Pauker Inquiry File, Executive Archive of the Central Committee of the R.C.P., p. 70.

11. Ibid.

12. Interrogation of Solomon Rabinsohn, March 3, 1953, ASRI, Fond P, Dosar 40009, Vol. 60, p. 29.

13. Declaration of Ana Toma, October 12, 1956, Ana Pauker Inquiry File, Executive Archive of the Central Committee of the R.C.P., p. 3.

14. Interrogation of Solomon Rabinsohn, March 3, 1953, ASRI, Fond P, Dosar 40009, Vol. 60, p. 29.

15. Shlomo Leibovici interview.

16. Ibid.; Mircu, *Ana Pauker și alții,* p. 137.

17. Shlomo Leibovici interview.

18. Shlomo Leibovici and Moses Rosen interviews; Mircu, *Ana Pauker și alții,* p. 137.

19. Moses Rosen interview.

20. Moses Rosen, *Primejdii, Incercări Miracole,* p. 116. An abbreviated version is found in the English edition of Rosen's memoirs (Moses Rosen, *Dangers, Tests and Miracles: The Remarkable Life Story of Chief Rabbi Rosen of Romania,* as told to Joseph Finklestone [London, 1990], pp. 75–76).

21. Moses Rosen interview.

22. Ibid.; Moses Rosen, *Primejdii, Incercări Miracole,* p. 116.

23. Shlomo Leibovici interview. Leibovici's source is Zalman Rabinsohn.

24. Interrogation of Solomon Rabinsohn, March 4, 1953, ASRI, Fond P, Dosar 40009, Vol. 60, p. 33; also see Moses Rosen, *Primejdii, Incercări Miracole,* p. 117.

25. Interrogation of Solomon Rabinsohn, February 18, 1953, ASRI, Fond P, Dosar 40009, Vol. 60, pp. 1–2; Synthesis of the Findings of the Inquiry of Solomon Rabinsohn, undated, ASRI, Fond P, Dosar 40009, Vol. 54, p. 61.

26. Answers given by Ana Pauker to questions put before her by an R.W.P. Commission, June 20, 1953, Ana Pauker Inquiry File, Executive Archive of the Central Committee of the R.C.P., p. 16.

27. Interrogation of Solomon Rabinsohn, February 18, 1953, ASRI, Fond P, Dosar 40009, Vol. 60, pp. 3–4; Interrogation of Solomon Rabinsohn, March 4, 1953, ASRI, Fond P, Dosar 40009, Vol. 60, p. 32.

28. Interrogation of Solomon Rabinsohn, February 18, 1953, ASRI, Fond P, Dosar 40009, Vol. 60, p. 4.

29. Ibid., p. 4.

30. Interrogation of Solomon Rabinsohn, March 4, 1953, ASRI, Fond P, Dosar 40009, Vol. 60, p. 32.

31. Ibid.

32. Interrogation of Vasile Luca, February 22, 1954, ASRI, Fond P, Dosar 40005, Vol. 2, p. 55.

33. Synthesis of the Findings of the Inquiry of Solomon Rabinsohn, undated, ASRI, Fond P, Dosar 40009, Vol. 54, p. 61; Interrogation of Solomon Rabinsohn, April 13, 1953, ASRI, Fond P, Dosar 40009, Vol. 60, p. 76.

34. Marie Birnbaum interview.

35. Tatiana Brătescu interview.

36. Marie Birnbaum interview.

37. Tatiana and Gheorghe Brătescu interview.

38. Interrogation of Solomon Rabinsohn, February 18, 1953, ASRI, Fond P, Dosar 40009, Vol. 60, p. 5. Dina Rabinsohn arrived in Romania in mid-Decem-

ber 1949 (Interrogation of Solomon Rabinsohn, March 4, 1953, ASRI, Fond P, Dosar 40009, Vol. 60, p. 34).

39. Interrogation of Solomon Rabinsohn, March 4, 1953, ASRI, Fond P, Dosar 40009, Vol. 60, p. 34; Declaration of Ana Toma, October 12, 1956, Ana Pauker Inquiry File, Executive Archive of the Central Committee of the R.C.P., pp. 3–4.

40. Interrogation of Solomon Rabinsohn, February 18, 1953, ASRI, Fond P, Dosar 40009, Vol. 60, p. 5; Interrogation of Solomon Rabinsohn, March 4, 1953, ASRI, Fond P, Dosar 40009, Vol. 60, p. 35.

41. Interrogation of Solomon Rabinsohn, March 4, 1953, ASRI, Fond P, Dosar 40009, Vol. 60, p. 32.

42. Interrogation of Solomon Rabinsohn, February 18, 1953, ASRI, Fond P, Dosar 40009, Vol. 60, p. 5.

43. Ibid., pp. 5–6; Answers given by Ana Pauker to questions put before her by an R.W.P. Commission, June 20, 1953, Ana Pauker Inquiry File, Executive Archive of the Central Committee of the R.C.P., pp. 15–16.

44. Interrogation of Solomon Rabinsohn, February 18, 1953, ASRI, Fond P, Dosar 40009, Vol. 60, p. 5.

45. Ibid., p. 6.

46. Elena Tudorache interview. At the time Tudorache was the Rabinsohns' downstairs neighbor.

47. Shlomo Leibovici interview.

48. Synthesis of the Findings of the Inquiry of Solomon Rabinsohn, undated, ASRI, Fond P, Dosar 40009, Vol. 54, p. 61.

49. Ibid., p. 62.

50. The Romanian Zionist leader A. L. Zissu even suggested to Rabinsohn in the spring of 1950 that he should probably return to Israel (Interrogation of Solomon Rabinsohn, April 6, 1953, ASRI, Fond P, Dosar 40009, Vol. 60, p. 64). Interrogation of Solomon Rabinsohn, March 10, 1953, ASRI, Fond P, Dosar 40009, Vol. 60, pp. 42, 45; Declaration of Melania Iancu, January 16, 1953, ASRI, Fond P, Dosar 40005, Vol. 160, p. 134; Interrogation of Marcu Cohin, August 10, 1953, ASRI, Fond P, Dosar 40009, Vol. 62, p. 304.

51. Moses Rosen, *Primejdii, Incercări Miracole,* p. 118.

52. Interrogation of Solomon Rabinsohn, June 18, 1953, ASRI, Fond P, Dosar 40009, Vol. 60, pp. 132, 135.

53. Ibid., p. 137; Interrogation of Solomon Rabinsohn, April 7, 1953, ASRI, Fond P, Dosar 40009, Vol. 62, p. 56.

54. Interrogation of Solomon Rabinsohn, June 18, 1953, ASRI, Fond P, Dosar 40009, Vol. 60, p. 137.

55. Ibid.; Interrogation of Solomon Rabinsohn, April 7, 1953, ASRI, Fond P, Dosar 40009, Vol. 62, p. 56.

56. Interrogation of Solomon Rabinsohn, June 18, 1953, ASRI, Fond P, Dosar 40009, Vol. 60, p. 139; Informative Note, April 24, 1953, ASRI, Fond P, Dosar 40009, Vol. 50, p. 140.

57. Interrogation of Solomon Rabinsohn, April 20, 1953, ASRI, Fond P, Dosar 40009, Vol. 62, p. 56; Interrogation of Solomon Rabinsohn, June 18, 1953, ASRI, Fond P, Dosar 40009, Vol. 60, p. 139.

58. Zalman suggested to the embassy that Israel should mellow its criticism of the RPR, for it was angering Romania's leaders. He based this on conclusions drawn from discussions with Ana Pauker, who told him "of the position and opinion of the RWP leaders towards the policies and manifestations of the Israeli government, a

matter that had repercussions towards the Zionists and emigration" (Interrogation of Solomon Rabinsohn, June 18, 1953, ASRI, Fond P, Dosar 40009, Vol. 60, p. 134; Interrogation of Solomon Rabinsohn, March 10, 1953, ASRI, Fond P, Dosar 40009, Vol. 60, pp. 46–47).

59. Declaration of Melania Iancu, January 16, 1953, ASRI, Fond P, Dosar 40005, Vol. 160, p. 133.

60. Yisrael Gutman interview; Interrogation of Solomon Rabinsohn, March 4, 1953, ASRI, Fond P, Dosar 40009, Vol. 60, p. 33.

61. Interrogation of Solomon Rabinsohn, February 25, 1953, ASRI, Fond P, Dosar 40009, Vol. 60, p. 15; Interrogation of Solomon Rabinsohn, March 10, 1953, ASRI, Fond P, Dosar 40009, Vol. 60, p. 42; Moses Rosen, *Primejdii, Incercări Miracole*, p. 119.

62. Declaration of Melania Iancu, January 16, 1953, ASRI, Fond P, Dosar 40005, Vol. 160, p. 134.

63. Interrogation of Solomon Rabinsohn, March 4, 1953, ASRI, Fond P, Dosar 40009, Vol. 60, pp. 36–37.

64. Interrogation of Solomon Rabinsohn, February 25, 1953, ASRI, Fond P, Dosar 40009, Vol. 60, p. 15.

65. Interrogation of Solomon Rabinsohn, March 4, 1953, ASRI, Fond P, Dosar 40009, Vol. 60, p. 37.

66. Zalman's close associate Rabbi Yitzchak Friedman later confirmed that Pauker inquired into the Zionists' condition at her brother's behest (Krivine, "Who Was Ana Pauker?" p. 9). Interrogation of Marcu Cohin, March 11–12, 1953, ASRI, Fond P, Dosar 40009, Vol. 62, p. 260(b); Interrogation of Leon Itzkar, April 29, 1952, ASRI, Dosar 16385, Vol. 44, pp. 300–301, cited in *Zionişti sub anchetă* [Zionists under Investigation] (Bucharest, 1993), p. 81.

67. Interrogation of Solomon Rabinsohn, February 25, 1953, ASRI, Fond P, Dosar 40009, Vol. 60, p. 16.

68. Ibid.; Interrogation of Solomon Rabinsohn, April 7, 1953, ASRI, Fond P, Dosar 40009, Vol. 60, p. 57.

69. Interrogation of Solomon Rabinsohn, February 25, 1953, ASRI, Fond P, Dosar 40009, Vol. 60, p. 16.

70. Declaration of Melania Iancu, January 16, 1953, ASRI, Fond P, Dosar 40005, Vol. 160, p. 134; Interrogation of Marcu Cohin, March 11–12, 1953, ASRI, Fond P, Dosar 40009, Vol. 62, p. 259(b).

71. Interrogation of Solomon Rabinsohn, March 10, 1953, ASRI, Fond P, Dosar 40009, Vol. 60, p. 42; Interrogation of Solomon Rabinsohn, June 18, 1953, ASRI, Fond P, Dosar 40009, Vol. 60, p. 132; Interrogation of Marcu Cohin, March 11–12, 1953, ASRI, Fond P, Dosar 40009, Vol. 62, pp. 259–263; Interrogation of Marcu Cohin, March 19, 1953, ASRI, Fond P, Dosar 40009, Vol. 62, pp. 264–266; Interrogation of Marcu Cohin, April 20, 1953, ASRI, Fond P, Dosar 40009, Vol. 62, pp. 267–269; Shlomo Leibovici and Israel Levanon interviews.

72. Interrogation of Solomon Rabinsohn, March 10, 1953, ASRI, Fond P, Dosar 40009, Vol. 60, p. 44; Interrogation of Solomon Rabinsohn, June 18, 1953, ASRI, Fond P, Dosar 40009, Vol. 60, p. 135.

73. Interrogation of Marcu Cohin, March 11–12, 1953, ASRI, Fond P, Dosar 40009, Vol. 62, p. 260.

74. Interrogation of Solomon Rabinsohn, March 10, 1953, ASRI, Fond P, Dosar 40009, Vol. 60, p. 43.

75. Interrogation of Marcu Cohin, March 19, 1953, ASRI, Fond P, Dosar 40009, Vol. 62, p. 266.

76. Interrogation of Solomon Rabinsohn, March 10, 1953, ASRI, Fond P, Dosar 40009, Vol. 60, p. 44.

77. Informative Note, June 21, 1953, ASRI, Fond P, Dosar 40009, Vol. 50, p. 368.

78. This was the case of the renowned Vishnitzer Rebbe, Rabbi Israel Hager, whose remains were taken off a ship headed for Israel when an accusation was made that jewels and money were hidden in his coffin. Pauker resolved the situation, intervening at the behest of Zalman and Chief Rabbi Moses Rosen (Interrogation of Solomon Rabinsohn, April 7, 1953, ASRI, Fond P, Dosar 40009, Vol. 60, p. 57; Moses Rosen, *Dangers, Tests and Miracles,* pp. 69–72). Pauker intervened again in a similar incident with the coffin of Rabbi Rosen's father in December 1951 (Rabbi Moses Rosen interview; also see Moses Rosen, *Dangers, Tests and Miracles,* pp. 72–76, and the Interrogation of Solomon Rabinsohn, April 7, 1953, ASRI, Fond P, Dosar 40009, Vol. 60, pp. 58–59).

79. Interrogation of Solomon Rabinsohn, June 18, 1953, ASRI, Fond P, Dosar 40009, Vol. 60, p. 137; Informative Note, June 13, 1953, ASRI, Fond P, Dosar 40009, Vol. 50, p. 346.

80. Interrogation of Solomon Rabinsohn, April 7, 1953, ASRI, Fond P, Dosar 40009, Vol. 62, p. 56.

81. Informative Note, June 13, 1953, ASRI, Fond P, Dosar 40009, Vol. 50, p. 346.

82. Ibid.

83. Synthesis of the Findings of the Inquiry of Solomon Rabinsohn, undated, ASRI, Fond P, Dosar 40009, Vol. 54, p. 65; Interrogation of Solomon Rabinsohn, March 26, 1953, ASRI, Fond P, Dosar 40009, Vol. 60, p. 54.

84. On the arrests in May and September, see the Interrogation of Marcu Cohin, March 11–12, 1953, ASRI, Fond P, Dosar 40009, Vol. 62, p. 260; Shlomo Leibovici interview. On those through the winter, see Sylvain, "Rumania," p. 540. On Georgescu, see the Interrogation of Solomon Rabinsohn, April 7, 1953, ASRI, Fond P, Dosar 40009, Vol. 60, p. 59.

85. Interrogation of Marcu Cohin, March 19, 1953, ASRI, Fond P, Dosar 40009, Vol. 62, p. 266. On Chişinevschi's anti-Zionist position, also see Interrogation of Solomon Rabinsohn, April 7, 1953, ASRI, Fond P, Dosar 40009, Vol. 60, pp. 57–58; Declaration of Melania Iancu, January 16, 1953, ASRI, Fond P, Dosar 40005, Vol. 160, p. 134; Declaration of Radu Robert Cohin (son of Marcu Cohin), February 5, 1953, ASRI, Fond P, Dosar 40005, Vol. 160, p. 188.

86. Peter Meyer, "Has Soviet Anti-Semitism Halted?" *Commentary,* July 1954, p. 7.

87. Ibid.; Rabbi Moses Rosen, *Dangers, Tests and Miracles,* pp. 115–117.

88. Boris Nicolaevsky, "The Meaning of Khrushchev's Victory," *New Leader,* September 2, 1957, p. 5; Benjamin Pinkus, *The Soviet Government and the Jews,* p. 238.

89. S. Avni, "Exodus from Romania," *Shoah* 11 (1983), p. 207, cited in Raphael Vago, "Jews in the Communist Regime, 1944–1948," p. 143.

90. Interrogation of Solomon Rabinsohn, June 18, 1953, ASRI, Fond P, Dosar 40009, Vol. 60, p. 141.

91. David Krivine, "Who Was Ana Pauker?" p. 9; David Krivine, personal correspondence with the author.

92. For Cohin's claims, see Interrogation of Marcu Cohin, April 20, 1953, ASRI, Fond P, Dosar 40009, Vol. 62, pp. 267–268; Minutes of the Interrogation of Marcu Cohin, March 19, 1953, ASRI, Fond P, Dosar 40009, Vol. 62, p. 265(b).

CHAPTER 8

1. Gyorgy Lazar (pen name), "Memorandum," in *Witnesses to Cultural Genocide: First-Hand Reports on Rumania's Minority Policies Today,* pp. 94–95.

2. Interrogation of Teohari Georgescu, July 4, 1955, ASRI, Fond P, Dosar 40009, Vol. 4, p. 237. The Secretariat appointed Moghioroş head of the Commission for the Verification of Cadres within the Central Committee on December 6, 1949, to be "assisted" by Ana Pauker; however, Pauker revealed that she no longer worked with him after her cancer operation in the summer of 1950 (Transcript of a Meeting of the Secretariat of the R.W.P., December 6, 1952, National Archives of Romania, Fond CC al PCR—Cancelarie, Dosar 105/1949, p. 24; Interrogation of Ana Pauker by a Party Commission of the R.W.P., June 12, 1953, Ana Pauker Inquiry File, Executive Archive of the Central Committee of the R.C.P., p. 64).

3. Mihai Alexandru, Jean Coler, Eugen Szabo, Cristina Boico, Charlotte Gruia, Ida Felix, and David Rotman interviews. On this phenomenon generally, see Sheila Fitzpatrick, "Stalin and the Making of a New Elite, 1928–1939," *Slavic Review* 38, no. 3 (September 1979), pp. 377–402.

4. Transcript of a Meeting of the Politburo of the R.W.P., March 12–14, 1961, Executive Archive of the Central Committee of the R.C.P., p. 164.

5. Tatiana and Gheorghe Brătescu interview.

6. Interrogation of Ana Pauker by a Party Commission of the R.W.P., June 12, 1953, Ana Pauker Inquiry File, Executive Archive of the Central Committee of the R.C.P., p. 77.

7. "Particularly in 1951," Pauker related, "I was unhappy that we weren't holding meetings, that problems weren't being discussed, and that I was being isolated and pushed aside." Important policy decisions, she added, were increasingly being made in "smaller committees" (Answers of Ana Pauker to the Questions Posed by the Party Commission of the R.W.P., June 12, 1953, Ana Pauker Inquiry File, Executive Archive of the Central Committee of the R.C.P., p. 16; Interrogation of Ana Pauker by a Party Commission of the R.W.P., June 12, 1953, Ana Pauker Inquiry File, Executive Archive of the Central Committee of the R.C.P., p. 77; Conversation of Ana Pauker and Two Party Leaders at a Party House in Otopeni, April 8, 1953, ASRI, Fond P, Dosar 40009, Vol. 68, p. 236).

8. Sorin Toma, Mircea Oprişan, Eduard Mezincescu, Jean Coler, Ida Felix, and Simion Bughici interviews.

9. Luca's syphilis was noted in a document dated 1933 of the Military Tribunal of the Romanian 5th Army Corp. It was also confirmed by Luca's personal physician, Dr. Sandu Liblich, who revealed to Dr. Gheorghe Brătescu that Luca had to be given daily injections to combat the symptoms of the syphilis (Stelian Tănase, "The Illnesses Appeared in Prison and Were Treated in Power," *Dosarele istoriei* 3, no. 4 [20] [1998], p. 43; Tatiana and Gheorghe Brătescu interview).

10. Interrogation of Interior Commerce Minister Vasile Malinschi by a Party Commission, June 5, 1952, National Archives of Romania, Fond 1, Dosar 254/1952, p. 164; Eduard Mezincescu interview.

11. Mihai Alexandru interview.

12. Radu Mănescu, written correspondence to the author, January 28, 1993 [emphasis added]. Also see the declaration of Zoltan Eidlitz, undated, ASRI, Fond P, Dosar 40005, Vol. 111, p. 111.

13. Luca revealed this to his friend Mihail Patriciu (Mihail Patriciu interview).

14. Interrogation of Ivan Solymos, February 9, 1953, ASRI, Fond P, Dosar 40005, Vol. 39, p. 157; Alexandru Nistor interview.

15. Transcript of the Plenary Meeting of the Central Committee of the R.C.P., January 25–28, 1946, National Archives of Romania, Fond 1, Dosar 1/1946, p. 3.

16. Alexandru Nistor interview.

17. Ibid. Luca did so, moreover, shortly after the CASBI leadership and a Soviet representative issued a report denouncing the Finance Ministry for refusing to sufficiently finance CASBI's investigations. Luca promptly summoned and harshly rebuked one of the signatories, Atanase Joja. "Luca told me," Joja declared, "that my attitude, particularly the fact that I signed a document with a representative of a foreign country, constituted an act of national treason" (Declaration of Atanase Joja, April 19, 1952, National Archives of Romania, Fond 1, Dosar 561/1952, p. 30; Declaration of Atanase Joja, October 18, 1952, ASRI, Fond P, Dosar 40005, Vol. 110, p. 80; Declaration of Mihail Maievschi, April 25, 1952, National Archives of Romania, Fond 1, Dosar 561/1952, p. 25).

18. Declaration of Mihail Maievschi, April 25, 1952, National Archives of Romania, Fond 1, Dosar 561/1952, p. 25.

19. Alexandru Nistor interview. Atanase Joja confirmed Pauker's backing of Luca on this issue (Declaration of Atanase Joja, Transcript of a Meeting of the Party Organization in the Foreign Ministry, June 16, 1952, National Archives of Romania, Fond CC al PCR—Cancelarie, Dosar 51/1952, p. 137).

20. Self-Criticism of Ana Pauker to the Politburo of the R.W.P., September 22, 1952, Ana Pauker Inquiry File, Executive Archive of the Central Committee of the R.C.P. Pauker's support for abolishing CASBI was in contrast to her position in the immediate postwar period, when she accused Ion Gheorghe Maurer of "nationalist tendencies" in 1945–46 for opposing the transfer to the Soviets of a certain annex of the Reșița industrial complex that they claimed had belonged to the Germans (Transcript of an Interrogation of Ana Pauker by a R.W.P. Commission, June 12, 1953, Ana Pauker Inquiry File, Executive Archive of the Central Committee of the R.C.P., p. 56; Transcript of an Interrogation of Ana Pauker by a R.W.P. Commission, July 29, 1953, Ana Pauker Inquiry File, Executive Archive of the Central Committee of the R.C.P., pp. 36–38).

21. Alexandru Nistor interview.

22. Ibid.

23. "Report Regarding Some Aspects of the Activities of the Reparations Administration in 1947–1948," May 14, 1952, National Archives of Romania, Fond 1, Dosar 561/1952, pp. 2–3.

24. Interrogation of Alexandru Iacob, April 4, 1952, ASRI, Fond P, Dosar 40005, Vol. 15, pp. 37–38.

25. Declaration of Zoltan Eidlitz, ASRI, Fond P, Dosar 40005, Vol. 111, p. 87; Alexandru Nistor interview.

26. Transcript of a Meeting of the Politburo of the R.W.P., May 26, 1952, National Archives of Romania, Fond CC al PCR—Cancelarie, Dosar 40/1952, pp. 41, 44; Declaration of Zoltan Eidlitz, ASRI, Fond P, Dosar 40005, Vol. 111, p. 87.

27. Transcript of the Plenary of the Central Committee of the R.W.P., May 27–29, 1952, National Archives of Romania, Fond CC al PCR—Cancelarie, Dosar 41/1952, p. 96; Transcript of a Meeting of the Politburo of the R.W.P., May 26, 1952, National Archives of Romania, Fond CC al PCR—Cancelarie, Dosar 40/1952, pp. 34, 44; Transcript of the Plenary of the Central Committee of the R.W.P., May 27–29, 1952, National Archives of Romania, Fond CC al PCR—Cancelarie, Dosar 41/1952, p. 9.

28. Interrogation of Teohari Georgescu, July 4, 1955, ASRI, Fond P, Dosar 40009, Vol. 4, p. 238; Transcript of the Plenary of the Central Committee of the

R.W.P., May 27–29, 1952, National Archives of Romania, Fond CC al PCR—Cancelarie, Dosar 41/1952, p. 9; Self-Criticism of Ana Pauker to the Politburo of the R.W.P., September 22, 1952, Ana Pauker Inquiry File, Executive Archive of the Central Committee of the R.C.P.

29. Victor Vezendean interview.

30. Ibid.

31. Ibid. Vezendean reported that both Dumitru Colu and Petre Borilă were also at the meeting.

32. Ibid.

33. Keleti revealed this to Wilhelm Einhorn (Einhorn interview).

34. An incriminating declaration of Keleti's, dated June 3, 1952, is in Iacob's Securitate file (ASRI, Fond P, Dosar 40005, Vol. 22, pp. 2–15).

35. Ro'i, *Soviet Decision Making in Practice*, pp. 357–358. Also see Checinski, *Poland: Communism, Nationalism, Anti-Semitism*, pp. 89–90; London, *The Confession*, p. 42; and Milovan Djilas, "Antisemitism," *Borba*, December 14, 1952.

36. Ivan T. Berend, *Central and Eastern Europe, 1944–1993: Detour from the Periphery to the Periphery* (Cambridge, 1996), pp. 70–71; Myron Rush, *How Communist States Change Their Rulers* (Ithaca, N.Y., 1974), pp. 40–41, 307 n. 16; Michael Checinski, "Soviet-Polish Relations and the Polish Jews," *Midstream*, May 1980, pp. 9–10.

37. Karel Kaplan, *London Times*, May 6, 1977; cited in Alex De Jonge, *Stalin* (New York, 1986), p. 467.

38. Eduard Ochab interview, in Teresa Toranska, *Them: Stalin's Political Puppets*, p. 46.

39. Roman Werfel interview, in Teresa Toranska, *Them: Stalin's Political Puppets*, p. 113.

40. Transcript of a Meeting of the Council of Ministers, December 18, 1951, National Archives of Romania, Fond Consiliul de Miniştri—Cabinetul, Dosar 9/1951, p. 124.

41. *Manchester Guardian*, June 2, 1952. Teohari Georgescu's reference in the Politburo to "certain manifestations [in 1951] in state enterprises and factories of discontented . . . workers and miners due to the difficult conditions everywhere" confirms this (Transcript of a Meeting of the Politburo, March 13, 1952, National Archives of Romania, Fond CC al PCR—Cancelarie, Dosar 19/1952, p. 48).

42. Theodor Lavi (Lowenstein), *Nu a fost pisica neagra* (Tel Aviv, 1979); cited in Mircu, *Ana Pauker şi alţii*, pp. 169–170; Yaffa Cuperman interview, December 20, 1991. Cuperman interviewed a significant number of the arrested Zionists for her study *Bi-tsevat ha-komunizm: ha-Histadrut ha-Tsiyonit be-Romanyah, 1944–1949* (Tel Aviv, 1995).

43. Interrogation of Elisabeta Luca, October 31, 1952, ASRI, Fond P, Dosar 40005, Vol. 13, pp. 75–79; Interrogation of Elisabeta Luca, March 5, 1953, ASRI, Fond P, Dosar 40005, Vol. 13, pp. 285–287.

44. Interrogation of Avram Isaevici Vaisman, June 8, 1949, ASRI, Fond P, Dosar 40005, Vol. 181, pp. 7–8.

45. Transcript of an Interrogation of Ana Pauker by an R.W.P. Commission, June 18, 1956, Ana Pauker Inquiry File, Executive Archive of the Central Committee of the R.C.P., pp. 17, 22.

46. Declaration of Gheorghe Pintilie, June 10, 1956, Ana Pauker Inquiry File, Executive Archive of the Central Committee of the R.C.P., p. 14.

47. Interrogation of Israel Pinhas, July 17–18, 1950, ASRI, Fond P, Dosar

40009, Vol. 61, p. 152; Interrogation of Israel Pinhas, August 4–5, 1950, ASRI, Fond P, Dosar 40009, Vol. 61, p. 146.

48. Declaration of Gheorghe Pintilie, June 10, 1956, Ana Pauker Inquiry File, Executive Archive of the Central Committee of the R.C.P., p. 14.

49. Arkady Vaksberg, *Stalin against the Jews* (New York, 1994), p. 193.

50. The Transylvanian Party leader writing under the pseudonym Gyorgy Lazar also made this point: "Being a woman was also a factor against the Jewish Pauker," enabling Dej to win Stalin's backing to purge her (Gyorgy Lazar [pen name], "Memorandum," pp. 96–97).

51. Transcript of the Plenary of the Central Committee of the R.W.P., May 27–29, 1952, National Archives of Romania, Fond CC al PCR—Cancelarie, Dosar 41/1952, p. 81.

52. Gheorghiu-Dej subsequently confirmed to the Politburo that Chişinevschi had accompanied him to this meeting with Stalin (Transcript of a Meeting of the Politburo of the R.W.P., April 17, 1952, National Archives of Romania, Fond CC al PCR—Cancelarie, Dosar 30/1952, p. 7). Moreover, Gheorghe Brătescu, then working in the Romanian embassy in Moscow, met Dej and Chişinevschi at the airport before their flight back to Bucharest—as did Miron Constantinescu, who was vacationing at the time in the Soviet Union. Upon arriving at the airport, Dej promptly informed Constantinescu, within earshot of Brătescu, that "he agreed to everything." Later, Constantinescu confirmed to his deputy, Mircea Oprişan, that Dej had indeed received Stalin's blessing for the purge at that meeting (Gheorghe Brătescu and Mircea Oprişan interviews).

53. Transcript of a Meeting of the Politburo of the R.W.P., February 21, 1952, National Archives of Romania, Fond CC al PCR—Cancelarie, Dosar 11/1952, pp. 107, 110.

54. Transcript of a Meeting of the Politburo of the R.W.P., February 26, 1952, National Archives of Romania, Fond CC al PCR—Cancelarie, Dosar 12/1952, p. 21.

55. Transcript of a Meeting of the Politburo of the R.W.P., February 21, 1952, National Archives of Romania, Fond CC al PCR—Cancelarie, Dosar 11/1952, pp. 107–108; Transcript of a Meeting of the Politburo of the R.W.P., March 13, 1952, National Archives of Romania, Fond CC al PCR—Cancelarie, Dosar 19/1952, pp. 27–28.

56. Declaration of Mihai Maievschi, May 10, 1952, National Archives of Romania, Fond 1, Dosar 563/1952, p. 28.

57. Transcript of a Meeting of the Politburo of the R.W.P., September 1, 1950, National Archives of Romania, Fond CC al PCR—Cancelarie, Dosar 54/1950, pp. 1–2.

58. Transcript of a Meeting of the Politburo of the R.W.P., February 26, 1952, National Archives of Romania, Fond CC al PCR—Cancelarie, Dosar 12/1952, p. 55; Transcript of a Meeting of the Politburo of the R.W.P., September 1, 1950, National Archives of Romania, Fond CC al PCR—Cancelarie, Dosar 54/1950, p. 2.

59. Transcript of a Meeting of the Politburo of the R.W.P., February 21, 1952, National Archives of Romania, Fond CC al PCR—Cancelarie, Dosar 11/1952, p. 79.

60. Ibid., p. 110. Also see the Declaration of Aurel Vijoli, March 11, 1952, National Archives of Romania, Fond 1, Dosar 512/1952, p. 53. For details of the Currency Reform, see Ionescu, *Communism in Romania,* pp. 203–204.

61. Transcript of a Meeting of the Politburo of the R.W.P., February 21, 1952, National Archives of Romania, Fond CC al PCR—Cancelarie, Dosar 11/1952, p. 110.

62. Transcript of a Meeting of the Politburo of the R.W.P., February 20, 1952, National Archives of Romania, Fond CC al PCR—Cancelarie, Dosar 11/1952, p. 94.

63. Transcript of a Meeting of the Politburo of the R.W.P., February 19, 1952, National Archives of Romania, Fond CC al PCR—Cancelarie, Dosar 11/1952, p. 65.

64. Memoir of Vasile Luca, November 5, 1954, ASRI, Fond P, Dosar 40005, Vol. 126, p. 51; Interrogation of Vasile Luca, February 19, 1953, ASRI, Fond P, Dosar 40005, Vol. 4, p. 449; Interrogation of Vasile Luca, February 22, 1953, ASRI, Fond P, Dosar 40005, Vol. 2, p. 58. Pauker confirmed that she opposed raising taxes on the peasants on the grounds "that they [couldn't] pay any more" (Transcript of an Interrogation of Ana Pauker by a Party Commission of the R.W.P., June 18, 1956, Ana Pauker Inquiry File, Executive Archive of the Central Committee of the R.C.P., p. 29).

65. Memoir of Vasile Luca, November 5, 1954, ASRI, Fond P, Dosar 40005, Vol. 126, p. 56. Pauker confirmed that she favored raising the price of cotton and other peasant produce, "for otherwise the peasants won't sell if we don't allow them high prices"; she also pushed for "giving advantages to the peasants so that they'll sell [their produce] to state buyers, so that we'll have food" (Transcript of an Interrogation of Ana Pauker by a Party Commission of the R.W.P., June 18, 1956, Ana Pauker Inquiry File, Executive Archive of the Central Committee of the R.C.P., p. 29; Transcript of an Interrogation of Ana Pauker by a Party Commission of the R.W.P., July 6, 1956, Ana Pauker Inquiry File, Executive Archive of the Central Committee of the R.C.P., p. 6).

66. Transcript of a Meeting of the Politburo of the R.W.P., February 19, 1952, National Archives of Romania, Fond CC al PCR—Cancelarie, Dosar 11/1952, p. 79; Transcript of a Meeting of the Politburo of the R.W.P., February 21, 1952, National Archives of Romania, Fond CC al PCR—Cancelarie, Dosar 11/1952, p. 110.

67. Declaration of Gheorghe Pintilie, June 10, 1956, p. 9; Transcript of a Meeting of the Politburo of the R.W.P., February 20, 1952, National Archives of Romania, Fond CC al PCR—Cancelarie, Dosar 11/1952, pp. 101–102.

68. Self-Criticism of Ana Pauker to the Politburo of the R.W.P., June 18, 1952, Ana Pauker Inquiry File, Executive Archive of the Central Committee of the R.C.P., p. 2.

69. The Politburo met on February 19, 20, 21, and 26 (National Archives of Romania, Fond CC al PCR—Cancelarie, Dosar 11/1952, pp. 1–131; Dosar 12/1952, pp. 3–73).

70. Transcript of an Interrogation of Ana Pauker by a Party Commission of the R.W.P., July 29, 1953, pp. 4, 14. Hence, the transcript of the meeting on February 26 notes the session was suddenly suspended in the middle of Chivu Stoica's remarks concurring with Moghioroș's proposal (Transcript of a Meeting of the Politburo of the R.W.P., February 26, 1952, National Archives of Romania, Fond CC al PCR—Cancelarie, Dosar 12/1952, p. 72).

71. Elisabeta Luca interview.

72. Notes of Teohari Georgescu on the Right Deviation, ASRI, Fond P, Dosar 40009/Annex, p. 1.

73. Elisabeta Luca interview.

74. Transcript of an Interrogation of Ana Pauker by a Party Commission of the R.W.P., July 29, 1953, Ana Pauker Inquiry File, Executive Archive of the Central Committee of the R.C.P., pp. 2–6.

75. Ibid., p. 4; Transcript of an Interrogation of Ana Pauker by a Party Commission of the R.W.P., June 12, 1953, Ana Pauker Inquiry File, Executive Archive of the Central Committee of the R.C.P., p. 64; Transcript of a Meeting of the Politburo,

March 13, 1952, National Archives of Romania, Fond CC al PCR—Cancelarie, Dosar 19/1952, p. 80; Transcript of an Interrogation of Ana Pauker by a Party Commission of the R.W.P., July 29, 1953, Ana Pauker Inquiry File, Executive Archive of the Central Committee of the R.C.P., pp. 8–9.

76. Transcript of a Meeting of the Politburo of the R.W.P., March 13, 1952, National Archives of Romania, Fond CC al PCR—Cancelarie, Dosar 19/1952, p. 62.

77. Transcript of an Interrogation of Ana Pauker by a Party Commission of the R.W.P., July 29, 1953, Ana Pauker Inquiry File, Executive Archive of the Central Committee of the R.C.P., pp. 5, 9, 11–14. The RWP leadership was later informed of Pauker's remarks (ibid., p. 35).

78. National Archives of Romania, Fond 1, Dosar 589/1952, p. 1.

79. ASRI, Fond P, Dosar 40009, Vol. 32, pp. 307–348.

80. Self-Criticism of Ana Pauker to the Politburo of the R.W.P., June 18, 1952, Ana Pauker Inquiry File, Executive Archive of the Central Committee of the R.C.P., p. 3.

81. Transcript of a Meeting of the Politburo, March 13, 1952, National Archives of Romania, Fond CC al PCR—Cancelarie, Dosar 19/1952, pp. 21–83.

82. Self-Criticism of Ana Pauker to the Politburo of the R.W.P., June 18, 1952, Ana Pauker Inquiry File, Executive Archive of the Central Committee of the R.C.P., p. 3; Interrogation of Vasile Luca, March 18, 1954, ASRI, Fond P, Dosar 40005, Vol. 2, p. 140.

83. Transcript of the Plenary of the Central Committee of the R.W.P., May 27–29, 1952, National Archives of Romania, Fond CC al PCR—Cancelarie, Dosar 41/1952, pp. 47–55, 75–76.

84. Hermina Tismăneanu interview. Tismăneanu was one of the translators.

85. Dej confirmed in a meeting of the Politburo that he was consulting with Mitin (Transcript of a Meeting of the Politburo of the R.W.P., April 17, 1952, National Archives of Romania, Fond CC al PCR—Cancelarie, Dosar 30/1952, p. 5). Also see Vladimir Tismaneanu, "The Tragicomedy of Romanian Communism," *Eastern European Politics and Societies* 3, no. 2 (Spring 1989), pp. 362–363. Tismaneanu learned of Mitin's connection to Dej from his aunt, Nehama Tismanetsky, who was personally close to Mitin's wife.

86. Netty Stachlovici, who worked as a typist at the Foreign Section in 1952, revealed this to her husband, Adam Feurştein (Iacob) (Adam Feurştein [Iacob] interview, June 25, 1991).

87. Ana Toma interview.

88. Transcript of the Declaration Given by Teohari Georgescu to the R.C.P. Commission, October 23, 1967, ASRI, Fond P, Dosar 40002, Vol. 203, p. 302.

89. Ibid.; Transcript of an Interrogation of Ana Pauker by a Party Commission of the R.W.P., July 29, 1953, Ana Pauker Inquiry File, Executive Archive of the Central Committee of the R.C.P., p. 15.

90. Transcript of a Meeting of the Politburo of the R.W.P., February 26, 1952, Fond CC al PCR—Cancelarie, Dosar 12/1952, p. 38.

91. Radu Mănescu interview. Mănescu was the deputy chief of the commission.

92. Declaration of Lt. Colonel Francisc Butyka, March 25, 1968, "Report Regarding the Trial of V. Luca," Executive Archive of the Central Committee of the R.C.P., No. 264/19, 18.02.1972, p. 90. Butyka headed the Luca inquiry in the Interior Ministry.

93. Remarks of Gheorghe Gheorghiu-Dej, Transcript of a Meeting of the Politburo of the R.W.P., November 29, 1961, Executive Archive of the Central Committee of the R.C.P., pp. 4–6. This meeting with Stalin took place soon after April 17,

1952, for Gheorghiu-Dej proposed to the Politburo on that date that Constantinescu, Apostol, and Moghioroş accompany him to the Kremlin (Transcript of a Meeting of the Politburo of the R.W.P., April 17, 1952, National Archives of Romania, Fond CC al PCR—Cancelarie, Dosar 30/1952, p. 7).

94. Interview of Gheorghe Apostol, recorded in April 1988, broadcast on BBC Radio April 25, 1990. Hence, Miron Constantinescu was designated to criticize Pauker at the Politburo meeting prior to the May 27–29 CC Plenary.

95. Self-Criticism of Ana Pauker to the Politburo of the R.W.P., September 22, 1952, Ana Pauker Inquiry File, Executive Archive of the Central Committee of the R.C.P.

96. Self-Criticism of Ana Pauker to the Politburo of the R.W.P., June 18, 1952, Ana Pauker Inquiry File, Executive Archive of the Central Committee of the R.C.P., p. 3.

97. Transcript of an Interrogation of Ana Pauker by a Party Commission of the R.W.P., July 29, 1953, Ana Pauker Inquiry File, Executive Archive of the Central Committee of the R.C.P., p. 36.

98. Leonte Răutu interview.

99. Ana Toma interview.

100. Transcript of an Interrogation of Ana Pauker by a Party Commission of the R.W.P., June 12, 1953, Ana Pauker Inquiry File, Executive Archive of the Central Committee of the R.C.P., pp. 71–72.

101. Declaration of Teohari Georgescu, May 23, 1956, Ana Pauker Inquiry File, Executive Archive of the Central Committee of the R.C.P., p. 11.

102. Georgescu revealed Dej's appeal to Alexandru Şiperco (Alexandru Şiperco interview).

103. "A Discussion with Alexandru Drăghici [and Teohari Georgescu]," April 20, 1968, Executive Archive of the Central Committee of the R.C.P., No. 264/18.02.1972, Vol. 7, p. 15.

104. Notes of Teohari Georgescu on the Right Deviation, ASRI, Fond P, Dosar 40009/Annex, p. 1.

105. Transcript of a Meeting of the Politburo of the R.W.P., May 26, 1952, National Archives of Romania, Fond CC al PCR—Cancelarie, Dosar 40/1952, p. 63.

106. Notes of Teohari Georgescu on the Right Deviation, ASRI, Fond P, Dosar 40009/Annex, p. 1.

107. Transcript of a Meeting of the Politburo of the R.W.P., May 26, 1952, National Archives of Romania, Fond CC al PCR—Cancelarie, Dosar 40/1952, pp. 31–32.

108. Sorin Toma interview.

109. Transcript of the Plenary of the Central Committee of the R.W.P., May 27–29, 1952, National Archives of Romania, Fond CC al PCR—Cancelarie, Dosar 41/1952, pp. 65, 81–83.

110. Ibid., p. 13.

111. "Report Regarding the Findings of the Inquiry of Ana Pauker," January 20, 1954, Ana Pauker Inquiry File, Executive Archive of the Central Committee of the R.C.P., pp. 1–2. Tatiana Brătescu's assertion is from her interview.

112. Tatiana and Gheorghe Brătescu interview.

113. Transcript of an Interrogation of Ana Pauker by a Party Commission of the R.W.P., July 6, 1956, Ana Pauker Inquiry File, Executive Archive of the Central Committee of the R.C.P., p. 24.

114. Transcript of a Meeting of the Politburo of the R.W.P., May 26, 1952, National Archives of Romania, Fond CC al PCR—Cancelarie, Dosar 40/1952, p. 86;

"Pentru Continua Intărire a Partidului" [For Continually Strengthening the Party], *Scânteia*, June 3, 1952; reprinted in *Rezoluții și Hotărîri ale Comitetului Central al Partidului Muncitoresc Român*, pp. 199–200.

115. Transcript of the Plenary of the Central Committee of the R.W.P., May 27–29, 1952, National Archives of Romania, Fond CC al PCR—Cancelarie, Dosar 41/1952, p. 69.

116. Ibid., p. 86.

117. "Pentru Continua Intărire a Partidului," p. 202.

118. Ana Toma interview.

119. Egon Balaş interview, April 18, 1997.

120. Dennis Deletant, *Ceaușescu and the Securitate: Coercion and Dissent in Romania, 1965–1989* (London, 1995), p. 16 n. 4; Victor Vezendean interview; Egon Balas, *Will to Freedom*, p. 241.

121. Transcript of a Meeting of the Party Organization in the Foreign Ministry, June 16, 1952, National Archives of Romania, Fond CC al PCR—Cancelarie, Dosar 51/1952, p. 168.

122. Carol Lustig interview.

123. Ibid.; Cristina Boico and Maria Sârbu interviews; Transcript of a Meeting of the Party Organization in the Foreign Ministry, June 12–13, 1952, National Archives of Romania, Fond CC al PCR—Cancelarie, Dosar 51/1952, pp. 4–5.

124. Egon Balaş interview.

125. Transcript of an Interrogation of Ana Pauker by a Party Commission of the R.W.P., July 29, 1953, Ana Pauker Inquiry File, Executive Archive of the Central Committee of the R.C.P., p. 11.

126. *New York Times*, July 7, 1952. According to Mihai Burcă, Kavtaradze was removed because he had tried to intervene on Pauker's behalf. Simion Bughici reported, moreover, that Kavtaradze provoked the wrath of his superiors by openly expressing his profound regret over her removal (Burcă and Bughici interviews).

127. Zandek Ellas and Joromir Netik, "Czechoslovakia," in William Griffith, ed., *Communism in Europe: Continuity, Change and the Sino-Soviet Dispute*, vol. 2 (Cambridge, Mass., 1966), p. 212; Shephard, *Russia's Danubian Empire*, p. 66 n. 2; *New York Times*, July 7, 1952.

128. *London Times*, July 8, 1952.

129. Transcript of a Meeting of the Politburo of the R.W.P., June 23, 1952, National Archives of Romania, Fond CC al PCR—Cancelarie, Dosar 56/1952, pp. 18–19.

130. Tatiana and Gheorghe Brătescu interview.

131. Transcript of a Discussion of Comrade Vințe with Ana Pauker, June 21, 1956, Ana Pauker Inquiry File, Executive Archive of the Central Committee of the R.C.P., p. 5.

132. Surveillance "through various means" began on September 16, 1952 (Note Regarding Certain Problems Emerging on How Ana Pauker was Investigated and Interrogated, April 9, 1968, Ana Pauker Inquiry File, Executive Archive of the Central Committee of the R.C.P., p. 2).

133. Declaration of Gheorghe Stoica, "A Discussion with Alexandru Drăghici," June 3, 1968, Executive Archive of the Central Committee of the R.C.P., No. 264/18.02.1972, Vol. 7, p. 2. Two exceptions from the Finance Ministry were Mihai Maievschi, the general secretary of the ministry and president of the Commission to Liquidate CASBI, who for some unknown reason was never arrested; and Marcel Balan, the director of the Administrative Directorate of the Finance Ministry, who killed himself in April 1952. An old-guard Communist who had been in prison for

most of the 1930s and World War II, Balan threw himself in front of a truck—leaving two small children (Alexandru Nistor interview).

134. Declaration of Lt. Colonel Francisc Butyka, March 25, 1968, "Report Regarding the Trial of V. Luca," Executive Archive of the Central Committee of the R.C.P., No. 264/19, 18.02.1972, pp. 90–91; Declaration of Lt. Colonel Francisc Butyka, June 18, 1968, ASRI, Fond P, Dosar 40005, Vol. 182a, p. 6.

135. Declaration of Gheorghe Stoica, "A Discussion with Alexandru Drăghici," June 3, 1968, Executive Archive of the Central Committee of the R.C.P., No. 264/ 18.02.1972, Vol. 7, p. 2.

136. Declaration of Lt. Major Gheorghe I. Enoiu, March 24, 1968, "Report Regarding the Trial of V. Luca," Executive Archive of the Central Committee of the R.C.P., No. 264/19, 18.02.1972, p. 118.

137. Declaration of Lt. Colonel Francisc Butyka, March 25, 1968, "Report Regarding the Trial of V. Luca," Executive Archive of the Central Committee of the R.C.P., No. 264/19, 18.02.1972, pp. 90–91; Declaration of Lt. Colonel Francisc Butyka, June 18, 1968, ASRI, Fond P, Dosar 40005, Vol. 182a, p. 6; Declaration of Petre M. Socol, March 24, 1968, "Report Regarding the Trial of V. Luca," Executive Archive of the Central Committee of the R.C.P., No. 264/19, 18.02.1972, pp. 106–107.

138. Iacob revealed this to his close friend Egon Balaş (Balaş, Will to Freedom, p. 241).

139. Declaration of Alexandru Iacob, June 18, 1968, ASRI, Fond P, Dosar 40005, Vol. 182a, p. 50; Interrogation of Alexandru Iacob, July 7, 1952, ASRI, Fond P, Dosar 40005, Vol. 15, p. 193.

140. Declaration of Alexandru Iacob, June 18, 1968, ASRI, Fond P, Dosar 40005, Vol. 182a, pp. 50–51.

141. Declaration of Iosif Bistran, "Report Regarding the Trial of V. Luca," Executive Archive of the Central Committee of the R.C.P., No. 264/19, 18.02.1972, p. 168.

142. Ibid.; Declaration of Gheorghe Stoica, "A Discussion with Alexandru Drăghici," June 3, 1968, Executive Archive of the Central Committee of the R.C.P., No. 64/18.02.1972, Vol. 7, pp. 14–15.

143. Transcript of the Interrogation of the Accused Iacob Alexandru, October 5, 1954, Supreme Court of the R.P.R., Military Board, Dosar N. 215/1954, ASRI, Fond P, Dosar 40005, Vol. 108, pp. 152–154.

144. Egon Balaş interview; Egon Balaş, Will to Freedom, p. 312.

145. Informative Note, May 20, 1961, Ministry of Internal Affairs, ASRI, Fond P, Dosar 40005, Vol. 180, p. 236.

146. Luca revealed this to his prison cell mate (Informative Note, May 1–15, 1955, Ministry of Internal Affairs, Văcăreşti Penitentiary, Bureau D, ASRI, Fond P, Dosar 40005, Vol. 154, p. 17).

147. "Report Regarding the Trial of V. Luca," Executive Archive of the Central Committee of the R.C.P., No. 264/19, 18.02.1972, p. 84.

148. Informative Note, May 20, 1961, Ministry of Internal Affairs, ASRI, Fond P, Dosar 40005, Vol. 180, p. 236.

149. Declaration of Mişu Dulgheru, April 24, 1967, ASRI, Fond P, Dosar 40002, Vol. 203, p. 69.

150. Declaration of Lt. Colonel Francisc Butyka, March 25, 1968, Documents Regarding the Trial of V. Luca, Executive Archive of the Central Committee of the R.C.P., No. 264/19, 18.02.1972, p. 91; Declaration of Lt. Colonel Francis Butyka, June 18, 1968, ASRI, Fond P, Dosar 40005, Vol. 182a, p. 6.

151. Declaration of Lt. Colonel Francisc Butyka, March 25, 1968, "Report Regarding the Trial of V. Luca," Executive Archive of the Central Committee of the R.C.P., No. 264/19, 18.02.1972, pp. 92, 95.

152. Gheorghe Brătescu interview.

153. Interrogation of Vasile Luca, October 7, 1952, ASRI, Fond P, Dosar 40005, Vol. 142, pp. 1–39; Interrogation of Vasile Luca, October 13, 1952, ASRI, Fond P, Dosar 40005, Vol. 143, pp. 12–27; Interrogation of Vasile Luca, October 15, 1952, ASRI, Fond P, Dosar 40005, Vol. 143, pp. 28–40.

154. Declaration of Lt. Colonel Francisc Butyka, March 25, 1968, "Report Regarding the Trial of V. Luca," Executive Archive of the Central Committee of the R.C.P., No. 264/19, 18.02.1972, pp. 91–92. Luca made his first admission September 29, 1952 (Declaration of N. Guină, "Transcript of a Discussion with Alexandru Drăghici," June 3, 1968, Executive Archive of the Central Committee of the R.C.P., No. 264/18.02.1972, Vol. 7, p. 9).

155. Declaration of Petre M. Socol, March 24, 1968, "Report Regarding the Trial of V. Luca," Executive Archive of the Central Committee of the R.C.P., No. 264/19, 18.02.1972, p. 113.

156. "Report Regarding the Trial of V. Luca," Executive Archive of the Central Committee of the R.C.P., No. 264/19, 18.02.1972, p. 36.

157. Declaration of Lt. Gheorghe Puşcoci, March 25, 1968, "Report Regarding the Trial of V. Luca," Executive Archive of the Central Committee of the R.C.P., No. 264/19, 18.02.1972, p. 129.

158. Ibid., p. 130.

159. In the car transporting them to Aiud, Luca complained to Iacob that "they didn't keep their word" and that "you were right to have been more firm" and not to have admitted everything at their trial. Luca also told him that, indeed, he had had some innocuous connections with the Siguranţă (such as, Iacob deduced, receiving permission to hold certain union meetings), but they had all been approved by the party leadership (Declaration of Alexandru Iacob, June 18, 1968, ASRI, Fond P, Dosar 40005, Vol. 182a, pp. 52–53).

160. Declaration of Lt. Gheorghe Puşcoci, March 25, 1968, "Report Regarding the Trial of V. Luca," Executive Archive of the Central Committee of the R.C.P., No. 264/19, 18.02.1972, p. 127. This is confirmed by Ana Pauker (Transcript of an Interrogation of Ana Pauker by a Party Commission of the R.W.P., June 18, 1956, Ana Pauker Inquiry File, Executive Archive of the Central Committee of the R.C.P., p. 20; Transcript of a Discussion of Comrade Vinţe with Ana Pauker, June 21, 1956, Ana Pauker Inquiry File, Executive Archive of the Central Committee of the R.C.P., p. 17).

161. Ro'i, Soviet Decision Making in Practice, pp. 341–342.

162. Kostyrchenko, Out of the Red Shadows, pp. 124–132. An additional 110 people arrested in connection with the case were sentenced in separate proceedings, of whom ten were executed, five died while being investigated, twenty-three received long prison terms, and the remainder were exiled for extended periods (ibid.).

163. George Garai, "Anti-Zionism in Hungary," Soviet Jewish Affairs 2, no. 2 (1982), p. 23.

164. Fejtö, History of the People's Democracies, p. 8. Slansky's codefendant Andrei Simone stated at the trial, "It is the duty of every Jew to support the Americans, even if he does not agree with every aspect of their policy" (Ibid.).

165. Peter Meyer, "Stalin Plans Genocide," New Leader, December 15, 1952, p. 4.

166. Ibid., p. 3; Gilboa, The Black Years of Soviet Jewry, p. 268; Rumanian

National Committee Information Bulletin, no. 46, January 1953, pp. 4–5. Pauker was also vulnerable due to her connections with Eugen Fried. According to Artur London, one of Slansky's codefendants, the Soviet advisers ordered the Czech interrogators to pursue questions on Fried. Moreover, at the trial Bedrich Geminder and Bedrich Reicin were questioned about Fried, whom they both depicted as a Trotskyist (Artur London, *The Confession,* pp. 147–148).

167. Mordechai Oren, *Reshimot asir Prag* [Political Prisoner in Prague] (Tel Aviv, 1960), p. 309.

168. Benjamin Pinkus, *The Jews of the Soviet Union,* p. 177; Gilboa, *The Black Years of Soviet Jewry,* p. 284. Also see Mihail Heller and Alexander Nekrich, *Utopia in Power: The History of the Soviet Union from 1917 to the Present* (New York, 1986), pp. 501–502.

169. Yakov Rapoport, *The Doctors' Plot of 1953* (Cambridge, Mass., 1991), pp. 84–85; Nadezhda Mandelshtam, *Hope Abandoned* (New York, 1974), p. 385; Kostyrchenko, *Out of the Red Shadows,* pp. 248–305; Heller and Nekrich, *Utopia in Power,* p. 503; Medvedev, *Let History Judge,* p. 495; De Jonge, *Stalin,* pp. 476–478.

170. Checinski, *Poland: Communism, Nationalism, Anti-Semitism,* p. 41; Jacob Berman interview, in Toranska, *Them: Stalin's Political Puppets,* p. 319; Garai, "Anti-Zionism in Hungary," pp. 28–29; Vaksberg, *Stalin against the Jews,* pp. 255–256; Hodos, *Show Trials,* pp. 125–126; Jeffrey Herf, *East German Communists and the Jewish Question: The Case of Paul Merker* (Washington, D.C., 1994), pp. 19–20.

171. See, for instance, Raphael Vago, in Pinkus, ed., *Yahadut Mizrach Europa ben Sho'ah li-tekumah,* p. 134.

172. Activity Report for 1952, Central Committee of the Jewish Democratic Committee, January 7, 1953, National Archives of Romania, Fond 37, Dosar 41, p. 28. Though the report added that measures were being taken to stop such practices, this proviso was written a week before the announcement of the Doctors' Plot, and thus before the anti-Semitic campaign's worst phase.

173. Rotman, "Romanian Jewry," p. 321.

174. Zeiger, "Certain Aspects of the Policies of the Party and State Leadership in Romania," p. 4; David Şerer interview.

175. David Rotman interview.

176. Victor Vezendean interview. Vezendean was quick to point out, however, that he was immediately appointed deputy mayor of Bucharest and that Vass was appointed to another high position on Gheorghiu-Dej's personal order. This suggested to him that the Soviets imposed the anti-Semitic campaign on the party and that Dej protected his protégés by assigning them to less conspicuous posts (ibid.).

177. The purges, one scholar observed, coincided with Pauker, Luca, and Georgescu's ouster, "which negatively influenced the evolution of Romanian university life as a whole. . . . Hence, the relative quiet that reigned at the university [of Iaşi] in November 1951 was violently shattered in May 1952, when the Dej group consolidated its position in Bucharest to the detriment of the 'deviationists.' No matter how much the Regional Committee worked to mask the repression in 1952, it became clear that the 'unmasking' meetings of reactionaries and deviationists in the academic world was identical to the political purges taking place within the Party leadership" (Dănuţ Doboş, "Purges at the University of Iaşi, 1949–1960," *Arhivele totalitarianismului,* anul II, no. 1–2, 1994, pp. 49–50).

178. Radu Bogdan, "A Witness to Socialist Realism," *Dilema* 3, no. 156 (January 5–11, 1996), p. 2; Radu Bogdan interview, October 1, 1994.

179. Radu Lupan interview, November 15, 1990.

180. *Scânteia,* January 15, 1953, p. 4 [emphasis added].

181. Regarding the distinction made in the Soviet Union between "cosmopolitanism" and "rootless," "passportless," or "countryless cosmopolitanism," see Benjamin Pinkus, *The Jews of the Soviet Union,* pp. 153–161, and Yehoshua A. Gilboa, *The Black Years of Soviet Jewry,* pp. 156–159.

182. *Scânteia,* January 18, 1953, p. 2; *Scânteia,* January 22, 1953, p. 3. Before, the Romanian press used only the term "cosmopolitanism" in its articles. For examples, see Aristide Burillianu's essay in Alexandre Cretzianu, ed., *Captive Romania* (London, 1956), pp. 155, 160; *Rumanian National Committee Bulletin,* no. 17, November 25, 1950, p. 2; *News from behind the Iron Curtain* 1, no. 3 (March 1952), p. 34, and 2, no. 1 (January 1953), p. 43.

183. *New York Times,* December 1, 1952. After the Prague trial the Romanian leadership made several statements obliquely linking the Pauker group with the Slansky prosecution. For example, Gheorghiu-Dej garnered international press attention with remarks he made on November 29 and rebroadcast a number of times on Radio Bucharest: "The rightist deviationist group disregarded the growing needs of the working class. . . . [O]nly through good decisions shall this be remedied. . . . As the trials in our own country and the recent Prague trial have shown, the activities of these traitors selected by the American imperialists end up by being discovered and punished, owing to the vigilance of the state organs and the entire working people" (cited in the *Rumanian National Committee Bulletin,* no. 46, January 1953, pp. 4–5). On December 31, Emil Bodnăraş also linked the Right Deviationists with the Slansky trial and hinted that their dismissal in May had not nearly ended their purge (*România liberă,* December 31, 1952; reprinted in the *Romanian Press Review,* December 31, 1952, annex, p. 9).

184. Meir Cotic, *The Prague Trial* (New York, 1987), p. 144.

185. Interrogation of Elisabeta Luca, September 4, 1952, ASRI, Fond P, Dosar 40005, Vol. 13, pp. 75–79; Interrogation of Elisabeta Luca, November 3, 1952, ASRI, Fond P, Dosar 40005, Vol. 13, pp. 83–88.

186. Interrogations of Elisabeta Luca, December 4, 1952, December 5, 1952, January 21, 1953, January 22, 1953, February 25, 1953, ASRI, Fond P, Dosar 40005, Vol. 13, pp. 98–100, 142–144, 179–184, 191, 274.

187. Interrogation of Lt. Colonel Laurian Zamfir, January 17, 1953, ASRI, Fond P, Dosar 40009, Vol. 14, pp. 270–271; Interrogation of Lt. Colonel Laurian Zamfir, January 29, 1953, ASRI, Fond P, Dosar 40009, Vol. 26, pp. 263–275; Interrogation of Major Octav Holban January 30, 1953, ASRI, Fond P, Dosar 40009, Vol. 26, pp. 286–289.

188. Pauker's arrest warrant can be found in ASRI, Fond P, Dosar 40009, Vol. 61, p. 31. Regarding Georgescu's arrest, see ASRI, Fond P, Dosar 40009, Vol. 1, p. 4.

189. Tatiana and Gheorghe Brătescu interview; Cristina Boico interview; Transcript of a Discussion of Comrade Vinţe with Ana Pauker, June 21, 1956, Ana Pauker Inquiry File, Executive Archive of the Central Committee of the R.C.P., p. 5.

190. "Note Regarding Certain Problems Emerging on How Ana Pauker was Investigated and Interrogated," April 9, 1968, Ana Pauker Inquiry File, Executive Archive of the Central Committee of the R.C.P., p. 2; Transcript of the Declaration Given by Comrade Miron Constantinescu Before the R.C.P. Commission, March 13, 1968, Executive Archive of the Central Committee of the R.C.P., No. 264/18.02.1972, Vol. 21, p. 156.

191. She told this to her family afterward (Tatiana and Gheorghe Brătescu interview).

192. Transcript of a Discussion of Comrade Vinţe with Ana Pauker, June 21, 1956, Ana Pauker Inquiry File, Executive Archive of the Central Committee of the R.C.P., pp. 5–6.

193. "Note Regarding Certain Problems Emerging on How Ana Pauker was Investigated and Interrogated," April 9, 1968, Ana Pauker Inquiry File, Executive Archive of the Central Committee of the R.C.P., p. 2.

194. Transcript of an Interrogation of Ana Pauker by a Party Commission of the R.W.P., July 29, 1953, Ana Pauker Inquiry File, Executive Archive of the Central Committee of the R.C.P., p. 30.

195. Conversation of Ana Pauker and Two Party Leaders at a Party House in Otopeni, April 8, 1953, ASRI, Fond P, Dosar 40009, Vol. 68, p. 232.

196. Ibid., p. 233.

197. Ibid., p. 232.

198. In 1956 Pauker insisted to a party commission that the Securitate's interrogators had subjected her to "physical and psychological pressure." Confirming this were Tatiana and Gheorghe Brătescu, who revealed that, when Pauker was released from prison, "she had a burn on the inside of her left hand. There were actually two marks," which they suspected had been caused by cigarette butts (Transcript of an Interrogation of Ana Pauker by a Party Commission of the R.W.P., June 18, 1956, Ana Pauker Inquiry File, Executive Archive of the Central Committee of the R.C.P., p. 38; Tatiana and Gheorghe Brătescu interview).

199. Conversation of Ana Pauker and Two Party Leaders at a Party House in Otopeni, April 8, 1953, ASRI, Fond P, Dosar 40009, Vol. 68, p. 228.

200. As Emil Bodnăraş revealed in 1961, Pauker was now accused of being "an agent . . . for International Zionism" and other services "leading right to the top" (Transcript of a Meeting of the Politburo of the R.W.P., March 12–14, 1961, Executive Archive of the Central Committee of the R.C.P., p. 166).

201. Remarks of Alexandru Drăghici, Transcript of the Plenary of the Central Committee of the R.W.P., December 5, 1961, Executive Archive of the Central Committee of the R.C.P., p. 448; "Synthesis of Material Gathered in the Period of Investigating Solomon Rabinsohn," undated, ASRI, Fond P, Dosar 40009, Vol. 54, p. 56.

202. Interrogation of Solomon Rabinsohn, February 20, 1953, ASRI, Fond P, Dosar 40009, Vol. 60, p. 8; Interrogation of Solomon Rabinsohn, February 22, 1953, ASRI, Fond P, Dosar 40009, Vol. 60, p. 10.

203. Interrogation of Solomon Rabinsohn, March 3, 1953, ASRI, Fond P, Dosar 40009, Vol. 60, p. 27; Interrogation of Solomon Rabinsohn, March 12, 1953, ASRI, Fond P, Dosar 40009, Vol. 60, p. 48; Interrogation of Solomon Rabinsohn, May 19, 1953, ASRI, Fond P, Dosar 40009, Vol. 60, pp. 110; Interrogation of Solomon Rabinsohn, May 25, 1953, ASRI, Fond P, Dosar 40009, Vol. 60, p. 119.

204. Interrogation of Solomon Rabinsohn, March 4, 1953, ASRI, Fond P, Dosar 40009, Vol. 60, pp. 36–37, 39; Interrogation of Solomon Rabinsohn, March 12, 1953, ASRI, Fond P, Dosar 40009, Vol. 60, p. 47; Synthesis of Material Gathered in the Period of Investigating Solomon Rabinsohn, undated, ASRI, Fond P, Dosar 40009, Vol. 54, p. 66.

205. Interrogation of Solomon Rabinsohn, March 10, 1953, ASRI, Fond P, Dosar 40009, Vol. 60, pp. 41–45; Interrogation of Solomon Rabinsohn, March 12, 1953, ASRI, Fond P, Dosar 40009, Vol. 60, p. 47; Interrogation of Solomon Rabinsohn, April 7, 1953, ASRI, Fond P, Dosar 40009, Vol. 60, pp. 57–60; Report on the Findings of the Inquiry of Ana Pauker, Former Secretary of the C.C. of the R.W.P. and Minister of External Affairs of the R.P.R., June 6, 1953, ASRI, Fond P, Dosar 40009, Vol. 173, p. 159; Interrogation of Marcu Cohin, March 11–12, 1953, ASRI,

Fond P, Dosar 40005, Vol. 62, pp. 259–261; Declaration of Radu Robert Cohin, February 5, 1953, ASRI, Fond P, Dosar 40005, Vol. 160, p. 188; Interrogation of Leon Itzkar, April 29, 1952, ASRI, Dosar 16385, Vol. 44, pp. 300–301, cited in *Zioniști sub anchetă* [Zionists under Investigation], p. 81; Interrogation of Marcu Cohin, March 11–12, 1953, ASRI, Fond P, Dosar 40005, Vol. 62, p. 260; Interrogation of Marcu Cohin, March 19, 1953, ASRI, Fond P, Dosar 40005, Vol. 62, pp. 265–266; Interrogation of Marcu Cohin, April 20, 1953, ASRI, Fond P, Dosar 40005, Vol. 62, pp. 267–268; Declaration of Melania Iancu, January 16, 1953, ASRI, Fond P, Dosar 40005, Vol. 160, p. 134; Report on the Findings of the Inquiry in the Case of the Former Minister of Internal Affairs — Teohari Georgescu, November 11, 1955, ASRI, Fond P, Dosar 40009, Vol. 21, p. 210; Synthesis of Material Gathered in the Period of Investigating Solomon Rabinsohn, undated, ASRI, Fond P, Dosar 40009, Vol. 54, p. 63.

206. Report on the Findings of the Inquiry of Ana Pauker, Former Secretary of the C.C. of the R.W.P. and Minister of External Affairs of the R.P.R., June 6, 1953, ASRI, Fond P, Dosar 40009, Vol. 173, p. 160.

207. Interrogation of Solomon Rabinsohn, June 18, 1953, ASRI, Fond P, Dosar 40009, Vol. 60, pp. 131–132; Report on the Findings of the Inquiry of Ana Pauker, Former Secretary of the C.C. of the R.W.P. and Minister of External Affairs of the R.P.R., June 6, 1953, ASRI, Fond P, Dosar 40009, Vol. 173, p. 160; Synthesis of Material Gathered in the Period of Investigating Solomon Rabinsohn, undated, ASRI, Fond P, Dosar 40009, Vol. 54, p. 63; Rabbi Moses Rosen interview.

208. Interrogation of Solomon Rabinsohn, May 25, 1953, ASRI, Fond P, Dosar 40009, Vol. 60, pp. 114–115.

209. Ibid., pp. 116–117.

210. Interrogation of Solomon Rabinsohn, May 19, 1953, ASRI, Fond P, Dosar 40009, Vol. 60, p. 111; Synthesis of Material Gathered in the Period of Investigating Solomon Rabinsohn, undated, ASRI, Fond P, Dosar 40009, Vol. 54, p. 68.

211. Interrogation of Solomon Rabinsohn, May 25, 1953, ASRI, Fond P, Dosar 40009, Vol. 60, p. 116.

212. Interrogation of Solomon Rabinsohn, February 18, 1953, ASRI, Fond P, Dosar 40009, Vol. 60, p. 5; Interrogation of Solomon Rabinsohn, May 25, 1953, ASRI, Fond P, Dosar 40009, Vol. 60, pp. 117–118.

213. Interrogation of Solomon Rabinsohn, April 9, 1953, ASRI, Fond P, Dosar 40009, Vol. 60, p. 63; Interrogation of Solomon Rabinsohn, May 19, 1953, ASRI, Fond P, Dosar 40009, Vol. 60, p. 112.

214. Interrogation of Solomon Rabinsohn, May 25, 1953, ASRI, Fond P, Dosar 40009, Vol. 60, p. 115.

215. Interrogation of Solomon Rabinsohn, May 19, 1953, ASRI, Fond P, Dosar 40009, Vol. 60, p. 112.

216. Eugen Szabo, who served in a senior position in the Interior Ministry during this period, insists that one could "absolutely" assume Rabinsohn was coerced while in custody (Eugen Szabo, personal communication with the author).

217. Interrogation of Solomon Rabinsohn, April 9, 1953, ASRI, Fond P, Dosar 40009, Vol. 60, p. 66(b); Interrogation of Solomon Rabinsohn, May 19, 1953, ASRI, Fond P, Dosar 40009, Vol. 60, pp. 110(b)–111; Synthesis of Material Gathered in the Period of Investigating Solomon Rabinsohn, undated, ASRI, Fond P, Dosar 40009, Vol. 54, p. 68.

218. Rosen, *Primejdii, Încercări Miracole*, pp. 122–123.

219. Israel Levanon and Shlomo Leibovici interviews.

220. Interrogation of Solomon Rabinsohn, April 9, 1953, ASRI, Fond P, Dosar

40009, Vol. 60, p. 63(b); Interrogation of Solomon Rabinsohn, June 18, 1953, ASRI, Fond P, Dosar 40009, Vol. 60, p. 134; Moses Rosen interview; Rosen, *Dangers, Tests and Miracles*, pp. 85–86.

221. Moses Rosen interview.

222. Interview of Chief Rabbi Moses Rosen, *Jerusalem Post*, June 24, 1988.

223. Synthesis of Material Gathered in the Period of Investigating Solomon Rabinsohn, undated, ASRI, Fond P, Dosar 40009, Vol. 54, p. 67.

224. Interrogation of Solomon Rabinsohn, June 18, 1953, ASRI, Fond P, Dosar 40009, Vol. 60, pp. 140–141.

225. Report on the Investigation of Ana Pauker, April 5, 1954, ASRI, Fond P, Dosar 40005, Vol. 173, pp. 185–186; Remarks of Gheorghe Gheorghiu-Dej, Transcript of a Meeting of the Politburo of the R.W.P., March 12–14, 1961, Executive Archive of the Central Committee of the R.C.P., p. 166.

226. Report on the Findings of the Inquiry of Ana Pauker, January 20, 1954, Ana Pauker Inquiry File, Executive Archive of the Central Committee of the R.C.P., p. 11; Transcript of an Interrogation of Ana Pauker by a Party Commission of the R.W.P., July 29, 1953, Ana Pauker Inquiry File, Executive Archive of the Central Committee of the R.C.P., pp. 17–29.

227. "Plan with the Principal Points for Orientating the Ana Pauker Inquiry," Chapter VI, Point 8, Ana Pauker Inquiry File, Executive Archive of the Central Committee of the R.C.P.

228. Interrogation of Vasile Luca, February 22, 1953, ASRI, Fond P, Dosar 40005, Vol. 2, p. 55.

229. Interrogation of Vasile Luca, February 19, 1953, ASRI, Fond P, Dosar 40005, Vol. 4, p. 448.

230. "Plan with the Principal Points for Orientating the Ana Pauker Inquiry," Chapter VI, Point 5, Ana Pauker Inquiry File, Executive Archive of the Central Committee of the R.C.P.; Interrogation of Vasile Luca, February 11, 1953, ASRI, Fond P, Dosar 40005, Vol. 4, p. 423; Interrogation of Vasile Luca, February 14, 1953, ASRI, Fond P, Dosar 40005, Vol. 4, p. 341(b).

231. For Luca's position on the Zionists, see Interrogation of Vasile Luca, February 22, 1954, ASRI, Fond P, Dosar 40005, Vol. 2, p. 55, and Interrogations of Anghel Dascalu, May 8 and May 11, 1953, ASRI, Fond P, Dosar 40005, Vol. 7, pp. 61, 70. The inquiry obtained a large number of declarations testifying to Luca's supporting Zionism and Israel, as well as his connections to certain prominent Zionists.

232. Synthesis of the Findings of the Investigation in the Case of Former Minister of Internal Affairs Teohari Georgescu, September 14, 1955, ASRI, Fond P, Dosar 40009, Vol. 21, pp. 147–149; Report on the Sending to Trial of Teohari Georgescu, February 4, 1956, ASRI, Fond P, Dosar 40009, Vol. 21, pp. 300–303.

233. Pacepa, *Moştenirea kremlinului*, pp. 72–77, 119–120.

234. On Roman, see "Regarding the Sanctioning of Valter Roman," p. 2; Interrogation of Vasile Luca, February 6, 1953, ASRI, Fond P, Dosar 40005, Vol. 4, p. 423. On Boico and Brill, see the Transcript of the Plenary of the Central Committee of the R.W.P., May 27–29, 1952, National Archives of Romania, Fond CC al PCR—Cancelarie, Dosar 41/1952, p. 151. Boico's inculpation would have probably included his wife, Cristina, who was a veteran of the French Resistance and Pauker's associate at the Foreign Ministry. On Patriciu, see Mihai Patriciu and Charlotte Gruia interviews. On Neumann, see the Report Regarding the Proposal of Arresting Carol Neuman, December 8, 1952, ASRI, Fond P, Dosar 40002, Vol. 108, pp. 1–4; Carol Neuman interview.

235. On Calmonovici, see Transcript of the Declaration Given by Teohari Georgescu to the R.C.P. Commission, October 23, 1967, ASRI, Fond P, Dosar 40002, Vol. 203, p. 302; Interrogation of Emil Calmanovici, March 6, 1953, ASRI, Fond P, Dosar 40002, Vol. 24, p. 1. On Dulgheru, see Transcript of a Discussion with Alexandru Drăghici, April 20, 1968, Executive Archive of the Central Committee of the R.C.P., No. 264/18.02.1972, Vol. 7, p. 19; Charlotte Gruia interview; Interrogation of Mişu Dulgheru, December 8, 1952, ASRI, Fond P, Dosar 40007, Vol. 2, p. 15; Plan of the Inquiry of Mişu Dulgheru, August 19, 1953, ASRI, Fond P, Dosar 40007, Vol. 12, pp. 86–87; Transcript of a Discussion with Alexandru Drăghici, April 20, 1968, Executive Archive of the Central Committee of the R.C.P., No. 264/ 18.02.1972, Vol. 7, p. 19.

236. Herbert (Belu) Zilber revealed that, in the renewed Patraşcanu inquiry beginning in August 1952, "[o]ne thing . . . was insisted on: to implicate Ana, Luca and Teo. That was always demanded of me" in his interrogations (Transcript of the Declaration Given by Herbert Zilber before the R.C.P. Commission, October 20, 1967, ASRI, Fond P, Dosar 40002, Vol. 202, p. 125). He did so, therefore, on February 23, 1953, when he provided details linking Pauker with Patraşcanu and stressing their supposed common political line (Interrogation of Herbert Zilber, February 23, 1953, ASRI, Fond P, Dosar 40002, Vol. 39, pp. 357–360). Moreover, Egon Balaş, of the Pauker-Luca case, was linked with Jacques Berman, implicated in the Patraşcanu inquiry, and Dinu Constantin, one of Luca's associates, was pressured to confess that he was an informer for Patraşcanu's "co-conspirator" Alexandru Ştefănescu (Report on Egon Balasz [Balaş], Arrested on August 12, 1952, October 20, 1954, ASRI, Fond P, Dosar 40005, Vol. 106, p. 412; Interrogation of Egon Balaş, May 21, 1953, ASRI, Fond P, Dosar 40005, Vol. 106, pp. 191–194; Interrogations of Dinu Constantin, January 18, March 10, and May 5, 1954, ASRI, Fond P, Dosar 40005, Vol. 74, pp. 4–6, 19–23, 37–40).

237. This apparent merging of the Pauker and Patraşcanu groups paralleled a strikingly similar development in Poland, where the Soviets in 1953 reportedly insisted on linking Gomulka's long-stalled prosecution with that of Jakub Berman, who has since been credited with having up to that point prevented Gomulka's trial (Checinski, *Poland: Communism, Nationalism, Anti-Semitism*, p. 82; Jakub Berman and Edward Ochab interviews, in Teresa Toranska, *Them: Stalin's Political Puppets*, pp. 112, 318–320).

238. Interrogation of Vasile Luca, March 5, 1953, ASRI, Fond P, Dosar 40005, Vol. 4, pp. 476–478, 481, 483, 486; Interrogation of Vasile Luca, March 12, 1953, ASRI, Fond P, Dosar 40005, Vol. 4, pp. 489–490; Interrogation of Vasile Luca, April 10, 1953, ASRI, Fond P, Dosar 40005, Vol. 4, pp. 519, 527–528.

239. Declaration of Lt. Gheorghe Puşcoci, March 25, 1968, "Report Regarding the Trial of V. Luca," Executive Archive of the Central Committee of the R.C.P., No. 264/19, 18.02.1972, p. 125; Jean Coler interview.

240. "Report of the Findings of the Inquiry Undertaken in the Case of Sandu Liblich," Ministry of Interior Affairs, November 14, 1953, Archive of the Romanian Justice Ministry, Dosar P17399, Vol. 6, pp. 9, 13; Declaration of Sandu Liblich, undated, Archive of the Romanian Justice Ministry, Dosar P17299, Vol. 5, p. 119.

241. Pacepa, *Moştenirea kremlinului*, pp. 72–77, 119–120.

242. Checinski, *Poland: Communism, Nationalism, Anti-Semitism*, p. 42.

243. Mihail Heller and Alexander Nekrich, *Utopia in Power*, p. 503. In 1956 Khrushchev confirmed the impending pogroms to the Polish Communist leadership (Stefan Staszewski interview, in Teresa Toranska, *Them: Stalin's Political Puppets*, p. 171).

244. Anton Antonov-Ovseyenko, *The Time of Stalin* (New York, 1981), p. 291.
245. Medvedev, *On Stalin and Stalinism*, p. 159; Vaksberg, *Stalin against the Jews*, p. 259. The quote is from Antonov-Ovseyenko, *The Time of Stalin*, p. 291.
246. On the planned Polish camps, see Jakub Berman interview, in Teresa Toranska, *Them: Stalin's Political Puppets*, p. 319.
247. Note Regarding Certain Problems Emerging on How Ana Pauker was Investigated and Interrogated, April 9, 1968, Ana Pauker Inquiry File, Executive Archive of the Central Committee of the R.C.P., pp. 2–3.
248. Transcript of the Declaration Given by Comrade Miron Constantinescu Before the R.C.P. Commission, March 13, 1968, Executive Archive of the Central Committee of the R.C.P., No. 264/18.02.1972, Vol. 21, p. 157.
249. Leonte Răutu interview.
250. On Zalman Rabinsohn, see Moses Rosen interview. On Georgescu, see Note Regarding the Arrest and Inquiry of Teohari Georgescu, April 14, 1968, Executive Archive of the Central Committee of the R.C.P., p. 4; Report Regarding Teohari Georgescu, March 19, 1956, ASRI, Fond P, Dosar 40009, Vol. 1, pp. 24–30. On Luca, see ASRI, Fond P, Dosar 40005, Vol. 173, pp. 4, 7; Nicholas Dima, *Journey to Freedom* (Washington, D.C., 1989), p. 84.
251. Transcript of a Discussion of Comrade Vinţe with Ana Pauker, June 21, 1956, Ana Pauker Inquiry File, Executive Archive of the Central Committee of the R.C.P., pp. 10, 35; Transcript of an Interrogation of Ana Pauker by a Party Commission of the R.W.P., July 6, 1956, Ana Pauker Inquiry File, Executive Archive of the Central Committee of the R.C.P., p. 35; Tatiana and Gheorghe Brătescu interview.

EPILOGUE

1. Tatiana and Gheorghe Brătescu interview.
2. ASRI, Fond P, Dosar 40009, Vol. 68, p. 188.
3. Tatiana and Gheorghe Brătescu interview.
4. The commission was comprised of Alexandru Moghioroş, Gheorghe Apostol, Petre Borilă, and Constantin Pârvulescu.
5. Tatiana and Gheorghe Brătescu interview.
6. Note Regarding Certain Problems Emerging on How Ana Pauker was Investigated and Interrogated, April 9, 1968, Ana Pauker Inquiry File, Executive Archive of the Central Committee of the R.C.P., p. 1. For instance, when interrogated by the party commission in June and July, Pauker reminded her inquisitors that both left and right deviations had been committed by people still "in the party leadership." She also refused to admit that she had been swayed by any "internal influences" (i.e., the Israeli embassy) when she released the seven Zionist emissaries. And in a discussion with commission members in Otopeni, Pauker denied responsibility for mass Jewish emigration and instead attributed it to, of all people, Iosif Chişinevschi—one of the more intransigent opponents of aliya and Zionism after Stalin's *volte face*—and Emil Bodnăraş. Pauker insisted that Chişinevschi was responsible for Jewish emigration through his connection, as the supervisor of the Foreign Section of the Central Committee, with the Zionist emissary Moshe Agami (Auerbach), and that Bodnăraş had a "permanent connection" with the Joint Distribution Committee and the Zionist representative Joseph Klarman. Actually, Luca confirmed to a prison cell mate that Agami's initial contact with the RWP leadership had been Chişinevschi; and actually, Bodnăraş did have connections with the JDC and Klarman. But both situations were in 1947 or earlier; that is, before the Soviet-imposed policy change on Israel (Transcript of an Interrogation of Ana Pauker by a Party Commission of the

R.W.P., July 29, 1953, Ana Pauker Inquiry File, Executive Archive of the Central Committee of the R.C.P., p. 20; Transcript of an Interrogation of Ana Pauker by a Party Commission of the R.W.P., June 12, 1953, Ana Pauker Inquiry File, Executive Archive of the Central Committee of the R.C.P., pp. 72, 82–83; Conversation of Ana Pauker and Two Party Leaders at the Party House in Otopeni, April 8, 1953, ASRI, Fond P, Dosar 40009, Vol. 68, pp. 229, 232; Declaration of Ana Pauker, April 20, 1953, Ana Pauker Inquiry File, Executive Archive of the Central Committee of the R.C.P., p. 3; Ministry of Internal Affairs, Văcărești Penitentiary, Bureau D, Informative Note, December 3 and 10, 1955, ASRI, Fond P, Dosar 40005, Vol. 154, pp. 1, 7; Memoir of Vasile Luca addressed to General Secretary Gheorghiu-Dej, February 3, 1957, Executive Archive of the Central Committee of the R.C.P., p. 9; David Giladi interview).

7. Note Regarding Certain Problems Emerging on How Ana Pauker was Investigated and Interrogated, April 9, 1968, Ana Pauker Inquiry File, Executive Archive of the Central Committee of the R.C.P., p. 3.

8. Transcript of an Interrogation of Ana Pauker by a Party Commission of the R.W.P., July 29, 1953, Ana Pauker Inquiry File, Executive Archive of the Central Committee of the R.C.P., pp. 29–30.

9. Tatiana Brătescu, "Ana Pauker: The Last Years," p. 5.

10. Pauker's superior at the publishing house was Leonte Tismăneanu, the deputy director (Note found in Ana Pauker's Inquiry File, Executive Archive of the Central Committee of the R.C.P.).

11. Transcript of a Meeting of the Politburo of the R.W.P., March 12–14, 1961, Executive Archive of the Central Committee of the R.C.P., p. 166. Mátyás Rákosi noted in his recently published memoirs that he also intervened with Gheorghiu-Dej on Pauker's behalf when he learned of her arrest (Mátyás Rákosi, *Visszaemlekezesek 1940–1956* [Remembrances, 1940–56], vol. 1 [Budapest, 1997], p. 62).

12. Mircu, *Ana Pauker și alții*, pp. 193–194.

13. Mordechai Resel, "The Daughter of a 'Shochet' Who Became the 'Iron Lady' of Romania," *Hatzofeh*, August 19, 1983.

14. Pauker's family, however, has no knowledge of her meeting either Rabinsohn or Dej (Tatiana and Gheorghe Brătescu interview).

15. Gheorghe Brătescu interview.

16. Transcript of an Interrogation of Ana Pauker by a Party Commission of the R.W.P., July 6, 1956, Ana Pauker Inquiry File, Executive Archive of the Central Committee of the R.C.P., pp. 13, 18, 32–33, 35–36; Transcript of an Interrogation of Ana Pauker by a Party Commission of the R.W.P., June 18, 1956, Ana Pauker Inquiry File, Executive Archive of the Central Committee of the R.C.P., p. 34.

17. Transcript of a Discussion of Comrade Vinte with Ana Pauker, June 21, 1956, Ana Pauker Inquiry File, Executive Archive of the Central Committee of the R.C.P., pp. 17–19.

18. Transcript of an Interrogation of Ana Pauker by a Party Commission of the R.W.P., July 6, 1956, Ana Pauker Inquiry File, Executive Archive of the Central Committee of the R.C.P., pp. 15–18, 21.

19. Buzatu, *Românii în arhivele kremlinului*, p. 156.

20. Transcript of a Discussion of Comrade Vinte with Ana Pauker, June 21, 1956, Ana Pauker Inquiry File, Executive Archive of the Central Committee of the R.C.P.

21. Gheorghe Brătescu interview.

22. Tatiana Brătescu, "Ana Pauker: The Last Years," p. 5; Tatiana and Gheorghe Brătescu interview.

23. Ibid. Maria Sârbu interview.

24. Ibid.

25. Tatiana and Gheorghe Brătescu interview.

26. Ibid.

27. Ibid.; Ana Toma and Elena Tudorache interviews.

28. Tatiana Brătescu, "Ana Pauker: The Last Years," p. 5; Tatiana and Gheorghe Brătescu interview; *Lichidarea lui Marcel Pauker: o anchetă stalinistă, 1937–1938,* p. 282.

29. Sorin Toma interview. Perhaps the source of this rumor was Lucrețiu Patrașcanu: according to Herbert (Belu) Zilber, Patrașcanu confided to him that he asked Ana Pauker about Marcel when they met in Moscow in September 1944 and Ana replied that Marcel was in a camp, sick with heart problems and near death (Declaration of Herbert [Belu] Zilber, February 23, 1950, ASRI, Fond P, Dosar 40002, Vol. 38, p. 124).

30. Declaration of Valter Roman, October 15, 1956, Ana Pauker Inquiry File, Executive Archive of the Central Committee of the R.C.P., p. 3.

31. Interrogation of Emil Pauker, May 4, 1953, ASRI, Fond P, Dosar 40009, Vol. 61, p. 31. She apparently continued to equivocate when Marcel's father demanded to know the truth while on his deathbed in 1947—leaving on one occasion muttering to herself, "I can't take it any more." But what she ultimately told him is unclear (ibid., p. 33).

32. Titi Pauker asserted this to Tatiana and Gheorghe Brătescu (interview). However, under interrogation in 1956, she maintained that Ana Pauker told her that Marcel was in fact dead (Interrogation of Emil and Titi Pauker, November 14, 1956, Ana Pauker Inquiry File, Executive Archive of the Central Committee of the R.C.P., p. 3).

33. Interrogation of Zalman Rabinsohn, March 26, 1953, ASRI, Fond P, Dosar 40009, Vol. 60, pp. 52–53. Tatiana and Gheorghe Brătescu interview; Ana Toma interview; Interrogation of Emil Pauker, May 5, 1953, ASRI, Fond P, Dosar 40009, Vol. 61, p. 40.

34. Mihai Alexandru interview.

35. Tatiana and Gheorghe Brătescu interview.

36. Ibid.; Tatiana Brătescu, "Ana Pauker: The Last Years," p. 5.

37. *New York Times,* June 15, 1960, p. 41.

38. Tatiana Brătescu, "Ana Pauker: The Last Years," p. 5; Tatiana and Gheorghe Brătescu interview.

39. Tatiana and Gheorghe Brătescu interview.

40. Michel Birnbaum interview, November 11, 1990.

41. Carol Luncea told them this (Tatiana and Gheorghe Brătescu interview).

42. Tatiana and Gheorghe Brătescu interview.

43. Ibid.

44. Marie Birnbaum interview.

45. Arthur Koestler, *The Invisible Writing: An Autobiography,* p. 88.

46. Wolfgang Leonhard, *Child of the Revolution,* pp. 51–52; Stefan Staszewski and Jakub Berman interviews, in Teresa Toranska, *Them: Stalin's Political Puppets,* pp. 128–129, 263, 265; Alfred Burmeister, *Dissolution and Aftermath of the Comintern,* p. 30.

47. Koestler, *The Invisible Writing: An Autobiography,* p. 88.

48. Sperber, *The Unheeded Warning,* p. 166.

49. Roman Werfel, interviewed by Teresa Toranska, *Them: Stalin's Political Puppets,* p. 100.

50. The quote is from Talmon, *Israel among the Nations,* p. 78.

51. Georg Lukacs, *Record of a Life: An Autobiographical Sketch,* edited by Istvan Eorsi (London, 1983), pp. 106–107.

52. Isaac Deutscher, "The Tragic Life of a Polrugarian Minister," in *Heretics and Renegades* (New York, 1969), p. 29.

53. Claudin, *The Communist Movement,* p. 312.

54. V. M. Molotov, *Molotov Remembers: Inside Kremlin Politics,* ed. Albert Resis (Chicago, 1993), p. 254.

55. Hugh Seton-Watson, "Thirty Years After," in Martin McCauley, ed., *Communist Power in Europe, 1944–1949* (London, 1979), p. 225.

56. Pauker herself denied that their power derived from the Soviet occupation in discussions with Romanian Social Democrats in 1946 (Transcript of a Meeting of the Politburos of the Central Committee of the Romanian Communist Party and the Social Democratic Party in Romania, January 14, 1946, National Archives of Romania, Fond CC al PCR—Cancelarie, Dosar 9/1946, pp. 21–22). On the desire for reform, see Charles Gati and Lezek Kolakowski interviews, in Michael Charlton, *The Eagle and the Small Birds* (Chicago, 1984), pp. 59, 88; Bela Szász, *Volunteers for the Gallows, Anatomy of a Show Trial* (New York, 1971), p. 223.

57. Ignazio Silone in Crossman, ed., *The God That Failed,* p. 91.

58. Alexander Weissberg, *The Accused,* p. 148.

59. Isaac Deutscher, "The Tragic Life of a Polrugarian Minister," p. 28.

60. Louis Frances Lubenz, *This Is My Story* (New York, 1947), p. 34.

61. Gheorghe Brătescu interview.

62. Stefan Staszewski interview, in Teresa Toranska, *Them: Stalin's Political Puppets,* p. 129.

63. Bela Szász, interviewed by Michael Charlton, *The Eagle and the Small Birds,* pp. 66, 68.

64. Sorin Toma interview. Also see Zbigniew K. Brzezinski, *The Soviet Bloc: Unity and Conflict,* rev. ed. (New York, 1963), pp. 27–32.

65. On the movement's lack of coordination, see Zubok and Pleshakov, *Inside the Kremlin's Cold War,* pp. 120, 129; Gaddis, *We Now Know,* pp. 40–41. On the Kremlin's postwar liberalism, see Burmeister, *Dissolution and Aftermath of the Comintern,* p. 39; Leonhard, *Child of the Revolution,* pp. 336, 338–339.

66. Koestler, *The Invisible Writing: An Autobiography,* pp. 154–155.

67. Boris Bazhanov, interviewed by George R. Urban, *Stalinism,* p. 24.

68. Marie Birnbaum interview.

69. Shephard, *Russia's Danubian Empire,* p. 39.

70. Koestler, *The Invisible Writing: An Autobiography,* pp. 30–31.

71. Leonard Schapiro, "Reflections on the Changing Role of the Party in the Totalitarian Polity," *Studies in Comparative Communism* 2, no. 2 (April 1969), p. 2.

72. Koestler, in Crossman, ed., *The God That Failed,* p. 58.

73. Jakub Berman interview, in Toranska, *Them: Stalin's Political Puppets,* p. 282.

74. Dorothy Healey and Maurice Isserman, *Dorothy Healey Remembers: A Life in the American Communist Party* (Oxford and New York, 1990), p. 150.

75. Tamas Aczel and Tibor Meray, *The Life of the Mind* (London, 1960), p. 13.

76. Eduard Goldstücker, interviewed by Michael Charlton, *The Eagle and the Small Birds,* pp. 93–94.

77. Aleksander Wat, *My Century,* pp. 14–15, 41–42.

78. Ignazio Silone, in Crossman, ed., *The God That Failed,* p. 88.

79. Stefan Staszewski interview, in Teresa Toranska, *Them: Stalin's Political Puppets*, pp. 128–129.

80. *Scaling the Wall, Talking to Eastern Europe: The Best of Radio Free Europe*, edited by George R. Urban (Detroit, 1964), pp. 100–101 [emphasis added].

81. Aleksander Wat, *My Century*, p. 14. Eduard Goldstücker also made this point (interview by Michael Charlton, *The Eagle and the Small Birds*, p. 93).

82. Tatiana Brătescu interview.

83. Gheorghe Brătescu interview.

84. Tatiana and Gheorghe Brătescu interview.

85. Aleksandr I. Solzhenitsyn, *The Gulag Archipelago*, part 2 (New York, 1975), p. 327.

86. On the topic in general, see Gail Kligman, *The Politics of Duplicity: Controlling Reproduction in Ceauşescu's Romania* (Berkeley and Los Angeles, 1998), pp. 13–15.

87. Declaration of Radu Robert Cohin [Marcu Cohin's son], February 5, 1953, ASRI, Fond P, Dosar 40005, Vol. 160, p. 188.

88. Ana Toma interview.

89. On the trend toward independence, see Inessa Iazhborovskaia, "The Gomulka Alternative: The Untravelled Road," and Igor Lukes, "The Czech Road to Communism," in Norman Naimark and Leonid Gibianskii, eds., *The Establishment of Communist Regimes in Eastern Europe, 1944–1949* (Boulder, Colo., 1997), pp. 123–138, 243–266; Krystyna Kersten, *The Establishment of Communist Rule in Poland, 1943–1948* (Berkeley, 1991); Imre Nagy, "Nagy Imre: Remarks on the Draft of the Economic Policy Guidelines of the H.C.P.," *Társadalmi Szemle* 7 (July 1989), pp. 55–61.

90. Wlodzimierz Brus, "Stalinism in the 'People's Democracies,'" in Robert C. Tucker, ed., *Stalinism* (Toronto, 1977), pp. 245–251; Leonid Gibianskii, "The Soviet-Yugoslav Split and the Cominform," in Norman Naimark and Leonid Gibianskii, eds., *The Establishment of Communist Regimes in Eastern Europe*, p. 307; Eduard Ochab and Jakub Berman interviews, in Toranska, *Them: Stalin's Political Puppets*, pp. 48, 203.

91. This contradicts the notion of the inherent mendaciousness of Stalinist purges. Though generalizing on the matter is impossible, Pauker's purge apparently was similar to those of Gomulka, Xoxe, Patraşcanu, and even Tito, in that the preliminary accusations at the time of dismissal (or expulsion in Tito's case) were distinguishable from those ultimately leveled at Stalinist show trials: while the latter as a rule were fraudulent and arbitrary, the former were actually more measured and closer to reality, being only the first step in a long series of escalating charges. On the Gomulka and Xoxe cases, see Hodos, *Show Trials*, pp. 5–12, 135–154; on Patraşcanu, see Ionescu, *Communism in Romania*, pp. 151–156; for the text of the June 28, 1948, Cominform resolution expelling Tito and the Yugoslav Communists from the Cominform, see *The Soviet-Yugoslav Dispute*, Royal Institute of International Affairs (London, 1948), pp. 62–70.

92. Tatiana and Gheorghe Brătescu interview; Ana Toma interview.

93. On Stalin's dinners, see Jakub Berman interview, in Toranska, *Them: Stalin's Political Puppets*, p. 236.

94. On Patraşcanu, see the Declaration of Elena Patraşcanu, March 9, 1950, ASRI, Fond P, Dosar 40002, Vol. 87, pp. 50, 59.

95. J. L. Talmon, *The Myth of the Nation and the Vision of Revolution*, p. 227.

96. Israel Getzler, "The Mensheviks," *Problems of Communism*, November–

December 1967, p. 26. Getzler's source regarding Dan was the latter's wife, Lydia Dan, interviewed in 1962.

97. Joseph Nedava, *Trotsky and the Jews* (Philadelphia, 1971), p. 120; Adam Ulam, *The Bolsheviks* (Toronto, 1965), p. 457 n. 7.

98. Zvi Y. Gitelman, *Jewish Nationality and Soviet Politics: The Jewish Sections of the C.P.S.U., 1917–1930* (Princeton, 1972), pp. 115–116.

99. Solomon M. Schwarz, *The Jews in the Soviet Union*, pp. 241–257; Solomon M. Schwarz, "The New Anti-Semitism of the Soviet Union," *Commentary*, January 1950, p. 40.

100. Transcript of a Meeting with Leading Activists of the Mass Organizations, October 5, 1945, National Archives of Romania, Fond CC al PCR—Cancelarie, Dosar 86/1945, p. 26.

101. Vladimir Tismaneanu, "The Ambiguity of Romanian Communism," pp. 71–72. Also see Attila Kovari, *The Antecedents of Today's National Myth in Rumania, 1921–1965* (Jerusalem, 1983), pp. 47–48.

102. Talmon, *The Myth of the Nation and the Vision of Revolution*, p. 181.

103. Robert S. Wistrich, *Revolutionary Jews from Marx to Trotsky* (New York, 1976), p. 88.

104. Haberer, *Jews and Revolution*, p. 174.

105. Interrogation of Marcu Cohin, March 11–12, 1953, ASRI, Fond P, Dosar 40009, Vol. 62, p. 262.

Bibliography

I. PRIMARY SOURCES

A. ARCHIVES

National Archives of Romania, Bucharest, Romania

Fond CC al PCR–Cancelarie (transcripts of meetings of the Secretariat and the Politburo of the Central Committee, and of plenaries of the Central Committee, of the Romanian Communist and Romanian Workers' Party).

Fond 1 (transcripts of meetings of leading bodies, and interrogations of special investigative commissions, of the Romanian Communist and Romanian Workers' Party).

Fond 18 (papers of the Central Committee of the Jewish Democratic Committee, 1945–1953).

Archives of the National Defense Ministry of Romania, Bucharest, Romania

Documents from the (former) Executive Archive of the Central Committee of the Romanian Communist Party.

The (former) Executive Archive of the Central Committee of the Romanian Communist Party, Bucharest, Romania

Official Dossier of the Inquiry of Ana Pauker (1952–1956) (obtained from Professor Vladimir Tismaneanu of the University of Maryland).

Documents of the 1967–1968 party commission investigating the Patrașcanu, Foriș, and Luca cases.

Archive of the Romanian Information Service (ASRI),
Bucharest, Romania

Fond P, Dosar 40002 (the Lucreţiu Patraşcanu case).
Fond P, Dosar 40005 (the Vasile Luca case).
Fond P, Dosar 40007 (the Mişu Dulgheru case).
Fond P, Dosar 40009 (the Teohari Georgescu case).
Fond P, Dosar 40009, Volumes 60–62 (the Zalman Rabinsohn case; documents on the Ana Pauker case).
Fond D, Dosar 4638, 4640, 9404 (material on collectivization).
Fond D, Dosar 9916, 10089, 10090 (documents of the leadership of the Ministry of Interior affairs—obtained from Mr. Marius Oprea, University of Bucharest, Romania).

Archive of the Academy of Sciences of Romania,
Bucharest, Romania

Documents of the former Central Archive of the Party Historical Institute Adjacent to the Central Committee of the RCP.

Archive of the Romanian Justice Ministry, Bucharest, Romania

Dosar P17299 (documents of the inquiry of Dr. Sandu Liblich).

Russian Center for the Preservation and Study of Documents
of Most Recent History (RTsKhIDNI), Moscow, Russia

Fond 495, Opis 255 (Ana Pauker's Comintern File).

B. INTERVIEWS

Note: For simplicity's sake, the dates listed here are those of the first interview. There were, however, often multiple follow-up interviews.

Alexandru, Mihai (July 11, 1991)
Alterescu, Sara (February 28, 1994)
Balaş, Egon (April 18, 1997)
Barbu, Cora (December 8, 1990)
Bălănescu, Mircea (July 16, 1991)
Belu, Nicolae (January 26, 1994)
Birnbaum, Marie (November 11, 1990)
Birnbaum, Michel (November 11, 1990)
Bîrladeanu, Victor (December 8, 1990)
Bogdan, Corneliu (August 8, 1989)
Bogdan, Radu (October 1, 1994)
Boico, Cristina (September 16, 1989)
Borilă, Katherina (July 17, 1991)
Brătescu, Gheorghe (November 11, 1990)
Brătescu, Tatiana (November 11, 1990)
Breban, Iosif (March 16, 1994)
Brill, Janetta (June 28, 1991)
Brucan, Silviu (November 25, 1993)

Bughici, Simion (July 11, 1991)
Bujes, Josef (September 12, 1990)
Burcă, Mihai (July 5, 1991)
Călin, Vera (September 18, 1990)
Coler, Jean (August 31, 1989)
Coposu, Corneliu (January 6, 1994)
Diamantshtein, Ella (August 28, 1989)
Dragan (Kajesco), Vilma (July 13, 1991)
Dumitrescu, Liuba (February 26, 1994)
Einhorn, Wilhelm (August 4, 1989)
Felix, Ida (December 24, 1993)
Feurştein (Iacob), Adam (June 25, 1991)
Finkelştein, Uşer (September 11, 1993)
Florescu, Mihai (July 12, 1991).
Gaston Marin, Gheorghe (June 27, 1991)
Giladi, David (July 29, 1989)
Gruia, Charlotte (July 15, 1991)
Kuller, Harry (January 11, 1994)
Leibovici, Shlomo (August 4, 1989)
Levanon, Israel (July 30, 1989)
Luca, Elisabeta (July 8, 1991)
Lupan, Radu (November 15, 1990)
Lustig, Carol (September 8, 1989)
Manea, Tudor (July 11, 1991)
Maurer, Ion Gheorghe (July 12, 1991)
Mănescu, Radu (August 28, 1989)
Mezincescu, Eduard (December 10, 1990)
Micu, Andre (April 14, 1994)
Mihail, David (July 19, 1991)
Neumann, Carol (December 6, 1990)
Nistor, Alexandru (January 22, 1994)
Olaru, Tudor (July 13, 1991)
Oprişan, Mircea (September 4, 1985)
Patriciu, Mihail (March 12, 1994)
Popescu, Ştefan (July 22, 1991)
Popper, Armand (December 6, 1990)
Răutu, Leonte (August 22, 1993)
Rojha, Gheorghe (July 16, 1991)
Rosen, Moses (August 7, 1989)
Rotman, David (December 7, 1990)
Rotman, Liviu (August 1, 1989)
Sauvard, Sanda (December 9, 1990)
Sârbu, Maria (December 7, 1990)
Sencovici, Alexandru (December 29, 1993)
Sevcenko, Sergiu (December 10, 1990)
Szabo, Eugen (July 24, 1991)
Şerer, David (July 22, 1991)
Şiperco, Alexandru (July 5, 1991)
Tismăneanu, Hermina (May 20, 1988)
Toma, Ana (November 16, 1990)
Toma, Sorin (August 25, 1989)

Tudorache, Elena (December 10 1990)
Vezendean, Victor (November 30, 1990)
Vrancea, Elena (December 26, 1991)
Wald, Henri (December 10, 1990)
Zaharescu, Barbu (December 7, 1990)
Zaharescu, Vladimir (July 10 1989)
Zaharia, Ilie (March 25, 1989)

II. SECONDARY SOURCES

A. .MICROFILM COLLECTIONS
Romainian Press Review (UCLA)

B. PERIODICALS AND NEWSPAPERS, 1945–1953
Bulletin of the Rumanian National Committee
Contemporanul
For a Lasting Peace, for a People's Democracy
Life
London Times
Lupta de clasă
Manchester Guardian
National-Zeitung
New York Herald Tribune
New York Times
News from behind the Iron Curtain
România liberă
Scânteia
Time
Viața sindicală

C. BOOKS, ARTICLES, AND UNPUBLISHED DISSERTATIONS
Abramsky, Chimen. "The Rise and Fall of Soviet Yiddish Literature." *Soviet Jewish Affairs* 12, no. 3 (1982).
Aczel, Tamas, and Tibor Meray. *The Life of the Mind.* London, 1960.
Agus, Jacob B. *Jewish Identity in an Age of Ideologies.* New York, 1978.
"Ana Pauker." *Current Biography,* 1948.
Ancel, Jean. *Yahadut Romanyah ben 23.8.1944 le-ven 30.12.1947* [Rumanian Jewry, August 23, 1944–December 30, 1947]. Ph.D. diss., Hebrew University, Jerusalem, 1979.
———. *"She'erit Hapletah* in Romania during the Transition Period to a Communist Regime, August 1944–December 1947." In Yisrael Gutman and Avital Saf, eds., *She'erit Hapletah, 1944–1948: Rehabilitation and Political Struggle.* Proceedings of the Sixth Yad Vashem International Historical Conference. Jerusalem, 1990.
———. "The Image of the Jew in the View of Romanian Anti-Semitic Movements: Continuity and Change." *Shvut: Jewish Problems in Eastern Europe* 16 (1993).
Anderson, Bonnie S., and Judith P. Zinnser. *A History of Their Own: Woman in Europe from Pre-History to the Present.* New York, 1988.

Andreski, Stanislav. "An Economic Interpretation of Antisemitism in Eastern Europe." *Jewish Journal of Sociology* 5, no. 2 (December 1963).

Angress, Werner T. *Stillborn Revolution: The Communist Bid for Power in Germany, 1921–1923.* Princeton, 1963.

Antonov-Ovseyenko, Anton. *The Time of Stalin.* New York, 1981.

Apostol, Gheorghe. Interviewed by BBC Radio. Recorded April 1988, broadcast April 25, 1990.

———. Interviewed in *Totuşi iubirea* 2, no. 18 (35) (May 1991).

Arendt, Hannah. *The Origins of Totalitarianism.* Cleveland and New York, 1958.

Armstrong, John A. *The Politics of Totalitarianism.* New York, 1961.

Arnon, Zeev Shlomo. *Ha-Yahas la-Yehudim shel ha-mimshal veha-tsibur be-Romanyah, ba-me'ah ha-19 (1812–1917)* [Attitudes and Relations to the Jews of the Public and Administration in Rumania during the Nineteenth Century, 1812–1917]. Ph.D. diss., Hebrew University, Jerusalem, May 1986.

Ascher, Abraham. *Pavel Axelrod and the Development of Marxism.* Cambridge, Mass., 1972.

Avriel, Ehud. *Open the Gates! A Personal Story of "Illegal" Immigration to Israel.* New York, 1975.

Balabanoff, Angelica. *Impressions of Lenin.* Ann Arbor, 1968.

Balaş, Egon. *Will to Freedom: A Perilous Journey through Fascism and Communism.* Syracuse, N.Y., 2000.

Bar-Avi, Israel. *O istorie a evreilor români* [A History of the Romanian Jews]. Vol. 3. Jerusalem, 1966.

Baron, Salo W. *The Russian Jew under Tsars and Soviets.* New York, 1964.

Bauman, Zygmunt, "Exit Visas and Entry Tickets: Paradoxes of Jewish Assimilation." *Telos*, no. 77, Fall 1988.

———. *Modernity and Ambivalence.* Oxford, 1991.

———. "The Literary Afterlife of Polish Jewry." *Polin: A Journal of Polish-Jewish Studies* 7 (1992).

Bazhanov, Boris. Interviewed by George R. Urban. *Stalinism.* London, 1982.

Beard, Miriam. "Anti-Semitism: Product of Economic Myths." In Isacque Graebner and Stewart Henderson Britt, eds., *Jews in a Gentile World: The Problem of Anti-Semitism.* New York, 1942.

Benjamin, Lya, ed. *Legislaţia antievreiască, evreii din România øntre anii 1940–1944* [Anti-Jewish Legislation: The Jews in Romania, 1940–1944]. Vol. 1. Bucharest, 1993.

Berend, Ivan T. "The Historical Evolution of Eastern Europe as a Region." *International Organization* 40, no. 2 (Spring 1986).

———. *Central and Eastern Europe, 1944–1993: Detour from the Periphery to the Periphery.* Cambridge, 1996.

Berger, Joseph. *Nothing but the Truth.* New York, 1971.

Berlin, Isaiah. *Against the Current: Essays in the History of Ideas.* Edited by Henry Hardy. New York, 1982.

Betea, Lavinia. *Maurer şi lumea de ieri, Mărturii Despre Stalinizarea României* [Maurer and Yesterday's World: Testimony on the Stalinization of Romania]. Arad, 1995.

Bîrladeanu, Alexandru. Interviewed in *Totuşi iubirea* 2, no. 6 (23) (February 1991).

———. Interviewed in *Totuşi iubirea* 2, no. 7 (24) (February 1991).

Bogdan, Radu. "A Witness to Socialist Realism." *Dilema* 3, no. 156 (January 5–11, 1996).

Boian, Ion. Interviewed by Dumitru Mitel Popescu. *Libertate cu dreptate* 1, no. 7 (March 14, 1990).

Borkenau, Franz. *European Communism*. London, 1951.

———. *World Communism: A History of the Communist International*. Ann Arbor, 1962.

Bossy, George H. "Transportation and Communications." In Stephen Fischer-Galati, ed., *Romania*. New York, 1957.

Brătescu, Tatiana. "Ana Pauker: ulteme ani" [Ana Pauker: The Last Years]. *Cotidianul*, Historical Supplement, 4, no. 10 (42) (October 27, 1995).

Brătescu, Tatiana and Gheorghe. Interview in *Dosarele istoriei* 2, no. 8 (13) (1997).

Brucan, Silviu. *Generaţia irosită* [The Wasted Generation]. Bucharest, 1992.

———. *The Wasted Generation: Memoirs of the Romanian Journey from Capitalism to Socialism and Back*. Boulder, 1993.

Bruchis, Michael. "The Jews in the Revolutionary Underground of Bessarabia and Their Fate after Its Annexation by the Soviet Union." In his *Nations-Nationalities-People*. New York, 1984.

Brus, Wlodzimierz. "Stalinism in the 'People's Democracies.' " In Robert C. Tucker, ed. *Stalinism*. Toronto, 1977.

Brzezinski, Zbigniew K. *The Soviet Bloc: Unity and Conflict*. Rev. ed. New York, 1963.

Buber-Neumann, Margarete. *Under Two Dictators*. London, 1949.

Burmeister, Alfred (alias for the Polish Communist Wanda Pampuch-Bronska). *Dissolution and Aftermath of the Comintern: Experiences and Observations, 1937–1947*. New York, 1955.

Butnaru, I. C. *The Silent Holocaust: Romania and Its Jews*. New York, 1992.

Buzatu, Gheorghe. *Românii în arhivele kremlinului* [The Romanians in the Kremlin Archives]. Bucharest, 1996.

Cahnman, Werner J. "Role and Significance of the Jewish Artisan Class." *Jewish Journal of Sociology* 7, no. 3 (December 1965).

Cang, Joel. *The Silent Millions*. New York, 1969.

Cantor, Aviva. *Jewish Women/Jewish Men: The Legacy of Patriarchy in Jewish Life*. New York, 1995.

Castro Delgado, Enrique. *Mi Fe Se Perdio en Moscu*. Barcelona, 1964.

Cârja, Ion. *Canalul morţii* [The Canal of Death]. Bucharest, 1993.

Charlton, Michael. *The Eagle and the Small Birds*. Chicago, 1984.

Checinski, Michael. "Soviet-Polish Relations and the Polish Jews." *Midstream*, May 1980.

———. *Poland: Communism, Nationalism, Anti-Semitism*. New York, 1982.

Claudin, Fernando. *The Communist Movement: From Comintern to Cominform*. Middlesex, England, 1975.

Cohen, Lloyd A. "The Jewish Question during the Period of the Romanian National Renaissance and the Unification of the Two Principalities of Moldavia and Wallachia, 1848–1866." In Stephen Fischer-Galati, Radu R. Florescu, and George R. Ursul, eds., *Romania between East and West: Historical Essays in Memory of Constantin C. Giurescu*. Boulder and New York, 1982.

Cohen, Mitchell. *The Wager of Lucien Goldmann: Tragedy, Dialectics, and a Hidden God*. Princeton, 1994.

Cohen, Stephen F. *Bukharin and the Bolshevik Revolution: A Political Biography, 1888–1938*. Rev. ed. Oxford, 1980.

"Comintern Reminiscences: Interview with an Insider." *Survey*, no. 32, April–June 1960.

Constante, Lena. *The Silent Escape: Three Thousand Days in Romanian Prisons.* Berkeley and Los Angeles, 1995.

Constantinescu, Miron, Constantin Daicoviciu, and Ştefan Pascu, eds. *Istoria României, Compediu.* Bucharest, 1971.

Conquest, Robert. *The Great Terror.* New York, 1968.

———. *The Great Terror: A Reassessment.* Oxford, 1990.

———. "The Somber Monster." *New York Review of Books,* June 8, 1995.

Coposu, Corneliu, with Vartan Arachelian. *Dialoguri.* Bucharest, 1993.

Cotic, Meir. *The Prague Trial.* New York, 1987.

Cretzianu, Alexandre, ed. *Captive Romania.* London, 1956.

Crossman, Richard, ed. *The God That Failed.* New York, 1950.

Cuperman, Yaffa. *Bi-tsevat ha-komunizm: ha-Histadrut ha-Tsiyonit be-Romanyah, 1944–1949.* Tel Aviv, 1995.

Danielopol, Dumitru G. "Romania at the Peace Conference, Paris 1946." Unfinished manuscript in the archives of the Hoover Institution on War, Revolution and Peace.

Davies, R. W. *The Socialist Offensive: The Collectivization of Soviet Agriculture, 1929–1930.* Cambridge, Mass., 1980.

De Jonge, Alex. *Stalin.* New York, 1986.

Deletant, Dennis. *Ceauşescu and the Securitate: Coercion and Dissent in Romania, 1965–1989.* London, 1995.

———. "New Light on Gheorghiu-Dej's Struggle for Dominance in the Romanian Communist Party." *Slavonic and East European Review* 73, no. 4 (October 1995).

Dench, Geoff. *Minorities in the Open Society.* London and New York, 1986.

Denize, Eugen Bernard. "Sephardic Culture in the Romanian Countries (1700–1821)." *Shvut: Jewish Problems in Eastern Europe* 16 (1993).

Deutscher, Isaac. *The Non-Jewish Jew and Other Essays.* Oxford, 1968.

———. "The Tragic Life of a Polrugarian Minister." In *Heretics and Renegades.* New York, 1969.

———. "The Tragedy of the Polish Communist Party." In Tamara Deutscher, ed., *Marxism in Our Time.* San Francisco, 1971.

Dima, Nicholas. *Journey to Freedom.* Washington, D. C., 1989.

Djilas, Milovan. "Antisemitism." *Borba,* December 14, 1952.

———. *Wartime.* New York, 1977.

———. *Rise and Fall.* San Diego, 1985.

Doboş, Dănuţ. "Purges at the University of Iaşi, 1949–1960." *Arhivele totalitarian-ismului* 2, no. 1–2 (1994).

Documents Concerning the Right Deviation in the Rumanian Workers' Party. Bucharest, 1952.

Drachkovitch, Milorad M., ed. *Marxism in the Modern World.* Stanford, 1965.

Drachkovitch, Milorad M., and Lazitch, Branko. "The Communist International." In Milorad M. Drachkovitch, ed., *The Revolutionary Internationals, 1864–1943.* Stanford, 1966.

Ehrenburg, Ilya. *Post-War Years.* New York, 1967.

Eidelberg, Phillip G. *The Great Rumanian Peasant Revolt of 1907.* Leiden, 1974.

Ellas, Zandek, and Joromir Netik. "Czechoslovakia." In William Griffith, ed., *Communism in Europe: Continuity, Change and the Sino-Soviet Dispute.* Vol. 2. Cambridge, Mass., 1966.

Eskenasy, Victor. "Moses Gaster and His Memoirs—the Path to Zionism." *Shvut: Jewish Problems in Eastern Europe* 16 (1993).

Ettinger, Shmuel. "The Origins of Modern Anti-Semitism." *Dispersion and Unity* 9 (1969).
———. "The Modern Period." In H. H. Ben Sasson, ed., *A History of Jewish People.* Cambridge, Mass., 1976.
———. "The Young Hegelians: A Source of Modern Anti-Semitism?" *Jerusalem Quarterly* 28 (Summer 1983).
Fast, Howard. *The Naked God: The Writer and the Communist Party.* New York, 1957.
Fejtö, Francios. *History of the People's Democracies.* New York, 1971.
Feuer, Lewis S. "The Socio-Psychological Transformations of Soviet Society." In Milorad M. Drachkovitch, ed., *Fifty Years of Communism in Russia.* Philadelphia, 1968.
Fischer, Ernst. *An Opposing Man: The Autobiography of a Romantic Revolutionary.* New York, 1974.
Fischer-Galati, Stephen. *The New Rumania: From People's Democracy to Socialist Republic.* Cambridge, Mass., 1967.
———. "Romanian Nationalism." In Peter F. Sugar and Ivo J. Lederer, eds., *Nationalism in Eastern Europe.* Seattle and London, 1969.
———. "Fascism, Communism, and the Jewish Question in Romania." In Bela Vago and George L. Mosse, eds., *Jews and Non-Jews in Eastern Europe, 1918–1945.* New York and Toronto, 1974.
———. "Jew and Peasant in Interwar Romania." *Nationalities Papers* 16, no. 2 (Fall 1988).
Fitzpatrick, Sheila. "Stalin and the Making of a New Elite, 1928–1939." *Slavic Review* 38, no. 3 (September 1979).
Fitzpatrick, Sheila, ed. *Cultural Revolution in Russia, 1928–1931.* Bloomington, Ind., 1984.
Frankel, Jonathan. *Prophecy and Politics: Socialism, Nationalism and the Russian Jews, 1862–1917.* Cambridge, 1981.
———. "Assimilation and the Jews in Nineteenth-Century Europe: Towards a New Historiography?" In Jonathan Frankel and Steven J. Zipperstein, eds., *Assimilation and Community: The Jews in Nineteenth-Century Europe.* Cambridge, 1992.
Frei, Bruno. "Marxist Interpretations of the Jewish Question." *Wiener Library Bulletin,* n.s., 28, no. 35/36 (1975).
Freytag, Gustav. *Debit and Credit (Soll und Haben).* New York, 1990.
Frunza, Victor. *Istoria stalinismului în România* [The History of Stalinism in Romania]. Bucharest, 1990.
Gaddis, John Lewis. *We Now Know: Rethinking the Cold War.* Oxford and New York, 1997.
Garai, George. "Anti-Zionism in Hungary." *Soviet Jewish Affairs* 2, no. 2 (1982).
Getzler, Israel. "The Mensheviks." *Problems of Communism,* November–December 1967.
Gheorghiu-Dej, Gheorghe. "The People's Revolutionary Vigilance." *Pravda,* no. 247 (12.084), September 4, 1951. Reprinted in *Scânteia,* September 6, 1951.
———. *Gh. Gheorghiu-Dej, Articole şi cuvântări* [Articles and Speeches]. Edition A III-a. Bucharest, 1952.
———. Speech to the National Meeting of Miners on June 27–28, 1952. *Scânteia,* July 2, 1952.
———. Report to the Plenary Meeting of the C.C. of the R.W.P., March 3–5, 1949. In *Gh. Gheorghiu-Dej, Articole şi cuvântări.* 3rd ed. Bucharest, 1953.

────. "Report of the Delegation of the Romanian Workers' Party to the 22nd Congress of the C.P.S.U. at the Plenary Meeting of the C.C. of the R.W.P., November 30–December 5, 1961." *Agerpres Information Bulletin,* no. 22–23, December 10, 1961.

Gibianskii, Leonid. "The Last Conference of the Cominform." In Giuliamo Procacci, ed., *The Cominform: Minutes of the Three Conferences, 1947/1948/1949.* Milan, 1994.

────. "The Soviet-Yugoslav Split and the Cominform." In Norman Naimark and Leonid Gibianskii, eds. *The Establishment of Communist Regimes in Eastern Europe, 1944–1949.* Boulder, 1997.

Gide, André. In Richard Crossman, ed., *The God That Failed.* New York, 1950.

Giladi, David. "In Bucharest: Ana Pauker at Israel's Independence Day Party." *Ma'ariv,* April 15, 1975.

Gilberg, Trond. "The Multiple Legacies of History: Romania in the Year 1990." In Joseph Held, ed., *The Columbia History of Eastern Europe.* New York, 1992.

Gilboa, Yehoshua A. *The Black Years of Soviet Jewry.* Boston, 1971.

Gilman, Sander L. *Jewish Self-Hatred.* Baltimore and London, 1986.

"A Girl Who Hated Cream Puffs." *Time,* September 20, 1948.

Gitelman, Zvi Y. *Jewish Nationality and Soviet Politics: The Jewish Sections of the C.P.S.U., 1917-1930.* Princeton, 1972.

────. *Anti-Semitism in the U.S.S.R.: Sources, Types, Consequences.* New York, 1974.

Gitlow, Benjamin. *The Whole of Their Lives.* New York, 1948.

Gluckstein, Ygael. *Stalin's Satellites in Europe.* London, 1952.

Goldhagen, Eric. "The Ethnic Consciousness of Early Russian Jewish Socialists." *Judaism* 23 (1974).

Goldstücker, Eduard. Interviewed by George R. Urban. *Communist Reformation.* London, 1979.

Gunther, John. *Behind the Curtain.* New York, 1949.

Haberer, Erich. *Jews and Revolution in Nineteenth-Century Russia.* Cambridge, 1995.

Halperin, Ernst. *The Triumphant Heretic.* London, 1957.

Handlin, Oscar. "Prejudice and Capitalist Exploitation: Does Economics Explain Racism?" *Commentary,* July 1948.

Hazard, Elizabeth W. *Cold War Crucible: United States Foreign Policy and the Conflict in Romania, 1943–1953.* Boulder, 1996.

Healey, Dorothy, and Maurice Isserman. *Dorothy Healey Remembers: A Life in the American Communist Party.* Oxford and New York, 1990.

Heller, Mihail, and Alexander Nekrich. *Utopia in Power: The History of the Soviet Union from 1917 to the Present.* New York, 1986.

Henry, Sondra, and Emily Taitz. *Written Out of History: A Hidden Legacy of Jewish Women Revealed through Their Writings and Letters.* New York, 1978.

Herf, Jeffrey. *East German Communists and the Jewish Question: The Case of Paul Merker.* Washington, D.C., 1994.

Hilberg, Raul. *The Destruction of the European Jews.* New York, 1973.

Hitchins, Keith. *Rumania, 1966–1947.* Oxford, 1994.

Hobsbawm, E. J. *The Age of Empire, 1875–1914.* New York, 1989.

Hodos, George. *Show Trials.* New York, 1987.

Hotărîrea plenarei a Comitetului Central al P.M.R., 3–5 martie, 1949 [The Resolution of the Plenary Meeting of the Central Committee of the R.W.P., March 3–5, 1949]. Bucharest, 1949.

Hyman, Paula E. *Gender and Assimilation in Modern Jewish History: The Roles and Representation of Women.* Seattle and London, 1995.

———. *The Jews of Modern France.* Berkeley and Los Angeles, 1998.

Iancu, Carol. *Les Juifs en Roumanie, 1866–1919, de l'exclusion à l'émancipation.* Aix-en-Provence, 1978.

Iazhborovskaia, Inessa. "The Gomulka Alternative: The Untravelled Road." In Norman Naimark and Leonid Gibianskii, eds. *The Establishment of Communist Regimes in Eastern Europe, 1944–1949.* Boulder, 1997.

Immigration to Israel: 1948–1972. Central Bureau of Statistics, Ministry of Immigrant Absorption, Jewish Agency of Aliya and Absorption Department. Special Series No. 489. Jerusalem, 1975.

"In New Romania." *Survey Reports,* June 15, 1953.

The Institute of Historical and Social-Political Study Next to the Central Committee of the P.C.R. *Istoria partidului comunist român* [The History of the Romanian Communist Party]. Documentary Synthesis, chapter 6, August 1944–December 1947. Bucharest, n.d.

Ioanid, Radu. *The Sword of the Archangel: Fascist Ideology in Romania.* Boulder and New York, 1990.

Ionescu, Ghita. *Communism in Romania.* London, 1964.

Israel, Gerard. *The Jews in Russia.* New York, 1975.

Jackson, George D., Jr. *Comintern and Peasant in East Europe, 1919–1930.* New York and London, 1966.

Jacobs, Jack. *On Socialists and "the Jewish Question" after Marx.* New York and London, 1992.

Jay, Martin. "Anti-Semitism and the Weimar Left." *Midstream,* January 1974.

Jelavich, Barbara. *History of the Balkans.* Vol. 2 of *Twentieth Century.* Cambridge, 1983.

Jewish Agency of Aliya and Absorption Department. *Immigration to Israel: 1948–1972.* Ministry of Immigrant Absorption, Central Bureau of Statistics, Special Series No. 489. Jerusalem, 1975.

The Jewish Encyclopedia. Vol. 10. New York and London, 1901–1906.

Judt, Tony. "Why the Cold War Worked." *New York Review of Books,* October 9, 1997.

Kahn, Lothar. "The Ugly Jew and the Cry for Normalcy: Jewish Self-Criticism at the Turn of the Century." *Judaism* 32, no. 2 (Spring 1983).

Kaplan, Karel. *Report on the Murder of the General Secretary.* Columbus, Ohio, 1990.

Karchmar, Lucien. "Communism in Romania, 1918–1921." In Ivo Banac, ed., *The Effects of WWI: The Class War after the Great War. The Rise of Communist Parties in East Central Europe, 1918–1921.* New York, 1983.

Katz, Jacob. *From Prejudice to Destruction: Anti-Semitism, 1700–1933.* Cambridge, Mass., 1980.

Kellogg, Fredrick. *The Road to Romanian Independence.* West Lafayette, Ind., 1995.

Kersten, Krystyna. *The Establishment of Communist Rule in Poland, 1943–1948.* Berkeley, 1991.

Khrushchev, N. *Khrushchev Remembers: The Glasnost Tapes.* Translated and edited by Jerrold L. Schecter with Vyacheslav V. Luchkov. Boston, 1990.

Kideckel, David A. "The Socialist Transformation of Agriculture in a Romanian Commune, 1945–62." *American Ethnologist* 9, no. 2 (May 1982).

King, Robert R. *History of the Romanian Communist Party.* Stanford, 1980.

Kligman, Gail. *The Politics of Duplicity: Controlling Reproduction in Ceauşescu's Romania.* Berkeley and Los Angeles, 1998.

Kochavi, Arieh J. "British Diplomats and the Jews in Poland, Romania and Hungary during the Communist Takeovers." *East European Quarterly* 29, no. 4 (Winter 1995).

Koenig, Ernest. "Collectivization in Czechoslovakia and Poland." In Irwin T. Sanders, ed., *Collectivization of Agriculture in Eastern Europe.* Lexington, Ky., 1957.

Koestler, Arthur. In Richard Crossman, ed., *The God That Failed.* New York, 1950.

———. *The Invisible Writing: An Autobiography.* Boston, 1954.

Korosi-Krizsan, Sandor. "Rumania and the Comintern." *East Europe,* no. 12, 1966.

Kostyrchenko, Gennadi. *Out of the Red Shadows: Anti-Semitism in Stalin's Russia.* Amherst, N.Y., 1995.

Kovari, Attila. *The Antecedents of Today's National Myth in Rumania, 1921–1965.* Jerusalem, 1983.

Kriegel, Annie, and Stéphane Courtois. *Eugen Fried, Le Grand Secret du PCF.* Paris, 1997.

Krivine, David. "Who Was Ana Pauker?" *Jerusalem Post Magazine,* December 26, 1975.

Kuusinen, Aino. *Before and After Stalin: A Personal Account of Soviet Russia from the 1920s to the 1930s.* Trans. by Paul Stevenson. London, 1974.

Laqueur, Walter. *A History of Zionism.* New York, 1976.

Lazar, Gyorgy (pen name). "Memorandum." In *Witness to Cultural Genocide: First-Hand Reports on Rumania's Minority Policies Today.* New York, 1979.

Lazitch, Branko. "Stalin's Massacre of the Foreign Communist Leaders." In Milorad M. Drachkovitch, ed., *The Comintern: Historical Highlights.* Stanford, 1966.

———. "Two Instruments of Control by the Comintern." In Milorad M. Drachkovitch, ed., *The Comintern: Historical Highlights.* Stanford, 1966.

Lazitch, Branko, with Milorad M. Drachkovitch. *Biographical Dictionary of the Comintern.* Rev. ed. Stanford, 1986.

Lehrman, Hal. "Hungary-Rumania: Crime and Punishment. Pages From a Correspondent's Notebook." *Commentary,* October 1946.

———. "Ana Pauker." *Life,* January 3, 1949.

Leonhard, Wolfgang. *Child of the Revolution.* Chicago, 1958.

———. *The Kremlin since Stalin.* New York, 1962.

Levy, Robert. "From the Secret Archives: New Revelations on the Purge of Lucreţiu Patraşcanu." *Sfera politicii,* no. 29–30, July–August 1995.

Lewin, Moshe. *Russian Peasants and Soviet Power: A Study of Collectivization.* New York and London, 1968.

———. "Society, State and Ideology." In Sheila Fitzpatrick, ed., *Cultural Revolution in Russia, 1928–1931.* Bloomington, 1984.

———*The Making of the Soviet System: Essays in the Social History of Interwar Russia.* New York, 1985.

Lichidarea lui Marcel Pauker, o anchetă stalinistă (1937–1938) [The Liquidation of Marcel Pauker: A Stalinist Inquiry, 1937–1938]. Trans. by G. Brătescu. Bucharest, 1995.

Lichtheim, George. "Social Democracy and Communism: 1918–1968." *Studies in Comparative Communism* 3, no. 1 (January 1970).

London, Artur. *The Confession.* New York, 1970.

Lubenz, Louis Frances. *This Is My Story.* New York, 1947.

Lukacs, Georg. *Record of a Life: An Autobiographical Sketch.* Edited by Istvan Eorsi. London, 1983.

Lukes, Igor. "The Czech Road to Communism." In Norman Naimark and Leonid Gibianskii, eds., *The Establishment of Communist Regimes in Eastern Europe, 1944–1949.* Boulder, 1997.

Mandelshtam, Nadezhda. *Hope Abandoned.* New York, 1974.

McCagg, William O., Jr. *Stalin Embattled.* Detroit, 1977.

McInnes, Neil. "The Labor Movement." In *The Impact of the Russian Revolution, 1917–1967.* London, 1967.

Medvedev, Roy A. *Let History Judge: The Origins and Consequences of Stalinism.* New York, 1971.

——. *On Stalin and Stalinism.* Oxford and New York, 1979.

Mendel, Hersh. *Memoirs of a Jewish Revolutionary.* London, 1989.

Mendelsohn, Ezra. *Class Struggle in the Pale: The Formative Years of the Jewish Workers' Movement in Czarist Russia.* Cambridge, 1970.

——. *The Jews of East Central Europe between the World Wars.* Bloomington, Ind., 1983.

Mendes-Flohr, Paul R. "The Throes of Assimilation: Self-Hatred and the Jewish Revolutionary." *European Judaism* 12, no. 1 (Spring 1978).

Meyer, Peter. "Stalin Plans Genocide." *New Leader,* December 15, 1952.

——. "Has Soviet Anti-Semitism Halted?" *Commentary,* July 1954.

Meyer, Peter, ed. *The Jews in the Soviet Satellites.* Syracuse, 1953.

Mezincescu, Eduard. "Detention without an Arrest Warrant." *Magazin istoric* 26, no. 6 (303) (June 1992).

——. "Procedural Gap or . . . Socialist Legality?" *Magazin istoric* 26, no. 7 (304) (July 1992).

Miles, Rosalind. *The Women's History of the World.* London, 1988.

Mircu, Marius. *Ana Pauker şi alţii* [Ana Pauker and the Others]. Bat Yam, Israel, 1989.

Moghioroş, Alexandru. "Speech of Comrade Alexandru Moghioroş to the Plenary Meeting of the C.C. of the R.W.P., November 30–December 5, 1961." *Scânteia,* no. 5380, December 16, 1961.

Molotov, V. M. *Molotov Remembers: Inside Kremlin Politics.* Edited by Albert Resis. Chicago, 1993.

Monnerot, Jules. *Sociology and Psychology of Communism.* Boston, 1953.

Montias, J. *Economic Development in Communist Rumania.* Cambridge, Mass., 1967.

Mosse, George L. "The Image of the Jew in German Popular Culture: Felix Dahn and Gustav Freytag." *Leo Baeck Institute Yearbook* 2. London, 1957.

Muraschko, Galina P., Albina F. Noskowa, and Tatjana W. Wolokitina. "Das Zentralkomitee der WKP(b) und das Ende der 'nationalen Wege zum Sozialismus.'" In *Jahrbuch für historische Kommunismus-forschung.* Akademie Verlag, 1994.

Muraschko, Galina P., Albina F. Noskowa, and Tatjana W. Wolokitina, eds. *Vostochnaia Evropa v dokumentakh arkhivov: 1944–1953* [Eastern Europe in the Documents of the Russian Archives, 1944–1953]. Vol. 1, Moscow, 1997. Vol. II, Moscow, 1998.

Nagy, Imre. "Nagy Imre—Remarks on the Draft of the Economic Policy Guidelines of the H.C.P." *Társadalmi Szemle* 7 (July 1989).

Namir, Mordechai. *Shelihut be-Moskvah* [Mission to Moscow]. Tel Aviv, 1971.

Nedava, Joseph. *Trotsky and the Jews.* Philadelphia, 1971.

"New Pieces in the 'Ana Pauker Dossier.'" *Magazin istoric* 26, no. 10 (307) (October 1992).

Nicolaevsky, Boris. "The Meaning of Khrushchev's Victory." *New Leader,* September 2, 1957.

Nollau, Gunther. *International Communism and World Revolution: History and Methods.* London, 1961.

Nove, Alec. *An Economic History of the USSR.* Rev. ed. London, 1976.

———. "Stalin and Stalinism—Some Introductory Thoughts." In *The Stalin Phenomenon.* New York, 1992.

Oelsner, Toni. "Wilhelm Roscher's Theory of the Economic and Social Position of the Jews in the Middle Ages: A Critical Examination." *Yivo Annual 1958–1959.*

———. "The Place of the Jews in Economic History as Viewed by German Scholars." *Leo Baeck Institute Yearbook,* 1962.

Oldson, William O. *A Providential Anti-Semitism, Nationalism and Polity in Nineteenth-Century Romania.* Philadelphia, 1991.

Onişoru, Gheorghe. "Propaganda and Counter-Propaganda: The Matter of Kolhozes, 1944–1949." In *Instaurarea comunismului—între rezistenţă şi represiune* [The Installation of Communism: Between Resistance and Repression]. Papers Presented at the Conference of Sighetu Marmaţiei (June 9–11, 1995). Analele Sighet 2. Bucharest, 1995.

Oprea, Marius. "Pagini din 'copilăria' Securităţii române" [Pages from the "Childhood" of the Romanian Securitate]. *Dosarele istoriei,* no. 5, 1996.

Oren, Mordechai. *Reshimot asir Prag* [Political Prisoner in Prague]. Tel Aviv, 1960.

Oren, Nissan. *Bulgarian Communism: The Road to Power.* New York, 1971.

———. *Revolution Administered: Agrarianism and Communism in Bulgaria.* Baltimore, 1973.

Pacepa, Ion Mihai. *Moiştenirea kremlinului* [The Kremlin's Legacy]. Bucharest, 1993.

Patraşcanu, Lucreţiu. "No Compromise on the Question of Transylvania." *Scânteia,* June 14, 1946.

Pauker, Ana. *Cuvânt de încheiere de Congresul Partidului Român din 21–23 februarie 1948* [Ana Pauker's Concluding Speech at the First R.W.P. Congress, February 23, 1948]. Bucharest, 1948.

Pinkus, Benjamin. *The Soviet Government and the Jews.* London, 1984.

———. *The Jews of the Soviet Union.* Cambridge, 1988.

Pippidi, Andrei. "The Mirror and behind It: The Image of the Jew in the Romanian Society." *Shvut: Jewish Problems in Eastern Europe* 16 (1993).

Pois, Robert A. "An Essay on the Jewish Problem in Marxist Historiography." *East European Quarterly* 11, no. 2 (1977).

Pokivailova, Tatiana A. "Tragica greşeală a lui Lucreţiu Patraşcanu" [The Tragic Mistake of Lucreţiu Patraşcanu]. *Magazin Istoric* 30, no. 9 (354) (September 1996).

Pons, Silvio. "The Twilight of the Cominform." In Giuliamo Procacci, ed., *The Cominform, Minutes of the Three Conferences 1947/1948/1949.* Milan, 1994.

Popescu, Dumitru. *Am fost şi cioplitor de himere.* Bucharest, 1994.

Rákosi, Mátyás. *Visszaemlekezesek 1940–1956* [Remembrances, 1940–56]. Budapest, 1997.

Rapoport, Yakov. *The Doctors' Plot of 1953.* Cambridge, Mass., 1991.

Raţiu, Anton. *Cumplita odisee a grupului Lucreţiu Pătrăşcanu* [The Terrible Odysscy of the Lucreţiu Patraşcanu Group]. 2 vols. Bucharest, 1996.

Redlich, Shimon. *Propaganda and Nationalism in Wartime Russia: The Jewish Antifascist Committee in the U.S.S.R., 1941–1948.* Boulder, 1982.

"Report of the Party Commission Established to Clarify the Situation of Lucreţiu Pa-traşcanu." Submitted to the Party Leadership on June 29, 1968, p. 29. Excerpts published in *Cuvîntul* nos. 38–44, 1992.

Resel, Mordechai. "The Daughter of a 'Shochet' Who Became the 'Iron Lady' of Romania." *Hatzofeh*, August 19, 1983.

Rezoluţii şi Hotărîri ale Comitetului Central al Partidului Muncitoresc Român [Resolutions and Decrees of the Central Committee of the Romanian Workers' Party]. Vol. 2, 1951–1953. Bucharest, 1954.

"The Rise and Fall of Ana Pauker." *News from behind the Iron Curtain*, July 1952.

Roberts, Henry L. *Rumania: Political Problems of an Agrarian State*. New Haven, 1951.

Robrieux, Philippe. *Histoire interieure du parti Communiste*. Paris, 1980.

Rodinson, Maxime. *Cult, Ghetto and State: The Persistence of the Jewish Question*. London, 1983.

Ro'i, Ya'acov. *Soviet Decision Making in Practice: The U.S.S.R. and Israel, 1947–1954*. New Brunswick, 1980.

———. "Soviet Policies and Attitudes toward Israel, 1948–1978: An Overview." *Soviet Jewish Affairs* 11, no. 2 (1981).

Rosen, Avram. "The Contribution of the Jews to the Industrial Development and Modernization of Romania, 1900–1938: The Case of Bucharest." *Shvut: Jewish Problems in Eastern Europe* 16 (1993).

Rosen, Moses. Interviewed by the *Jerusalem Post*, June 24, 1988.

———. *Dangers, Tests and Miracles: The Remarkable Life Story of Chief Rabbi Rosen of Romania*. As told to Joseph Finklestone. London, 1990.

———. *Primejdii, incercări, miracole* [Dangers, Tests, and Miracles]. Bucharest, 1991.

Roske, Octavian. *Dosarul colectivizării agriculturii în România, 1949–1962* [The Dossier of the Collectivization of Agriculture in Romania, 1949–1962]. Bucharest, 1992.

———. "Colectivizarea agriculturii în România, 1949–1962" [The Collectivization of Agriculture in Romania, 1949–1962]. *Arhivele totalitarismului* 1, no. 3 (1993).

———. "Colectivizarea agriculturii, Represiunea totală, 1957–1962" [The Collectivization of Agriculture, Total Repression, 1957–1962]. *Arhivele totalitarismului* 3, nos. 1 and 2 (1995).

Rotman, Liviu. "Mental and Cultural Structures of Romanian Jews at the Turn of the Century." *Shvut: Jewish Problems in Eastern Europe* 16 (1993).

———. "Romanian Jewry: The First Decade after the Holocaust." In Randolph L. Braham, ed., *The Tragedy of Romanian Jewry*. New York, 1994.

Royal Institute of International Affairs. *The Soviet-Yugoslav Dispute*. London, 1948.

Ruben, David. "Marxism and the Jewish Question." *The Socialist Register*, 1982.

Rubin, Jacob H. *I Live to Tell: The Russian Adventures of an American Socialist*. New York, 1934.

Rubin, Reuven. *My Life My Art*. New York, 1969.

Rush, Myron. *How Communist States Change Their Rulers*. Ithaca, 1974.

Ryker, T. W. *The Making of Roumania*. London, 1931.

Safran, Alexandre. *Resisting the Storm: Romania, 1940–1947. Memoirs*. Edited by Jean Ancel. Jerusalem, 1987.

Sanders, Irwin T., ed. *Collectivization of Agriculture in Eastern Europe*. Lexington, Ky., 1957.

Schapiro, Leonard. "Reflections on the Changing Role of the Party in the Totalitarian Polity." *Studies in Comparative Communism* 2, no. 2 (April 1969).

Schatz, Jaff. *The Generation: The Rise and Fall of the Jewish Communists of Poland.* Berkeley and Los Angeles, 1991.

Schwarz, Solomon M. "The New Anti-Semitism of the Soviet Union." *Commentary,* January 1950.

———. *Jews in the Soviet Union.* New York, 1951.

Scurtu, Ioan. "PMR și 'criza iugoslavă'" [The R.W.P. and the "Yugoslav Crisis"]. *Dosarele istoriei,* no. 3 (19), 1998.

Scurtu, Ioan, ed. *România, viața politică în documente 1946* [Romania: Political Life in Documents, 1946]. Bucharest, 1996.

Serge, Victor. *Memoirs of a Revolutionary, 1901–1941.* Trans. and edited by Peter Sedgwick. London, 1963.

Seton-Watson, Hugh. *The East European Revolution.* New York, 1962.

———. *Eastern Europe between the Wars, 1918–1941.* New York, 1967.

———. "Thirty Years After." In Martin McCauley, ed. *Communist Power in Europe, 1944–1949.* London, 1979.

Shafir, Michael. *Romania, Politics, Economics and Society.* Boulder, 1985.

Shephard, Gordon. *Russia's Danubian Empire.* London, 1954.

Silberner, Edmund. "German Social Democracy and the Jewish Problem Prior to World War I." *Historica Judaica* 15, part 1 (April 1953).

Silone, Ignazio. In Richard Crossman, ed., *The God That Failed.* New York, 1950.

———. *Emergency Exit.* London, 1969.

Skerpan, Alfred A. "Aspects of Soviet Antisemitism." *Antioch Review* 12, no. 3 (September 1952).

Solzhenitsyn, Aleksandr I. *The Gulag Archipelago.* New York, 1975.

The Soviet-Yugoslav Dispute. London, 1948.

Sperber, Manes. *The Unheeded Warning.* New York, 1991.

Spulber, Nicolas. "Collectivization in Hungary and Romania." In Irwin T. Sanders, ed., *Collectivization of Agriculture in Eastern Europe.* Lexington, Ky., 1957.

———. *The State and Economic Development in Eastern Europe.* New York, 1966.

Stalin, Joseph V. *Selected Works.* Davis, Calif., 1971.

Stampfer, Shaul. "Gender Differentiation and Education of the Jewish Woman in Nineteenth-Century Eastern Europe." *Polin: A Journal of Polish-Jewish Studies* 7 (1992).

Stanislawski, Michael. Introduction to Emil Dorian, *The Quality of Witness: A Romanian Diary, 1937–1944.* Edited by Marguerite Dorian. Philadelphia, 1982.

Stănescu, Marin C. *Moscova, Cominternul, filiera comunistă balcanică și România (1919–1944)* [Moscow, the Comintern, the Balkan Communist Channel and Romania, 1919–1944]. Bucharest, 1994.

Stillman, Edmund O. "The Collectivization of Bulgarian Agriculture." In Irwin T. Sanders, ed., *Collectivization of Agriculture in Eastern Europe.* Lexington, Ky., 1957.

Stryjkowski, Julian. "'A Writer Not a Hero': An Interview with Julian Stryjkowski." Translated by Ursula Phillips. *East European Jewish Affairs* 25, no. 1 (Summer 1995).

Suciu, Mircea, and Mircea Chirițoiu. "Ana Pauker: Repere pentru o biografie neretusată" [Ana Pauker: Landmarks of a Real Biography]. *Dosarele istoriei* 2, no. 8 (13) (1997).

Sugar, Peter F. "Roots of Eastern European Nationalism." In Peter F. Sugar and Ivo J. Lederer, eds., *Nationalism in Eastern Europe.* Seattle and London, 1969.

Surpat, Gheorghe, ed. *România în anii socialismului 1948–1978* [Romania in the Years of Socialism, 1948–1978]. Bucharest, 1980.

Sylvain, Nicolas. "Rumania." In Peter Meyer, ed., *The Jews in the Soviet Satellites.* Syracuse, 1953.

Szász, Bela. *Volunteers for the Gallows: Anatomy of a Show Trial.* Translated by Kathleen Szász. New York, 1971.

Şerbulescu, Andrei (Belu Zilber). *Monarhia de drept dialectic.* Bucharest, 1991.

Talmon, J. L. *Israel among the Nations.* New York, 1970.

———. *The Myth of the Nation and the Vision of Revolution.* London, 1981.

Tănase, Stelian. "The Illnesses Appeared in Prison and Were Treated in Power." *Dosarele istoriei* 3, no. 4 (20) (1998).

Teller, Judd. *Scapegoat of Revolution.* New York, 1954.

———. *The Kremlin, the Jews, and the Middle East.* New York, 1957.

Tismaneanu, Vladimir. "The Ambiguity of Romanian Communism." *Telos,* no. 60, Summer 1984.

———. "Ceauşescu's Socialism." *Problems of Communism* 34, no. 1 (January– February 1985).

———. "The Tragicomedy of Romanian Communism." *East European Politics and Societies* 3, no. 2 (Spring 1989).

Toranska, Teresa. *Them, Stalin's Political Puppets.* New York, 1987.

Traverso, Enzo. *The Marxists and the Jewish Question: The History of a Debate, (1843–1943).* Translated by Bernard Gibbons. Atlantic Highlands, N. J., 1994.

Troncotă, Cristian. "Colonia de muncă" [The Work Colony]. *Arhivele totalitaris- mului* 1, no. 1 (1993).

Tucker, Robert C. *Stalin as Revolutionary, 1879–1929: A Study in History and Per- sonality.* New York, 1973.

Ulam, Adam. *The Bolsheviks.* Toronto, 1965.

———. "Titoism." In Milorad M. Drachkovitch, ed., *Marxism in the Modern World.* Stanford, 1965.

———. *Stalin: The Man and His Era.* New York, 1973.

———. Interviewed by George R. Urban. *Stalinism.* London, 1982.

The Universal Jewish Encyclopedia. Vol. 9. New York, 1943.

Urban, George R., ed. *Scaling the Wall, Talking to Eastern Europe: The Best of Ra- dio Free Europe.* Detroit, 1964.

———. *Communist Reformation.* London, 1979.

———. *Stalinism.* London, 1982.

Vago, Bela. *The Shadow of the Swastika: The Rise of Fascism and Anti-Semitism in the Danubian Basin, 1936–39.* London, 1975.

Vago, Raphael. "Jews in the Communist Regime, 1944–1948." In Benjamin Pinkus, ed., *Yahadut Mizrach Europa ben Sho'ah li-tekumah, 1944–1948* [Eastern Eu- ropean Jewry from the Holocaust to Redemption, 1944–1948]. Sde Boker, Is- rael, 1987.

———. "The Traditions of Antisemitism in Romania." *Patterns of Prejudice* 27, no. 1(1993).

Vaksberg, Arkady. *Hotel Lux.* Paris, 1993.

———. *Stalin against the Jews.* New York, 1994.

Veiga, Francisco. *Istoria gărzii de fier 1919–1941.* Bucharest, 1993.

Viola, Lynne. *Peasant Rebels under Stalin.* New York and Oxford, 1996.

Vital, David. *The Origins of Zionism.* Oxford, 1975.

Volokitina, T. V., G. P. Muraschko, and A. F. Noskova. *Narodnaia demokratiia, mif ili realnost? Obshchestvenno-politicheskie protessy v Vostochnoi Evrope, 1944– 1948* [Popular Democracy: Myth or Reality? Sociopolitical Processes in Eastern Europe, 1944–1948]. Moscow, 1993.

Volovici, Leon. *Nationalist Ideology and Antisemitism: The Case of Romanian Intellectuals in the 1930s*. Oxford, 1991.
Wat, Aleksander. *My Century: The Odyssey of a Polish Intellectual*. New York, 1988.
Weber, Eugen. *Varieties of Fascism*. New York, 1964.
———. "Romania." In Hans Rogger and Eugen Weber, eds., *The European Right*. Berkeley and Los Angeles, 1966.
———. "Jews, Antisemitism, and the Origins of the Holocaust." *Historical Reflections* 5, no. 1 (Summer 1978).
———. "The Men of the Archangel." In George L. Mosse, ed., *International Fascism: New Thoughts and New Approaches*. London, 1979.
Weinryb, Bernard. "The Economic and Social Background of Modern Antisemitism." In Koppel S. Pinson, ed., *Essays on Antisemitism*. New York, 1942.
Weissberg, Alexander. *The Accused*. New York, 1951.
Wistrich, Robert S. *Revolutionary Jews from Marx to Trotsky*. New York, 1976.
———. *Socialism and the Jews: The Dilemmas of Assimilation in Germany and Austria-Hungary*. East Brunswick, N.J., 1982.
Wolfe, Bertram D. "Marxism and the Russian Revolution." In Milorad M. Drachkovitch, ed., *Fifty Years of Communism in Russia*. London, 1968.
Wolff, Robert Lee. *The Balkans in Our Time*. Cambridge, Mass., 1974.
World Jewish Congress. "The Persecution of Jews in Rumania." *Congress Weekly* 21, no. 20 (May 24, 1954).
Yahadut Romanyah bi-tekumat Yisrael [Rumanian Jewry during the Revival of Israel]. Vol. 2, *Prisoners of Zion*. Tel Aviv, 1994.
Ypsilon [pseud.]. *Pattern for World Revolution*. Chicago, 1947.
Zeiger, Simion. "Certain Aspects of the Policies of the Party and State Leadership in Romania towards the Jewish Population in the First Years after Taking Power." Unpublished manuscript, n.d.
Zilber, Herbert (Belu). *Actor în procesul Pătrășcanu, prima versiune a memorilor lui Belu Zilber* [Actor in the Patrașcanu Trial: The First Version of Belu Zilber's Memoirs]. Edited by G. Brătescu. Bucharest, 1997.
Zioniști sub anchetă [Zionists under Investigation]. Bucharest, 1993.
Zubok, Vladislav, and Constantine Pleshakov. *Inside the Kremlin's Cold War: From Stalin to Khrushchev*. Cambridge, Mass., 1996.

Index

Text:	10/13 Sabon
Display:	Sabon
Composition:	G & S Typesetters, Inc.
Printing and binding:	Malloy Lithographing, Inc.